T0178207

Lecture Notes in Computer Science 12756

More information about this subseries at http://www.springer.com/series/7410

Leyla Bilge · Lorenzo Cavallaro ·
Giancarlo Pellegrino · Nuno Neves (Eds.)

Detection of Intrusions and Malware, and Vulnerability Assessment

18th International Conference, DIMVA 2021
Virtual Event, July 14–16, 2021
Proceedings

Editors
Leyla Bilge
NortonLifeLock Research Group
Biot, France

Lorenzo Cavallaro
King's College London
London, UK

Giancarlo Pellegrino
CISPA Helmholtz Center for Information Security
Saarbrücken, Germany

Nuno Neves
University of Lisbon
Lisbon, Portugal

ISSN 0302-9743 ISSN 1611-3349 (electronic)
Lecture Notes in Computer Science
ISBN 978-3-030-80824-2 ISBN 978-3-030-80825-9 (eBook)
https://doi.org/10.1007/978-3-030-80825-9

LNCS Sublibrary: SL4 – Security and Cryptology

This Springer imprint is published by the registered company Springer Nature Switzerland AG
The registered company address is: Gewerbestrasse 11, 6330 Cham, Switzerland

Preface

We would like to welcome you once again to the proceedings of the virtual edition of DIMVA 2021 – the 18th Conference on Detection of Intrusions and Malware and Vulnerability Assessment.

This year, despite the impact of the ongoing COVID-19 pandemic, we received a higher number of submissions compared to last year. We were excited about the program that the Program Committee put together. DIMVA 2021 received 65 valid submissions from academic and industrial organizations from more than 114 different institutions across 38 countries. Each submission was carefully reviewed by three Program Committee members or external experts. The final selection of papers was decided by Program Committee members during online discussions, in lieu of our traditional physical meeting. Our Program Committee members put a tremendous effort into the reviewing and paper discussion process. As a result, we selected 18 full papers and 1 short paper for presentation at the conference and publication in the proceedings, resulting in an acceptance rate of 27.9%.

We would like to express our appreciation to the Program Committee members and external reviewers for the time spent reviewing papers, participating in the online discussion, and shepherding some of the papers to ensure the highest quality possible. This was clearly a difficult time for everybody, but the Program Committee did a great job. We also deeply thank the members of the Organizing Committee and the Steering Committee for their hard work and responsiveness during this crisis. We are wholeheartedly thankful to our sponsors, Fachgruppe Sidar of the German Informatics Society and Lasige, Ciancias ULisboa, for generously supporting DIMVA 2021.

Our final thanks go to all participants, authors, and attendees, who are at the core of our conference - thank you so much for making DIMVA 2021 such an interesting and beautiful conference.

June 2021

Leyla Bilge
Lorenzo Cavallaro

Organization

General Chair

Nuno Neves	University of Lisbon, Portugal

Program Committee Chair

Leyla Bilge	NortonLifeLock Research Group, France

Program Committee Co-chair

Lorenzo Cavallaro	King's College London, UK

Publications Chair

Giancarlo Pellegrino	CISPA Helmholtz Center for Information Security, Germany

Publicity Chair

Daniel Kats	NortonLifeLock Research Group, USA

Sponsor Chair

Andrew Paverd	Microsoft Research Cambridge, UK

Local Arrangements Chair

Ibéria Medeiros	University of Lisbon, Portugal

Steering Committee Chairs

Ulrich Flegel	Infineon Technologies, Germany
Michael Meier	University of Bonn and Fraunhofer FKIE, Germany

Steering Committee Members

Magnus Almgren	Chalmers University of Technology, Sweden
Sébastien Bardin	CEA, France
Gregory Blanc	Télécom SudParis, France
Herbert Bos	Vrije Universiteit Amsterdam, the Netherlands
Danilo M. Bruschi	Università degli Studi di Milano, Italy
Roland Bueschkes	RWE AG, Germany
Juan Caballero	IMDEA Software Institute, Spain
Lorenzo Cavallaro	King's College London, UK
Hervé Debar	Télécom SudParis, France
Sven Dietrich	City University of New York, USA
Cristiano Giuffrida	Vrije Universiteit Amsterdam, the Netherlands
Bernhard Haemmerli	Acris GmbH and HSLU Lucerne, Switzerland
Thorsten Holz	Ruhr-University Bochum, Germany
Marko Jahnke	CSIRT, German Federal Authority, Germany
Klaus Julisch	Deloitte, Switzerland
Christian Kreibich	ICSI, USA
Christopher Kruegel	University of California, Santa Barbara, USA
Pavel Laskov	University of Liechtenstein, Liechtenstein
Federico Maggi	Trend Micro Research, Italy
Clémentine Maurice	CNRS and IRISA, France
Roberto Perdisci	University of Georgia and Georgia Institute of Technology, USA
Michalis Polychronakis	Stony Brook University, USA
Konrad Rieck	Technische Universität Braunschweig, Germany
Jean-Pierre Seifert	Technical University Berlin, Germany
Robin Sommer	ICSI and LBNL, USA
Urko Zurutuza	Mondragon University, Spain

Program Committee

Magnus Almgren	Chalmers University of Technology, Sweden
Daniel Arp	Technische Universität Braunschweig, Germany
Tiffany Bao	ASU, USA
Sébastien Bardin	CEA LIST, France
Antonio Bianchi	Purdue University, USA
Gregory Blanc	Télécom SudParis, France
Juan Caballero	IMDEA Software Institute, Spain
Sven Dietrich	City University of New York, USA
Brendan Dolan-Gavitt	New York University, USA
Ulrich Flegel	Infineon Technologies AG, Germany
Yanick Fratantonio,	Cisco Talos, USA
Chris Gates	NortonLifeLock, USA
Mariano Graziano	Cisco Talos, USA
Christophe Hauser	University of Southern California, USA

Alexandros Kapravelos	North Carolina State University, USA
Vasileios Kemerlis	Brown University, USA
Johannes Kinder	Bundeswehr University Munich, Germany
Erik van der Kouwe	Vrije Universiteit Amsterdam, the Netherlands
Platon Kotzias	NortonLifeLock, Greece
Christopher Kruegel	VMWare, USA
Pierre Laperdrix	CNRS and Lille University, France
Pavel Laskov	University of Liechtenstein, Liechtenstein
Federico Maggi	Trend Micro, Italy
Michael Meier	University of Bonn and Fraunhofer FKIE, Germany
Marius Muench	Vrije Universiteit Amsterdam, the Netherlands
Anita Nikolich	Illinois Institute of Technology, USA
Giancarlo Pelegrino	CISPA Helmholtz Center for Information Security, Germany
Roberto Perdisci	University of Georgia and Georgia Tech, USA
Fabio Pierazzi	King's College London, UK
Fabio Pagani	University of California, Santa Barbara, USA
Christian Rossow	CISPA Helmholtz Center for Information Security, Germany
Deborah Shands	SRI International, USA
Seungwon Shin	KAIST, South Korea
Yan Shoshitaishvili	Arizona State University, USA
Gianluca Stringhini	Boston University, USA
Juan Tapiador	Universidad Carlos III, Spain
Sam Thomas	University of Birmingham, UK
Gang Wang	University of Illinois at Urbana-Champaign, USA
Christian Wressnegger	Karlsruhe Institute of Technology, Germany

Additional Reviewers

Kevin Roundy
Gibran Gómez
Avinash Sudhodanan
Soheil Khodayari
Sergej Epp
Yufei Han
Andrea Marcelli
Xabier Ugarte-Pedrero
Michaël Marcozzi
Matthieu Lemerre
Lesly-Ann Daniel
Thomas Papastergiou
Kleanthis Karakolios

Sponsors

GERMAN
INFORMATICS SOCIETY

LASIGE driven by excellence

Contents

You've Got (a Reset) Mail: A Security Analysis of Email-Based Password Reset Procedures

Tommaso Innocenti[1(✉)], Seyed Ali Mirheidari[2(✉)], Amin Kharraz[4(✉)], Bruno Crispo[2,3(✉)], and Engin Kirda[1(✉)]

[1] Northeastern University, 360 Huntington Avenue, Boston, MA 02115, USA
{innocenti.t,e.kirda}@northeastern.edu
[2] University of Trento, via Calepina, 14, 38122 Trento, Italy
{seyedali.mirheidari,Bruno.crispo}@unitn.it
[3] KU Leuven, Oude Markt 13, 3000 Leuven, Belgium
[4] Florida International University, 11200 SW 8th Street, Miami, FL 33199, USA
ak@cs.fiu.edu

Abstract. The password recovery process is a critical part of a website's functionality. Many websites that provide online services to their users also need to solve the problem of allowing their users to reset their passwords (e.g., if they have forgotten it). A popular, established technique for allowing a user to recover a lost account is to allow her to send a reset link to her own account via email. Although it might seem easy at a first glance, the security requirements of the password recovery process require web sites to carefully design each step of the process to be resilient even in the presence of an attack. In this paper, we present an in-depth security analysis of the email-based recovery mechanisms of a wide range of web applications. By manually registering accounts and triggering the password recovery process for each website, we were able to study the password reset mechanisms of web sites from three different groups in the Alexa Top 5K (i.e., popular sites, medium popular sites, low popular sites). In this work, we show that the lack of standards in the password recovery process plagues many websites with security weaknesses, and negatively influences the security of the reset process itself. We also show that concrete password-recovery reset attacks can be launched against a high percentage of websites that might even lead to account takeover.

Keywords: Web applications · Account recovery · Password resets

1 Introduction

Web applications have been historically an attractive target for adversaries. They are often open to the public-facing Internet and are designed to handle critical tasks and valuable data [27]. Therefore, any flaws in their identity and account

L. Bilge et al. (Eds.): DIMVA 2021, LNCS 12756, pp. 1–20, 2021.
https://doi.org/10.1007/978-3-030-80825-9_1

access management can have a significant impact on the integrity and confidentiality of the protected resources. This paper primarily focuses on the security of the account recovery process, a set of steps users have to follow to re-gain access to their accounts. We provide an empirical study on what is missing in the current implementation of account recovery mechanisms and how some of the flaws introduce significant risks with consequential impacts.

Account management has never been an easy task for normal users. Reports show that users, on average, possess 80 accounts [12]. Hence, it is not very surprising if users lose their access to their accounts and generate password recovery requests from time-to-time [21]. Although modern password managers [25] have shown to be effective in facilitating account management, the need to have a well-designed recovery mechanism has not been diminished. Users may need to update their accounts and change their passwords for many reasons. Consequently, having a robust password recovery is undeniably a critical service to maintain the security posture of web applications and protect users' accounts from unauthorized access.

Despite the importance of password recovery, the necessary details to implement and enforce the mechanism do not seem to be sufficient. The main source of guidance is OWASP [26] which mainly focuses on general requirements without providing specifics on how to implement or assess the security of the procedure. Consequently, little knowledge is available to web developers on how to create a secure and usable account recovery process. This lack of guidance has provided a unique opportunity for adversaries [7,8,11] to steal sensitive information.

Our work is guided by three primary research questions. First, how do websites implement the account recovery process? Second, how prevalent are account recovery problems? And third, what are the immediate threats of misconfigured recovery processes? To answer these questions, we built an analysis pipeline to collect a real-world dataset of the account recovery process in 366 websites in the Top 5K Alexa list.[1] This dataset includes information about the login page, password reset request page, and recovery link. We defined eight implementation controls in account recovery based on OWASP guidelines and ran a semi-automated experiment to empirically analyze if websites satisfy these requirements.

Our analysis shows that insecure practices are prevalent. Our measurements revealed that the account recovery mechanism in 72% of the websites is affected by at least one implementation weakness. For instance, 147 (40%) of the websites were generating multiple valid tokens, providing an opportunity to issue unauthorized password reset requests. Among all websites, 163 (45%) did not send password change request notifications to the account owner, leaving users with no warning in case of unauthorized password reset. We also found that 82 (22%) websites suffering from login CSRF, where users can be tricked into performing the password reset and get authenticated as the attacker, allowing the attacker to observe all user's interactions with the site. Despite the broad

[1] Our data collection infrastructure will be made open source.

set of sites analyzed, our measurement findings represent a lower bound of the potential weaknesses in the wild.

Our analysis also shows that OWASP guidelines are only partially deployed in practice. Since there was no concrete implementation standard for account recovery, we used the OWASP guidelines as the "metric" to determine the adherence of websites to these basic security recommendations. Our results show that only 13% of the websites were following the OWASP guidelines. We observed that 82% of the password reset procedures on the test websites were based on sending reset links. In most cases, we observed violations of OWASP guidelines. For instance, 52 websites were sending the tokens via insecure links, 75 websites had a very long link expiration window (i.e., more than 24 h). We were able to use the reset links after 24 h. We also observed that in 21 websites, the generated token could be used multiple times. Among other empirical evidence, our data shows that the security controls in account recovery mechanisms are almost missing – leaving significant opportunities for abuses.

Finally, our experiments reveal that the weaknesses in the account recovery process can have consequential impacts on the security posture of the websites. For instance, we observed that attackers can mislead the remote server to generate poisoned reset mails during the password reset request. Users can be tricked to click on the poisoned reset link providing an opportunity for attackers to launch login CSRF attacks where they can collect the user's reset token and potentially perform an account takeover. Moreover, it also allows the adversary to retrieve almost all the activities on the target account (e.g., message exchange, credit card entry) by misleading the victim to reset an attacker-controlled account.

While the weaknesses mentioned in this paper may not always result in blatant security vulnerabilities, they are indicators that developers are failing to follow robust practices, leading to a more fertile environment for adversarial operations. We provide an empirical look at the security consequences of these unsavory practices such as login CSRF and header manipulation. We hope that this work serves to raise awareness about the importance of defining reliable mechanisms for the account recovery in the web ecosystem. We also hope our approach will prove useful to the web security community and open the door for future solutions.

This paper's contributions are summarized as follows.

- We propose a methodology to identify weakness in email-based password recovery process.
- We present a measurement of common weaknesses in password recovery among the Alexa Top 5K.
- We study a set of web-based attack scenarios on email-based password recovery, and quantify the prevalence of them among high-profile sites.

The remainder of this paper is structured as follows. In Sect. 2, we present the related work. In Sect. 3, we provide the background information introducing the OWASP guidelines and the related threat model. In Sect. 4, we explain the adopted methodology and the data collection infrastructure used to conduct the study. In Sect. 5, we present our findings.

2 Related Work

The security community has introduced several fallback authentication mechanisms for account recovery, ranging from knowledge-based authentication (e.g., security questions) to possession-based authentication (e.g., OAuth, tokens, security cards, and email verification). In the following, we will discuss works that primarily focus on the security of account recovery mechanisms.

Password Reset via Email Verification. Although email-based account recovery [4] has reached a wide adoption among sites [29], the procedures to deploy the mechanism is not very well-defined [3,13,14,28–30]. The motivation for some of the prior work was to analyze the effectiveness of account recovery emails [1,2,15,20]. The research showed that malformed recovery emails that do not inform users of the reset link's validity time, or that do not warn users about keeping the link confidential may introduce a vulnerability. In a different approach, Raponi et al. [29] proposed a technique to protect users from service provider-level attacks. Despite the open-source availability of the solution, the study is limited in scope and the vulnerabilities covered in the work. In our work, we investigated eight common weaknesses and attack scenarios based on OWASP guidelines [26] as described in Sect. 4.

Password Reset via SMS OTP. Researchers have also performed several security analyses of the implication of SMS OTP methods in the authentication process [10,19,22,24,33]. For instance, AUTH-EYE [22] proposed an automated approach to detect implementation flaws in the authentication modules of a program. The analysis showed that in 98.5% of the test cases, the applications violated different security rules in generating (OTP randomness, length) and verifying the SMS OTP code (e.g., allowed retry attempts and renewal interval). In a similar study, Mulliner et al. [24] conducted a measurement study of the SMS OTP security architecture by introducing several weaknesses and attack scenarios. They demonstrated that intruders could obtain the SMS OTP utilizing SIM swapping or the wireless interception attacks. Dmitrienkoet et al. [10], investigated two-factor authentications of high profile Internet service providers and discovered several weaknesses which could be exploited to circumvent SMS-based authentication in four larges online banks applications as well as Google. In a recent study, Zeyu Lei et al. [19] performed a systematic study on mobile apps' authentication schemes based on SMS OTP. Their study not only discovered vulnerable mobile apps with hundreds of millions of installations, but also revealed several flaws in core API implementations of mobile operating systems.

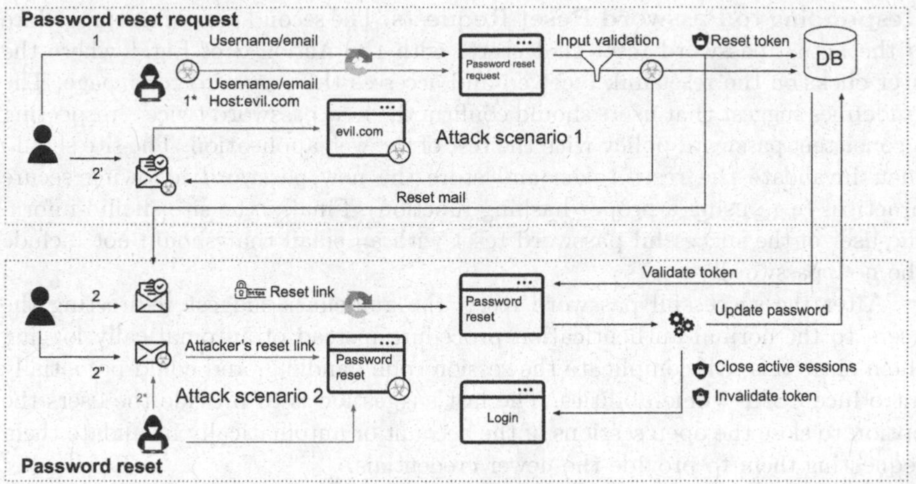

Fig. 1. Password reset flow

3 Background

In this section, we first discuss the OWASP guidelines [26] for resetting user passwords. Then, we provide information on the attack scenarios that we used as complementary security checks for our measurement.

3.1 OWASP Guidelines

The main reference that is publicly available for password reset is provided by OWASP. The guideline divides the password reset process into two parts; (1) initiating the password reset request, (2) processing the password reset request. In the following, we briefly describe each step.

Initiating the Password Reset Requests. The first part of the procedure is to initiate the password reset as presented in Fig. 1. For this step, the OWASP guidelines suggest providing to the users a consistent message for existing and non-existing accounts with a constant time for each reply. This approach reduces the risk of classic timing side-channel attacks on password management [5] and also protect websites from possible user enumeration attacks [4,6]. Malicious web bots can target the password reset mechanism. To reduce the impact of such adversarial attempts on the password reset, the guidelines suggest the implementation of a protection mechanism against automated submission as CAPTCHA or other rate-limiting controls [34]. Moreover, before processing the request, the received input should be properly sanitized with an input validation alongside an SQL injection prevention method that will protect the website's database. After the input validation, the website first stores the generated reset token in a database and then includes it in the reset link. Finally, a reset email containing the reset link is sent to the user.

Responding to Password Reset Requests. The second part of the procedure is the actual password reset that starts with the Action 2 of Fig. 1 where the user clicks on the reset-link received and accesses the password reset page. The guidelines suggest that users should confirm the new password twice – respecting a consistent password policy with the rest of the web application. The site should then invalidate the reset token and store the new password following secure practices (e.g., using a proper hashing function). Finally, the site should inform the user of the successful password reset with an email that should not include the new password.

After the successful password reset, the guidelines suggest redirecting the users to the normal authentication procedure instead of automatically logging them since this will complicate the session code handling, and could potentially introduce CSRF vulnerabilities. The last suggestion is to provide the users the option to close the open sessions of the account or automatically invalidate them requesting them to provide the newer credentials.

3.2 Attack Scenarios

The attack scenarios presented are derived from the OWASP guidelines [26]. These attacks are directly related with email-based password recovery process that represent the majority of the recovery methods adopted in the wild. With the studied attack scenarios, we demonstrated how misconfigurations in the recovery process could be used to directly target a website's users. We first explain header manipulation issues, and then discuss login CSRF problems.

Header Injection. The first attack scenario starts at the initiation of the password reset procedure [16–18] due to improper processing of the network headers. That is, the attacker sends a poisoned password reset request marked as 1* in Fig. 1 and manipulates the host field in the network header of the requests. This can mislead the site's server that, without a proper sanitization, will generate the reset link using the poisoned field. As a result, the attacker without needing any interaction with the victim, mislead the websites' server to send a poisoned reset mail to the victim. The only information the attacker needs to initiate the attack is the victim email. This attack thanks to the generation of the poisoned email by the website's server will easily bypass victims' inbox spam filter. Moreover, since most of the resetlink included in reset mail is hide behind a button, the poisoned email generated can easily mislead the victim in click the malicious link (Action 2') increasing the chance of a successful attack.

Login CSRF. As depicted in Fig. 1, a user would choose a new password in the final step of the password reset process. Since the user is expected to submit a valid reset link that is confidential, some applications immediately set an authorization cookie and redirect the user to the dashboard, bypassing the normal authentication. Skipping the authentication phase occurs in many applications as they presume that only the valid user would have access to this concrete reset link. Unfortunately, this assumption creates a security risk. In login CSRF attacks, an attacker would request a password reset link for its own account, and then send this link to the victims (Action 2*), encouraging them to click on the link to update the password.

The application would then validate the password reset token, and would set the proper authorization cookie associated with the reset token. This process is very dangerous since the victims (Action 2") use the attacker's authorization cookies (i.e., the owner of the reset link) to interact with the website. In fact, the application recognizes the victim as the account owner because of the possession of the password reset link. As a result, any of the user's activities in the attacker's account (e.g., web search history, exchanged messages, etc.), can later be accessed by the attacker. Moreover, if the user saves any personally-identifiable or financial information (e.g., credit card numbers), this information would be accessible to the attacker as it is saved in an account under the attacker's control.

Motivating Example. It is critical to evaluate how websites initiate and process account recovery requests. Account recovery problems are less well-studied security issues with significant impact. For instance, springer.com, a well-known scientific publisher, has multiple issues in initiating the password requests. We observed that password reset tokens in this website do not expire. OWASP strictly suggests single-use reset tokens to minimize the risk of account takeover and the abuse of the reset mechanism. We also observed that users are provided with no notification about the password recovery requests. The notification allows users to identify unauthorized attempts for hijacking accounts. As other examples, Seattlenews.com, a very popular news website in the US Northwest region, and rakuten.co.jp, a known Japanese shopping website all suffer from similar types of account recovery problems. The examples we discussed here are among the most popular websites with a significant number of users and web traffic. Consequently, issues in password recovery can have consequential impacts on the security of users as well as the web application. Our experiments, discussed at length in Sect. 5, show that these issues occur frequently. In Sect. 4, we describe eight different classes of weaknesses in the account recovery mechanism, and incorporate them to evaluate the security of real-world recovery mechanisms.

4 Methodology

This section introduces our data collection infrastructure, and the methodology we used to study the security of the password reset procedure in real-world websites.

4.1 Measurement Setup

The initial step of the measurement is to select websites and form a test corpus. We selected 900 websites from the Alexa Top 5,000 websites. We divided the sites into three groups based on their popularity. As presented in Sect. 5.3, this site selection enabled us to analyze the behavior of each site group allowing us to identify how sites with different popularity exhibit similar results.

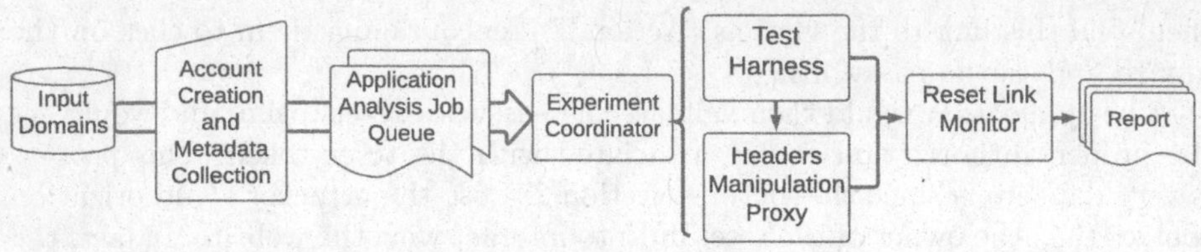

Fig. 2. Data collection infrastructure.

However, we were able to create accounts only on 513 websites since for some websites, we were not able to provide all the required information during the account creation process. For instance, some websites did not have a public login page or required a pre-approval process such as bank account information. Also, some of the 900 sites required a specific class of data such as a local phone number or a Social Security Number (SSN). In some cases, the confirmation link was not received during the account generation process. To measure the security of the password reset procedure, we created a user account for each site under test. During our measurements, we observed that some data deduplication was necessary. That is, institutions such as Google Inc. had several websites with different Country Code Top-Level Domains (ccTLDs) where the reset link was redirected to the main domain. For instance, the password reset requests on google.es or google.it were redirected to google.com. We removed these cases from our analysis which were 147 websites to avoid identical measurements. This initial setup allowed us to collect metadata for each site under test such as the presence of CAPTCHAs. The metadata helped us in the account recovery process where we could decide how to interact with the target websites. Figure 2 shows the overall data collection pipeline.

4.2 Data Collection Infrastructure

As presented in Fig. 2, the data collection infrastructure is coordinated by the *Experiment coordinator* that takes as input the filtered domains and performs test probes using several high-level components: (1) the *test harness*, (2) the *reset link monitor*, and (3) the *header manipulation proxy*.

Test Harness. Is in charge of managing all the *account interfaces* and communicating with the header manipulation proxy to generate the *manipulated account reset*. This component is responsible for reproducing the user's interaction with the website. The interaction with the website was done by writing a Python script based on Selenium Chrome web driver. The crawler uses *CSS selectors* to identify the login element in the page and issue the password reset request. To verify the correct validation of a correct login, a visual check was performed to make sure that the browsing session works well in practice. Moreover, we note that 44 sites were using CAPTCHA services in their login page and that 90 sites require an explicit CAPTCHA verification before initiating the password reset request. Since automatic interaction was not possible in these cases, we manually ran the experiment to find and reset the password.

Header Manipulation Proxy. Is in charge of modifying the request generated by the test harness. The header manipulation proxy modifies the generated requests from the test harness including markers in two different header types: Host header and non-Standard Headers. The markers are used to modify the requests that are subsequently used by the reset link monitor to pinpoint the creation of a poisoned reset mail from the web applications.

Reset Link Monitor. Monitors email accounts corresponding to user accounts created in the setup step. Received emails are scanned using a combination of regular expressions and inspection of HTML mail body to extract all links contained in the message body and check the presence of injected markers. The extracted links are then filtered using a keyword heuristic to retain password reset links and discard all others.

4.3 Password Reset Testing Methodology

Using OWASP guidelines [26] as a benchmark, we derived the following tests to evaluate the OWASP adherence of the website's recovery process.

Reset Link Validity Window ($\mathbf{T}_W$). The length of time a reset link is valid after being issued can have security consequences. A long validity window can introduce opportunity for an attacker to abuse a stolen link. That being said, there is also an inherent usability trade-off in this mechanism. That is, a too short validity window makes it difficult to legitimately use a link before it expires. Since OWASP guidelines only suggest an "appropriate time validity", we chose 24 h as a reasonable trade-off between reset link validity window security and usability. To test the validity window T_W for a site s, a fresh link l is requested. This reset link is then stored for 24 h before it is used to attempt a password reset. Effectively, the test determines whether or not $T_W(s) > 24\,\text{h}$.

Multi-Use Reset Links ($\mathbf{T}_U$). Another security-relevant property of reset links is whether the reset links are valid for multiple uses. OWASP strictly suggests a single use reset link for each reset token. This prevents, for example, an attacker from gaining access to an email account containing older reset links and reusing them to perform a password reset without generating new reset link emails. This test measures whether a site s allows resetting links to be used multiple times, denoted by T_U. First, a reset link l is requested. Then, we attempt to use it to perform a password reset twice in succession. If the second attempt succeeds, then s does not invalidate l on first use and so $T_U(s) > 1$.

No Password Change Confirmation ($\mathbf{T}_C$). As suggested by OWASP, websites should notify users after a successful password change. These notifications allow users to recognize when an attacker is attempting an account takeover via password reset requests. Since these notifications are sent as a password change confirmation email, we measure this property for each website. The test measures whether a site s confirms password changes, denoted by T_C. To carry out the test, we first request a reset link l and then use it to perform a password reset. Next, the email monitor waits to receive a confirmation email. If one is not received within 1 h, we consider the test to have failed, i.e., $T_C(s) = \mathsf{false}$.

No Session Invalidation ($\mathbf{T}_I$). After a password reset has been performed, OWASP suggests allowing the users to shutdown all the account's active sessions. This is a useful practice because if a password reset was requested due to an account compromise, failing to invalidate existing sessions would allow an attacker to maintain persistence. Hence, we tested which websites by default do not close the account's active session after a password reset. To measure whether the website s invalidates existing sessions after a password reset (T_I), a reset link l is requested. Then, a fresh session is created by authenticating to s. In a *separate* unauthenticated browser instance, l is used to reset the account's password. Then, we check whether u_1 is still authenticated to s. If so, then $T_I(s) = \mathsf{true}$. To prove that the site s closes the session u_1, we performed a manual verification interacting with the open session for a maximum of 60 s. The manual verification is necessary due to the heterogeneous behavior of websites where in some cases a page refresh would invalidate the session and in some others, a more complex interaction with the site is needed for session invalidation.

Insecure Reset Link ($\mathbf{T}_S$). OWASP suggests that all the reset links should use HTTPS. Otherwise, users run the risk of falling victim to several attacks. For instance, an attacker could act as a man-in-the-middle and intercept the new account password. Furthermore, a passive network attacker could sniff the new account password if HTTPS redirection is not performed and subsequent requests are transmitted in the clear. This test, which we denote T_S, simply involves checking whether a reset link l for site s uses the HTTPS scheme. If not, then $T_S(s) = \mathsf{true}$.

Multiple Valid Reset Links ($\mathbf{T}_N$). If a site receives multiple password reset requests, it may issue multiple reset links.[2] However, each new reset link represents another opportunity for leakage and abuse by an attacker. Thus, although not specified in the OWASP guideline [26], from a security perspective, it is preferable to limit the number of reset links that are valid at any point in time, ideally to one. This test measures whether a site s allows multiple, simultaneously valid reset links; we denote the number of simultaneously valid links allowed by a site as T_N. First, two reset links l_1, l_2 are requested. Then, we attempt to use l_1 to initiate a password reset. If the reset succeeds, then this indicates that $T_N(s) > 1$. In particular, it means that s does not invalidate older links when a new one is issued.

HTTP Header Injection ($\mathbf{T}_H$). As suggested by OWASP, websites should validate the user's input before processing it. This includes secure handling of HTTP headers since malicious content injection of various kinds could be reflected in reset emails. These vulnerabilities can enable several distinct attacks.

[2] In principle, a site could also refuse to issue a new reset link while prior links are still valid. In our experiments, we never observed this to occur.

For instance, if a site uses a password reset request's Host header to generate reset links, an attacker could explicitly set the Host header when issuing a reset request to point to an attacker-controlled origin. This would allow the attacker to phish victims and intercept both the old and new account passwords. Alternatively, arbitrary content injection vulnerabilities could be abused to carry out XSS attacks against victims that receive reset emails.

To test whether a site s is vulnerable to HTTP header injection (T_H), we used our test harness to issue a password reset request, but this time, using the Headers manipulation proxy, we intercept it, inject unique markers and then send it to the site s. In particular, we selected a number of standard and non-standard HTTP headers to inject markers into. These headers include Host, Origin, Referer, X-Host, X-Forwarded-Host, X-Forwarded-For, X-Forwarded-Server, Proxy-Host, Destination, True-Client-IP, Client-IP, X-Client-IP, X-Real-IP, X-Originating-IP, CF-Connecting-IP, X-Original-URL, X-HTTP-DestinationURL, X-Arbitrary, X-Forwarded-Proto, Proxy, Contact, From, Forwarded, X-Wap-Profile, and Profile. The email monitor collects the password reset email. Once it is received, it is scanned for the presence of an injected marker. If one is found, then the site is considered to be *conditionally* vulnerable to HTTP header injection; that is, $T_H(s) = \mathsf{true}$. The reset email is flagged for later manual confirmation.

Login CSRF($\mathbf{T}_L$). Immediate redirection of a user to the authenticated page after a successful password reset without an intervening re-authentication represents a potential login CSRF vulnerability. For this reason, OWASP suggests redirecting users to the login process instead of automatically logging in users. In fact, by targeting a vulnerable site, an attacker could send a password reset email to a victim for an attacker-controlled account. If the victim is tricked into performing the password reset, she will be authenticated as the attacker, allowing the attacker to observe all of the victim's interactions with the site. To test for the presence of a login CSRF vulnerability at site s, we request a rest link l and then use it to perform a password reset. After the password, reset we manually verify if the site si, without requesting the new password, automatically logs in the user. If so, then $T_L(s) = \mathsf{true}$.

4.4 Limitations

Due to the inherent limitations of the proposed approach, the reported findings and results in this paper should be considered as a lower bound. For instance, we exclude websites that require entering the social security numbers, corporate email addresses, or credit card information. Furthermore, in the header manipulation assessment, our crawler tested only fifteen popular HTTP headers, while the origin server might be still vulnerable to other headers which have not been tested in our methodology. Since our crawler should send a new request for each test case, some websites blocked our test accounts after a number of password reset attempts. We stopped testing these websites. However, the implementations of these websites might still be vulnerable.

4.5 Ethical Considerations

We defined a set of security controls in our experiments to make sure that the measurements will not cause any damage to the sites under analysis. For instance, we ran a minimum number of password reset requests to limit the amount of traffic generated by our measurement tools. During our measurements, we never injected any malicious code in the network traffic, nor tried to access accounts that were not under our control. Since our study measures the actual presence of weaknesses in real-world websites, we did not publicly disclose the vulnerable websites and contacted the vulnerable websites directly.

We followed the recommendations proposed by works such as [23,31,32]. We first used an open-source vulnerability disclosure and bug bounty program database to obtain the sites' contact [9]. From the database, we were able to obtain the contact information of 62 vulnerable sites. In addition, we identified sites that use a broker (e.g., HackerOne or Bugcrowd) as a designed channel to disclose vulnerabilities. We then manually contacted each site following the platforms' processes.

Unfortunately, not all the vulnerable sites we identified were included in the database. For the remaining 200 sites, we used the WhoisXML API to gather the sites' contact associated with the registered domain. Once we obtained all sites' contact information, we used these as input for our automated email script to automatically generate and send a custom email for each site. In the communication, we used a verified mail account, as well as our contact information and a method to verify our identity. Along with the weakness that afflicted each site, we included a link to the OWASP guidelines used to measure the process security.

Of all the contacted sites, we received an acknowledgment from 38 sites (14.5%). The sites contacted by email showed lower responsiveness compared to the sites that used a broker. In fact, we received 19 replies out of 243 sites. 8 sites reported the issue to their dev team and another 8 marked our report as informative. 3 sites fixed the issue that we reported.

All the 19 sites contacted through a broker replied to our report, with 8 of them marking our report as duplicated. Some of the duplicated reports were dated as far back as 2014 – indicating that the website lacked a fix. A known site of video streaming confirmed that they will fix the issue. The remaining sites acknowledged the issue, but due to restricted bug bounty program scope, our report was marked as informative without providing any information about possible future fixes.

5 Security Measurement

In this section, we provide the result of our measurement, and present the security implications of our findings.

5.1 Account Recovery Implementation

Password Recovery Type. Since analyzing email-based recovery processes are the main focus of this work, the first step is to identify the recovery methods adopted by the selected websites. The most reliable way to discover the recovery method is to perform a password reset request on each of the selected websites. This step of the initial filtration, described in Sect. 4.1, allowed us to remove websites that do not provide a password recovery mechanism as well as websites that consisted of multiple domains. The output of the setup is **366 websites** that constitute our study's site seed. A summary of the password recovery type discovery is presented in Table 1. Our dataset's analysis confirms the findings of [4] that the majority of websites adopt an email-based password recovery procedure. Moreover, it answers our first research question by defining how many websites implement the account recovery process. In fact, the email-based recovery type (361 websites) represents 98.6% of the whole recovery types with only **five** websites that adopt *SMS* as the primary recovery method.

Table 1. Recovery types summary

Recovery type	Channel	# Sites
Text-Msg	SMS	5 (1.4%)
Original Password	E-mail	7 (1.9%)
One-time Security Code	E-mail	27 (7.4%)
Temporary Password	E-mail	25 (6.8%)
Password Reset Link	E-mail	302 (82.5%)
Total		366 (100%)

Table 2. Common weaknesses statistics

Weakness	All sites
No Change Notification (NCN)	163 (44.5%)
Multiple Valid Tokens (MVT)	147 (40.2%)
No Session Termination (NST)	139 (38.0%)
Login CSRF (LC)	82 (22.4%)
No Expiration (NE)	75 (20.5%)
Insecure Reset Link (IRL)	52 (14.2%)
Multi Use Token (MUT)	21 (5.7%)
Headers Manipulation (HM)	6 (2.0%)
Total	262 (71.6%)

5.2 Recovery Procedure Analysis

Since 302 sites (82.5%) used the reset-link as the recovery method, we focused on the security implementation of the reset tokens included in the reset-link.

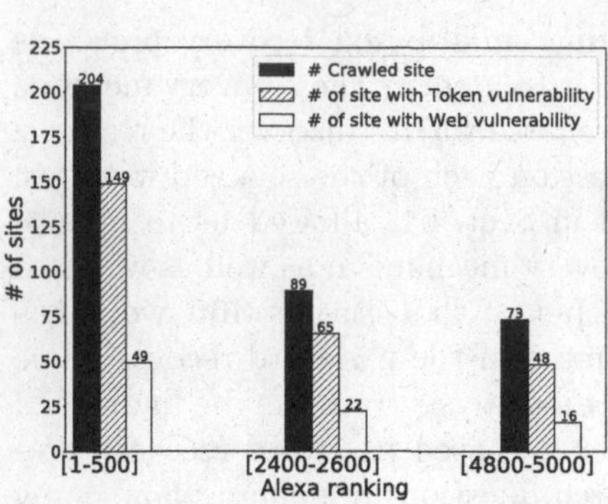

Fig. 3. Sites distribution in Alexa ranking

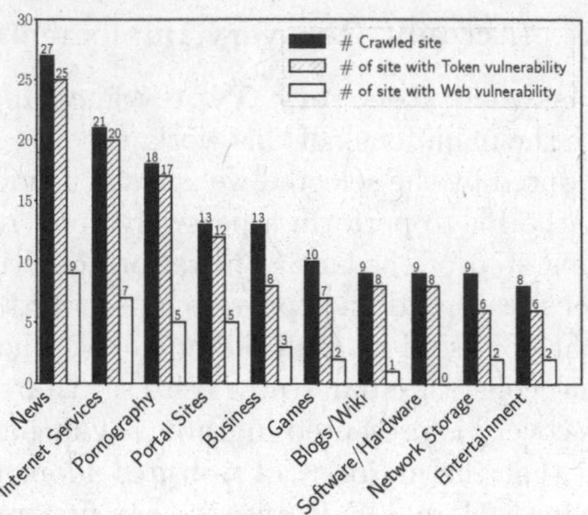

Fig. 4. Top 10 categories

The reset token is a secret code generated by the website, and included in the reset-link. The token allows opening a temporary session to reset the account's password. Due to its central role, the reset token's security checks play a fundamental part in ensuring the password reset procedure's security. Hence, we allocated four out of six implementation checks to verify its correct implementation and the remaining two to verify a correct implementation after password reset (i.e., no session termination, no change notification). The result of our measurement are presented in Table 2.

Combining the result of Table 2 with the data of Fig. 6 shows that 57.7% of websites (211 websites out of 366) misimplemented a security check on reset token. For the remaining two implementation checks, we found that 54.0% (198 out of 366 websites) of websites wrongly managed the active sessions after a password reset, or missed a confirmation email after a successful password reset. The tests performed show a large diffusion of misimplementation of the password reset procedure among websites. Moreover, the widespread number of websites with at least one weakness (i.e., 262 out of 366 – 71.6%) answers the second research question affirmatively; That is, the missing of a standard clearly causes a degradation of the password reset procedure's implementation security on websites. The diffusion of weaknesses among websites is a clear indicator of a much-needed strict regulation of this critical procedure urging a practical effort from websites to the research community to solve this overlooked problem.

5.3 Weakness Analysis

Alexa Ranking. As presented in Fig. 3, the percentage of websites affected by a weakness is, in the first group, **97%** (198 sites) of the most popular websites, **97.7%** (87 sites) for the second group and, **87.7%** (64 sites) for less popular websites. The result of our measurement shows an homogeneous diffusion of weaknesses among all three different groups.

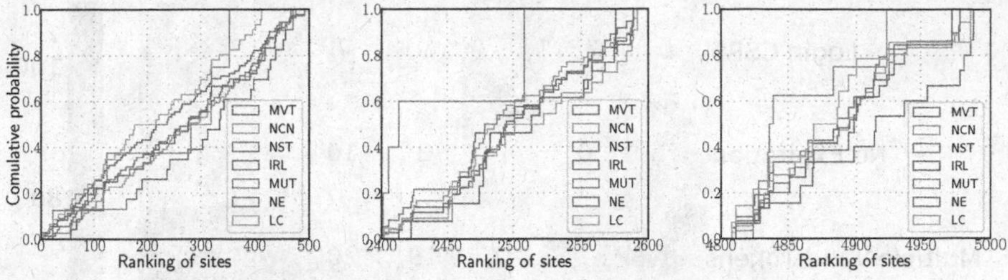

Fig. 5. CDF weaknesses comparison

Category. The analysis of the website categories reveals that all the categories have at least 60% of websites that are vulnerable, with six categories that have at least 89% of the websites that are vulnerable. As presented in Fig. 4, from the composition of the sites' weaknesses, it is clear that token weaknesses have a higher incidence with respect to the web vulnerabilities. Even though some categories showed a lower percentage in weaknesses, the result obtained shows how the weaknesses we analyzed affect all the website categories indiscriminately, reinforcing the conclusion that the security of password reset procedure is an open and widespread problem.

Weakness Distribution. Figure 5 shows the cumulative distribution of websites that exhibit an implementation weakness. For each weakness measured, we represent here the distribution of vulnerable sites in all three sites bucket. A more inclined line shows that a particular weakness affects more popular sites than less popular sites. As shown in the graph, the majority of the weaknesses show a similar trend among sites. Further analyzing the distribution of each bucket of sites, we performed a Mann-Whitney U test and, with a p-value of 0.01, we cannot reject the null hypothesis that all three buckets belongs to the same distribution. This result suggests a counter-intuitive result; that websites are affected regardless of their ranking and popularity.

Furthermore, we investigated the diffusion of weaknesses among websites with the co-occurrence matrix presented in Fig. 6. The matrix shows three weakness clusters: Multiple Valid Token, No Change notification, and No Session Termination. These clusters suggest that websites that did not pass one of the security checks have a higher chance of having issues in other security check implementations. The consequence is that even a single misimplementation could endanger the security of the reset procedure. However, websites that expose multiple weaknesses enable the chaining of weaknesses, considerably increasing the severity of the problems.

5.4 Attack Scenarios

In this section, we present the result of our attack scenarios investigation. While our analysis represents a lower bound of vulnerable sites, it still shows an urgent

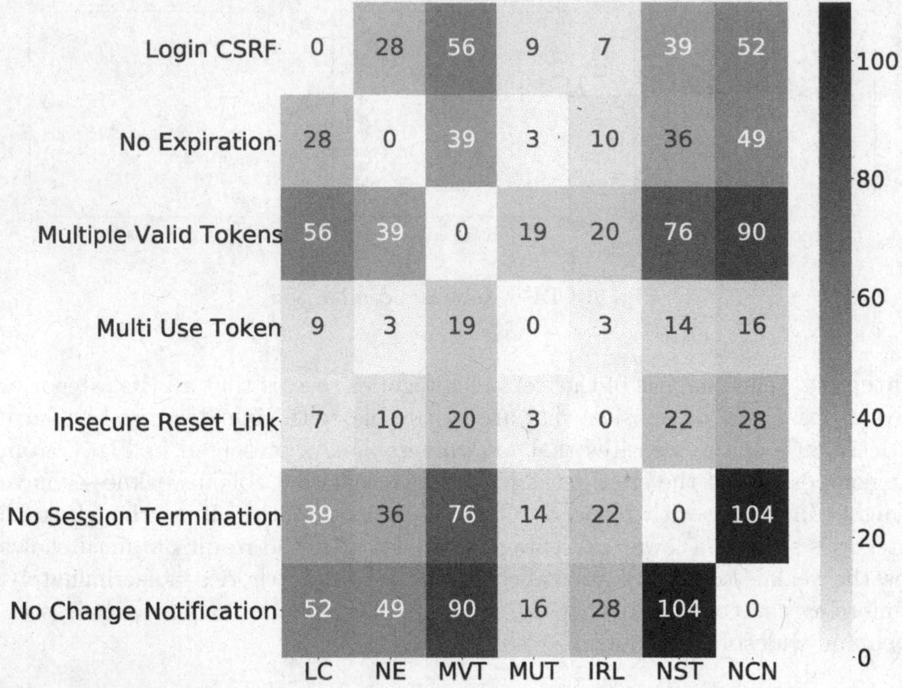

Fig. 6. Co-occurence matrix

need for a better password reset procedure implementation. Furthermore, sites should account for every potential attack when designing their recovery procedure to reduce the risk that malicious actors could exploit security assumptions.

Header Injection. In this experiment, our proxy, in two separate account reset requests, manipulated Host header as well and fifteen standard and Non-Standard HTTP headers through injecting specific values. We later investigated all reset email contents and reset links for the presence of a marker (manipulated headers value). Our crawler discovered 6 out of 366 (2.0%) websites echoed our injected marker either in reset link, or inside email contents. The details of each category are described below.

Host Header Injection. In the first step, our proxy replaced the `Host` header in all password reset requests with a specific marker. By investigating all reset emails, our crawler discovered 3 out of 366 (1.0%) websites to be vulnerable, i.e., the generated password reset link pointed to the injected domain name by the crawler. It is noteworthy that our crawler did not detect any changes in the content of the password reset email, which implies `Host` header manipulation would only affect reset links. Leveraging this vulnerability enables an attacker to steal the password reset token and compromise user's accounts. Our results show that only 66 out of 366 (18%) websites accepted password reset requests with manipulated `Host` header and sent the password reset emails, whereas only 3 were found to be vulnerable. For the rest of the websites, our crawler recorded three different behaviors. 96 websites handled requests properly and redirected our crawler to custom error pages. 70 websites returned different 400 error codes (mostly `403 Not Found`), and 8 websites returned `500 Internal Server Error`. For websites that do not accept password reset requests, it is plausible that a variety of middle HTTP components (e.g., Load balancer, Web application firewall, etc.) have blocked requests with manipulated `Host` header and do not route the request to the server. Then, the presented result in this section should be considered as a lower bound because the server can still be vulnerable, but other in the middle protections avoid the server's exposure to vulnerability.

Other HTTP Headers Injection. In the final step, our proxy manipulated the password reset requests by adding fifteen standard and Non-Standard HTTP headers and discovered 3 out of 366 (1.0%) websites to be vulnerable. During the measurement, 198 websites out of 366 (54%) accepted our poisoned request showing a lower bouncing rate compared to the host headers poisoning an older and better documented vulnerability. The lower popularity and documentation of Non-Standard HTTP headers open the door to unexplored weakness as showed by the result of our measurement. Two of three cases were vulnerable to `X-Forwarded-Host` header, and the servers used these header values to create a password reset link. Obtaining the password reset link would enable the attacker to steal the password reset token and perform an account take over.

The third site was exploited with manipulation of a different header, namely `x-originating-ip`, while the site was vulnerable to altering neither `Host` nor `X-Forwarded-Host` headers. The result of manipulating `x-originating-ip` was notable in that the marker we injected in the field was echoed in the contents of the email. Therefore, it would be possible to inject arbitrary phishing contents in the password reset email. Another notable observation was specifically observed in `anonymous.com` site, which was including not only the password reset link in the password reset email, but also the IP address of the requester. This IP address would be set as the value of `x-originating-ip` header. Interestingly, when we populated `x-originating-ip` with our marker, this value was the one which was shown in the anonymous password reset email. We think this observation could be justified with assuming the existence of some middle network components or servers, which are responsible to find the requester's IP and then append that IP address to the header, without overwriting the value we set. When the results are sent to the server, it shows the first value of `x-originating-ip`, which had been set by us. These results confirmed our hypothesis that manipulating Non-Standard headers are an effective variation of header manipulation and can target password reset processes either by reset link poisoning or email content manipulation.

Login CSRF. The attack scenario presented in Sect. 3.2 is a variation of the well-known Login CSRF (i.e., Auth-CSRF). Login CSRF was first introduced in

2009 [15]. In the attack, an attacker forces the victim to login to the attacker's account by sending a forged authentication request with the attacker's credentials through the victim's browser. As described in Sect. 4.3, after completing the password reset process, we manually investigated the landing pages to verify if the browser session is authenticated. In case of an authentication landing page, the site would be tagged as vulnerable. As a result of our experiments, 82 out of 366 (22.4%) websites were vulnerable to login CSRF.

6 Conclusions

One of the most security-critical aspects of a website's functionality is the password recovery service. It has been long known that malicious actors often target the password recovery process to hijack a victim's account (e.g., by guessing their secret recovery questions). A popular, established technique for allowing a user to recover a lost account is to allow her to send a reset link to her account via email. The security requirements of the password recovery process requires web sites to carefully design each step of the process to be resilient even in the presence of an attack.

This paper presented a security analysis of the email-based recovery mechanisms of a wide range of web applications from the Alexa Top 5K. We studied groups of popular, medium popular, and low popular websites, and manually registered accounts on these websites. Our work shows that the lack of standards in the password recovery process plagues many websites with security weaknesses, and also negatively influences the security of the reset process itself. We also show that concrete password-recovery reset attacks (e.g., login CSRF, header manipulation) can be launched against a significant number of websites that might even lead to account takeover. We hope that this paper will pave the way in highlighting the importance of improving the email-based account recovery mechanisms in real-world websites.

Acknowledgments. We would like to thank anonymous reviewers for reading the paper carefully and making helpful comments. This work was supported by National Science Foundation under grant CNS-1703454. This work was also partially supported by Secure Business Austria.

References

1. Al Maqbali, F., Mitchell, C.J.: Email-based password recovery-risking or rescuing users? In: 2018 International Carnahan Conference on Security Technology (ICCST), pp. 1–5. IEEE (2018)
2. Maqbali, F.A., Mitchell, C.J.: Web password recovery: a necessary evil? In: Arai, K., Bhatia, R., Kapoor, S. (eds.) FTC 2018. AISC, vol. 881, pp. 324–341. Springer, Cham (2019). https://doi.org/10.1007/978-3-030-02683-7_23
3. Bonneau, J., Bursztein, E., Caron, I., Jackson, R., Williamson, M.: Secrets, lies, and account recovery: lessons from the use of personal knowledge questions at google. In: Proceedings of the 24th International Conference on World Wide Web, pp. 141–150 (2015)

4. Bonneau, J., Preibusch, S.: The password thicket: technical and market failures in human authentication on the web. In: WEIS (2010)
5. Cao, Y., Chen, Z., Li, S., Wu, S.: Deterministic browser. In: Proceedings of the 2017 ACM SIGSAC Conference on Computer and Communications Security, pp. 163–178 (2017)
6. Chen, S., Wang, R., Wang, X., Zhang, K.: Side-channel leaks in web applications: a reality today, a challenge tomorrow. In: 2010 IEEE Symposium on Security and Privacy, pp. 191–206. IEEE (2010)
7. Conikee, C.: Case study: exploiting a business logic flaw with github's forgot password workflow, December 2019. https://medium.com/@chetan_conikee/case-study-exploiting-a-business-logic-flaw-with-githubs-forgot-password-workflow-discovered-d4d36ee3dd16
8. Corporation, T.M.: CWE-640: weak password recovery mechanism for forgotten password. https://cwe.mitre.org/data/definitions/640.html
9. Disclose.io: Open-source tools to help hackers and organizations make the internet safer, together. https://disclose.io. Accessed 20 Feb 2021
10. Dmitrienko, A., Liebchen, C., Rossow, C., Sadeghi, A.R.: Security analysis of mobile two-factor authentication schemes. Intel Technol. J. **18**(4) (2014)
11. Gracey, J.: Hacking github with unicode's dotless 'i', November 2019. https://eng.getwisdom.io/hacking-github-with-unicode-dotless-i/
12. Hanamsagar, A., Woo, S.S., Kanich, C., Mirkovic, J.: Leveraging semantic transformation to investigate password habits and their causes. In: Proceedings of the 2018 CHI Conference on Human Factors in Computing Systems, pp. 1–12 (2018)
13. Jakobsson, M., Stolterman, E., Wetzel, S., Yang, L.: Love and authentication. In: Proceedings of the SIGCHI Conference on Human Factors in Computing Systems, pp. 197–200 (2008)
14. Just, M.: Designing and evaluating challenge-question systems. IEEE Secur. Priv. **2**(5), 32–39 (2004)
15. Karlof, C., Tygar, J.D., Wagner, D.A.: Conditioned-safe ceremonies and a user study of an application to web authentication. In: NDSS (2009)
16. Kettle, J.: Practical http host header attacks, May 2013. https://www.skeletonscribe.net/2013/05/practical-http-host-header-attacks.html
17. Kettle, J.: Cracking the lens: targeting http's hidden attack-surface, July 2017. https://portswigger.net/research/cracking-the-lens-targeting-https-hidden-attack-surface
18. Kettle, J.: Collaborator everywhere, May 2018. https://github.com/PortSwigger/collaborator-everywhere
19. Lei, Z., Nan, Y., Fratantonio, Y., Bianchi, A.: On the insecurity of SMS one-time password messages against local attackers in modern mobile devices. In: Proceedings of the 2021 Network and Distributed System Security (NDSS) Symposium (2021)
20. Li, Y., Wang, H., Sun, K.: Email as a master key: analyzing account recovery in the wild. In: IEEE INFOCOM 2018-IEEE Conference on Computer Communications, pp. 1646–1654. IEEE (2018)
21. Lovisotto, G., Malik, R., Sluganovic, I., Roeschlin, M., Trueman, P., Martinovic, I.: Mobile biometrics in financial services: a five factor framework. University of Oxford, Oxford, UK (2017)
22. Ma, S., et al.: An empirical study of SMS one-time password authentication in android apps. In: Proceedings of the 35th Annual Computer Security Applications Conference, pp. 339–354 (2019)

23. Mirheidari, S.A., Arshad, S., Onarlioglu, K., Crispo, B., Kirda, E., Robertson, W.: Cached and confused: web cache deception in the wild. In: 29th {USENIX} Security Symposium ({USENIX} Security 2020), pp. 665–682 (2020)
24. Mulliner, C., Borgaonkar, R., Stewin, P., Seifert, J.-P.: SMS-based one-time passwords: attacks and defense. In: Rieck, K., Stewin, P., Seifert, J.-P. (eds.) DIMVA 2013. LNCS, vol. 7967, pp. 150–159. Springer, Heidelberg (2013). https://doi.org/10.1007/978-3-642-39235-1_9
25. Oesch, S., Ruoti, S.: That was then, this is now: a security evaluation of password generation, storage, and autofill in browser-based password managers. In: USENIX Security Symposium (2020)
26. OWASP: Forgot password cheat sheet. https://cheatsheetseries.owasp.org/cheatsheets/ForgotPasswordCheatSheet.html
27. Preibusch, S., Bonneau, J.: The password game: negative externalities from weak password practices. In: Alpcan, T., Buttyán, L., Baras, J.S. (eds.) GameSec 2010. LNCS, vol. 6442, pp. 192–207. Springer, Heidelberg (2010). https://doi.org/10.1007/978-3-642-17197-0_13
28. Rabkin, A.: Personal knowledge questions for fallback authentication: security questions in the era of Facebook. In: Proceedings of the 4th Symposium on Usable Privacy and Security, pp. 13–23 (2008)
29. Raponi, S., Di Pietro, R.: A longitudinal study on web-sites password management (in) security: evidence and remedies. IEEE Access **8**, 52075–52090 (2020)
30. Schechter, S., Brush, A.B., Egelman, S.: It's no secret. Measuring the security and reliability of authentication via "secret" questions. In: 2009 30th IEEE Symposium on Security and Privacy, pp. 375–390. IEEE (2009)
31. Stock, B., Pellegrino, G., Li, F., Backes, M., Rossow, C.: Didn't you hear me? - Towards more successful web vulnerability notifications. In: Proceedings of the 2018 Network and Distributed System Security (NDSS) Symposium (2018)
32. Stock, B., Pellegrino, G., Rossow, C., Johns, M., Backes, M.: Hey, you have a problem: on the feasibility of large-scale web vulnerability notification. In: 25th {USENIX} Security Symposium ({USENIX} Security 2016), pp. 1015–1032 (2016)
33. Yoo, C., Kang, B.T., Kim, H.K.: Case study of the vulnerability of OTP implemented in internet banking systems of South Korea. Multimedia Tools Appl. **74**(10), 3289–3303 (2015)
34. Zhang, Y., Gao, H., Pei, G., Luo, S., Chang, G., Cheng, N.: A survey of research on captcha designing and breaking techniques. In: 2019 18th IEEE International Conference on Trust, Security and Privacy in Computing and Communications/13th IEEE International Conference on Big Data Science and Engineering (TrustCom/BigDataSE), pp. 75–84 (2019). https://doi.org/10.1109/TrustCom/BigDataSE.2019.00020

The Full Gamut of an Attack: An Empirical Analysis of OAuth CSRF in the Wild

Michele Benolli, Seyed Ali Mirheidari, Elham Arshad(✉), and Bruno Crispo

University of Trento, Trento, Italy
{seyedali.mirheidari,elham.arshad,bruno.crispo}@unitn.it

Abstract. OAuth 2.0 is a popular and industry-standard protocol. To date, different attack classes and relevant countermeasures have been proposed. However, despite the presence of guidelines and best practices, the current implementations are still vulnerable and error-prone. In this research, we focus on OAuth Cross-Site Request Forgery (OCSRF) as an overlooked attack scenario.

We studied one of the most recurrent types of OCSRF attacks by proposing several novel attack strategies based on different status of the victim browser. In order to validate them, we designed a repeatable methodology and conducted a large-scale analysis on 314 high-ranked sites to assess the prevalence of OCSRF vulnerabilities. Our automated crawler discovered about 36% of targeted sites are still vulnerable and detected about 20% more well-hidden vulnerable sites utilizing the novel attack strategies. Although our experiment revealed a significant increase in the number of OCSRF protection compared to the past scale analyses, over one-fourth are still vulnerable to at least one proposed attack strategy.

1 Introduction

OAuth 2.0 is an industry-standard protocol for authorization. It was released in 2012 as RFC 6749 and nowadays is pervasively used to manage authorization flows in web, desktop, mobile applications, and in smart devices. The protocol has been widely studied, and its theoretical and practical security has been covered extensively by the literature. OAuth was designed to enhance several aspects of the former client-server authorization model.

The OAuth 2.0 Threat Model and Security Considerations [26] and OAuth 2.0 Security Best Current Practice [16] documents are published to address the most common security issues and vulnerability scenarios discovered within concrete implementations of the protocol. However, despite the rich guidelines and the many mitigation proposed over time, several OAuth-based services are still subject to a wide range of security flaws. This because, those guidelines are not detailed enough to consider all possible settings that can lead to an attack, especially for what relates client-side parameters.

L. Bilge et al. (Eds.): DIMVA 2021, LNCS 12756, pp. 21–41, 2021.
https://doi.org/10.1007/978-3-030-80825-9_2

As reported by [23] CSRF vulnerabilities related to authentication and identity management services are extremely pervasive, even among the top-ranked domains. Our paper is mainly focused on a specific vulnerability, the CSRF attack against the `redirect_uri` [26], since it's one of the most popular concrete attack in OAuth implementations. The attack is well documented in the Threat Model document and it can lead to serious consequences, ranging from the disclosure of sensitive information to a malicious user [3] to the complete account takeover [10]. Our work extensively covers the details of this security threat, with a systematic analysis of its root causes and practical impact. We built an automated testing framework to evaluate the presence of the aforementioned vulnerability in a large number of popular sites that implement the Facebook login service. The rationale of our approach is to help developers to avoid implementation mistakes by providing the most comprehensive set of attack strategy such that developers are aware what implementation settings to avoid.

The outcome of our large-scale analysis is that more than a third of the tested sites were found vulnerable to at least one of the proposed attack strategy.

We selected only one attack because the purpose of the paper is not to find the highest number of vulnerabilities, but rather to demonstrate how to build a comprehensive set of attack strategies for an attack, considering scenarios and configurations that have been so far ignored or overlooked in the literature, This based on the wrong assumptions those scenarios were not significant. Our analysis proved they are indeed significant and contributed to find 20% additional vulnerabilities.

The paper makes the following contributions:

- To the best of our knowledge, we present the most comprehensive set of test cases to exploit OCSRF vulnerabilities, including novel attack strategies that stress all possible client-side status. They complement and integrate the guidelines provided by documents such as [16,26] in helping OAuth developers to mitigate implementation mistakes.
- We designed a repeatable methodology and conducted an automated and large-scale analysis on 314 high-ranked sites to assess the prevalence of CSRF attack against the `redirect_uri` in OAuth implementations.
- The analysis discovered that about 36% of targeted sites are still vulnerable and detected about 20% more well-hidden vulnerable sites utilizing the novel attack strategies.

2 Background

This work primarily focuses on a specific OAuth vulnerability, that can lead to a cross-site request forgery attack. For a thorough understanding of the risks and consequences related to this vulnerability, this section provides a brief background on OAuth and CSRF attacks in the context of OAuth. Threat model and its impact are described as well.

2.1 OAuth

OAuth is an authorization protocol and does not handle user authentication. However, authentication protocols can be built on top of it [19]. Many identity providers (IdP) such as Google and Facebook use OAuth to allow their users to share identity and personal information with third-party websites and applications (clients).

The OAuth 2.0 specification describes different methods for a client application to obtain an access token and consequently the access to user's protected resources. The four grant types are authorization code, implicit, resource owner password credentials, and client credentials. Each grant type is optimized for a particular use case. In this research, we are only concerned with the authorization code and implicit grant flows.

2.2 Login CSRF

In a login cross-site request forgery, the attacker deceives the victim into executing a cross-site request to the login endpoint of a target website. The attacker uses its own credentials to forge the login request. If the attack succeeds, the server issues a session cookie for the browser of the victim. As a result, the victim is logged into the target website with the account of the attacker [3]. There has been several studies [13,21,23,30] analysing the login CSRF attacks.

At first sight, the attack may appear quite innocuous. Generally, a cross-site request forgery attack concerns operations performed on the victim's protected resources. In the login CSRF, the attacker exploits an application flaw to deceive the users into performing some unintended operations inside the attacker's account. The browser state is changed after the execution of the attack, and the victims may be completely unaware of the fact they are using an account owned by someone else. As a result, they may upload sensitive documents, share credit card numbers and other personal data with a malicious user.

2.3 State Parameter

According to OAuth 2.0 specification [9], the client must implement CSRF protection for its redirection URI. Any request sent to the redirection endpoint must include a value that binds to the user-agent's authenticated state. This value `state` parameter which can be performed in OAuth 2.0 flow. The state parameter, to prevent CSRF attacks, should be a non-guessable randomly generated sequence of characters. However, the presence of the parameter does not guarantee the security of the client against a CSRF attack. A wrong validation or a mishandling of the parameter may lead to the vulnerability of the application, as evidenced in [30].

3 OAuth Cross Site Request Forgery

In the context of OAuth 2.0, a successful cross-site request forgery can allow an attacker to obtain authorization to resources protected by the protocol, without the consent of the user. A recurrent type of login OCSRF is the OCSRF attack against `redirect_uri` [26], where the victim is logged into an account controlled by the attacker. As a direct consequence, all the operations performed by the victim are unconsciously accomplished inside the attacker's session and the result of these actions can potentially be disclosed to the attacker.

3.1 Threat Model

Figure 1 represents the main steps of the OCSRF attack against `redirect_uri` considered in our large-scale analysis. The attack starts with the victim's browser opening a malicious web page (1). At the loading page, the crafted request is generally launched by the browser automatically (2). The OAuth flow, initiated by the attacker, is then completed on the victim's side. The identity provider exchanges the received code for an access token and returns it to the client (4). At this point, the client can use the token to access the information needed to authenticate the user. Since the flow is initiated by the attacker, the login is performed using the attacker's account.

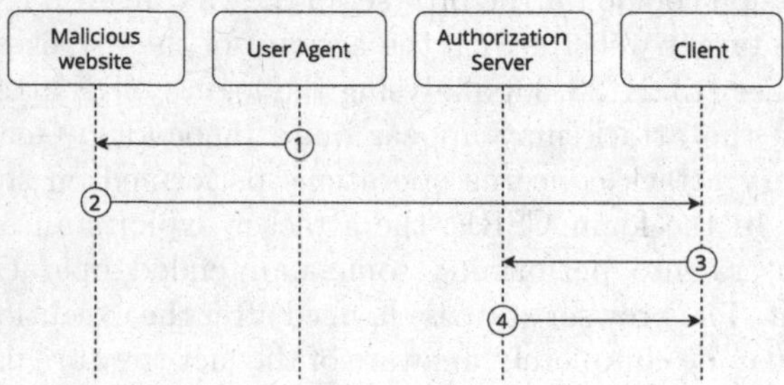

Fig. 1. Main steps involved in the OCSRF attack against `redirect_uri`

3.2 Impact

Some sites allow their users to register several OAuth provider logins, linked to the principal account. It represents an alternative and simpler way to access the application. In this scenario, if one of the implemented OAuth flows is insecure, a login OCSRF attack may lead to an account takeover. The account linking feature can be exploited to gain full access to the victim's data. The attack flow was first discussed by Egor Homakov [10]. The attack is possible only if certain preconditions are satisfied. The attack can only be executed against a registered user on the target site. At the end of the attack, the account owned by the attacker is linked to the victim's account. As a result, the attacker can access the victim's account on the client with the identity provider's profile used in the attack.

3.3 Enabling Factors

Several factors can influence the success rate of the OCSRF attack against `redirect_uri`. What happens if the victim is registered to the vulnerable application? Is the attack feasible even if the user never visited the domain before? If the victim is already authenticated to the website, is the attack prevented? Having these questions answered is important to better understand the impact of OCSRF in real-life scenarios. To be exploitable, the OCSRF attack against `redirect_uri` does not require the victim to be authenticated on the target application. Frequently the attack works even if the victim never visited the site before. However, the presence of cookies, previously set by the target site in the browser, can alter the outcome of the attack. In our analysis, we investigated this hypothesis running all the test scenarios with three different victim browser status as follows: a) No cookie, b) Visitor (unauthorized) cookies and c) Authorized cookies. We designed different attack strategies utilizing above-mentioned victim browser status which would be discussed in detail in Sect. 5.3. In the rest of the paper, for brevity, OCSRF attack refers to the OCSRF attack against `redirect_uri`.

4 Related Work

The security of OAuth 2.0 has been widely examined in the literature. Several theoretical studies (e.g. [2,7,20,29]) use abstract models to evaluate the security of the OAuth protocol. A downside of theoretical approach is that it does not allow to discover the vulnerabilities resulting from implementation errors.

Many empirical works have been done on the security of OAuth-SSO (e.g., [1,5,6,18,25,28,31]) either by developing web-based tools or evaluating the risk in real-world implementations.

A similar approach is employed by Li and Mitchell [13] to analyse the security of SSO implementations based on OAuth 2.0. Regarding the CSRF attack against the `redirect_uri`, authors found a significant fraction of clients are not implementing any countermeasure. The detected security issues were manually inspected and led to the generation of several case studies.

Sumongkayothin et al. present OVERSCAN [24], a security scanner able to identify missing parameters within the OAuth 2.0 protocol, analysing the traffic between the browser and the web application. Part of this analysis required manual inspection. The main limitation of the manual approach is scalability. The lack of automation makes the inspection process extremely time consuming and the limited size of the resulting sample makes it difficult to generalize the findings and distill error patterns.

Calzavara et al. [4] designed and implemented a browser-side security monitor for web protocols, called WPSE, to prevent nine attacks violating the security properties of OAuth. However, WPSE cannot prevent certain classes of attacks, including automatic login CSRF attacks, network attacks which are not observable by the browser and impersonation attacks.

Yang et al. [30] propose a model-based approach for the automated discovery of vulnerabilities in OAuth 2.0 implementations, called OAuthTester. To overcome the limitations of previous theoretical approaches, OAuthTester starts building a state machine from the protocol specifications, but then enhance the state machine and fills the gaps due to the ambiguities of the specification by observing traffic traces of the OAuth flow and the server state. However, as said by the authors, they can observe only traffic over HTTP, so they cannot gain the all knowledge we used in our approach to design the attack strategies. As a results they do not detect vulnerabilities that we detect with our analysis.

Shernan et al. [21] perform a large-scale analysis to assess the presence of CSRF vulnerabilities in real-world deployments of OAuth. The analysis on the Alexa Top 10K sites reveals that 25% of sites using OAuth were vulnerable to CSRF attacks. A significant limitation of this approach is represented by the metric used to assess the occurrence of CSRF vulnerabilities. A lot of sites were excluded from the analysis simply because of the existence of the `state` parameter in the authorization URL. As we show in this paper, the mere presence of the `state` value does not guarantee protection against CSRF attacks.

Sudhodanan et al. [23] present a comprehensive study on the different types of authentication CSRF reported in the literature. For identification of strategies in order to detect and reproduce each vulnerability, they used the same browser to simulate the interaction between the attacker and the victim, which led to missing some additional scenarios regarding to victim's browser states at the time of the attack. Our approach consider additional attack strategies. Instead of using the same browser, we totally separated the environment in which attacker and victim operate. In place of performing the attack only in a clean browser session, we also performed tests in presence of visitor and authorized cookies; which is not considered in their analysis.

5 Methodology

We designed a repeatable methodology to discover and validate OCSRF vulnerabilities in targeted sites. As depicted in Fig. 2, our methodology has three phases: 1. target selection, 2. measurement setup 3. OCSRF detection. We developed a tool based on Python-Selenium to automatically select targets and test different OCSRF scenarios.

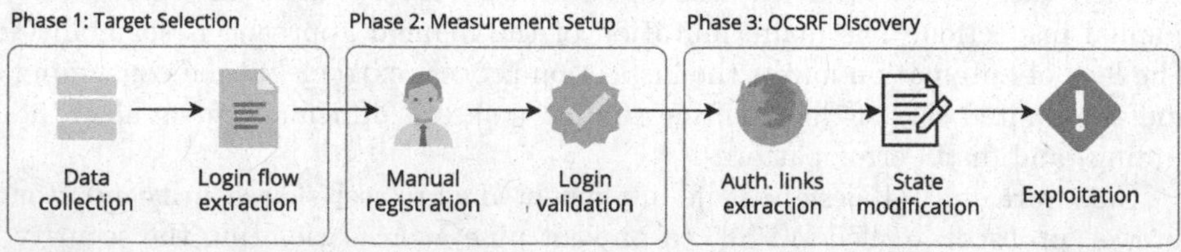

Fig. 2. Abstract view of OCSRF detection methodology.

5.1 Phase 1: Target Selection

Step 1: OAuth Login Detection. For extracting the initial seed set of candidate sites using OAuth login, we develop a browser-based crawler to visit sites in the initial seed set (e.g., Alexa Top 50K) in April 2020. The crawler is designed in a way that extracts initial OAuth login links for specific popular providers via checking the presence of OAuth standard parameters in all extracted links.: `response_type`, `client_id`, and `oauth`. The string «`oauth`» is commonly contained in the URL of authorization endpoints and its presence is a good indicator of the existence of an OAuth-based process. All these parameters are used by the crawler in the detection phase, to classify the links and identify the different login systems built on top of the OAuth protocol. Since many sites use JavaScript which requires interaction with users to trigger OAuth login, we develop a browser-based crawler to increase the detection rate.

Step 2: OAuth Flow Extraction. In order to remove false positives and extract OAuth redirection flows properly, the crawler follows all extracted and selected links. If the crawler lands on any well-known identity provider we will add the site to our candidate list, which would be later used to test our OCSRF attack strategies. A keyword-based approach is used to detect the Login/Sign-in buttons (these elements usually contain some known keywords to identify the login action and the identity provider). Extracted flows would later fed into next phases.

5.2 Phase 2: Measurement Setup

Step 1: Manual Registration. We follow the extracted OAuth links and create two sets of test accounts (victim and attacker) for each targeted site. Since the information provided by the external identity provider is not sufficient for the account creation process in many targeted sites, manual data entry is necessary. We adopt previously proposed technique [17] to populate attacker and victim accounts with unique information (e.g., name, email, user identifier, phone number, profile logo, etc.) and use them in next steps as `markers`.

Step 2: Login Validation. To verify the login steps, the crawler uses the login information gathered in the first phase to initiate the OAuth login trail. It reaches the authentication page and enters the credential automatically. At this point the flow is complete, and the browser is redirected to the target site's landing page.

OCSRF attack detection requires a victim to login as an attacker to the targeted site. The detection crawler should be capable of detecting the forged login to the attacker's account. In this regard, a learning process is developed for the crawler to automatically complete and learn the login processes for both attacker and user accounts. In the learning process, the crawler scans the HTML code of the landing page and looks for specific user-related strings. We presume the presence of some predefined unique `markers`, visible only as a result of a valid login to each account (which is populated to each account in registration step).

5.3 Phase 3: OCSRF Discovery

The main goal of this phase is to discover exploitable sites. The crawler is designed in a way to discover various implementation flaws in `state` validation (described in the step 2). In the first step, the crawler follows the OAuth flow, logs into the attacker account and extracts the authorization response links. In the second step, the crawler applies different modifications based on five attack strategies on the extracted authorization link. In the last step, the different victim browser status is exploited with modified links.

Step 1: Authorization link Extraction. Since the successful exploitation of OCSRF needs an attacker authorization response link including authorization code, `state` etc., the crawler initially follows OAuth login and obtains an attacker authorization response from the identity provider. We develop a browser extension to allow the crawler to record the attacker authorization link from the identity provider and halt the OAuth flow immediately. In other words, the generated authorization link is recorded and the OAuth flow is stopped before redirection to the target site. The extracted link will be modified in the next steps to discover vulnerable sites.

Step 2: `state` Modification. The extracted authorization link would be modified via going through five attack strategies. All attack strategies are performed mainly based on modifications on `state`, as a result of which attack URLs would be created. The first scenario is applied to the subset of sites in which a `state` is not present in the authorization link. In other scenarios, attack strategy would build further attack URLs by manipulating the `state` value as enumerated as follows.

0. **No `state`.** The link is sent unaltered to the victim if the original link does not contain a `state`.
1. **Empty `state`.** The `state` value is replaced with an empty string.
2. **Lack of `state` validation.** The value of the `state` is replaced with a randomly generated string.
3. **Unlinked `state`.** The link including `state` is sent unaltered to the victim.
4. **Missing `state`.** The `state` is removed.

In the first attack strategy, the authorization response link obtained at the first stage remains unchanged. In order to build other test cases, the testing strategy would manipulate the value of `state` value by either replacing it with an empty string, substitute it with a randomly generated string or keep the same value. Last attack strategy would completely remove the `state` parameter. In both strategies 0 and 3 the attacker would deliver the attack link unchanged to the victim. The strategies 1 and 2 rely on different alterations of the `state` value. In strategy 1, the content of the parameter is replaced with an empty string while attack strategy 2 replaces the value with random string. Finally, in the last strategies the `state` value and parameter name is completely removed.

Step 3: Exploitation. Each of the attack URLs generated in the previous step would be opened in a separate browser. We propose several OCSRF test cases based on above strategies to determine whether a site is exploitable or not. In this regard, above strategies assess various victim browser status. Each of them is performed on three different victim browser status:

(a) **Status A. No Cookie,** when the victim opens the attack URL, there is no cookie related to the targeted site in the victim browser. In other words, either victim never visited the targeted site in the past or uses a new/history-cleared browser. Obviously, no cookies will be sent to the server when attack URLs are requested.
(b) **Status B. Visitor Cookies,** If the victim visited the targeted site in the past and visitor or unauthorized cookies have been set in the browser, the victim browser adds them to all requests. In this case, the crawler visits the first page of candidate site and stores all cookies before requesting the attack URLs.
(c) **Status C. Authorized Cookies,** If the victim is already authenticated to the targeted site, authorized cookies have been set on the victim browser. To simulate this test case, the victim has been authenticated by our crawler through logging in the victim's account, before requesting the attack URLs.

Each of the created attack URLs, obtained from applying previously-mentioned strategies, would be tested on each and every browser status defined above. As we have five different attack strategies and three possible victim browser status, we would end up with 15 test cases which would be exploited for each site. We later open all attack URLs inside victim browsers. We consider a test case to be successful if the attacker's marker is observed inside the victim's browser.

In a nutshell, each test case could be considered as the following three-step process.

1. Extract an attacker valid authorization response.
2. `state` parameter modification based on attack strategies.
3. Simulation of OCSRF attack on one of victim browser's status

5.4 Ethical Consideration

All test cases were performed with accounts specifically generated for this purpose. We never tried to exploit user accounts outside of our control. In all vulnerability assessment phases, our crawler never injected, sent or stored any malicious payload to candidate sites. In order to evade detection by bots detector [27], less than 100 pages of each candidate site was visited slowly in the data collection phase. We also developed Selenium crawler to complete the authentication steps and simulate a real user browser session. The number of requests involved in all test cases are significantly low, and the examined websites did not suffer from excessive bandwidth consumption. Moreover, all tests were conducted on the entire set of candidate sites therefore none of them has repeatedly been scanned in a short period of time.

Responsible Disclosure. Since the impact of the discovered vulnerabilities are severe, we reported the site owners using recommended notification techniques [12,22]. Additionally, we tried to disclose the vulnerabilities to those sites for which a centralized reporting system such as Hackerone [8] can be used, as these promise an increased success rate over attempting direct notification.

6 Analysis

In this section, we present the results of the empirical analysis and discuss them in detail. We also independently evaluate the results of each attack strategy and test case. This approach gives us the opportunity to properly focus on individual case studies among exploitable sites. The section would be concluded with the presentation of noteworthy observations.

6.1 Measurement Overview

Dataset. We fed our crawler with the Alexa Top 50K sites and analyzed the first page of them to extract the list of candidate sites with OAuth login. Since most of the discovered sites support different identity providers in their authentication pages, we only targeted one of their implementations and selected the most popular one, Facebook. The crawler discovered 539 sites with Facebook login. In the next step, we tried to create two sets of accounts (victim and attacker) and recorded the successful OAuth flow on each site. We narrowed down the dataset to 314 due to exclusion of sites with incomplete account registration (e.g., Social Security Number, credit card, etc.) and unsuccessful account verification.

Alexa Ranking. Our crawler analyzed all fifteen proposed test cases on target dataset and discovered 114 out of 314 (%36.3) sites to be exploitable by at least one test case. Given the distribution of the targeted and vulnerable sites across the Alexa Top 50K, it is noteworthy that about 32% of the sites among the Top Alexa 1K are vulnerable. Sites with higher Alexa ranking are slightly more vulnerable, but no specific major correlation among different buckets has been observed.

Categories Based on Presence of `state`. The candidate sites have been categorized based on absence or presence of `state` parameter within the recorded authorization request. For the former category, as mentioned in Sect. 5.3, our crawler directly exploit site without `state` and no modification applied on the attack URLs. However, on the latter category, due to presence of state parameter, 15 different attack scenarios have been tested. We will discuss the result of both categories in Sect. 6.2 in detail.

1. The first category, 44 out of 314 (14.0%) sites, do not use `state`, which shows a significant increase in utilization of `state` compare to past large scale analyses [3,11,14].

2. The second category, 270 out of 314 (85.9%) sites, are using `state`. Although, this indicates a significant increase in OCSRF protection compared to the past studies [3, 11, 14, 15], our crawler detected 73 out of 270 (27.0%) exploitable sites utilizing different test cases.

Table 1. Number of exploitable sites in Facebook by OCSRF for each attack strategies

#	No cookies (a)	Visitor cookies (b)	Auth. cookies (c)	All
0	33 (10.5%)	41 (13.1%)	23 (7.3%)	41 (13.1%)
1	34 (10.8%)	33 (10.5%)	23 (7.3%)	41 (13.1%)
2	30 (9.6%)	40 (12.7%)	23 (7.3%)	40 (12.7%)
3	49 (15.6%)	63 (20.1%)	36 (11.5%)	64 (20.4%)
4	33 (10.5%)	34 (10.8%)	24 (7.6%)	40 (12.7%)
Total	91 (29.0%)	105 (33.4%)	62 (19.7%)	114 (36.3%)

Attack Strategies. Table 1 shows the number of exploitable sites to each attack strategy. As shown, the «attack strategy 3: Unlinked `state`» has the highest success rate (20.4%) in all victim browser status. In this attack strategy, as previously described in Sect. 5.3, the victim visited a crafted attack URL with an attacker's valid and unused `state`. It means lack of proper relation between the victim browser and generated `state` is the most common implementation mistake. Interestingly «attack strategy 1: Empty state» has the second rank which means some sites mistakenly accept the authorization link with a null `state` value.

Test Cases. Since visitor cookie is the most vulnerable status which makes highest success rate (20.4%) and «attack strategy 3: Unlinked `state`» is the most effective attack strategy, test case «3b» has the highest detection rate. Our crawler detected 63 out of 270 (20.1%) sites to be exploitable with it. Test cases «1c» and «2c» had the lowest detection rates, most probably because targeted sites do not accept new OAuth login when user is authenticated.

Table 2. Classification of exploitable sites in Facebook by OCSRF - The first category of candidates (with Absence of `state` parameter)

#	0a	0b	0c	Sites
1	●	●	●	17 (38.6%)
2	●	●	○	16 (36.4%)
3	○	●	●	6 (13.6%)
4	○	○	○	3 (6.8%)
5	○	●	○	2 (4.5%)
Total	33	41	23	44

Victim Browser Status. We tested each attack strategy with three different victim browser status. Our crawler detects unique exploitable cases in each browser status. Previous researches only test the OCSRF in a clean browser without presence of any cookie [23] or only with visitor cookie [30]. In this research, our crawler was able to detect 23 out of 114 (20.2%) more exploitable OCSRF cases compared to test case «a: No cookies» through utilizing different browser status and 9 out of 114 (7.9%) compared to test case «b: Visitor cookies». Applying all of the browser status together with attack strategies have been done for the first time to the best of our knowledge.

Based on our results presented in Table 1, the presence of visitor cookie in victim browser increases the chance of finding exploitable cases significantly. Even though it is common that sites with authorization cookies are less vulnerable, we observed test cases that unexpectedly were vulnerable only in this specific test cases, which would be discussed in Sect. 6.2.

Table 3. Classification of exploitable sites in Facebook by OCSRF - The second category of candidates (with Presence of `state` parameter)

#	1a	1b	1c	2a	2b	2c	3a	3b	3c	4a	4b	4c	Sites	Sites/Const state
1	○	○	○	○	○	○	○	○	○	○	○	○	197 (73.0%)	1 (5.9%)
2	●	●	●	●	●	●	●	●	●	●	●	●	18 (6.7%)	4 (23.5%)
3	○	○	○	○	○	○	●	●	●	○	○	○	11 (4.1%)	5 (29.4%)
4	●	●	○	●	●	○	●	●	○	●	●	○	7 (2.6%)	0
5	○	○	○	○	○	○	●	●	○	○	○	○	6 (2.2%)	1 (5.9%)
6	○	●	○	○	●	○	○	●	○	○	●	○	5 (1.9%)	1 (5.9%)
7	○	○	○	○	○	○	○	●	○	○	○	○	4 (1.5%)	3 (17.6%)
8	●	○	○	○	○	○	○	○	○	●	○	○	4 (1.5%)	0
9	○	○	○	●	●	●	●	●	●	○	○	○	3 (1.1%)	0
10	○	○	○	○	●	○	○	●	○	○	○	○	3 (1.1%)	0
11	●	○	○	○	○	○	○	○	○	○	○	○	2 (0.7%)	0
12	●	○	●	○	○	○	○	○	○	●	○	●	2 (0.7%)	0
13	○	○	○	●	●	○	●	●	○	○	○	○	2 (0.7%)	0
14	○	●	●	○	●	●	○	●	●	○	●	●	2 (0.7%)	1 (5.9%)
15	○	○	○	○	○	○	●	●	●	●	●	●	1 (0.4%)	1 (5.9%)
16	○	○	○	○	○	○	●	○	○	○	○	○	1 (0.4%)	0
17	●	●	●	○	○	○	○	○	○	●	●	●	1 (0.4%)	0
18	○	○	○	○	○	○	○	●	●	○	○	○	1 (0.4%)	0
Total	34	33	23	30	40	23	49	63	36	33	34	24	270	17

6.2 `state` Parameter

As mentioned, there are two categories of candidates based on the presence of `state` parameter within the recorded authorization request, which would be analysed and explained separately in this section.

Absence of state. Interestingly, 44 out of 314 (14.0%) of sites do not set `state` and our crawler detected 33 (75.0%), 41 (93.1%) and 23 (52.2%) sites are vulnerable to test cases «0a», «0b» and «0c» respectively. In some cases, the absence of visitor cookies led to errors in the OAuth login flow, and this contributes to explain the lower number of vulnerabilities found in status «a» than «b».

Interestingly, all exploitable sites are also exploitable to «b» while about half of them are not exploitable when there is an authorized cookie. The classification of exploitable sites are listed in Table 2. Each row represents one pattern w.r.t different test cases (1a, 1b, etc.). A filled circle in each entry indicates successful exploitation. The `Sites` column shows the total number of sites which have been found exploitable via the indicated pattern in corresponding row. For example, 3 out of 44 sites were not exploitable to any of test cases, so on. While only 17 sites are vulnerable to all three test cases, there are two sites that are only exploitable when the visitor cookies are present. It means successful exploitation of them requires the victim browser to add only unauthorized cookies in the Attack URL.

In contrast to other researches, absence of `state` does not guarantee success exploitation of OCSRF, as other enabling factors can prevent targets from being exploited. In order to remove the false positives, our crawler analyzed all 44 sites in the first category of candidates. Unexpectedly, 3 sites were not exploitable. Two out of three sites use encoded and nonstandard parameters in the `redirect_uri` and implement proper validation to check if the OAuth flow initiated with the same browser. At the time of writing this paper, Facebook doesn't allow developers to set arbitrary parameters to `redirect_uri` as the full redirect URL should be reserved and the OAuth flow is blocked if there is any change in `redirect_uri`. It seems Facebook still allows old implementations to use nonstandard parameters in `redirect_uri`, probably for backward compatibility reasons. Anyhow, further investigation into the exceptions of the Facebook OAuth implementation is beyond the scope of this research.

The third secure expects the flow to be completed in a popup window, which is not opened by the crawler during the attack execution. The JavaScript code running on the client-side fails due to the absence of an opener parent window and the attack is consequently blocked in the browser. We consider this site as a secure one despite the absence of adequate protection against OCSRF. We will discuss related case studies in Sect. 6.4.

Presence of state Attack. Presence of the `state` does not mitigate OCSRF vulnerabilities. We summarized each exploitable pattern which was observed during our experiment on 270 sites in our candidate set in Table 3. About 73% of sites are not exploitable to any of the proposed test cases. In many sites, this is due to a correct implementation of the OAuth flow. Some secure instances notify the user about the OCSRF attack, others simply display a generic authorization error or do not perform any action. It should be noted that the group of 197 site marked as not exploitable by the crawler may contain a small fraction of false negatives. This hypothesis is supported by some evidence presented later in the analysis. For this reason, the number of vulnerabilities identified in our tests must be considered as a lower bound. Details would be discussed in the following section.

6.3 Case Studies

In this section, different test cases used during this research would be explained along with notable case studies of each attack strategy. It is worth mentioning that in this section the second category, presence of `state` parameter, is studied.

Empty and Missing `state`. In attack strategy 1, the value of the `state` in the authorization response is replaced with an empty string. At the beginning of the flow, the site generates a valid `state` to identify the authorization request. If the authorization response contains an empty `state` value, the application is supposed to not accept it and block the OAuth flow. The same approach applies to attack strategy 4, in which the `state` parameter – not only its value – is entirely removed from the authorization response URL. One of the manually analyzed sites has been discovered to be exploitable only to attacks 1 and 4, as illustrated in Table 3, classification 17. This result shows that when the parameter is present, `state` is handled supposedly and would be verified by the application. However, when the `state` value is empty or the parameter is missing, the validation would be bypassed and the flow successfully be accepted. The application source code is not directly available. However, we can get an insight into the internal logic of the `state` validation algorithm by analyzing the site reactions in response to different inputs.

A couple of sites are exploitable only via attack strategy 1 but not the 4th (Refer to Table 3, classification 11). The validation process checks the presence of a parameter called `"state"` in the authorization response and blocks the flow if it is not found. However, an empty `state` is accepted as valid and leads to the flow completion. The reverse is still possible when a site is exploitable with attack 4 and not to 1 (Refer to Table 3, classification 15). As an instance, we found a case study in which the verification succeeds only in presence of a valid `state`, while it could be bypassed if the parameter was not provided. The empty `state` supplied in the first test scenario was considered invalid by the application and caused the flow to be halted. Furthermore, we also found 6 exploitable sites in which the only performed validation is related to the presence of the `state` parameter inside the authorization response (Table 3, classification 9 and 10). The client application does not accept requests with a missing or empty `state` parameter, but even a random value is enough to bypass the validation.

The difference between attack strategy 1 and 4 is subtle and the results are almost overlapping. But the insight provided by above-mentioned unexpected results would be to take both attack strategies into account to discover related vulnerabilities to a great extent.

Lack of `state` Validation. In attack 3, the authorization response received by the attacker is maintained unchanged and sent to the victim. The test is performed to assess the absence of a valid relation between the `state` and the user's session. If the `state` is not handled properly during the generation of the authorization request, the application does not have enough information to perform correct validation in the subsequent steps of the flow. The site is not able to understand whether the authorization response was issued by the identity provider for the current user or if someone else initiated the request. As a result, the client may accept all the `state` values produced by the application as valid.

As illustrated in Table 1, attack strategy 3 is the most successful one. More than 20% of the candidate site are vulnerable to scenario «3a», «3b», or «3c». This can be justified by the inherent complexity of implementing a valid relation between the browser session and the `state`, which requires to generate and store a random token and proper management of that in the validation phase. Even though the RFC clearly describes the role and operation of the `state` parameter, the documentation provided by different identity providers are not often sufficiently precise and detailed. 23 out of 114 (20.2%) exploitable sites are only vulnerable to attack strategy 3 (Table 3, classifications 3, 5, 7, 16, and 18). For these applications, arbitrary `state` values are correctly rejected by the validation method, but valid states with incorrect associated to user sessions are erroneously not refused. Eleven sites are vulnerable to all configurations of attack strategy 3 (Table 3, classifications 3).

Unlinked `state`. In attack strategy 2, the `state` parameter produced by the client application is replaced with another string which is a random permutation of the initially generated value. The new parameter has the same length as the original and the same character set. The purpose of this strategy is to understand if using an invalid `state` is sufficient to bypass the OCSRF protections implemented by the examined sites. Our crawler detects total number of 30 out of 114 (26.3%), 40 out of 114 (35.1%) and 23 out of 114 (20.2%) exploitable sites to be vulnerable to test cases «2a»,«2b», and «2c». Presence of visitor cookies increases the attack success rate similar to other attack strategies.

It can be easily noticed from Table 3 that the results of attack strategies 2 and 3 are strongly related. There are no sites discovered to be vulnerable only to 2, and the sites vulnerable to this attack constitute a proper subset of the ones vulnerable to the third scenario. Although it does not add any item to the set of vulnerable domains, the second scenario gives remarkable indications about the nature of the validation performed. For instance, looking at the attack results reveals the possibility of a completely incorrect validation from a session association issue. A particular case in attack 2 is represented by sites that use a `state` consisting of a single character, or a sequence of N identical characters. In this scenario, the generation of a different permutation of the original string is not feasible and the attack cannot be performed as originally described. Among the samples considered, there are two sites with `state` of length one. The characters used are underscore «_» and slash «/», respectively. The site using «/» was found vulnerable to attack 3b. The attack succeeded even if «/» is substituted with a different arbitrary character. In the other site, the replacement of «_» with a random character prevented the attack from being executed successfully.

Based on above-mentioned implementation mistakes, we recommend to use a `state` value which is not guessable and is randomly produced. Moreover, it is required `state` to be in correct association with the user session in order to avoid OCSRF vulnerability.

6.4 Notable Observations

Constant `state`. The OAuth 2.0 specification clearly states that the `state` parameter must be one time use and a random string. This requirement is necessary to protect applications from brute-force attack. Some sites do not follow these instructions and include a fixed and constant `state` in the OAuth authorization request which would not change for different users and browser sessions. These websites are not able to distinguish between a legitimate authorization response created for the victim and a response forged by the attacker. We visited all candidate sites twice from two different browser sessions and compared the `state` values in order to identify this implementation problem. If the `state` remains unchanged, the site is potentially vulnerable to a "state reuse" attack. Our crawler collected and stored all authorization requests. We later extracted the `state` values from the URL and compared them to each other. The analysis disclosed 17 out of 270 (6.3%) sites reusing the same `state` values. Table 3 in the last column shows the number of discovered test cases with constant `state` parameter for each classification. 16 out of 17 (94.1%) were found vulnerable to the CSRF against `redirect-uri`. A manual analysis showed that the use of a popup-based login prevented the completion of OCSRF attack.

The presence of a constant `state` value does not provide any additional protection to the OAuth flow as a malicious user can easily assess the existence of a "state reuse" vulnerability and include the same unchanged parameter in every attack attempt. Finally, a web application was classified as not vulnerable by the crawler (Table 3, classification 7).

Popup-Based Login. Some sites open a popup window during the login process. The developed crawler correctly handles the opening of multiple browser windows, switching the control from one to the other. Selenium has the capability to check if a secondary window is opened or closed and deal with it properly.

In some cases, the usage of a popup provides unintended protection against OCSRF attack. As an instance, we discovered one application which is not exploitable. In that case, a popup window is opened when the «Login with Facebook» button is clicked. Our crawler correctly extracts the authorization response generated for the attacker. When the URL is opened within the victim's browser session, the redirection endpoint on the target site is reached. The page response contains a few lines of JavaScript in which a function of the `window.opener` object is invoked. Since the attack URL is called directly from the address bar of the victim's browser and there is no `opener` window, an error is generated and the attack would not be completed.

However, this login architecture cannot be considered as an effective OCSRF mitigation because it does not prevent the attack from being executed with other techniques. For instance, the domain with the constant `state` appears to be vulnerable to a specifically crafted attack using a POST request. When the login popup calls the JavaScript function in the main window, a script generates a POST request to an internal endpoint, providing the authorization code as a body parameter. The client subsequently continues the flow, contacting the authorization server to receive a valid access token. To bypass the error and complete the attack, it is sufficient to replicate the POST request using a form from a domain which is under the attacker's control. Therefore, popup-based logins do not always prevent our crawler from successfully performing attacks. We found evidence of several sites using this access strategy and many of them were exploited successfully using simple techniques.

6.5 Limitations

Some technologies built specifically to detect bots and crawlers and to interfere with their operation. We found evidence of several protections implemented by the sites tested to prevent automated login and browsing, such as CAPTCHA and similar human verification systems. An attack could fail due to the presence of a properly implemented OCSRF protection or because of the sporadic intervention of a bot detection system. However, this does not undermine the presented results as they indicate a notable lower bound for vulnerable sites.

The performed tests were not exempt from false positives. Our analysis revealed that marker information is sometimes present even if the login was not performed correctly. We verified all successful attacks by manual analysis in order to avoid including false positives which were mistakenly considered as successful in our automated crawler. Another source of errors in testing is the occurrence of temporary service unavailability. Even a highly available system has periods of downtime, for instance due to system failures, bad network conditions, or scheduled maintenance. We manually assessed the presence of these classification errors. For all the reasons outlined above, the sites classified as vulnerable by the crawler do not represent a comprehensive list but only a reasonably lower bound for the number the vulnerable sites in our analyzed candidate sites including high profile sites. This indicates the requirements of OCSRF countermeasures and the significance of the implementation mistakes which have been captured through our carefully designed attack strategies.

7 Mitigation

The OAuth 2.0 standard clearly states that developers must implement CSRF protection, by using a value that binds the authorization request to the browser session. For this purpose, the use of the state parameter is strongly recommended. The empirical evidence gathered in our work suggests that still today many OAuth implementations are vulnerable due to the absence of the state value (13%). Even when the parameter is correctly included inside the authorization URI, often it is not properly handled and validated (27%). Additionally, more than 5% of the applications tested reuse the same constant string.

Lack of adherence to the standard leaves a significant portion of websites using the OAuth 2.0 flow vulnerable to OCSRF attacks. Undeniably, identity providers have the responsibility to request the inclusion of suitable security measures. In Facebook Login the state parameter is not mandatory, and the flow works correctly also without it. The provided documentation does not help developers understand the importance of this security countermeasure and the absolute need to introduce it. At the time of writing, the examples provided do not mention that the parameter must be a random string. It is not specified how its value should be generated and there are no details about the validation process. The state value used in the practical examples is `"state123abc"`, which is also misleading as it does not help developers understand the need to make the parameter not guessable. The documentation provided by Facebook is not sufficient for a developer to build a working and secure login flow.

Alternative mitigations to OCSRF attacks involve the analysis of HTTP headers. Li et al. [14] proposed a technique based on the analysis of the Referer header field. Their strategy involves the introduction of an additional validation that must be performed by the relying party. When the client application receives the authorization response from the identity provider, it must analyse the Referer header. If the address contained in the field belongs to the relying party or to the identity provider domain, the authorization response is considered legitimate, otherwise it is discarded. The technique allows preventing the execution of OCSRF initiated from domains under the control of an attacker.

This mitigation was used inside a browser extension named OAuthGuard [15], a vulnerability scanner developed with the aim of providing real-time protection against common OAuth vulnerabilities to end-users. Even if this solution is technically valuable and relatively easy to implement, its real impact in protecting against the perils of OCSRF attacks is directly related to the number of users who employ it. From the perspective of a developer who is made aware of the threats associated with OCSRF attacks, focusing on generating a secure flow that involves the use of the `state` parameter represents probably still the best solution.

8 Conclusions

Our work is mainly focused on the analysis of the CSRF attack against `redirect_uri`, a well-known and documented OAuth 2.0 vulnerability. Our security assessment revealed that many actual implementations of OAuth-based SSO services are vulnerable to the considered attack. The reason behind the prevalence of this class of vulnerabilities is related to the complexity of implementing effective mitigations and to the absence of tools to reliably detect the threats. As a future work, we plan to test similar strategies also for other OCSRF attacks.

We designed a wide range of different, including novel, attack strategies, considering different possible implementation weaknesses and the state of the victim's browser at the time of the attack. Our analysis showed that several enabling factors influence the feasibility of the attack and play a major role in preventing it or increasing its chances of success, augmenting the overall risk. We inspected several under-explored aspects of the vulnerability, trying to cover different areas of interest, and to expand our knowledge and understanding about the impact of the attack in different scenarios. The large number of considered test cases helped us to discover numerous well-hidden vulnerabilities and implementation mistakes. We conducted a large-scale analysis based on the approach presented, to assess the presence of OCSRF vulnerabilities in more than 300 sites implementing the Facebook Login flow. More than a third of them were found vulnerable to at least one of the designed attack scenarios. This result demonstrates that this security threat still represents a critical problem for OAuth-based authentication systems and that it probably deserves more attention from researchers and developers.

References

1. Bai, G., et al.: Authscan: automatic extraction of web authentication protocols from implementations. In: NDSS (2013)
2. Bansal, C., Bhargavan, K., Delignat-Lavaud, A., Maffeis, S.: Discovering concrete attacks on website authorization by formal analysis 1. J. Comput. Secur. **22**(4), 601–657 (2014)
3. Barth, A., Jackson, C., Mitchell, J.C.: Robust defenses for cross-site request forgery. In: Proceedings of the 15th ACM Conference on Computer and Communications Security, pp. 75–88 (2008)
4. Calzavara, S., Focardi, R., Maffei, M., Schneidewind, C., Squarcina, M., Tempesta, M.: {WPSE}: fortifying web protocols via browser-side security monitoring. In: 27th {USENIX} Security Symposium ({USENIX} Security 2018), pp. 1493–1510 (2018)
5. Farooqi, S., Zaffar, F., Leontiadis, N., Shafiq, Z.: Measuring and mitigating oauth access token abuse by collusion networks. In: Proceedings of the 2017 Internet Measurement Conference, pp. 355–368 (2017)
6. Fett, D., Küsters, R., Schmitz, G.: SPRESSO: a secure, privacy-respecting single sign-on system for the web. In: Proceedings of the 22nd ACM SIGSAC Conference on Computer and Communications Security, pp. 1358–1369. ACM (2015)
7. Fett, D., Küsters, R., Schmitz, G.: A comprehensive formal security analysis of OAuth 2.0. In: Proceedings of the 2016 ACM SIGSAC Conference on Computer and Communications Security, pp. 1204–1215. ACM (2016)
8. HackerOne: Hackerone bug bounty platform (2020). https://www.hackerone.com/
9. Hardt, D.: The OAuth 2.0 authorization framework. RFC 6749, RFC Editor, October 2012. http://www.rfc-editor.org/rfc/rfc6749.txt. http://www.rfc-editor.org/rfc/rfc6749.txt
10. Homakov, E.: The most common OAuth2 vulnerability. His Blog at (2012)
11. Kerschbaum, F.: Simple cross-site attack prevention. In: 2007 Third International Conference on Security and Privacy in Communications Networks and the Workshops-SecureComm 2007, pp. 464–472. IEEE (2007)
12. Li, F., et al.: You've got vulnerability: exploring effective vulnerability notifications. In: 25th {USENIX} Security Symposium ({USENIX} Security 2016), pp. 1033–1050 (2016)

13. Li, W., Mitchell, C.J.: Security issues in OAuth 2.0 SSO implementations. In: Chow, S.S.M., Camenisch, J., Hui, L.C.K., Yiu, S.M. (eds.) ISC 2014. LNCS, vol. 8783, pp. 529–541. Springer, Cham (2014). https://doi.org/10.1007/978-3-319-13257-0_34
14. Li, W., Mitchell, C.J., Chen, T.: Mitigating CSRF attacks on OAuth 2.0 and OpenID connect. arXiv preprint arXiv:1801.07983 (2018)
15. Li, W., Mitchell, C.J., Chen, T.: Oauthguard: protecting user security and privacy with OAuth 2.0 and OpenID connect. In: Proceedings of the 5th ACM Workshop on Security Standardisation Research Workshop, pp. 35–44 (2019)
16. Lodderstedt, T., Bradley, L.F.: draft-ietf-oauth-security-topics-15 (2020). https://tools.ietf.org/html/draft-ietf-oauth-security-topics-15
17. Mirheidari, S.A., Arshad, S., Onarlioglu, K., Crispo, B., Kirda, E., Robertson, W.: Cached and confused: web cache deception in the wild. In: 29th {USENIX} Security Symposium ({USENIX} Security 2020), pp. 665–682 (2020)
18. Mladenov, V., Mainka, C., Schwenk, J.: On the security of modern single sign-on protocols: second-order vulnerabilities in openid connect. arXiv preprint arXiv:1508.04324 (2015)
19. OAuth.net: User authentication with OAuth 2.0 (2020). https://oauth.net/articles/authentication/. Accessed 30 July 2020
20. Pai, S., Sharma, Y., Kumar, S., Pai, R.M., Singh, S.: Formal verification of OAuth 2.0 using alloy framework. In: 2011 International Conference on Communication Systems and Network Technologies, pp. 655–659. IEEE (2011)
21. Shernan, E., Carter, H., Tian, D., Traynor, P., Butler, K.: More guidelines than rules: CSRF vulnerabilities from noncompliant OAuth 2.0 implementations. In: Almgren, M., Gulisano, V., Maggi, F. (eds.) DIMVA 2015. LNCS, vol. 9148, pp. 239–260. Springer, Cham (2015). https://doi.org/10.1007/978-3-319-20550-2_13
22. Stock, B., Pellegrino, G., Rossow, C., Johns, M., Backes, M.: Hey, you have a problem: on the feasibility of large-scale web vulnerability notification. In: 25th {USENIX} Security Symposium ({USENIX} Security 2016), pp. 1015–1032 (2016)
23. Sudhodanan, A., Carbone, R., Compagna, L., Dolgin, N., Armando, A., Morelli, U.: Large-scale analysis & detection of authentication cross-site request forgeries. In: 2017 IEEE European Symposium on Security and Privacy (EuroS&P), pp. 350–365. IEEE (2017)
24. Sumongkayothin, K., Rachtrachoo, P., Yupuech, A., Siriporn, K.: OVERSCAN: OAuth 2.0 scanner for missing parameters. In: Liu, J.K., Huang, X. (eds.) NSS 2019. LNCS, vol. 11928, pp. 221–233. Springer, Cham (2019). https://doi.org/10.1007/978-3-030-36938-5_13
25. Sun, S.T., Beznosov, K.: The devil is in the (implementation) details: an empirical analysis of OAuth SSO systems. In: Proceedings of the 2012 ACM Conference on Computer and Communications Security, pp. 378–390 (2012)
26. Lodderstedt, T.: OAuth 2.0 threat model and security considerations. RFC 6819, RFC Editor, January 2013. https://www.rfc-editor.org/rfc/rfc6819.txt. https://www.rfc-editor.org/rfc/rfc6819.txt
27. Wang, D.Y., Savage, S., Voelker, G.M.: Cloak and dagger: dynamics of web search cloaking. In: Proceedings of the 18th ACM Conference on Computer and Communications Security, pp. 477–490 (2011)
28. Wang, R., Chen, S., Wang, X.: Signing me onto your accounts through facebook and google: a traffic-guided security study of commercially deployed single-sign-on web services. In: 2012 IEEE Symposium on Security and Privacy, pp. 365–379. IEEE (2012)

29. Wang, R., Zhou, Y., Chen, S., Qadeer, S., Evans, D., Gurevich, Y.: Explicating SDKS: uncovering assumptions underlying secure authentication and authorization. In: 22nd {USENIX} Security Symposium ({USENIX} Security 2013), pp. 399–314 (2013)
30. Yang, R., Li, G., Lau, W.C., Zhang, K., Hu, P.: Model-based security testing: an empirical study on OAuth 2.0 implementations. In: Proceedings of the 11th ACM on Asia Conference on Computer and Communications Security, pp. 651–662 (2016)
31. Zhou, Y., Evans, D.: SSOScan: automated testing of web applications for single sign-on vulnerabilities. In: 23rd {USENIX} Security Symposium ({USENIX} Security 2014), pp. 495–510 (2014)

Detecting and Measuring In-The-Wild DRDoS Attacks at IXPs

Karthika Subramani[1(✉)], Roberto Perdisci[1,2], and Maria Konte[2]

[1] University of Georgia, Athens, USA
{ks54471,perdisci}@uga.edu
[2] Georgia Institute of Technology, Atlanta, USA
mkonte@gatech.edu

Abstract. Distributed reflective denial of service (DRDoS) attacks are a popular choice among adversaries. In fact, one of the largest DDoS attacks ever recorded, reaching a peak of 1.3 Tbps against GitHub, was a memcached-based DRDoS attack. More recently, a record-breaking 2.3 Tbps attack against Amazon AWS was due to a CLDAP-based DRDoS attack. Although reflective attacks have been known for years, DRDoS attacks are unfortunately still popular and largely unmitigated.

In this paper, we measure in-the-wild DRDoS attacks as observed from a large Internet exchange point (IXP) and provide a number of security-relevant insights. To enable our measurements, we first developed IXmon, an open-source DRDoS detection system specifically designed for deployment at large IXP-like network connectivity providers and peering hubs. We deployed IXmon at Southern Crossroads (SoX), an IXP-like hub that provides both peering and upstream Internet connectivity services to more than 20 research and education (R&E) networks in the South-East United States. In a period of about 21 months, IXmon detected more than 900 DRDoS attacks towards 31 different victim ASes. An analysis of the real-world DRDoS attacks detected by our system shows that most DRDoS attacks are short lived, lasting only a few minutes, but that large-volume, long-lasting, and highly-distributed attacks against R&E networks are not uncommon. We then use the results of our analysis to discuss possible attack mitigation approaches that can be deployed at the IXP level, before the attack traffic overwhelms the victim's network bandwidth.

Keywords: DDoS attack · DRDoS attack · IXP · Traffic analysis

1 Introduction

Large-scale distributed denial of service (DDoS) attacks pose an imminent threat to the availability of critical Internet-based operations [35], and have become part of sophisticated cyber-warfare arsenals [52]. DDoS attacks can take many different forms [43], and leverage weaknesses that span from the application-layer to the physical-layer. In particular, recent incidents have demonstrated that *bandwidth exhaustion* DDoS attacks are capable of bringing down even the most well-provisioned Internet services, such as highly popular websites (e.g., Twitter, Netflix, etc.) and cybersecurity services [27,39,49,67]. Among bandwidth exhaustion

L. Bilge et al. (Eds.): DIMVA 2021, LNCS 12756, pp. 42–67, 2021.
https://doi.org/10.1007/978-3-030-80825-9_3

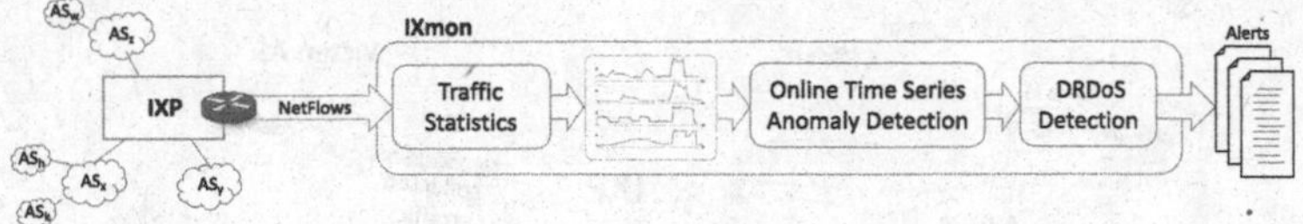

Fig. 1. IXmon system overview

attacks, distributed reflective denial of service (DRDoS) attacks are a popular choice among adversaries [44]. In fact, one of the largest DDoS attacks ever recorded, reaching a peak of 1.3 Tbps against GitHub, was a memcached-based DRDoS attack [20]. More recently, a record-breaking 2.3 Tbps attack against Amazon AWS was due to a CLDAP-based DRDoS attack [51] and attackers have started exploiting Microsoft's RDP for DDoS attacks [63].

Although reflective attacks have been known for years [54] and could be mitigated in part by filtering/throttling traffic to/from some UDP services (e.g., filtering memcached traffic at the edge of a network [23]), DRDoS attacks are unfortunately still popular [33] and largely unmitigated. At the same time, while some information about DRDoS attacks can be found in blog posts or white papers from security vendors (e.g., [22]), there is a lack of systematic studies that provide an in-depth measurement of the properties of *in-the-wild* DRDoS attacks, such as occurrence frequency, the distribution of their sources, duration, volume, targets, and what mitigation steps could be applied to combat them.

In this paper, we aim to partly fill this gap by measuring real-world DRDoS attacks as observed from a large Internet exchange point (IXP)[1]. IXPs are high-density peering and connectivity hubs that provide infrastructure used by autonomous systems (ASes) to interconnect with each other (e.g., public or private peering and other connectivity agreements). Because IXPs provide an increasingly large portion of the global Internet infrastructure used by ASes to exchange traffic, they can play a key role in detecting and mitigating DDoS attacks.

To enable our measurements, we first develop IXmon, an open-source DRDoS detection system specifically designed for deployment at large IXP-like network connectivity providers and peering hubs. While there exists several DDoS detection and mitigation solutions, such as *traffic scrubbing* services [12,21], these are typically expensive third-party commercial services. In addition, they are not designed for detecting DRDoS attacks at IXPs, and are instead more focused on inline DDoS traffic detection and traffic filtering. On the other hand, our IXmon system is fully open-source[2], can be deployed at large IXPs, and can also be used to enable IXP-based DDoS mitigations. IXmon's goal is not only to detect the occurrence of a DRDoS attack very early after its inception, but also to identify ASes that host the reflectors used in the attack. This capability could be used

[1] Whereas others may define IXPs purely as facilitating public peering, we refer to IXPs more broadly as hubs that facilitate both peering and commercial connectivity (e.g., transit) services.

[2] https://github.com/perdisci/IXmon.

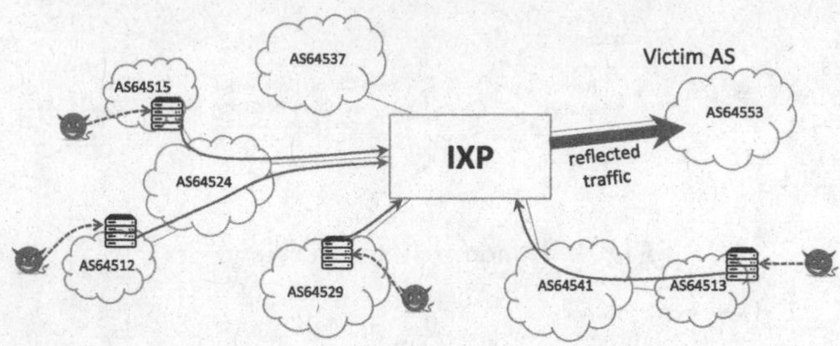

Fig. 2. Example of reflection attack traffic flowing through an IXP

to enable filtering of DRDoS attack traffic at IXP level before it is routed to the victim, thus preventing the victim's network bandwidth from being exhausted.

Figure 1 provides an overview of our IXmon system, whereas Fig. 2 shows an example of how reflected traffic belonging to a DRDoS attack may traverse an IXP's fabric to reach the victim network. To detect DRDoS attacks, IXmon takes in input network flow summaries (e.g., using Cisco's NetFlow v9 format [19]), which report flow statistics for all traffic from any source IP to a any destination IP that crosses the IXP. Because IXmon aims to detect DRDoS attacks, we focus on UDP flows whose source port is associated with services that can be abused for amplification attacks, such as *DNS*, *NTP*, *memcached*, *CLDAP*, etc. [54] (see Sect. 3 for a complete list). Given a specific service (e.g., *memcached*), we then aggregate all related UDP flows directed to each destination AS and compute the overall traffic volume of all flows belonging to the same (service, dstAS) pair. We update these aggregate flow statistics in an online fashion at regular (small) time intervals, and perform online time series anomaly detection to detect highly anomalous increases in traffic volume. Finally, every time an anomalous traffic volume increase is detected for a (service, dstAS) pair, we pass this information to the DRDoS detection module, which applies additional checks to filter out possible false positives and only issue an alert for events that are highly likely associated with actual DRDoS attacks. Additionally, the DRDoS detection module identifies the source ASes involved in an attack, and ranks them according to the attack traffic volume they contribute. By knowing the UDP source port number, the destination AS (i.e., the victim network), and the source ASes that contribute the highest amount of attack traffic, an IXP could then deploy traffic filtering rules to mitigate the attack in its very early stages. In fact, this filtering rule deployment process could be automated by automatically deriving BGPFlowSpec rules [1] from IXmon's alerts.

Notice that while time-series analysis has been previously used in other contexts to detect DDoS attacks and other network traffic anomalies [10,40,62], the contributions of our approach stems from adapting previous approaches to modeling IXP-level traffic and to measuring in-the-wild DDoS attacks at a real-world IXP.

We have deployed IXmon at Southern Crossroads (SoX) [60], an IXP-like hub that provides both peering and upstream Internet connectivity services to more than 20 research and education (R&E) networks in the South-East United States. In a period of about 21 months, IXmon detected more than 900 DRDoS attacks towards 31 different victim ASes. In Sect. 4, we study the characteristics of these attacks and present a number of insights regarding their duration and intensity, what services are most abused, what networks are more often targeted, and whether the victim networks took action to mitigate the attacks.

In summary, we make the following contributions:

- To measure in-the-wild DDoS attacks, we develop IXmon, an open-source DRDoS detection system (available after publication) specifically designed to be deployed at large IXP-like peering and connectivity hubs.
- We deploy IXmon at a large IXP-like R&E peering and connectivity hub located in the South-East United Sates for a period of about 21 months, where we detected a large number and variety of real-world DRDoS attacks in near real time.
- We analyze the real-world DRDoS attacks detected by our system and report a number of security-relevant measurements and insights. For instance, we show that most DRDoS attacks are short lived, lasting only a few minutes, but that large-volume, long-lasting, and highly-distributed attacks against R&E networks are not uncommon.

2 Background on IXPs

IXPs have been traditionally established as infrastructures that primarily offer peering services. The primary role of an IXP is to serve as a physical exchange point to facilitate the exchange of Internet traffic between different autonomous systems (ASes). The minimum number of ASes that interconnect at an IXP should be at least three and there must be a clear and open policy for other ASes to join [4]. The ASes interconnect through a shared switching fabric that the IXPs offer. This interconnection infrastructure can vary widely in complexity. Some infrastructures can be very simple and minimal (as a single switch), or very complex (as a large scale distributed infrastructure that includes remote peering) [45].

Since their initial establishment, the role of IXPs has been evolving along with their offered services. Some services are offered as free value-added services and others are paid services. Many IXPs offer both public peering and private peering, multi-lateral and bi-lateral peering, data center services, multiple network management and other services including route servers, SDN-based network management, traffic engineering, and traffic blackholing.

IXPs have been recently further evolving towards becoming major peering and connectivity hubs, claiming a central role as part of the Internet's core infrastructures [11,16,53]. There are currently hundreds of IXPs worldwide, with more than 200 just in Europe [3]. IXP membership and traffic growth show their dynamic and evolving role in the Internet ecosystem. Some of the largest IXPs have several hundreds members, while they carry as much traffic as some of the largest global Tier-1 ISPs [3]. It should also be noted that IXPs may serve different roles in different regions of the world. For example, there exist significant differences between traditional European IXP models and US-based IXPs [9]. In addition, non-profit, EDU-oriented IXPs such as SoX [60] exist with the purpose of helping EDU networks interconnect directly with each other (as in typical IXP peering) but also connect with upstream providers (i.e., providing an exchange point for access to upstream services). In this work, we refer to IXPs in this latter broader sense, as exchange points in which multiple ASes peer with each other and can also connect to upstream Internet connectivity services.

3 IXmon System

In this section, we describe how IXmon's components work, following the high-level overview shown in Fig. 1. It worth noting that IXmon relies on time-series analysis as a component of our detection pipeline. While time-series analysis been previously used in other contexts to detect DDoS attacks and other network traffic anomalies [10,40,62], the contributions of our approach stems from adapting previous approaches to modeling IXP-level traffic and to measuring in-the-wild DDoS attacks at a real-world IXP, as explained below.

Approach Overview: IXmon is designed to detect DRDoS attacks in near *real time* (e.g., with a delay of only one minute) in IXP-like network environments. Given the traffic towards a specific AS, A, to detect DRDoS attacks against A we look for the following factors:

1. Focus on traffic coming from a UDP source port typically associated with a service that can be abused for attack amplification.
2. For each of those source ports, has the traffic volume towards A increased in a highly anomalous way?
3. Is the anomalous traffic distributed across several contributing source ASes?

As an example, assume that a destination AS A usually receives very low amounts of traffic from source port UDP 123, which is typically associated with the NTP service. We monitor all traffic from port UDP 123 that flows towards A through IXP's fabric. All of a sudden, at time t we detect a spike in incoming NTP traffic, and notice that several different source AS numbers are contributing in a coordinated way to this traffic spike. This scenario meets the "recipe" for a DRDoS attack, which IXmon aims to detect automatically. Next, we explain how we translate the above high-level approach into a concrete DRDoS detection system.

3.1 Aggregate Traffic Statistics

IXmon is designed to monitor network traffic at large real-world IXP-like peering and connectivity hubs. Due to the sheer amount of traffic observed from such a vantage point, efficiency is a high priority goal. In particular, memory consumption is a main concern, given the large amount of network traffic statistics that we need to track over all possible targets and sources of DRDoS attacks visible from an IXP. To this end, our first step is to condense detailed information about network flows crossing the IXP into *traffic sketches* containing aggregated traffic statistics.

IXmon receives network flow statistics as input. While our current implementation supports and has been tested only on Cisco NetFlow versions 9 and 10 [18], it is designed to also support other formats, including sFlow [48]. For simplicity, in the following we will simply use the term *flow* to refer to a network flow in NetFlow format. While NetFlow flows include many details about how the related network packets traversed the IXP (e.g., including the network interfaces involved in routing the flow), we will only refer to the properties that are used by our system. Let the tuple

$$f_i = (srcIP_i, srcPort_i, dstIP_i, dstPort_i, protocol_i, packets_i, bytes_i) \quad (1)$$

represent a network flow, where $packets_i$ and $bytes_i$ represent the number of packets and overall number of bytes sent from the source to the destination IPs/ports that have been "captured" by flow f_i.

The IXP collects all flows crossing its infrastructure by implementing a uniform packet sampling policy to reduce load on its routers and sends them to IXmon in a *stream* (flows are sent out when they are closed by a FIN packet, in case of TCP, or after a configurable timeout managed by the IXP operators). IXmon mines this stream of traffic flows to detect DRDoS attacks in near real time. Given our focus on DRDoS attacks, we keep only flows whose protocol is UDP and whose source port is related to a service that is known to be vulnerable to be used for attack amplification. The set of source port numbers and related UDP services we use in our current configuration of IXmon is inspired by previous work [54, 66] and listed in Table 1.

Table 1. List of monitored UDP source ports

Service	Port	Bandwidth amplification factor
DNS	53	28 to 54
NTP	123	556.9
CLDAP	389	56 to 70
CharGen	19	358.8
Memcached	11211	10,000 to 51,000
SunRPC	111	7 to 28
SSDP	1900	30.8
SNMP	161	6.3
SRCDS	27005	–
Call of Duty	20800	–
NETBIOS	137	3.8
RIP	520	131.24
Quake	27960	63.9
Steam	29015	5.5
QOTD	17	140.3

To analyze the continuous large stream of UDP flows received by IXmon, we proceed as follows. First, IXmon partitions time into intervals of fixed length Δt (one minute, in our experiments). Given the set of all flows received during an interval Δt, we map *srcIP* and *dstIP* to their respective AS numbers, *srcAS* and *dstAS* (e.g., using RouteViews data [7]). This gives us flows:

$$F_i(t) = (srcAS_i, srcPort_i, dstAS_i, dstPort_i, packets_i(t), bytes_i(t)) \quad (2)$$

where t indicates the start of a time interval Δt, *protocol* is omitted since it is constant (always UDP), and the packets and bytes counts vary in time while the other flow parameters are fixed for a given subscript index. Then, given a time interval Δt, we aggregate all flows $F_i(t)$ that share the same source port and destination AS numbers, and sum up all of their bytes. More formally, we obtain aggregate *sketch* flows of this form:

$$A_k(t) = (srcPort_k, dstAS_k, bytes_k(t)) \tag{3}$$

where $bytes_k(t)$ is the sum of the byte counts contributed by all flows aggregated into $A_k(t)$.

Notice that, given a fixed pair of source port, $srcPort_k$, and destination AS, $dstAS_k$, the AS-level flows $A_k(t)$ give us a time series of total traffic volume (i.e., $bytes_k(t)$) flowing through the IXP that originated from $srcPort_k$ (from any source IP) and destined towards $dstAS_k$ (to any destination IP belonging to that AS and any destination UDP port). Also, while not represented in the above *sketch*, for simplicity, we keep track of the contribution (in terms of total bytes) to flow $A_k(t)$ of each $srcAS_i$ whose traffic is aggregated into the sketch.

3.2 Online Time Series Anomaly Detection

Given a stream of flow sketches $A_k(t)$ related to a $(srcPort_k, dstAS_k)$ pair, we detect anomalous increases in traffic volume by performing an online analysis of the time series represented by $bytes_k(t)$. Specifically, we maintain a time series model consisting of an exponentially-weighted moving average and variance [29], as follows:

$$\mu(t) = \alpha \cdot \mu(t-1) + (1-\alpha) \cdot b(t) \tag{4}$$

$$\sigma^2(t) = (1-\alpha) \cdot (\sigma^2(t) + \alpha \cdot (b(t) - \mu(t-1))^2) \tag{5}$$

where α is a constant and where we omitted the subscript k and used $b(t)$ in place of $bytes_k(t)$, for brevity. Then, given the moving average, $\mu_k(t)$, and variance $\sigma_k^2(t)$ computed at time t for $A_k(t)$, we compute an anomaly (or *deviation*) score as:

$$\delta_k(t) = \max\left(0, \frac{b_k(t) - (\mu_k(t) + \theta \cdot \sigma_k(t))}{b_k(t) + \varepsilon}\right) \tag{6}$$

where θ is a tunable parameter (set to 3 in our experiments) and ε is a small constant (e.g., 10^{-6}) that is only needed to avoid division by zero. Essentially, $\delta_k(t)$ tells us how much $b_k(t)$ deviates (on the positive side) from the moving average plus a tolerance factor proportional to the standard deviation. Notice that $\delta_k(t) \in [0,1]$, which we use as an anomaly score. The larger $\delta_k(t)$, the more strongly the current reading of A_k's traffic volume, $b_k(t)$, deviates from the expected value plus some tolerance that takes natural variations into account. If $\delta_k(t) > \tau$, where τ is a tunable detection threshold (set to 0.5 in our experiments), we say that the current reading of the traffic volume for the flows aggregated by A_k is anomalous.

Notice that anomalies can be detected in real time, enabling a rapid detection (and a potential automated mitigation) of DRDoS attacks.

Additional Details: At every new time interval, we use Eqs. 4 and 5 to update our time series model. However, once an anomaly is detected, we stop updating the model until the new traffic volume measurements go back to pre-anomaly levels. More formally, assume t_d is the first time in which an anomaly is detected, we do *not* use the new measurement at time t_d to compute $\mu(t_d+1)$ and $\sigma^2(t_d+1)$. Now, let

$$\delta_k(t+n,t) = \max\left(0, \frac{b_k(t+n) - (\mu_k(t) + \theta \cdot \sigma_k(t))}{b_k(t+n) + \varepsilon}\right) \tag{7}$$

and $t_d = t+1$. In other words, at the time when the anomaly is detected, $n = 1$. At the next time slot, $n = 2$, we compare the latest measurement of the traffic volume $b_k(t+n)$ to the time series model that was last updated at time t. If $\delta_k(t+n,t) > \tau$ this means that the anomalous traffic is still present at time $t+n$, and we continue to keep the same model computed at time t. Let us now assume that at $n = m$ the anomalous levels of traffic revert back to normal. Namely, $\delta_k(t+m,t) \leq \tau$. Then, we use $b_k(t+m)$ to update the values of μ_k and σ_k and keep updating the model at the following time intervals, until another anomaly is identified.

This approach of updating the average and standard deviation only during "normal times" allows us to more easily determine when a traffic volume anomaly, which may represent a DRDoS attack, starts and ends. Specifically, in the example above we can determine that the anomaly started at time $t+1$ and ended at time $t+m$.

3.3 Attack Detection

Let $A_k(t)$ be a traffic sketch time series, and assume that t_d is the time interval in which a time series anomaly has been detected using the approach described in Sect. 3.2. To detect DRDoS attacks in real time while filtering out possible traffic volume anomalies unrelated to reflection attacks, we introduce two additional conditions:

- *Minimum traffic volume*: Given the last aggregate traffic volume measurement, $b_k(t_d)$, we discard the detected anomaly if $b_k(t_d) < \nu$ (in our experiments we set ν to 5 Mbps). The reason is that if the aggregate traffic volume is very low, either the anomaly is not caused by an attack, or the effects of the attack on the target AS's bandwidth are negligible and can be ignored.
- *Source AS volume entropy*: Since we focus on DRDoS attacks, we expect the anomalous traffic volume increase to be distributed across multiple reflectors located in different source ASes.

To compute the source AS volume entropy, we first consider the set of source ASes whose traffic is aggregated into A_k, and take into account the overall number of bytes sent from each of this sources ASes to A_k's destination AS (i.e., the potential victim network). Let $S_k(t_d) = \{s_1, s_2, \ldots, s_n\}$ represents the set of traffic volume amounts contributed by each source AS at time t_d. We then normalize each element in the set as $s'_i = \frac{s_i}{\sum_{j=1}^{n} s_j}$. Finally, we treat s'_i as the probability of "observing" the i-th source AS as contributor to A_k's aggregate traffic, and compute the entropy $\mathcal{H}(S'_k(t_d))$ of the set $S'_k(t_d) = \{s'_1, s'_2, \ldots, s'_n\}$. If $\mathcal{H}(S'_k(t_d)) = 1$, it means that the traffic from port $srcPort_k$ to $dstAS_k$ is evenly distributed across the contributing source ASes. On the other hand, low values of $\mathcal{H}(S'_k(t_d))$ mean that most of the traffic is contributed by only one (or very few) source ASes. Therefore, we set a threshold h so that traffic volume anomalies are labeled as DRDoS attacks only when $\mathcal{H}(S'_k(t_d)) > h$ (in our experiments, we use $h = 0.4$).

All time series anomalies detected based on the algorithm described in Sect. 3.2 that also meet the two above conditions are labeled as DRDoS attacks. Correspondingly, a DRDoS attack alert is issued, which contains all details of the attack as measured at time t_d, including the destination AS number, source port, current aggregate attack volume, and distribution of traffic amounts from the contributing source ASes. A new alert is issued for every new time interval $t_d + n$ for which the attack is sustained, allowing a network operator to identify whether the attack is still ongoing or has terminated (when no new alert is issued). On the other hand, time series anomalies that do not pass the checks discussed above are logged and can be sent to network operators but are not labeled as DRDoS attacks.

4 Analysis of In-the-Wild Attacks

In this section we provide some background information about SoX, describe how we setup and deployed IXmon at SoX, and present our measurements and analysis of the in-the-wild DRDoS attacks we detected during our deployment period. SoX's customer ASes rely on the IXP's infrastructure for both peering with each other and upstream connectivity. Therefore, SoX provided us with an important vantage point for measuring DRDoS attacks.

Notice that because sizable ground truth datasets of IXP traffic with labeled DRDoS attacks are very difficult to come by (we are not aware of any publicly available dataset of this kind), to tune IXmon's detection parameters we rely on domain knowledge and a manual analysis of IXmon's logs during the preliminary phases of our deployment. In addition, during our preliminary deployment phase we also contacted SoX and its participants to verify some of the attacks detected by IXmon, and we received positive confirmation from network operators that in fact the victim network identified by IXmon was under attack at the time when the alerts were issued. In practice, to tune our systems' detection parameters we take a conservative approach that favors minimizing possible false detections (see Sect. 4.1). While this may cause us to miss some smaller (i.e., lower volume and duration), more subtle DRDoS attacks, these attacks are unlikely to have a significant impact on their target networks.

One possible valuable alternative to enable gathering more ground truth could be to correlate our findings with traffic from DRDoS honeypots [38,64]. At the same time, concurrent work has found that the intersection between attacks observed at IXPs and attacks observed from DRDoS honeypots may be limited [37]. We plan to investigate the overlap between attacks detected by IXmon and DRDoS honeypots in followup work.

In the following analysis we anonymize all AS numbers related to autonomous systems involved in the detected DRDoS attacks, as some of this information may be sensitive (e.g., some of SoX's members may not want to publicly disclose how many attacks their network received and if/how they mitigated them). For instance, we replace AS 10490 with a consistent but randomly chosen identifier of the form "Anon.XXX" (where XXX is a positive integer).

4.1 IXmon Implementation and Setup

We implemented IXmon's flow parsing and traffic aggregation modules in C++, leveraging an open-source tools named FastNetMon [47]. FastNetMon is a DDoS detection system mainly geared towards enterprise networks or single ASes. Its detection approach is not designed to detect and track DRDoS attacks related to many possible large networks and involving large numbers of source and destination ASes, making it unusable for our purposes. For instance, we found that in FastNetMon one would need to explicitly specify all subnets that should be considered as DRDoS attack targets, and that attack detection is done per IP address. In an IXP environment in which many large ASes are the potential targets, in which there can be many sources of attack, and in which we are interested in tracking if the IXP customers are either victims or potentially contributors to DRDoS attacks, we found that FastNetMon would use an exceedingly large amount of resources. Therefore, while we leveraged and adapted the NetFlow parsing module of FastNetMon, we designed and implemented our own open-source IXP-focused online time series anomaly detection and DRDoS detection algorithms using Python. Our IXmon system code can be found on GitHub[3].

As explained in Sect. 3, the mining and aggregation of the NetFlow traffic, which are implemented in C++, allow IXmon to be scalable and process large volumes of traffic typically observed at IXPs (in the order of hundreds of Gbps). During our experiments, IXmon has had no issue keeping up with the large traffic volumes received from SoX, thanks to the use of efficient flow aggregation.

IXmon's online anomaly detection and DRDoS detection algorithms include a few tunable parameters (see Sect. 3). As mentioned earlier, to set our systems' parameters we take a conservative approach that favors minimizing possible false detections. We set the length of the time interval for traffic aggregation $\Delta t = 1$ minute. This interval is long enough to accumulate sufficient aggregate data from the stream of flows related to each $(srcPort_k, dstAS_k)$ pair and to compute meaningful traffic sketches, and at the same time it enables *near real-time* DRDoS detection. Specifically, after traffic sketches are computed they are immediately analyzed and an alert is triggered immediately as attacks are detected in the data stream.

In Eq. 6, we set the parameter $\theta = 3$. Essentially, θ controls how much the traffic volume can deviate from the mean, before an anomaly is detected. The value of $\theta = 3$ is quite conservative, and is inspired by the fact that for Gaussian distributions $Pr(\mu - 3\sigma \leq X \leq \mu + 3\sigma) \approx 99.73\%$. In addition, we set the anomaly

[3] https://github.com/perdisci/IXmon.

detection threshold $\tau = 0.5$. In other words, we tune the system to detect large anomalies, as compared to historic traffic volumes modeled by moving average and standard deviations. While this may cause us to miss small (i.e., low volume) attacks, it makes sure that the anomalies we detect are in fact highly likely related to attacks. This is further reinforced by additional constraints explained in Sect. 3.3.

As for the parameters defined in Sect. 3.3, we set $\nu = 5$ Mbps because DRDoS attacks whose peak traffic is lower are unlikely to cause much disruption to institutional networks (such networks typically have Internet connectivity bandwidth ranging from hundreds of Mbps to tens of Gbps). Finally we set the source AS entropy threshold $h = 0.4$. We tuned this threshold based on a data collected during a preliminary deployment of IXmon, and is meant to capture attacks whose traffic is fairly distributed across multiple sources, rather than all coming mostly from one single source AS.

An additional "operational" parameter is related to the packet sampling rate used by the network operator that provides the raw flows. In IXmon, we take the sampling rate into account, and adjust our traffic measurements accordingly (e.g., we adjust the average traffic volume measured per minute of observation).

4.2 Data Collection at SoX

As mentioned earlier, we deployed IXmon at a large IXP called SoX (AS 10490) that provides peering and Internet connectivity services to several research and education networks. Specifically, we deployed IXmon at one of two routers operated by SoX that enables peering among educational networks and upstream connectivity to Internet2 [5]. This provided us with visibility on most of the traffic crossing the SoX infrastructure (though not all).

Based on public data on AS-to-AS relationships provided by CAIDA [14,41], SoX has more than 20 direct customer networks (also called the IXP *members* or *participants*), peers with 9 other large ASes, and is connected to 5 upstream providers. Furthermore, SoX serves as upstream provider for a variety of smaller ASes that are reachable through it from the rest of the Internet. This study is based on data collected between *April,2018 - April,2020* (due to interruptions due to operational reasons, our traffic monitoring was only active during part of this time period). Overall, we collected traffic information for 634 days. During this period, the source/destination traffic crossing the IXP's fiber was related to a total of *5212* different autonomous systems.

4.3 Attack Measurements and Analysis

In this section, we present an analysis of the DRDoS attacks detected by IXmon to understand their behavior and gain insights that could prove useful for mitigating future attacks. As an example of the attacks that are included in the analysis provided below, Fig. 3 shows a snapshot of two different DRDoS attacks detected by IXmon. Notice that IXmon detected the represented attacks in near real-time (within about one minute from the attack inception). However, the plots in Fig. 3

are formed post-detection stage by combining consecutive attack alerts, and are shown here to visualize the intensity and duration of the attacks as a whole. The x axis shows the time window within which the attack occurred (including a duration of 30 min prior to and after the attack), whereas the y axis shows the volume of traffic contributed by each source AS involved in the attack (the graph is limited to the top 10 source ASes by volume). Each line in the graph represents the traffic sent to the victim AS from a single source AS. For instance, Fig. 3a (top) shows a DRDoS attack that leverages the CLDAP service (source port 389) directed towards AS Anon.2371. The aggregate traffic for the attack, which sums the contribution of all source ASes that sent traffic to AS Anon.2371 from UDP port 389 reached a peak of ≈210 Mbps. It is interesting to notice that before and after the attack there was little or no traffic sent by those source ASes to the destination AS from port 389. Then, all of a sudden all the source ASes start sending high volumes of traffic in a coordinated way, which is a telltale sign of an ongoing DRDoS attack. After all, inter-AS CLDAP use is rarely needed or justified, and it is therefore natural to have very low or no inter-AS CLDAP traffic outside of DRDoS attacks. In addition, having many source ASes sending CLDAP traffic to a common destination AS would be quite a big coincidence for this to be explained by normal activities.

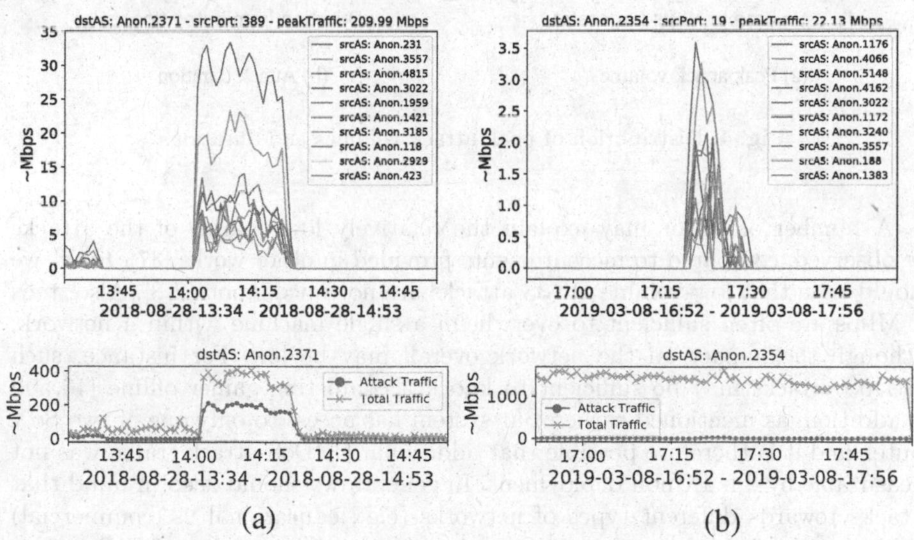

Fig. 3. Two examples of DRDoS attacks detected by IXmon. The top figures show the attack traffic contributed by the top 10 source ASes, while the bottom figures show the overall attack traffic volume compared to all traffic (TCP and UDP) flowing towards the destination AS. Notice also that while these figures span a large time window, IXmon detected the attacks in near real-time.

Volume and Duration. While large DDoS attacks have caught the attention of bloggers and news media, there is limited publicly available data on the overall distribution and characteristics of in-the-wild DRDoS attacks (some information can be found in a 2017 blog post by Cloudflare [22]).

To better understand in-the-wild DRDoS attacks, we analyze the characteristics of all attacks detected by IXmon. Specifically, during our deployment period IXmon detected 987 attacks. We use this large number of attacks to measure the distribution of the volume and duration of in-the-wild DRDoS attacks, which are reported in Figs. 4a and 4b. It can be seen that most of the observed attacks ($\approx$ 80%) have a duration of less than 10 min, whereas the median peak attack volume is less than 20 Mbps. Overall, only $\approx$ 8% of the attacks reach a peak volume of more than 100 Mbps with a few attacks reaching peaks above 1 Gbps (the highest attack volume we observed was *1.5 Gbps*).

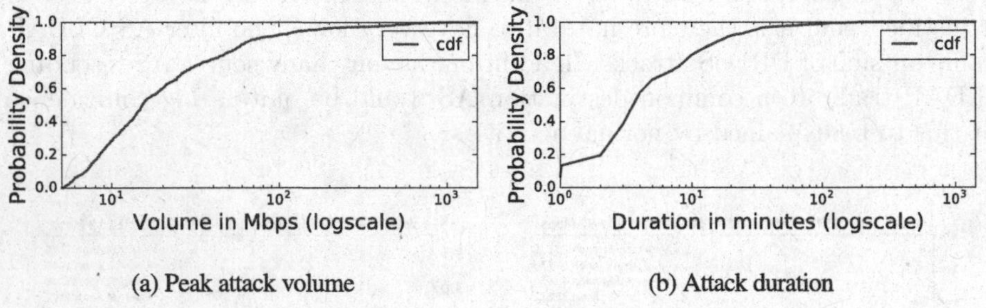

(a) Peak attack volume

(b) Attack duration

Fig. 4. Distribution of peak attack volumes and durations

A number of factor may explain the relatively low volume of the attacks we observed, compared to measurements provided in other works [37]. First, we should note that low-volume DDoS attacks are not uncommon [2,8]. Also, tens of Mbps are often sufficient to overwhelm a single machine within a network, although the impact on the network overall may be low. For instance, such DRDoS attacks may be sufficient to knock a competing gamer offline [46,50]. In addition, as mentioned earlier, our system has access to only one of two SoX router and it is therefore possible that additional DRDoS attack traffic was not measurable by our IXmon deployment. In general, we should keep in mind that attacks towards different types of networks (e.g., educational vs. commercial) and measured from different vantage points (e.g., different types of IXPs), may present different characteristics.

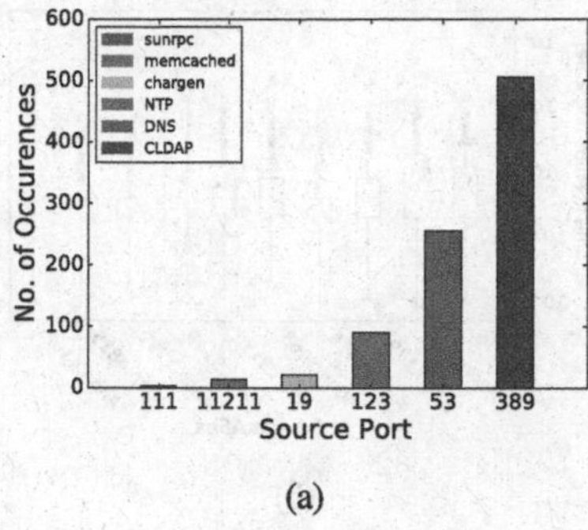

(a)

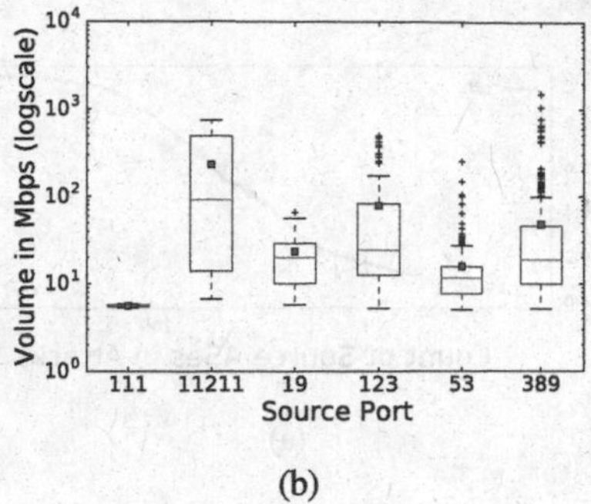

(b)

Fig. 5. (a) Number of attack instances per (reflection) source port (b) Distribution of attack volume per (reflection) source port

Services Abused for Attack Amplification. IXmon monitors traffic from the UDP ports listed in Table 1. However, only some of these ports were used in DRDoS attacks visible from SoX. Figure 5a shows the distribution of source ports (ab)used for reflecting traffic against DRDoS victims, with the y axis showing the number of attacks in which a given port was used. As can be seen, CLDAP (port 389) appears to be the most abused service for attack amplification, followed by DNS (port 53) and NTP (port 123). Figure 5b reports a boxplot showing the distribution of peak attack volume per port (the red line represents the median, while the red square shows the average value). This shows that some CLDAP-based attacks reached peak volumes above 1 Gbps.

Multi-vector Attacks. DRDoS attacks can be launched by abusing more than one UDP service at a time. Currently, IXmon separately tracks traffic from a given source port and detects DRDoS attacks independently for each abused service. However, attackers can abuse multiple services at the same to increase the number of reflectors to be aimed against the victim and thus further amplify the attack bandwidth. To analyze these attacks in our alerts dataset, we can retrieve DRDoS attacks related to individual source ports that have a common destination AS and that overlap in time. By doing so, we found 36 multi-vector attack instances (out of 987) involving up to 4 different source ports simultaneously.

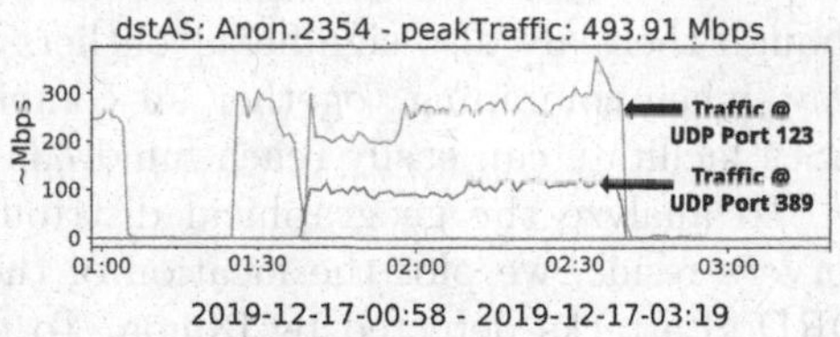

Fig. 6. Example of a multi-vector attack

Figure 6 shows an example of attack detected by IXmon that simultaneously leverages NTP (port 123) and CLDAP (port 389) to reflect the attack traffic towards AS Anon.2354. A coordinated surge in traffic volume can be seen from both source ports, clearly indicating a multi-vector attack.

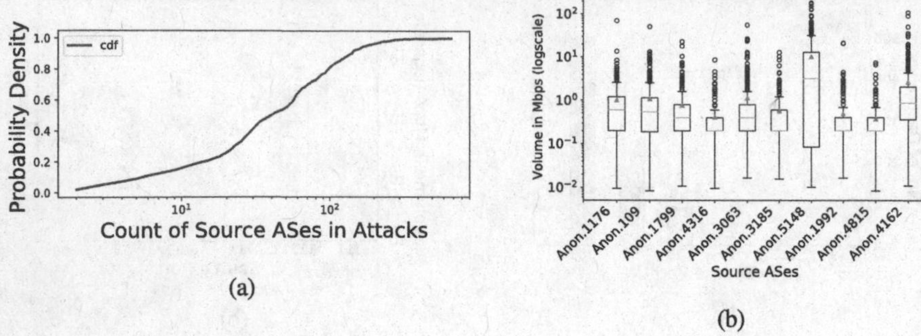

Fig. 7. (a) Distribution of number of source ASes involved in attacks (b) Distribution of peak traffic volume contributed by the top 10 Source ASes in Attacks

Distribution of Reflectors. DRDoS attacks are executed by exploiting a (at times large) number of publicly reachable reflection servers. In this section, we analyze where reflected attack traffic originates from. Figure 7a shows the distribution of the number of different source ASes that contribute to each attack (notice that, due to packet sampling, reflectors that only contribute very low amounts of traffic may not be visible in our data). The median is 40, indicating that at least half of all attacks are highly distributed across many different source networks that are themselves abused to reflect and amplify attack traffic. In Fig. 7b we show the distribution of peak traffic contributed to different attacks by the top 10 source ASes (ranked based on the number of DRDoS attacks each source AS participates to). As can be seen, the median (red line) peak volume for reflected traffic from each AS is relatively limited, typically around ≈ 1 Mbps, though there are also significant outliers with high peak traffic volumes. Either way, when combining together all contributing source ASes the attacks these ASes facilitate can easily reach hundreds of Mbps.

To analyze the geographical distribution of the networks where reflection servers reside, we plot the location of the source ASes that contributed to the DRDoS attacks detected by IXmon. To map the geolocation of a given AS we first obtain the prefixes owned by the AS, based on BGP traffic from the day before the AS participated in an attack. Next, we select a random IP address belonging to one of the prefixes and map the IP address to its geolocation via a IP geolocation API [6]. While this is only an approximate method for determining the geolocation of an AS (some AS numbers span multiple regions), it gives an idea of how geographically distributed the reflectors typically are.

As an example, Fig. 8 shows the geolocation of both destination ASes (i.e., the victims) and source ASes (i.e., the networks that host the servers abused for reflection and amplification) related to NTP-based attacks detected by IXmon. Naturally, given the fact that SoX serves as a peering hub for research and education networks in the South-East USA, the destination ASes are clustered in that region. It is easy to see that the sources of NTP traffic are distributed widely across the world. This is evidently anomalous, in that in normal (i.e., non-attack) cases the vast majority of NTP responses would be coming from NTP servers that are geographically closer to the requesting IP address. Combined with the fact that no NTP requests are sent from a victim AS to those reflection servers, this lack of "locality" could be used as a way to develop an attack mitigation strategy.

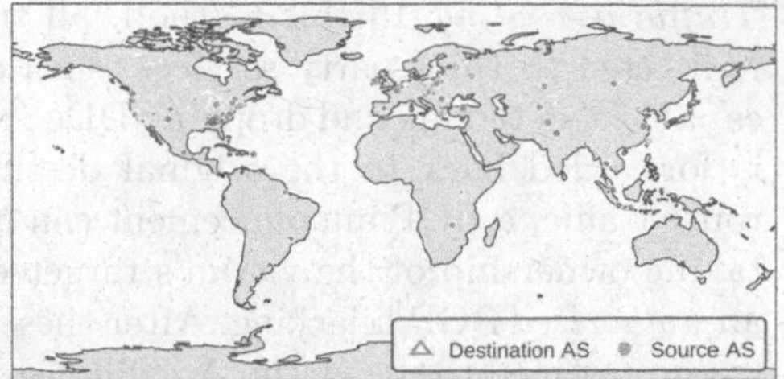

Fig. 8. Geo-locations of source and destination ASes for NTP-based DRDoS attacks

4.4 Attack Mitigation

We now analyze whether the operators of the victim networks attempted to mitigate the attacks detected by IXmon. Specifically, we focus on mitigations that require BGP actions. Afterwards, we discuss how IXmon could help mitigate future attacks by (a) detecting DRDoS attacks in near real time (with a delay of about $\Delta t = 1$ min); (b) determining the AS being targeted by the attack and what service (i.e., source UDP port) is being abused to reflect/amplify attack traffic; and (b) identifying the source ASes that contribute the most to the attack, so that attack traffic originating from those ASes can be filtered out.

Mitigation Strategies. Multiple ways exist to respond to DDoS attacks [55]. However, as we focus on bandwidth exhaustion DRDoS attacks, we ignore mitigations implemented locally at the victim network. Instead, we focus on mitigations that are implemented upstream, with the help of third-party networks such as traffic providers or scrubbing centers, and that make use of BGP to drop or redirect traffic before it reaches the victim network:

- *Blackholing*: BGP-based blackholing redirects all traffic towards a victim AS (both legitimate and malicious traffic) into a null interface, or "blackhole." Although multiple variations of blackholing exist, they are primarily achieved by adjusting the next-hop attribute and BGP communities in BGP announcements [36]. The next-hop method involves the trigger source sending a BGP update to the edge routers with the next-hop attribute set to an IP address that is pre-configured to a *null* interface. The most commonly used next-hop IP for blackholing is 192.0.2.1, which is reserved by IANA for test networks [15].

- *Traffic re-routing*: In this method, all traffic towards the victim network is redirected to third-party services, such as a traffic scrubbing center that is capable of detecting and dropping DDoS attack traffic. Then, legitimate traffic is forwarded back to the original destination (i.e., the victim AS). To re-route traffic, a BGP announcement can be issued by the scrubbing center AS taking ownership of the victim's targeted IP prefixes, essentially performing an *authorized* BGP hijacking. After these BGP announcements propagate, all traffic destined to the victim AS will instead reach the scrubbing center. After the attack has ended, another BGP messages can be issued to reinstate the original IP prefix ownership and again route all traffic to the true destination.

Detecting BGP-Based DRDoS Mitigations. To detect whether mitigations were put into place to counter the attacks detected by IXmon, we perform an analysis of BGP announcements related to the victim ASes before, during and after a DRDoS attack occurrence. To this end, we leverage routing information from RouteViews [7], as explained below:

- *Blackholing*: To detect the use of blackholing mitigations, we monitor the BGP updates involving all IP prefixes owned by a victim AS, and check if any of these updates announce the next-hop to be 192.0.2.1. In addition, we look for BGP updates with a community value set to 666, which is commonly used to implement balckholing [36].
- *Traffic re-routing*: To detect cases in which traffic is re-routed to a third-party AS (e.g., to a scrubbing center), we gather all BGP updates made around a DRDoS attack time window and consider all updates related to IPs that fall within the victim's network ownership. Then, for each such BGP update, we check if the origin AS (extracted from RIB records) has changed, compared to before the attack (e.g., compared to the previous day). If the origin AS in the BGP updates observed during the attack does not match the previously seen origin AS, we mark this as a temporary change in ownership, and check whether future BGP messages also show another change of AS ownership from the third-party AS back to the previous origin AS. We implement this approach using `PyBGPStream` library and Routeview data.

Measuring In-the-Wild Mitigations. Using the BGP-based analysis explained earlier, we measure whether a mitigation effort was deployed for the DRDoS attacks detected by IXmon. With respect to mitigating attacks via traffic re-routing traffic, we found 56 BGP relevant announcements that occurred during 3 different DRDoS attacks. These BGP announcements effectively changed the origin AS of IP prefixes owned by the victim network and redirected traffic to a known traffic scrubbing provider. All of these mitigation efforts were related to attacks directed towards AS Anon.2354, with traffic being re-routed to the AS Anon.1890. All 3 attacks for which mitigation was deployed had a duration greater than 30 min. With respect to mitigation via BGP-based blackholing, we did not find any evidence that blackholing was used for remediating any of the DRDoS attacks we detected.

Figure 9 shows an example of DRDoS attack for which a traffic rerouting mitigation was implemented. As can be seen, in this case the attack had been ongoing for around 45 min, before traffic was re-routed to a scrubbing center. Traffic rerouting is identified by the BGP announcements to change origin (as seen in Fig. 9) of the victim prefix to scrubbing center's AS Anon.1890. Considering this specific AS Anon.2354 that had employed scrubbing services, we performed an experiment to test if our system had missed any attacks for which similar mitigation by re-routing traffic was deployed. To this end, we collected BGP updates for a period of 6 months related to prefixes belonging to our victim AS Anon.2354 whose origin was changed to the scrubbing AS Anon.1890. However, we did not find any evidence in BGP updates to denote an attack that our system missed.

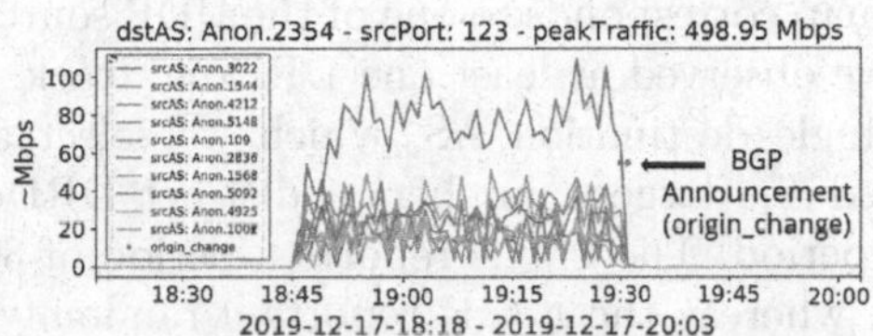

Fig. 9. Example of DRDoS attack and traffic re-routing mitigation

While it was a bit surprising that only 3 attacks and only one network operator used attack mitigation, personal communications with the SoX operators confirmed that only that one member network made use of a DDoS mitigation plan available to all of SoX's customers/members. Another surprising observation is that only long-lived attacks are considered for mitigation. It is possible that one of the main issue is that currently DDoS detection happens "manually," once the attack has started to cause noticeable disruption and perhaps network users start complaining to the operators. Our IXmon system can reduce such detection delay significantly, by performing DRDoS attack detection in near real time with an inexpensive open-source solution.

Improving Attack Mitigation at IXPs. While re-routing traffic to third-party scrubbing services is a commonly used strategy for mitigating DDoS attacks, it can become a quite expensive depending on the size and duration of the attack that a victim is trying to defend against. Another possibility for mitigation is to rely on IXPs and upstream ISPs to implement traffic blackholing. However, as explained earlier, currently blackholing is either an "all or nothing" or very coarsely selective strategy that can cause significant collateral damage [30,59], because it filters out both legitimate and attack traffic. In this section, we discuss how IXmon could enable IXPs to help their customer/members who fall victim of DRDoS attacks, by making traffic blackholing more "surgical" so that only traffic associated with specific services and with specific attack-contributing source ASes is blocked. This has the potential of significantly reducing collateral damage.

The strategy we propose is the following. Let V be the victim AS of a DRDoS attack detected by IXmon, p be the source UDP port abused for reflecting attack traffic towards V, and $S = \{s_1, s_2, \ldots, s_n\}$ be the set of source ASes that send traffic from port p to V during the attack. The IXP could implement a filtering rule that only blocks all traffic from each source AS s_i and port p directed towards V. Because all information necessary to create these filtering rules is contained in IXmon's DRDoS alerts, it would be possible to simply automatically translate each alert into a BGP Flowspec rule that can be propagated to the IXP's routers thus greatly reducing the mitigation time compared to manual intervention.

To understand what is the potential impact to the above strategy, we investigate the extent of the "collateral damage" (i.e., blocked non-DRDoS traffic) a target network may incur. To this end, let us consider the measurements shown in Fig. 10. Each heatmap corresponds to one of the UDP source ports reported in Fig. 5a, from which we observed at least one DRDoS attack. All four heatmaps are related to one single destination AS, which we select as the AS number for which we observed the largest number of distinct DRDoS attacks, during IXmon's deployment period. The x axis reports a period of 30 consecutive days of traffic monitoring, whereas the y axis reports a randomly selected set of 20 source ASes. These source ASes were selected among all source ASes that during the 30 days period in the x axis sent at least some traffic from any of the six source UDP ports. The color of each heatmap cells indicates the total number of MBytes sent by a source AS to the destination AS during each day. Gray cells indicate zero bytes, whereas other cell colors indicated the "intensity" of the daily traffic. From all these graphs we exclude attack traffic detected by IXmon. The reason is that we want to highlight the volume of normal (i.e., non-DRDoS attack) traffic typically sent by any source AS to a destination AS, as seen from the vantage point of an IXP.

Let us consider first Fig. 10a, which is related to CLDAP traffic (port 389). As we can see, it is rare to observe any inter-AS traffic for this service. This makes sense, in that CLDAP is primarily meant as an authentication protocol to be used within a local network. Similarly, ports 19, 111, and 11211 are unlikely to be used for legitimate inter-AS communication purposes. Therefore, blocking inter-AS traffic from these ports at the IXP level is unlikely to cause much collateral damage at all. Services such as NTP (port 123) and DNS (port 53) have a different traffic profile. Inter-AS traffic in these cases is not uncommon, though the overall volume can be quite low, and therefore traffic filtering can produce some observable collateral damage. For example, filtering all source port 53 traffic towards a destination AS may impact DNS resolutions for domains whose authoritative name servers are located within the destination AS. However, let us assume IXmon detects an attack related to one of these ports/services. A BGP Flowspec rule automatically derived from IXmon's DRDoS alert would suggest that the IXP filter all traffic coming from the identified attack source port directed to the victim network. In addition the filtering rule would specify what source ASes are contributing to the attack, so that the IXP could block only traffic from a specific source port and a specific subset of source ASes, thus

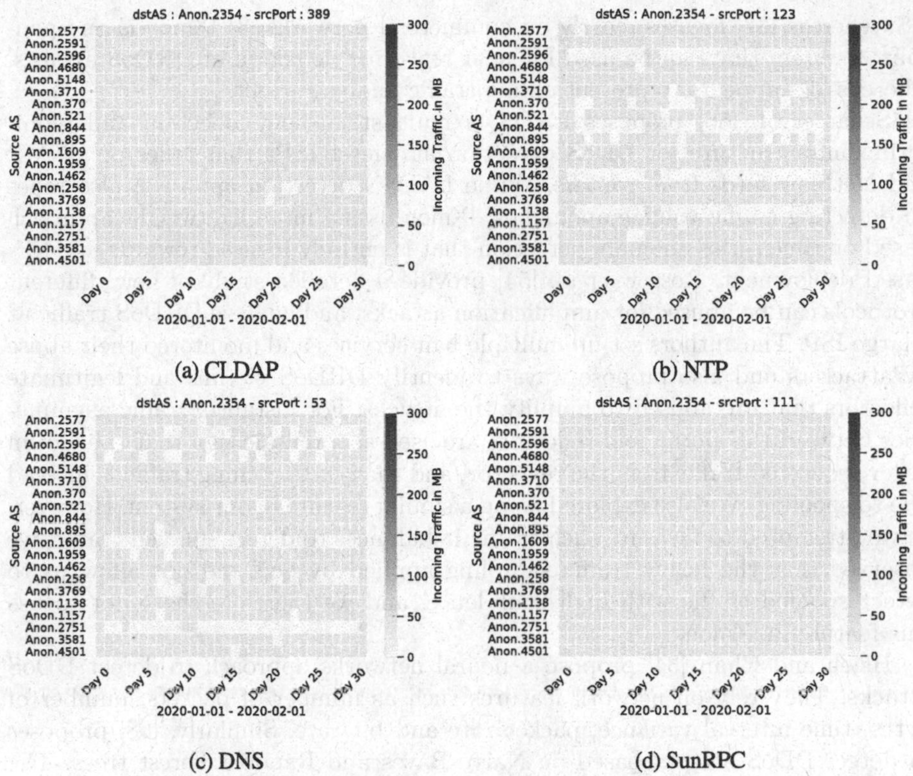

(a) CLDAP (b) NTP

(c) DNS (d) SunRPC

Fig. 10. Daily traffic (in MBytes per day) to destination AS Anon.2354 from a set of 20 legitimate ASes not involved in DRDoS attacks.

further limiting possible collateral damage. Furthermore, filtering could be limited to the duration of the attack. As soon as IXmon detects that the DRDoS attack is over, a new BGP Flowspec rule could be issued so that the IXP would stop filtering any traffic towards the target AS. This approach could help IXPs protect their downstream customer/member networks from bandwidth exhaustion DRDoS attacks with minimal collateral damage.

5 Related Work

In this section we are presenting prior work in the area of DDoS detection and mitigation both in the context of IXPs and large Tier-1 ISPs.

Detection: Concurrently to our work, Kopp et al. [37] also studied amplification attacks from an IXP. Many of our findings agree with their results [37]. However, our work differs from [37] in the following ways: 1) IXmon can detect low volume attacks, whereas [37] only focuses on attacks with volume ≥ 1 Gbps; 2) IXmon provides insights into traffic from research and education networks in the

US, whereas [37] focuses mostly on commercial networks; 3) IXmon is an open-source system that can be used for near real-time detection of DRDoS attacks, whereas [37] appears to present offline traffic analysis results.

Sekar et al. [56] proposes LADS, a multi-stage flow collection and monitoring infrastructure for DDoS detection at Tier-1 ISPs that relies on SNMP and NetFlow feeds from routers. While LADS's detection approach also relies on detecting traffic volume anomalies, IXmon uses a more lightweight approach based on time series anomaly detection that is entirely focused towards an IXP-based deployment. Rossow et al. [54] provide a detailed study of how different protocols can be abused for amplification attacks, and analyze DRDoS traffic at a large ISP. The authors set up multiple bait services and monitored their abuse by attackers and also propose ways to identify DRDoS victims and legitimate reflectors that are abused to amplify the attacks. For instance, traffic asymmetries between the victim and reflectors are used as a telltale sign that the victim never requested traffic from the reflector, and that the incoming traffic is instead due to spoofing. We also explored using a similar feature in our system. However, as we attempted to measure such traffic imbalances to detect spoofed traffic, we observed that the heavy traffic sampling applied by SoX did not allow us to detect spoofed traffic with high confidence, and we therefore chose not to use this feature in IXmon.

Hsieh and Chan [34] propose a neural networks approach to detect DDoS attacks. They rely on network features such as number of packets, number of bytes, time interval variance, packet rate and bit rate. Similarly, [68] proposes to detect DDoS attacks based on Naive Bayes and Random Forest trees. The drawback of these approaches is that they are not designed for real-time traffic analysis and deployment at large IXPs. Furthermore, they require large volumes of historical labeled data for reliable model training, which is often difficult to collect.

BGP-Based Mitigation: Past research [26,30] has developed BGP-based techniques that an infrastructure operator can use to mitigate DDoS attacks. These techniques work in the premise that a network operator has already deployed a tool to detect DDoS attacks. Once a DDoS attack is detected then the network operator can inform an upstream provider, for example, a higher-tier ISP or an IXP, to enforce BGP-based rules and redirect the attack traffic away from the victim network. The techniques are primarily based on: a) BGP Blackholing, and b) BGP Flowspec rules. [25,30,44] offer a detailed description and measurements of the BGP blackholing technique that has become popular and is offered as a service at many IXPs. [1] offers an example application of BGP Flowspec rules. Another study [57,58,65] proposes an additional BGP-based technique, called BGP poisoning, to filter out attack traffic. Our work differs from these approaches because we focus on designing a detection system that can be deployed at IXPs to enable the measurement of DRDoS attack characteristics and that could also be used to enable faster and more selective attack mitigation.

SDN-Based Mitigation: Previous works propose systems that leverage the capabilities of Software Defined Networking (SDN) technologies and Network Functions Virtualization (NFV) to detect and mitigate DDoS attacks. To overcome BGP-based mitigation techniques [13,61], Fayaz et al. [28] propose an OpenDayLight [42] controller and a network of Virtual Machines (VMs) for increased scalability. The controller is designed to route the traffic through the VMs to scrub the traffic. Gupta et al. [17,31,32] and Dietzel et al. [24] have proposed SDN enabled applications as a network management solution for IXPs. Our approach is not based on the SDN and NVF paradigms. Instead, our system can complement these approaches because it can be deployed on infrastructures that do not have SDN-based capabilities, and could be adapted to work with SDN-based traffic routing infrastructure at IXPs to mitigate DRDoS attacks in a very selective way with low collateral damage.

6 Conclusion

In this paper, we studied in-the-wild DRDoS attacks as seen from a large Internet exchange point (IXP). To enable this study, we first developed IXmon, an open-source DRDoS detection system specifically designed for deployment at large IXP-like network connectivity providers and peering hubs. We then deployed IXmon at Southern Crossroads (SoX), an IXP-like hub that provides both peering and upstream Internet connectivity services to more than 20 research and education (R&E) networks in the South-East United States. In a period of about 21 months, IXmon detected more than 900 DRDoS attacks towards 31 different victim ASes. An analysis of the real-world DRDoS attacks detected by our system shows that most DRDoS attacks are short lived, lasting only a few minutes, but that large-volume, long-lasting, and highly-distributed attacks against R&E networks are not uncommon. We then used the results of our analysis to discuss possible attack mitigation approaches that can be deployed at the IXP level, before the attack traffic overwhelms the victim's network bandwidth.

Acknowledgments. We would like to thank the anonymous reviewers for their constructive comments and suggestions on how to improve this paper, and Prof. Christian Rossow for serving as our shepherd. Also, many thanks to the SoX network operators for their help with IXmon's deployment. This material is based in part upon work supported by the National Science Foundation (NSF) under grants No. 1741607 and 1741608. Any opinions, findings, and conclusions or recommendations expressed in this material are those of the authors and do not necessarily reflect the views of the NSF.

References

1. BGP flowspec. https://archive.nanog.org/sites/default/files/wed.general.trafficdiversion.serodio.10.pdf
2. DDoS attack frequency grows 40%, low volume attacks dominate. https://www.helpnetsecurity.com/2018/09/13/ddos-attack-frequency-grows/

3. Euro IX- internet exchange points. https://www.euro-ix.net/media/filer_public/d5/84/d584495f-b8ae-4f24-b589-7b9efed3594b/ixp_report_2018-2019-final.pdf
4. European internet exchange association 2012 report on European IXPs. https://www.euro-ix.net/documents/1117-Euro-IX-IXP-Report-2012-pdf
5. Internet2: Regional research and education networks. https://internet2.edu/network/state-and-regional-r-e-networks/
6. IP geolocation mappingk. https://ipgeolocation.io/ip-location-api.html
7. Routeviews project. http://www.routeviews.org/routeviews/
8. Threat actors target remote learning during COVID-19. https://www.netscout.com/blog/threat-actors-target-remote-learning-during-covid-19
9. The U.S. vs. European internet exchange point models. http://drpeering.net/HTML_IPP/chapters/ch12-9-US-vs-European-Internet-Exchange-Point/ch12-9-US-vs-European-Internet-Exchange-Point.html
10. Fouladi, R.F., Ermiş, O., Anarim, E.: A DDoS attack detection and defense scheme using time-series analysis for SDN. J. Inf. Secur. Appl. **54**, 102587 (2020). https://doi.org/10.1016/j.jisa.2020.102587
11. Ager, B., Chatzis, N., Feldmann, A., Sarrar, N., Uhlig, S., Willinger, W.: Anatomy of a large European IXP. In: Proceedings of the ACM SIGCOMM 2012 Conference on Applications, Technologies, Architectures, and Protocols for Computer Communication, pp. 163–174 (2012)
12. Akamai: Why Akamai cloud security for DDoS protection? https://www.akamai.com/us/en/solutions/products/cloud-security/ddos-protection-service.jsp
13. Butler, K., Farley, T.R., McDaniel, P., Rexford, J.: A survey of BGP security issues and solutions. Proc. IEEE **98**(1), 100–122 (2010)
14. CAIDA: As relationship. http://data.caida.org/datasets/as-relationships/
15. Network Startup Resource Center: Remote blackhole filtering lab. https://nsrc.org/workshops/2019/mnnog1/riso/networking/routing-security/en/labs/RTBH-local.html
16. Chatzis, N., Smaragdakis, G., Feldmann, A., Willinger, W.: There is more to IXPs than meets the eye. ACM SIGCOMM Comput. Commun. Rev. **43**(5), 19–28 (2013)
17. Chiesa, M., et al.: Inter-domain networking innovation on steroids: empowering IXPs with SDN capabilities. IEEE Commun. Mag. **54**(10), 102–108 (2016)
18. CISCO: Netflow layer 2 and security monitoring exports. http://www.cisco.com/c/en/us/td/docs/ios-xml/ios/netflow/configuration/12-4/nf-12-4-book/nf-lay2-sec-mon-exp.html
19. CISCO: Netflow v9. https://www.cisco.com/en/US/technologies/tk648/tk362/technologies_white_paper09186a00800a3db9.html
20. CloudFlare: Famous DDoS attacks learning objectives. https://www.cloudflare.com/learning/ddos/famous-ddos-attacks/
21. Cloudflare: How cloudflare's architecture allows us to scale to stop the largest attacks. https://blog.cloudflare.com/how-cloudflares-architecture-allows-us-to-scale-to-stop-the-largest-attacks/
22. CloudFlare: Reflections on reflection (attacks) (2017). https://blog.cloudflare.com/reflections-on-reflections/
23. CloudFlare: Memcrashed - major amplification attacks from UDP port 11211 (2018). https://blog.cloudflare.com/memcrashed-major-amplification-attacks-from-port-11211/
24. Dietzel, C., Antichi, G., Castro, I., Fernandes, E.L., Chiesa, M., Kopp, D.: SDN traffic engineering and advanced blackholing at IXPs. In: Proceedings of the Symposium on SDN Research (2017)

25. Dietzel, C., Feldmann, A., King, T.: Blackholing at IXPs: on the effectiveness of DDoS mitigation in the wild. In: Proceedings of Passive and Active Measurement: 17th International Conference, PAM 2016, Heraklion, Greece, 31 March–1 April 2016 (2016)
26. Dietzel, C., Wichtlhuber, M., Smaragdakis, G., Feldmann, A.: Stellar: network attack mitigation using advanced blackholing. In: Proceedings of the 14th International Conference on emerging Networking EXperiments and Technologies, pp. 152–164 (2018)
27. Digital Attack Map: DDoS attacks worldwide. http://www.digitalattackmap.com
28. Fayaz, S.K., Tobioka, Y., Sekar, V., Bailey, M.: Bohatei: flexible and elastic DDoS defense. In: 24th USENIX Conference on Security Symposium. USENIX Association, USA (2015)
29. Finch, T.: Incremental calculation of weighted mean and variance (2009). https://fanf2.user.srcf.net/hermes/doc/antiforgery/stats.pdf
30. Giotsas, V., Smaragdakis, G., Dietzel, C., Richter, P., Feldmann, A., Berger, A.: Inferring BGP blackholing activity in the internet. In: 2017 Internet Measurement Conference (2017)
31. Gupta, A., et al.: An industrial-scale software defined internet exchange point. In: 13th {USENIX} Symposium on Networked Systems Design and Implementation ({NSDI} 2016), pp. 1–14 (2016)
32. Gupta, A., et al.: SDX: a software defined internet exchange. ACM SIGCOMM Comput. Commun. Rev. **44**(4), 551–562 (2014)
33. Hao, M.: DDoS attack landscape (2020). https://nsfocusglobal.com/ddos-attack-landscape-3/
34. Hsieh, C., Chan, T.: Detection DDoS attacks based on neural-network using apache spark. In: 2016 International Conference on Applied System Innovation (ICASI), pp. 1–4 (2016)
35. Kang, M.S., Lee, S.B., Gligor, V.D.: The crossfire attack. In: Proceedings of the 2013 IEEE Symposium on Security and Privacy (2013). http://dx.doi.org/10.1109/SP.2013.19
36. King, T., Dietzel, C., Snijders, J., Doering, G., Hankins, G.: Blackhole BGP community for blackholing. https://tools.ietf.org/html/draft-ietf-grow-blackholing-00
37. Kopp, D., Dietzel, C., Hohlfeld, O.: DDoS never dies? An IXP perspective on DDoS amplification attacks. In: Hohlfeld, O., Lutu, A., Levin, D. (eds.) PAM 2021. LNCS, vol. 12671, pp. 284–301. Springer, Cham (2021). https://doi.org/10.1007/978-3-030-72582-2_17
38. Krämer, L., et al.: AmpPot: monitoring and defending against amplification DDoS attacks. In: Bos, H., Monrose, F., Blanc, G. (eds.) RAID 2015. LNCS, vol. 9404, pp. 615–636. Springer, Cham (2015). https://doi.org/10.1007/978-3-319-26362-5_28
39. Krebs, B.: Krebsonsecurity hit with record DDoS. https://krebsonsecurity.com/2016/09/krebsonsecurity-hit-with-record-ddos/
40. Li, D., Chen, D., Goh, J., kiong Ng, S.: Anomaly detection with generative adversarial networks for multivariate time series (2019)
41. Luckie, M., Huffaker, B., Dhamdhere, A., Giotsas, V., Claffy, K.: As relationships, customer cones, and validation. In: 2013 Conference on Internet Measurement Conference (2013). https://doi.org/10.1145/2504730.2504735
42. Medved, J., Varga, R., Tkacik, A., Gray, K.: Opendaylight: towards a model-driven SDN controller architecture. In: Proceeding of IEEE International Symposium on a World of Wireless, Mobile and Multimedia Networks 2014, pp. 1–6. IEEE (2014)
43. Mirkovic, J., Reiher, P.: A taxonomy of DDoS attack and DDoS defense mechanisms. SIGCOMM Comput. Commun. Rev. **34**(2), 39–53 (2004)

44. Nawrocki, M., Blendin, J., Dietzel, C., Schmidt, T.C., Wählisch, M.: Down the black hole: dismantling operational practices of BGP blackholing at IXPs. In: Proceedings of the Internet Measurement Conference, pp. 435–448. Association for Computing Machinery, New York (2019)
45. Norton, W.: The Internet Peering Playbook: Connecting to the Core of the Internet. DrPeering Press (2011). https://books.google.com/books?id=rkDz6fvX_XkC
46. NSFOCUS: Have rich game customers who suffered DDoS attacks turned to you? https://nsfocusglobal.com/have-rich-game-customers-who-suffered-ddos-attacks-turned-to-you/
47. Odintsov, P.: Fastnetmon - very fast DDoS analyzer with sflow/netflow/mirror support. https://github.com/pavel-odintsov/fastnetmon
48. Phaal, P., Lavine, M.: sFlow version 5. http://sflow.org/sflow_version_5.txt
49. Prince, M.: The DDoS that knocked spamhaus offline. https://blog.cloudflare.com/the-ddos-that-knocked-spamhaus-offline-and-ho/
50. Radware: 3 attack surfaces that can take your game offline. https://blog.radware.com/security/ddosattacks/2020/10/3-attack-surfaces-that-can-take-your-game-offline/
51. Computer Business Review: AWS hit with a record 2.3 Tbps DDoS attack. https://www.cbronline.com/news/record-ddos-attack-aws
52. Richards, J.: Denial-of-service: the Estonian cyberwar and its implications for U.S. National Security. http://www.iar-gwu.org/node/65
53. Richter, P., Smaragdakis, G., Feldmann, A., Chatzis, N., Boettger, J., Willinger, W.: Peering at peerings: on the role of IXP route servers. In: Proceedings of the 2014 Conference on Internet Measurement Conference, pp. 31–44 (2014)
54. Rossow, C.: Amplification hell: revisiting network protocols for DDoS abuse. In: Proceedings of the 2014 Network and Distributed System Security (NDSS) Symposium, February 2014
55. Ryba, F.J., Orlinski, M., Wählisch, M., Rossow, C., Schmidt, T.C.: Amplification and DRDoS attack defense - a survey and new perspectives (2015)
56. Sekar, V., Duffield, N.G., Spatscheck, O., van der Merwe, J.E., Zhang, H.: Lads: large-scale automated DDoS detection system. In: USENIX Annual Technical Conference (2006)
57. Smith, J.M., Schuchard, M.: Routing around congestion: defeating DDoS attacks and adverse network conditions via reactive BGP routing. In: 2018 IEEE Symposium on Security and Privacy (2018)
58. Smith, J., Birkeland, K., McDaniel, T., Schuchard, M.: Withdrawing the BGP re-routing curtain: understanding the security impact of BGP poisoning through real-world measurements (2020)
59. Snijders, J.: DDoS damage control, cheap and effective. https://ripe68.ripe.net/presentations/176-RIPE68_JSnijders_DDoS_Damage_Control.pdf
60. SoX: Southern crossroads. https://www.sox.net/
61. Streibelt, F., et al.: BGP communities: even more worms in the routing can. In: Proceedings of the Internet Measurement Conference 2018, pp. 279–292 (2018)
62. Tabatabaie Nezhad, S.M., Nazari, M., Gharavol, E.A.: A novel DoS and DDoS attacks detection algorithm using Arima time series model and chaotic system in computer networks. IEEE Commun. Lett. **20**(4), 700–703 (2016). https://doi.org/10.1109/LCOMM.2016.2517622
63. arsTECHNICA: DDoSers are abusing Microsoft RDP to make attacks more powerful. https://arstechnica.com/information-technology/2021/01/ddosers-are-abusing-microsoft-rdp-to-make-attacks-more-powerful/

64. Thomas, D.R., Clayton, R., Beresford, A.R.: 1000 days of UDP amplification DDoS attacks. In: 2017 APWG Symposium on Electronic Crime Research (eCrime), pp. 79–84 (2017)
65. Tran, M., Kang, M.S., Hsiao, H., Chiang, W., Tung, S., Wang, Y.: On the feasibility of rerouting-based DDoS defenses. In: 2019 IEEE Symposium on Security and Privacy (SP) (2019)
66. US CERT: UDP-based amplification attacks. https://www.us-cert.gov/ncas/alerts/TA14-017A
67. York, K.: DYN statement on 10/21/2016 DDoS attack. http://dyn.com/blog/dyn-statement-on-10212016-ddos-attack/
68. Zhang, B., Zhang, T., Yu, Z.: DDoS detection and prevention based on artificial intelligence techniques. In: 2017 3rd IEEE International Conference on Computer and Communications (ICCC), pp. 1276–1280 (2017)

Digging Deeper: An Analysis of Domain Impersonation in the Lower DNS Hierarchy

Florian Quinkert(✉), Dennis Tatang, and Thorsten Holz

Ruhr University Bochum, Bochum, Germany
{florian.quinkert,dennis.tatang,thorsten.holz}@rub.de

Abstract. Attackers use various techniques to lure victims to malicious domains. A typical approach is to generate domains which look similar to well-known ones so that a confused victim is tricked into visiting the domain. An important attack technique in practice is the *impersonation* of domains in the lower DNS hierarchy as *subdomains* of otherwise unsuspiciously looking domains, such as *paypal.com.foo.example.com*.

In this paper, we present an in-depth, empirical measurement study of low-level domain impersonations to understand their prevalence and provide a basis for the development of corresponding countermeasures. We introduce a generic measurement approach to find and analyze such domains in phishing feeds from three large anti-phishing vendors (PhishLabs, Phishtank, and OpenPhish) covering multiple years and a data set consisting of one and a half years of certificate transparency logs (CTL). In our measurement study, we discovered more than 122,000 cases of domain impersonations detected during the last seven years in PhishLabs, almost 3,000 in Phishtank, and a couple of hundred instances in OpenPhish. Additionally, we compared the usage of low-level domain impersonation with other well-known domain squatting techniques and find that low-level domain impersonation is among the most popular squatting techniques in the wild.

1 Introduction

Domain names, or short domains, are an important building block of today's Internet because they allow users to use easily recognizable strings to access websites and other resources instead of difficult to remember IP addresses. However, attackers utilize domains to maintain their attack infrastructure, e.g., to switch seamlessly between multiple IP addresses. Furthermore, attackers register domains similar to well-known ones to use them, e.g., in e-mails they send to potential victims as part of spearphishing [19] and similar attacks. Creating such domains is often referred to as *domain squatting* [18] and has been studied multiple times before [10,20,22,28]. But it is possible to detect such malicious domains in (almost) real-time by monitoring newly registered domains and comparing them to a set of benign reference domains [10,20,22].

L. Bilge et al. (Eds.): DIMVA 2021, LNCS 12756, pp. 68–87, 2021.
https://doi.org/10.1007/978-3-030-80825-9_4

To avoid the early detection, an attacker can initially register an unsuspiciously looking domain and, afterwards, create subdomains which contain a well-known domain that she wants to impersonate. For example, an attacker registers the legitimate domain *example.com* and creates a subdomain for malicious purposes, e.g., ***secure.paypal.com***.*example.com*. We refer to such domains as *low-level domain impersonation* (LLDI) because the impersonated domain is added in the lower level of the domain within the DNS hierarchy. In contrast to other domain squatting techniques, the registered domain does not reveal the malicious purpose, i.e., it is not possible to detect such domains by examining registered domains and other similar detection techniques. Additionally, *defensive registrations* (i.e., the legitimate owner of a second-level domain registers potential domain squatting names in advance) are not possible, rendering an important, practical defense mechanism futile. Nowadays, the technique is even more effective because many users access websites via mobile browsers on devices with a limited screen width so that only the well-known part of the domain is visible [26]. Even the Advanced Persistent Threat (APT) group *Silent Librarian* uses this attack technique to create targeted phishing e-mails for universities [17].

In this paper, we introduce a generic approach, independent of a predefined list of well-known domains, to find domains which potentially use this technique. Moreover, we present the results of a long-term, empirical measurement study using this approach to attract attention and better understand this domain squatting technique. We analyze LLDIs in phishing feeds and newly issued certificates (*Certificate Transparency Logs (CTL)*) to provide a comprehensive overview and dissect the structure of domains using LLDIs. The phishing feeds contain multiple years of malicious domains collected by PhishLabs [6], a commercial anti-phishing company, and multiple months of malicious domains collected by the two anti-phishing initiatives Phishtank [7] and OpenPhish [4]. These data feeds serve as a ground truth on phishing attacks and enable us to comprehensively study LLDI in the wild. In addition, we compare LLDI with common domain squatting vectors to demonstrate that the number of LLDIs is comparable with these techniques. The CTLs cover a period of 18 months and contain almost two billion entries. Since CTLs contain the domain for which a certificate is issued and almost 70% of all phishing sites nowadays use TLS [5], we can use this data set to investigate LLDIs.

In our empirical measurement study, we discovered more than 122,000 LLDIs during the last seven years in PhishLabs. Additionally, we found almost 3,000 domains in Phishtank since August 2018 and a couple of hundred ones since February 2019 in OpenPhish. Our results show that especially big technology companies (e.g., *facebook*) as well as financial companies (e.g., *paypal*) face LLDIs. However, our generic approach also identified smaller companies as targets, such as regional banks (e.g., the Belgian bank *kbc*). Furthermore, our results show that most domains start with the impersonated brand name but often use suitable terms, e.g., *login* or *secure*, to lure a victim. Analyzing the CTLs revealed that many more LLDIs are used in the wild which further emphasizes the need for proper countermeasures.

2 Background and Related Work

2.1 Structure of Domains

In networks, domains are used to provide easy access to resources which otherwise would require hard to remember, plain IP addresses. A domain is a sequence of labels separated by dots with each label defining a namespace (see RFC 1035 [27]). The domain is also referred to as *fully qualified domain name* (FQDN). The rightmost label is called *top-level domain* (TLD) and with the next label to the left *second-level domain.* A user registers a second-level domain, e.g., *example.com*, and can add an arbitrary number of lower-level labels, e.g., *test.example.com*, which is called *subdomain.* We refer to the *level* of a subdomain as the number of labels, i.e., a subdomain *www.appleid* has level two.

2.2 Certificate Transparency Logs (CTLs)

A domain owner can obtain a digital certificate from a certificate authority (CA) for a registered domain and use it to secure the connection to the resource associated with the domain. Especially in case of applications requiring the input of sensitive information (e.g., passwords or personal details), the usage of secured connections and certificates is nowadays inevitable. Because users expect a connection to be secured, attackers generate certificates for their malicious domains, too [2]. A couple of years ago, multiple certificate authorities were compromised [13,15], leading to the establishment of certificate transparency logs (CTLs) [9] which store details about every issued certificate. CTLs aim at detecting maliciously issued certificates faster by making newly issued certificates publicly available, hence enabling more transparency.

2.3 Related Work

Domain Squatting. Attackers use multiple techniques to create believable domains. In a *homograph domain*, the attacker replaces characters in a well-known domain with visually similar ones, e.g., from different alphabets [14,20, 24,31,34]. In *typosquatting*, attackers register well-known domains with a common typing error, e.g., *faecbook.com* instead of *facebook.com* [10,35].

Combosquatting is a popular phishing technique, in which an attacker adds suitable words to a well-known domain to obtain a new domain which still looks legitimate, e.g., *facebook-security.com* [21]. Additionally, attackers use randomly occurring bit errors to redirect victims to domains under their control [29] as well as domains which sound similar to well-known domains (e.g., *jutube.com* instead of *youtube.com*) [28].

In case of *shadow domains*, an attacker gains access to legitimate domains, e.g., via phishing, and registers additional subdomains for malicious purposes [25]. In contrast, we do not focus only on subdomains an attacker created when she gained access to a second-level domain, but focus on *all* subdomains containing a well-known domain, regardless of how the second-level domain was generated.

Malicious Domain Detection. Researchers introduced multiple approaches to detect malicious domain usage as early as possible. In 2011, Bilge et al. proposed a system called EXPOSURE which analyzes passive DNS data and detects malicious domains based on the domain itself and the way it is requested [12]. Antonakakis et al. presented a similar system called KOPIS [11]. In contrast to EXPOSURE, KOPIS uses DNS data from the upper DNS hierarchy, e.g., from authoritative nameservers, which allows a more global perspective. Hao et al. developed PREDATOR, a system detecting malicious domains at the time of registration based on typical characteristics, such as a high number of registrations almost at the same time or registration of similar domains [16]. Tian et al. identified phishing domains by taking both the domain itself and the visual appearance of the website into consideration [36]. They detected 1,175 phishing domains, out of which more than 90% were not added to well-known blacklists within a month. Roberts et al. also analyzed the usage of well-known domains in subdomains [32]. In contrast to our approach, they used a fixed set of well-known domains and searched for them in certificate transparency logs only.

3 Measurement Setup

3.1 Input Data

Our measurement setup works with every kind of data source that provides access to subdomains. In this work, we focus on phishing feeds from three different vendors as they represent a ground truth for our analysis, and complement our study with data obtained from certificate transparency logs.

Phishing Feeds. We use phishing feeds from security company PhishLabs [6] and two data sets collected from OpenPhish [4] and Phishtank [7]. Detecting LLDI in these verified sources of phishing domains demonstrates that attackers use this attack vector in the wild.

We analyzed 1,410,201 domains collected by PhishLabs during a period of about seven years between 2012/06/12 and 2019/07/31. This high-quality data source enables us to study LLDIs in detail and provides a broad overview of all domain squatting techniques in recent years. Phishtank is an anti-phishing website that collects URLs involved in phishing and updates its database hourly. We collected all available phishing domains on an hourly basis for about one year between 2018/08/10 and 2019/07/31. Afterwards, we extracted the distinct fully qualified domain names (FQDNs), leading to 103,147 distinct domains, which we use as input for our analysis pipeline. Similarly, we collected all available phishing domains from OpenPhish, another initiative to collect phishing domains, on an hourly basis for about half a year between 2019/02/12 and 2019/07/31, leading to 36,351 FQDNs.

Certificate Transparency Logs (CTLs). In 2018, Scheitle et al. already briefly discussed the benefits of CTLs to detect phishing domains [33]. The CTL ecosystem consists of multiple log files to which everybody can submit certificates. The certificates contain FQDNs so that they are especially interesting to detect LLDIs. Collecting data from CTLs requires maintaining a list of active log files, collecting and parsing the data, and removing duplicates. To overcome these challenges, we use CertStream [1], an aggregated, real-time feed of newly added certificates provided by security company Calidog. CertStream contains the date and time as well as the FQDN for which a certificate is issued, without additional certificate information. However, our analysis needs only the FQDNs as input data. We collected the CTLs from CertStream for almost one and a half years between 2018/02/02 and 2019/07/31 and gathered almost two billion entries in total.

3.2 Analysis Pipeline

Next, we describe the analysis pipeline used in our measurement study. First, we define the three terms *test domain*, *candidate domain*, and *reference domain*. A *test domain* is an FQDN from the three phishing feeds and CTLs, which we use as input. A *candidate domain* is a test domain which contains a domain in the subdomain part, e.g., *secure.**paypal.com**.account.example.com* contains *paypal.com*. A candidate domain consists of a prefix, a reference brand, a TLD, a suffix, and a second-level domain: <prefix>.<reference-brand>.<top-level-domain>.<suffix>.<second-level-domain>. In the previous example, *secure* is the prefix, *paypal* the reference brand, *com* is the TLD, *account* the suffix, and *example.com* the second-level domain. Prefix and suffix can also be empty. We refer to the reference brand plus top-level domain (TLD) as *reference domain*.

Identification of Candidate Domains. Our approach to identify candidate domains among test domains consists of three steps. As example test domain, we continue to use *secure.**paypal.com**.account.example.com*. First, we split each test domain at the dots to obtain a list of labels, ignoring the test domain's TLD. In our example, this leads to: [secure, paypal, com, account, example] Afterwards, we search for labels consisting of a valid TLD or starting with a valid TLD plus a hyphen. For that purpose, we compiled a list of 258 country-code TLDs and the four generic TLDs *com*, *net*, *org*, and *edu*. We ignored the newly introduced generic TLDs because they often consist of generic terms which can lead to false positives. Furthermore, well-known brands do not use these TLDs. If a list of labels does not contain such a TLD or a label starting with a TLD plus hyphen, we reject it as candidate domain. However, our example list of labels contains the label *com* so that we continue.

Second, we collect the previously identified top-level domain along with the label before as possible reference domain. In our example, this leads to *paypal.com*. Next, we send a DNS A resource record request to the possible reference domain to check whether it is an actual registered domain or just a coincidental finding. If a DNS A resource record exists, which is the case for *paypal.com*, we continue with step three.

Third, even a registered domain can still be rather a coincidental finding than an interesting reference domain. Thus, we additionally send an HTTP GET request secured via a TLS connection to the possible reference domain, based on the assumption that connections to banks, companies, and other interesting phishing targets are TLS secured nowadays [2]. In our example, we send a request to https://paypal.com and discover that the connection is properly secured.

In summary, we refer to a test domain as candidate domain, if it contains a registered domain (i.e., it has a valid A resource record) in the subdomain part, which is reachable via an HTTPS connection.

4 Measurement Study

In this section, we evaluate the previously introduced approach to detect reference domains. Afterwards, we analyze LLDIs utilizing the phishing feeds and compare it to other domain squatting techniques. Subsequently, we describe our findings in the CTL data set.

4.1 Reference Domain Evaluation

We use a generic approach to automatically detect reference domains instead of using a predefined list of reference domains (see Sect. 3). In this section, we first show the feasibility of our approach and second compare the selected reference domains with 500 and 1,000 static reference domains from the Tranco list [23].

Quality of Identified Reference Domains. Step one of our approach identified 3,313 reference domains in test domains from the PhishLabs data set. In this section, we assess how well steps two and three of our approach are able to tell apart actual reference domains from coincidental findings. For that purpose, a human annotator visits each in step one identified reference domain and decides whether it is a valid reference domain, e.g., because it contains input forms or belongs to a well-known brand. The manual annotation is not part of our approach but only done to show the feasibility of our approach.

Table 1 shows a comparison between the approach's and the human annotator's results. True positive (TP) means both the approach and the human annotator classified a reference domain as valid reference domain. This category contains mostly domains of well-known brands, such as *facebook.com*, *paypal.com*, or *apple.com*. The connections to these domains are TLS secured and display meaningful content. In case of true negative (TN), both the approach and the human annotator considered a reference domain as invalid reference domain. This category contains often typo- or combosquatted variants of well-known brands, e.g., *appleid.com* or *mobile-facebook.com*. In addition, it contains domains consisting of common words, for example, *confirm.eu*. The connections to these domains are neither TLS secured, nor is the content meaningful. The combination of TPs and TNs contains 85% of the reference domains, which are responsible for almost 98% of the candidate domains. That is, the vast majority

Table 1. Overview of reference domain evaluation results showing that reference domains responsible for 98% of the candidate domains were classified correctly.

	Reference domains	Candidate domains
True positives	666 (20%)	121,113 (87%)
True negatives	2,155 (65%)	14,831 (11%)
False positives	348 (10%)	1,593 (1%)
False negatives	144 (5%)	2,259 (1%)
Precision	0.66	0.99
Recall	0.82	0.98
F-score	0.73	0.98

of candidate domains are classified correctly. Similarly, false positive (FP) means the human annotator considered a domain not to be a reference domain while the approach did so. In those cases, the domains had a valid certificate issued, but the human annotator did not consider the domains as relevant. Example domains include *support.com* or *service.com.* On the contrary, false negative (FN) means the human annotator considered a domain to be a reference domain while the approach did not. This category includes domains which are not considered by the approach because they forward to another valid domain, e.g., *fb.com* which forwards to *facebook.com.* However, in case of both FP and FN, the number of affected candidate domains is minimal (about 2%). The reference domains' precision is 0.657, recall is 0.822, and F-score is 0.730. For the candidate domains, we calculated a precision of 0.987, a recall of 0.982, and an F-score of 0.984. The reference domains' precision is comparatively low because it classifys some reference domain wrong. However, this metric does not consider the different number of candidate domains for each reference domain. In contrast, the candidate domains' precision shows that we classify the vast majority of candidate domains correctly. Hence, our evaluation confirms that our generic automated approach works in a reasonably precise way.

Comparison with Static Reference Domains List. Multiple recent publications studying domain squatting used fixed sets of 1,000 or less reference domains [10,21,29]. Therefore, we downloaded the top one million Tranco list [23] on 2019/09/11 and compared the 1,014 reference domains our approach identified with the top 500 and top 1,000 domains on the Tranco list: the top 500 contain only 71 reference domains of the 1,014 ones our approach identified, i.e., we would have missed 943 reference domains responsible for 28,108 candidate domains (about 23% of all candidate domains), including noteworthy examples like *capitalone.com*, *bankofamerica.com*, or *rbcroyalbank.com.*

The top 1,000 contain 102 of the reference domains identified by our approach so that still 912 reference domains with 18,074 candidate domains would be missing (about 15% of all candidate domains), such as westernunion.com,

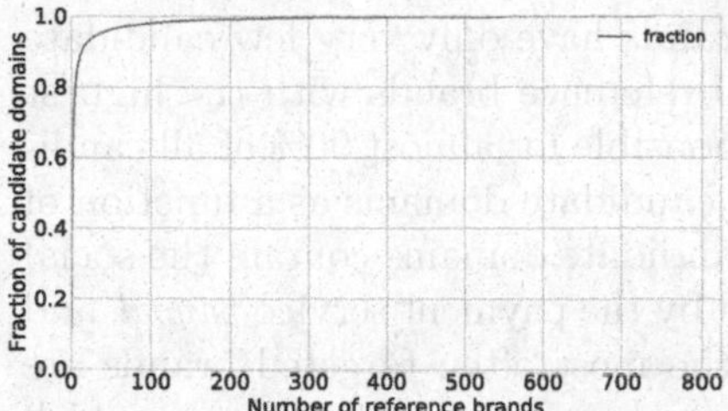

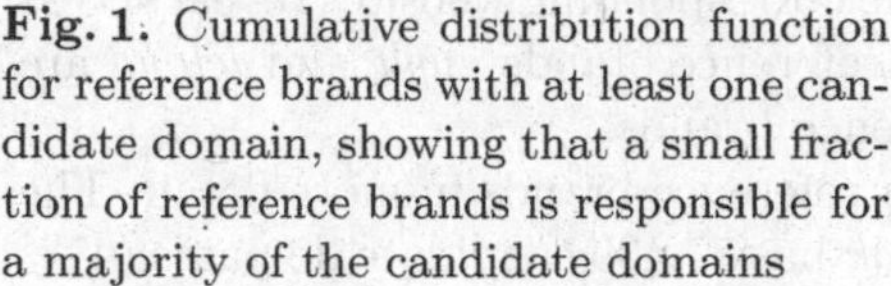

Fig. 1. Cumulative distribution function for reference brands with at least one candidate domain, showing that a small fraction of reference brands is responsible for a majority of the candidate domains

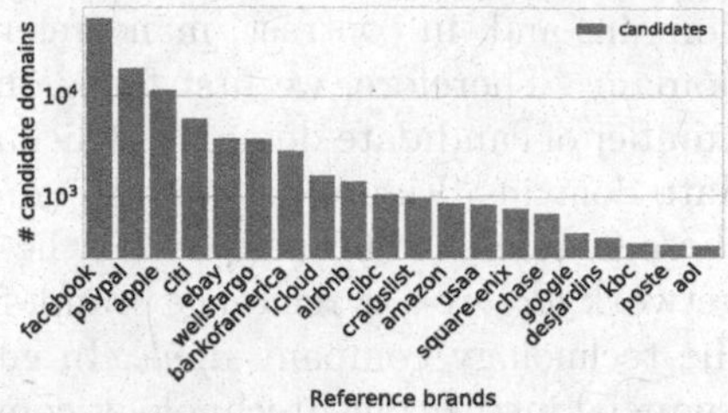

Fig. 2. Number of candidate domains as a function of the top 20 reference brands. Big tech and financial companies are targeted

scotiabank.com, or intesasanpaolo.com. The results show that our generic approach is capable of detecting important reference domains which would otherwise be missing. In addition, our approach will identify reference domains in future without having to modify a static list of reference domains.

4.2 Analysis of Phishing Feeds

In this section, we analyze LLDI in phishing feeds and start with an overview of our findings. Afterwards, we analyze each part of a candidate domain to provide information for the development of countermeasures. We focus on the PhishLabs data set because it covers by far the longest time period.

Overview. In the PhishLabs data set, our approach identified 122,707 candidate domains for 1,014 distinct reference domains (true positives plus false positives in Table 1). The oldest LLDIs date back to 2012. Additionally, the usage slightly increased over the years with a higher number of candidate domains in 2015. In the Phishtank data set, we identified 2,920 candidate domains for 258 reference domains and in the OpenPhish data set 424 candidate domains for 47 reference domains. That is, other phishing feeds detect LLDI as well.

Subsequently, we analyze each part of a candidate domain based on the structure: <prefix>.<reference-brand>.<top-level-domain>.<suffix>.<second-level-domain>. The goal is to understand how attackers use this type of impersonation in the wild. We start with the reference brand part because it is most important to understand which brands are affected.

Reference Brand. The 122,707 candidate domains in the PhishLabs data set target 1,014 distinct reference domains. Figure 1 depicts a cumulative distribution function for reference brands with at least one candidate domain. Only a small number of reference brands is responsible for the vast majority of candidate domains and, in contrast, many reference brands have only very few candidate domains. Therefore, we first focus on the 20 reference brands with the highest number of candidate domains, which are responsible for almost 90% of all candidate domains. Figure 2 shows the number of candidate domains as a function of these 20 reference brands. By far the most candidate domains contain the social network *facebook* as reference brand, followed by the payment service *paypal*, and the technology company *apple*. In general, the most often targeted brands are financial institutions, technology companies, and e-commerce businesses, which is as anticipated because the accounts at the corresponding websites reveal access to sensitive information. Interestingly, the reference brands *apple* and *icloud* are both among the most often targeted reference brands.

In the following, we analyze interesting reference brands in more detail: The most often targeted reference brand *facebook* has 57,439 candidate domains (47% of all candidate domains). Interestingly, the vast majority of candidate domains (97%) starts with *facebook*, i.e., they do not have additional characters or words before the reference brand starts. Facebook is one of the most popular websites so that the high number of candidate domains is not surprising. Additionally, we found candidate domains on 499 distinct days during our evaluation period with the first occurrence in September 2012 and the last occurrence in March 2019. This leads to the conclusion that a company like Facebook constantly faces LLDIs, and it is crucial to develop proper countermeasures.

The second most-often targeted reference brand is *paypal*. It has 18,543 candidate domains (15% of all candidate domains). In contrast to *facebook*, only about 40% of the candidate domains start with *paypal* itself. However, almost the same number of candidate domains starts with the equally well-known *www.paypal* (37%) so that victims again get the impression that the domain is legitimate. Furthermore, we detected candidate domains on almost every day (more than 2,000 days out of about 2,200 days covered by PhishLabs). The reference brand *paypal* was the most often targeted in the OpenPhish data set, too (192 candidate domains) with almost all candidate domains starting with *paypal* and being detected through the whole evaluation time period.

The reference brand *square-enix*, a video game company, has 758 candidate domains and differs from the other reference brands, which mainly target well-known tech companies or financial institutions. All candidate domains either start with the term *secure* or *support.na*, followed by *square-enix.com*, followed by a short randomly looking second-level domain or a second-level domain which contains additional terms like *oauth*, *login*, or *account*. The domains frequently use the free subdomain *usa.cc* (499 candidate domains) or the uncommon top-level domain *asia* (114 candidate domains). The subdomain *secure.square-enix.com* is the login page to the Square Enix account, while *support.na.square-enix.com* is Square Enix' support page for North America. Hence, scammers use valid subdomains as beginning for their own subdomains. Phishlabs detected the candidate domains on 199 days between 2013 and 2016, i.e., the campaign was active for a very long time. Furthermore, it shows how difficult it is to detect and protect against LLDIs.

Another example emphasizing the necessity to understand LLDI better is the reference brand *runescape*, which is an online game. PhishLabs identified 241 candidate domains on 150 days between 2012 and 2018. All candidate domains for *runescape* either start with the term *secure* or *services*, followed by *runescape*, followed by a second-level domain which starts with *com-* and ends with up to three random letters or numbers and a rather unusual top-level domain, like for example *ml* (56 candidate domains) or *ga* (45). Further research revealed a common phishing scheme [8] in which attackers generate such domains, create videos on the popular streaming website *twitch.tv*, and promise users a reward if they log in to lure them to the phishing website, which is hosted on the previously generated domain. Surprisingly, the reference brand *runescape* is the most often targeted brand in the Phishtank data set (816 candidate domains).

In summary, our analysis shows that big financial and technology brands are predominantly targeted. Further analyses of the four most often targeted reference brands *facebook*, *paypal*, *apple*, and *citi* revealed that the candidate domains for each reference brand often share a common domain beginning. In contrast, the number of active days differed in some cases. Additionally, the examples of *square-enix* and *runescape* demonstrate that smaller vendors should pay attention to how their domains are used, too.

Candidate Domain Prefix. It is crucial to either start with the reference brand or with a suitable prefix to trick the victim into thinking this is a legitimate domain. Therefore, we analyzed the prefixes and found that the PhishLabs candidate domains on average have a prefix of length three before the reference brand starts. Overall, we discovered 3,951 distinct prefixes for the 122,707 candidate domains. A small number of prefixes is used by many candidate domains, while many other prefixes are used by only one or very few candidate domains. 61% of the candidate domains start with the reference brand and do not have a prefix at all. The most popular prefix is the common *www* (13,732 candidate domains, 11%). The prevalence of no prefix and *www* is as expected because both guarantee a believably impersonated domain. Additionally common are generic prefixes like *online* (6,695, 5%), *signin* (2,931, 2%), or *secure* (1678, 1.4%). Those prefixes can help to convince a victim to click on a domain because they let a domain look believable. Furthermore, the prefixes *appleid* (4,308, 4%) and *www.appleid* (538, 0.4%) were among the top ten prefixes, which is explained by the brand *apple* being one of the most prevalent reference brands. In contrast, the term *mobile*, which is often used for mobile websites, was less prevalent (120 candidate domains). The more generic *m* had 1,367 of the candidate domains as prefix. Moreover, the prefixes have on average two levels with one and two being by far the most prevalent levels. We found the same structure (high number of candidate domains without a prefix and generic terms as prefixes) when analyzing the Phishtank and OpenPhish data sets, i.e., it is common for LLDIs.

Top-Level Domain. In total, we discovered the use of 90 distinct top-level domains. Table 2 provides an overview of the five most often observed top-level

Table 2. Five most often used top-level domains along with top ranked reference brands and number of candidate domains

.com	.co.uk	.de	.ca	.nl
facebook	paypal	ebay	paypal	apple
57,439	2,403	2,121	2,192	613
paypal	apple	amazon	scotiabank	isccards
13,086	806	462	58	239
apple	ebay	paypal	interac	rabobank
9,180	237	304	37	66
citi	barclays	account	bell	abnamro
5,896	157	53	27	38
wellsfargo	amazon	postbank	bmo	wunion
3,741	114	36	26	26

domains. International companies, such as *facebook*, *paypal*, or *ebay* are usually top-ranked. However, attackers not only focus on globally-known brands but target locally-known brands as well, which further demonstrates the importance of our generic approach because those regional reference brands are usually not among the globally top ranked domains. For example, we found the british bank *barclays* in *.co.uk*, the german bank *postbank* in *.de*, the canadian bank *scotiabank* in *.ca*, and the dutch bank *rabobank* in *.nl*.

We found 77 reference brands with at least two different top-level domains among our candidate domains. Furthermore, the reference brands *apple* and *paypal* have 20 different top-level domains. This shows that it is not sufficient to use only the *.com* address of a brand name to get a comprehensive overview.

The top-level domain *.com* was also predominantly used by the candidate domains we identified in the Phishtank data set which is as expected because it is the most often used top-level domain. Subsequently, candidate domains used as well country-code top-level domains, such as *.co.uk* or *.de*.

Candidate Domain Suffix. A victim usually focuses on the beginning of the generated domain. Nevertheless, using a prefix to separate the reference brand further from the often obviously not legitimate second-level domain is reasonable. In total, we found 96,505 distinct suffixes. 17,949 of the 122,707 candidate domains do not have a suffix (15%), i.e., the reference domain is immediately followed by the second-level domain. The most prevalent suffixes usually contain, comparable to the prefixes, terms which suggest the candidate domain is valid, such as *login* (191 candidate domains), *signin* (36), or *support* (20). In 1,687 candidate domains, attackers used suffixes starting with at least two dashes (--) to shift away the second-level domain.

In the Phishtank data set, more than 70% of candidate domains do not have a suffix. While this might be confusing, the reference brand *runescape* is by far the most often targeted one. These candidate domains do not use a suffix, explaining the prevalence of candidate domains without a suffix.

Table 3. Characteristics of LLDI shared by the three phishing feeds.

Characteristic	PhishLabs	Phishtank	OpenPhish
Start date	12/06/12	18/08/10	19/02/12
End date	19/07/31	19/07/31	19/07/31
Candidate domains	122,707	2,919	424
Targeted brands	823	227	41
Targeted brand #1	facebook	runescape	paypal
Targeted brand #2	paypal	paypal	facebook
Targeted brand #3	apple	apple	apple
Predominant TLD	com	com	com
Most often prefix	no prefix	no prefix	no prefix
Most often suffix	no suffix	no suffix	no suffix

Second-Level Domain. An attacker can use a second-level domain only very few times for malicious actions because it will be blacklisted by security tools. Therefore, we expected a low number of candidate domains per second-level domain. The 122,707 candidate domains have 29,634 distinct second-level domains, i.e., on average a second-level domain has two candidate domains. In addition, 424 second-level domains were discovered by PhishLabs within less than 10 days (average 1.9 days, median 1 day). For the remaining second-level domains, there were often multiple years between the detections so that we assume the second-level domains were re-registered.

An analysis of the Phishtank candidate domains further supported our assumption (1.3 candidate domains per second-level domain). Nevertheless, we found 552 second-level domains in the PhishLabs data set with more than ten candidate domains. However, the majority of those second-level domains was detected within a short period of time, i.e., attackers use a second-level domain multiple times but in a short period of time.

Summary. Table 3 summarizes the key characteristics of LLDIs. The three phishing feeds cover different time periods, but the candidate domains share common characteristics and target the same brands. Surprisingly, only PhishLabs and Phishtank share 521 candidate domains, while PhishLabs and OpenPhish as well as PhishTank and OpenPhish do not share any candidate domains. In general, the overlap between the data sources is higher. For our data collection time periods, PhishLabs and Phishtank shared 30,079 FQDNs, PhishLabs and OpenPhish 5,303 FQDNs, and Phishtank and OpenPhish 9,537 FQDNs. Comparing the overall overlap with the overlap in case of LLDI shows that there is room for improvement in the detection of LLDIs. Furthermore, it shows that using additional phishing feeds broaden the analysis.

Table 4. Comparison of different domain squatting techniques. Examples with reference domain *paypal.com*. Note that the number of combosquatting domains is an upper bound (see Sect. 4.3 for details)

Type	Example	# candidate domains
LLDI	paypal.com.foo.com	122,707
Typosquatting	aypal.com	2,503
Combosquatting	paypal-login.com	394,471
Wrong TLD	paypal.top	3,290
Homograph domains	päypal.com	139

4.3 Other Domain Squatting Techniques

In the following, we compare our findings of LLDIs with the prevalent domain squatting techniques typosquatting [10], combosquatting [21], the usage of a wrong top-level domain (wrong TLD) [3], and homograph domains [20]. We used the PhishLabs data set because it covers by far the longest time period and provides a good overview of the domain squatting landscape. Table 4 shows an example as well as the number of candidate domains for each domain squatting technique. LLDI and combosquatting have by far the most candidate domains, while typosquatting, wrong TLD, and homograph domains have a negligible number of candidate domains.

Figure 3 visualizes the fraction of LLDI (red) in comparison with typosquatting, combosquatting, wrong TLD, and homograph domains (green) for the top five reference brands we identified as using LLDI. Up to 98% of the candidate domains utilize LLDI, i.e., the share is comparably high among the analyzed reference brands. It is remarkable that combosquatting is by far the most often used domain squatting technique besides LLDI. In particular, almost 99% of the non-LLDI candidate domains belong to combosquatting. The reference brand *apple* is special because it consists of a common word. Therefore, Kintis et al. excluded it in their study on combosquatting [21]. However, we did not remove common words from our list of reference brands to keep it as comparable as possible. The lower part of the Fig. 3 shows the same comparison for the total amount of reference brands. This reveals that LLDI is used in about one third of all domain squatting candidate domains. Next, we analyze the different domain squatting techniques in more depth.

Typosquatting. In typosquatting, an attacker uses a domain which differs from a well-known domain by a typical typing error [10]. We took the 1,014 reference domains identified in the PhishLabs data set and created the 58,290 possible typosquatting domains according to the five rules of Wang et al. [37]: ① Missing dot between *www* and reference brand: *wwwexample.com* ② Omit character: *xample.com* ③ Swap neighboring characters: *xeample.com* ④ Substitute character

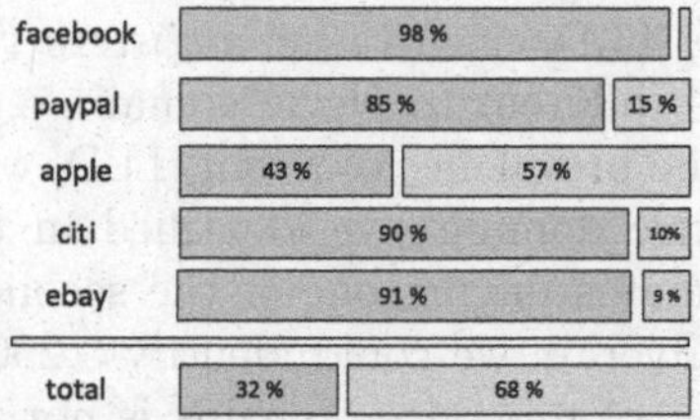

Fig. 3. Fraction of LLDI (red) in comparison with the other domain squatting techniques (green) for the top five reference brands in LLDI. The lower part shows this regarding all reference brands. (Color figure online)

with neighboring character on qwerty keyboard: *wxample.com* ⑤ Duplicate character: *eexample.com*

Afterwards, we searched for test domains which ended with one of the typosquatted reference domains and found 2,503 such domains targeting 402 unique reference domains. The number of possible typosquatting domains is limited so that the low number of typosquatting domains is not surprising. Furthermore, a lot of possible typosquatting domains do not look convincing and are therefore unlikely to be used, e.g., *bay.com* instead of *ebay.com*. The number of typosquatted domains increased between 2012 and 2016 from about 100 per year to about 500 per year and remains constant since then. It is easy to defend against typosquatting by registering the domains in advance.

Combosquatting. In combosquatting, an attacker registers a well-known domain with added suitable terms (e.g., login-paypal.com) or random characters (e.g., abcpaypal.com) to get a not yet registered domain which looks still similar to the original one [21]. Kintis et al. already mentioned that combosquatting is hard to detect if the reference domains are too short or consist of common words [21]. Eventually, they selected only 246 domains for their study. To keep the combosquatting results, at least to a certain degree, comparable to the other domain squatting techniques, we did not remove reference domains from the list of 1,014 reference domains we identified in the PhishLabs data set. Instead we used the second-level labels and searched for test domains which end with a second-level label and at least one additional character plus a valid top-level domain. Given that some of the second-level labels are short or consist of common words, the 394,471 candidate domains (254,011 unique fqdns because some fqdns contain more than one reference domain) are an upper bound. Especially among the most often targeted reference domains are many which are most likely candidate domains because they are common words often used in phishing domains, e.g., *service.com* or *account.co.jp*. However, we found many examples for well-known reference domains, such as *icloud.com* (6,142), *paypal.com* (3,127), or *wellsfargo.com* (1,946).

Wrong TLD. In wrong TLD, an attacker registers the second-level label of a well-known domain in a different top-level domain, e.g., *paypal.top* instead of *paypal.com*. To measure the prevalence of wrong TLD, we took the 1,014 second-level labels of the reference domains we identified in the PhishLabs data set and searched for test domains having one of the second-level labels but a different top-level domain. Overall, we could identify 3,290 wrong TLD candidate domains. However, our set of reference domains is not perfectly suited for this experiment because it contains, for example, the domain *home.ge*, a georgian real estate portal. We found 451 candidate domains ending with the general term *home* plus another top-level domain than *ge*. But it is unlikely that all these domains target the real estate portal. Nevertheless, we found interesting examples, e.g., the canadian bank *cibc.com* (72 candidate domains), *airbnb.com* (43), and *icloud.com* (35). The usage of wrong TLD is limited by the number of available top-level domains, and a legitimate domain owner can defend herself by registering such domains in advance.

Homograph Domains. A homograph domain is a domain using a well-known domain as template and replacing one or multiple characters with similar looking Unicode characters [20]. For example, *paypal.com* and *paypal.com* differ in the usage of a Cyrillic *a* in the first domain. Similarly to Quinkert et al. [31], we created a list of pairs of Latin characters and similarly looking Unicode characters. We searched for test domains in the PhishLabs data set differing from one of the 1,014 reference domains by one or multiple pairs in our list.

In total, we identified 139 domains as homograph domains targeting 27 unique reference domains, which is a comparatively low number but in line with recent publications [20,24,31]. The most often targeted reference domains include the two crypto currency related websites *myetherwallet.com* (26 candidate domains) and *poloniex.com* (17). The majority of candidate domains was identified in recent years, showing at least a small increase of homograph domain usage. Compared to LLDIs, the usage of homograph domains is complicated because the attacker has to select a suitable replacement and make sure that it looks similar in different browsers. Modern browsers often display the homograph domain in an encoded form, e.g., the aforementioned *paypal.com* as *xn--pypl-53dc.com*. The resulting domain does not look like the original domain at all, further explaining the little usage of homograph domains.

4.4 Certificate Transparency Logs (CTLs)

Besides phishing feeds, we used Certificate Transparency Logs (CTLs) from CertStream as additional input for our analysis pipeline. In total, we identified 1,260,639 candidate domains. A closer examination of these candidate domains revealed that in some cases either the selected reference domains are not relevant or the second-level domains are clearly not malicious. For example, universities provide their students access to scientific newspapers using domains like *wiley.com.lib-ezproxy.<university>.edu*. While *wiley.com* is a legitimate domain and a valid reference domain, *university.edu* is a legitimate second-level domain and not an impersonation attempt.

In the following, we focus on the 20 most often targeted reference brands in the PhishLabs data. We identified 102,509 candidate domains for these 20 reference brands with 246 distinct reference domains in CTLs. Note that 1.5 years of CTLs already contain almost as many candidate domains for these 20 reference domains as seven years of PhishLabs' data. In addition, only 4,415 of the 102,509 candidate domains in CTLs are already included in PhishLabs, indicating that many LLDIs are not properly identified by phishing feeds. Next, we analyze each part of the candidate domains, similarly to the phishing feeds.

Candidate Domain Prefix. Overall, we identified 37,787 distinct prefixes which is a lot higher than the 20,386 in PhishLabs identified prefixes, even though the number of candidate domains is comparable. A closer look revealed that the fraction of candidate domains without a prefix is considerably smaller than in the PhishLabs candidate domains (19% vs. 56%). The prefix *www* is similarly common (12% vs 8%), and we found suitable terms like *accounts* (0.5%), *support* (0.5%), or *maps* (0.3%) among the most often used prefixes. In conclusion, our results show that the prefix structure of the examined candidate domains is similar to the PhishLabs candidate domains' prefix structure.

Reference Brand. In general, bigger brands like *apple* or *google* have more candidate domains than less well-known brands like *desjardins* or *kbc*. We found only one candidate domain for the reference brand *square-enix*. However, the candidate domains in PhishLabs were all detected between 2013 and 2016, while our CTL data set covers February 2018 through July 2019 so that the low number of candidate domains is as expected.

Besides the 20 most often targeted reference brands, we also analyzed the previously discussed reference brand *runescape*. Surprisingly, we found more than 5,000 candidate domains for this reference brand in CTLs (compared to 241 candidate domains identified between 2012 and 2018 by PhishLabs). The vast majority of these candidate domains follows a very similar structure than the candidate domains identified by PhishLabs. More than 3,000 candidate domains start with *secure* or *www.secure* and more than 1,500 candidate domains start with *service* or *www.service*. Additionally, we could find prefixes like *webmail.secure* or *mail.services* showing that attackers change the particular subdomains.

Our results show that phishing feeds cover LLDI usage to a certain extent. However, the number of domains possibly used in the wild is far higher so that better detection mechanisms are necessary to identify the domains early on. Instead of using our generic method, which we used to get a broad overview of LLDIs, a domain owner can use our technique to monitor a limited, predefined set of domains she owns.

Top-Level Domain. We identified 136 distinct top-level domains being used with the previously mentioned reference brands. However, only 20 top-level domains are used in more than 96% of the candidate domains with the generic top-level domain *.com* being the by far most often used top-level domain (85%). Subsequently, country code top-level domains like *.co.uk*, *.co.jp*, or *.de* are used to a lesser degree. These results are similar to the PhishLabs results, even though the particular country code top-level domains following *.com* changed slightly.

Candidate Domain Suffix. In total, we identified 9,870 distinct suffixes, which is about 10% of the number of suffixes we identified in the PhishLabs candidate domains. The vast majority of candidate domains does not have a suffix, followed by short suffixes or suffixes with terms like *admin*, *support*, or *manage*. A candidate domain with a suffix starting with -- is a good way to separate the reference domain from the rest. In contrast to the PhishLabs data set, we found only a very limited number of candidate domains which used this technique.

Second-Level Domain. The 102,509 candidate domains use 33,198 second-level domains which is comparable to the 29,634 second-level domains used by the PhishLabs candidate domains. Similarly, the vast majority of the second-level domains is used for less than ten candidate domains. In addition, we found 218 candidate domains starting with *com-* (19 in PhishLabs) and one with *de-* (0 in PhishLabs). The usage of suitable terms is more common in the CTL data set. We found especially *account* (2,812), *secure* (1,148), and *support* (1,024) being used. To a lesser degree, *sign* (689) and *verification* (542) were used.

5 Limitations

Our approach to detect reference domains performs well on phishing feeds because domains in the subdomain part are impersonated with malicious intent. In contrast, on CTLs we encountered challenges deciding whether a possible reference domain is impersonated with malicious intent or an accidental finding. Using a fixed set of reference domains instead of our approach to discover reference domains works better as long as the reference domains are well-known and often impersonated. While this is the case for a list containing a limited number of well-known reference domains, e.g., the top 500 or top 1,000 Tranco domains, increasing the number of domains so that less well-known domains are included will lead to the same problem we faced with our approach. Additionally, legitimate usage of domains in the subdomain part (e.g., magazine websites in subdomains of university libraries) is an issue both our approach and the usage of a fixed set of reference domains have. A possible mitigation is to check the domain's reputation to decide whether it is a legitimate second-level domain. The generic approach offers interesting insights because it enables us to find small and often overlooked phishing targets. Therefore, we decided to use the generic approach and focus our analysis on the phishing feeds. This study is a first step to show how prevalent LLDI is and to discuss the structure of the domains.

We do not know how the phishing feeds are created so that we cannot assess their completeness. To address this, we used three different phishing feeds for the evaluation of our approach. Thus, we are confident to get the best possible overview of phishing domains and the used domain squatting techniques.

6 Conclusion and Recommendations

In this paper, we presented a generic approach to identify LLDIs in phishing feeds and CTLs to understand their usage and provide a basis to develop proper countermeasures. In a comprehensive measurement study, we identified more than 122,000 domains in PhishLabs showing that attackers use LLDIs for at least seven years. Additionally, we discovered almost 3,000 domains in Phishtank and a few hundred ones in OpenPhish. In contrast to other domain squatting studies, our generic approach does not rely on a predefined list of reference domains so that we identified not only big technology companies or financial institutions as victims, but also locally operating companies, such as regional banks. Our analysis of LLDI's structure revealed that attackers start with the impersonated brand or use suitable terms to convince victims of the domain's legitimacy. Additionally, we compared LLDI with other domain squatting techniques and found that it exceeds many of them. Hence, this attack technique needs more attention from academics and practitioners. An analysis of one and a half years of CTL data demonstrated an even greater usage of LLDI in the wild.

Our results show that domain owners should closely pay attention in which context their domains are used to detect potential attacks early on. Since traditional detection (e.g., analyzing newly registered domains) and prevention mechanisms (e.g., defensive registrations) are not capable of defending against LLDIs, our results emphasize a need to understand the technique better and develop proper countermeasures. We consider a combination of two countermeasures as most promising: first, awareness trainings for users, and second, identification and proper representation of such domains in browsers. Recently, Quinkert et al. showed teaching users how domain squatting works improves their capability to identify malicious domains [30]. We analyzed the structure of candidate domains to show characteristics, e.g., typical prefixes or the position of reference brands in candidate domains. Our structural analysis can be a basis for awareness campaigns to teach users how LLDI works and what characteristics are important to detect it. We recommend browser vendors should clearly mark the second-level domain (the trend to display the subdomain part in gray and the second-level domain in black points in the right direction) and display a warning if, for example, a well-known brand name is used in the subdomain part.

References

1. CertStream. https://certstream.calidog.io/. Accessed 06 Apr 2020
2. Half of all Phishing Sites Now Have the Padlock. https://krebsonsecurity.com/2018/11/half-of-all-phishing-sites-now-have-the-padlock/comment-page-1/. Accessed 06 Apr 2020

3. LEGO vs Cybersquatters: The burden of new gTLDs. https://news.netcraft.com/archives/2017/04/14/lego-vs-cybersquatters-the-burden-of-new-gtlds.html. Accessed 06 Apr 2020
4. OpenPhish. https://openphish.com. Accessed 06 Apr 2020
5. Phishing Activity Trends Report, 3rd Quarter 2019. https://docs.apwg.org/reports/apwg_trends_report_q3_2019.pdf. Accessed 06 Apr 2020
6. PhishLabs. https://www.phishlabs.com. Accessed 06 Apr 2020
7. Phishtank. https://www.phishtank.com/. Accessed 06 Apr 2020
8. Twitch Phishing - 182 Phishing Streams In 2 Weeks (2018). https://www.reddit.com/r/runescape/comments/8in1r0/twitch_phishing_182_phishing_streams_in_2_weeks/. Accessed 06 Apr 2020
9. What is Certificate Transparency? (2018). https://www.certificate-transparency.org/what-is-ct. Accessed 06 Apr 2020
10. Agten, P., Joosen, W., Piessens, F., Nikiforakis, N.: Seven months' worth of mistakes: a longitudinal study of typosquatting abuse. In: Network and Distributed System Security Symposium (NDSS) (2015)
11. Antonakakis, M., Perdisci, R., Lee, W., Vasiloglou, N., Dagon, D.: Detecting Malware Domains at the Upper DNS Hierarchy. In: USENIX Security Symposium (2011)
12. Bilge, L., Kirda, E., Kruegel, C., Balduzzi, M.: EXPOSURE: finding malicious domains using passive DNS analysis. In: Network and Distributed System Security Symposium (NDSS) (2011)
13. blog.comodo.com: Comodo SSL Affiliate The Recent RA Compromise (2011). https://blog.comodo.com/other/the-recent-ra-compromise/. Accessed 06 Apr 2020
14. Chiba, D., Akiyama, A.H., Koide, T., Sawabe, Y., Goto, S., Akiyama, M.: DomainScouter: understanding the risks of deceptive IDNs. In: Research in Attacks, Intrusions, and Defenses (RAID) (2019)
15. Fisher, D.: Attackers Obtain Valid Cert for Google Domains, Mozilla Moves to Revoke It (2011). https://threatpost.com/attackers-obtain-valid-cert-google-domains-mozilla-moves-revoke-it-082911/75590/. Accessed 06 Apr 2020
16. Hao, S., Kantchelian, A., Miller, B., Paxson, V., Feamster, N.: PREDATOR: proactive recognition and elimination of domain abuse at time-of-registration. In: Conference on Computer and Communications Security (CCS) (2016)
17. Hassold, C.: Silent Librarian: More to the Story of the Iranian Mabna Institute Indictment (2018). https://info.phishlabs.com/blog/silent-librarian-more-to-the-story-of-the-iranian-mabna-institute-indictment. Accessed 06 Apr 2020
18. Hatch, O.G.: The Anticybersquatting Consumer Protection Act (1999). https://www.gpo.gov/fdsys/pkg/CRPT-106srpt140/html/CRPT-106srpt140.htm. Accessed 06 Apr 2020
19. Ho, G., Sharma, A., Javed, M., Paxson, V., Wagner, D.: Detecting credential spearphishing in enterprise settings. In: USENIX Security Symposium (2017)
20. Holgers, T., Watson, D.E., Gribble, S.D.: Cutting through the confusion: a measurement study of homograph attacks. In: USENIX Annual Technical Conference (2006)
21. Kintis, P., et al.: Hiding in plain sight: a longitudinal study of combosquatting abuse. In: Conference on Computer and Communications Security (CCS) (2017)
22. Lauinger, T., Chaabane, A., Buyukkayhan, A.S., Onarlioglu, K., Robertson, W.: Game of registrars: an empirical analysis of post-expiration domain name takeovers. In: Usenix Security Symposium (2017)

23. Le Pochat, V., Van Goethem, T., Tajalizadehkhoob, S., Korczynski, M., Joosen, W.: TRANCO: a research-oriented top sites rankinghardened against manipulation. In: Network and Distributed System Security Symposium (NDSS) (2019)
24. Liu, B., et al.: A reexamination of internationalized domain names: the good, the bad and the ugly. In: International Conference on Dependable Systems and Networks (DSN) (2018)
25. Liu, D., Li, Z., Du, K., Wang, H., Liu, B., Duan, H.: Don't let one rotten apple spoil the whole barrel: towards automated detection of shadowed domains. In: Conference on Computer and Communications Security (CCS) (2017)
26. Luo, M., Starov, O., Honarmand, N., Nikiforakis, N.: Hindsight: understanding the evolution of UI vulnerabilities in mobile browsers. In: Conference on Computer and Communications Security (CCS) (2017)
27. Mockapetris, P.: RFC 1035 - Domain Names - Implementation and Specification (1987). https://tools.ietf.org/html/rfc1035. Accessed 06 Apr 2020
28. Nikiforakis, N., Balduzzi, M., Desmet, L., Piessens, F., Joosen, W.: Soundsquatting: uncovering the use of homophones in domain squatting. In: International Conference on Information Security (ISC) (2014)
29. Nikiforakis, N., Van Acker, S., Meert, W., Desmet, L., Piessens, F., Joosen, W.: Bitsquatting: exploiting bit-flips for fun, or profit? In: International World Wide Web Conference (WWW) (2013)
30. Quinkert, F., Degeling, M., Blythe, J., Holz, T.: Be the phisher - understanding users' perception of malicious domains. In: ASIA Conference on Computer and Communications Security (ASIACCS) (2020)
31. Quinkert, F., Lauinger, T., Robertson, W., Kirda, E., Holz, T.: It's not what it looks like: measuring attacks and defensive registrations of homograph domains. In: Conference on Communications and Network Security (CNS) (2019)
32. Roberts, R., Goldschlag, Y., Walter, R., Chung, T., Mislove, A., Levin, D.: You are who you appear to be: a longitudinal study of domain impersonation in TLS Certificates. In: Conference on Computer and Communications Security (CCS) (2019)
33. Scheitle, Q., et al.: The rise of certificate transparency and its implications on the internet ecosystem. In: Internet Measurement Conference (IMC) (2018)
34. Suzuki, H., Chiba, D., Yoneya, Y., Mori, T., Goto, S.: ShamFinder: an automated framework for detecting IDN homographs. In: Internet Measurement Conference (IMC) (2019)
35. Szurdi, J., Kocso, B., Cseh, G., Spring, J., Felegyhazi, M., Kanich, C.: The long "Taile" of typosquatting domain names. In: USENIX Security Symposium (2014)
36. Tian, K., Jan, S.T.K., Hu, H., Yao, D., Wang, G.: Needle in a haystack: tracking down elite phishing domains in the wild. In: Internet Measurement Conference (IMC) (2018)
37. Wang, Y.M., Beck, D., Wang, J., Verbowski, C., Daniels, B.: Strider typo-patrol: discovery and analysis of systematic typo-squatting. In: USENIX Workshop on Steps Reducing Unwanted Traffic on the Internet (SRUTI) (2006)

Help, My Signal has Bad Device!

Breaking the Signal Messenger's Post-Compromise Security Through a Malicious Device

Jan Wichelmann(✉), Sebastian Berndt, Claudius Pott, and Thomas Eisenbarth

University of Lübeck, Lübeck, Germany
{j.wichelmann,s.berndt,c.pott,thomas.eisenbarth}@uni-luebeck.de

Abstract. In response to ongoing discussions about data usage by companies and governments, and its implications for privacy, there is a growing demand for secure communication techniques. While during their advent, most messenger apps focused on features rather than security, this has changed in the recent years: Since then, many have adapted end-to-end encryption as a standard feature. One of the most popular solutions is the Signal messenger, which aims to guarantee forward secrecy (i. e. security of previous communications in case of leakage of long-term secrets) and future secrecy (i. e. security of future communications in case of leakage of short-term secrets). If every user uses exactly one device, it is known that Signal achieves forward secrecy and even post-compromise security (i. e. security of future communications in case of leakage of *long*-term secrets). But the Signal protocol also allows for the use of multiple devices via the Sesame protocol. This multi-device setting is typically ignored in the security analysis of Signal.

In this work, we discuss the security of the Signal messenger in this multi-device setting. We show that the current implementation of the device registration allows an attacker to register an own, malicious device, which gives them unrestricted access to all future communication of their victim, and even allows full impersonation. This directly shows that the current Signal implementation does not guarantee post-compromise security. We discuss several countermeasures, both simple ones aiming to increase detectability of our attack, as well as a broader approach that seeks to solve the root issue, namely the weak device registration flow.

1 Introduction

Messenger apps like Whatsapp, WeChat or Telegram have become a cornerstone of person-to-person communication in the past decade. To meet users demand for privacy and to protect their right for freedom of expression, many messengers now employ end-to-end encryption (E2EE) to ensure message privacy. E2EE also ensures that operators cannot pry on users communication and thus poses new challenges to government surveillance. With the popularity and better protection of communication, governments and their police forces fear *going blind* and try to regain access via jurisdiction and/or improved technical capabilities. For example, Russia banned Telegram for several years, due to its use

L. Bilge et al. (Eds.): DIMVA 2021, LNCS 12756, pp. 88–105, 2021.
https://doi.org/10.1007/978-3-030-80825-9_5

of E2EE [23]. But political will to push regulation and/or improve technical capabilities also exist in the US [19] and the EU [8].

One messenger and its same-named secure communication protocol stands out: Signal. The Signal protocol has received great scrutiny by the crypto community and is widely accepted as providing a very high level of security. In fact, Whatsapp adopted the Signal protocol to restore user trust after being bought by Facebook in 2014. One of the features that make the Signal protocol special is its *future secrecy* property, which—in addition to protecting all communication completed *before* a breach of local credentials—also provides security guarantees in case the *short-term keys* of a system were leaked [25]. Furthermore, the specification states that the protocol achieves some sort of security against passive attackers that were able to compromise one of the parties, but not against active attackers [27]. This is a weaker notion than that of *post-compromise security*, which also protects all communication if the *long-term keys* are leaked [16]. Post-compromise security seems particularly desirable in a world where governments invest heavily in the ability to intercept messenger communication. But it can also restore trust in cases where long-term secrets have been compromised due to a malware infection, leakage of backups, or legal reasons [12,17]. For most messengers, even a short-term compromise results in insecure subsequent communication if long-term keys could be leaked (see e. g. the comparison in [18]). Most of the messengers that restore security toward a broad class of adversaries even with compromised secrets are based on the Signal protocol. Furthermore, it was shown that Signal does indeed guarantee the stronger notion of post-compromise security, in the one-device-per-user use case [9,15].

Multi-device support is handled by the Sesame sub-protocol in Signal. Sesame adds a new level of complexity to the protocol, which is often not reflected in current cryptographic analysis [9,15]. Unlike other parts of the Signal protocol, the Sesame specification is less precise and leaves a lot of freedom to the actual implementation of the protocol. Whether Signal achieves post-compromise security in the general case of users having multiple devices is thus not as clear. In [16], the authors state that TextSecure—the predecessor of Signal—might not achieve post-compromise security due to its implementation of the handling of multiple devices. The authors of [15] state that the post-compromise security of Signal depends on subtle details related to device state reset and the handling of multiple devices, but that Signal could achieve some form of it.

Just recently, the question whether implementations of the Signal protocol do have post-compromise security was answered in [18]: The authors argue that the Signal *protocol* does guarantee post-compromise security, but several prominent implementations either do not guarantee it at all (e. g. WhatsApp and Facebook Secret Conversations) or only partially (e. g. Signal messenger), due to their problematic handling of desynchronization scenarios. More concretely, the authors clone a device and later try to use this clone. Whenever the clone sends a message, the receiving party just displays a message "Bad encrypted message". Similarly, whenever this clone receives a message, only the message "Bad encrypted message" is displayed. In both cases, the sending party does not receive any notification about this. This behavior means that the cloned device can impersonate the original device, but can not be used to send or receive messages, making it rather useless.

In this work, we present an attack on the post-compromise security of the Signal messenger that allows to stealthily register a new device via the Sesame protocol. In contrast to the attack in [18], this new device can *send and receive messages* without raising any "Bad encrypted message" errors. Our attack thus shows that the Signal messenger does not guarantee post-compromise security at all in the multi-device setting.

1.1 Our Contribution

This work analyzes the Sesame protocol as it is implemented in the current version of the Signal messenger. As many parts of Sesame are not specified out, we reverse-engineer specific implementation details of Sesame in the Signal messenger. With those gaps in the Sesame specification filled, we analyze the *post-compromise security* property of the Signal protocol, which indeed holds in the single-device per user scenario [15]. However, we show that the current implementation of the Signal messenger, due to unfortunate choices in the Sesame realization, undermines the post-compromise security and may ease interception of messenger communication. We further point out how simple changes in the realization of Sesame can be used to close these existing gaps. In summary, we

- give an overview of the Signal protocol suite, and discuss its security in case one of a user's devices gets temporarily compromised;
- highlight security-critical steps that have been declared implementation details and thus were left out from the protocol specification;
- show that in the current implementation, an attacker can fully break post-compromise security by leaking only two long-term secrets, and using these to register a new device;
- discuss several mitigations to help users detect our attack, and to fix the underlying issue in order to allow secure registration of devices.

1.2 Responsible Disclosure

We disclosed our findings to the Signal organization on October 20, 2020, and received an answer on October 28, 2020. In summary, they state that they do not treat a compromise of long-term secrets as part of their adversarial model. Therefore, they do not currently plan to mitigate the described attack or implement one of the proposed countermeasures.

2 Background

We always denote key-pairs by capital letters. For a key-pair IK, we denote the secret key by $\mathrm{sec}(IK)$ and the public key by $\mathrm{pub}(IK)$. Symmetric keys are denoted by lowercase letters, e.g. sk.

Nowadays, instant messaging is omnipresent and such messengers often even replace the use of e-mail in companies (examples include Slack [4], Microsoft Teams [2], or Webex Teams [6]). Over the last decades, many different cryptographic protocols for secure messaging were developed. Due to the rapid technical development, many new features were added to the applications implementing these protocols, but their security guarantees were rarely updated as well. Two common features leading to security problems are *group communication* and *multi-device communication* (see also the discussion in [13] for important differences between these scenarios). In the case of group communication, multiple users want to communicate in a group. Furthermore, these groups are typically dynamic, i. e. the users in a group can and do change relatively often. To circumvent the arising problems with group communication, the *Messaging Layer Security (MLS)* protocol was introduced and is currently in the standardization process [5,14]. In the case of multi-device communication, two users want to communicate, but each of them may use different devices (such as a laptop, a smartphone, and a tablet). Furthermore, users typically want to register new devices, transfer old messages, and have a synchronized status on all of their devices. To the best of our knowledge, there is no proposal for a unified handling of multiple devices.

In this work, we only consider the multi-device setting and the problems arising in this scenario. For simplicity, we focus on two-user communication, i. e., two users A (or Alice) and B (or Bob) communicate, but each of the users owns several devices.

2.1 Post-Compromise Security

Modern cryptographic protocols aim to achieve different security guarantees, depending on their use case. One of those guarantees is the security in case the long term keys of a party are leaked. Two important notions dealing with this are *forward secrecy* and *post-compromise security*: Forward secrecy (typically achieved by the use of ephemeral keys) guarantees that *previous* communication is still confidential, even if the long-term keys of the parties are leaked (see Fig. 1a).

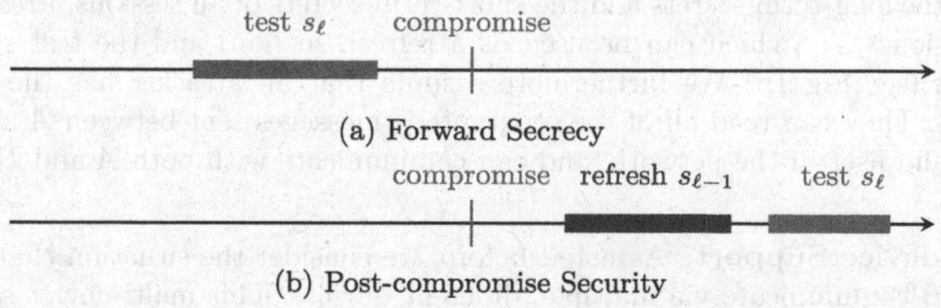

Fig. 1. Schematic representation of forward secrecy and post-compromise security.

In contrast, post-compromise security guarantees that leakage of the long-term keys does not break the confidentiality of *future* communication (see Fig. 1b). Clearly, the general goal of universal post-compromise security is not achievable. If A and B have not communicated before, an attacker knowing the long-term identity key $\mathrm{sec}(IK_A)$ of A can perfectly impersonate A and is thus able to perform a man-in-the-middle attack, breaking the confidentiality of the communication between A and B. But, only slightly weaker guarantees are still possible: If A and B have already communicated before, they might have agreed on an (ephemeral) key $EK_{A,B}$ during this session. Whenever A and B now want to resume their communication, A uses both $\mathrm{sec}(IK_A)$ and $EK_{A,B}$ to authenticate themselves. Clearly, having only access to the long-term key $\mathrm{sec}(IK_A)$ is thus not sufficient to break the confidentiality of the communication in this scenario.

In [16], Cohn-Gordon, Cremers, and Garratt formalized this above intuition both about the impossibility of universal post-compromise security, but also on the possibility of slightly weaker versions. Informally, they show that even if all but one exchange of messages before the secure session are compromised, post-compromise security can still be achieved.

Note that post-compromise security can be useful for a wide range of situations, not only for a complete breach of a device: For example, an old backup containing the long-term keys might have been leaked (see e. g. [3]), malware was present on the device (see e. g. [1]), parts of the implementation were manipulated (see e. g. [10,11]), or a secondary device might have been stolen.

Attacker Model. Here, we only give an informal discussion about the formalization of post-compromise security and refer the interested reader to [16] for formal definitions. Alice and Bob communicate via a sequence of *sessions*, which can be thought of as runs of an authenticated key exchange protocol. Each session s has its own *local state*, which includes e. g. the session key EK_s, the parties A and B, the randomness used in s, and all messages exchanged during the session. The parties A and B have a *global state*, which includes e. g. the long-term secrets IK and the public keys of all other parties.

Now, consider a sequence of sessions $s_1, s_2, \ldots, s_\ell$ between A and B, where the final session s_ℓ is the *test session*. The goal of an attacker is to break the confidentiality of this test session. To do so, we assume that an attacker can obtain the long-term secrets and the short-term secrets of all sessions, *except* for the session $s_{\ell-1}$ (which can be used as a refresh session) and the test session s_ℓ itself (see Fig. 1b) We furthermore assume that an attacker has the usual abilities: They can read all of the (encrypted) messages sent between A and B, are a valid user in the network, and can communicate with both A and B.

Multi-device Support. As noted before, we consider the situation that both A and B communicate via multiple, different devices. This multi-device setting already leads to non-trivial problems with regard to post-compromise security. Consider a single-device communication protocol Π that has post-compromise security. In order to adapt Π to a multi-device setting, several questions arise:

- How to synchronize the different devices of a single user?
- How to register a new device?

To still guarantee the post-compromise security of the multi-device protocol, these questions (and many more) need to be answered carefully.

To handle the synchronization of the different devices of a single user (and also handle asynchronous messaging), one could make use of a server. For each user A of the system, this server manages a *mailbox*, which stores all messages sent to A, all messages received by A, and all registered devices of A. The messages are stored encrypted. Now, whenever A uses one of their devices to send a message to B, the device would put this message in the mailbox of A and in the mailbox of B, if this device was successfully registered for A. To synchronize received messages, every successfully registered device of A could obtain and decrypt the content of the mailbox of A.

A straight-forward way to register a new device would be using the long-term secret key $\mathrm{sec}(IK_A)$ to add the new device to the device list of the mailbox of A. Unfortunately, such a strategy might already break the post-compromise security of the protocol: If, apart from knowing $\mathrm{sec}(IK_A)$, no further verification from A is required for such a registration, an attacker knowing $\mathrm{sec}(IK_A)$ can register a new device without alerting A. From this point on, the attacker would be able to observe the complete communication of A, thus breaking the post-compromise security of the protocol. The Sesame protocol used by Signal to handle multiple devices roughly follows this approach and, as we will show, is thus not post-compromise secure.

3 The Signal Protocol

The *Signal* (formerly *Axolotl*) protocol [26] provides end-to-end encryption for text messages and multimedia files. It is widely used in different communication applications such as WhatsApp [33], Skype [24] and the Signal messenger itself. The protocol is based on the Double Ratchet algorithm and uses a triple Elliptic-curve Diffie–Hellman handshake (X3DH) to initiate new conversations. The Sesame protocol is used to enable multi-device support. Signal uses a number of cryptographic primitives including

- Elliptic Curve Diffie-Hellman functions (implemented by X25519 or X448 [21]);
- a signature scheme called XEdDSA producing EdDSA-compatible signatures from X25519 or X448 using the hash function SHA-512 [26];
- a hash function (implemented by SHA-256/SHA-512);
- a key derivation function KDF based on the HKDF algorithm [20];
- an authenticated encryption (AEAD) scheme [31,32]. Concretely, KDF is used to produce an encryption key, an authentication key, and an initialization vector (IV). The plaintext is then encrypted with AES-256 in CBC mode. Finally, HMAC with the hash function and the authentication key is used on the authenticated data.

We continue by giving an overview over the three protocol parts that jointly form the Signal protocol. For the remainder of this paper we use the term *user* for one communicating entity that usually is a single person. Note, that one user may have multiple devices, that they use for their communication. The term *party* on the other hand is used more abstractly on the protocol level for one side of the communication, usually represented by a single device or server.

3.1 X3DH [29]

In order to setup a secure session, all parties have to agree on a key. Usually, this is done via a Diffie-Hellman key exchange, but this does not work well in a messenger setting, which heavily relies on asynchronous communication. If party A wants to send a message to party B, but party B is offline, party A needs a way to derive a shared secret key sk without any interaction with party B.

The X3DH protocol aims to solve that problem, by allowing B to store a set of public keys in a public location, which A can subsequently use for a Diffie-Hellman computation. In order to provide authentication and freshness, B offers their public identity key and a set of *prekeys*. A retrieves B's public keys and computes DH key exchanges with their own secret identity key and an ephemeral key. To allow B to later derive the same shared key, A subsequently sends their public identity key and the public ephemeral key. A can now encrypt messages with the shared key and send them to B. As soon as B gets online again, they can use A's public keys to derive the same shared secret and decrypt A's messages. In order to encrypt and send messages to A, B executes the same protocol steps as A, deriving another shared secret for the other direction of communication.

3.2 Double Ratchet [27]

While agreement on a shared secret key is sufficient for A and B to exchange encrypted messages, it is quite vulnerable against possible compromise: As soon as the shared key gets leaked, an attacker gains full access to all past and future communication between A and B. To avoid this, the shared key needs to be refreshed in regular intervals, to add new randomness and narrow down the possible damage from a leaked secret.

The Double Ratchet protocol solves this by introducing four cryptographic chains. The first one, the *Diffie-Hellman (DH) chain*, consists of an alternating series of public and private ephemeral keys, where the private part is provided by the local party, and the public part comes from the remote party. Ideally, each message sent from A to B also contains a new public ephemeral key from A, and vice versa. Each time a party receives a new public ephemeral key, they advance their local DH chain by one step.

The shared secret from the DH chain is then fed into a symmetric *root chain*, which is initialized with the initial secret from the X3DH key exchange. On each step of the DH chain, the root chain is advanced by one step as well. The root chain uses a keyed hash function to generate a *root key*, which is used as key for the next root chain step, and a *chain key* for sending or receiving. Each chain key spawns a new sending or receiving chain, which is in turn used to derive the keys for encrypting or decrypting messages. Since all chain keys are derived using a keyed hash function, an attacker cannot compute their predecessors, so the protocol grants forward secrecy.

Note that each DH chain step leads to a new sending or receiving chain. Thus, if a sending or receiving chain key gets compromised, only the messages encrypted with that particular chain are affected. The same holds for the root chain: If a root key gets compromised, only the immediate sending or receiving chain and its associated messages are affected. The next step of the root chain can be considered secure again, as it incorporates fresh randomness from the DH chain. In case a long-term secret (e.g., the private identity key) gets leaked, the confidentiality of future messages from existing Double Ratchet sessions is still preserved, as long as the attacker does not also gain access to all new private ephemeral keys. Thus, intuitively, the Double Ratchet protocol also provides post-compromise security. For a formal security proof of Signal's forward secrecy and post-compromise security we refer to [15].

3.3 Sesame [28]

In order to allow users to send and receive messages from multiple devices, the Sesame protocol was introduced. The protocol describes two scenarios: A *per-user* scenario, where a single identity key is used on all the user's devices, and a *per-device* scenario, where each device has its own identity key. Both scenarios are handled in a similar fashion by the Sesame protocol, since the only difference is the location where the identity keys are stored – either in the user records or in the device records.

On the highest level, each device stores a list of users that it knows, including its owner. For each of these users, a non-empty list of their devices is stored, which in turn is associated with a list of Double Ratchet sessions. Additionally, each device has its own *mailbox* on the server, which is used to asynchronously fetch encrypted messages from other devices and which only contains messages that weren't yet received. For each device, exactly one session is *active* at a time, while the other ones are *stale* and only kept in case delayed messages arrive.

Whenever a device of user A sends a message to user B, it sends this message to each device associated with B, either via its current active session or by initializing a new session via X3DH. Additionally, the message is sent to all devices of A, using the same mechanism. The server then puts the messages into the respective mailboxes, where the receiving devices can obtain their messages from and then decrypt them using the corresponding session keys.

While Sesame describes how messages are kept synchronized on all devices in a multi-device scenario, it does not cover the registration of new devices: These details are fully left to the implementation, excluding them from considerations regarding Sesame's security. In Sect. 4, we show that the current implementation in the Signal messenger is indeed vulnerable, and allows an attacker to impersonate their victim.

4 Signal Implementation in the Signal Messenger

While the specification of the X3DH key exchange and the Double Ratchet are rather specific, Signal's multi-device extension Sesame only describes a high-level view of exchanging messages between multiple devices and sessions (compare e. g. [27] and [28]). Many important details, most notably the registration of new devices, are left to the programmer, and are thus not included in any security proofs. In this section, we take a closer look at these implementation details and show how these allow an attacker to work around Signal's post-compromise guarantees, gaining unconstrained access to a user's future communication. Our attack shows that the Signal messenger currently does not guarantee post-compromise security. Furthermore, in contrast to [18], our attack allows us to completely break the privacy of the communication, as it allows us to both send and receive messages.

For simplicity, we assume a single user with identity key *IK* and who uses the Signal app *A*. The device registration aims to add a new device *D*.

4.1 Reverse Engineering the Protocol Implementation

Since the device registration protocol is not specified anywhere, we had to analyze how it is implemented in the Signal messenger. Unfortunately, there is neither an official API specification nor any documentation of the procedure, so we had to dive into the implementation and try to piece together the relevant bits in order to get a full view of the device registration protocol and do a security analysis.

For our analysis, we checked out the source repositories of Signal's Android app (commit `fc41fb5`[1]) and Desktop client (commit `a1721ed`[2]). Apart from occasional source code comments, both implementations are almost entirely undocumented, and it proved difficult for us to get an overview by inspecting the various subfolders/packages. In order to roughly locate the relevant code parts, we searched for various strings which are shown in the UI, and then followed the call traces.

There is no built-in means for exporting sent/received packets in debug mode; Signal does certificate pinning with a custom TLS root certificate, which we weren't able to circumvent without losing connectivity, so setting up a proxy for intercepting the network communication was not an option. Thus, we mostly resorted to static analysis in order to understand what data is sent across the network, along with some custom debug outputs. Studying the server implementation[3] helped us infer the higher level information flow.

We lay out our reverse engineering results in the following section, where we explain the device registration process and the involved secrets.

---

1 https://github.com/signalapp/Signal-Android/tree/fc41fb5.

2 https://github.com/signalapp/Signal-Desktop/tree/a1721ed.

3 https://github.com/signalapp/Signal-Server.

4.2 Device Registration

Prerequisites. To register a new device, several private and public values are required, which may be partially known to an attacker:

- The (private) identity key *IK*: As described in Sect. 3.1, this long-term key is required to setup new prekeys and start new conversation sessions. It is only stored on the user's device.
- The phone number *pn*: As, for the current implementation, the phone number is the only means for creating and identifying user accounts, it can be assumed to be known to the attacker.
- The app's API username un_A and password pw_A: These are used in HTTP authentication when communicating with the server. The username directly depends on the phone number and the device ID (which is constant for the primary device), and can thus be easily guessed; the password is random and needs to be leaked. Since the authentication data is sent in the clear, but inside the TLS layer, the attacker may either exfiltrate it through the same channel as the identity key, or by gaining (limited) access to the server, which is assumed untrusted by the Signal protocol.
- The profile key *pk*: The profile key allows accessing certain meta information, like the user's display name and their avatar image. It usually is transmitted when starting a new conversation, to allow the other peer to download and decrypt the user's profile information, so the attacker may have already gained access to that key by communicating with their victim at an earlier point of time. Anyway, we found that sending the profile key is optional for device registration, and does not influence detectability of our attack.

Adversarial Scenario. We now concretize our generic attacker model, which we presented earlier. Throughout the rest of the paper, we assume an adversary who at some point managed to obtain the private identity key *IK*, the phone number *pn*, the API username un_A, and the password pw_A. After all of these information are retrieved, the attacker does not interact directly with the victim or interferes with their communication. Instead, the adversary will only interact with the public Signal servers once during the compromise stage, using these cloned credentials of the victim to impersonate the victim towards the server (but not toward any of the communication partners of the victim). Once registered, the adversary performs direct communication with a party (the Signal server), to collect messages from their mailbox. This corresponds to the scenario described in [18], where an attacker was able to clone the complete smartphone and uses this cloned copy at a later time.

The PIN. Another secret, which is only known to the user, is the PIN *pin*: Signal PINs were introduced in 2020 [30], and are designed as a means for storing private information in an untrusted location. This information may be later used to recover key material and the contact list, e.g., after losing the primary phone (*Secure Value Recovery* [22]). The PIN cannot be acquired by breaking into the

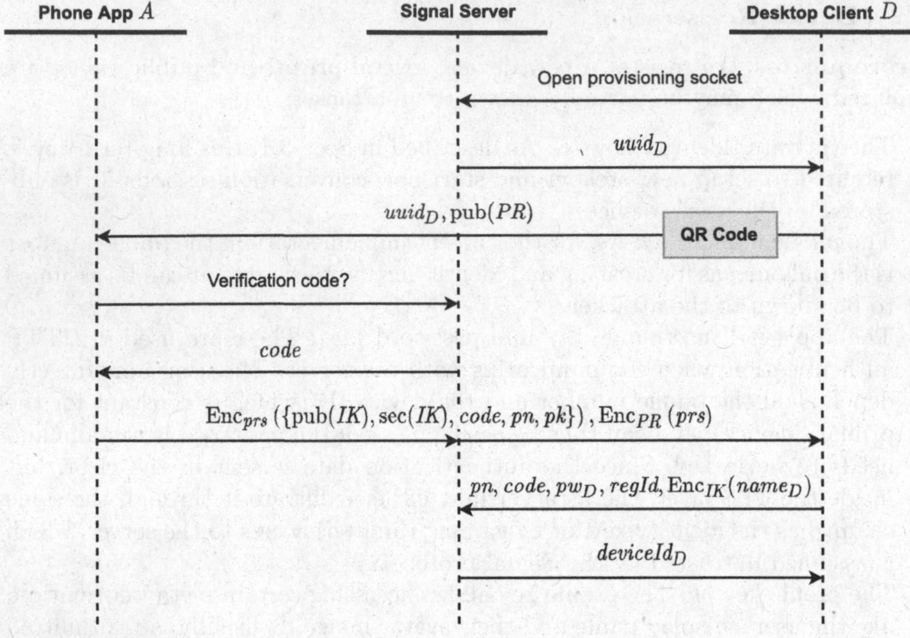

Fig. 2. The Signal device provisioning protocol. The user registers a new device D with their primary device A.

server, as it is claimed to be secured by an SGX Enclave, which only permits a small number of guesses. However, the current implementation of the app offers a PIN "reminder" feature, which asks the user to enter the PIN in regular intervals. This feature compares the hash of the entered PIN to a locally stored value, in order to avoid accidentally using up the number of allowed guesses on the server side. If an attacker manages to retrieve this hash value, e.g. by dumping the memory of the app, they may be able to determine the (likely short) PIN through an offline brute-force attack. However, knowing the PIN is not required for our attack, except if the attacker wants to obtain the full contact list of their victim.

Device Provisioning Protocol. The protocol for registering a new device, called *provisioning* by the Signal implementation, is illustrated in Fig. 2. As stated before, we use A to denote the phone (primary) instance of the user's Signal account, and D to denote the desktop client instance which the user tries to register as a new device.

Upon start of the desktop client, the software will open a *provisioning* WebSocket to the Signal servers, which will generate and send a random device UUID $uuid_D$. The desktop client then generates a provisioning key pair PR and encodes $uuid_D$ and $\mathrm{pub}(PR)$ into a QR code, which is presented to the user.

After the user scanned the QR code using the Signal app, the app will first request a verification code *code* from the server, and then encrypt some of the app's private data with a random AES key *prs*:

$$\mathsf{Enc}_{prs}\left(\{\text{pub}(IK), \text{sec}(IK), code, pn, pk\}\right)$$

The encrypted data and the encrypted key $\mathsf{Enc}_{PR}(prs)$ is sent to the server, which relays it via the provisioning socket to the desktop client. The desktop client uses the private provisioning key $\text{sec}(PR)$ to obtain *prs* and thus decrypt the data packet sent by the app.

The desktop client registers with the Signal servers by sending a packet containing the phone number *pn*, the string *code* for verification, a random password pw_D, a random registration ID *regId*, and the device name $name_D$, which is chosen by the user and is encrypted using the identity key *IK*. Upon receiving the registration packet, the servers return a new device ID $deviceId_D$, completing the protocol.

Since the Signal servers require HTTP authentication, the desktop client will include the username $un_D := pn.deviceId$ and the password pw_D in any future communication.

After the registration is done, the desktop client requests the current list of conversations, which is implemented via a hidden Double Ratchet session between the desktop client and the app. This "shadow" session is also used to synchronize messages sent by the user between their devices. There is no notification to the user that a device requested their conversations. Note that only the conversation metadata and the lists of participants are transmitted; the data does not include the chat history prior to device registration.

4.3 Registering a Malicious Device

If an attacker manages to temporarily compromise the victim's primary device in a fashion that reveals certain private values, namely the victim's identity key *IK* and the API password pw_A, they can simulate a device registration and add a malicious device.

As illustrated in Fig. 2, the only points where the primary device interacts with the server during the device registration are requesting a verification code and sending the encrypted private data. The former only requires API credentials, while the latter additionally requires the private identity key. Since we assume that the attacker has gained access to these values, they can fully emulate the protocol and set up the new device, without any interaction from the victim or their app.

To demonstrate malicious device registration, we created a simple dummy app[4] in C#, which takes the private identity key and the API credentials, and

[4] Code is available on GitHub: https://github.com/balasdansb/signal-attack.

then runs the described API calls. For testing, we started a new instance of the official desktop client, extracted the contents of the displayed QR code, and fed these into our dummy app. As soon as the API calls were completed, the desktop client started downloading the conversations from the victim's phone app. As the phone app happened to be up and online, all contacts and groups were successfully retrieved, without showing any notification to the victim (Fig. 3). After the registration was completed, the victim and their peers started to forward new messages and conversations to the forged device as well, giving the attacker full access to their communication.

Since the server manages a list of all registered devices, the forged device will appear in the victim's device list, if they access it in their app. However, in case the attacker has some level of control over the (untrusted) server, they can easily manipulate the returned list to exclude their forged device, making the attack almost undetectable.

4.4 Implications for Post-compromise Security

The newly added device gives the attacker a high level of access to all communications of the victim.

According to the Sesame specification, new messages shall be sent to the active sessions of each of the peers' devices, so each device can display the entire chat history from the point of device registration, even if the user switches their active device in between. Thus, the attacker receives all new communication directed to their victim, as well as all messages sent by the victim to other devices, as chat history is kept synchronous between all devices of a user.

The attacker may also impersonate the victim and send messages on their behalf. As sending such a message is easily detectable by other synchronized devices, one might suppress the synchronization to the victim's other devices. However, this may be detected as soon as one of the peers responds, since an answer will be sent to all registered devices, including the victim's own ones.

In summary, our attack shows that compromising just two secret values leads to a full disclosure of all future communications. Previously, it was only known that a cloned devices could be used, but this device was not able to send or receive messages [18]. In contrast, our attack shows that leaked long-term keys of Signal can directly be used to completely break the post-compromise security, both in theory *and* in practice. While Double Ratchet itself has strong post-compromise guarantees, this is subverted by the weak device registration and synchronization procedure in Signal's implementation of the Sesame protocol.

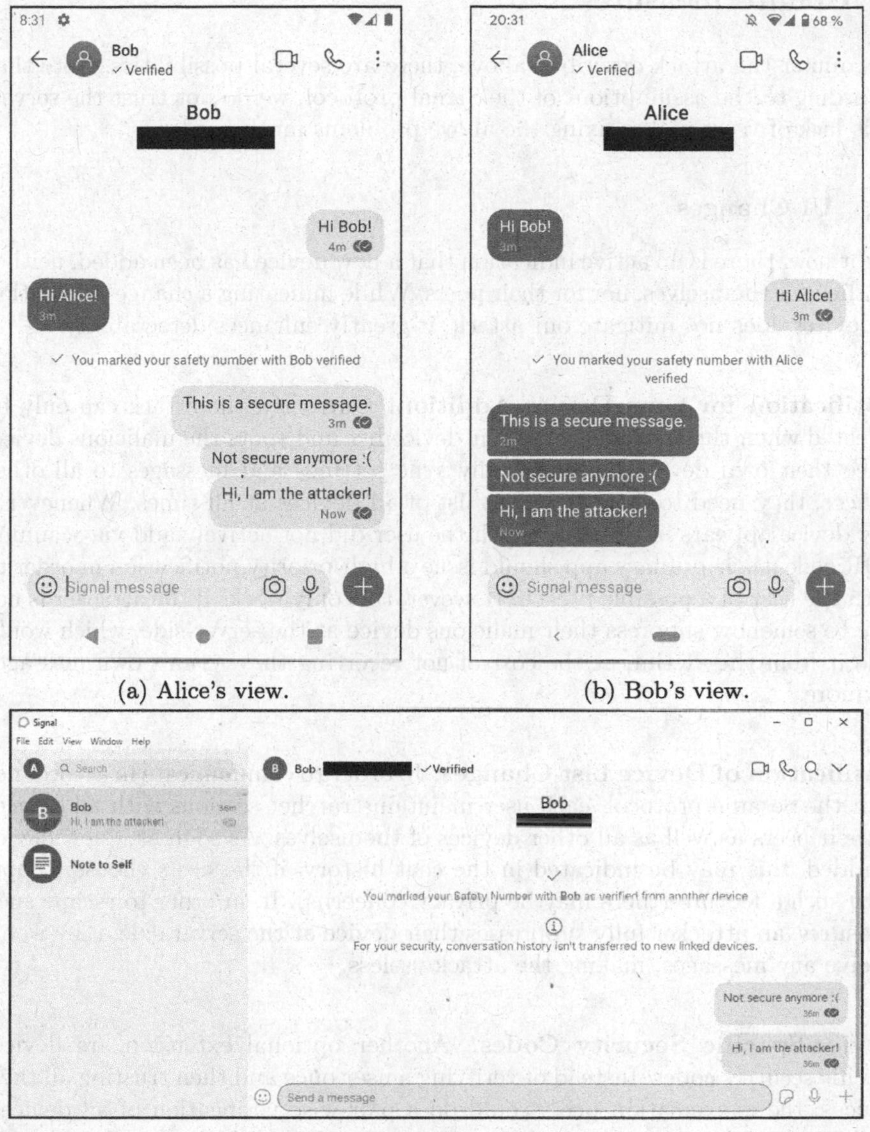

(a) Alice's view. (b) Bob's view.

(c) Attacker's view.

Fig. 3. View of a conversation between Alice and Bob (screenshots (a) and (b) slightly shortened to save space, by removing the user icons). After Alice initiated the conversation and Bob answered, both verified their safety numbers. After another message ("This is a secure message"), Alice's account got compromised. The attacker installed another device, and was able to read Alice's last message ("Not secure anymore"). Finally, the attacker impersonated Alice and sent a message on her behalf. There is no indication to Bob or Alice that a new device was added to the conversation, or which device authored a given message.

5 Countermeasures

To counter the attack described above, there are several possibilities. Note that according to the assumptions of the Signal protocol, we do not trust the server. This lack of trust makes fixing the above problems much harder.

5.1 UI Changes

Right now, there is no active indication that a new device has been added, neither for the user themselves, nor for their peers. While indicating a change or addition of devices does not mitigate our attack, it greatly enhances detectability.

Notification for Own Device Addition. Currently, the attack can only be detected when the victim checks their device list and spots the malicious device. Since their own devices automatically sync settings and messages to all other devices, they need to have a current list of all devices at all times. Whenever a new device appears in this list, which the user did not actively add via scanning a QR code, their primary app should issue a high-priority notification in order to warn the user of a possible breach. However, this only works if the attacker is not able to somehow suppress their malicious device at the server-side, which would hide it from the victim, at the cost of not receiving the victim's own messages anymore.

Notification of Device List Changes. In order to communicate in accordance with the Sesame protocol, each user maintains ratchet sessions with all devices of their peers as well as all other devices of themselves. As soon as a new device is added, this may be indicated in the chat history, if the users choose to opt-in to such a feature (there may be privacy concerns). If, in order to escape such measures, an attacker fully suppresses their device at the server-side, they won't receive any messages, making the attack useless.

Device-Specific Security Codes. Another optional extension are device-specific security codes: Instead of verifying a user once and then trusting all their devices, the conversation peers could do a pair-wise verification of all devices. In this setting, messages are only sent to authenticated devices, and a warning is issued whenever a non-verified device is present. This approach is taken e.g. by the Matrix messenger platform [7], which allows either a device-based or a user-based verification.

5.2 Alternative Multi-device Protocols

An alternative, more radical approach would be replacing the Sesame protocol itself. Just recently, Campion, Devigne, Duguey, and Fouque devised a replacement protocol for Sesame [13]. While Sesame realizes multi-device support by opening separate Signal channels between all devices used by the two communicating parties, the approach presented in [13] uses a single Signal channel for all communication between two users A and B. The usage of multiple devices on A's side is therefore transparent to B (and vice versa), meaning that higher privacy guarantees are achieved. A's devices can only use the same Signal channel to communicate with B, if all of them use the same double ratchet session, which can only be achieved when they synchronize the used ratchet key. In order to achieve such a synchronization the authors introduce the Ratcheted Dynamic Multicast (RDM). Based on asymmetric keys that are renewed regularly (hence ratcheting), this allows every device of A to use a non-interactive multicast channel to send session updates to all other devices owned by A, while providing forward secrecy and post-compromise security (called healing properties in [13]).

In our attack we exploited the device registration and management, which are mostly handled by the Signal server. The device registration presented in [13] enforces the use of another already registered device. This is possible because the registered devices of a user keep track of all other registered devices in a decentralized fashion. If A wants to register a new device, they must use one of their registered devices, which in turn uses the RDM to notify all other devices of A about the new device. Note that the RDM can only be used if the current ephemeral keys are known, which means that an attacker who has only extracted long-term secrets is not able to register a new device.

6 Conclusion

In this work, we presented a security analysis of the Sesame protocol and its current implementation in the Signal messenger, with focus on post-compromise security. To enable a detailed security analysis, we first had to reverse-engineer several implementation details of the Signal messenger. Based on the detailed knowledge, we showed that the multi-device support of the Signal messenger can be abused to eavesdrop on all communication after a one-time credential breach. Thus, currently, the Signal messenger does not provide message privacy in the post-compromise security scenario. We further discussed possible mitigations of the described attack, where some are easy to implement and have minimal impact on the user experience of the Signal messenger, while providing enhanced detectability of our attack.

Acknowledgements. This project was funded by the Deutsche Forschungsgemeinschaft (DFG) under Grant No. 427774779 and through the ERDF project EMSIK.

References

1. Barcode Scanner app on Google Play infects 10 million users with one update. https://blog.malwarebytes.com/android/2021/02/barcode-scanner-app-on-google-play-infects-10-million-users-with-one-update/. Accessed 22 Feb 2021
2. Microsoft Teams. https://teams.microsoft.com. Accessed 22 Feb 2021

3. More Keys Than A Piano: Finding Secrets in Publicly Exposed Ebs Volumes. https://www.defcon.org/html/defcon-27/dc-27-speakers.html#Morris. Accessed 22 Feb 2021
4. Slack. https://slack.com/. Accessed 22 Feb 2021
5. The Messaging Layer Security (MLS) Protocol (11). https://tools.ietf.org/id/draft-ietf-mls-protocol-11.html. Accessed 22 Feb 2021
6. Webex Teams. https://teams.webex.com. Accessed 22 Feb 2021
7. Matrix. https://matrix.org/. Accessed 16 Feb 2021
8. Council resolution on encryption. Council of the European Union, November 24 (2020). https://data.consilium.europa.eu/doc/document/ST-13084-2020-REV-1/en/pdf. Accessed 22 Feb 2021
9. Alwen, J., Coretti, S., Dodis, Y.: The double ratchet: security notions, proofs, and modularization for the signal protocol. In: Ishai, Y., Rijmen, V. (eds.) EUROCRYPT 2019. LNCS, vol. 11476, pp. 129–158. Springer, Cham (2019). https://doi.org/10.1007/978-3-030-17653-2_5
10. Bellare, M., Jaeger, J., Kane, D.: Mass-surveillance without the state: strongly undetectable algorithm-substitution attacks. In: Proceedings of the CCS. pp. 1431–1440. ACM (2015)
11. Bellare, M., Paterson, K.G., Rogaway, P.: Security of symmetric encryption against mass surveillance. In: Garay, J.A., Gennaro, R. (eds.) CRYPTO 2014. LNCS, vol. 8616, pp. 1–19. Springer, Heidelberg (2014). https://doi.org/10.1007/978-3-662-44371-2_1
12. Bergman, R., Fassihi, F.: Iranian hackers found way into encrypted apps, researchers say (2020). https://www.nytimes.com/2020/09/18/world/middleeast/iran-hacking-encryption.html. Accessed 13 Oct 2020
13. Campion, S., Devigne, J., Duguey, C., Fouque, P.-A.: Multi-device for signal. In: Conti, M., Zhou, J., Casalicchio, E., Spognardi, A. (eds.) ACNS 2020. LNCS, vol. 12147, pp. 167–187. Springer, Cham (2020). https://doi.org/10.1007/978-3-030-57878-7_9
14. Cohn-Gordon, K., Cremers, C., Garratt, L., Millican, J., Milner, K.: On ends-to-ends encryption: asynchronous group messaging with strong security guarantees. In: CCS, pp. 1802–1819. ACM (2018)
15. Cohn-Gordon, K., Cremers, C.J.F., Dowling, B., Garratt, L., Stebila, D.: A formal security analysis of the signal messaging protocol. In: EuroS&P, pp. 451–466. IEEE (2017)
16. Cohn-Gordon, K., Cremers, C.J.F., Garratt, L.: On post-compromise security. In: CSF, pp. 164–178. IEEE Computer Society (2016)
17. Cox, J.: How police secretly took over a global phone network for organized crime. Motherboard Tech by VICE, July 2 (2020). https://www.vice.com/en/article/3aza95/how-police-took-over-encrochat-hacked. Accessed 13 Oct 2020
18. Cremers, C., Fairoze, J., Kiesl, B., Naska, A.: Clone detection in secure messaging: improving post-compromise security in practice. In: CCS, pp. 1481–1495. ACM (2020)
19. Feiner, L.: Republican senators introduce bill that tech advocates have warned would weaken privacy. CNBC, June 24 (2020). https://www.cnbc.com/2020/06/24/gop-senators-introduce-bill-that-would-create-a-backdoor-for-encryption.html. Accessed 22 Feb 2021
20. Krawczyk, H., Eronen, P.: Hmac-based extract-and-expand key derivation function (HKDF). RFC **5869**, 1–14 (2010)
21. Langley, A., Hamburg, M., Turner, S.: Elliptic curves for security. RFC **7748**, 1–22 (2016)

22. Lund, J.: Technology Preview for secure value recovery. https://signal.org/blog/secure-value-recovery/ (2019). Accessed 15 Feb 2021
23. Meyer, D.: Russia's online censorship machine is no longer running smoothly. FORTUNE, June 24 (2020). https://fortune.com/2020/06/24/russia-online-censorship-faltering-telegram-kasparov/. Accessed 22 Feb 2021
24. Microsoft: Skype private conversation (2018). https://az705183.vo.msecnd.net/onlinesupportmedia/onlinesupport/media/skype/documents/skype-private-conversation-white-paper.pdf. Accessed 29 Sept 2020
25. Open Whisper Systems: Advanced cryptographic ratcheting. https://signal.org/blog/advanced-ratcheting/. Accessed 16 Feb 2021
26. Open Whisper Systems: Signal Protocol Specifications. https://signal.org/docs/. Accessed 29 Sept 2020
27. Open Whisper Systems: The Double Ratchet Algorithm. https://signal.org/docs/specifications/doubleratchet/. Accessed 28 Sept 2020
28. Open Whisper Systems: The Sesame Algorithm: Session Management for Asynchronous Message Encryption. https://signal.org/docs/specifications/sesame/. Accessed 28 Sept 2020
29. Open Whisper Systems: The X3DH Key Agreement Protocol. https://signal.org/docs/specifications/x3dh/. Accessed 28 Sept 2020
30. Randall: Introducing Signal PINs. https://signal.org/blog/signal-pins/ (2020). Accessed 15 Feb 2021
31. Rogaway, P.: Authenticated-encryption with associated-data. In: ACM Conference on Computer and Communications Security, pp. 98–107. ACM (2002)
32. Rogaway, P., Shrimpton, T.: A provable-security treatment of the key-wrap problem. In: Vaudenay, S. (ed.) EUROCRYPT 2006. LNCS, vol. 4004, pp. 373–390. Springer, Heidelberg (2006). https://doi.org/10.1007/11761679_23
33. WhatsApp: Whatsapp encryption overview (2017). https://www.whatsapp.com/security/WhatsApp-Security-Whitepaper.pdf. Accessed 28 Sept 2020

Refined Grey-Box Fuzzing with SIVO

Ivica Nikolić[1(✉)], Radu Mantu[2], Shiqi Shen[1], and Prateek Saxena[1]

[1] School of Computing, NUS, Singapore, Singapore
inikolic@nus.edu.sg
[2] University Politehnica of Bucharest, Bucharest, Romania

Abstract. We design and implement from scratch a new fuzzer called SIVO that refines multiple stages of grey-box fuzzing. First, SIVO refines data-flow fuzzing in two ways: (a) it provides a new taint inference engine that requires only logarithmic number of tests in the input size to infer dependency of many program branches on the input bytes, and (b) it employs a novel method for inverting branches by solving a systems of inequalities efficiently. Second, our fuzzer refines accurate tracking and detection of code coverage with simple and easily implementable methods. Finally, SIVO refines selection of parameters and strategies by parameterizing all stages of fuzzing and then dynamically selecting optimal values during fuzzing. Thus the fuzzer can easily adapt to a target program and rapidly increase coverage. We compare our fuzzer to 11 other state-of-the-art grey-box fuzzers on 27 popular benchmarks. Our evaluation shows that SIVO scores the highest both in terms of code coverage and in terms of number of found vulnerabilities.

1 Introduction

Fuzzing is the automatic generation of test inputs for programs with the goal of finding bugs. With increasing investment of computational resources for fuzzing, tens of thousands of bugs are found in software each year today. We view fuzzing as the problem of maximizing coverage within a given computational budget. The coverage of all modern fuzzers improves with the computation budget allocated. Therefore, we can characterize the quality of a fuzzer on its *rate of coverage increase*, the average number of new control-flow edges exercised per CPU cycle.

Broadly, there are three types of fuzzers. Black-box fuzzers do not utilize any knowledge of the program internals, and are sometimes referred to as undirected fuzzers. White-box fuzzers perform intensive instrumentation, for example, enabling dynamic symbolic execution to systematically control which program branches to invert in each test. Grey-box fuzzers introduce low-overhead instrumentation into the tested program to guide the search for bug-triggering inputs. These three types of fuzzers can be combined. For instance, recent hybrid fuzzers selectively utilize white-box fuzzers in parallel to stand-alone grey-box fuzzers. Of the three types of fuzzers, grey-box fuzzers have empirically shown promising cost-to-bug ratios, thanks to their low overhead techniques, and have seen a flurry of improved strategies. For example, recent grey-box fuzzers have

L. Bilge et al. (Eds.): DIMVA 2021, LNCS 12756, pp. 106–129, 2021.
https://doi.org/10.1007/978-3-030-80825-9_6

introduced many new strategies to prioritize seed selection, byte mutations, and so on during fuzzing. Each of these strategies works well for certain target programs, while being relatively ineffective on others. There is no dominant strategy that works better than all others on all programs presently.

In this paper, we present the design of a new grey-box fuzzer called SIVO that *generalizes* well across many target programs. SIVO embraces the idea that there is no one-size-fits-all strategy that works universally well for all programs. Central to its design is a "parameterization-and-optimization" engine where many specialized strategies and their optimization parameters can be specified. The engine dynamically selects between the specified strategies and optimizes their parameters on-the-fly for the given target program based on the observed coverage. The idea of treating fuzzing as an optimization problem is not new—in fact, many prior fuzzers employ optimization either implicitly or explicitly, but they do so *partially* [4,22,30,35]. SIVO differs from these works conceptually in that it treats parameterization as a first-class design principle—all of its internal strategies are parameterized. The selection of strategies and determination of all parameter values is done dynamically. We empirically show the power of embracing *complete parameterization* as a design principle in grey-box fuzzers.

SIVO introduces 3 additional novel refinements for grey-box fuzzers. First, SIVO embodies a faster approximate taint inference engine which computes taint (or sensitivity to inputs) for program branches during fuzzing, using number of tests that are only logarithmic in the input size. Such taint information is helpful for directed exploration in the program path space, since inputs influencing certain branches can be prioritized for mutation. Our proposed refinement improves exponentially over a recent procedure to calculate taint (or data-flow dependencies) during fuzzing [12]. Second, SIVO introduces a light-weight form of symbolic interval reasoning which, unlike full-blown symbolic execution, does not invoke any SMT/SAT solvers. Lastly, it eliminates deficiencies in the calculation of edge coverage statistics used by common fuzzers (e.g. AFL [37]), thereby allowing the optimization procedure to be more effective. We show that each of these refinements improves the rate of coverage, both individually and collectively.

We evaluate SIVO on 27 diverse real-world benchmarks comprising several used in recent work on fuzzing and in Google OSS-fuzz [15]. We compare SIVO to 11 other state-of-the-art grey-box fuzzers. We find that SIVO outperforms all fuzzers in terms of coverage on 25 out of the 27 benchmarks we tested. Our fuzzer provides 20% increase in coverage compared to the next best fuzzer, and 180% increase compared to the baseline AFL. Furthermore, SIVO finds most vulnerabilities among all fuzzers in 18 of the benchmarks, and in 11 benchmark programs finds unique vulnerabilities. This provides evidence that SIVO generalizes well across multiple programs according to multiple metrics. We have released our fuzzer publicly and open-source [25].

2 Problem

Fuzzers look for inputs that trigger bugs in target programs. As the distribution of bugs in programs is unknown, fuzzers try to increase the chance of finding bugs by constructing inputs that lead to maximal program code execution. The objective of fuzzers is thus to construct inputs, called *seeds*, that increase the amount of executed program code, called *code coverage*. The coverage is measured based on the control-flow graph of the executed program, where nodes correspond to basic blocks (sets of program statements) and edges exist between sequential blocks. Some of the nodes are conditional (e.g. correspond to if and switch statements) and have multiple outgoing edges. Coverage increases when at some conditional node, called a *branch*, the control flow takes a new edge which is not seen in previous tests—this is called *inverting* or *flipping* a branch.

Grey-box fuzzers assess code coverage by instrumenting the programs and profiling coverage data during the execution of the program on the provided inputs. They maintain a pool of seeds that increase coverage. A grey-box fuzzer selects one seed from its pool, applies to it different operations called *mutations* to produce a new seed, and then executes the program on the new seed. Those new seeds that lead to previously unseen coverage are added to the pool. To specify a grey-box fuzzer one needs to define its seed selection, the types of mutations it uses, and the type of coverage it relies on. All these fuzzing components, we call *stages* or *subroutines* of grey boxes. We consider a few research questions related to different stages of fuzzing.

RQ1: Impact of Complete Parameterization? Fuzzers optimize for coverage. There is no single fuzzing strategy that is expected to work well across all programs. So, the use of multiple strategies and optimization seems natural. Existing fuzzers do use dynamic strategy selection and optimize the parameter value selection. For example, MOpt [22], AFLFast [4], and EcoFuzz [35] use optimization techniques for input seed selection and mutations. But, often such parameterization comes with internal constants, which have been hand-tuned on certain programs, and it is almost never applied universally in prior fuzzers. The first question we ask is what would be the result of complete parameterization, i.e., if we encode all subroutines and their built-in constants as optimization parameters.

The problem of increasing coverage is equivalent to the problem of inverting more branches. In the initial stage of fuzzing, when the number of not yet inverted branches is high, AFL mutation strategies (such as mutation of randomly chosen bytes) are successful and often help to invert branches in bulk. However, easily invertible branches soon become exhausted, and different strategies are required to keep the branch inversion going. One way is to resort to targeted inversion. In targeted inversion, the fuzzer chooses a branch and mutates input bytes that influence it. The following two questions are about refining target inversion in grey-box fuzzing.

RQ2: Efficient Taint Inference? Several fuzzers have shown that taint information, which identifies input bytes that influence a given variable, is useful to targeted branch inversion [2,6,8,12,26,34]. If we want to flip a particular branch, the input bytes on which the branch condition variables depend should be mutated while keeping the other bytes unchanged. The main challenge, however, is to efficiently calculate the taint information. Classical methods for dynamic taint-tracking incur significant instrumentation overheads whereas static methods have false negatives, i.e. they miss dependencies due to imprecision. The state-of-the-art fuzzers aim for light-weight techniques for dynamically inferring taint during fuzzing itself. Prior works have proposed methods which require number of tests linear in n, the size of the seed input [12]. This is extremely inefficient for programs with large inputs. This leads to our second question: Can we compute useful taint information but with exponentially fewer tests?

RQ3: Efficient Constraint-Based Reasoning? Taint only captures whether a change in certain values of an input byte may lead to a change in the value of a variable. If we are willing to compute more expressive symbolic constraints, determining the specific input values which cause a program branch to flip is possible. The challenge is that computing and solving expressive constraints, for instance first-order SAT/SMT symbolic formulae, is computationally expensive. In this work, we ask: Which symbolic constraints can be cheap to infer and solve during grey-box fuzzing?

RQ4: Precise Coverage Measurement? Grey-box fuzzers use coverage information as feedback to guide input generation. AFL, and almost all other fuzzers building on it, use control-flow edge counts as a common metric. Since there can be many control-flow edges in the program, space-efficient data structures for storing runtime coverage data are important. Recent works have pointed out AFL's hash-based coverage map can result in collisions [13], which has an unpredictable impact on the resulting optimization. How do we compute compressed edge counts with high precision using standard compilers for instrumentation?

3 Overview of SIVO

Grey-box fuzzers instrument the target program to gather runtime profiling data, which in turn guides their seed generation strategies. The objective of SIVO is to generate seeds that increase code coverage by using better and more of the profiling data. SIVO addresses the four research questions with four refinements.

Parametrize-Optimize Approach (RQ1). SIVO builds on the idea of complete parameterization of all fuzzing subroutines and strategies, i.e. none of the internal parameters are hard-coded. SIVO selects strategies and parameter values dynamically based on the observed coverage statistics, using a standard optimization algorithm. Such complete parameterization and optimization inherently makes SIVO adaptable to the target program and more general, since specialized strategies that work best for the program are prioritized. To answer RQ1, we empirically show in our evaluation that this design principle individually helps SIVO outperform other evaluated fuzzers across multiple target programs.

Fast Approximate Taint Inference (RQ2). We devise a fast and approximate taint inference engine TaintFAST based on probabilistic group testing [10]. Instead of testing individually for each input byte, TaintFAST tests for carefully chosen groups of bytes and then combines the results of all tests to infer the taint for each individual byte. This helps to reduce the test complexity of taint inference from $O(n)$ to $O(\log n)$ executions of the program, where n is the number of input bytes. Thus the fuzzer can infer useful taint dependency even for very large inputs using TaintFAST.

Symbolic Interval Constraints (RQ3). We propose inferring symbolic interval constraints that capture the relationship between inputs and variables used in branch conditions only. Instead of deductively analyzing the semantics of executed instructions, we take an optimistic approach and infer these constraints from the observed values of the inputs and branch conditional variables. The value-based inference is computationally cheap and tailored for a common case where values of the variables are direct copies of the inputs and when branches have comparison operations $(=, \neq, <, \leq, >, \geq)$. We show that such a constraint system can be solved efficiently as well without the use of SAT/SMT solvers.

Compressed and Precise Edge Count Recording (RQ4). We tackle both the collision problem and the compressed edge count problem in tracking coverage efficiently during grey-box fuzzing. For the former, we show a simple strategy based on using multiple basic block labels (rather than only one as in AFL) and reduce or entirely eliminate the collisions. For the later, to improve the prospect of storing important edge counts we propose temporary coverage flushing (i.e. resetting the coverage to zero). Although this may appear to be a minor refinement in grey-box fuzzing, we find that it has a noticeable impact experimentally.

4 Design

We present the details of our four refinements in Sects. 4.1–4.4 and then show the complete design of SIVO in Sect. 4.5.

4.1 The Parametrize-Optimize Paradigm

The SIVO grey-box fuzzer aims to increase the code coverage in the fuzzed programs. Two points are central to this goal. First, fuzzed programs come in different flavors, hence the fuzzer should be flexible and adaptive. We tackle the first point with *parametrization*, i.e. by expanding the choice of available fuzzer subroutines. Second, a fuzzer has a few stages (i.e., selection of seeds, choice of mutations and their parameters, etc.), and each one of them can be optimized. To address this point, we apply a complete *optimization* of all available parameters.

Parametrization. The more fuzzing subroutines are available, the higher the chance that some of them may be optimal for fuzzing the targeted program. Thus it is useful to expand the set of available fuzzing subroutines. To do so, we:

- *Add many fuzzing subroutines.* For instance, in addition to the AFL-style *vanilla* mutations that do not require any dependency information (e.g. mutate random bytes), we implement *data-flow* strategies that utilize input dependency of program branches (e.g., mutation of dependent bytes). Besides adding new mutations, we also add more seed prioritization methods that determine how to sample a seed from the pool.

- *Introduce variations in each subroutines.* Often this can be done by varying internal hard-coded parameters in subroutines. For instance, in the mutation of random bytes, instead of changing a single byte, SIVO can change 1, 2, 4, 8, 16, 32, or 64 bytes at once. The exact number of bytes is considered an input parameter; it can take one of the above 7 values (and the choice of value potentially can be optimized). Not all variations in subroutines are effected with changing integer parameters. For instance, the seed selection criterion is based on speed, number of repetitions, length of seed, and so on. These variations are enumerated and serve as an input parameter to the seed criterion. All such parameters to subroutines are optimized per program.

As a result, across the whole fuzzer, there are 17 different fuzzing subroutines with 68 variations. In comparison, the baseline AFL has around 15 different subroutines with around 45 variations[1].

Optimization. The parametrization increases the chance that potentially optimal subroutines are chosen for each program. The next step is to select which subroutines are turned on for a given program. It is critical to understand that we are not dealing with a single optimization problem. Fuzzing is a continuous process, composed of iterations that select a seed and a mutation, apply the mutation to the seed, and check on coverage increase. Thus, in each iteration we need to optimize the selection of fuzzing subroutines several times—for example, the used seed criterion and class, the mutation strategy, (potentially a number of) mutations sub-strategies, the inputs to the mutation strategy, and so on. For this purpose, we use multi armed bandits (MAB), a simple reinforcement learning algorithm. Given a set of choices, each choice providing a certain reward when selected, MAB helps to select the choices such that their accumulative rewards are maximized. The rewards are unknown and stochastic, and the selection process is continuous. Note, after MAB selects a choice, it needs to receive as a feedback the obtained reward to update its choice selection strategy.

Reducing the selection of fuzzing subroutines to MAB problem is straightforward. First, note that we consider each selection as an independent MAB problem, for instance, the optimal number of random bytes to mutate is one MAB problem. Our objective is to maximize the coverage, hence it is natural to use the additional coverage acquired from executing the choice as the MAB *reward*. However, this metric alone may not be accurate because some choices incur higher computational costs. Therefore, we use the *additional coverage per time unit* as the reward. In the conventional MAB, the distributions of rewards are stationary with some unknown mean. In our case, as the fuzzer progresses, it requires more computational effort to reach the remaining unexplored code and increase coverage. In other words, the rewards for the selection choices monotonically decrease over time. Therefore, we model our problem as MAB with *non-stationary* rewards and use discounting to solve it [19]. For more details on application of MAB in SIVO, we refer the reader to Algorithm 1 and Sect. 4.5.

[1] Despite having comparable numbers, SIVO and AFL use mostly different mutations and thus subroutines.

4.2 Fast Approximate Taint Inference

To infer dependency of branches on input bytes, earlier fuzzers relied on the truth value of branch conditions: if changing the value of a particular byte changes the truth value of a branch, then it is inferred that the branch depends on this byte. For instance, in Fig. 1, to correctly infer the dependency of the branch at line 6, the engine first needs to select for mutation the input byte `x[100]` and then to change its value from any other than 40 to 40. GreyOne [12] proposed so-called *fuzzing-driven taint inference* FTI by switching the focus from the truth value of a branch to the value of the variables used in the branch. For instance, FTI determines the dependency of branch at line 6 on `x[100]` as soon as this input bytes is mutated, because this will lead to a change of the value of the variable A that is used in the branch. FTI is sound (no over-taint) and incomplete (some under-taint). Exact reasoning with provable soundness or completeness is not a direct concern in fuzzers, since they only use it to generate tests which are concretely run to exhibit bugs.

```
1 //input is uint8_t x[1024]
2 A = x[100] + 10;
3 B = (uint32_t *)x[200];
4 C = (uint32_t *)x[236];
5 ...
6 if ( A == 50)
7   ...
8 if( B + C < 200 )
9   ...
10 if( C  > 200 ) {
11   ...
12   if( A + C < 400 )
13     ...
14 }
```

Fig. 1. Branches with dependent input bytes.

The prime issue with FTI, which improves significantly over many other prior data-flow based engines, is efficiency. The taint is inferred by mutating bytes one-by-one in FTI. Thus, to infer the full dependency on all input bytes, the engine will require as many executions as the number of bytes. A seed may have tens of KBs, and there may be thousands of seeds, therefore the full inference may quickly become a major bottleneck in the fuzzer. On the other hand, precise or improved branch dependency may not significantly boost fuzzer bug-finding performance, thus long inference time may be unjustified. Hence, it is critical to reduce the inference time.

The TaintFAST Engine. We use *probabilistic group testing* [10] to reduce the required number of test executions for potential full inference from $O(n)$ to $O(\log n)$, where n is the number of input bytes. Instead of mutating each byte individually followed by program execution (and subsequent FTI check for each branch condition if any of its variables has changed), we simultaneously mutate multiple bytes, and then execute the program with the FTI check. We choose the mutation positions non-adaptively, according only to the value of n. This assures that dependency for many branches can be processed simultaneously.

Consider the code fragment at Fig. 1 (here $n = 1024$). We begin the inference by constructing 1024-bit binary vectors V_i, where each bit corresponds to one of the input bytes. A bit at position j is set iff the input byte j is mutated (i.e. assigned a value other than the value that has in the seed). Once V_i is built, we execute the program on the new input (that corresponds to V_i) and for each branch check if any of its variables changed value (in comparison to the values produced during the execution of the original seed). If so, we can conclude that the branch depends on some of the mutated bytes determined by V_i. Note, in all prior works, the vectors V_i had a single set bit (only one mutated byte). As such, the inference is immediate, but slow. On the other hand, we use vectors with $\frac{1024}{2} = 512$ set bits and select $2 \cdot \log_2 1024 = 20$ such vectors. Vectors $V_{2 \cdot j}, V_{2 \cdot j+1}$ have repeatedly 2^j set bits, followed by 2^j unset bits, but with different starts. For instances, the partial values of the first 5 vectors V_i are given below on the right.

$$
\begin{aligned}
V_0 &= 10101010101010101010\ldots \\
V_1 &= 01010101010101010101\ldots \\
V_2 &= 11001100110011001100 11\ldots \\
V_3 &= 00110011001100110011 00\ldots \\
V_4 &= 11110000111100001111 00\ldots \\
&\ldots
\end{aligned}
$$

We execute the resulting 20 inputs and for each branch build 20-bit binary vector Y. The bit i in Y is set if any of the branch values changed after executing the input that corresponds to V_i. For instance, for the branch at line 6 of Fig. 1, $Y = 10100110100101101010$. Finally, we decode Y to infer the dependency. To do so, we initialize 1024-bit vector D that will hold the dependency of the branch on input bytes—bit i is set if the branch depends on the input byte i. We set all bits of D, i.e. we start by guessing full dependency on all inputs. Then we remove the wrong guesses according to Y. For each unset bit j in Y (i.e. the branch value did not change when we mutated bytes V_j), we unset all bits in D that are set in V_j (i.e. the branch does not depend on any of the mutated bytes V_j).

After processing all unset bits of Y, the vector D will have set bits that correspond to potential dependent input bytes. Theoretically, there may be under and over-taint, according to the following information-theoretic argument: Y has 20 bits of entropy and thus it can encode at most 2^{20} dependencies, whereas a branch may depend on any of the 1024 input bytes and thus it can have 2^{1024} different dependencies. In practice, however, it is reasonable to assume that most of the branches depend only on a few input bytes[2], and in such a case the inference is more accurate. For branches that depend on a single byte, the correctness of the inference follows immediately from group testing theory[3]. For instance, the branch at line 6 of Fig. 1 will have correctly inferred dependency only on byte `x[100]`. For branches that depend on a few bytes, we can reduce (or entirely prevent) over-taint by repeating the original procedure while permuting the vectors V_i. In such a case, each repeated inference will suggest different candidates, except the truly dependent bytes that will be suggested by all procedures. These input bytes then can be detected by taking intersection of all the suggested candidates. For instance, for the branch at line 8 (that actually depends on 8 bytes), a single execution of the procedure will return 16 byte candidates. By repeating once the procedure with randomly permuted positions of V_i, with high probability only the 8 actual candidates will remain.

The above inference procedure makes the implicit assumption that *same branches are observed across different executions.* Otherwise, if a branch is not

---

[2] C-type branches that contain multiple variables connected with AND/OR statements, during compilation are split into subsequent independent branches. Our inference is applied at assembly level, thus most of the branches depend only on a few variables.

[3] The matrix with rows $V_0, V_1, \ldots$ is 1-disjunct and thus it can detect 1 dependency.

observed during some of the executions, then the corresponding bit in Y will be undefined, thus no dependency information about the branch will be inferred from that execution. For some branches the assumption always holds (e.g. for branches at lines 6,8 in Fig. 1). For other branches, the assumption holds only with some probability that depends on their branch conditions. For instance, the branch at line 12 may not be seen if the branch at line 10 is inverted, thus any of the 20 bits of Y may be undefined with a probability of $\frac{200}{2^{32}}$. In general, for any branch that lies below some preceding branches, the probability that bits in Y will be defined is equivalent to the probability that none of the above branches will inverted by the mutations[4]. As a rule of thumb, the deeper the branch and the easier to invert the preceding branches are, the harder will be to infer the correct dependency. To infer deeper branches, we introduce a modification based on forced execution. We instrument the code so the executions at each branch will take a predefined control-flow edge, rather than decide on the edge according to the value of the branch condition. This guarantees that the target branches seen during the execution of the original seed file (used as a baseline for mutation), will be seen at executions of all subsequent inputs produced by mutating the original seed. We perform forced execution dynamically, with the same statically instrumented program, working in two modes. In the first mode, the program is executed normally, and a trace of all branches and their condition values is stored. In the second mode, during execution as the branches emerge, their condition values are changed to the stored values, thus the execution takes the same trace as before. No other variables aside from the condition values are changed. Note that our procedure aims to infer taint dependencies fast and optimistically; we refer readers to Sect. 4.6 for a discussion on these aspects.

4.3 Solving System of Intervals

It was noted in RedQueen [2], that when branches depend trivially on input bytes (so-called direct copies of bytes) and the branch condition is in the form of equality (either = or $\neq$), then such branches can be solved trivially. For instance, the branch at line 1 of Fig. 2, depends trivially on the byte `x[0]` and its condition can be satisfied by assigning $x[0] = 5$ (or inverted by assigning $x[0] \neq 5$).

```
1 if ( x[0] == 5 )
2   ...
3 if( x[1] < 100 )
4   ...
5 if( x[2]  > 10 ) {
6   ...
7   if( x[2] <=  200 )
8     ...
9     if( foo(x[2]) ==  0 )
10      ...
11 }
```

Fig. 2. Branches and systems of intervals.

Thus it is easy to satisfy or invert such branches, as long as the dependency is correctly inferred and the branch condition is equality. Similar reasoning, however, can be applied when the condition is in the form of inequality over integers. Consider the branch at line 3 of Fig. 2, that depends trivially on the input byte $x[1]$. From the type of inequality (which can be obtained from the instruction code of the branch), and the correct dependency on the input byte $x[1]$ and the

[4] This holds even in the case of FTI. However, the probabilities there are higher because there is a single mutated byte.

constant 100, we can deduce the branch form $x[1] < 100$, and then either satisfy it resulting in $x[1] \in [0, 99]$, or invert it, resulting in $x[1] \in [100, 255]$. In short, we can represent the solution in the form of integer intervals for that particular input byte.

Often to satisfy/invert a branch we need to take into account not one, but several conditions that correspond to some of the branches that have common variables with the target branch. For instance, to satisfy the branch at line 7, we have two inequalities and thus two intervals: $x[2] \in [0, 200]$ corresponding to target branch at line 7 and $x[2] \in [11, 255]$ corresponding to branch at line 5. Both share the same input variable $x[2]$ with the target branch. A solution ($x[2] \in [11, 200]$) exists because the intersection of the intervals is not empty.

In general, SIVO builds a system of such constraints starting from the target branch, by adding gradually preceding branches that have common input variables with the target branch. Each branch (in)equality is solved independently immediately, resulting in one or two intervals (two intervals only when solving $x \neq value$, i.e. $x \in [0, value-1] \cup [value+1, maxvalue]$), and then intersection is found with the previous set of intervals corresponding to those particular input bytes. Keeping intervals sorted assures that the intersection will be found fast. Also, each individual intersection can increase the number of intervals at most by 4. Thus the whole procedure is linear in the number of branches along the executed path. As a result, we can efficiently solve these type of constraints and, thus, satisfy or invert branches that depend trivially on input bytes.

Even when some of the preceding branches do not depend trivially on input bytes, solving the constraints for the remaining branches gives an advantage in inverting the target branch. In such a case, we repeatedly sample solutions from the solved constraints and expect that the non-inverted branch constraints will be satisfied by chance. As sampling from the system requires constant time (after solving it), the complexity of branch inversion is reduced only to that of satisfying non-trivially dependent branches. For instance, to reach line 10, we first solve the lines 5, 7 to obtain $x[2] \in [11, 200]$, and then keep sampling $x[2]$ from this interval and hope to satisfy the branch at line 9 by chance.

4.4 More Accurate Coverage

AFL uses a simple and an elegant method to record the edges and their counts by using an array showmap. First, it instruments all basic blocks B_i of a program by assigning them a unique random label L_i. Then, during the execution of the program on a seed, as any two adjacent basic blocks B_j, B_k are processed, it computes a hash of the edge (B_j, B_k) as $E = (L_j \ll 1) \oplus L_k$ and performs showmap[E]++. New coverage is observed if the value $\lfloor \log_2 \text{showmap[E]} \rfloor$ of a non-zero entry showmap[E] has not been seen before. If so, AFL updates its coverage information to include the new value, which we will refer to as the logarithmic count.

Prevent Colliding Edge Hashes. CollAFL [13] points out that when the number of edges is high, their hashes will start to collide due to birthday paradox, and showmap will not be able to signal all distinct edges. Therefore, a fuzzer will fail to detect some of the coverage. We propose a simple solution to the collision problem. Instead of assigning only one label L_i to each basic block B_i, we assign several labels $L_i^1, \ldots, L_i^m$, but use only one of them during an execution. The index of the used label is switched occasionally for all blocks simultaneously. The switch assures that with a high chance, each edge will not collide with any other edge at least for some of the indices. The number of labels required to guarantee that all edges will be unique with a high chance at some switch depends on the number of edges. Due to space restrictions we omit the combinatorial analysis. In our actual implementation the size of the showmap is 2^{16} and we use $m = 4$ labels per basic block – on average this allows around 8,000 edges to be mapped uniquely (and even 20,000 with less than 100 collisions), which is sufficiently high quantity for most of the programs considered in our experiments. By default, the index is switched once every 20 min.

Improve Compressed Edge Counts. The logarithmic count helps to reduce storing all possible edge counts, but it may also implicitly hinder achieving better coverage. This is because certain important count statistics that have the same logarithmic count as previously observed during fuzzing might be discarded.

For instance, if the for loop in Fig. 3 gets executed 13 times, then AFL will detect this as a new logarithmic count of $\lfloor \log_2 13 \rfloor = 3$, it will update the coverage, save the seed in the pool, and later when processing this seed, the code block $F1()$ will be executed as soon as the condition $C1$ holds. On the other hand, afterwards if the for loop gets executed 14 times, then the same logarithmic count $\lfloor \log_2 14 \rfloor = 3$ is achieved, thus the new seed will not be stored, therefore the chance of executing the code block $F2()$ is much lower. In other words, to reach $F2()$, simultaneously the for loop needs to be executed 14 times and $C2$ condition needs to hold. Hence, $F1()$ and $F2()$ cannot be reached with the same ease despite having similar conditional dependency, only because of AFL's logarithmic count mechanism.

```
count = 0;
for(i=0; i< x; i++)
  count++;

if( 13 == count && C1 )
  F1();
else if( 14 == count && C2 )
  F2();
```

Fig. 3. The effects of AFL's edge count compression.

To avoid this issue, we propose flushing the coverage information periodically. More precisely, periodically we store the current coverage information, then reset it to zero, and during some time generate new coverage from scratch. After exhausting the time budget on new coverage, we keep only the seeds that increase the stored coverage, and continue the fuzzing with the accumulated coverage.

4.5 Design of the Whole Fuzzer SIVO

SIVO implements all the refinements mentioned so far. It uses the standard grey-box approach of processing seeds iteratively. In each iteration, it selects a seed, mutates it to obtain new seeds, and stores those that increase coverage.

Algorithm 1: OneIterationSIVO (Seeds, Coverage)

```
use_class ← MAB_select( Seed_class )                       // choose seed class with MAB
use_crit ← MAB_select( Seed_criterion )                        // choose seed criterion
seed ← Sample( use_class , use_crit, Seeds )                // sample seed from the pool
use_strategy ← MAB_select( Fuzzer_strategy )           // choose Data-flow or Vanilla
if use_strategy == Data-flow then
    Taint_inference(seed)                               // if Data-flow then infer dependency
tot_cov_incr ← 0
while time budget left do
    use_mut ← MAB_select( strategy )                              // choose one mutation
    use_mut_params ← MAB_select( use_mut )                     // choose its params
    new_seed ← Mutate( seed, use_mut, use_mut_params )          // apply mutation
    new_coverage ← ProduceCoverage(new_seed)
    cov_increase ← || new_coverage \ Coverage ||                        // new coverage?
    if cov_increase > 0 then
        Seeds ← Seeds ⋃ new_seed                                 // add new seed to the pool
        Coverage ← Coverage ⋃ new_coverage                           // update coverage
    // feedback cov/sec to MAB to update the effectiveness of the chosen
    mutation and its params
    MAB_update( [use_mut , use_mut_params], cov_increase, while_time )
    tot_cov_incr += cov_increase
// feedback total cov/sec to MAB to update the effectiveness of the chosen
seed class/criterion and fuzzing strategy
MAB_update( [use_class,use_crit,use_strategy] , tot_cov_incr , iter_time)
```

In SIVO (refer to the pseudo-code in Algorithm 1), the seed selection is optimized: first with MAB the currently best class and best criterion are selected, and then a seed is sampled from the pool according to the chosen class and criterion. Afterwards, the fuzzer with the help of MAB decides on the currently optimal fuzzing strategy, either vanilla (apply mutations that do not require dependency information) or data-flow (require dependency). If latter, SIVO first infers the dependency (as a combination of FTI and TaintFAST). Then, according to the chosen fuzzing strategy the fuzzer again uses MAB to select one optimal mutation strategy. The vanilla fuzzing strategy allows a choice of 3 different mutations: 1) mutation of random bytes, 2) copy/remove of byte sequence of current seed, and 3) concatenation of different seeds. On the other hand, data-flow fuzzing strategy consists of 5 mutations: 1) mutation of dependent bytes, 2) branch inversion with system solver, 3) branch inversion by minimizing objective function, 4) branch inversion by mutation of their dependent bytes, and 5) reusing previously found bytes from other seeds to current seed. Most mutations have sub-versions or parameters which are also chosen with MAB. For instance, mutation of random bytes supports two versions: it can use heuristics to determine the positions of the bytes (choice 1), or use random byte positions (choice 2). If choice 1, then it needs to select the number of mutated bytes (1, 2, 4, 8, 16, 32, or 64). Both of these selections are determined with MAB. Each mutation is applied to the chosen seed to obtain a new seed, and then the seed is executed.

Algorithm 2: SIVO

```
Seeds ← Initial_seeds
Coverage ← ProduceCoverage(Seeds)
while true do
    OneIterationSIVO ( Seeds, Coverage );
    if time_to_switch_index then
        SwitchIndexInCoverage()
        Coverage ← ProduceCoverage( Seeds )
    if time_to_start_flush then
        Old_coverage, Old_seeds ← Coverage, Seeds
        Seeds ← Initial_seeds
        Coverage ← ProduceCoverage( Seeds )
    if time_to_stop_flush then
        New_coverage ← Coverage \ Old_coverage
        Coverage ← Coverage ⋃ Old_covarege
        Seeds ← Old_seeds ⋃ GetSeedsThatProduceCov(Seeds, New_coverage)
```

The coverage update information is fed back to the MAB, thus assuring that MAB can further optimize the selections.

SIVO runs the iterations and occasionally executes the code coverage refinements – refer to Algorithm 2. We implement the whole fuzzer from scratch in C++ with around 20,000 lines of code [25].

4.6 Limitations of SIVO

The taint engine TaintFAST relies on forced execution, which by definition is not sound, thus the inference is approximate. It means, the engine may introduce false positives/negatives, i.e. it may suggest dependencies of branches on incorrect input bytes. This, however, is not a real concern in fuzzing because later it leads solely to mutating incorrect input bytes, hence potentially it has only impact on efficiency[5], and does not affect the correctness of the fuzzer in any other way. The accuracy of the engine varies between programs. In certain cases (of particular traces), the forced execution crashes the program, and thus the inference has lower accuracy (because the corresponding Y bit is undefined). In our actual implementation of TaintFAST, we prevent some of the crashes by detecting with binary search sequences of input bytes that lead to crashes, and later eliminate them from consideration.

The refinement based on system of intervals is neither sound nor complete. Problems may appear due to incorrect inference of the intervals as well as due to the fact that the system describes only a partial dependency of the target branch on input bytes, i.e. includes only branches that can be presented in the form of integer intervals. Therefore, one may not assume that all of the branches can be properly inverted using this refinement.

[5] The impact can be reduced with various methods, e.g., the MAB-based optimization presented in this paper.

The remaining two refinements do not have apparent limitations, aside from affecting the efficiency in some cases.

5 Evaluation

We show that SIVO performs well on multiple benchmarks according to the standard fuzzing metrics such as code coverage (Sect. 5.2) and found vulnerabilities (Sect. 5.3). We evaluate the performance of each refinement in Sect. 5.4.

5.1 Experimental Setup

Experiment Environment. For all experiments we use the same box with Ubuntu Desktop 16.04, two Intel Xeon E5-2680v2 CPUs @2.80 GHz with 40 cores, 64 GB DDR3 RAM @1866 MHz and SSD storage. All fuzzers are tested on the same programs, provided with only one initial seed, randomly selected from samples available on the internet. To keep experiments computationally reasonable, while still providing a fair comparison of all considered fuzzers, we performed a two-round tournament-like assessment. In the first round, all fuzzers had been appraised over the course of 12 h. This interval is chosen based on Google's FuzzBench periodical reports, which shows that 12 h is sufficient to decide the ranking of the fuzzers usually [15]. The top 3 fuzzers from the first round that perform the best on average over all evaluated programs progress to the second round, in which they are run for 48 h.

Baseline Fuzzers. We evaluate SIVO in relation to 11 notable grey-box fuzzers. In addition to AFL [37], we take the extended and improved AFL family: AFLFast [4], FairFuzz [20], LAF-Intel [1], MOpt [22] and EcoFuzz [35]. Moreover, we include Angora [6] for its unique mutation techniques, Ankou [23] for its fitness function, and a few fuzzers that perform well on Google's OSS-Fuzz [15] platform such as Honggfuzz [32], AFL++ and AFL++_mmopt [11] (version 2.67c). To prevent unfair comparison, we omit from our experiments two categories of fuzzers. First, we exclude popular grey-box fuzzers that do not have an officially available implementation, such as CollAFL [13] and GreyOne [12]. We did not implement these fuzzers from scratch due to the complexity of such a task (e.g. the authors of GreyOne report 20K LoC implementation). Second, we exclude hybrid fuzzers because their approach is basically orthogonal to traditional grey-box fuzzers and thus they can be combined. For instance, the well-known hybrid fuzzer QSYM [36] inverts branches with symbolic execution and is built on top of AFL. With minor modification, QSYM could be built on top of SIVO instead of AFL, and this hybrid may lead to an even better performance.

Programs. Our choice of programs was influenced by multiple factors, such as implementation robustness, diversity of functionality, and previous analysis in other works. Our main goal of the evaluation is comparison of fuzzers according to a few criteria (including discovery of bugs), thus we use versions of programs that have already been tested in prior fuzzer evaluations on similar criteria. Due to limited resources, we did not run the fuzzers on the latest versions to look for actual

CVEs. Our final selection consists of 27 programs including: binutils (e.g.: readelf, nm), parsers and parser generators (e.g.: bson_to_json@libbson, bison), a wide variety of analysis tools (e.g.: tcpdump, exiv2, cflow, sndfile-info@libsndfile), image processors (e.g.: img2txt), assemblers and compilers (e.g.: nasm, tic@libncurses), compression tools (e.g.: djpeg, bsdtar), the LAVA-M dataset [9], etc. A complete list of the programs and their version under test is given in Table 1.

Efficiency Metrics. We use two metrics to compare the efficiency of fuzzers: edge coverage and the number of found vulnerabilities. To determine the coverage, we use the logarithmic edge count because this number is the objective in the fuzzing routines of the AFL family of fuzzers (simple count of unique edges leads to similar results which we omit due to space restrictions). To measure the total number of distinct vulnerabilities found by each fuzzer, first we confirm the reported vulnerabilities, i.e. we take all seeds generated by a fuzzer and keep those that trigger a crash by any of the sanitizers ASAN [28], UBSAN [27] and Valgrind [24]. Then, for each kept seed, we record the program source line where the crash triggers and count each such distinct source line as a vulnerability.

5.2 Coverage

We run all 12 fuzzers for 12 h each, and record the coverage discovered during the fuzzing. The results are reported in Fig. 4. We can see that at the end, SIVO provides the best coverage for 25 out of the 27 programs. On average SIVO produces 11.8% higher coverage than the next best fuzzer when analyzed individually for each program. In direct comparison to fuzzers, SIVO outperforms the next best fuzzer MOpt by 20.2%, and EcoFuzz by 30.6%, and outperforms the baseline AFL by producing 180% increase in coverage. For most of the programs, our fuzzer very soon establishes as the top fuzzer. In fact, the time frame needed to create advantage is so short, that the improved coverage refinement of Sect. 4.4 has still not kicked in, whereas the MAB optimization of Sect. 4.1 had barely any time to feed enough data back to the MABs. Thus, arguably the early advantage of SIVO is achieved due to the parametrize paradigm, as well as the remaining two refinements (TaintFAST and the system solver method).

We test the top three fuzzers SIVO, MOpt, and EcoFuzz on 48-h runs and report the obtained coverage in Fig. 5. We see that SIVO is the top fuzzer for 24 of the programs, with 13.4% coverage increase on average with respect to the next best fuzzer for each program, and 15.7%, and 28.1% with respect to MOpt and EcoFuzz. In comparison to the 12-h runs, the other two fuzzers managed to reduce slightly the coverage gap, but this is expected (given sufficient time all fuzzers will converge). However, the gap is still significant and SIVO provides consistently better coverage.

5.3 Vulnerabilities

We summarize the number of vulnerabilities found by each fuzzer on 25 programs during the 12-h runs in Table 1. (We removed two programs from Table 1, as none

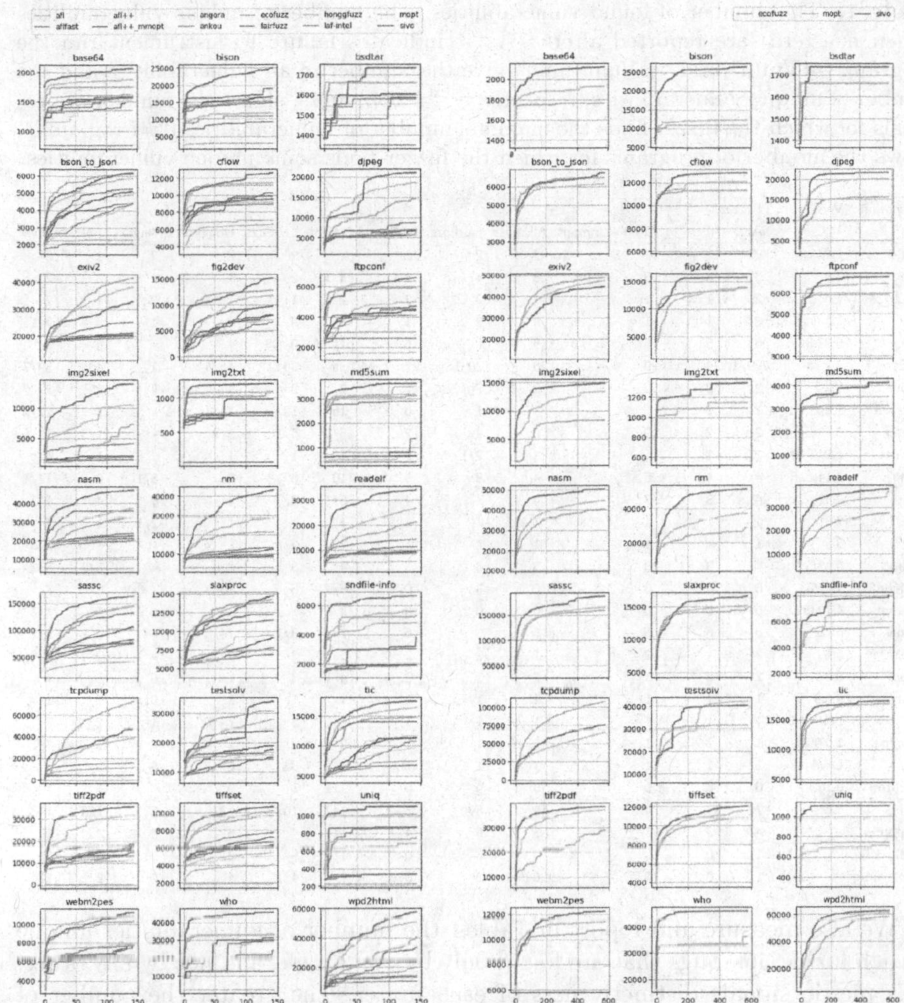

Fig. 4. Coverage for all fuzzers during 12 h of fuzzing (in 5 min increments).

Fig. 5. Coverage for top three fuzzers SIVO, MOpt, EcoFuzz during 48 h of fuzzing.

of the fuzzers finds vulnerabilities for them.) Out of 25 evaluated programs, SIVO is able to find the maximal number of vulnerabilities in 18 programs (72%). For comparison, the next best fuzzer MOpt holds top positions in 11 programs (44%) in terms of vulnerability discovery. This indicates that SIVO is significantly more efficient at finding vulnerabilities than the remaining candidate fuzzers. However, SIVO achieves less top positions in discovery of vulnerabilities compared to code coverage, but this is not unusual as the objective of our fuzzer is code coverage, and the correlation between produced coverage and found vulnerabilities is not necessarily strong [17,18].

Table 1. The number of found vulnerabilities. The number of unique vulnerabilities (when non-zero) are reported after "/". "-" indicates failure to instrument/run the program. "#Vuln." and "#Vuln. uniq" give the number of all vulnerabilities and the number of unique vulnerabilities, respectively. "#Top vuln." shows the number of programs for which the fuzzer finds the maximal number of vulnerabilities. "#Prog. uniq" shows the number of programs for which the fuzzer finds some unique vulnerabilities.

Application	Version	Fuzzer											
		AFL	AFL++	AFL++_mmopt	AFLFast	FairFuzz	LAF-Intel	MOpt	EcoFuzz	Honggfuzz	Angora	Ankou	SIVO
base64	LAVA-M	2	2	2	2	2	2	2	2	2	2	1	2
bison	3.0.5	3	3	3	3	4/1	3	4/1	2	2	1	3	2
bson_to_json	1.8	2	1	1	1	2	2	2	1	1	2	1	2
cflow	1.5	2	1	1	2	2	1	5	3	2	1	3	6/1
exiv2	0.27.3	6	5	6	5	6	6	11/3	0	-	-	8	8
Fig.2dev	3.2.7a	29/1	24	29	26	30/1	22	35	30/2	43/4	1	40	59/7
ftpconf	3.2.2	2	2	2	2	2	2	2	2	2	2	2	2
img2sixel	1.8.2	1	1	1	1	1	0	16/1	12/1	15/3	-	7	22/6
img2txt	0.99beta19	2	2	2	0	4	2	8/2	5/1	3	-	7/3	10/5
md5sum	LAVA-M	1	1	1	1	2/1	1	1	1	1	1	1	1
nasm	2.14rc15	4	4	5	4	8	4	10	8	2	5/1	9	13/1
nm	2.31	4	3	3	4	4	4	6/1	5	3	0	4	6/1
readelf	2.31	1	1	1	1	1	1	1	1	1	2/1	1	1
sassc	3.5	1	1	1	1	2	1	2	2	1	-	1	5/3
slaxproc	0.22.0	4	3	3	3	3	3	4	3	3	-	6/2	5/1
sndfile-info	1.0.28	0	0	0	0	3	0	8/2	6	13/6	-	1	7
tcpdump	4.10.0rc1	0	0	0	0	0	0	3	1	1	-	1	7/3
testsolv	0.7.2	6	6	6	6	6	6	7	8/1	14/8	-	6	9/2
tic	6.1	2	1	2	1	2	2	3	2	2	-	0	3
tiff2pdf	4.0.9	2	2	1	2	1	2	4	3	1	0	3	4
tiffset	4.0.9	1	1	1	1	1	1	1	1	1	0	1	1
uniq	LAVA-M	1	1	1	1	1	1	2	3	7	1	2	7
webm2pes	1.0.0.27	1	1	1	1	1	1	2	2	1	-	1	3/1
who	LAVA-M	1	1	1	1	1	1	7	3	6	0	3	7
wpd2html	0.10.1	0	0	0	0	0	0	1/1	1	0	-	1	1
#Vuln.		78	67	74	69	89	68	147	107	127	18	113	193
#Top vuln.		4	3	3	3	6	4	11	4	6	4	4	18
#Vuln. uniq		1	0	0	0	3	0	11	5	21	2	5	31
#Prog. uniq		1	0	0	0	3	0	7	4	4	2	2	11

We also measure and report in Table 1 the number of vulnerabilities unique to each fuzzer, i.e. bugs that are found only by one fuzzer, and not by any other. This metric signals distinctiveness of each fuzzer—the greater the number of unique vulnerabilities, the more distinct the fuzzer is on vulnerability detection. Out of 25 programs, SIVO discovers at least one unique vulnerability in 11 programs. In total, SIVO finds 31 unique vulnerabilities, while the next best fuzzer is Honggfuzz [32] with 21 vulnerabilities.

5.4 Performance of Refinements

We evaluate the four refinements individually, in terms of their impact and necessity. To assess the impact of a refinement, i.e. to estimate how much it helps to advance the fuzzer, we compare the performance of the baseline version of SIVO (where all four refinements have been removed) to the baseline version with the one refinement added on. On the other hand, to assess the necessity of a refinement, i.e. to estimate how irreplaceable in comparison to the other three refinements it is, we compare the full version of SIVO to the version with a single refinement removed. We note that all refinements aside for the Parametrize-Optimize strategy, can be assessed reasonably well because it is easy to switch them on or off in the fuzzer. The same holds for Optimize, but not for Parametrize. As SIVO is built from scratch with many new fuzzing subroutines that are not necessarily present in AFL, it is not clear which fuzzing subroutines and which of their variations need to be removed in the baseline. Therefore, we only assess Optimize, and consider Parametrize to be part of the baseline.

We fuzz the 25 programs (on which SIVO outperformed all other 11 fuzzers) for 12 h, and compare the found coverage to the coverage produced by the complete version of SIVO. In Table 2, we provide the comparisons (as a percentage drop of the coverage) of the versions. We also give the data about the performance of the best non-SIVO fuzzer for each program (see the column Best NoneSivo). In the last row of the table we summarize the number of programs on which the considered version of the fuzzer is able to out-perform all of the remaining 11 none-SIVO fuzzers (for reference, for SIVO this number is 25).

A few observations are evident from the Table 2:

Table 2. Percentage drop in coverage of fuzzers in comparison to SIVO. When no drop occurs, the cells are empty.

Application	Fuzzer									
	Best NoneSivo	SivoBase	SivoBase+Opt	SivoBase+FI	SivoBase+SI	SivoBase+AC	Sivo-Opt	Sivo-FI	Sivo-SI	Sivo-AC
base64	9.1	7.2	2.4	7.2	4.7	7.2	3.3	3.3	8.4	1.7
bison	23.9	23.1		23.1	23.1	23.1	33.4			4.9
bsdtar	4.1						0.4	0.4	0.4	
bson_to_json	0.8	18.9	3.0	18.9	16.1	18.9	17.1		4.6	2.9
cflow	9.5	10.9	4.6	10.9	10.9	10.9	13.4		3.8	5.0
djpeg	11.9	23.9	23.9	23.9	23.9	21.2	33.7		15.4	22.0
fig2dev	15.9	13.3		13.3	13.3	13.3	23.0		1.8	6.1
ftpconf	3.5	10.5	0.6	9.8	9.9	10.5	12.3			1.4
img2sixel	24.7	21.9	8.0	21.5	15.9	21.9	19.9	3.8	7.7	0.6
img2txt	9.8	9.3	9.3	9.3	9.3	8.9	8.6	8.9	7.9	10.3
md5sum	2.9	14.8	14.2	14.8	0.6	6.4	4.6		12.3	
nasm	20.3	27.7	0.5	27.7	27.0	27.7	39.8		3.7	0.6
nm	33.6	11.8	11.8	11.8	6.6	11.8	15.9	43.6	27.4	18.8
readelf	22.0	15.2		7.7	5.0	7.1	7.8	1.9	0.1	
sassc	10.9	25.4		25.4	21.5	23.5	34.6			
slaxproc	3.3	34.9		31.1	28.0	30.3	38.5		1.9	
sndfile-info	16.2	17.2	10.8	17.2	11.7	17.2	6.6		18.6	1.7
testsolv	9.4	43.0	33.1	42.3	10.9	24.6	33.3	34.3	37.2	10.6
tic	6.0	16.9		16.9	16.7	13.7	19.7			0.1
tiff2pdf	10.5	2.4	2.4	2.4	2.0	0.3	3.7			
tiffset	4.4	8.9	7.8	8.9	8.9			0.3		
uniq	7.8	16.4	0.4	16.4	3.1	16.4		0.2	4.8	
webm2pes	3.0	14.0		12.6	14.0	14.0	12.2	7.1	6.6	
who	27.3	29.3	13.6	23.3	17.4	27.6	2.7	9.5	35.9	10.5
wpd2html	11.8	27.1	13.6	27.1	27.1	27.1	48.9	6.4	0.3	5.2
Top positions		9	19	11	13	9	11	22	18	21

- **Parametrize alone is valuable**. The baseline SivoBase, i.e. the version of the fuzzer that does not have any of the four refinements aside from Parametrize, already performs well. It is able to achieve the most coverage for 9 of the 25 considered programs. Hence, just by introducing new fuzzing subroutines and their variations, the fuzzer is able to outperform in terms of coverage the other 11 fuzzers on 36% of the fuzzed programs.
- **Optimize has a strong impact**. Among the four refinements, Optimize has the strongest impact. It helps the baseline fuzzer to add 10 top stops resulting in 19 top positions (refer to SivoBase+Opt column in Table 2), thus leading to most coverage in comparison to the other 11 none-SIVO fuzzers on 76% of the programs. On the other hand, SIVO without Optimize (refer to SIVO-Opt), loses 14 top positions, i.e. the fuzzer loses the top spot for 56% of the programs. Moreover, this refinement effects all of the fuzzed programs, with the exception of a few. The effect is significant—the coverage drop when this refinement is not present is at least 10% and sometimes more than 30%.
- **TaintFAST has a moderate to low impact**. This refinement, denoted as FI in the Table 2, helps the baseline fuzzer to add two top spots. On the other hand, SIVO without TaintFAST, i.e. with only the FTI engine present, loses three top spots. TaintFAST has a strong variance (refer to the Sivo-FI column) in terms of providing additional coverage and most fuzzed programs either benefit largely, or have no benefit at all. This is not unexpected, because the true benefit of TaintFAST is manifested in programs that accept large inputs and that have branches that depend on all of those inputs.
- **Solving systems of interval (SI) has a strong to moderate impact**. It adds 4 top stops to the baseline, and removes 7 top spots from the complete version of SIVO. It provides consistent benefits to the fuzzer – for most of the fuzzed programs SI produces extra coverage. Presumably, this is based on the fact that most programs do have branches based on integer inequalities and that use direct copy of input bytes.
- **Accurate coverage (AC) has a moderate to low impact**. This refinement does not have a strong impact on providing top positions (no jumps after adding it to the baseline, and lost 4 positions when removing it from SIVO), but it gives well balanced improvements in coverage to the fuzzer.

5.5 The Cause of Observed Benefits

It is important to understand and explain why certain fuzzing techniques (or in our case refinements) work well. In Sect. 5.4 we speculate about the type of programs that can be fuzzed well with some of the refinements. Showing this conclusively, however, is difficult. Table 2 shows the percentage drop in coverage observe, per application, obtained by adding and removing one-by-one each of our proposed refinements. However, attributing the cause of improved performance to individual refinements based on such coarse empirical data could be misleading. This is because we are measuring the joint outcome of mutually-dependent fuzzing strategies. We cannot single out the cause of an observed outcome and attribute it to each strategy, since the strategies mutate the internal state that others use. We thus only coarsely estimate their impact via our empirical findings and speculate that these results extend to other programs.

6 Related Work

Grey-box fuzzers, starting from the baseline AFL [37], have been the backbone of modern, large-scale testing efforts. The AFL-family of fuzzers (e.g. AFLGo [3], AFLFast [4], LAF-Intel [1], MOpt [22], and MTFuzz [30]) improve upon different aspects of the baseline fuzzer. For instance, instead of randomly selecting mutation strategy, MOpt [22] uses particle swarm optimization to guide the selection. MTFuzz [30] trains a multiple-task neural network to infer the relationship between program inputs and different kinds of edge coverage to guide input mutation. Similarly, for the seed selection, AFLFast [4] prioritizes seeds that exercise low-probability paths, CollAFL [13] prioritizes seeds that have a lot of not-yet inverted branches, and EcoFuzz [35] uses multi-armed bandits to guide the seed selection. Common feature for all current fuzzers from the AFL-family is that they optimize at most one of the fuzzing subroutine[6]. In contrast, SIVO first parameterizes all aspects, i.e. introduces many variations of the fuzzing subroutines, and then tries to optimize all the selection of parameters. Even the seed selection subroutines of EcoFuzz and SIVO differ, despite both using multi-armed bandits: EcoFuzz utilizes MAB to select candidate seed from the pool, whereas SIVO uses MAB to decide on the selection criterion and the pool of seeds.

Several grey-box fuzzers deploy data-flow fuzzing, i.e. infer dependency of branches on input bytes and use it to accomplish more targeted branch inversion. VUzzer [26], Angora [6], BuzzFuzz [14] and Matryoshka [7] use a classical dynamic taint inference engine (i.e. track taint propagation) to infer dependencies. Fairfuzz [20], ProFuzzer [34], and Eclipser [8] use lighter engine and infer partial dependency by monitoring the execution traces of the seeds. RedQueen [2] and Steelix [21] can infer only dependencies based on exact (often called direct) copies of input bytes in the branches, by mutating individual bytes. Among grey boxes, the best inference in terms of speed, type, and accuracy is achieved by GreyOne [12]. Its engine called FTI is based on mutation of individual bytes (thus fast because it does not track taint propagation) and can detect dependencies of any type (not only direct copies of input bytes). FTI mutates bytes one by one and checks on changes in variables involved in branch conditions (thus accurate because it does not need for the whole branch to flip, only some of its variables). SIVO inference engine TaintFAST improves upon FTI and provides exponential decrease in the number of executions required to infer the full dependency, at a possible expense of accuracy. Instead of testing bytes one by one, TaintFAST uses probabilistic group testing and reduces the number of executions.

Data-flow grey boxes accomplish targeted branch inversion by randomly mutating the dependent bytes. A few fuzzers deploy more advanced strategies:

[6] This refers to optimization only – some fuzzers improve (but not optimize) multiple fuzzing subroutines.

Angora [6] uses gradient-descent based mutation, Eclipser [8] can invert efficiently branches that are linear or monotonic, and GreyOne [12] inverts branches by gradually reducing the distance between the actual and expected value in the branch condition. Some fuzzers, such as RedQueen and Steelix invert branches by solving directly the branch conditions based on equality (called magic bytes). SIVO can solve more complex branch inversion conditions that involve inequalities, without the use of SAT/SMT solvers. On the other hand, white boxes such as KLEE [5], and hybrid fuzzers such as Driller [31] and QSYM [36], use symbolic execution that relies on SMT solvers (thus it may be slow) to perform inversions in even more complex branches. The hybrid fuzzer Pangolin [16] uses linear approximations of branch constraints (thus more general than our intervals) called polyhedral path abstraction and later it utilizes them to efficiently sample solutions that satisfy path constraints. To infer the (more universal) linear approximations, Pangolin uses a method based on SMT solver. On the other hand, SIVO infers the (less universal) intervals with a simpler method.

The AFL-family of fuzzers as well as many other grey boxes track *edge coverage*. In addition, the AFL-family uses bucketization, i.e. besides edges, they track the counts of edges and group them in buckets that have ranges of powers of two. For practical purposes AFL does not record the precise edges (this will require storing whole execution traces which may be slow), but rather it works with hashes of edges (which is quite fast). The process of hashing may introduce collisions as noted by CollAFL [13]. To avoid such collisions, CollAFL proposes during compilation to choose the free parameters of the hashing function non-randomly, and according to a specific strategy. AFL++ [11] uses a similar idea and provides an open-source implementation based on link-time instrumentation. In addition, AFL++, LibFuzzer [29], and Honggfuzz [32] use so-called sanitizer coverage available in LLVM starting from version 11 to prevent collisions by assigning the free parameters during runtime. On the other hand, SIVO solution is to switch between different hashing functions during the fuzzing (i.e. at run-time). Instead of tracking edge coverage, a few fuzzers such as Honggfuzz [32], VUzzer [26] and LibFuzzer [29] track block coverage. Moreover, the grey-box fuzzer TortoiseFuzz [33] uses alternative coverage measurement metric (assigns different weights to edges based on their potential security impact) to prioritize testcases, and achieves higher rate of vulnerability detection.

7 Conclusion

We have presented four refinements for grey-box fuzzers that boost different fuzzing stages, specifically: (a) a faster dynamic taint dependency inference engine, (b) an integer inequality constraint learner and inference engine, (c) improved coverage tracker, and (d) complete parameterization of the strategies which can be optimized for dynamically. We have implemented the refinements in a fuzzer called SIVO. In comparison to 11 other popular grey-box fuzzers, SIVO scores highest with regards to coverage and number of vulnerabilities found.

Acknowledgments. We thank our shepherd Erik van der Kouwe for his helpful feedback. Abhik Roychoudhury, Zhijingcheng Yu, Shin Hwei Tan, Lu Yan, Andrea Fioraldi, and the anonymous reviewers gave us valuable comments and improvements on this work, for which we are thankful. All opinions expressed in this paper are solely those of the authors. This research is supported in part by the Crystal Centre at NUS and by the research grant DSOCL17019 from DSO in Singapore.

References

1. Circumventing fuzzing roadblocks with compiler transformations (2016). https://lafintel.wordpress.com/
2. Aschermann, C., Schumilo, S., Blazytko, T., Gawlik, R., Holz, T.: Redqueen: fuzzing with input-to-state correspondence. NDSS. **19**, 1–15 (2019)
3. Böhme, M., Pham, V.T., Nguyen, M.D., Roychoudhury, A.: Directed greybox fuzzing. In: Proceedings of the 2017 ACM SIGSAC Conference on Computer and Communications Security, pp. 2329–2344 (2017)
4. Böhme, M., Pham, V.T., Roychoudhury, A.: Coverage-based greybox fuzzing as Markov chain. IEEE Trans. Softw. Eng. **45**(5), 489–506 (2017)
5. Cadar, C., Dunbar, D., Engler, D.R., et al.: Klee: unassisted and automatic generation of high-coverage tests for complex systems programs. OSDI **8**, 209–224 (2008)
6. Chen, P., Chen, H.: Angora: efficient fuzzing by principled search. In: 2018 IEEE Symposium on Security and Privacy (SP), pp. 711–725. IEEE (2018)
7. Chen, P., Liu, J., Chen, H.: Matryoshka: fuzzing deeply nested branches. In: Proceedings of the 2019 ACM SIGSAC Conference on Computer and Communications Security (2019)
8. Choi, J., Jang, J., Han, C., Cha, S.K.: Grey-box concolic testing on binary code. In: 2019 IEEE/ACM 41st International Conference on Software Engineering (ICSE), pp. 736–747. IEEE (2019)
9. Dolan-Gavitt, B., et al.: Lava: large-scale automated vulnerability addition. In: S&P (2016)
10. Du, D., Hwang, F.K., Hwang, F.: Combinatorial group testing and its applications, vol. 12. World Scientific (2000)
11. Fioraldi, A., Maier, D., Eißfeldt, H., Heuse, M.: Afl++: combining incremental steps of fuzzing research. In: 14th USENIX Workshop on Offensive Technologies WOOT) (2020)
12. Gan, S., et al.: Greyone: data flow sensitive fuzzing. In: 29th USENIX Security Symposium (USENIX Security 20). USENIX Association, Boston, MA (2020). https://www.usenix.org/conference/usenixsecurity20/presentation/gan
13. Gan, S., et al.: CollAFL: path sensitive fuzzing. In: 2018 IEEE Symposium on Security and Privacy (SP), pp. 679–696. IEEE (2018)
14. Ganesh, V., Leek, T., Rinard, M.: Taint-based directed whitebox fuzzing. In: 2009 IEEE 31st International Conference on Software Engineering, pp. 474–484. IEEE (2009)
15. Google: OSS-Fuzz - continuous fuzzing of open source software (2020). https://github.com/google/oss-fuzz
16. Huang, H., Yao, P., Wu, R., Shi, Q., Zhang, C.: Pangolin: incremental hybrid fuzzing with polyhedral path abstraction. In: 2020 IEEE Symposium on Security and Privacy (SP), pp. 1613–1627. IEEE (2020)

17. Inozemtseva, L., Holmes, R.: Coverage is not strongly correlated with test suite effectiveness. In: Proceedings of the 36th International Conference on Software Engineering, pp. 435–445 (2014)
18. Klees, G., Ruef, A., Cooper, B., Wei, S., Hicks, M.: Evaluating fuzz testing. In: Proceedings of the 2018 ACM SIGSAC Conference on Computer and Communications Security, pp. 2123–2138 (2018)
19. Kocsis, L., Szepesvári, C.: Discounted UCB. In: 2nd PASCAL Challenges Workshop, vol. 2 (2006)
20. Lemieux, C., Sen, K.: Fairfuzz: a targeted mutation strategy for increasing greybox fuzz testing coverage. In: Proceedings of the 33rd ACM/IEEE International Conference on Automated Software Engineering, pp. 475–485 (2018)
21. Li, Y., Chen, B., Chandramohan, M., Lin, S.W., Liu, Y., Tiu, A.: Steelix: program-state based binary fuzzing. In: Proceedings of the 2017 11th Joint Meeting on Foundations of Software Engineering, pp. 627–637 (2017)
22. Lyu, C., Ji, S., Zhang, C., Li, Y., Lee, W.H., Song, Y., Beyah, R.: MOPT: optimized mutation scheduling for fuzzers. In: 28th USENIX Security Symposium (USENIX Security 2019), pp. 1949–1966 (2019)
23. Manès, V.J., Kim, S., Cha, S.K.: Ankou: guiding grey-box fuzzing towards combinatorial difference. In: Proceedings of the ACM/IEEE 42nd International Conference on Software Engineering, pp. 1024–1036 (2020)
24. Nethercote, N., Seward, J.: Valgrind: a framework for heavyweight dynamic binary instrumentation. In: PLDI (2007)
25. Nikolic, I., Mantu, R.: Sivo: Refined gray-box fuzzer. https://github.com/ivicanikolicsg/SivoFuzzer
26. Rawat, S., Jain, V., Kumar, A., Cojocar, L., Giuffrida, C., Bos, H.: Vuzzer: application-aware evolutionary fuzzing. NDSS **17**, 1–14 (2017)
27. Ryabinin, A.: Ubsan: run-time undefined behavior sanity checker (2014). https://lwn.net/Articles/617364/
28. Serebryany, K., Bruening, D., Potapenko, A., Vyukov, D.: Addresssanitizer: a fast address sanity checker. In: USENIX ATC (2012)
29. Serebryany, K.: Continuous fuzzing with libfuzzer and addressanitizer. In: 2016 IEEE Cybersecurity Development (SecDev), pp. 157–157. IEEE (2016)
30. She, D., Krishna, R., Yan, L., Jana, S., Ray, B.: Mtfuzz: fuzzing with a multi-task neural network. In: FSE (2020)
31. Stephens, N., et al.: Driller: augmenting fuzzing through selective symbolic execution. NDSS **16**, 1–16 (2016)
32. Swiecki, R.: Honggfuzz: Security oriented software fuzzer. supports evolutionary, feedback-driven fuzzing based on code coverage (SW and HW based) (2020). https://honggfuzz.dev/
33. Wang, Y., et al.: Not all coverage measurements are equal: fuzzing by coverage accounting for input prioritization. NDSS (2020)
34. You, W., et al.: Profuzzer: On-the-fly input type probing for better zero-day vulnerability discovery. In: 2019 IEEE Symposium on Security and Privacy (SP), pp. 769–786. IEEE (2019)
35. Yue, T., et al.: Ecofuzz: adaptive energy-saving greybox fuzzing as a variant of the adversarial multi-armed bandit. In: 29th USENIX Security Symposium (USENIX Security 20) (2020)

36. Yun, I., Lee, S., Xu, M., Jang, Y., Kim, T.: QSYM: a practical concolic execution engine tailored for hybrid fuzzing. In: 27th USENIX Security Symposium (USENIX Security 2018), pp. 745–761 (2018)
37. Zalewski, M.: American fuzzy lop (2.52b) (2019). https://lcamtuf.coredump.cx/afl/

SCRUTINIZER: Detecting Code Reuse in Malware via Decompilation and Machine Learning

Omid Mirzaei[1(✉)], Roman Vasilenko[2], Engin Kirda[1], Long Lu[1], and Amin Kharraz[3]

[1] Northeastern University, Boston, USA
{o.mirzaei,e.kirda,l.lu}@northeastern.edu
[2] VMware, Boston, USA
rvasilenko@vmware.com
[3] Florida International University, Miami, USA
ak@cs.fiu.edu

Abstract. Growing numbers of advanced malware-based attacks against governments and corporations, for political, financial and scientific gains, have taken security breaches to the next level. In response to such attacks, both academia and industry have investigated techniques to model and reconstruct these attacks and to defend against them. While such efforts have been all useful in mitigating the effects of modern attacks, automated malware code reuse inspection and campaign attribution have received less attention.

In this paper, we present an automated system, called SCRUTINIZER, to identify code reuse in malware via a novel machine learning-based encoding mechanism at the function-level. By creating a large knowledge base of previously observed and tagged malware campaigns, we can compare unknown samples against this knowledge base and determine how much overlap exists. SCRUTINIZER leverages an unsupervised learning approach to filter out irrelevant functions before code reuse detection. It provides two valuable capabilities. First, it identifies ties between an unknown sample and those malware specimens that are known to be used by a specific campaign. Second, it inspects if specific tools or functionalities are used by a campaign. Using SCRUTINIZER, we were able to identify 12 samples that were previously unknown to us and that we were able to correctly assign to well-known APT campaigns.

Keywords: Malware analysis · Code reuse detection

1 Introduction

Recent reports show that advanced malware-based breaches are increasing in volume and impact [68]. Companies are frequently becoming the targets of financially and politically-motivated attackers. For example, very recently, several biotech

L. Bilge et al. (Eds.): DIMVA 2021, LNCS 12756, pp. 130–150, 2021.
https://doi.org/10.1007/978-3-030-80825-9_7

research firms experienced crippling targeted attacks during the COVID19 pandemic [14,54]. Despite more attention on advanced attacks recently [25,27,28,30, 40,48] and their significant effects [3], there has been little investigation into how to automatically detect and identify specific advanced malware campaigns at scale when looking at large volumes of incoming malware samples.

The security community has extensively investigated how unknown attacks can be detected based on code similarity. Previous work studied binary and source code similarity testing detection [18,63,71], clone detection [4,5,35,37,42] and (fuzzy) hashing [38,41,58,67]. Very recently, the community has also begun to explore the use of modern machine learning approaches to detect more sophisticated malware attacks such as APTs [27]. While these efforts have been useful in identifying some forms of attacks, the challenge of detecting more interesting samples (e.g., APTs) in large volumes of incoming malware data is still an open challenge. Existing approaches are inadequate for characterizing malicious code reuse and campaign attribution in modern malware attacks for two primary reasons: First, relevant data about advanced (e.g., APT) samples is scarce. Hence, in real-world deployments, this limitation makes common machine learning techniques such as supervised machine learning significantly less effective in finding specific types of malware. Second, current static code similarity testing approaches are ineffective in locating previously unknown threats due to the intense use of evasive techniques by malware authors, rendering almost all of the existing static analysis approaches ineffective in practice (and hence, making dynamic analysis often necessary).

The core insight behind of our work is that almost all malware-based attacks (including advanced, targeted attacks such as APTs) follow practically proven patterns to deliver the actual malicious payload. Malware is rarely written from scratch and often depends on an existing code base or on specific, unique code bases (e.g., Mimikatz). Thus, if we accurately create a knowledge base of a large corpus of known, malicious source code snippets (some of them being known APT activity) observed in modern malware attacks, we can then compare unknown samples against this dataset and identify code similarities.

One major challenge when analyzing malware samples is the lack of source code. Hence, the malware binary needs to be analyzed and understood. While binary comparisons between malware samples are possible, in practice, even small differences between the files can lead to major reported differences even though the samples might belong to the same campaign. To be able to build an effective, accurate code similarity detection approach that works on real-world malware binaries, in the first step, we need to use dynamic analysis techniques that can execute the code and then create process snapshots of the running sample. In the second step, we need to be able to reconstruct the corresponding high-level source code from the memory dumps, and automatically locate segments of the code that are highly likely used in the malicious operation. This second step is more challenging, and has not been addressed to date.

In this work, we partnered with a well-known anti-malware company to run and extract run-time memory snapshots from 12,450 real-world malware samples.

We then built tools to analyze the process snapshots and to reconstruct the source code of the actual malicious payloads, and retrieve the corresponding function code snippets. Armed with a large set of decompiled code samples from a wide-range of malware specimens, in this paper, we propose a novel encoding mechanism to perform automated code similarity analysis. We developed a python-based framework to post-process run-time memory snapshots, and extract source code in order to be able to translate an arbitrary malware sample into a set of encoded functions that are representative of the functionality of the code. To achieve this, we take advantage of advances from the field of document classification by treating each function in the decompiled code as a sequence of words. We incorporate Siamese Neural Networks (SNNs) [9] to vectorize the functions and build the encoding model to be able to perform similarity testing. We applied our proposed similarity testing approach on 44,015 recent benign and malicious samples we received from the anti-malware company. The knowledge base we generated contains 1,734,992 clusters of extracted functions that were determined to be similar.

The automated code similarity comparison system that we built, called SCRUTINIZER, was used to analyze 3,000 random samples submitted to the anti-malware company in the summer of 2020. We could automatically identify and assign unknown samples to already known APT campaigns using function-level similarities. Evaluating advanced malware (e.g., APT) in the real-world is a great challenge because of the lack of ground truth. However, we were able to manually verify our detection results for 12 different, unknown samples by comparing our findings with those of other security vendors. Also, on average, SCRUTINIZER was able to discard on average 56% of the code of the unknown samples because it was determined to be uninteresting. Hence, SCRUTINIZER also proved to be useful during binary analysis as a filtering mechanism.

Contributions. In summary, this paper makes the following main contributions:

- We propose a machine-learning-based system, called SCRUTINIZER, to detect code reuse in malware samples. SCRUTINIZER relies on an unsupervised learning algorithm to filter out less relevant functions to malicious code samples.
- To our knowledge, we are the first to extract and use high-level source code from adversarial malware samples for performing automated malware campaign attribution. We were able to identify 12 samples that were previously unknown to us and that we were able to correctly assign to well-known APT campaigns.
- We have created a large knowledge base which contains more than 1.7M clusters of function encodings obtained from a large-scale analysis of 44K real-world advanced malware and benign samples. Both filtering and code reuse detection rely on this knowledge base to discard noisy functions and to identify code reuse.
- We release our code, our findings and other relevant information to foster the research in this area [64].

2 Approach

In this section, we describe our approach for performing automated code analysis. Building of a solution that serves this goal requires extracting the unpacked version of a given payload for decompilation, developing an efficient encoding mechanism on decompiled code for similarity testing, and constructing an unsupervised model to run code analysis on an unknown sample. The overall architecture of the proposed system for both the modeling and testing phases is shown in Fig. 1. In this section, we describe SCRUTINIZER's architecture in detail and our approach to implement each part.

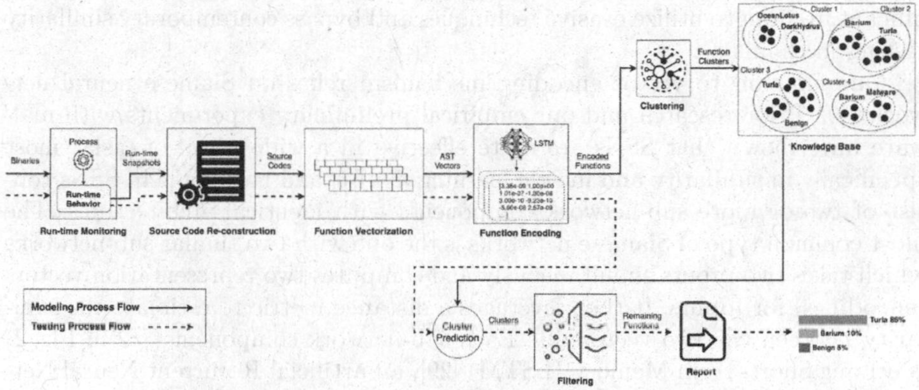

Fig. 1. Overall architecture of the proposed system and steps of modeling (i.e., solid arrows) and testing (i.e., dashed arrows) phases.

2.1 Decompilation

The first step in our pipeline involves binary decompilation to generate the unpacked version of the given payload. To this end, our approach relies on existing dynamic analysis techniques where the given binary is executed in an advanced sandbox developed by Lastline [39], to load and unpack the payload and record the run-time behavior. The sandbox acts as a universal unpacker by running the sample inside a guest operating system.

The dynamic analysis engine produces multiple process dumps (or snapshots) at critical points during different stages of the analysis. An analysis stage is known to be critical if one of these conditions are met: 1) when sensitive APIs are executed, causing a new process creation (e.g., CreateProcess), a new file creation (e.g., CreateFile) or privilege escalation (e.g., AdjustTokenPrivileges), 2) when execution happens outside of the original PE image, and 3) when the original PE image changes. The process dumps contain run-time information about loaded code and memory blocks of the binary under analysis. These snapshots, taken at different stages of the analysis, are then saved under a single analysis subject when the engine detects a suspicious behavior (e.g., a sensitive API call from an untrusted memory region). We parse these snapshots and run a post-process analysis to reconstruct the program's source code in C/C++. To this end, we developed a plugin for Ghidra [24] to map the memory regions from snapshots into Ghidra's virtual memory space and decompile the code found in memory.

2.2 Func2vec Encoding

The second step in the analysis pipeline is designed to perform code similarity testing across malicious payloads. Our analysis on existing similarity testing techniques on source code [4,5,18,35,37,42,63,71] revealed that these approaches are too sparse to such an adversarial landscape where malicious operators have significant freedom to utilize evasive techniques and bypass contemporary similarity testing mechanisms.

Our function to vector encoding mechanism relies on Siamese neural networks [9]. Prior research and our empirical preliminary experiments with malware have shown that SSNs are quite effective in a wide range of tasks, most specifically in similarity and metric learning [56,57] and hashing [44]. SSNs consist of two or more sub-network components with identical architectures. The most common type of Siamese networks is the one with two similar sub-networks which takes two inputs simultaneously and computes two representation vectors (encodings) for inputs. It then leverages a distance metric to estimate the similarity between the two vectors [9]. Each sub-network component (#2 in Fig. 2) is a Long Short-Term Memory (LSTM) [29], an artificial Recurrent Neural Network (RNN) architecture, that has shown to be efficient on a variety of tasks such as anomaly detection [21] and forecasting time series data [26]. LSTMs are also capable of learning long-term dependencies which is not quite possible in other types of networks due to the vanishing gradient problem [7]. To vectorize functions and feed them as inputs to the Siamese network, we rely on Abstract Syntax Trees (ASTs). In particular, we map each function to a flattened version of its AST node types (#1 in Fig. 2). Finally, to compare the final hidden states of two LSTM layers, we leverage the Manhattan distance metric (#5 in Fig. 2), which turns our Siamese network to be of a MaLSTM [52] variant.

To find similar functions across decompiled samples, we start by extracting n-grams of each function vector (i.e., a sequence of AST nodes). We then hash all extracted functions by applying the Locality Sensitive Hashing (LSH) algorithm [33] to these n-grams. LSH can map similar functions to the same hash code which is referred to as a bucket. At the end of the analysis, buckets that contain only a single function are incorporated as dissimilar functions. We then select all permutations of these functions as dissimilar pairs. We have observed that relying on LSH alone normally introduces false positives, especially in cases where functions are extracted from decompiled codes and they have major differences. For this reason, we leverage this hashing mechanism along with two verification techniques to discard false positives and come up with an ML-based hashing mechanism.

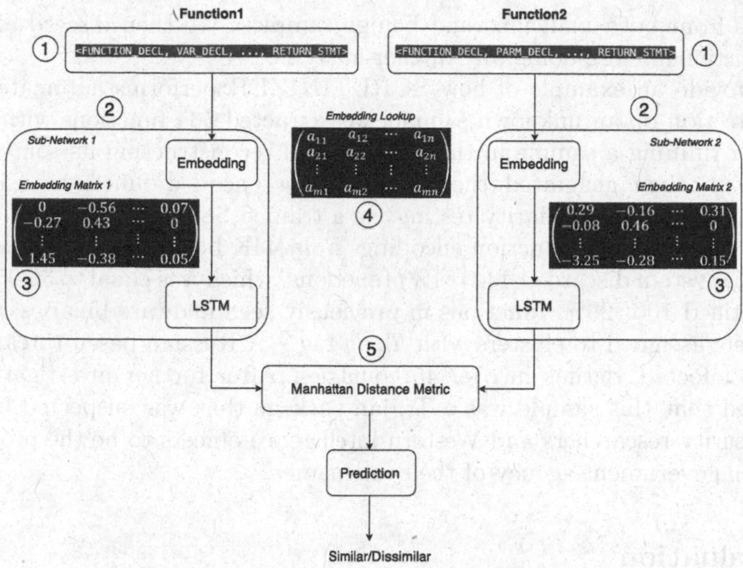

Fig. 2. Overall architecture of Siamese network.

2.3 Encoding Clustering

The primary goal of our analysis pipeline is to provide insights on a previously unknown binary. To this end, we begin by incorporating a trained Siamese network (see Sect. 2.2) to encode functions, and then, leverage an unsupervised learning approach to cluster similar functions from different code samples together. The generated clusters form our knowledge base to locate code reuse in a previously unknown sample and reason about the potential behavior of the sample. That is, the sample is converted to a set of encoded functions which are compared against clusters of hundreds of thousands of encoded functions that correspond to previously detected campaigns or malware families.

For each cluster, we generate a unique dictionary tag by maintaining the occurrence frequency of each function observed in different decompiled code samples. The tag of each cluster reveals the usage or popularity of the clustered functions in malware samples used by one or more campaigns. We have also tags for functions that were used mainly for benign code samples.

Malicious and benign binaries share significant volumes of code samples based on our observations. For instance, statically-linked standard library functions, global variable initialization code, and import resolution code are significantly common in both types. Therefore, a function cannot be simply labeled as malicious if it is observed in malware. Benign code samples could be identified as malicious only because they share several lines of code with malicious binaries. Thus, in this work, we rely on clusters of function encodings and automatically tag new functions as noisy if they are assigned to a mixed cluster that contains functions from both malicious and benign samples. We then discard all these noisy functions before doing any further analysis.

To provide an example of how SCRUTINIZER performs automated code reuse detection on an unknown sample, we extracted 534 functions with 45,902 LoC after running a sample in the sandbox and reconstructing its source code. The system then generated the corresponding encoded functions using the func2vec method for similarity testing via a trained SSN and a knowledge base of approximately 1.7M function encodings from 44K benign and malicious payloads. The system discarded 434 (81%) functions, which was equal to 36,957 LoC, and identified 100 (29%) functions in previously seen malware binaries, most of which were assigned to clusters with *Turla* tag – A Russian-based threat group that has infected victims in over 45 countries. After further investigation, we discovered that this sample was a Trojan package that was suspected by computer security researchers and Western intelligence officers to be the product of a Russian government agency of the same name.

3 Evaluation

In this section, we evaluate our system and discuss the results. In particular, we will explain our experimental setting, the encoding mechanism used to cluster similar functions. We will also provide details on the real-world deployment of SCRUTINIZER and our results in malware campaign analysis.

3.1 Experimental Setting and Dataset

SCRUTINIZER is implemented in Python. We have leveraged a library for parallel computing, called Dask [15], to improve the execution speed of our scripts. The experiments are conducted on a 2.2 GHz Intel Xeon Ubuntu server with 20 CPUs and 276 GB of RAM. We have used two distinct and non-overlapping datasets for the modeling and testing phases (see Table 1). To create a model, we have relied on 31,475 benign and 12,540 malware samples. Benign samples are different versions of Windows DLL files crawled from a website [17] in around one week. Table 1 shows the average size for each type of binary, and also, the average Lines of Code (LoC) and cyclomatic complexity [45] of their decompiled codes. Malicious samples (shown in Fig. 3) are both regular malware (12,253 samples) and those that have been used in advanced (i.e., APT) attacks (287 samples) according to the APT notes and threat intelligence of MITRE ATT&CK [50], FireEye [22], Kaspersky [36] and ThreatMiner [66][1]. To test our system, we have increased the malware-to-benign ratio and have evaluated its performance on unknown samples (See Sect. 3.4).

[1] We plan to release a labeled dataset of malware binaries that have been used by different APT campaigns that we have access to.

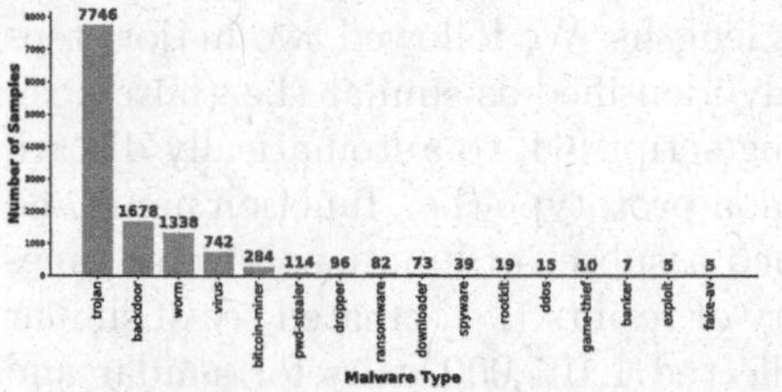

(a) Distribution of malware samples in different types.

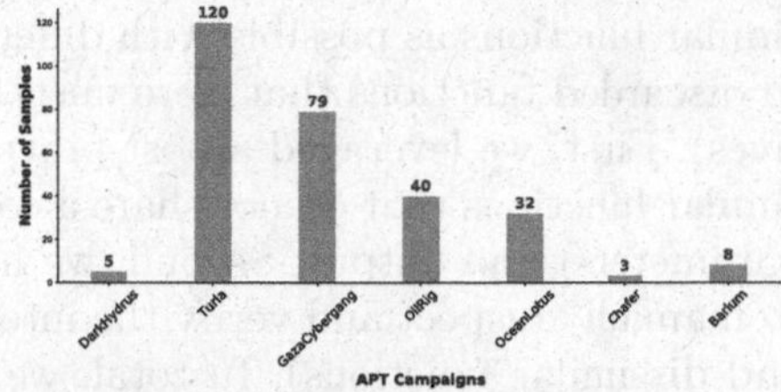

(b) Distribution of malware samples in different APT campaigns [65]

Fig. 3. Distributions of malware in our dataset.

Table 1. Overview of the dataset used in this work. The size (in MB) and cyclomatic complexity are given on average per sample. Avg_LOC is the average lines of code per sample and per function.

Phase	Data type	#Samples	Size	Avg_LOC	Complexity
Modeling	Malware [39]	12,540	0.55	106.21	11.05
	Benign [17]	31,475	0.31	35.73	5.80
Total		44,015			
Testing	Malware [39]	500	0.38	95.47	10.21
	Benign [39]	2,500	0.29	33.25	5.76
Total		3,000			

3.2 Function Encoding

This section particularly deals with answering two important questions: 1) How is a model is trained to embed functions?, and 2) How can the system leverage this encoding method to perform similarity testing? To perform training experiments, we first decompile each binary using a Ghidra[2] post-processing script [64] as discussed in Sect. 2.1. We then leverage Clang[3] to map each function to a flattened AST vector. Our choice of Clang is motivated by the fact that it is less sensitive to code artifacts commonly produced by decompilation tools. To make our AST construction more precise, we replace each function or API call (`CALL_EXPR` node in AST) in the vector by the exact name of a function or API call. This allows us to differentiate between calls to functions authored by the coders and APIs.

We then train the MaLSTM network to identify pairs of similar and dissimilar functions by mapping their AST vectors into an embedding space. We relied on the MinHashing implementation of Locality Sensitive Hashing (LSH) [33], and hashed functions based on the n-grams of their AST vectors. The parameters of fuzzy hashing were chosen very loosely so that we could come up with as many

[2] Version 9.1.2 with SHA-256: ebe3fa...ecac61.

[3] Version 10.0.0: https://releases.llvm.org/10.0.0/tools/clang.

similar functions as possible with different lengths. We followed two major steps to discarded functions that were mistakenly identified as similar (i.e., false positives). First, we leveraged a post-processing script [64] to automatically discard similar functions that do not share a common prototype (i.e., function name and parameters) and output. Second, we hashed a subset of functions several times to manually inspect and verify the integrity of results (i.e., created set of similar and dissimilar functions). In total, we collected 1,105,000 pairs for similar and dissimilar functions from both malicious and benign samples.

The accuracy of the trained network is evaluated via non-stratified 5-fold cross-validation. In particular, the dataset was first split into 5 folds of approximately equal size. Next, in each of the 5 iterations, we trained our system on 4 folds, and then, evaluated it on the remaining fold. The average, median and standard deviation of prediction errors (shown in Table 2) are 0.082, 0.097, 0.056, and 0.061 for malware and benign function vectors respectively that show our system works well. Moreover, we have randomly selected 1,000 function encodings and have manually checked the integrity of the results. Our manual inspection confirms the integrity and accuracy of the encoding mechanism and that similar AST nodes are properly placed close to each other in the latent space.

Table 2. Prediction error statistics after 5-fold cross-validation using only malware, only benign vectors, and a combination of both.

Type	Mean	Standard deviation	Median
Malware	0.082	0.097	0.031
Benign	0.056	0.061	0.004
Both	0.058	0.071	0.017

We also leveraged cross-validation to confirm the optimal value of embedding dimension and to tune the network's hyper-parameters, and in particular, the number of hidden layers. Due to time limit and the number of samples, we evaluated the performance of our system with 5 different dimensions and 3 networks with different numbers of hidden layers. Our results confirmed that an embedding size of 128 yields to higher F1 scores for all three settings.

3.3 Cluster Analysis

Equipped with a precise function-level encoding mechanism and similarity testing, we now hash each function to an encoding of a particular dimension (i.e., Func2vec encoding). To achieve this goal, we process all samples in our dataset and extract their functions and their AST vectors initially. We then generate the encodings of the functions using one of the sub-networks (i.e., LSTM) of our Siamese network (i.e., MaLSTM), cluster them into groups, and use these clusters to discard noisy functions and keep the ones that had been seen mainly in malware samples.

We leveraged the HDBSCAN clustering algorithm [13,46] to group function encodings in different clusters due to its superior performance over other algorithms for big data [59]. This algorithm is a variant of a popular density-based clustering algorithm, known as DBSCAN [20]. It requires no parameter tuning, runs faster and consumes less memory compared to the regular DBSCAN algorithm due to the way it has been implemented. To speed up the clustering process, we have reduced the dimension of our function encodings from 128 to 8 using Principal Component Analysis (PCA). Also, we experimentally tested and approved that reducing the dimension of the data would not significantly impact the clustering result, and most specifically, the number of clusters.

Our system could find a total number of 1,734,992 clusters based on the above parameters and clustering algorithm. Each cluster contains functions whose encodings resemble each other. From this number, 91% of clusters are completely benign, 3.2% are completely malicious, and 5.88% of clusters are mixed. The biggest cluster in our dataset has 14,406 similar function encodings, while the average size of clusters is around 5.

After clustering similar functions together, we generate a dictionary tag for each cluster based on the occurrence frequency of the observed functions in decompiled code samples. The occurrence frequency of a function is shown in Eq. 1. We maintain the occurrence frequency of each function during the modeling phase, and eventually, generate a dictionary tag of all the possible use cases of the function. For instance, the function that we described in Sect. 2.3 was automatically assigned to a cluster that had the following cluster tag:

$$tag = [benign = 12.5, Turla = 87.5] \tag{1}$$

The cluster tags created during clustering are used later for filtering and code reuse detection. To show the performance of SCRUTINIZER in these two tasks, we have applied it on real-world data. Specifically, we first show the efficiency of the filtering process, and then, we discuss how it can improve the accuracy of a malware detection system. Finally, we show how the proposed system could be leveraged to identify code reuse among malware samples that have been used by APT campaigns.

3.4 Real-World Deployment

We received 3,000 previously unknown samples collected by a well-known anti-malware company in the summer of 2020 to test the effectiveness of SCRUTINIZER. Note that based on our empirical analysis, each sample contained on average of 485 functions. This makes code similarity testing a significantly expensive process. More importantly, malware and benign samples share large volumes of standard code. This overlap could potentially introduce many false positives in malware detectors. Thus, we first filter noisy functions that are common in both malware and benign samples, and then, rely on the remaining functions of each sample to perform similarity analysis. In the following, we provide more details on each step as well as the summary of our experiments.

Filtering. The filtering process is applied by relying on cluster tags that are created during the clustering process (see Sect. 3.3). After the cluster assignment, the system discards functions if the cluster tag indicates that all or the majority of the functions (enforced by δ) in the assigned cluster are observed in the benign samples. It is worth mentioning that δ is customizable. Therefore, a higher value would only discard functions that were seen in benign clusters. We set the δ value to 0.5 to discard functions because this threshold value left us with more functions in malicious clusters on average. The summary of the filtering experiment is quite promising (See Fig. 4). The analysis shows that the samples in the previously unknown dataset have a median of 199 functions where the system was able to filter a median of 126 functions (63%) from those samples. This was equal to removing approximately 11,476 (56%) lines of code from the given code.

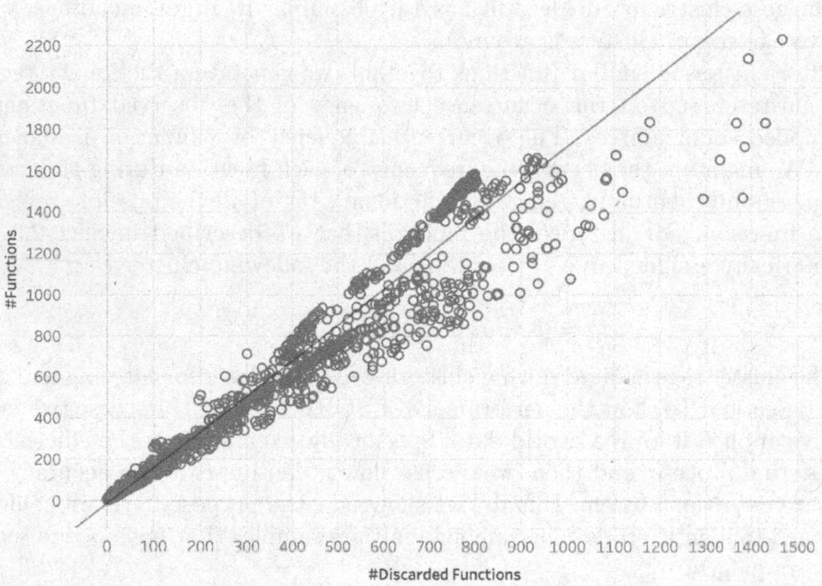

Fig. 4. The result of the filtering phase on the unknown sample set. Our analysis suggests that the filtering mechanism works well in practice by filtering a median of 126 functions of the input samples.

The filtering process had a significant impact on the performance of our system. To confirm this, we deployed SCRUTINIZER to detect unknown malware. Here, the system was tuned to label any incoming unknown sample as malware when malicious functions outnumbered benign ones, and the similarity of the sample to any previously known samples was more than a threshold, ranging from 0 to 100%. The experimental results show that the true positive rate increased from 82% to 92% after filtering the functions that were common in both malware and benign samples. At the same time, the false positive rate decreased from 10% to around 1.2%. In other words, as shown in Fig. 5, the Area Under the Curve (AUC) score, ranging from 0 (worst classifier) to 1 (perfect classifier), improved from 0.88 to 0.95 when the filtering was applied. In Sect. 3.4, we explain how the output of this section helped us to conduct the malware similarity analysis on this dataset.

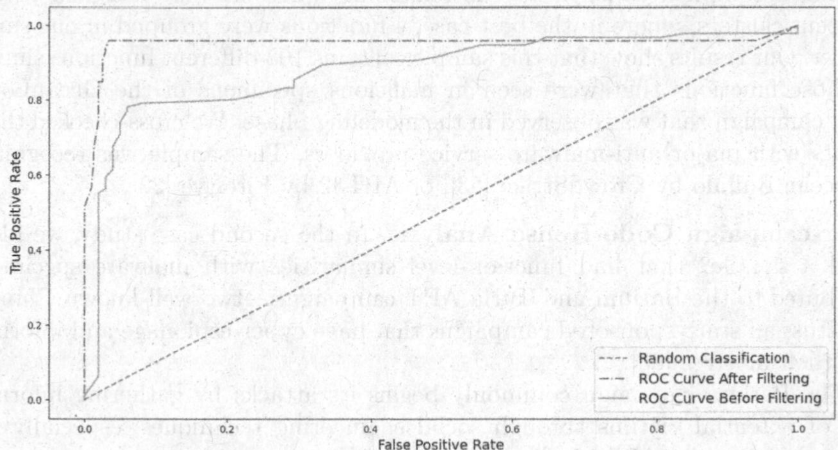

Fig. 5. Classification performance before and after filtering process. The results suggest that the applied filtering mechanism improves the TPR by 10% and decreases the FPR by 8.8%.

Code Reuse Analysis on APT Campaigns. One of our motivations behind developing SCRUTINIZER was to enhance contemporary techniques to perform malware similarity analysis on unknown samples. In this experiment, we tested SCRUTINIZER by using all the 3,000 unknown samples we discussed in Sect. 3.4. We followed the steps we described in Sect. 2 to perform this experiment. In this Section, we discuss two case studies: 1) a scenario where chunks of codes were identified by our system to be shared by malware samples that had been used by one single APT campaign, and 2) a scenario were code was shared and re-used by multiple APT campaigns.

Intra-campaign Code Reuse Analysis. In the first case study, we discuss how SCRUTINIZER can incorporate function-level similarity testing and automatically reason about code reuse in a given sample. In our analysis, we found a case[4] which was identified to have function-level similarities with malware specimens attributed to OceanLotus Vietnamese APT campaign.

The very initial malicious operation of this cyber-theft and espionage APT campaign dates back to 2014, where a European corporation was compromised [55]. Since then, this campaign has been continuously active with the maximum number of operations in 2018. The most recent and known activity of

[4] MD5: fcd7227891271a65b729a27de962c0cb.

this campaign has been focused on targeting the Wuhan government and Chinese ministry of emergency management to steal COVID-19 related findings via sending phishing emails [54].

Our automated system found 377 different functions from this sample with 18,125 lines of code. From this amount, SCRUTINIZER could discard 247 noisy functions which were up to 8,720 lines of code - i.e., around 48% of the original decompiled code. Next, the remaining functions were assigned to 109 different clusters, where in the best case, 4 functions were grouped in one single cluster. Our results show that this sample contains 105 different functions similar to those functions that were seen in malicious specimens of the OceanLotus APT campaign that was observed in the modeling phase. We cross-checked these results with major anti-malware service providers. The sample was recognized as Ocean Buffalo by CrowdStrike [53], or APT32 by FireEye [22].

Inter-campaign Code Reuse Analysis. In the second case study, we identified a sample[5] that had function-level similarities with malware specimens attributed to the Barium and Turla APT campaigns – two well-known Chinese and Russian state-sponsored campaigns that have cyber-espionage and information theft motives [65].

The Barium campaign commonly begins its attacks by gathering information of potential victims through social engineering techniques, especially via online social media. Multimedia and online game companies were attacked more frequently by this campaign. The Turla campaign, also known as Waterbug by Symantec [70], has targeted a wider range of users and sectors in over 45 different countries. The threat intelligence report also shows that this campaign is one of the most sophisticated APT campaigns that relies on a wide range of tools to deliver its attacks [65].

Our system found 971 functions from this sample with 74,309 lines of code overall. Also, it discarded 767 noisy functions which corresponded to 59,976 lines of code (≈81% of the original decompiled code). Next, the remaining 204 functions were assigned to 163 different clusters. Experimental results show that this sample has 22 functions that are syntactically similar to those of malware samples attributed to both the Barium and Turla campaigns. After further investigation, we discovered that this sample contains an open-source hacking code known as Mimikatz [49] that has not only been used by these two campaigns, but also by a number of other advanced malware campaigns [65].

Summary. Table 3 shows the list of all binaries that our system reported to have similarities with specimens that were known from each advanced malware (i.e., APT) campaign that existed in our knowledge base. We could verify the veracity of our results by consulting online AV scanners and threat intelligence reports. Some of these binary hashes were already reported as IoCs of known APT campaigns. Others were cross-checked by retrieving the name of the malicious operation or malware family and consulting the recent APT threat ency-

---

[5] MD5: 276c28759d06e09a28524fffc2812580.

clopedia [65]. The results included in Table 3 confirm that our tool can reason about code reuse in unknown samples by relying on function-level similarities.

Specifically, a similarity score presented for each sample by our tool shows how many functions an unknown sample has in common with already known malware instances. Moreover, this score represents how frequently a function is observed in each campaign. A low similarity score for an unknown malicious binary shows that it has less shared functions with known malware specimens of a specific campaign. On the other hand, a high similarity score indicates that the unknown binary has more functions in common with known malware samples that have been used by a malware campaign. Thus, the proposed approach to perform similarity testing can be used in different ways depending on the goal of the analysis. That is, if a human analyst aims at locating new and emerging trends in malware samples, a lower score is more preferable. If, however, the analyst is looking for code reuse in unknown samples, a higher score is an indicator of more overlaps.

Table 3. Campaign analysis result for a subset of samples that we could manually verify using online threat reports and AV scanners.

MD5	#Functions	Discarded functions (%)	Assigned campaign: similarity (%)	Real campaign
22d01fa2725ad7a83948f399144563f9	763	81.9	Turla: 58.0	Turla [69]
0d07422ba42d4a548e807b0298e372c7	225	55.1	GazaCybergang: 73.0	GazaCybergang [51]
655f56f880655198962ca8dd746431e8	188	66.5	GazaCybergang: 64.0	GazaCybergang [51]
ff8d92dfbcda572cf97c142017ccc658	144	70.1	Barium: 38.5	Barium [65,69]
c11dd805de683822bf4922aecb9bfef5	220	65.9	Barium: 38.4	Barium [65,69]
aae531a922d9cca9ddca3d98be09f9df	558	61.6	OilRig: 43.7	OilRig [65,69]
6a7bff614a1c2fd2901a5bd1d878be59	588	59.0	OilRig: 40.6	OilRig [65,69]
a921aa35deedf09fabee767824fd8f7e	44	68.2	GazaCybergang: 41.5	GazaCybergang [65,69]
0e441602449856e57d1105496023f458	73	61.6	Turla: 35.3	Turla [69]
7f05d410dc0d1b0e7a3fcc6cdda7a2ff	220	65.9	Barium: 38.4	Barium [65,69]
557ff68798c71652db8a85596a4bab72	144	70.1	Barium: 38.5	Barium [65,69]
b0877494d36fab1f9f4219c3defbfb19	144	70.1	Barium: 38.5	Barium [65,69]

4 Discussion

In this section, we discuss the accuracy, robustness and potential deployment costs of our approach.

Accuracy. The very first step of our pipeline involves mapping memory regions from snapshots taken during dynamic analysis into Ghidra's virtual memory space and use this tool to decompile the code found in memory. Thus, any issues that may happen during this step could impact the accuracy of our tool. In addition, like any other machine learning approach, the accuracy of SCRUTINIZER depends on the quantity of the data that is used to build the detection models. In particular, a prerequisite in training a Siamese network is the availability of a large number of function pairs from different binaries. This process requires extracting the corresponding syntactical features after constructing the decompiled version of the binary. However, collecting a large volume of relevant data is a non-trivial task since binary decompilation is an error-prone process on malware binaries, and it could contribute to lower accuracy. Furthermore, our experiments show that the AST construction method we used in this project can also produce false positives. In particular, we empirically found that in specific cases, ASTs produced by Clang showed similarities that were false positives. As a result, there might be noise in the training data and this might affect the function encoding process. To cope with this problem, we leveraged a post-processing mechanism to carefully inspect the result of the encoding process, and we performed hyper-parameter tunings to prefilter false positives. We note that in practice, the post-processing operation needs to be constantly visited and updated to keep the false positive rate in a manageable range.

Analysis Costs and Potential Bottlenecks. Our analysis of the performance overhead revealed three sources of potential bottlenecks in the process. Recall that our analysis relies on dynamic analysis which is inherently an expensive operation in code analysis. Common evasion techniques could even increase this cost by inserting stalling code or logic bombs and make the dynamic analysis significantly less effective. The analysis framework we used in this project allowed us to record the actual malicious behavior even with the presence of logic and time bombs. However, this is a best-effort approach, and requires constant improvement to maintain effectiveness which outside of the scope of this paper. The second expensive task in this process is related to constructing the training data for the Siamese network. This phase requires performing pair-wise similarity testing across all the decompiled code instances. The similarity testing on all functions in 1,000 decompiled code samples required around 4 h. However, note that this process needs to be performed once in order to build the training dataset, and subsequent incremental updates would not introduce signification overhead. The third potential computational cost is related to the training process where several parameters such as hyper-parameters and epochs need to be considered for constructing the model. In this work, each of the sub-networks were trained in 5 epochs in parallel, and the training process on around 1M pairs of functions took approximately 36 min. We observed that the processing time can dramatically increase when we incorporated larger pairs of functions. However, the results do suggest that a larger number of pairs (e.g., 10M) did not necessarily contribute to significantly more accurate results.

Practical Deployment. We posit that a number of useful activities can be performed with our tool such as approximating the prevalence of emerging advanced malware threats, filtering previously known binaries, or identifying the adoption of new attack techniques across different campaigns. The proposed approach to perform code reuse analysis would allow human analysts to locate emerging trends by looking for code samples with lower similarity scores. For instance, we automatically identified several variants of OceanLotus campaign by simply looking for code samples with similarity score less than 15%. Furthermore, by applying a higher similarity score, it is possible to perform scalable unsupervised learning and group more relevant code based on their function-level similarity.

We empirically showed that this approach works well in practice by analyzing 3,000 previously unknown samples (see Sect. 3).

5 Related Work

Binary Code Similarity Detection. Binary code similarity detection has been applied to many applications, including code plagiarism detection [43,62], malware family and lineage analysis [6,34], and vulnerability analysis [10] to name a few.

State-of-the-art BCSD solutions heavily rely on a specific syntactic feature of binary code extracted via static analysis such as control flow graphs (CFGs) [8,19,23,60]. The majority of these solutions have low accuracy, especially when it comes to advanced malware that leverages several anti-analysis techniques to circumvent the static analysis. On the other hand, few solutions are proposed that are more resilient against anti-analysis techniques such as obfuscation and have considered semantics of binary codes to identify possible similarities. Nevertheless, they have not been applied to malicious binaries. Contrary to these solutions, SCRUTINIZER relies on syntactic features that are extracted from decompiled memory snapshots taken during dynamic analysis.

Authorship Attribution. Previous studies have also explored different ways through which users can be deanonymized based on their coding styles. Two broad categories of methods have been investigated in academia to address this problem that work either at the binary-level [11,47,61] or at the source code level [1,12,16]. Binary-level methods, while fast and useful, work under the assumption that a toolchain provenance is used to generate the binary, including a specific compiler, operating system and source language. In contrast, code-level methods are more flexible, specifically because coding styles of authors at the source code level are not lost during compilation. Recent works have relied on coding style features and have leveraged machine learning to develop more robust mechanisms for code authorship attribution. For example, Abuhamad et al. [1] have proposed a system that attributes code at a large scale effectively using deep neural networks. Caliskan-Islam et al. have relied on random forests and syntactic features from ASTs to de-anonymize code authors based on their coding styles [2,12]. While these approaches are effective in attributing code to specific authors, they are less effective when dealing with adversarial code that has been decompiled and where coding style features such as the naming conventions for variables have been lost. In comparison to existing authorship attribution work, our work fills the gap and addresses the code similarity detection problem in code that is only available as binary, and where source code needs to be extracted.

Malware Clustering. Automated malware clustering has received well-deserved attention in the past as it helps to identify the type and severity of the threat that each malware specimen constitutes. Also, it is useful in tracing new trends in malware samples and creating detection signatures and removal procedures. These approaches can be categorized into three main groups depending on their feature extraction strategy. The first category of approaches rely on features that are extracted statically before the binary is executed. For example, MutantX-S [32] is an automated tool that relies on code instruction sentences to cluster malware samples. The second category of approaches leverage features that are extracted at run-time, normally by running the sample in an emulated environment. As an example, Bayer et al. [6] run each binary in a sandbox and cluster malware specimens based on their behavioral profiles and how they interact with the operating system. Finally, the third category makes use of features that are extracted before and after the execution time. An example includes DUET [31], a tool that relies on both static and dynamic features to cluster malware binaries. Note that these tools are primarily interested in automatically identifying to what family an unknown, obfuscated (or encrypted) sample belongs to. They are not focused on coding patterns to be able to determine campaign similarity or potential attribution.

6 Conclusion

In this paper, we presented an automated system for malicious code similarity identification and campaign attribution. The system decompiles binaries of both malicious and benign applications and encodes their functions using Siamese networks. It then clusters function encodings into different groups and leverages cluster tags created during clustering to facilitate the analysis of new samples that anti-malware companies rccive every day. We deployed SCRUTINIZER in a real-world setting and it proved to be useful in both function filtering (i.e., reverse engineering) and code reuse analysis on APT campaigns. Using this system, we were able to identify 12 samples that were previously unknown to us and that we were able to correctly assign to well-known APT campaigns.

Acknowledgement. This work was partially-supported by National Science Foundation (NSF) under grant CNS-1703454, and the Office of Naval Research (ONR) under the "In Situ Malware" project. This work was also partially-supported by Secure Business Austria.

References

1. Abuhamad, M., AbuHmed, T., Mohaisen, A., Nyang, D.: Large-scale and language-oblivious code authorship identification. In: Proceedings of the 2018 ACM SIGSAC Conference on Computer and Communications Security, pp. 101–114 (2018)
2. Afroz, S., Islam, A.C., Stolerman, A., Greenstadt, R., McCoy, D.: Doppelgänger finder: taking stylometry to the underground. In: 2014 IEEE Symposium on Security and Privacy, pp. 212–226. IEEE (2014)
3. APT trends report Q1 2020 (2020). https://securelist.com/apt-trends-report-q1-2020/96826/. Accessed 05 July 2020
4. Baker, B.S.: On finding duplication and near-duplication in large software systems. In: Proceedings of 2nd Working Conference on Reverse Engineering, pp. 86–95. IEEE (1995)

5. Baxter, I.D., Pidgeon, C., Mehlich, M.: DMS/SPL REG: program transformations for practical scalable software evolution. In: Proceedings of 26th International Conference on Software Engineering, pp. 625–634. IEEE (2004)
6. Bayer, U., Comparetti, P.M., Hlauschek, C., Kruegel, C., Kirda, E.: Scalable, behavior-based malware clustering. In: NDSS, vol. 9, pp. 8–11. Citeseer (2009)
7. Bengio, Y., Simard, P., Frasconi, P.: Learning long-term dependencies with gradient descent is difficult. IEEE Trans. Neural Netw. **5**(2), 157–166 (1994)
8. Bindiff: a comparison tool for binary files. https://www.zynamics.com/bindiff.html (2020). Accessed 05 May 2020
9. Bromley, J., Guyon, I., LeCun, Y., Säckinger, E., Shah, R.: Signature verification using a "siamese" time delay neural network. In: Advances in Neural Information Processing Systems, pp. 737–744 (1994)
10. Brumley, D., Poosankam, P., Song, D., Zheng, J.: Automatic patch-based exploit generation is possible: Techniques and implications. In: 2008 IEEE Symposium on Security and Privacy (SP 2008), pp. 143–157. IEEE (2008)
11. Caliskan, A., et al.: When coding style survives compilation: de-anonymizing programmers from executable binaries. arXiv preprint arXiv:1512.08546 (2015)
12. Caliskan-Islam, A., et al.: De-anonymizing programmers via code stylometry. In: 24th USENIX Security Symposium (USENIX Security 2015), pp. 255–270 (2015)
13. Campello, R.J.G.B., Moulavi, D., Sander, J.: Density-based clustering based on hierarchical density estimates. In: Pei, J., Tseng, V.S., Cao, L., Motoda, H., Xu, G. (eds.) PAKDD 2013. LNCS (LNAI), vol. 7819, pp. 160–172. Springer, Heidelberg (2013). https://doi.org/10.1007/978-3-642-37456-2_14
14. APT Groups Target Healthcare and Essential Services. https://us-cert.cisa.gov/ncas/alerts/AA20126A (2020). Accessed 05 May 2020
15. Dask: A flexible library for parallel computing in python. https://docs.dask.org (2018). Accessed 05 May 2020
16. Dauber, E., et al.: Git blame who?: stylistic authorship attribution of small, incomplete source code fragments. Proc. Privacy Enhanc. Technol. **2019**(3), 389–408 (2019)
17. DLL Files. https://www.dll-files.com (2020). Accessed 14 Mar 2020
18. Ducau, F.N., Rudd, E.M., Heppner, T.M., Long, A., Berlin, K.: SMART: semantic malware attribute relevance tagging. CoRR abs/1905.06262 (2019). http://arxiv.org/abs/1905.06262
19. Eschweiler, S., Yakdan, K., Gerhards-Padilla, E.: discovre: efficient cross-architecture identification of bugs in binary code. In: NDSS (2016)
20. Ester, M., Kriegel, H.P., Sander, J., Xu, X., et al.: A density-based algorithm for discovering clusters in large spatial databases with noise. KDD **96**, 226–231 (1996)
21. Feng, C., Li, T., Chana, D.: Multi-level anomaly detection in industrial control systems via package signatures and LSTM networks. In: 2017 47th Annual IEEE/IFIP International Conference on Dependable Systems and Networks (DSN), pp. 261–272. IEEE (2017)
22. Advanced Persistent Threat Groups. https://www.fireeye.com/current-threats/apt-groups.html (2020). Accessed 14 Mar 2020
23. Gao, D., Reiter, M.K., Song, D.: BinHunt: automatically finding semantic differences in binary programs. In: Chen, L., Ryan, M.D., Wang, G. (eds.) ICICS 2008. LNCS, vol. 5308, pp. 238–255. Springer, Heidelberg (2008). https://doi.org/10.1007/978-3-540-88625-9_16
24. Ghidra: A software reverse engineering (SRE) suite of tools developed by NSA's Research Directorate. https://ghidra-sre.org (2020). Accessed 14 Mar 2020

25. Graziano, M., et al.: Needles in a haystack: mining information from public dynamic analysis sandboxes for malware intelligence. In: 24th USENIX Security Symposium (USENIX Security 2015), pp. 1057–1072 (2015)
26. Guo, T., Xu, Z., Yao, X., Chen, H., Aberer, K., Funaya, K.: Robust online time series prediction with recurrent neural networks. In: 2016 IEEE International Conference on Data Science and Advanced Analytics (DSAA), pp. 816–825. IEEE (2016)
27. Han, X., Pasquier, T., Bates, A., Mickens, J., Seltzer, M.: UNICORN: runtime provenance-based detector for advanced persistent threats. In: NDSS (2020)
28. Hardy, S., et al.: Targeted threat index: Characterizing and quantifying politically-motivated targeted malware. In: 23rd USENIX Security Symposium (USENIX Security 2014), pp. 527–541 (2014)
29. Hochreiter, S., Schmidhuber, J.: Long short-term memory. Neural Comput. **9**(8), 1735–1780 (1997)
30. Hossain, M.N., et al.: SLEUTH: real-time attack scenario reconstruction from COTS audit data. In: 26th USENIX Security Symposium (USENIX Security 2017), pp. 487–504 (2017)
31. Hu, X., Shin, K.G.: Duet: integration of dynamic and static analyses for malware clustering with cluster ensembles. In: Proceedings of the 29th Annual Computer Security Applications Conference, pp. 79–88 (2013)
32. Hu, X., Shin, K.G., Bhatkar, S., Griffin, K.: Mutantx-s: scalable malware clustering based on static features. In: 2013 USENIX Annual Technical Conference (USENIX ATC 2013), pp. 187–198 (2013)
33. Indyk, P., Motwani, R.: Approximate nearest neighbors: towards removing the curse of dimensionality. In: Proceedings of the Thirtieth Annual ACM Symposium on Theory of Computing, pp. 604–613 (1998)
34. Jang, J., Woo, M., Brumley, D.: Towards automatic software lineage inference. In: 22nd USENIX Security Symposium (USENIX Security 2013), pp. 81–96 (2013)
35. Jiang, L., Misherghi, G., Su, Z., Glondu, S.: Deckard: scalable and accurate tree-based detection of code clones. In: 29th International Conference on Software Engineering (ICSE 2007), pp. 96–105. IEEE (2007)
36. Targeted Cyberattacks Logbook. https://apt.securelist.com/#!/threats/ (2018). Accessed 14 Mar 2020
37. Komondoor, R., Horwitz, S.: Using slicing to identify duplication in source code. In: Cousot, P. (ed.) SAS 2001. LNCS, vol. 2126, pp. 40–56. Springer, Heidelberg (2001). https://doi.org/10.1007/3-540-47764-0_3
38. Kornblum, J.: Identifying almost identical files using context triggered piecewise hashing. Digit. Invest. **3**, 91–97 (2006)
39. Lastline. https://www.lastline.com (2021). Accessed 04 May 2021
40. Le Blond, S., Uritesc, A., Gilbert, C., Chua, Z.L., Saxena, P., Kirda, E.: A look at targeted attacks through the lense of an NGO. In: 23rd USENIX Security Symposium (USENIX Security 2014), pp. 543–558 (2014)
41. Li, Y., et al.: Experimental study of fuzzy hashing in malware clustering analysis. In: 8th Workshop on Cyber Security Experimentation and Test (CSET 2015) (2015)
42. Li, Z., Lu, S., Myagmar, S., Zhou, Y.: CP-miner: a tool for finding copy-paste and related bugs in operating system code. OSdi **4**, 289–302 (2004)
43. Luo, L., Ming, J., Wu, D., Liu, P., Zhu, S.: Semantics-based obfuscation-resilient binary code similarity comparison with applications to software plagiarism detection. In: Proceedings of the 22nd ACM SIGSOFT International Symposium on Foundations of Software Engineering, pp. 389–400 (2014)

44. Masci, J., Bronstein, M.M., Bronstein, A.M., Schmidhuber, J.: Multimodal similarity-preserving hashing. IEEE Trans. Pattern Anal. Mach. Intell. **36**(4), 824–830 (2013)
45. McCabe, T.J.: A complexity measure. IEEE Trans. Softw. Eng. **4**, 308–320 (1976)
46. McInnes, L., Healy, J.: Accelerated hierarchical density based clustering. In: 2017 IEEE International Conference on Data Mining Workshops (ICDMW), pp. 33–42. IEEE (2017)
47. Meng, X., Miller, B.P., Jun, K.-S.: Identifying multiple authors in a binary program. In: Foley, S.N., Gollmann, D., Snekkenes, E. (eds.) ESORICS 2017. LNCS, vol. 10493, pp. 286–304. Springer, Cham (2017). https://doi.org/10.1007/978-3-319-66399-9_16
48. Milajerdi, S.M., Gjomemo, R., Eshete, B., Sekar, R., Venkatakrishnan, V.: Holmes: real-time apt detection through correlation of suspicious information flows. In: 2019 IEEE Symposium on Security and Privacy (SP), pp. 1137–1152. IEEE (2019)
49. Mimikatz: an open-source application for veiwing and saving authentication credentials (2014). https://github.com/gentilkiwi/mimikatz. Accessed 05 May 2020
50. MITRE ATT&CK: a globally-accessible knowledge base of adversary tactics and techniques based on real-world observations (2020). https://attack.mitre.org/. Accessed 14 Mar 2020
51. Moonlight - Targeted attacks in the Middle East (2016). https://tinyurl.com/45m3jtx8. Accessed 05 July 2020
52. Mueller, J., Thyagarajan, A.: Siamese recurrent architectures for learning sentence similarity. In: Thirtieth AAAI Conference on Artificial Intelligence (2016)
53. Meet the threat actors: List of APTs and adversary groups (2019). https://www.crowdstrike.com/blog/meet-the-adversaries/. Accessed 05 May 2020
54. Vietnamese Threat Actors APT32 Targeting Wuhan Government and Chinese Ministry of Emergency Management in Latest Example of COVID-19 Related Espionage (2020). https://tinyurl.com/7whx7ecr. Accessed 05 May 2020
55. Cyber espionage is alive and well: Apt32 and the threat to global corporations (2017). https://tinyurl.com/54eact6v. Accessed 05 May 2020
56. Oh Song, H., Jegelka, S., Rathod, V., Murphy, K.: Deep metric learning via facility location. In: Proceedings of the IEEE Conference on Computer Vision and Pattern Recognition, pp. 5382–5390 (2017)
57. Oh Song, H., Xiang, Y., Jegelka, S., Savarese, S.: Deep metric learning via lifted structured feature embedding. In: Proceedings of the IEEE Conference on Computer Vision and Pattern Recognition, pp. 4004–4012 (2016)
58. Oliver, J., Cheng, C., Chen, Y.: TLSH-a locality sensitive hash. In: 2013 Fourth Cybercrime and Trustworthy Computing Workshop, pp. 7–13. IEEE (2013)
59. Benchmarking performance and scaling of python clustering algorithms (2020). https://hdbscan.readthedocs.io/en/latest/performance_and_scalability.html. Accessed 05 May 2020
60. Pewny, J., Garmany, B., Gawlik, R., Rossow, C., Holz, T.: Cross-architecture bug search in binary executables. In: 2015 IEEE Symposium on Security and Privacy, pp. 709–724. IEEE (2015)
61. Rosenblum, N., Zhu, X., Miller, B.P.: Who wrote this code? Identifying the authors of program binaries. In: Atluri, V., Diaz, C. (eds.) ESORICS 2011. LNCS, vol. 6879, pp. 172–189. Springer, Heidelberg (2011). https://doi.org/10.1007/978-3-642-23822-2_10
62. Sæbjørnsen, A., Willcock, J., Panas, T., Quinlan, D., Su, Z.: Detecting code clones in binary executables. In: Proceedings of the Eighteenth International Symposium on Software Testing and Analysis, pp. 117–128 (2009)

63. Schleimer, S., Wilkerson, D.S., Aiken, A.: Winnowing: local algorithms for document fingerprinting. In: Proceedings of the 2003 ACM SIGMOD International Conference on Management of Data, pp. 76–85 (2003)
64. Scrutinizer: Detecting code reuse in malware via decompilation and machine learning (2021). https://github.com/OMirzaei/SCRUTINIZER. Accessed 04 May 2021
65. THREAT GROUP CARDS: A threat actor encyclopedia (2019). https://tinyurl.com/bb8mt23k. Accessed 05 Oct 2019
66. ThreatMiner: Data Mining for Threat Intelligence (2020). https://www.threatminer.org/index.php. Accessed 14 Mar 2020
67. Upchurch, J., Zhou, X.: Variant: a malware similarity testing framework. In: 2015 10th International Conference on Malicious and Unwanted Software (MALWARE), pp. 31–39. IEEE (2015)
68. Verizon's 2020 data breach investigations report (2020). https://tinyurl.com/56m7m9ym. Accessed 05 May 2020
69. VirusTotal (2020). https://www.virustotal.com/gui/home/search. Accessed 05 June 2020
70. Waterbug: Espionage Group Rolls Out Brand-New Toolset in Attacks Against Governments (2020). https://tinyurl.com/92s76xdn. Accessed 05 May 2020
71. Xu, X., Liu, C., Feng, Q., Yin, H., Song, L., Song, D.: Neural network-based graph embedding for cross-platform binary code similarity detection. In: Proceedings of the 2017 ACM SIGSAC Conference on Computer and Communications Security, pp. 363–376 (2017)

SPECULARIZER: Detecting Speculative Execution Attacks via Performance Tracing

Wubing Wang[1], Guoxing Chen[1], Yueqiang Cheng[3], Yinqian Zhang[2(✉)], and Zhiqiang Lin[1]

[1] The Ohio State University, Columbus, OH 43210, USA
wang.11488@osu.edu, chen.4329@osu.edu, zlin@cse.ohio-state.edu
[2] Southern University of Science and Technology, Shenzhen, Guangdong 518055, China
yinqianz@acm.org
[3] NIO Security Research, San Jose, CA 95134, USA
yueqiang.cheng@nio.io

Abstract. This paper presents SPECULARIZER, a framework for uncovering speculative execution attacks using performance tracing features available in commodity processors. It is motivated by the practical difficulty of eradicating such vulnerabilities in the design of CPU hardware and operating systems and the principle of defense-in-depth. The key idea of SPECULARIZER is the use of Hardware Performance Counters and Processor Trace to perform lightweight monitoring of production applications and the use of machine learning techniques for identifying the occurrence of the attacks during offline forensics analysis. Different from prior works that use performance counters to detect side-channel attacks, SPECULARIZER monitors triggers of the critical paths of the speculative execution attacks, thus making the detection mechanisms robust to different choices of side channels used in the attacks. To evaluate SPECULARIZER, we model all known types of exception-based and misprediction-based speculative execution attacks and automatically generate thousands of attack variants. Experimental results show that SPECULARIZER yields superior detection accuracy and the online tracing of SPECULARIZER incur reasonable overhead.

1 Introduction

Speculative execution attacks exploit micro-architectural design flaws and side channels in modern processors and enable unprivileged processes to exfiltrate sensitive information across security boundaries. These attacks have seriously undermined the fundamental security assumptions made in the design of the operating systems and have been in the spotlight since their very first public disclosure in early 2018. The most prominent examples of speculative execution attacks are Meltdown [27] and Spectre [23], and later variants, such as Foreshadow [41], Micro-architectural Data Sampling (MDS) [31,37,43], Load Value Injection (LVI) [42] are also well-known examples of such attacks.

In this paper, we apply the principle of defense-in-depth and propose SPECULARIZER[1], a software framework for uncovering speculative execution attacks using hardware performance tracing features available in commodity processors, *i.e.*, hardware

[1] SPECULARIZER is a portmanteau of "Speculative" and "Polarizer".

Y. Cheng—This work was mainly done at Baidu Research.

L. Bilge et al. (Eds.): DIMVA 2021, LNCS 12756, pp. 151–172, 2021.
https://doi.org/10.1007/978-3-030-80825-9_8

performance counters (HPC) and processor trace (PT). SPECULARIZER complements existing defenses against speculative execution attacks, by offering a capability of logging both architectural and micro-architectural behaviors of the monitored software to enable forensic analysis and offline attack detection.

In contrast to prior work that detects cache side channels to identify speculative execution attacks [19], which can be easily circumvented by attacks using alternative side channels, SPECULARIZER is inspired by the following key observations: Although speculative execution attacks may leverage a variety of micro-architectural side channels (*e.g.*, TLBs, caches) to leak secrets from speculatively executed instructions, the invariant of these attacks is the method with which the speculative execution can be triggered. In exception-based attacks, speculative execution is triggered by exceptions, which are either handled or suppressed; in misprediction-based attacks, speculative execution is triggered either by control-flow misprediction or by misprediction in the memory disambiguation. Therefore, SPECULARIZER utilizes the inevitable execution patterns of exceptions and mispredictions as signatures.

We identify PT packets and HPC events that can reveal crucial information necessary for attack detection, such as control-flow transfers for exception handling and TSX aborts, mispredicted branch instructions, machine clears due to memory order conflicts, *etc.* While each type of PT or HPC record alone is insufficient for reconstructing all attack activities, collectively they offer greater insight into the micro-architectural level behavior of the monitored applications. Therefore, we develop techniques to combine HPC and PT data to construct execution traces. With these traces, we build classification models using the Long Short Term Memory (LSTM) network to perform the classification of attack and benign programs.

SPECULARIZER consists of two components: an online trace collection component that is integrated into the operating system of a production machine, on which the monitored application runs, and an offline attack detection component that performs HPC and PT records parsing, trace processing, and trace classification, which are time-consuming and hard to finish in real-time. In fact, rarely do HPC or PT-based monitoring systems perform real-time analysis [14,51]. As such, SPECULARIZER is best suited for VM or container-based cloud systems, where suspicious workloads from untrusted cloud tenants are monitored on cloud servers and forensic analyses are performed on separate servers to detect attack activities. While deferred attack detection does not prevent the attacks from happening, it can trigger further investigation of attacks to identify their sources and assess their consequences.

We have implemented a prototype of SPECULARIZER and evaluated its effectiveness and efficiency in a lab setting. Specifically, to evaluate SPECULARIZER, we develop parameterized models for each type of the speculative execution attacks we aim to detect, and then automatically generate thousands of attack variants by tuning the parameters of these models. With the data sets collected from both benign and attack samples, the evaluation of SPECULARIZER suggests it has promising detection accuracy while inducing reasonable performance overhead. The evaluation results also indicate that SPECULARIZER significantly raises the bar for performing speculative execution attacks even if the attackers understand the detection mechanism.

Contributions. The paper makes the following contributions: ① SPECULARIZER is the software tool that detects speculative execution attacks, by their triggers of speculative execution rather than specific covert channels. ② SPECULARIZER provides new insights of combined use of multiple performance tracing hardware features, *e.g.*, PT and HPCs, in the context of offline attack detection. ③ The paper presents parameterized models of speculative execution attacks and methods to automatically generate attack variants with varying attack success rates. ④ The paper presents a prototype implementation of SPECULARIZER and empirically evaluates its selection of parameters, its effectiveness, and performance overhead.

2 Background

Speculative Execution Attacks. A speculative execution attack contains the following components [3]: *Speculation primitive* triggers speculative execution of instructions. *Disclosure gadget* transmits information through a side channel. *Disclosure primitive* reads the side-channel information that was transmitted by the disclosure gadget. As such, a speculative execution attack can be performed in the following steps: ① executes the *speculation primitive* to trigger speculative execution of instructions. ② utilizes the speculative instructions (including the *speculation primitive* itself) to access secrets across the security boundary; ③ speculatively executes the *disclosure gadget* to encode the secret value into the cache states; ④ uses the *disclosure primitive* to decode the secret data from cache states.

According to the *speculation primitives*, we classify speculative execution attacks into the following three categories [11]. Misprediction-based attacks leverage branch, Store-To-Load (STL), and memory-order buffer mispredictions as the *speculation primitive* and performs attacks before the correct target is resolved. Exception-based attacks and assistance-based attacks use exceptions (*e.g.* Page fault, General Protection fault, *etc.*) and microcode assists (*e.g.* line-fill buffer, store buffer, and load port conflict [1], *etc.*) as *speculation primitive*, respectively, and speculatively execute instructions before they are handled by the processor.

Performance Tracing Hardware. Intel PT is a hardware feature available in Intel processors since Broadwell. It is designed to record the information regarding the control-flow transfers of software programs with very low performance overhead. The PT hardware generates PT packets to reconstruct the timestamped control flow for a program [17,45]. HPCs are a set of model-specific registers that can be used to count user-selected processor architectural or micro-architectural events. Each HPC register can be configured to count a specific event supported by the processor. At runtime, when the specified event happens, the corresponding HPC counter will be incremented.

The HPCs have two different approaches for software to collect event samples. First, when the performance monitor interrupt (PMI) is enabled in a specific counter, a PMI will be triggered when the counter overflows, which provides the software with an opportunity to handle the HPCs data [7]. However, the large volume of interrupts dramatically increases the performance overhead. Second, to address the performance issues, Intel introduces Precise Event-Based Sampling (PEBS), which can store the events in a buffer (dubbed *Debug Store* (DS) area). Only one interrupt is triggered when the buffer is almost full (determined by a threshold).

3 Threat Model and SPECULARIZER Overview

Threat Model. All misprediction-based and exception-based attacks are in-scope of this paper. Our method detects these two types of attacks by monitoring its execution of the *speculation primitives*, which are either a branch instruction that takes time to resolve its target address or a memory load that accesses data across the security boundary. We consider MDS and LVI attacks that are triggered by exceptions, which are the most common cases in current state-of-the-art attack examples, as exception-based attacks, and hence SPECULARIZER will detect those attacks.

SPECULARIZER Architecture. The overall architecture of SPECULARIZER is shown in Fig. 1, which consists of two components: *Online Trace Collection* and *Offline Attack Detection*. *Online Trace Collection* is an online component that runs on a production system, running as system programs, which produces execution traces collected using PT and HPC. *Offline Attack Detection* is a component that runs offline that includes two parts (*i.e. Trace Processing* and *Attack Detection*), possibly on a separate machine, and performs analysis of the collected traces to identify speculative execution attacks.

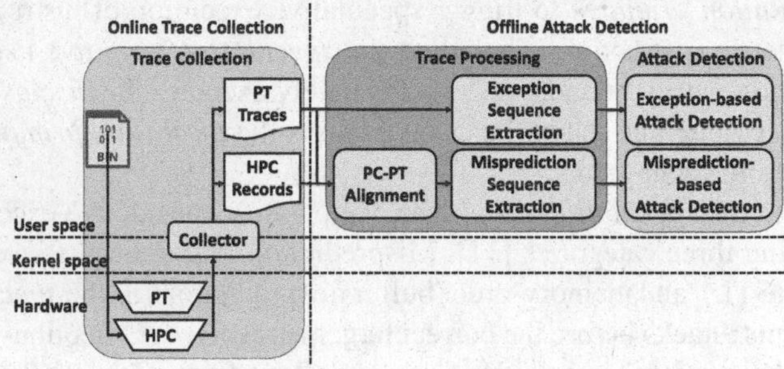

Fig. 1. Architectural of SPECULARIZER.

Online Trace Collection. To detect exception-based speculative execution attacks, SPECULARIZER monitors exceptions using PT. When the attacks use TSX to suppress exceptions, PT packets can record TSX aborts; when the attacks handle the exceptions directly, PT packets can record control-flow transfers that correspond to exception handling.

To detect misprediction-based attacks, SPECULARIZER needs to monitor the pattern of mispredictions, which includes misprediction in control-flow predictors (branch prediction units like BTB, PHT, and RSB) and data-flow predictors (the memory disambiguator in load/store buffers). However, PT is insufficient to monitor these microarchitectural events. HPCs are utilized instead. The limitation of using HPCs to monitor misprediction is that they are asynchronous with execution context, which is insufficient for detecting misprediction-based attacks. To address this problem, SPECULARIZER utilizes Intel PT to provide the execution contexts.

Offline Attack Detection. During the execution of benign programs, exceptions, TSX transaction aborts, and misprediction in control-flow and data loading is normal. There-

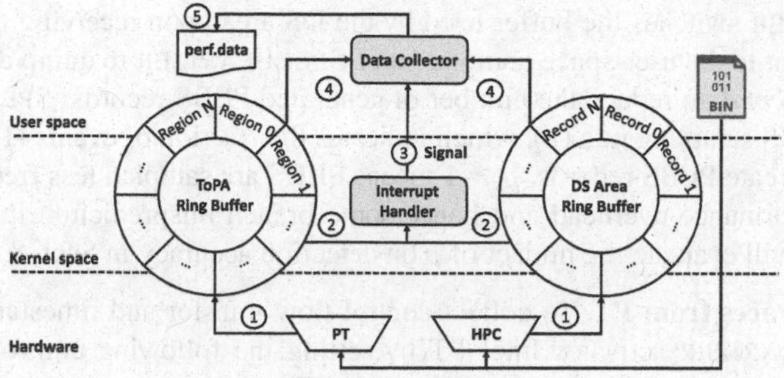

Fig. 2. Architectural and workflow of trace collection.

fore, we cannot simply detect speculative execution attacks using exception handling/-suppressing and branch/data misprediction as signatures. Instead, patterns of exceptions and mispredictions must be learned from both benign and attack programs and utilized to detect attacks in the program to be monitored.

4 Trace Collection

The overall workflow of trace collection (shown in Fig. 2) is as follows: ① SPECULARIZER enables PT and HPC to monitor the execution of the target program and specify the memory buffer to record the execution traces. ② When the memory buffer is full, an interrupt is triggered. ③ After replacing the full buffer with an empty one for the hardware to continue recording data, the interrupt handler sends a signal to the userspace data collector. ④ Upon receiving the signal, the data collector reads data from the full buffer. ⑤ Finally, the data collector saves the collected data into files.

Collecting Traces from HPC. To gain visibility into micro-architectural events, SPECULARIZER activates HPCs to monitor branch mispredictions (*e.g.* direct, indirect branches) and machine clear events caused by *memory order conflicts* by activating the events `BR_MISP_RETIRED.ALL_BRANCHES` and `MACHINE_CLEARS.MEMORY_ORDERING`. SPECULARIZER uses the PEBS to monitor the branch misprediction event and PMI to monitor the memory order conflict event, as the memory order conflict event is not available in PEBS mode. These two events are monitored simultaneously on different HPCs. When monitoring in the PMI mode, the overhead mainly comes from PMI handling. When monitoring in the PEBS mode, although the interrupts are significantly reduced, there are still two sources of overhead: First, writing each PEBS record into the DS area takes about 200 ns [8]. Second, DS-area-overflow interrupts need to be generated when the DS area is full (maximum size is 4 MB). Thousands of interrupts need to be generated during trace collection for one application.

Two performance optimization were implemented: *First*, SPECULARIZER implements a ring buffer [51] to cache the data in the DS area. Specifically, SPECULARIZER allocates two buffers for the DS area to reduce the overhead introduced by dumping data inside the interrupt handler. When the data in one of the buffers reaches the threshold,

SPECULARIZER switches the buffer used by the DS area upon receiving the interrupt. A signal is sent to the user-space component of SPECULARIZER to dump data from the full buffer. *Second*, to reduce the number of generated PEBS records, SPECULARIZER tunes the PEBS sampling rate (ρ), which indicates the fraction of events ($1/\rho$) sampled by PEBS to create PEBS records. $\rho > 1$ means PEBS are sampled less frequently with a higher performance overhead and hence some branch mispredicition information is missing. We will evaluate the impact of ρ on detection accuracy in Sect. 8.

Collecting Traces from PT. To collect control-flow transfer and timestamp information, SPECULARIZER activates Intel PT by setting the following control bits of the MSR `IA32_RTIT_CTL`: `TraceEn` (to enable PT), `BranchEn` (to generate control-flow related packets, *e.g.*, TNT, TIP & FUP), `OS & User` (to monitor both user-mode processes kernel threads), `TSCEn, MTCEn & CYCEn` (to generate timestamp related packets, *e.g.* TSC, MTC & CYC).

The overhead incurred in generating PT packets is negligible. The main overhead comes from handling the memory buffer that stores the PT packets when it is full. Unlike PEBS's DS area, which has a fixed size (*i.e.*, 4 MB), the memory buffer used by PT can vary. Specifically, PT uses a Table of Physical Addresses (ToPA) to store all generated packets, which is a linked list that links multiple output regions. Therefore, the total size of the ToPA is flexible, and the number of generated interrupts can be controlled to decrease the runtime performance overhead.

5 Trace Processing

SPECULARIZER processes HPC events and PT packets offline, possibly on a machine that is different from the host that implements the SPECULARIZER monitors. The exception-based output sequences are generated using PT traces only, and the misprediction-based output sequences are extracted with information from both PT traces and HPC records.

5.1 Processing Exceptions

Among the three approaches to tackling exceptions in exception-based speculative execution attacks, namely handling exceptions, suppressing exceptions with TSX, and suppressing exceptions with branch misprediction, the first two cases trigger an indirect control-flow transfer. Therefore, SPECULARIZER extracts exception-triggered control flow transfers in collected PT records. The third case is categorized as misprediction-based and discuss later.

Extracting Addresses of Exceptions. When the exception is handled by exception handlers, the control flow will transfer from user space to kernel space. With the PT packets, we can extract all *kernel traces*—a sequence of instructions in the kernel space. Afterwards, by comparing those traces with the kernel symbol table, the *kernel traces* can be used to identify different types of exceptions.

When the exception is suppressed by TSX transactions, the exception type is not revealed through *kernel traces*. Nevertheless, the exception is recorded by the MODE packet which has a field called TXAbort, with its value as 1. The addresses of the instructions that trigger TXAbort are recorded by the FUP packet that follows.

Extracting Timestamps of Exceptions. PT can be used to recover the timestamp of exceptions, as PT records the following time-related packets: Timestamp Counter (TSC) packets provide the wall-clock time (`wc`); Mini Time Counter (MTC) packets are generated periodically based on the core-crystal clock (`ccc`); a TMA packet is generated immediately after each TSC packet, with a common timestamp copy (`ctc`) value in its payload; a Cycle Accurate (CYC) packet is generated immediately preceding TIP packets and provides the accurate `ctc` value since the last CYC packet. To extract exception timestamp, SPECULARIZER calculates `ccc` for each TIP packet based on the relationship between these time-related packets [7], as PT generates a TIP packet when an exception is raised.

Output. SPECULARIZER analyzes each PT trace offline, identifies and records all exceptions, the virtual address of the instruction that triggers it, as well as the timestamps of the identified exceptions. Two parameters, δ and μ, were involved in the data output: PT traces are segmented into windows of δ CPU cycles, and the attack detection algorithm runs over the traces in each window.

The output of this step is a set of sequences of two tuples, which is denoted as $X_{e_k} = [(c_1, t_1), (c_2, t_2), \cdots, (c_n, t_n)]$, where e_k is the virtual address of the instruction that triggers the exception, c_i indicates whether exists an exception of the ith occurrence of the virtual address e_k, t_i is the timestamp of its occurrence, and μ is the length of each sequence, which is the input of attack detection model in Sect. 6. For each δ-cycle window, one or multiple sequences are gathered: if the total number of exceptions is greater than μ, a new sequence is created; a sequence less than μ is padded to μ with $(0, 0)$. We will evaluate the impact of different values of δ and μ on the effectiveness of the detection algorithm in Sect. 8.

5.2 Identifying Branch and Data Misprediction

SPECULARIZER identifies branch and data misprediction from the recorded HPC events. Particularly, SPECULARIZER first extracts the timestamp of each misprediction event from the HPC records, then extracts the timestamp of each branch instruction from the PT traces. Finally, by aligning the timestamp information from the HPC records and PT traces, SPECULARIZER outputs traces of correctly predicted and mispredicted branches for attack detection.

HPC Records Parsing. SPECULARIZER parses the HPC records and identifies the records that are related to either branch misprediction or data misprediction, and then outputs a sequence of two tuples: $[(c_1, t_1), (c_2, t_2), \cdots, (c_n, t_n)]$, where c_i is the event (*i.e.*, the branch misprediction or data misprediction) of the ith occurrence of the misprediction and t_i is its timestamp. The accuracy of misprediction information could depend on the PEBS overflow threshold ρ discussed in Sect. 4.

PT Trace Reconstruction. SPECULARIZER first reconstructs the program execution trace and the timestamp value of each branch with packets generated by the PT hardware. Meanwhile, PT timestamp packets are used to reconstruct the timestamp of each branch instruction using the method described in Sect. 5.1. By combining program execution trace with the timestamp information, SPECULARIZER outputs a sequence of two tuples: $[(b_1, t_1), (b_2, t_2), \cdots, (b_n, t_n)]$, where b_i is the virtual address of the ith occurrence of the branch and t_i is the timestamp when the branch is executed.

HPC and PT Alignment. SPECULARIZER aligns HPC records with the control-flow transfer information collected from PT to attribute HPC records to a specific branch of the program. The alignment can be performed by matching the timestamp value t_i in the two sequences. Particularly, for each element (c_k, t_k) in the HPC sequence, we search the PT sequence to find an element with index i that satisfies $t_i \leq t_k < t_{i+1}$. Then we associate (c_k, t_k) with b_i.

Output. For each δ-cycle window, each branch instruction b_k, SPECULARIZER outputs a set of sequences of two tuples, which is denoted as $X_{b_k} = [(c_1, t_1), (c_2, t_2), \cdots, (c_n, t_n)]$, where t_i is the timestamp when the ith execution of the branch b_k, c_i indicates whether there is a misprediction and the misprediction type (*i.e.* branch or data) in the ith execution of this branch, and μ is the length of the sequences.

6 Attack Detection

Given the traces produced in the previous section, SPECULARIZER uses the LSTM to extract the temporal information of the traces for attack detection. SPECULARIZER uses four detection models to detect four different attack types, which are exception-based attacks, misprediction-based attacks exploiting BTB/PHT, RSB, and memory disambiguator, respectively. These four detection models share the same layout: one LSTM layer and one Dense layer. Particularly, the detection model inputs the traces to the LSTM layer and outputs the likelihood for the trace to be an attack (between 0 and 1) from the Dense layer.

An end-to-end construction of SPECULARIZER, therefore, works as follows: (1) for every program monitored, both HPC and PT traces are collected and processed; (2) all processed traces for the program are classified by all four models. If one of the models classifies any of the traces as "attack" with a likelihood higher than a threshold α, the program is labeled by SPECULARIZER as performing speculative execution attacks.

7 Attack Variants Generation

To systematically evaluate how accurate SPECULARIZER can detect speculative execution attacks, we produce a data set of attack variants. To do so, we first propose parameterized models for speculative execution attacks and then systematically tuning the parameters of these models to generate a set of attack variants.

7.1 Exception-Based Attack Variants

Modeling Attacks. The attack model of exception-based speculative execution attacks is described in Fig. 3 (a), which depicts the timestamps of exceptions that happened at

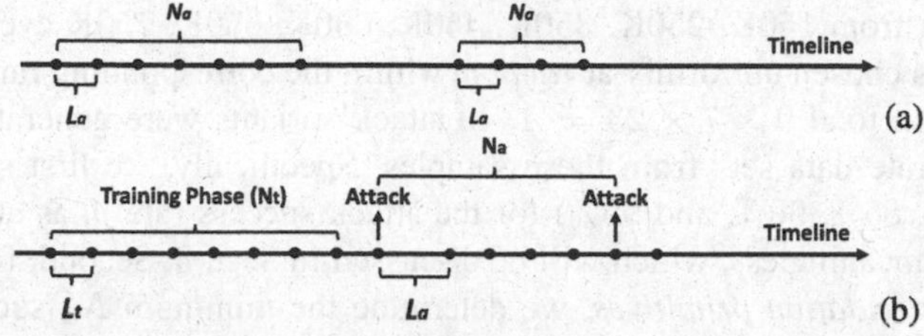

Fig. 3. Attack models for (a) exception-based attacks and (b) misprediction-based attacks.

Table 1. Relationship between N_a and p in exception-based attacks.

Success	Exception type								
rate (p)	US	RW	NM	BR	GP	P	LFB	LP	LVI
10%	1	1	17,000	1	10,000	300	3	1	4,000
30%	1	1	80,000	1	18,000	30,000	3	1	15,000
50%	2	1	130,000	1	58,000	60,000	3	1	28,000
80%	2	1	300,000	1	120,000	140,000	3	2	68,000
85%	3	1	400,000	1	140,000	180,000	3	2	86,000
90%	3	1	1,000,000	1	180,000	240,000	4	4	110,000
95%	4	1	1,300,000	1	300,000	400,000	8	6	140,000

a specific virtual address of the monitored program; each dot on the timeline represents the occurrence of an exception. N_a is the number of exceptions in a cluster that any two consecutive exceptions are no more than L_a cpu cycles apart.

To understand the practical implication of N_a and L_a, we performed an empirical evaluation of these two parameters using the Proof-of-Concept (PoC) code provided by Canella *et al.* [11]. We executed each of the PoC 10,000 times when the system is idle and report the relationship between minimum N_a and the success rate (p) in Table 1. When the system is busy, the N_a increases for the same p. Therefore, we only present the data when the system is idle in Table 1. As we see from the result, when utilizing different *speculation primitives*, to have $p \geq 95\%$, N_a ranges from 1 to 1,300,000.

We also measured the relationship between L_a and p. When $FLUSH+RELOAD$ is selected as the *disclosure primitive*, it takes at least 150,000 CPU cycles to finish reloading 255 elements (the minimum for encoding one byte). Therefore, with $N_a = 100$, we select L_a from 150K, 250K, 350K, 450K, 550K, 650K, 750K cycles. The experiment results suggest that the variation of L_a does not have an observable effect on p.

Generating Attack Variants. For each type of *speculation primitives* (*e.g.* #PF, #GP, *etc.*), we generate one attack variant for each of the following 23 value ranges for N_a: {[1, 1], [2, 2], [3, 3], [4, 4], [5, 5], [6, 6], [7, 7], [8, 8], [9, 9], [10, 10], [11, 20], [21, 30], [31, 40], [41, 50], [51, 60], [61, 70], [71, 80], [81, 90], [91, 100], [1,000, 10,000], [10,001, 100,000], [100,001, 1,000,000], [1,000,001, 2,000,000]}. In all attack variants,

L_a was chosen from 150K, 250K, 350K, 450K, 550K, 650K, 750K cycles. For each variant, N_a was chosen uniformly at *random* within the corresponding range.

Therefore, in total $9 \times 7 \times 23 = 1449$ attack variants were generated. Then we created 3 separate data sets from these samples. Specifically, we first selected three thresholds (*i.e.*, 85%, 90%, and 95%) for the attack success rate p, as attack variants with low p are meaningless, which will be discussed in Sect. 8. Second, for each p and each type of *speculation primitives*, we determine the minimum N_a such that attack variants with equal or greater N_a yield attack success rates larger than the corresponding p (from Table 1). As such, the three data sets have 476, 448, and 399 attack variants, respectively.

7.2 BTB/PHT Misprediction Variants

Modeling Attacks. To perform a successful misprediction-based speculative execution attack against BTB (*e.g.*, *Spectre-BTB*) and PHT (*e.g.*, *Spectre-PHT*), one needs to train (poison) the prediction unit in a loop multiple times before performing the attack to retrieve one byte of data [23]. This training can be performed either from the same address space or cross different address spaces [11]; moreover, the training can be performed either in-place or out-of-place [11]. Our detection target is the process that per-

Table 2. The success rate of misprediction-based attacks.

BTB/PHT											
N_t	L_t					N_a	L_a				
	350	450	550	650	750		150K	250K	350K	450K	550K
1	0.13	0.46	0.52	0.65	0.38	**1**	0.20	0.21	0.20	0.21	0.25
2	0.72	0.95	0.99	0.99	0.98	**3**	0.48	0.87	0.90	0.86	0.89
3	0.81	0.99	0.99	0.99	0.98	**5**	0.46	0.87	0.89	0.91	0.92
4	0.81	0.99	0.98	0.99	0.98	**10**	0.49	0.90	0.91	0.94	0.95
5	0.83	0.99	0.98	0.98	0.98	**30**	0.52	0.96	0.96	0.95	0.95
6	0.80	0.99	0.99	0.98	0.97	**50**	0.57	0.96	0.95	0.96	0.95
7	0.81	0.99	0.99	0.99	0.98	**100**	0.51	0.95	0.94	0.96	0.96
RSB						STL					
N_a	L_a					N_a	L_a				
	150K	250K	350K	450K	550K		150K	250K	350K	450K	550K
10	0.00	0.00	0.00	0.00	0.00	**10**	0.00	0.00	0.00	0.00	0.00
100	0.00	0.00	0.00	0.05	0.06	**100**	0.00	0.00	0.01	0.01	0.02
1,000	0.13	0.25	0.30	0.33	0.33	**1,000**	0.07	0.17	0.14	0.05	0.05
10,000	0.47	0.81	0.94	0.96	0.96	**10,000**	0.19	0.30	0.62	0.67	0.74
20,000	0.83	0.96	0.97	0.98	0.98	**20,000**	0.72	0.86	0.90	0.90	0.91
30,000	0.91	0.97	0.98	0.98	0.98	**30,000**	0.90	0.95	0.97	0.97	0.96
50,000	0.97	0.98	0.98	0.98	0.97	**50,000**	0.98	0.99	0.99	0.98	0.98

forms the training, regardless of whether it aims to perform same-address-space/cross-address-space or in-place/out-of-place attacks.

Therefore, the attack model of different types of misprediction-based speculative execution attacks is described in Fig. 3(b), which depicts the timestamps of branch/data prediction happened at a specific virtual address of the monitored program; each dot on the timeline represents the occurrence of one prediction. There are four parameters: N_a is the total number of attack attempts, L_a is the time interval between an attack attempt and the next training phase (in cpu cycles), N_t is the number of training attempts in each training phase, and L_t is the time interval between two consecutive training attempts.

To measure the parameters of the model, we used the PoC from Kocher *et al.* [23] and Canella *et al.* [11]. First, we tested the relationship between the occurrence of branch misprediction when the "attack" is performed and the success rate of the attack by leveraging the HPC event. The result shows that whenever the branch misprediction occurs, the attack can always have a 100% attack success rate. This is because the speculative window caused by BTB/PHT misprediction is large enough to load secret into the microarchitecture [52]. Therefore, an occurrence of a branch misprediction is equivalent to a successful attack.

Next, we evaluate how N_t and L_t affect the success rate of triggering branch misprediction. In the experiments described below, $N_a = 1$ and $L_a = 150$K cycles, and the result is shown in the BTB/PHT portion of Table 2. Each L_t is the CPU cycles (starting from the minimum value 350) and N_t enumerates each integer between 1 and 7 (inclusive). Each number in the table is the attack success rate in $10,000$ trials. As we see from the table, when $L_t \geq 450$ and $N_t \geq 2$, p is greater than 95%.

Finally, we evaluated how N_a and L_a affect the attack success rate (p). In these experiments, we set $N_t = 1$ and $L_t = 350$ cycles, because this pair of N_t and L_t has the worst p, which is the best scenario for analyzing the effects of N_a and L_a. The result in Table 2 shows that larger N_a has greater p. L_a has very little impact on p: For L_a between 250k and 550k CPU cycles, p is greater than 95% when $N_a > 30$. When L_a is large enough (*e.g.* $L_a >$ 450k CPU cycles), L_a has no observable effect on p.

Generating Attack Variants. For each type of *speculation primitives* (*e.g.*, BTB sa-ip, PHT ca-ip, *etc.*), we generate one attack variant for each combination of N_t, N_a, L_t, and L_a. The values of N_t and N_a are sampled uniformly at random from the following 14 value ranges: {[1, 1], [2, 2], [3, 3], [4, 4], [5, 5], [6, 6], [7, 7], [8, 8], [9, 9], [10, 10], [11, 20], [21, 30], [31, 50], [51, 100]}; The values of L_t are chosen from {350, 450, 550, 650, 750} CPU cycles; and the values of L_a are chosen from: {150K, 250K, 350K, 450K, 550K} CPU cycles. Therefore, in total $14 \times 14 \times 5 \times 5 \times 2 \times 4 = 39,200$ attack variants were generated. With the similar approach described in Sect. 7.1, we created 3 separate data sets with 37,904, 37,544, and 36,968 attack variants, respectively.

7.3 RSB and STL Misprediction Variants

Modeling Attacks. Spectre-RSB [11] and spectre-STL [11] exploits RSB and the memory disambiguator to trigger misprediction. In these two attacks, because RSBs can be poisoned by *push* and *pop* instructions, which is difficult to monitor using HPC and PT, and the memory disambiguator can be triggered simply by *load* instructions, which does not need training phase. Therefore, we use the model described in Fig. 3(a) to model these attacks.

To measure the impact of the parameters of the model on the success rate of the attacks, we used the PoC released with the published paper [11]. Using HPC events, we tested the relationship between p with N_a and L_a, respectively. Tested L_a and N_a start from the minimum ones, 150K and 1, respectively. The results are shown in Table 2. For Spectre-RSB, the value of N_a must be greater than $10,000$ for p to be larger than 90%. For Spectre-STL, the value of N_a must be greater than $20,000$ to achieve a similar success rate. For both attacks, L_a does not seem to play a significant role.

Generating Attack Variants. For each of RSB and memory disambiguator, we generated one attack variant for each of the following 15 value ranges for N_a:{[1, 10], [11, 100], [101, 1,000], [1,001, 2,000], [2,001, 3,000], [3,001, 4,000], [4,001, 5,000], [5,001, 6,000], [6,001, 7,000], [7,001, 8,000], [8,001, 9,000], [9,001, 10,000], [10,001, 20,000], [20,001, 30,000], [30,001, 50,000]} and 5 values for L_a: {150K, 250K, 350K, 450K, 550K}. In each variant, N_a was chosen uniformly at random during run-time with the corresponding value range. Therefore, in total $15 \times 5 \times 2 = 150$ attack variants were generated. With the similar approach described in Sect. 7.1, we created 3 separate data sets with 21, 20 and 14 attack variants, respectively.

8 Evaluation

In this section, we evaluate the detection accuracy and performance of SPECULARIZER. The data sets used in the evaluation are collected in the following approaches: The benign programs are selected from GNU Binutils[2] and SPEC benchmark 2006. The attack samples are drawn from the attack variants discussed in Sect. 7. The experiments were conducted on desktops with Intel Core i7-7700 Processors and 32 GB RAMs. 64-bit Ubuntu 16.04.6 LTS operating systems with the kernel version 5.4.0 were installed on the desktops.

8.1 Evaluation of SPECULARIZER's Parameters

There are a few parameters that can be tuned for SPECULARIZER: ① In the collection phase, the PEBS sampling rate (ρ) specifies the accuracy of branch misprediction records. We collected traces with 4 different ρ values: 1, 3, 5, 10. ② In the trace processing phase, the window size δ and trace length μ determine how the collected HPC and PT data are segmented for the LSTM algorithm to work on. We particularly picked two window sizes δ, 10 million CPU cycles and 100 million CPU cycles, and two trace lengths, 500 and 1000 data points. ③ The parameter we use to select *training data set* is the success rate p of the attack variants, which can be chosen from 85%, 90%, and 95%.

[2] https://www.gnu.org/software/binutils/.

Table 3. Data sets for parameter evaluation.

Index	Window size δ	Trace length μ	Sample ρ	Success rate p
1	10M	1000	1	95%
2	100M	1000	1	95%
3	100M	500	1	95%
4	100M	1000	3	95%
5	100M	1000	5	95%
6	100M	1000	10	95%
7	100M	1000	1	90%
8	100M	1000	1	85%

In this section, we analyze how these parameters affect the detection results. We created 8 data sets, whose parameter configuration is shown in Table 3. Each data set contains four groups of traces; each group is used to evaluate one LSTM model, as specified in Sect. 6. In each group, around 30,000 benign traces and 30,000 attack traces were collected. Then the traces in each group are randomly split into the training set (80%) and a testing set (20%).

By running the LSTM classification, the algorithm outputs a class label ("benign" or "attack") for each trace together with the likelihood between 0 and 1. We selected a threshold α of the likelihood, such that SPECULARIZER alerts the detection of an "attack" trace when the LSTM classifier outputs "attack" with a likelihood greater than α. Two values were selected for α, 0.5 and 0.75. The accuracy is evaluated using the F1 scores when $\alpha = 0.5$ and when $\alpha = 0.75$. A high F1 score suggests a balanced precision and recall. Here recall is defined as the percentage of detected attack traces in all attack traces and precision is defined as the percentage of correctly detected attack traces in all detected attack traces.

PEBS Sampling Rate ρ. We only evaluated ρ for misprediction-based attacks, because the detection of exception-based attacks does not need HPC. The data sets we used in this test are (2), (4), (5), and (6) (as shown in Table 3), where the window size (δ) is selected as 100 million cycles, trace size (μ) is selected as 1000, and $p > 95\%$ for attack variants selected in the training/testing set. The result is shown in Table 4. We see from the table that ρ only affects the detection of BTB/PHT-based attacks. Specifically, only when $\rho \leq 3$, F1 scores yield good detection accuracy (F1 score greater than 90%). In contrast, regardless of the ρ value, the detection accuracy for RSB and STL-based attacks is high. This is because losing branch misprediction information due to larger ρ values is more critical to detecting attacks that require training.

Window Size δ. To evaluate the effect of δ, we used data set (1) and (2), where for both data sets $\rho = 1$, $p > 95\%$, and $\mu = 1000$. For each window size (δ), we evaluate the F1 score when the threshold is 0.5 and 0.75 and the result is shown in Table 5, which suggests δ does not have a strong impact on the detection accuracy.

Table 4. Impact of PEBS sample rate ρ.

Misprediction-based	PEBS sampling rate ρ							
	1		3		5		10	
	F1 (0.5)	F1 (0.75)	F1 (0.5)	F1 (0.75)	F1 (0.5)	F1 (0.75)	F1 (0.5)	F1 (0.75)
BTB/PHT	0.977	0.977	0.910	0.909	0.716	0.715	0.593	0.593
RSB	1.0	1.0	1.0	1.0	1.0	1.0	1.0	1.0
STL	0.993	0.991	0.974	0.971	0.955	0.954	0.913	0.911

Table 5. Impact of window size δ, trace length μ and threshold of attack success rate p.

		Window Size δ (CPU Cycles)				Trace length μ (elements)				Attack Success Rate Threshold p					
		10M		100M		500		1000		0.85		0.90		0.95	
		F1 (0.5)	F1 (0.75)	F1 (0.5)	F1 (0.75)	F1 (0.5)	F1 (0.75)	F1 (0.5)	F1 (0.75)	F1 (0.5)	F1 (0.75)	F1 (0.5)	F1 (0.75)	F1 (0.5)	F1 (0.75)
Misprediction-based	BTB/PHT	0.963	0.962	0.977	0.977	0.969	0.970	0.977	0.977	0.976	0.976	0.976	0.975	0.977	0.977
	RSB	0.992	0.992	1.0	1.0	0.997	0.997	1.0	1.0	1.0	1.0	1.0	1.0	1.0	1.0
	STL	0.992	0.993	0.993	0.991	0.994	0.995	0.993	0.991	0.991	0.991	0.990	0.989	0.993	0.991
Exception-based		0.945	0.937	0.960	0.955	0.936	0.938	0.960	0.955	0.961	0.960	0.959	0.956	0.960	0.955

Trace Length μ. The evaluation utilized data set (2) and (3), with $\rho = 1$, $p \geq 95\%$ and $\delta = 100$M cycles. The result is presented in Table 5, which means $\mu = 500$ or $\mu = 1000$ does not affect the detection accuracy dramatically.

Success Rate Threshold p. The data sets used in this evaluation are (2), (7), and (8), with $\rho = 1$, $\mu = 1000$ and $\delta = 100$M cycles. The result shown in Table 5 suggests that p does not have much impact on the detection accuracy.

Classification Likelihood Threshold α. The result shown in Table 4 and Table 5 suggests that $\alpha = 0.5$ or $\alpha = 0.75$ does not affect F1 score. Thus, we chose $\alpha = 0.5$ for the following evaluation.

Summary: In parameters ρ, δ, μ, p, and α; only ρ has a significant impact on detection accuracy of attacks that exploit BTB/PHT.

8.2 Evaluation of Detection Accuracy

We evaluated the detection accuracy of the LSTM models trained using data set (4) in Table 3. Using these parameters, in the following experiments, we evaluate the models' capability of detecting various attack variants. Because the traces that are classified as benign all have a precision that is close to 100%, the F1 score does not provide more information than recall, or true positive rate (TPR). Therefore, we use TPR as the metric for evaluating detection accuracy, which is defined as the percentage of correctly classified traces among all traces that are classified as attacks. The results are represented in Fig. 4, while the blue line is the TPR and the red line is the attack success rate p. In the cases where TPR $> p$ means the probabilistic to detect the attack is higher than the secret been leaked.

Exception-Based Attacks. We collected 11,700 traces from all types of exception-based variants we generated and split them into separate groups according to their N_a

value. Then we perform classification on each of the groups and show the results in Fig. 4(a). In this figure, the X-axis is the value of N_a, the red line is the attack success rate p and the blue line is the TPR. When $N_a = 4$, TPR $= 99.1\%$; when $N_a > 10$, TPR $\geq 99.9\%$; but when $N_a \leq 3$, TPR drops to 0, which means we were not able to detect exception-based attacks with fewer than 4 attempts within a time window of 100 million CPU cycles.

Misprediction-Based Attacks on BTB/PHT. We collected 980,000 traces from the BTB/PHT attack variants. To evaluate SPECULARIZER with varying N_t, N_a, L_t, and L_a values, we split the traces accordingly. The results are shown in Fig. 4 (b), Fig. 4 (d), Fig. 4 (c) and Fig. 4 (d), respectively. As we see from these figures, SPECULARIZER can detect attack variants with $N_t \geq 2$, $N_a \geq 3$, $350 \leq L_t \leq 750$ CPU cycles, and 150K $\leq$ $L_a \leq$ 550K CPU cycles with TPR $\geq 90\%$.

Misprediction-Based Attacks on RSB and Memory Disambiguator. We collected 7,500 traces from attack variants exploiting RSB and memory disabmiguators. To evaluate SPECULARIZER with varying L_a and N_a values, we split the traces accordingly. The results are presented in Fig. 4 (g), Fig. 4 (i), Fig. 4 (f), and Fig. 4 (h), respectively. As we see from these figures, SPECULARIZER can detect attack variants with 150K $\leq L_a \leq$ 550K cpu cycles with TPR $> 80\%$. TPR increases almost monotonically when N_a increases. SPECULARIZER can detect attack variants when $N_a > 3000$ with TPR $> 80\%$. It is worth noting that when TPR $< 80\%$ for both attacks, the success rate of these attacks goes below 30%, which suggests that the adversary needs to balance the attack efficiency with the risk of detection.

Summary: With the selected parameters, SPECULARIZER can detect most of the attack traces we collected from the generated attack variants with high recalls. However, In cases where the detection is less accurate, p of these attack variants is also low.

8.3 End-to-End Evaluation

In practice, SPECULARIZER monitors the execution of a program and raises alarms if any of the traces collected from the program is detected as "attacks". To perform end-to-end evaluation, we use the same model as trained using data set (4).

The data set we used has 26 benign programs collected from GNU Binutils and SPEC benchmark 2006, and randomly selected 160 attack variants we generated (*i.e.* 40 variants for each attack type). Each of the 186 programs was examined using all the four LSTM models. Among the 41 benign programs, only one (*gobmk*) is falsely classified as BTB/PHT misprediction attacks and four benign programs (*i.e.*, *ld*, *perlbench*, *sophlex*, and *gobmk*) were misclassified as exception-based attacks. However, in all these misclassified cases, less than 3 traces (out of over 1000 traces) extracted from each program were indeed misclassified, which means these false detections can be prevented if SPECULARIZER only raises alarms when multiple traces (*e.g.*, > 3) were detected as attacks, which can be another parameter the user of SPECULARIZER could tune. Nevertheless, all attack variants are successfully detected by their corresponding LSTM classifier. The BTB/PHT classifier also detects 117 out of 120 other attack variants, because these attack variants also exhibit this type of branch misprediction.

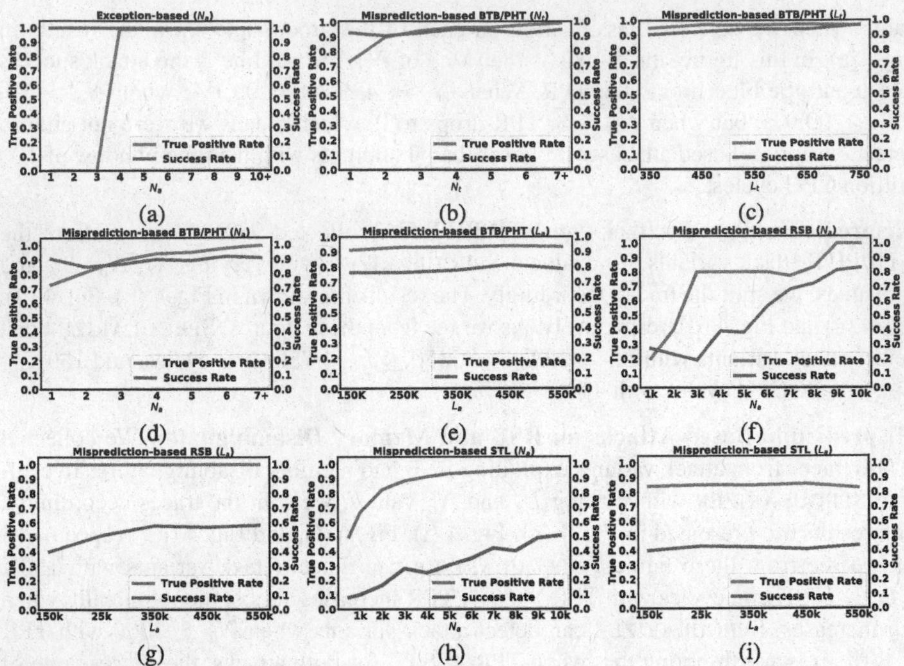

Fig. 4. Accuracy of attack detection (recall). (a) N_a in exception-based attacks, (b) N_t in BTB/PHT misprediction attacks, (c) L_t in BTB/PHT misprediction attacks, (d) N_a in BTB/PHT misprediction attacks, (e) L_a in BTB/PHT misprediction attacks, (f) N_a in RSB misprediction attacks, (g) L_a in RSB misprediction attacks, (h) N_a in STL attacks, (i) L_a in STL attacks. (Color figure online)

8.4 Performance Analysis

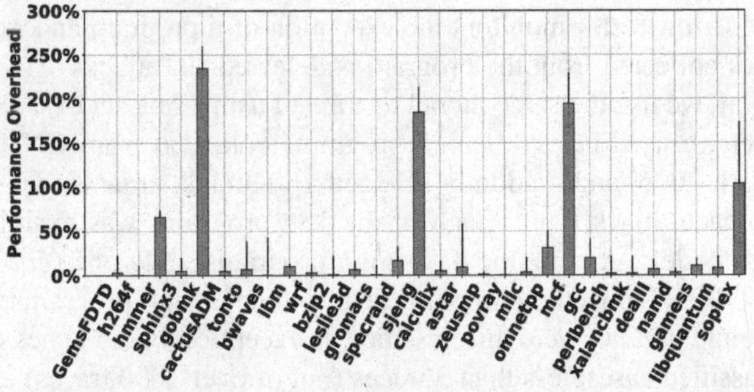

Fig. 5. The performance overhead of online trace collection.

Overhead of Online Trace Collection. In our experiments, SPECULARIZER enabled trace collection of both HPC and PT, with the HPC events and MSR configurations

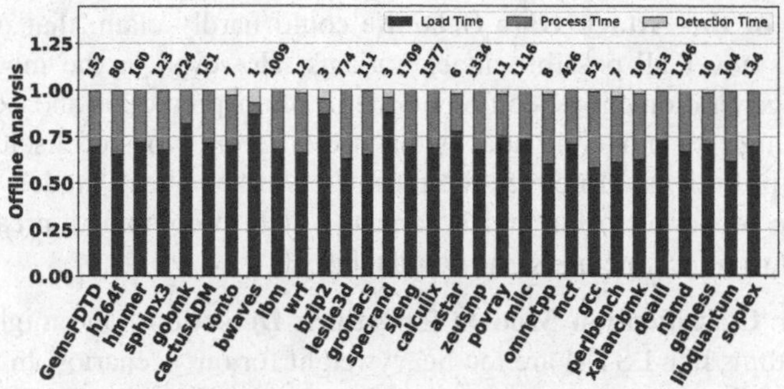

Fig. 6. Running time of offline attack detection.

specified in Sect. 4. The ρ was set to 3. The experiments on LMbench [29] show the runtime overhead on I/O is negligible. The results of the SPEC benchmark are shown in Fig. 5. The runtime overhead was introduced from 0.038% to 231.42%, with a geometric mean of 14.36%. Some of the benchmark programs (*e.g.* mcf, gobmk, and sjeng) had high performance overhead; as their execution triggers a lot of branch misprediction. We note that the performance can be reduced with Intel's new feature that redirects PEBS's sampling output to PT packets [7], as PT packet generation introduces much less overhead [16]. We leave this evaluation to future work.

Running Time of Offline Attack Detection. Figure 6 shows the running time of offline attack detection. The number above each bar is the average running time (of 1000 trials) of the offline analysis for each SPEC benchmark (in seconds), which ranges from 3 s to 1709 s with PT trace files between 13M bytes and 13G bytes. More specifically, the offline analysis includes three phases: trace loading, trace processing, and attack detection. On average, they account for 70.01%, 29.85%, and 0.14% of the entire running time. One reason for the long-running time for trace loading/processing (99.86%) is that PT generates a large number of packets, which takes a long time to parse and analyze. The attack detection phase typically takes less than 1s. Finally, it is worth noting our offline analyses were performed within a single thread with limited memory, which can be further optimized using multi-threading and larger memory. And for applications such as forensics, the overhead of offline analysis is not critical.

9 Discussion

Detecting Assistance-Based Attacks. Microcode assist was exploited in some recent works [31,37,42,43]. However, there is no systematic study of these microcode assists yet. It is not clear how many methods can trigger microcode assists and how many of them can be exploited in speculative execution attacks by unprivileged programs. Without such systematic exploration, an ad-hoc detection technique is likely to be bypassed. We leave the detection of assistance-based attacks to future work.

Completeness of the Attack Data Sets. We could hardly claim that our generated attack data sets cover all possible attack variants. However, as the models used for attack variants generation only specify the patterns of misprediction and exception, they are general enough for modeling attacks that use different types of disclosure gadgets and disclosure primitives. Moreover, the parameters in the attack models can be tuned to alter specific properties of an attack variant, which in combination can be used to approximate most attack methods one could think of.

Using Simpler Classification Models for Attack Detection. One might think deep learning algorithms like LSTM are too heavyweight for our scenarios. In fact, we have also tested multiple alternatives, such as decision trees, K-means, random forest, *etc.* However, we found those models very fragile for any practical use. In contrast, LSTM offers an automated selection of parameters and thresholds, greatly reducing the subjectivity in the selection of classification models.

Adversarial Machine Learning (AML). SPECULARIZER is vulnerable to AML-based techniques that generate carefully crafted attack variants to evade detection. As shown in Fig. 4, in general, attack code that evades detection is likely to have a lower success rate. In that sense, SPECULARIZER makes speculative execution attacks harder to perform, but may not eliminate the threats. However, we note this arms race is common in all machine-learning-based defense systems [14,32].

Real-Time Attack Detection. Ideally, attack detection should be performed in real-time and for all programs. However, as parsing PT packets and processing the traces are time-consuming (as shown in Fig. 6), it is very challenging to do so in practice. Moreover, enabling whole system monitoring with PT will drastically increase the overhead of trace parsing and analysis. These are common issues for PT/HPC-based monitoring systems [39,51].

10 Related Work

Detecting Speculative Execution Attacks. Prior works on detecting speculative execution attacks mainly focus on the detection of *disclosure primitives*, such as the Flush+Reload cache side channels [19]. In contrast, SPECULARIZER detects the speculative execution attacks by monitoring its root cause—the *speculation primitives*. Close to our work is due to [25,44] who also leverages HPC to detect speculative execution attacks. However, as their approach only uses HPC, it omits the context of program execution in the detection of attacks. Therefore, their approach is less accurate and only applicable to simple proof-of-concept attacks.

Mitigating Speculative Execution Attacks. Software solutions provide temporary mitigation of the threats, which are reactive to only known attacks and ad hoc. For instance, page table isolation (*e.g.*, KPTI of Linux) PTE inversion, and L1d flush [5], compiler-based mitigation [12,23,30,40] provides generic solutions for exception-based and misprediction-based speculative execution attacks. *SPECCFI* [24], *ConTExT* [36] mitigates a specific type of speculative attack. Furthermore, many works focus on detecting the code gadget of speculative execution attacks [13,18,20,28,33,47].

Proposals from the computer architecture research community mitigate speculative execution attacks with more dramatic revision on the micro-architectural level [2,4, 6,9,10,15,21,22,26,34,35,38,43,46,48–50]. While these approaches may be efficient in addressing the targeted problems, however, it may take a longer time before these academic proposals can be adopted by the industry.

11 Conclusion

In this paper, we present SPECULARIZER, a software tool for uncovering speculative execution attacks using performance tracing hardware features (PT and HPCs). SPECULARIZER monitors the execution of the inspected applications in an online mode, introducing modest runtime performance overhead, and then performs attack detection in an offline analysis using LSTM networks. Empirical evaluation of SPECULARIZER suggests that the proposed approach leads to high detection accuracy with reasonable overhead, particularly suitable for offline forensic analysis.

References

1. Deep dive: Intel analysis of microarchitectural data sampling (2019). https://software.intel.com/security-software-guidance/insights/deep-dive-intel-analysis-microarchitectural-data-sampling
2. Intel analysis of speculative execution side channels. Revision 4.0. Accessed July 2018
3. Mitigating speculative execution side channel hardware vulnerabilities (2018). https://msrc-blog.microsoft.com/2018/03/15/%20mitigating-%20speculative-%20execution-%20side-%20channel-%20hardware-%20vulnerabilities/
4. Speculative execution side channel mitigations (2018). http://kib.kiev.ua/x86docs/SDMs/336996-001.pdf. Revision 1.0, January 2018
5. Deep dive: Intel analysis of l1 terminal fault (2019). https://software.intel.com/security-software-guidance/insights/deep-dive-intel-analysis-l1-terminal-fault
6. Engineering new protections into hardware (2019). https://www.intel.com/content/www/us/en/architecture-and-technology/engineering-new-protections-into-hardware.html
7. Intel® 64 and IA-32 architectures software developer's manual (2019). https://software.intel.com/sites/default/files/managed/39/c5/325462-sdm-vol-1-2abcd-3abcd.pdf. January 2019
8. Akiyama, S., Hirofuchi, T.: Quantitative evaluation of intel PEBS overhead for online system-noise analysis. In: 7th International Workshop on Runtime and Operating Systems for Supercomputers (ROSS). ACM (2017)
9. Barber, K., Bacha, A., Zhou, L., Zhang, Y., Teodorescu, R.: SpecShield: shielding speculative data from microarchitectural covert channels. In: 28th International Conference on Parallel Architectures and Compilation Techniques (PACT). IEEE (2019)
10. Bourgeat, T., Lebedev, I., Wright, A., Zhang, S., Devadas, S.: Mi6: secure enclaves in a speculative out-of-order processor. In: 52nd Annual IEEE/ACM International Symposium on Microarchitecture (2019)
11. Canella, C.: A systematic evaluation of transient execution attacks and defenses. In: 28th USENIX Security Symposium (2019)
12. Carruth, C.: Speculative load hardening (2018)

13. Chen, G., Chen, S., Xiao, Y., Zhang, Y., Lin, Z., Lai, T.H.: Stealing intel secrets from SGX enclaves via speculative execution. In: IEEE European Symposium on Security and Privacy, June 2019
14. Chen, L., Sultana, S., Sahita, R.: HeNet: a deep learning approach on intel® processor trace for effective exploit detection. In: IEEE Security and Privacy Workshops (SPW). IEEE (2018)
15. Fustos, J., Farshchi, F., Yun, H.: SpectreGuard: an efficient data-centric defense mechanism against Spectre attacks. In: 56th Annual Design Automation Conference (2019)
16. Ge, X., Cui, W., Jaeger, T.: GRIFFIN, guarding control flows using intel processor trace. ACM SIGPLAN Not. (2017)
17. Gu, Y., Zhao, Q., Zhang, Y., Lin, Z.: PT-CFI: transparent backward-edge control flow violation detection using intel processor trace. In: 7th ACM on Conference on Data and Application Security and Privacy (2017)
18. Guarnieri, M., Köpf, B., Morales, J.F., Reineke, J., Sánchez, A.: Spectector: principled detection of speculative information flows. In: IEEE Symposium on Security and Privacy (SP) (2020)
19. Gulmezoglu, B., Moghimi, A., Eisenbarth, T., Sunar, B.: FortuneTeller: predicting microarchitectural attacks via unsupervised deep learning (2019). arXiv preprint arXiv:1907.03651
20. Guo, S.: SpecuSym: speculative symbolic execution for cache timing leak detection (2019). arXiv preprint arXiv:1911.00507
21. Khasawneh, K.N., Koruyeh, E.M., Song, C., Evtyushkin, D., Ponomarev, D., Abu-Ghazaleh, N.: SafeSpec: banishing the spectre of a meltdown with leakage-free speculation (2018). arXiv preprint arXiv:1806.05179
22. Kiriansky, V., Lebedev, I.A., Amarasinghe, S.P., Devadas, S., Emer, J.: DAWG: a defense against cache timing attacks in speculative execution processors. IACR Cryptology ePrint Archive (2018)
23. Kocher, P., et al.: Spectre attacks: exploiting speculative execution. In: 40th IEEE Symposium on Security and Privacy (S&P) (2019)
24. Koruyeh, E.M., Shirazi, S.H.A., Khasawneh, K.N., Song, C., Abu-Ghazaleh, N.: SPECCFI: mitigating Spectre attacks using CFI informed speculation (2019). arXiv preprint arXiv:1906.01345
25. Li, C., Gaudiot, J.-L.: Detecting malicious attacks exploiting hardware vulnerabilities using performance counters. In: 43rd Annual Computer Software and Applications Conference (COMPSAC). IEEE (2019)
26. Li, P., Zhao, L., Hou, R., Zhang, L., Meng, D.: Conditional speculation: an effective approach to safeguard out-of-order execution against Spectre attacks. In: IEEE International Symposium on High Performance Computer Architecture (HPCA). IEEE (2019)
27. Lipp, M., et al.: Meltdown: reading kernel memory from user space. In: 27th USENIX Security Symposium (2018)
28. Mambretti, A., Neugschwandtner, M., Sorniotti, A., Kirda, E., Robertson, W., Kurmus, A.: Speculator: a tool to analyze speculative execution attacks and mitigations. In: 35th Annual Computer Security Applications Conference (2019)
29. McVoy, L.W., Staelin, C., et al.: lmbench: portable tools for performance analysis. In: USENIX Annual Technical Conference (1996)
30. Miller, M.: Mitigating speculative execution side channel hardware vulnerabilities. Microsoft Security Response Center (MSRC) (2018)
31. Minkin, M., et al.: Fallout: reading kernel writes from user space (2019)
32. Moosavi-Dezfooli, S.-M., Fawzi, A., Fawzi, O., Frossard, P.: Universal adversarial perturbations. In: IEEE Conference on Computer Vision and Pattern Recognition (2017)
33. Oleksenko, O., Trach, B., Silberstein, M., Fetzer, C.: SpecFuzz: bringing spectre-type vulnerabilities to the surface. In: 29th USENIX Security Symposium (2020)

34. Saileshwar, G., Qureshi, M.K.: CleanupSpec: an "undo" approach to safe speculation. In: 52nd Annual IEEE/ACM International Symposium on Microarchitecture (2019)
35. Sakalis, C., Kaxiras, S., Ros, A., Jimborean, A., Själander, M.: Efficient invisible speculative execution through selective delay and value prediction. In: 46th International Symposium on Computer Architecture. ACM (2019)
36. Schwarz, M., Lipp, M., Canella, C., Schilling, R., Kargl, F., Gruss, D.: ConTexT: a generic approach for mitigating Spectre. In: Network and Distributed System Security Symposium (NDSS) (2020)
37. Schwarz, M., et al.: ZombieLoad: cross-privilege-boundary data sampling (2019). arXiv:1905.05726
38. Taram, M., Venkat, A., Tullsen, D.: Context-sensitive fencing: securing speculative execution via microcode customization. In: 24th International Conference on Architectural Support for Programming Languages and Operating Systems. ACM (2019)
39. Thalheim, J., Bhatotia, P., Fetzer, C.: INSPECTOR: data provenance using intel processor trace (PT). In: 36th International Conference on Distributed Computing Systems (ICDCS). IEEE (2016)
40. Turner, P.: Retpoline: a software construct for preventing branch-target-injection (2018). https://support.google.com/faqs/answer/7625886
41. Van Bulck, J: Foreshadow: extracting the keys to the Intel SGX kingdom with transient out-of-order execution. In: 27th USENIX Security Symposium (2018)
42. Van Bulck, J.: LVI: hijacking transient execution through microarchitectural load value injection. In: 41th IEEE Symposium on Security and Privacy (S&P) (2020)
43. van Schaik, S.: RIDL: rogue in-flight data load. In: IEEE Symposium on Security and Privacy (S&P) (2019)
44. Wang, H., Sayadi, H., Rafatirad, S., Sasan, A., Homayoun, H.: SCARF: detecting side-channel attacks at real-time using low-level hardware features. In: 26th International Symposium on On-Line Testing and Robust System Design (IOLTS). IEEE (2020)
45. Wang, W., Zhang, Y., Lin, Z.: Time and order: towards automatically identifying side-channel vulnerabilities in enclave binaries. In: 22nd International Symposium on Research in Attacks, Intrusions and Defenses (RAID) (2019)
46. Weisse, O., Neal, I., Loughlin, K., Wenisch, T.F., Kasikci, B.: Nda: preventing speculative execution attacks at their source. In: 52nd Annual IEEE/ACM International Symposium on Microarchitecture (2019)
47. Xiao, Y., Zhang, Y., Teodorescu, R.: Speechminer: a framework for investigating and measuring speculative execution vulnerabilities. In: Network and Distributed System Security Symposium (NDSS) (2020)
48. Yan, M., Choi, J., Skarlatos, D., Morrison, A., Fletcher, C.W., Torrellas, J.: InvisiSpec: making speculative execution invisible in the cache hierarchy. In: International Symposium on Microarchitecture (2018)
49. Yu, J., Hsiung, L., Hajj, M.E., Fletcher, C.W.: Data oblivious ISA extensions for side channel-resistant and high performance computing. In: Network and Distributed System Security Symposium (NDSS) (2019)
50. Yu, J., Yan, M., Khyzha, A., Morrison, A., Torrellas, J., Fletcher, C.W.: Speculative taint tracking (STT) a comprehensive protection for speculatively accessed data. In: 52nd Annual IEEE/ACM International Symposium on Microarchitecture (2019)
51. Zhang, T., Jung, C., Lee, D.: ProRace: practical data race detection for production use. ACM SIGOPS Oper. Syst. Rev. **51**(2), 149–162 (2017)
52. Zhang, Z., Cheng, Y., Zhang, Y., Nepal, S.: GhostKnight: breaching data integrity via speculative execution (2020). arXiv preprint arXiv:2002.00524

Aion Attacks: Manipulating Software Timers in Trusted Execution Environment

Wei Huang[1(✉)], Shengjie Xu[1], Yueqiang Cheng[2], and David Lie[1]

[1] University of Toronto, Toronto, Canada
{wh.huang,shengjie.xu}@mail.utoronto.ca, lie@eecg.toronto.edu
[2] NIO, San Jose, USA
yueqiang.cheng@nio.io

Abstract. Side-channel attacks are a threat to secure software running in a Trusted Execution Environment (TEE). To protect Intel SGX applications from these attacks, researchers have proposed mechanisms to detect cache-probing and repeated interrupts that these attacks rely on. These defenses often rely on high-resolution timers. However, since there is no trusted high-resolution timer hardware module, developers have resorted to software timers, which unfortunately underestimate the scope of possible attacks. In this paper, we propose *Aion* attacks that manipulate the speed of a reference software timer to subvert defensive mechanisms against SGX side-channel attacks. Specifically, we introduce a CPU thermal attack that leverages the thermal management mechanism to change the execution speed of the timer thread, and a cache eviction attack that evicts the target timer counters and forces the system to load them from memory instead of cache. We evaluated the above Aion attacks and introduced an analytical model and show that software timers cannot be improved to fit the defenders under our attacks.

1 Introduction

The threat model of Intel SGX assumes that only CPUs are trustworthy, placing code and data of protected applications in a secure enclave isolated from other system software. However, the protection guaranteed by SGX does not take into account an attacker who monitors information leakage via side-channels. As a result, various defense mechanisms have been proposed [5,17] to defend against side-channel attacks on SGX applications [1,3,4,7,8,10,15,19,25].

Many of these defenses rely on the ability to measure the frequency and duration of certain events, such as cache access and code execution time, or the number of asynchronous enclave exits. Since SGX does not provide a trusted hardware timer, these defenses instead use high-resolution software timers to measure the passage of time. All software timers make assumptions about the processor they are executing on: They assume that 1) CPU instructions execute at a relatively constant speed, and that 2) the clock frequency the CPU operates at stays within a well-defined range. For example, they acknowledge

L. Bilge et al. (Eds.): DIMVA 2021, LNCS 12756, pp. 173–193, 2021.
https://doi.org/10.1007/978-3-030-80825-9_9

that SGX must defend against an adversary who might modify the processor clock frequency. Thus, they are resilient to an adversary who can slow down the clock frequency by a factor of 3.25–4.25×, as this is the typical ratio between the maximum and minimum operating clock frequency of modern processors.

In this paper, we show that both of these assumptions can be broken by a significant margin. We present *Aion* attacks, which can be mounted by both privileged and unprivileged attackers, and enable an adversary to tamper with software timer accuracy by 2.5–202×. We also build a model of software timers and show empirically that secure software timers are not possible on current architectures. This renders all current software-timer-based SGX side-channel defenses useless.

Our Aion attacks use two mechanisms to break the assumptions made by software timers. The first attack manipulates the thermal management facilities of the processor to cause execution slowdown below that of the lowest supported clock frequency of the processor, violating the assumption that slowdowns are bounded by the lowest clock frequency. As far as we are aware, this is the first instance of a security attack that abuses CPU thermal management, and does not actually need to physically overheat or damage the CPU in any way. Instead, we trigger thermal management features using software-only attacks. The second attack generates cache evictions to slow down the execution of instructions in the software timer, violating the assumption that the execution time of instructions is relatively constant. We show these attacks can compromise the security properties of applications running in SGX enclaves, and can allow existing side-channel attacks to evade detection by existing defenses. We implement a prototype of Aion attacks and evaluate them in a real-world environment. We make the following contributions in this paper:

- We propose an analytical model which suggests that no existing software timers used in SGX enclaves are reliable, meaning that current SGX side-channel defences are ineffective if timers are manipulated by attackers.
- We present two generic Aion attacks and show that they are able to effectively exploit all existing SGX software timers, invalidating current defense mechanisms.
- We evaluate two prototypes of Aion attacks on two different CPUs. Experimental results indicate that both are able to consistently break the desired properties of the software timers. With our mechanism, an end-to-end attack is demonstrated where existing side-channel attacks can evade detection.
- We prove that, under our attack model, it is impossible to build a software timer immune to Aion attacks, motivating the need for hardware support.

The remainder of this paper includes: Sect. 2 provides related backgrounds. We propose our analytical system model in Sect. 3 and describe our attack design in Sect. 4, implementation in Sect. 5, and evaluations in Sect. 6. We finally conclude the paper in Sect. 7.

2 Background and Related Work

2.1 Intel SGX and TSX

Intel Software Guard Extensions (SGX) [6,11] is an instruction set extension introduced in 2015 to the Intel architecture. SGX is designed for security and system properties such as confidentiality, execution isolation, memory integrity, and verifiability. It provides a trusted execution environment (TEE) for user-level applications to securely run in a shielded environment called an enclave. Security properties are guaranteed by putting application code and data into the processor reserved memory (PRM) which is isolated from the main memory and transparently encrypted by the memory encryption engine (MEE). Secure applications in enclaves can be interrupted by other applications outside the enclave, triggering an asynchronous enclave exit (AEX) event.

Intel Transactional Synchronization Extensions (TSX) [11] is an Intel ISA extension for hardware transactional memory. It ensures that when a sequence of instructions is executed, either the execution is completed without interruption or memory read-write conflicts (i.e., concurrent access to the same data where at least one access is a write) with other threads, or the transaction is aborted and the execution is rolled back. The original purpose of TSX was to speed up multi-threaded applications by reducing locking, while recent work has leveraged it to notify secure enclaves about interruptions by other threads [20] and protect cryptographic keys against memory disclosure attacks [9].

2.2 Power and Thermal Management of Intel CPU

Recent CPUs have power and thermal management features for energy efficiency and protection of the processors from overheating. For example, Intel has several digital thermal sensors (DTS) in each CPU package to monitor processor temperature [11], and the results can be retrieved from model-specific registers (MSRs) or the platform environment control interface (PECI). When a certain temperature limit is reached, a thermal control circuit (TCC) will be activated and it may take following three actions: 1) Reducing core frequencies so the clock runs slower, 2) Reducing the core voltages to make the processors use less power and generate less heat, and 3) Forcing one or more cores to enter a hardware duty cycling (HDC) mode, in which the processor forces its components in the physical package into the idle state for a certain fraction of time. The TCC can be configured by privileged system administrators to automatically activate under certain circumstances. Such thermal events can also be triggered by software, trapping the CPU into a mode where processors reduce their power consumption by clock modulation.

To the best of our knowledge, our attack is the first academic work to use CPU thermal management features for SGX defence exploitation. We point out that if this thermal management feature is maliciously used, CPU execution speed can be a target that is easily manipulated without being detected by threads running on the controlled core.

2.3 Cache-Based Side-Channel Attacks and Defences in SGX

Cache-based side-channel attacks on SGX are based on general timing attacks on cache like Prime+Probe [16] and Flush+Reload [26]. The basic idea is to measure the access times to a series of specific addresses, and use the information to infer whether or not the victims have accessed data in related addresses. With this knowledge of the victim's memory access patterns, attackers can retrieve confidential data like private keys. General defence mechanisms have also been proposed for detection and prevention of side-channel attacks like CacheD [23], CaSym [2] and CEASER [18].

Cache-based attack methods have been commonly used in exploiting SGX applications. Malware Guard Extension [19] and CacheZoom [15] develop Prime+Probe type of attacks with the help of a high-resolution timer to distinguish cache hits and misses, and uses the LLC cache channel. Other side-channel attacks [1,7,8,24] are based on similar methods, with the common strategy of using a high-resolution timer to measure the access latency when probing the victim enclave application's cache and infer secret data from the enclave.

Defensive mechanisms against side-channel SGX attacks also depend on high-resolution software timers inside the SGX enclave. Varys [17] defends cache-based side-channel attacks by enforcing that security-sensitive threads be reserved on the same CPU physical cores and detecting attacker threads that attempt to access shared CPU resources. Déjà Vu [5] measures application execution time with a more complex software timer using Intel TSX, but not all of the timer thread is under TSX's protection because some parts of the timer need to be shared across threads. Vulnerabilities in these designs will be further discussed in Sect. 3 and 4.

3 System Model

3.1 Model of Software Timers

To establish a software timer model, we first define a concept of *wall time*, denoted T_w, as an imaginary clock that is always accurate and up-to-date with physical time in the real world. We assume that all software timer designs should serve the same purpose: to track the wall time as accurately as possible and provide the current time to software that needs it. Since there is no dedicated hardware available in the enclaves for time, we assume that any software timer would need to use a sequence of instructions to track wall-time and use them to mimic an ordinary clock's behavior. To achieve this, a software timer should maintain a *clock time* T_c, and make it available to other threads that need to learn what the current time is.

In the ideal case, the wall time is proportional to clock time by some constant factor, so the clock time can emulate the wall time by executing a sequence of instructions, and the constant factor is decided by how much time the sequence of instructions take to run. This is the best that a software timer could do since a program inside an SGX enclave has no access to a high-resolution hardware timer that can directly provide wall time. We measure its margin of error from wall-time, and define a measure M_t that indicates how accurate the software timer is comparing with the absolute time:

$$\frac{|\Delta t_c - \Delta t_w|}{\Delta t_w} < M_t \tag{1}$$

In the above form, the clock-time at t_1 and t_2 are T_{c1} and T_{c2}, the wall-times are T_{w1} and T_{w2}, with the times passing by Δt_c and Δt_w respectively. M_t is generally assumed to be so small in practice that $\Delta t_c \approx \Delta t_w$, and is affected by the execution speed of the sequence of instructions, which is in turn affected by CPU execution speed and memory/cache access speed, so the timer model can take this into account by adjusting the measure M_t.

We can now construct a generalized software timer with the above concepts, and use a global variable V_G to simulate the clock ticks. We call V_G the "clock variable". As different machines have different micro-architectures and speed of operations and accesses to cache, for the same timer algorithm, we use a varying parameter I_c to reflect the relation between variable increase and the clock time. I_c represents how much the clock time increases per tick of V_G in average. With this model, the problem of simulating a dedicated timer is transformed to the problem of using an increasing clock variable to indicate the current time, where the parameter I_c makes it generally adaptable under different settings of different machines.

In this way, when a user or an application needs to measure some Δt_w and since $\Delta t_c \approx \Delta t_w$ (previously assumed due to small M_t), then they can just measure Δt_c to learn how much time it passes in the clock-time and will get the result in the form of:

$$\begin{aligned} \Delta t_c &= T_{c2} - T_{c1} \\ &= I_c \cdot (V_{G2} - V_{G1}) \end{aligned} \tag{2}$$

Where V_{G1} and V_{G2} are the value of V_G at time t_1 and t_2. In this software model, the key problem for system developers is how to determine the value of I_c, and all current software timer approaches assume the value to be relatively stable as it would result in a small accuracy measure M_t. From our previous empirical findings, we have:

$$I_c \propto \frac{T_{Inc(V_G)}}{F_{CPU}} \tag{3}$$

Thus, the value I_c is proportional to $T_{Inc(V_G)}$, the time taken to increment V_G, and reciprocal to F_{CPU}, the CPU speed, which we may estimate to be the average clock frequency of the CPU during the time measured.

To summarize, the software timer model measures the accuracy M_t of a software timer by comparing the clock time it generates with the wall time. The accuracy is affected by an intermediate parameter I_c, which depends on the execution speed of the CPU (F_{CPU}) and the time $T_{Inc(V_G)}$ it needs to increment a global variable. To slow down a software timer, Eq. 2 says the adversary should make I_c larger, so that it takes longer to increment the clock variable by some amount. To increase I_c, Eq. 3 tells us that the adversary may either make the execution of instructions take longer, or reduce the speed of the CPU.

With these components modeled, we next need to take a look at the victims: The enclave applications and defenders, and how they use the software timers.

3.2 Defender Model

The goal of an SGX side-channel defender is to recognize attacks. A number of defenses do this by measuring the rates or latency of certain events, so they depend on a software timer. As an example, we here consider two strategies taken by previous work [5,17] that use the rate or the execution time of a measured event as a component of an SGX side-channel defense:

- Cache hit time: The Prime+Probe cache channel attacks on SGX enclaves require the adversary code to run on the same physical core with the victim thread [17], because they have to share the L1/L2 cache to perform the probe. Thus, one method for preventing this attack is filling a core entirely with the application's own threads. To confirm that two threads share the same physical core, we can measure and compare the time that the two threads take to access a shared variable in the L1/L2 cache: if it is an L1/L2 cache hit, the access time should be within around 10 cycles, which implies they share a physical CPU core. A software timer must be used for this measurement.
- Counting Asynchronous Enclave Exits (AEXs): To perform the Prime+Probe cache channel attacks, which give the adversary a fine-grained cache channel for probing, the adversary actively and frequently preempts the target SGX enclave using, for example, the high-precision Advanced Configuration and Power Interface (ACPI) or the High Precision Event Timer (HPET). The preemptions trigger an AEX every time they interrupt the victim enclave, which is an indicator of side-channel attacks if it happens too frequently. The defensive mechanisms can count the number of AEX events during a period of time or measure the time that a certain known sequence of executions takes [5,17] and decide whether the rate of AEX events is too high to raise an alert of side-channel attacks.

In general, these methods all attempt to measure the delay or frequency of some phenomenon. For example, they may monitor whether there is an *irregular* rate of events N_{Ev} (such as AEXs) that happen during a certain period of time. Similarly, the delay of a variable access can be viewed as just the inverse of the number of times the variable is accessed within some period of time. Thus, all tests essentially compare some measured rate of events, N_{Ev}, against a threshold, N_{Th} to detect whether an attack is taking place or not in one of the possible scenarios:

$$N_{Ev} > N_{Th} : attack = true \tag{4}$$

One dilemma that the defender faces is the choice of threshold: Setting N_{Th} too high will result in missed attacks or false negatives, while setting N_{Th} too low will result in false alarms or false positives. The usual solution is to set it according to a calibration run, during which the system is assumed to not be under the influence of an attacker.

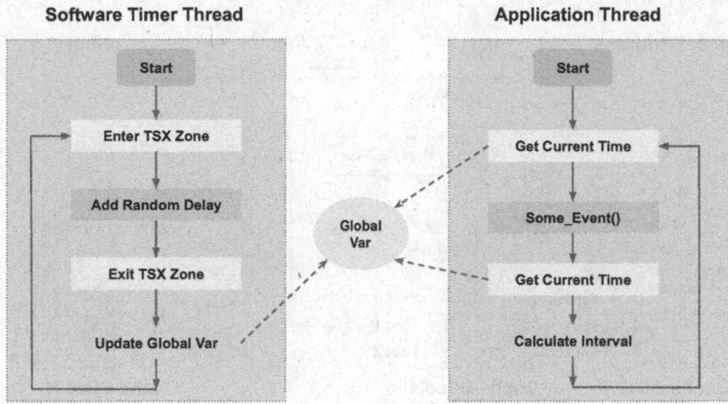

Fig. 1. A model of how a software timer works and is used by an application thread.

However, even then, the defense mechanism must still account for the fact that the measured rate of events N_{Ev} is dependent on both the true rate of events and the ratio between the wall clock and the rate of increment of the clock variable:

$$N_{Ev} = \frac{\Delta t_w}{\Delta t_c} \cdot R_{Ev} \tag{5}$$

where R_{Ev} is the true rate of events according to the wall clock. Normally, we expect that $\Delta t_w \approx \Delta t_c$, so $N_{Ev} \approx R_{Ev}$. However, recall that Δt_c is proportional to I_c in Eq. 3. Even under benign conditions, there is some variability to I_c, which may result in some number of false positives and false negatives—typically N_{Th} is set slightly higher so as to bias the detection method for fewer false positives. However, so long as I_c is similar to the value of I_c during calibration when N_{Th} is set, this will constrain R_{Ev} to be roughly N_{Ev}. Since R_{Ev} corresponds to how fast an attacker is able to read a side-channel, constraining R_{Ev} effectively slows the rate of information leakage to the attacker. However, if the attacker is able to arbitrarily increase I_c, then she can also arbitrarily increase the true rate of events R_{Ev} without being detected. This allows her to probe the side-channel faster and thus reduces the time taken for the attack to extract sensitive information from the enclave.

With this general model of a software timer thread, we now discuss why a best-effort software timer design is still vulnerable to attacker manipulation.

3.3 Timer Countermeasures

We illustrate the general structure of a software timer in Fig. 1. A software timer thread updates a global clock variable, which is read by application threads to the current time.

An attacker that wants to tamper with the timer might attempt to interrupt the timer so as to make the difference between Δt_c and Δt_w arbitrarily large. To defend against this, both Déjà Vu and Varys use TSX to detect if the timer

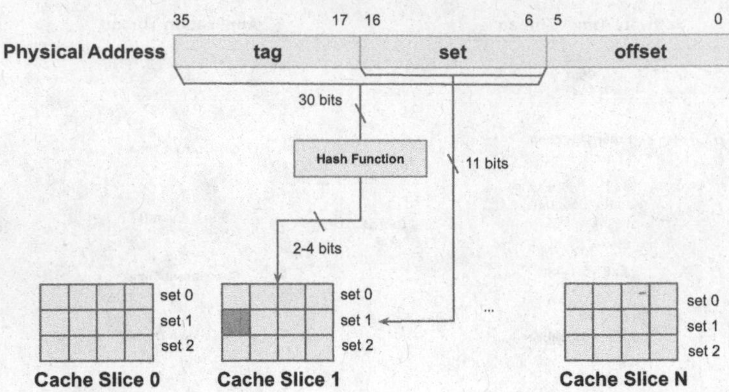

Fig. 2. Illustration of Intel cache slice and cache set structure.

has been interrupted. However, TSX can only protect the component of the loop that generates the delay Δt_c, and can not protect the update of the global clock variable, as the clock variable is simultaneously accessed by both the timer thread and application threads. As a result, the update of the global clock variable must be outside the TSX-protected region.

To prevent an attacker from interrupting and delaying the thread as it updates the global variable, TSX is combined with a randomized delay function inside the TSX region, and the global clock variable is updated with the randomized delay. This makes it hard for an attacker to guess when the timer thread is outside of the TSX region and can be interrupted without detection. Thus, we summarize that a secure timer that provides a timing service to other secure application threads needs to include at least the following parts:

1. A global clock variable V_G inside the secure enclave that records the current clock time. The clock time can be read from the clock variable by other threads in the same enclave.
2. A timer loop that increments the clock variable by an amount assumed to be proportional to the amount of time that has passed.
3. A protection mechanism that can either prevent the timer loop from being interrupted or detect if the loop has been interrupted. An example of such a mechanism is TSX.
4. If the entire loop cannot be protected from interruption, a random delay element such that the attacker cannot predict when the timer is in the unprotected region of execution, i.e., right before the clock variable is incremented.

As we can see, a TSX-protected timer should ideally spend a minimal amount of time outside the TSX region. In other words, the only action taken outside of the TSX region should be to increment the clock variable.

With the extra protection of the software timer loop, trivial attacks that manipulate the software timer by interrupting it frequently and/or deprioritizing the timer thread in an OS thread scheduler to make the software timer deviate from the wall clock would not work. Such scheduler attacks that have OS-level privilege would attempt to preempt the timer thread, which requires interrupting into it. This interruption would be easily caught by the TSX mechanism and the interrupted transaction would be aborted and detected by the defender.

4 Attack Design

4.1 Aion-1: CPU Thermal and Frequency Attack

The *Aion-1* attack manipulates the rate of increase of the clock variable indicating the internal time in the software timer thread, i.e., the F_{CPU} in Eq. 3 of our software timer model in Sect. 3.1. Intuitively, this can be done by changing the CPU working frequency via the CPU power management modules of the operating system kernel, such that the clock variable increases out of sync with wall time. The strawman method of simply changing CPU frequencies has been described [5], where $procfs$ is used to control the CPU frequency from userspace in on-demand mode, and its effect was generally considered to be bounded by CPU frequency scaling. Taking the Intel i7-6600U as an example: The processor base frequency (PBF) is 2.6 GHz; the max turbo frequency (MTF) is 3.4 GHz. If the attacker obtains control of a CPU power management module, the minimum controllable frequency of a single core is 800 MHz. Thus, it was generally believed that the maximum achievable scale-down of CPU frequency $\Delta t_w/\Delta t_c$ was between 3.25× and 4.25×, a value that most previous defenses could tolerate and still prevent an adversary from mounting an effective attack.

However, our attack can break the above assumptions using CPU thermal management features. As mentioned in Sect. 2, Intel CPU thermal management is controlled by a thermal control circuit, whose settings are controlled by a software adaptive thermal monitor. We find that an attacker with root privileges can trigger a thermal event on the CPU thermal control circuit using only software. This not only causes the CPU core frequency and voltage to be throttled down, but can also force the processor into the HDC mode where CPUs are paused for part of the clock duty cycle. Thus, while the clock frequency does not change in HDC mode, the effective execution speed of the CPU is lowered below that of the minimum clock speed, as the CPU is effectively idle for a fraction of the clock cycles. By doing this, we can make the effective execution speed of a CPU approximately equivalent to that of a 100 MHz CPU.

According to our software timer model in Sect. 3, the accuracy of a software timer depends on the execution speed of the CPU core that the software timer thread runs on. In side-channel defensive mechanisms, the defenders need to make sure the secure enclave has occupied both hyper-threads on the same physical core, such that they do not share L1/L2 cache with other, potentially malicious threads. They do this by measuring the access latency of a shared variable to see if it hits the L1/L2 cache, since if both threads can hit the cache of the same clock variable within around 10 cycles, they must share the same physical core. To evade detection, the Aion-1 attacker only needs to slow down the software timer to make the tester believe that the cache hit time is within 10 cycles in its calibration run, even if it actually hits LLC and takes around 40 cycles or more. It can also do the reverse, depending on which thread the attacker wants to slow down. In this way, any secure application that uses the software timer will read values inconsistent with wall time. This tricks the defender into thinking that the variable access has hit in the L1 cache when it could have hit in the L2 or higher.

The effectiveness of this attack depends on the highest and lowest possible processor execution speed on a single CPU core. The processor execution speed can be regarded as equivalent to the average core frequency during a period of time. When the attack is being mounted, the core that the software timer thread runs on should be set to the lowest possible running speed, and other threads, including the attacker threads, should be set to the highest running speed (or the other way around, when needed). Without the ability to know its own clock speed reliably, the software timer can unknowingly run slower or faster than the original settings. This type of attack also has some limitations, including:

- The attack can only happen if the attackers are able to access CPU MSRs, requiring kernel privileges. In SGX applications on a multi-tenant cloud scenarios, an attacker may not be able to get such privileges as they would need to compromise the hypervisor.
- The attack also assumes the CPU should support thermal control features including clock modulation via MSRs to issue a software signal that activates the TCC. Most of the Intel CPUs available on the market support these features, but not all of them do.

Due to these limitations of privilege and feature availability, we present another attack that uses cache eviction to achieve the goal of manipulating the software timer, possibly as an unprivileged attacker.

4.2 Aion-2: Cache Eviction Attack

The *Aion-2* attack directly targets the clock variable used in the secure software timer thread using an attacker thread in user space. We call this a cache eviction attack, as it slows down the speed of the reference software clock by evicting the clock variable from the CPU cache to DRAM. According to the software timer model in Sect. 3, this attack exploits the stability assumption of the cache/memory access speed of the clock variable, i.e., the $T_{Inc(V_G)}$ in Eq. 3.

Intel L1/L2 caches are shared by two logical threads on the same physical core, and all threads share the LLC. Because most Intel CPUs use an inclusive cache policy between different levels of cache, evicting the cache line containing the clock variable from LLC would also evict it from L1 and L2 cache. In this way, whenever the software timer thread needs to increment the clock variable, the thread has to wait for extra cycles to complete the request because it has to be served from DRAM. From our experimental results, it takes almost the same number of clock cycles (though not the same wall time) for accessing the same level of cache, and the DRAM access time is about 150 cycles on average, which means the attacker knows how much she can slow down the increment of the clock variable by each eviction. For the rest, the only job that the attacker threads in the user space need to do is to evict the cache line where the clock variable is located. Note that since the clock variable indicating the internal time in the software timer thread is not protected by TSX transactions, access to the clock variable does not trigger a transaction abort, regardless of whether it hits cache or DRAM.

To perform the attack, the attacker threads need a minimum cache eviction set. A minimum cache eviction set is a set of virtual addresses with which a user thread can make sure the target cache line is evicted out of the cache. For example, if the virtual address of the clock variable address on a CPU with 4-way associative LLC is `0x00007E30`, then the attacker could find an eviction set of addresses that shares the same cache set: {`0x00013D30`, `0x00026A30`, `0x000E2730`, `0x0009AB30`}, and according to the Intel cache structure, this means they should also reside on the same LLC cache slice. The allocation of LLC matters because cache entries on different cache slices do not belong to the same cache set. After finding the eviction set, to make sure that the clock variable is evicted from all levels of cache, one just needs to access all the addresses in the eviction set. Once the cache entry is successfully evicted, the secure timer thread needs to hit the DRAM to read or write to the clock variable, which slows down the increment speed of the software timer ticks.

We now explain how the cache eviction set can be found. As in Fig. 2, the physical address of each memory request is decomposed into three parts when mapping the address to an LLC cache line. The part with the lowest bits of the address indicates the offset in the line, and the set bits decide which cache set it is mapped to. In recent Intel CPUs, LLC are further divided into slices, and an undocumented hash function maps the set and tag bits of the addresses to a specific LLC cache slice. While the hash function itself is undocumented, there have been attempts [14] to reverse-engineer it. Alternatively, other methods [22] can successfully find a minimum eviction set with user-level programs with high probability. We adopt existing methods for finding an LLC eviction set and use them for our attack.

After finding a cache eviction set, as shown in Fig. 3, the attacker thread can then access all the virtual addresses in the eviction set of the clock variable in the software timer thread, so that the clock variable is evicted from the cache and the incrementing speed is much slower. The attacker can repeatedly access the eviction set and keep evicting the clock variable in a loop, so that whenever the software timer thread accesses the clock variable again and makes it cached, the cache entry will actively be evicted by the attacker again.

Because the attacker thread runs concurrently with the software timer thread, the eviction of the cache line containing the clock variable is probabilistic without the knowledge of the exact hardware cache replacement algorithm used by the CPU. However, the attacker can also improve the chance of cache eviction by parallelizing the accesses to the cache eviction set. The attackers can distribute the elements of the cache eviction set to different threads that are controlled by

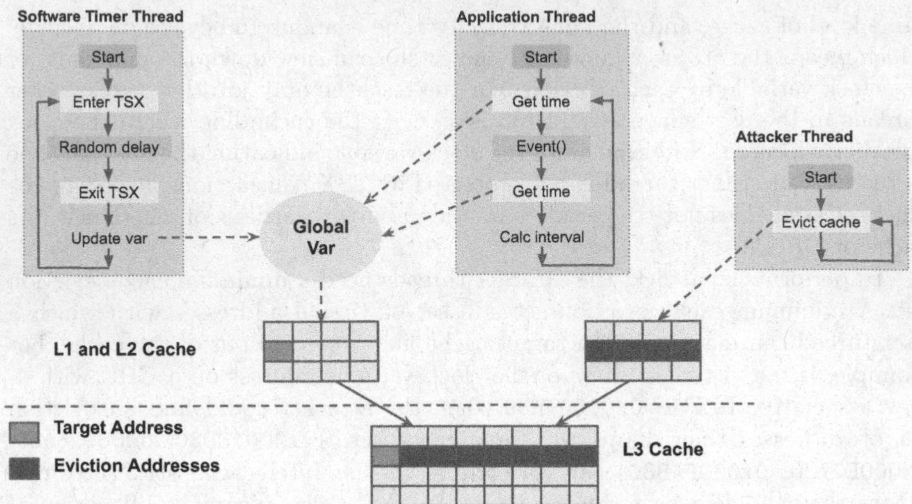

Fig. 3. Illustration of Aion-2: Cache eviction attack.

the attacker, preferably filling all the rest of available CPU cores with attacker threads. This approach turns the single-threaded attack into a multi-threaded coordinated attack and gives the attacker a better chance to evict the target victim cache entry more efficiently.

The attacker achieves the maximum timer slow-down effect by ideally forcing every increment of the clock variable to miss all levels of cache and hit DRAM. In this way, the software timer runs slower in comparison with the wall time at the maximum limit, which is the theoretical worst case for the reference timer. However, due to the nature of multi-core and scheduler, it is difficult for an attacker with only user-level privilege, to achieve this guarantee. We will show in the evaluation section how practical the attack is and describe our results.

To summarize, the target of both types of the Aion attacks is to manipulate the accuracy of the software timer, either to slow it down or speed it up without being noticed by the victim system. According to our software timer model, it is the accuracy measure M_t that the attacker focuses on. To attack M_t, the malicious party may either change the execution speed of CPU F_{CPU}, or the time $T_{Inc(V_G)}$ needed to increase the global clock variable.

5 Implementation

5.1 Reference Software Timer

In our experiments on Aion attacks, we use a real-world software timer as an implementation of the general model described in Sect. 3. We choose the software timer implementation from Déjà Vu [5], because (1) it has high accuracy for event rate measurement, and (2) it can detect repeated interruptions and protect itself from malicious preemptions from privileged threads. It not only includes an essential loop that increments the clock variable, but also additional defense code using Intel TSX that protects the software timer threads from frequent interruptions by malicious attackers as shown in Listing 1.1:

```
1  while (infinite_loop_flag) {
     if (_xbegin() == _XBEGIN_STARTED) {  /* TSX begins */
3      __asm volatile {
         "rdrand %0\n\t"
5        :"=r"(rand)
       };
7      rand = (rand & 0x7) + 1;
       for (i = 0; i < rand; i++) {
9        for (k = 0; k < 5; k++)
           my_udelay(1);
11     }
       _xend();           /* TSX ends */
13   } else {
       int_flag++;
15   }
     current_time = current_time + rand;
17 }
```

Listing 1.1: Reference Timer Thread Implementation in C

L1: The timer thread starts an infinite loop from an SGX enclave.

L2: It enters into a TSX-protected zone, where any interruption to the middle of the TSX zone will fall into a trap, generate an exception, and rollback to the beginning of the entry point.

L3–7: It generates a random integer number between 1 and 8. Here the randomness is provided by `rdrand` as the original authors use it, while other pseudo-random functions could also work.

L8–11: This is a loop creating a delay proportional to the generated random value, so it is harder for attackers to guess when TSX protection covers the thread execution.

L12 and **L**16: The code leaves the TSX-protected region and the clock variable is updated. As mentioned in Sect. 4, the reason for ending the TSX zone before the timer tick number is updated is that the clock variable is intended to be read from other threads concurrently. If the update is in TSX zone then any concurrent read will abort the transaction and roll back the timer thread.

The clock variable (`current_time` in **L**16) is exposed to both the timer thread and the application threads. With some randomness, the timer thread periodically increment the clock variable. When the application thread needs to take a high-resolution time measurement of a particular event, it first retrieves the clock variable's value before the event and reads the same variable again afterward to calculate the interval. In this standard procedure, the TSX protection does not apply to the clock variable. Thus, theoretically, anyone can access it without triggering the TSX or SGX trap as long as they are in the enclave. However, the accuracy of the timer is questionable for two reasons. First, the thread execution speed is relevant to the CPU clock speed, because the real-world time of instructions being processed by the CPU and on which the clock speed is not known or controlled by the enclave applications. Secondly, the time of access of the clock variable, whether from the timer thread or any other thread, cannot be assumed to be constant because there is no guarantee of which level of cache or memory it may hit. Therefore, the software timer is not as reliable and secure as was thought, even if it is running in an SGX enclave.

5.2 Implementing Aion-1: CPU Thermal and Frequency Attack

This type of attack focuses on changing the speed of targeted CPU cores. The two methods manipulating CPU core speed include triggering thermal events to force a core into HDC mode, and adjusting CPU frequency directly via the power control module of the OS. Because HDC mode stops a CPU core from running in a certain percentage of the time, and therefore both methods can be regarded equivalent to making a CPU core running at a certain frequency, we refer to it as the "equivalent frequency" later in this section.

The thermal management attack needs to be implemented in a thread with root privilege. We trigger thermal events by changing the respective MSRs: IA32_CLOCK_MODULATION and operate on the programmable bits of [3:1]. For direct frequency adjustment, there are three kernel modules we can use for scaling the CPU core frequencies: `intel_pstate`, `acpi-cpufreq`, and `p4-clockmod`. We have tested them all and found that 1) `intel_pstate` as a new power management module cannot achieve per-core frequency scaling, and 2) `p4-clockmod` as a relative last-generation kernel driver has dependency on the Intel `speedstep-lib` driver which is not compatible with our test CPUs. We therefore chose `acpi-cpufreq` as the driver that facilitates the attacker thread.

We set the kernel driver to use a "userspace" power governor, so that a user-level application with root privilege can configure any CPU core to run at a specified frequency. In this case, it is the attacker thread that controls the CPU core frequency of the software timer thread and other threads. Many methods can be used to trigger CPU thermal events, such as configuring TCC offset of CPU, increasing CPU workloads to stress out the cores, blocking physical airflow or stopping case fan from working, and sending software signal to CPU to force clock modulation. We choose the last approach that only requires a write to an MSR register `0x19A` for implementation, however, we believe that an attacker can use various creative approaches to generate thermal events.

In the attacker thread, we set the target execution speed for the software timer thread to F_c and other threads to F_x. The attacking thread first gets the information of which CPU core the software timer thread executes on, and then runs in a loop while `Loop_Flag` is `TRUE` to set the frequencies of the software timer thread and other threads. The attacker thread stops when `Loop_Flag` is changed to `FALSE`.

5.3 Implementing Aion-2: Cache Eviction Attack

The cache eviction attack needs the address of the timer variable used in the software timer thread to find the cache eviction set. We here assume that the image of the victim SGX application is openly available to all, which makes sense because it is supposed to be loaded by the OS into an SGX enclave. The address can be determined by doing a binary analysis on the application image.

Once the address `Addr_t` is found after loading the SGX application, the attack can start to slow down the software timer: First, the attacker thread finds a cache eviction set for `Addr_t`. This can be done by an unprivileged user-level process using a group reduction algorithm [22], or like in our experiment for the ease of implementation, use the page map and get the physical address `Addr_p` of `Addr_t` to find the cache eviction set directly.

As is shown in Listing 2, with the physical address, the undocumented hash function is required to determine which LLC cache slice an address belongs to. We obtain the hash function by reverse engineering using the algorithms mentioned in previous work [14]. Then, with the cache eviction set `EV_t` in hand, the attacker thread can loop accessing the addresses in the eviction set to keep evicting the software timer thread's clock variable out of all levels of cache. This will then slowing down the timer because every time it increments the clock variable, it should hit DRAM instead of the cache.

We have optimized the attack by parallelizing the attacking loop: the addresses in the eviction set `EV_t` can be further divided and assigned to multiple threads. The attacker threads can keep accessing the addresses in the same eviction set and evicting the target clock variable from the cache faster, because the multithreaded attacker still shares the same LLC and it should take less time for all addresses in `EV_t` to be accessed to evict the target address `Addr_t`.

6 Evaluation

6.1 Purpose and Experiment Setup

We conduct all experiments on two machines with different CPUs: (1) Intel i7-6700K with 4 cores; and (2) Intel Xeon E3-1230 v6 with 4 cores. For the system software environment setup, we use Intel SGX v2.11 SDK on top of Linux with kernel v5.4, and all of the machines have hyper-threading enabled. The experiments in this section are conducted to demonstrate the following:

- Software timers in SGX enclaves are vulnerable to Aion attacks, which can manipulate the reported clock time from outside the enclave.
- Without compromising the software timer of the defender, a representative cache-based side-channel attack will be detected and prevented from exploiting the victim applications.
- With the help of Aion attacks, the same side-channel attacks can evade detection by the defender.

Table 1. Results of software timer readings affected by the Aion attacks.

Random Func (+CPU Thermal)	Xeon E3-1230v6				i7-6700K			
	RD	RD+TA	TF	TF+TA	RD	RD+TA	TF	TF+TA
Baseline	**256.3**	7.0 (37×)	**337.4**	8.7 (39×)	**225.9**	5.8 (39×)	**302.5**	7.9 (38×)
Single-thread (Cache Eviction)	156.2 (1.6×)	5.2 (49×)	181.5 (1.9×)	6.1 (55×)	148.9 (1.5×)	4.7 (48×)	148.1 (2.0×)	4.1 (73×)
Multi-thread (Cache Eviction)	94.3 (2.7×)	2.3 (111×)	54.6 (6.2×)	1.8 (187×)	90.6 (2.5×)	1.9 (120×)	41.7 (7.3×)	1.5 (202×)

In the remaining parts of this section, we first demonstrate experiments and results that show that Aion attacks can successfully manipulate software timers in SGX enclaves. We then present an end-to-end attack to show that our attacks can facilitate an existing cache-based side-channel attack on SGX enclaves, evading the detection of a defender based on a software timer.

6.2 Aion Attack Evaluation

Both types of Aion attacks have the same goal of manipulating the running speed of the software timer, and their effectiveness will be evaluated in this section. As we previously analyzed, Aion attacks can assist the side-channel attackers in evading the detection of existing defensive mechanisms that rely on the software timer to be accurate. We evaluate the extent to which our attacks can speed up or slow down the software timer, as this determines the probability of a successful side-channel attack.

We combine the two types of Aion attacks and demonstrate their effectiveness in manipulating the software timer as a unit test. We test the reduction rate (how much the attack can slow down the software timer) by the CPU thermal attack and cache eviction attack under different settings.

The baseline workload runs in an SGX enclave as a simple loop that runs operations from AES encryption. We compare the time intervals under different scenarios in Table 1, including: a) the baseline scenario where the timer is not under attack, and only affected by the thermal attack at the row of "baseline"; b) a single-thread attacker scenario where only one attacking thread of Aion-2 attack is running; and c) a multi-thread attackers scenario where the number of Aion-2 attacking threads is the `(# of total hyper threads - 2)`, and the other two threads are taken by the software timer thread and the application thread.

Another variant we are comparing in the evaluation shown in Table 1 is the different random functions used in the software timer thread. Because randomness is not free of cost, all random number generators take different amounts of execution time which may affect how much time the software timer thread spends in a loop to increment the clock variable. We use four different sets of functions for randomness generation and combined them with or without CPU core execution speed manipulation by the thermal attack: (1) `RD`: `RDRAND` instruction; (2) `RD+TA`, which combines CPU thermal attack and use it under (1)'s settings of RDRAND instruction; (3) TF, which is a simple pseudo-random number generator called T-Function [12]; and (4) TF+TA, which combines the CPU thermal attack and uses it under the same settings of (3) for the evaluation. We note here that since the T-Function() is so cheap in execution costing less than 30 cycles after optimization, that we did not repeat a separate evaluation with no randomness generated, which also makes sense in the scenario of real defence. Again, we make sure that the software timer thread, the application thread, and the attacking thread(2) in our evaluation do not share the same core to avoid them from competing for the same processor resource. After each number, the number in a bracket (e.g., 202×) indicates its slow-down factor comparing with the baseline.

From the above results, we can see that under various settings, the CPU thermal attack is powerful and can achieve 30–40× slow-down on its own. Also, both single-threaded and multi-threaded attacking methods can effectively slow down the software timer via the cache eviction attack, and in all but the RD case, achieve a slow down that exceeds the range of slowdowns that previous systems claim to be able to defend. Moreover, when combined with the core frequency manipulation attack, the effectiveness is further improved, in total slowing down the software timer by a factor greater than 200 for software timer using T-function() under both types of Aion attacks, and by a factor about 120 for software timer using RDRAND instruction under both types of Aion attacks.

6.3 End-to-End Attack Evaluation

We previously showed how much the Aion attacks can slow down the software timer, but the timer slow-down ratio alone may not be enough evidence to prove that the software timer slow-down rate can effectively assist other side-channel attacks to go undetected by SGX side-channel defenders. Therefore, for a full evaluation, we have mounted an end-to-end attack to demonstrate the complete procedure, combining the traditional SGX side-channel attack and our Aion attacks to defeat the software timer that defenders rely on. The end-to-end attack experiments consist of three parts: (1) a known side-channel attack on SGX; (2) a defender used to detect the side-channel attack in (1); and (3) our Aion attacks that can compromise the defensive mechanism in (2).

In our experiments, the side-channel attack is implemented based on the SGX-Step framework [21] and uses a Prime+Probe [13] type cache-based side-channel attack to extract an AES key that is used to do encryption operations repeatedly inside an SGX enclave. We use the OpenSSL 0.9.7a library, which is known to be vulnerable against cache timing attacks and is also known to work in the environment of SGX, as a proof-of-concept demonstration. The ratio of successful key extractions of the attack on our Intel i-7 6700K machine is above 98.4% under 100K rounds of victim encryption operations.

For the defender, we have tested our implementation of SGX side-channel attack defender based on the defense paper [5]. Our results are comparable to the evaluation data shown in the original work: the defender can successfully

Table 2. End-to-end evaluation of Aion attacks against existing defences.

Benchmark	Baseline defence			Defence under Aion attack		
	Threshold	Acc %	FP%	Threshold	Acc % (E3)	Acc % (i7)
Numeric sort	4	100	97	4	95	94
	40	100	40	40	17	15
	80	**95**	**3**	**80**	**2**	**2**
	160	87	2	160	1	0
	320	40	0	320	0	0
	640	9	0	–	–	–
	1280	3	0	–	–	–
Fourier	4	100	98	4	95	92
	40	100	46	40	19	18
	80	**96**	**4**	**80**	**2**	**1**
	160	74	2	160	0	0
	320	30	0	320	0	0
	640	10	0	–	–	–
	1280	2	0	–	–	–

detect at least 95% of the basic SGX side-channel attacks under a trained threshold value δ. The threshold value is gathered and calculated by running normal applications in SGX enclaves without being attacked, so it counts and tracks the normal number of AEX events happening and decides to trigger the alarm when there is a burst of an abnormal amount of such events. The results with the Intel i7-6700K machine environment are shown in the column of Baseline Defence in Table 2 with the randomness generator of `RDRAND` in its software timer loop.

Distinct from the previous evaluation that shows the effect of Aion attacks on the software timer, the evaluation with end-to-end attacks combines our two types of Aion attacks with the basic side-channel attacks, and the SGX side-channel attack defender. We measure how effectively our attacks can assist the base side-channel attack to evade detection of the defender. Experiments run on two of the machines with SGX with the defender using `RDRAND` as the randomness generator, using both types of Aion attacks combined, and results are shown in Table 2. From the results, we can see that under Aion attacks, the defender identifies less than 2% of the side-channel attacks in its normal setting of the threshold value 80. For the threshold value of 40, the accuracy is less than 15–19%, however, without the knowledge of the ongoing Aion attacks, the defender would not choose to use a low threshold value by taking the risk of a high false-positive rate. The results demonstrate that the combined Aion attacks can effectively assist the base side-channel SGX attack to make it undetectable by the SGX defensive software that is based on a software timer.

To summarize our findings, software timer-based defenses are not viable in the face of tampering of timers from Aion attacks. Comparing the left part of

Table 2, which shows false positive rates under benign conditions at various E_{th} thresholds, with the right part of Table 2, which shows detection accuracy after tampering with the Aion attack, we can see that the detection rate is on the order of the false positive rate. At threshold 80, both of the false positive rates in benign conditions are 3–4% while the detection rates under attack are 1–2%. Even if we decrease the threshold to 40, the detection rates only range from 14–19% while the false positive rates have increased to 40–46%. As a result, it is not possible for the defender to select a threshold that permits good detection when under attack, but still keeps false positives at acceptable levels. We see this trend holds for all thresholds. As a result, our empirical analysis shows that it is not possible to use a software timer in any defense due the adversary's ability to manipulate the timer.

7 Conclusion

Side-channel attacks are major threats that TEEs currently face, including Intel SGX. Although software-based defences have been proposed for detection and prevention of cache-based side-channel attacks, the lack of a reliable hardware timer for secure applications to use inside the enclave makes such solutions vulnerable against Aion attacks. In this paper, we design and implement two types of Aion attacks, one based on manipulating the software timer thread execution speed by triggering CPU thermal events, and the other focusing on cache eviction to slow down the rate at which the target timer is increased, both of which can effectively change the how fast the software timer in an SGX enclave runs and invalidate the defensive approaches that rely on accurate high-resolution software timers. We also argue that in our general software timer model, there is no way to design a reliable timer purely in software that makes the defense usable and effective in detecting side-channel attacks, unless the defence can tolerate up to 200x slowdown of their timer, but this is unlikely.

The core of the problem we show through our model analysis is that when system designers use a software timer to measure the time certain critical events take, they made an invalid assumption: That the increment speed of the variable used in the software timer is nearly constant, and can not be significantly altered by an adversary. However, this fails to account for dramatic changes in execution speed when accessing a global variable that can occur when the CPU frequency varies or when cache behaviour is manipulated. By breaking the high-resolution measurement of time, Aion attacks are able to exploit existing defences.

Acknowledgement. We would like to thank Professor Yinqian Zhang, Dr. Sanchuan Chen and Oleksii Oleksenko for their help in SGX defensive frameworks. We appreciate Dr. Lianying Zhao, Tony Liao and colleagues from Baidu Research for their valuable advice on this paper.

References

1. Brasser, F., Müller, U., Dmitrienko, A., Kostiainen, K., Capkun, S., Sadeghi, A.R.: Software grand exposure: SGX cache attacks are practical. In: Proceedings of USENIX WOOT, Vancouver, Canada (2017)
2. Brotzman, R., Liu, S., Zhang, D., Tan, G., Kandemir, M.: CaSym: cache aware symbolic execution for side channel detection and mitigation. In: Proceedings of IEEE S&P, San Fransico, USA (2019)
3. Bulck, J.V., et al.: Foreshadow: extracting the keys to the intel SGX kingdom with transient out-of-order execution. In: Proceedings of USENIX Security, Baltimore, USA, August 2018
4. Bulck, J.V., Weichbrodt, N., Kapitza, R., Piessens, F., Strackx, R.: Telling your secrets without page faults: stealthy page table-based attacks on enclaved execution. In: Proceedings of USENIX Security, Vancouver, Canada (2017)
5. Chen, S., Zhang, X., Reiter, M.K., Zhang, Y.: Detecting privileged side-channel attacks in shielded execution with Déjà Vu. In: Proceedings of ASIA CCS, Abu Dhabi, UAE (2017)
6. Costan, V., Devadas, S.: Intel SGX explained. Cryptology ePrint Archive, Report 2016/086 (2016). https://ia.cr/2016/086
7. Dall, F., et al.: CacheQuote: efficiently recovering long-term secrets of SGX EPID via cache attacks. In: Proceedings of CHES, Amsterdam, Netherlands (2018)
8. Gözfried, J., Eckert, M., Schinzel, S., Müller, T.: Cache attacks on Intel SGX. In: Proceedings of EuroSec, Belgrade, Serbia (2017)
9. Guan, L., Lin, J., Luo, B., Jing, J., Wang, J.: Protecting private keys against memory disclosure attacks using hardware transactional memory. In: Proceedings of IEEE S&P, San Jose, USA (2015)
10. Hähnel, M., Cui, W., Peinado, M.: High-Resolution side channels for untrusted operating systems. In: Proceedings of USENIX ATC, Santa Clara, USA (2017)
11. Intel Corporation: Intel 64 and IA-32 Architectures Software Developer's Manual (2021)
12. Klimov, A., Shamir, A.: A new class of invertible mappings. In: Proceedings of CHES, San Francisco Bay, CA, USA (2002)
13. Liu, F., Yarom, Y., Ge, Q., Heiser, G., Lee, R.B.: Last-level cache side-channel attacks are practical. In: Proceedings of IEEE S&P, San Jose, USA (2015)
14. Maurice, C., Scouarnec, N., Neumann, C., Heen, O., Francillon, A.: Reverse engineering intel last-level cache complex addressing using performance counters. In: Proceedings of RAID, Kyoto, Japan (2015)
15. Moghimi, A., Irazoqui, G., Eisenbarth, T.: CacheZoom: how SGX amplifies the power of cache attacks. In: Proceedings of CHES, Taipei, Taiwan (2017)
16. Neve, M., Seifert, J.P.: Advances on access-driven cache attacks on AES. In: Proceedings of SAC Workshop, Montreal, Canada, pp. 147–162 (2006)
17. Oleksenko, O., Trach, B., Krahn, R., Martin, A., Fetzer, C., Silberstein, M.: Varys: protecting SGX enclaves from practical side-channel attacks. In: Proceedings of USENIX ATC, Boston, USA (2018)
18. Qureshi, M.K.: CEASER: mitigating conflict-based cache attacks via encrypted-address and remapping. In: Proceedings of IEEE MICRO, Fukuoka, Japan (2018)
19. Schwarz, M., Weiser, S., Gruss, D., Maurice, C., Mangard, S.: Malware guard extension: using SGX to conceal cache attacks. In: Proceedings of DIMVA, Bonn, Germany (2017)

20. Shih, M.W., Lee, S., Kim, T., Peinado, M.: T-SGX: eradicating controlled-channel attacks against enclave programs. In: Proceedings of NDSS, San Diego, USA (2017)
21. Van Bulck, J., Piessens, F., Strackx, R.: SGX-Step: a practical attack framework for precise enclave execution control. In: Proceedings of SysTEX, Shanghai, China (2017)
22. Vila, P., Kopf, B., Morales, J.F.: Theory and practice of finding eviction sets. In: Proceedings of IEEE S&P, San Francisco, USA, pp. 39–54 (2019)
23. Wang, S., Wang, P., Liu, X., Zhang, D., Wu, D.: CacheD: identifying cache-based timing channels in production software. In: Proceedings of USENIX Security, Vancouver, Canada (2017)
24. Wang, W., et al.: Leaky cauldron on the dark land: understanding memory side-channel hazards in SGX. In: Proceedings of CCS, Dallas, USA (2017)
25. Xu, Y., Cui, W., Peinado, M.: Controlled-channel attacks: deterministic side channels for untrusted operating systems. In: Proceedings of IEEE S&P, San Jose, USA (2015)
26. Yarom, Y., Falkner, K.: Flush+Reload: a high resolution, low noise, L3 cache side-channel attack. In: Proceedings of USENIX Security, San Diego, USA (2014)

THIRD-EYE: Practical and Context-Aware Inference of Causal Relationship Violations in Commodity Kernels

Chuhong Yuan, Dong Du, and Haibo Chen(✉)

Shanghai Jiao Tong University, Shanghai, China
{chyuan,Dd_nirvana,haibochen}@sjtu.edu.cn

Abstract. A causal relationship implies that a function call should follow another function call. However, causal relationships can be implicit in practice and therefore often missed and violated by developers, causing many serious risks such as memory leaks and crashes. Although a set of works are proposed to mitigate the issue, they fall short in solving two main challenges: the contradiction between bugs in specific paths and intra-function path-explosion, and missing contextual constraints of causal relationships, which leads to high performance cost or failing to detect context-related bugs.

This paper proposes THIRD-EYE, a practical static analysis tool that infers causal relationship violations for commodity kernels like Linux. THIRD-EYE leverages the intersection-based call sequence building algorithm to cope with intra-function path-explosion, which can reduce the number of paths while collecting callee information as much as possible. Besides, THIRD-EYE detects causal relationship violations context-sensitively based on a statistical method. Our experiments show THIRD-EYE is effective and efficient—successfully identified 60 bugs in Linux 5.3. Of them, 41 have been confirmed and fixed by Linux developers (The accepted patches are in https://ipads.se.sjtu.edu.cn:1312/opensource/third-eye.).

Keywords: Static analysis · Operating system kernel · Causal relationship

1 Introduction

The causal relationship is a programming pattern that means `b()` must follow `a()`. A well-known example from Linux is that `spin_unlock()` should be called after `spin_lock()`. Violating causal relationships in kernels will lead to severe consequences like memory leaks, DoS, and even crashes.

However, causal relationships are often implicit because of the lack of documentation or comments. For example, `alloc_workqueue()` and `destroy_workqueue()` have a causal relationship but neither of their comments

L. Bilge et al. (Eds.): DIMVA 2021, LNCS 12756, pp. 194–214, 2021.
https://doi.org/10.1007/978-3-030-80825-9_10

mentions the relationship with the other [1,2]. Also, causal relationships usually have contextual constraints, which makes the patterns more complex. For example, in a function, `kfree()` should be called after a successful `kmalloc()` if the caller fails. Hence, here the successful `kmalloc()` and the failure are the contextual constraints of this causal relationship. Due to the two reasons, many violations of causal relationships pop up in commodity kernels.

Since violations of causal relationships in commodity kernels may cause fatal errors, many works tried to detect them. First, static analysis tools, e.g., APISan [29] and PR-Miner [16], utilize the statistical method [11] to infer causal relationships but face a tradeoff between performance and accuracy. For example, APISan [29] can infer causal relationships where the second function's invocation relies on the first function's return value. However, it needs to search through all intra-function paths, and then it suffers from **intra-function path-explosion** with large performance cost (14 h with 32-core CPU and 256 GB RAM) [29]. PR-Miner [16] discards intra-function path information for better performance, but it achieves worse accuracy—cannot detect the bugs that exist in specific paths, i.e., some paths in a function violate causal relationships while others do not. Moreover, it does not consider **contextual constraints**.

Besides, dynamic analysis tools like Perrocotta [28] mine causal relationships from execution traces while the dynamic methods fall short in achieving high code coverage. Furthermore, works like PF-Miner [19], PairMiner [17], and PairDyn [3] only focus on specific scopes like error handlers and driver interfaces. Other works like WoodPecker [10], IMChecker [13], and WYSIWIB [14] need known causal patterns, while the patterns are often implicit.

To overcome the implicitness of causal relationships and achieve high code coverage, we use static analysis based on a statistical method, which needs no previous knowledge by regarding major patterns as rules. Here, to avoid searching through the call graph, we only perform intra-procedural analysis. However, by summarizing the limitations of previous works, we face two main challenges in inferring causal relationship violations in commodity kernels.

C1: Contradiction Between Bugs in Specific Paths and Intra-function Path-Explosion. Since every path needs to satisfy causal relationships, we have to traverse each path in functions to learn causal relationships and detect violations. Also, there are indeed bugs in specific paths as our example (Sect. 2.1) and survey (Sect. 2.2) show, so keeping path information is necessary. Unfortunately, commodity kernels have severe intra-function path-explosion. According to our study (Sect. 2.1), there are about 3000 functions with more than 5000 internal execution paths (after unrolling loops) in Linux. Hence, without reducing the number of paths, it took us 25 min to consume all 32 GB memory and only analyze 0.27% of functions in Linux. For a static analysis tool, a large time cost caused by intra-function path-explosion will both delay tests of kernels and the evolution of the tool, while the tool needs to collect path information in functions. Moreover, as we do not know the causal patterns in the beginning, previous methods [10,12,13] that use known patterns to remove unrelated paths are not applicable. Thus, the contradiction is a crucial challenge for our work.

C2: Missing Contextual Constraints. Causal relationships often exist depending on contextual constraints such as failed checks. Therefore, tools need to be context-aware to identify such constraints, otherwise, we will obtain both false positives and false negatives because of imprecise learned rules. Unfortunately, few previous tools consider contextual constraints when inferring violations of causal relationships. APISan [29] considers one case of contextual constraints—the return value of the first function in a causal relationship, but it will miss other kinds of contextual constraints, like failures in a process.

In this paper, we develop THIRD-EYE, an effective and context-sensitive static analysis tool based on LLVM to detect violations of causal relationships in commodity kernels. We use two novel techniques to address the two challenges.

T1: Intersection-Based Call Sequence Building. To address the first challenge (**C1**), we utilize two observations. First, for a causal relationship `A()` and `B()`, if `A()` is called, then in all paths after `A()`'s call, `B()` should be called. Therefore, the intersection of callees in the paths after `A()`'s call should still contain `B()`. Hence, we can merge the paths to their **intersection** to mitigate intra-function path-explosion. However, paths with different execution results may need to satisfy different causal relationships so we cannot merge them directly. Hence, we use the second observation that paths with different execution results can be distinguished by the *exits* that they end with. For example, normal paths return zero while failed paths return error codes.

Based on the two observations, we develop the ***intersection-based*** *call graph building.* This method merges paths leading to the same exit to their intersection and preserves paths with different exits. It can both eliminate intra-function path-explosion and collect path information as much as possible. Also, this method of removing paths does not rely on known patterns.

T2: Context-Sensitive Statistical Analysis. Considering that causal relationships are usually implicit and context-related, we propose the *context-sensitive statistical analysis* to learn causal relationships and detect violations within kernels. Our algorithm extracts contextual constraints from conditional statements and attaches them to the learned causal relationships. Then, when detecting violations, we only apply the causal relationships when all attached contextual constraints are satisfied.

We use THIRD-EYE to statically analyze the Linux kernel 5.3. We find 60 bugs in total and 41 fixes have been accepted by Linux maintainers. It takes 34 min to analyze Linux 5.3, which is much faster than the 14 h cost by APISan [29]. Furthermore, we find 18 bugs under contextual constraints other than the return value of the first function in a causal relationship. These bugs will be missed by APISan [29]'s strategy of mining contextual constraints.

In short, our contributions are:

- We study intra-function path explosion in Linux and find the problem is severe. Moreover, we study the patterns of causal relationships' violations in kernels to show their major characteristics. (Sect. 2)
- We develop THIRD-EYE, a novel static analysis tool to infer violations of causal relationships in kernels. (Sect. 3)

```
//drivers/infiniband/core/cma.c
static int __init cma_init(void)
{
  int ret;

  cma_wq = alloc_ordered_workqueue(...);
  if (!cma_wq)
    return -ENOMEM;

  ret = register_pernet_subsys(...);
  if (ret) // registration fails
    goto err_wq; // not need to undo here
  ...
  register_netdevice_notifier(...);

  ret = ib_register_client(...);
  if (ret) // meet failures afterwards
    goto err;

  ret = cma_configfs_init();
  if (ret)
    goto err_ib;

  return 0;

  err_ib:
    ib_unregister_client(...);
  err:
    unregister_netdevice_notifier(...);
    ...
    // lack of unregister_pernet_subsys() here.
  err_wq:
    destroy_workqueue(cma_wq);
  return ret;
}
```

Listing 1.1. A detected example of violating a causal relationship.

- We design two new techniques to cope with the challenges in inferring violations of causal relationships. In particular, the intersection-based call sequence building algorithm allows detecting bugs in specific paths without severe intra-function path-explosion when collecting callees in paths. Context-sensitive statistical analysis can mine causal relationships with their contextual constraints and infer violations under certain contexts (Sect. 4).
- We detect 60 bugs in total. Of them, 41 fixes have been accepted by the Linux community. (Sect. 6)

2 Motivation

In this part, we motivate our work based on a typical bug example and a study on violations of causal relationships in the Linux kernel.

To simplify our illustration, we define several terminologies. We name two functions with a causal relationship *pair functions* while naming the function called earlier *pre-function*, the later one *post-function*.

2.1 An Example of Violating Causal Relationship

Listing 1.1 shows an example of violating a causal relationship in Linux 5.3 to illustrate our motivation. This bug is detected by our tool.

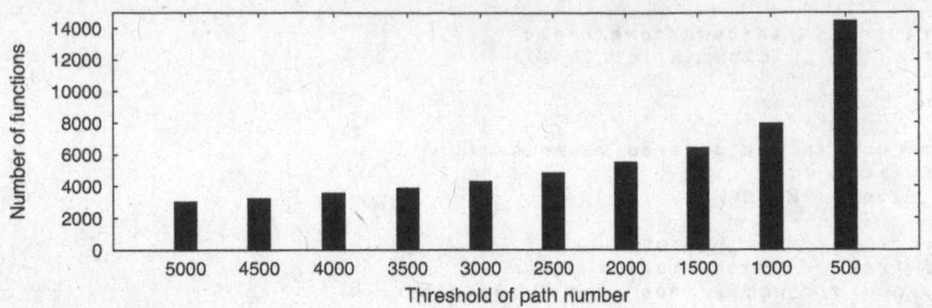

Fig. 1. Number of functions with path number beyond certain thresholds.

Here, `err` block (line 28) forgets to release the memory resource acquired by `register_pernet_subsys()` (line 10) with `unregister_pernet_subsys()` when `cma_init()` fails, which can lead to memory leak and DoS. The causal relationship between the two functions relies on two contextual constraints – a successful registration and a failure after it, like the failure of `ib_register_client()` (line 16). Therefore, if the registration fails or there is no failure after the successful registration, `cma_init()` does not need to release the resources.

This example illustrates two features of violations of causal relationships.

First, it shows that some bugs exist **in specific paths**. The bug in the example only exists in the paths which contain the `err` (line 28) block. Thus, we need to collect path information of all paths to detect the bug. Hence, the strategy of PR-Miner [16], which ignores path information, is insufficient.

Nonetheless, collecting path information has the problem of intra-function path-explosion. We **study the severity of intra-function path-explosion** in the Linux kernel by an LLVM pass. We use the DFS algorithm to traverse all paths after unrolling loops in Linux 5.3. To avoid too much time cost from path-explosion, we search until the branch depth reaches 14. As shown in Fig. 1, about 3000 functions have more than 5000 paths. As we count, the total number of intra-function paths is over 2 billion. Therefore, the severe issue of intra-function path-explosion makes tracing all paths infeasible.

Based on the result of this study and the pattern shown by the example, we confirm that the contradiction between intra-function path-explosion and bugs in specific paths indeed exists (***C1***).

Also, the example indicates that some bugs relate to **contextual constraints**. In the example, if we miss the contextual constraints of the violated causal relationship, we will regard the normal path (line 24) as a violation then get a false positive. Moreover, as the statistical method regards major patterns as causal relationships, without considering contextual constraints, we will confuse cases under different contexts. Then the causal relationships with certain contextual constraints may not reach the majority and therefore they are missed. As a result, we will get a false negative in the `err` block (line 28). Besides, this example has two constraints, so only considering the return value of the pre-function as a contextual constraint like APISan [29] is not sufficient.

2.2 Study of Violations in the Linux Kernel

To check whether the patterns shown in Sect. 2.1 are common in kernels and to further learn the patterns of causal relationships' violations, we collected the commits from Linux 4.19 to 5.4 and used keywords like "Merge" to filter unrelated commits, then we manually picked out the commits of fixing causal relationship violations. We found 92 commits in total.

60 violations (65.2%) exist only in specific paths. 57 violations (62%) only exist under certain contexts. Moreover, we find 54 bugs (58.7%) that both exist in specific paths and under certain contextual constraints.

Then we get two conclusions based on the major characteristics of the bugs. First, it is important to collect callee information in paths to detect bugs in specific paths, while intra-function path-explosion is severe (***C1***). Also, context-sensitive analysis is necessary for detecting context-related bugs (***C2***).

3 Overview

Figure 2 shows the structure of THIRD-EYE, which takes IR files of a kernel as its input, and analyzes the files through three phases: preparation, analysis, and post-processing. In the end, THIRD-EYE outputs bug reports.

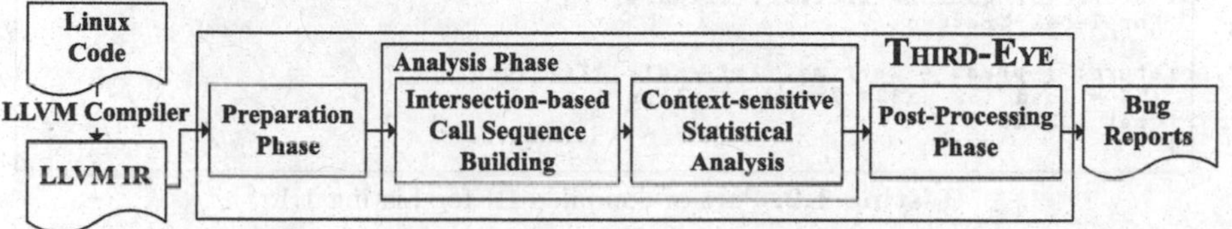

Fig. 2. The structure of THIRD-EYE. It has three phases: preparation phase, analysis phase, and post-processing phase. In the analysis phase, it has two key techniques: *intersection-based call sequence building* and *context-sensitive statistical analysis*.

We briefly introduce the three phases here. First, in the preparation phase, THIRD-EYE collects necessary information, e.g. targets of indirect calls, for later analysis. We will discuss the details in Sect. 5.

In the analysis phase, we use two key techniques to infer violations of causal relationships. We first leverage the *intersection-based call sequence building* to build call sequences. This algorithm merges paths with the same exit while keeping paths with different exits, which both eliminates intra-function path-explosion and records path information as much as possible. Then we perform the *context-sensitive statistical analysis* to infer causal rules with their contextual constraints and detect violations. We illustrate the key techniques in Sect. 4.

Last, in the post-processing phase, we filter the result to mitigate false positives and rank the bug reports. The details of this phase are shown in Sect. 5.

4 Key Techniques

4.1 Intersection-Based Call Sequence Building

Main Ideas. We observe that for pair functions `A()` and `B()`, if `A()` is called, then in all subsequent paths `B()` should be called. Therefore, if no violation exists, the intersection of all paths after `A()`'s call should still contain `B()`. Otherwise, at least one violation exists. Hence, we can **merge paths within a function to their intersection** to reduce the number of paths for mitigating intra-function path-explosion. Additionally, to record more information in paths, when one path is the other path's subset, we use the superset path as the result.

```
define internal i32 @cma_init() {
  ...
if.then: ; return -NOMEM;
  store i32 -12, i32* %retval, align 4
  br label %return
  ...
if.end13: ; return 0;
  store i32 0, i32* %retval, align 4
  br label %return
  ...
err_ib: ; err_ib
  ...
err: ; err
  ...
err_wq: ; err_wq, return ret;
  ...
  %5 = load i32 i32* ret, align 4
  store i32 %5 i32* %retval, align 4
  br label %return

return: ; preds = %err_wq, %if.end13, %if.then
  %6 = load i32, i32* %retval, align 4
  ret i32 %6
}
```

Listing 1.2. Part of compiled IR for Listing 1.1.

However, we cannot merge all paths within a function because different paths can have different execution results, so they need to obey different rules. For example, failed paths in functions usually call error handlers, while the normal paths do not. Thus, we will lose the error handlers if we merge the two kinds of paths together. If so, we cannot detect the causal relationships between failed functions and their error handlers like the example in Listing 1.1. To cope with this problem, we observe that exits of functions usually represent execution results. For example, normal paths can return zero while failed paths return error codes. Therefore, we can **merge paths with the same exit, while preserving paths with different exits**. By this, we can both eliminate intra-function path-explosion and keep path information as much as possible. Also, this method does not rely on known rules as it only utilizes a feature of causal relationships.

We implement this based on LLVM IR (intermediate representation). In IR, to reach the return block (the block with a return instruction) of a function, one of its predecessors must be reached first. We find that each predecessor usually corresponds to one exit of the function in the source code. Based on this observation, we merge paths that reach the same predecessor of the return block,

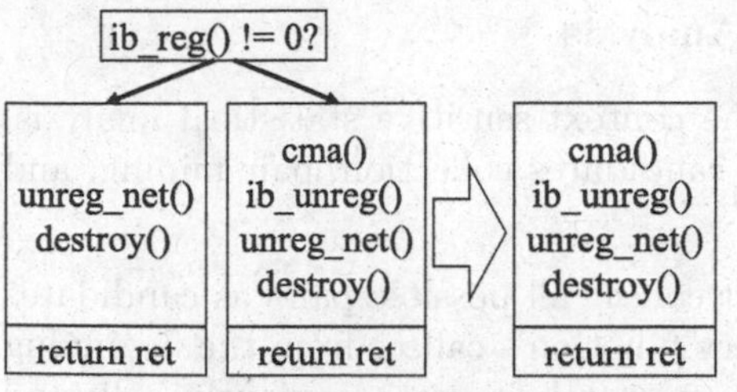

(a) Merging paths with the same exit.

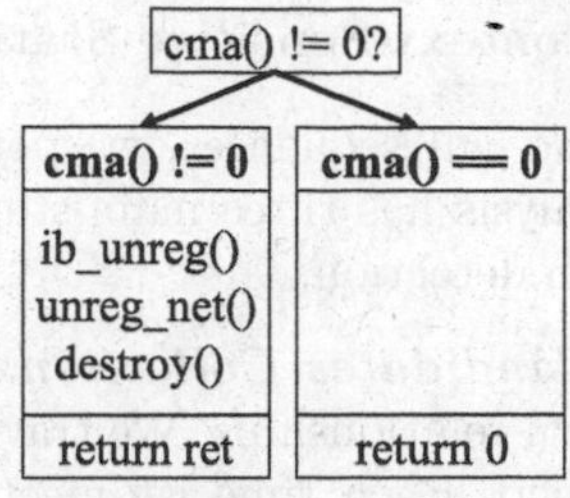

(b) Preserving paths with different exits.

Fig. 3. Part of the process of the intersection-based call sequence building on Listing 1.1. `ib_reg()` = `ib_register_client()`, `cma()` = `cma_configfs_init()`, `ib_unreg()` = `ib_unregister_client()`, `unreg_net()` = `unregister_netdevice_notifier()`, and `destroy()` = `destroy_workqueue()`.

while preserving paths that end with different predecessors. Listing 1.2 shows the compiled IR of Listing 1.1, here the three predecessors of the return block exactly correspond to the three exits in the source code.

Process. For a function, the algorithm firstly uses DFS from the head block to visit all basic blocks (after unrolling loops and it visits each block only once) and records callees of the blocks. Then it merges branches from the end block, appends the result to the predecessor blocks until the head block so that it gets a complete list of callees and contextual constraints of the function.

Figure 3 shows part of the process of intersection-based call sequence building for Listing 1.1. Due to the space limitation, we simplify the functions' names as the caption shows. In Listing 1.1, after `ib_register_client()` (line 16), two failed paths exist. One fails immediately after a failed check (line 18), and the other fails after `cma_configfs_init()`'s failure (line 22). Figure 3(a) shows the two paths. Since they have the same exit, the tool merges them together. Because one path is the other's subset, the result is the superset. In comparison, Fig. 3(b) shows the two paths after `cma_configfs_init()` (line 20), while one is a normal path and the other is a failed one. Since they have different exits, the tool preserves both. Also, for paths with different exits, the tool records their preconditions as contextual constraints.

In this process, we discard some branches which have no benefit for us, such as `BUG_ON()` failure which leads to panic. For a loop, we unroll it by first merging paths within the body of the loop, then appending the merged exit paths.

Furthermore, we collect function calls' arguments and return values during the process. We use the alias analysis provided by LLVM to check whether the values are aliases, if so (all results except `NoAlias`), we mark the values with the same ID. We also check whether two values are loaded from the same variable, if so, we also mark them with the same ID.

4.2 Context-Sensitive Statistical Analysis

With the call sequences, we perform the context-sensitive statistical analysis. The analysis has three main steps: pair candidates collection, pair mining, and violation detection.

Pair Candidates Collection. We first collect all possible pairs as candidates for causal relationships. We traverse every function's callees from the beginning to the end. Each time we meet a call, we match it with previously collected called functions to get function pairs. The matching has six rules:

- *RM1:* A function cannot match itself.
- *RM2:* A post-function cannot match one pre-function more than once.
- *RM3:* A pre-function cannot match one post-function more than once.
- *RM4:* A post-function prefers to match a nearer pre-function.
- *RM5:* The resulted pair includes all contextual states of the pre-function.
- *RM6:* The post-function should share arguments or return values with the pre-function.

RM1 is to prevent self-matched pairs. *RM2* and *RM3* are because multiple identical causal relationships cannot share pre-functions or post-functions. For example, one check function cannot check multiple return values. *RM4* is because pair functions usually obey a LIFO pattern (e.g. lock/unlock) or a post-function should be called as soon as a pre-function returns (e.g. checking a return value). *RM5* is to get all possible contextual constraints for the collected pairs. *RM6* is because functions with causal relationships usually share arguments or return values (e.g. use the same lock, check the pre-function's return value).

Each time we meet a contextual constraint, we append it to the visited functions' contextual states. The appending has three rules:

- *RA1:* The process keeps all existed states.
- *RA2:* If a new constraint is the same as the last one in the *opcode* and the *operand*, do not append it.
- *RA3:* If a new constraint's checked value is not returned by the pre-function, delete the *returned by which function* field.

We use *RA1* to get all possible contextual constraints of pre-functions. *RA2* is since the same constraints usually have the same meaning (e.g. *less than zero* usually represents error) and therefore they are duplicated. *RA3* is because the *returned by which function* field can be unnecessary if it is not the pre-function. For example, in Listing 1.1, the causal relationships do not care which function causes an error (denoted by a failed check), but only care whether there is a failure. However, if the checked value is returned by the pre-function, it may represent whether the pre-function succeeds, so it is necessary.

We use the path which has an error handler in Listing 1.1 to show the process, which is shown in Table 1. We simplify the path to make the illustration clearer. Also, due to the space limitation, we simplify the functions' names as the caption

Table 1. The simplified process of collecting pair candidates in Listing 1.1's error path. `alloc()` = `alloc_ordered_workqueue()`, `reg_per()` = `register_pernet_subsys()`, `cma()` = `cma_configfs_init()`, `destroy()` = `destroy_workqueue()`. Callees with the same argument ID have shared arguments or return values, otherwise have no shared argument nor return value.

#	Callee Info	Current State Func	Current State Context	Candidates Pair	Candidates Context
0	alloc(0) alloc() != 0 reg_per(1) cma(1) cma() != 0 destroy(0)	alloc(0) alloc(0)	∅ alloc() != 0		
1	alloc(0) alloc() != 0 reg_per(1) cma(1) cma() != 0 destroy(0)	alloc(0) alloc(0)	∅ alloc() != 0		
2	alloc(0) alloc() != 0 reg_per(1) cma(1) cma() != 0 destroy(0)	alloc(0) alloc(0) reg_per(1) reg_per(1) cma(1) cma(1)	∅ alloc() != 0 ∅ != 0 ∅ cma() != 0	reg_per(),cma()	∅
3	alloc(0) alloc() != 0 reg_per(1) cma(1) cma() != 0 destroy(0)	alloc(0) alloc(0) reg_per(1) reg_per(1) cma(1) cma(1)	∅ alloc() != 0 ∅ != 0 ∅ cma() != 0	reg_per(),cma() alloc(),destroy() alloc(),destroy()	∅ ∅ alloc() != 0

illustrates. Furthermore, we use numbered IDs to represent the arguments and return values. Calls that have the same ID share arguments or return values, otherwise no such sharing. Each row in the table represents a step in the analysis.

Each time we meet a function, we add it to visited functions (column **Func** of **Current State** in Table 1). Each time we meet a contextual constraint, we append it to visited functions' contextual states (column **Context** of **Current State** in Table 1) based on *RA1*–*RA3*.

In row #0, we append the contextual constraint to `alloc()`. Because of *RA1*, `alloc()` gets two states. In row #1, we match `reg_par()` with `alloc()`. However, `alloc()` does not share arguments or return value with it, so due to *RM6*, we get no candidate. In row #2, we have got one candidate. Besides, because of *RA3*, we delete the *returned by which function* field of `cma() != 0` for `reg_per()`. Also, considering *RA2*, since `cma() != 0` is the same as `alloc()`'s last condition (`alloc() != 0`) in opcode and operand, we do not append it. Although this seems wrong since the two conditions do not have the same semantics, we get fewer false negatives comparing to the strategy of appending the new constraint. We guess this is because the constraints after the pre-function's success are more critical for causal relationships, and the pre-functions' return values are not checked in many cases. In row #3, because of *RM6*, we can match `destroy()` with `alloc()`, so we get two candidates with different contextual constraints as *RM5*. Finally, we get three candidates from this path.

Pair Mining. We use a statistical method to determine whether a candidate pair has a causal relationship so that we do not need kernel-specific knowledge. The formula is shown as Formula (1). N_{pair} means the number of a pair's appearances. N_{pre} means the number of appearances of the pre-function in the pair. If Formula (1) is satisfied for a pair, it is regarded as a causal relationship.

$$\frac{N_{pair}}{N_{pre}} \geq threshold(N_{pre}) \tag{1}$$

A constant threshold is inappropriate for all pairs since for a frequently called function, the proportion of correct cases should be higher because normally, violations will not increase linearly with the total number. Therefore, the threshold should be higher for functions with more invocations. Hence, we use the Logistic Function to calculate the threshold as Formula (2).

$$threshold(x) = \frac{1}{1 + e^{-alog_2 x - b}} \tag{2}$$

a and b can be set to adjust the threshold. To get a and b, in practice, we first set two points in Formula 2, then calculate the parameters by solving binary linear equations. To set proper parameters, users can adjust the two points until getting ideal results. Section 6.4 shows this process for evaluation.

The Logistic Function is suitable since, first, it increases with the total number's increasing. Second, it increases slower when the total number is larger, as if the number of violations is invariable, the increasing of the matched pairs' ratio gets slower when the total number grows. We study the effect of different parameters and compare Formula (2) with constant thresholds in Sect. 6.4.

After mining pairs, we refine the constraints by removing them one by one from back to front. If after removing a constraint, the pair still exists, we delete the original one. Otherwise, if no simpler form of the pair exists, we keep it.

Violations Detection. To detect violations in paths, we match function pairs in each path with the mined causal relationships.

To begin with, we introduce the concept of ***mutual exclusion***. If the post-function of a pair cannot share multiple causal relationships simultaneously, this pair is mutually exclusive (ME), otherwise non-mutually exclusive (NME). For example, a check function cannot check multiple return values, so it cannot be shared. Hence, the causal relationships are mutually exclusive here. However, in a workflow which has several allocation and releasing functions, each releasing function can match several allocation functions, so the causal relationships are non-mutually exclusive. If we do not distinguish these two kinds of causal relationships, we will get false negatives or false positives. For example, if we regard return value checking as non-mutually exclusive, we will match one check with several functions, so if one function lacks checking, we will miss that.

We run two rounds for violations detection.

In the first round, we decide **whether each pair is mutually exclusive**. We firstly assume all pairs are mutually exclusive, then for each pair, we check whether the pair is satisfied in each path where it exists. If the pair can be

Table 2. The simplified process of detecting violations in Listing 1.1's error path. `alloc()` = `alloc_ordered_workqueue()`, `reg_per()` = `register_pernet_subsys()`, `cma()` = `cma_configfs_init()`, `destroy()` = `destroy_workqueue()`, `unreg_per()` = `unregister_pernet_subsys()`.

Rules					
Pair		**Context**		**Mutually Exclusive**	
alloc(),destroy()		alloc() != 0		Yes	
reg_per(),unreg_per()		!= 0		No	
#	**Callee Info**	**Current State: Func**	**Current State: Context**	**Matching Result: Pair**	**Matching Result: Context**
0	alloc() alloc() != 0 reg_per() cma() cma() != 0 destroy()	alloc() alloc()	Ø alloc() != 0		
1	alloc() alloc() != 0 reg_per() cma() cma() != 0 destroy()	alloc() alloc() reg_per()	Ø alloc() != 0 Ø		
2	alloc() alloc() != 0 reg_per() cma() cma() != 0 destroy()	alloc() alloc() reg_per() reg_per() cma() cma()	Ø alloc() != 0 Ø != 0 Ø cma() != 0	alloc(),destroy()	alloc() != 0
Violations					
Func			**Context**		
reg_per()			!= 0		

satisfied beyond a certain threshold of the paths, it will be identified as mutually exclusive, otherwise non-mutually exclusive. For simplicity, the threshold is also calculated by Formula (2) and the parameters are unchanged.

In the second round, we match pairs in each path and **detect unmatched pre-functions as violations**. We match pairs under six rules. *RM1* to *RM3* are the same as *RM2* to *RM4* in collecting candidates, so we do not list them here. Moreover, since when collecting candidates, we only consider pairs that share arguments or return values, we do not have mined pairs that do not have such matching. Therefore, we discard arguments and return values here.

- *RM4:* Matched mutually exclusive pairs stop matching.
- *RM5:* Mutually exclusive pairs cannot share post-functions.
- *RM6:* Only apply a causal relationship when the pre-function has a state which is the same as the contextual constraints.

Since mutually exclusive pairs cannot share post-functions with others, if a post-function has been matched to a mutually exclusive pair, it cannot be matched to other pre-functions, so the match will stop as *RM4*. If a post-function has been matched to a causal relationship, even if the pair is non-mutually exclusive, other mutually exclusive pairs cannot use this post-function, so we have *RM5*. To make the analysis context-sensitive, we only apply a rule if all its contextual constraints have been satisfied by a pre-function, so we have *RM6*.

Appending contextual constraints has the same rules as collecting candidates (*RA1* to *RA3*), so we do not list them here.

Table 2 illustrates the process of detecting violations with the same path in Table 1. The simplification of functions' names is shown in the caption. Each row represents a step in the process. We visit the callees in a path from beginning to end like collecting candidates.

In row #0, we meet `reg_per()` and two pre-functions exist, but no rule is applicable, so there is no result. In row #1, we meet `cma()`, but no rule is applicable, too. In row #2, we meet `destroy()`, and we can match it with `alloc()`. According to *RM6*, we demand the pre-function to satisfy the contextual constraints, and a suitable one exists, so we match `destroy()` with the `alloc()` which has the contextual constraint, `alloc() != 0`. Moreover, when finishing the match, we find that the `reg_per()` which has a contextual constraint `!= 0` is a pre-function in the mined rules, but it fails to match any post-function. Therefore, we record it as a violation.

5 Implementation

We implement THIRD-EYE as LLVM passes with clang 9.0. Since Sect. 4 has introduced the analysis phase, we now focus on the implementation details in the preparation phase and the post-processing phase.

5.1 Preparation Phase

To provide needed data for filters (Sect. 5.2), we collect field information of global variables and analyze targets of indirect calls. For global variable analysis, we collect global variables' fields which are function pointers, then record their indices and the functions which are assigned to the fields. For indirect call analysis, we adopt a simplified version of the two-layer type analysis proposed by CRIX [20] and finally output the targets of indirect calls.

5.2 Post-processing Phase

Customized Filters. After analysis, the tool generates initial inferred violations. A violation report consists of the unmatched pre-function, the missed post-function, and the function where the violation appears (we call it *bug place*). Since statistical analysis uses major patterns as rules and the analysis limits to intra-procedural, there are many non-violation reports. To prune these reports, users can implement *customized filters* to filter the result.

As Listing 1.3 shows, to write a new filter, users need to define a subclass of `Filter`, then implement the interface `filterViolation()`. The filter can utilize the methods and data provided by the analysis passes. We have implemented two filters as Table 3 shows. Both filters do not need kernel-specific knowledge since they only contain general program analysis or string analysis.

```
class Filter {
  public:
  virtual bool
  filterViolation(const VioCase* vio) const = 0;
  protected:
  CrossCheckingPass* pass;
}
```

Listing 1.3. Definitions of filter classes and interfaces.

Table 3. Implemented customized filters.

Filter	Description
LayerFilter	Look for the missed post-function in the callees of three directions: the bug place's Callees, the bug place's callers, and the bug place's callers' callees
MacroFilter	Filter the mined pairs which are caused by macros

Ranking. To help manual verification of bug reports, we rank all reported potential bugs in the result. A report with a lower ratio of bugs in the unmatched pre-function's appearances will rank higher. A lower ratio of bugs means the violated pattern appears more in all uses of the pre-function, so the confidence that the pattern is a real one is higher. Therefore, the confidence that the violations of the pattern are real also becomes higher.

6 Evaluation

We perform the evaluation on a machine with Intel i7-8700 CPU (3.2 GHz, 6 cores), 32 GB RAM, Ubuntu 20.10. The used LLVM version is LLVM 9.0. To evaluate the effectiveness and scalability of THIRD-EYE, we run it on Linux kernel 5.3.0 (configured with *allyesconfig* while debug options are unchecked).

As for the threshold, based on the result of Sect. 6.4, we use $a = 0.02948$ and $b = 1.6072$ (see Formula (2)) ($x = 20, threshold = 0.85$; $x = 1000, threshold = 0.87$). The threshold is used for evaluating mining pairs (Sect. 6.1) and **the final bug reports** (Sect. 6.2, Sect. 6.3, Sect. 6.5, Sect. 6.6).

6.1 Mine Pair Functions

One important stage of THIRD-EYE is to mine pair functions. Therefore, we evaluate our tool on the identified 59 pairs in the 92 studied commits (Sect. 2.2) to check whether it can mine these pairs.

We run our tool on Linux 5.3 and successfully find 16 pairs of the 59 identified ones. In the remaining 43 pairs, 4 are not in our compiled IR code. So we find $16/55 = 29.1\%$ pairs in the compiled kernel. The undetected 39 pairs' intra-procedural appearances are not often enough, so our statistical method cannot identify them. In comparison, APISan [29] detected 37 of 187 causal relationships (19.8%) in OpenSSL, which is comparable with us.

6.2 Detect Bugs

We have identified 60 bugs during our process of development. This does not represent all bugs in the reports since we only checked about 33% of the final reports due to time limitation. Besides the 9 ones that have been fixed or removed in the upstream, we reported 51 ones to the Linux community, and 41 of them have been confirmed. Furthermore, we have got 1 CVE assigned (CVE-2019-20810, severity is medium).

Features. In the bugs, 26 (43.3%) are in specific paths (so they cannot be detected by the path-insensitive tool, PR-Miner [16]) and 21 (35%) are context-related (18 ones have contextual constraints other than the return value of the pre-function, so they cannot be detected by APISan [29]), which proves the effectiveness of our design.

Security Impact. 19 (31.7%) bugs may lead to memory leaks due to missing freeing memory, 29 (48.3%) may cause a crash because of missing checks, and 7 (11.7%) bugs can cause DoS because of missing releasing resources, which shows their criticalness. The average time length of the bugs' existence is about 4.25 years and even 6 bugs have existed for more than 10 years.

6.3 False Positive and False Negative

We rank the final reports and select the top 300 bugs in the final report to measure false positives. It cost one researcher about 2 h to manually check the reports. We choose the top 300 reports because prior works like APISan [29] and PR-Miner [16] both use the top reports to evaluate, so only the top reports' data is comparable to theirs. The result is shown in Table 4.

Table 4. False positives in the top 300 ranked bug reports.

	Num	Ratio	Reason	Num (Ratio)
Bugs	21	7%	–	–
Specifications	166	55.3%	Inter-procedure	53 (31.9%)
			Alternative pattern	49 (29.5%)
			Missed context	42 (25.3%)
			Mutual exclusion	5 (3%)
			Others	17 (10.2%)
False positives	113	37.7%	Statistical method	113 (100%)
Total	300	100%	–	–

Although filters have pruned a lot of non-violation reports, such reports still exist. However, the result is acceptable as comparing with previous tools. Since we do not have PR-Miner [16]'s source code and we fail to run APISan [29] on Linux 5.3 due to compatibility problems, we use the data in their papers here. PR-Miner [16] has 44 non-violation reports in top 60 (73.3%), and it only mines pairs which appear more than 15 times, while we do not have such a limitation. Also, it cannot detect context-related bugs and bugs in specific paths. APISan [29] has 391 non-violation reports in the top 445 (87.9%). Although this data is from detecting missing-check bugs, as all bugs are found by the same method, we think the result of causal relationship violations is similar to this value. Therefore, considering our method is more general and it can find more complex bugs, we think that our result is comparable with previous tools.

Although non-violation reports cannot directly lead to bug fixes, as suggested by PR-Miner [16], some of them are still meaningful because they reflect the right causal patterns and then they can be used as specifications for the development of other tools, such as filters for our tool and automatic checkers. Because of the benefits of these reports, we separate them from meaningless false positives as PR-Miner [16] does. We use *specifications* in Table 4 to represent them.

Table 4 lists the reasons for non-violations reports. *Inter-procedure* means that the post-function exists outsides the pre-function's caller and our filter's search depth is insufficient. *Alternative pattern* means that the post-function is replaced by another function with a similar functionality. *Missed context* means that the post-function is only called under certain context but we do not detect it. This is mainly due to the refinement of contextual constraints. *Mutual exclusion* means that we incorrectly regard some causal relationships as mutually exclusive, so they prevent other pre-functions to match, which leads to non-violation reports. *Others* include minor reasons like assert functions that break paths, continue statements that break loops, etc. *Statistical method* means that these cases have no specific reason to be mined besides their frequent appearances.

Moreover, we randomly selected 200 reports from all ones (12859 in total) and checked them, while 167 (83.5%) are false positives and 1 bug (0.5%) exists, which reflects the whole situation and shows the efficiency of ranking.

False Negatives. Some false negatives can be caused by not mined pairs as Sect. 6.1 shows. Furthermore, in the bugs found in our development, some of them are missed in the final bug report due to the thresholds or some techs of our tool. We count these cases and analyze the causes of them.

8 bugs in the found 60 (13.3%) are missed in the final report. The high threshold leads to 7 of them. Merged post-function makes the pair missed and then causes 1 false negative. This post-function relates to debugging and we discard it since paths with the same exit can have different debugging functions, while this method may break subset relations and lead to the lost of callees.

6.4 Result Variation

The values of parameters in Formula (2) affect pair mining largely, so we test the results with different a and b, then see their variation. To make the results more intuitive, we set two points of Formula (2), calculate a and b, then test the results. The two points are $(x_1 = 20, y_1)$ and $(x_2 = 1000, y_2)$. With different y_1

and y_2, we use the total number of bug reports, the number of false positives, and the number of false negatives in the found 60 bugs to evaluate the efficiency. Since the bug reports are too many, we randomly select 200 reports to evaluate false positives and false negatives. Figure 4 shows the results.

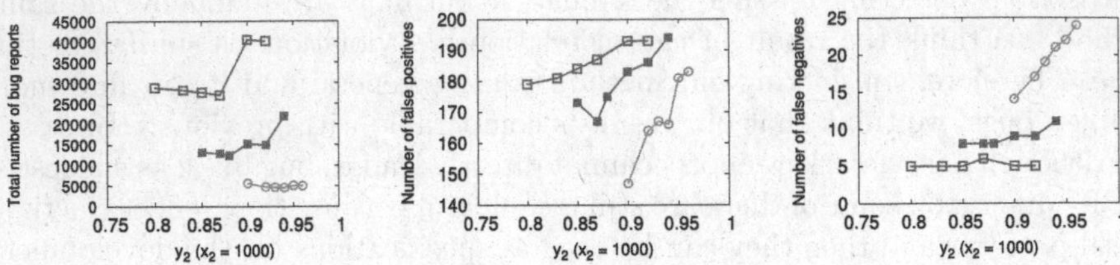

(a) Total number of bug reports. **(b)** Number of false positives. **(c)** Number of false negatives

Fig. 4. Result variation with different thresholds.

We have two findings. First, by comparing different lines, when the threshold is higher, the total number and the false positives are less while the false negatives become more. Furthermore, by comparing points in each line, the difference between y_1 and y_2 significantly affects the results. When the difference is larger, the threshold of x which is smaller than 20 becomes lower. Therefore, the tool mines more minor pairs and leads to more bug reports and false positives. As for the false negatives, it increases as the threshold gets higher.

Furthermore, we compare all points and find the threshold under (20,0.85) and (1000, 0.87) has relatively fewer bug reports and false positives/negatives, so we use it for the final report. Also, we compare this threshold with constant thresholds including 0.8, 0.85, and 0.9 (by setting y_1 and y_2 the same value). As the figures show, 0.8 and 0.85 have more reports and false positives, while 0.9 has too many false negatives, so the Logistic Function is better.

6.5 Sensitivity Analysis

Intersection-Based Call Sequence Building. We write a pass to build call sequences for all functions while it does not merge paths into their intersections. After 25 min, the pass only analyzed 1,126 functions and it has consumed all memory (32 GB), so it was blocked. In comparison, the original pass only needs 13 m 30 s to analyze 422,318 functions and it only uses 8.6 GB of memory. Hence, the intersection-based call sequence building can both save space and time.

Context-Sensitive Statistical Analysis. To show the importance of context-sensitive analysis, we remove all contextual constraints in the call sequences, then do the statistical analysis. The context-insensitive analysis misses 25 bugs in the found 60 ones, which is worse than the context-sensitive version (8 ones in the final report). Therefore, context-sensitive analysis is necessary.

Also, we test without checking mutual exclusion. When regarding all pairs as mutually exclusive, the tool has 176,902 reports before filtering, while the final report only has 27,106 without filters, so there should be too many false positives. When regarding all pairs as non-mutually exclusive, the result has 2 more false negatives. Hence, distinguishing mutual exclusion is meaningful.

Filters. Without filters, there are 18,158 bug reports after merging the same ones (12,859 with filters), and only 14 bugs exist in the top 300 (21 with filters), so filters are useful.

6.6 Performance

The tool uses eight threads for mining pairs, checking violations, and filtering, while a single thread for other works. The total time cost is 34m34s and it is acceptable considering the size of the Linux kernel.

Besides, the analysis costs 7.5 GB RAM for statistical analysis for call sequences (6 million lines) and collected candidates (3 million). The cost is due to using complicated map data structures to accelerate the process.

In comparison, PR-Miner [16] runs on Linux 2.6.11 (3 million LoC). It costs 1 m 26 s and 441 MB for detecting violations without recording path information. However, we work on Linux 5.3 (18 million LoC counted by *cloc*) and detect violations on paths with different exits, which has more workload. APISan [29] runs on Linux 4.5-rc4 (11 million LoC counted by *cloc*). It costs 14 h and generates a 300 GB database for detection with a 32-core CPU and 256 GB RAM, which is worse than us.

7 Discussion and Related Work

Limitation Discussion. We have four limitations: (1) merging branches will lead to the loss of callees, which can cause false negatives; (2) the lack of inter-procedural analysis will miss causal relationships and fail to filter non-violation reports; (3) the high non-violation report rate; and (4) the lack of dynamic verification of the detected bugs. We will address them in our future work.

Violations of Causal Relationships Detection. Without the knowledge of rules, previous works use various methods to mine rules and detect violations. Static analysis [4,11,16,18,19,23,26], including symbolic execution [29] is widely used, while they fail to cope with the two main challenges.

Dynamic methods analyze runtime traces to get rules [7,8,28]. However, dynamic methods meet difficulties in code coverage and hardware requirements (like drivers), while static methods can cover most subsystems in kernels.

Some tools use known rules to check violations [3,10,13,14], while we use a statistical method to mine implicit rules, so we do not need specific knowledge.

Bug Detection in Kernels. Various projects aim to detect bugs in kernels. Methods, like static analysis [5,6,11,13–17,19,21,22,25], dynamic analysis [3,4,7,8,18,28], fuzzing [9,24] and symbolic execution [27,29] are involved.

CRIX [20] develops the two-layer type analysis to find targets of indirect calls, which we adopt in our tool. Also, it uses the types of opcode and operand to represent conditional statements, which inspires us in mining contextual constraints. Dr. Checker [21] performs a soundy general bug finding in Linux kernel drivers with pointer and taint analysis, but it will miss improper API usage bugs like violations of causal relationships. K-Miner [12] uses partitioning to analyze only a part of the kernel to avoid path-explosion, while we need to analyze the whole kernel and we do not have known rules, so the method is not applicable.

8 Conclusion

This paper presents THIRD-EYE, a novel, practical, and context-sensitive static analysis tool to detect causal relationship violations (41 fixes accepted) in commodity kernels. The tool utilizes the intersection-based call sequence building to deal with the contradiction between bugs in specific paths and intra-function path-explosion, performs context-sensitive statistical analysis to mine pairs with contextual constraints, and successfully detects context-related violations.

Acknowledgment. We thank the anonymous reviewers for their insightful comments. This work is supported by the National Natural Science Foundation of China (No. 61925206).

References

1. Code of include/linux/workqueue.h in linux 5.3. https://git.kernel.org/pub/scm/linux/kernel/git/torvalds/linux.git/tree/include/linux/workqueue.h?h=v5.3
2. Code of kernel/workqueue.c in linux 5.3. https://git.kernel.org/pub/scm/linux/kernel/git/torvalds/linux.git/tree/kernel/workqueue.c?h=v5.3
3. Bai, J., Liu, H., Wang, Y., Hu, S.: Runtime checking for paired functions in device drivers. In: 2014 21st Asia-Pacific Software Engineering Conference, vol. 1, pp. 407–414, December 2014. https://doi.org/10.1109/APSEC.2014.66
4. Bai, J., Wang, Y., Liu, H., Hu, S.: Automated resource release in device drivers. In: 2015 IEEE 26th International Symposium on Software Reliability Engineering (ISSRE), pp. 172–182, November 2015. https://doi.org/10.1109/ISSRE.2015.7381811
5. Bai, J.J., Lawall, J., Tan, W., Hu, S.M.: DCNS: automated detection of conservative non-sleep defects in the Linux kernel. In: Proceedings of the Twenty-Fourth International Conference on Architectural Support for Programming Languages and Operating Systems, ASPLOS 2019, New York, NY, USA, pp. 287–299. ACM (2019). https://doi.org/10.1145/3297858.3304065. http://doi.acm.org/10.1145/3297858.3304065
6. Bai, J.J., Wang, Y.P., Lawall, J., Hu, S.M.: DSAC: Effective static analysis of sleep-in-atomic-context bugs in kernel modules. In: 2018 USENIX Annual Technical Conference (USENIX ATC 2018), Boston, MA, pp. 587–600. USENIX Association, July 2018. https://www.usenix.org/conference/atc18/presentation/bai
7. Bai, J.J., Wang, Y.P., Liu, H.Q., Hu, S.M.: Mining and checking paired functions in device drivers using characteristic fault injection. Inf. Softw. Technol. **73**, 122–133 (2016)

8. Bai, J.J., Wang, Y.P., Yin, J., Hu, S.M.: Testing error handling code in device drivers using characteristic fault injection. In: 2016 USENIX Annual Technical Conference (USENIX ATC 2016), Denver, CO, pp. 635–647. USENIX Association, June 2016. https://www.usenix.org/conference/atc16/technical-sessions/presentation/bai
9. Corina, J., et al.: Difuze: interface aware fuzzing for kernel drivers. In: Proceedings of the 2017 ACM SIGSAC Conference on Computer and Communications Security, CCS 2017, New York, NY, USA, pp. 2123–2138. ACM (2017). https://doi.org/10.1145/3133956.3134069. http://doi.acm.org/10.1145/3133956.3134069
10. Cui, H., Hu, G., Wu, J., Yang, J.: Verifying systems rules using rule-directed symbolic execution. In: Proceedings of the Eighteenth International Conference on Architectural Support for Programming Languages and Operating Systems, ASPLOS 2013, New York, NY, USA, pp. 329–342. ACM (2013). https://doi.org/10.1145/2451116.2451152. http://doi.acm.org/10.1145/2451116.2451152
11. Engler, D., Chen, D.Y., Hallem, S., Chou, A., Chelf, B.: Bugs as deviant behavior: a general approach to inferring errors in systems code. In: Proceedings of the Eighteenth ACM Symposium on Operating Systems Principles, SOSP 2001, New York, NY, USA, pp. 57–72. ACM (2001). https://doi.org/10.1145/502034.502041. http://doi.acm.org/10.1145/502034.502041
12. Gens, D., Schmitt, S., Davi, L., Sadeghi, A.R.: K-miner: Uncovering memory corruption in Linux. In: NDSS (2018)
13. Gu, Z., Wu, J., Li, C., Zhou, M., Jiang, Y., Gu, M., Sun, J.: Vetting API usages in c programs with imchecker. In: 2019 IEEE/ACM 41st International Conference on Software Engineering: Companion Proceedings (ICSE-Companion), pp. 91–94, May 2019. https://doi.org/10.1109/ICSE-Companion.2019.00046
14. Lawall, J.L., Brunel, J., Palix, N., Hansen, R.R., Stuart, H., Muller, G.: Wysiwib: a declarative approach to finding API protocols and bugs in linux code. In: 2009 IEEE/IFIP International Conference on Dependable Systems Networks, pp. 43–52, June 2009. https://doi.org/10.1109/DSN.2009.5270354
15. Lawall, J.L., Muller, G., Palix, N.: Enforcing the use of API functions in linux code. In: Proceedings of the 8th Workshop on Aspects, Components, and Patterns for Infrastructure Software, ACP4IS 2009, New York, NY, USA, pp. 7–12. ACM (2009). https://doi.org/10.1145/1509276.1509279. http://doi.acm.org/10.1145/1509276.1509279
16. Li, Z., Zhou, Y.: PR-Miner: automatically extracting implicit programming rules and detecting violations in large software code. In: Proceedings of the 10th European Software Engineering Conference Held Jointly with 13th ACM SIGSOFT International Symposium on Foundations of Software Engineering, ESEC/FSE-13, New York, NY, USA, pp. 306–315. ACM (2005). https://doi.org/10.1145/1081706.1081755. http://doi.acm.org/10.1145/1081706.1081755
17. Liu, H., Bai, J., Wang, Y., Bian, Z., Hu, S.: PairMiner: mining for paired functions in kernel extensions. In: 2015 IEEE International Symposium on Performance Analysis of Systems and Software (ISPASS), pp. 93–101, March 2015. https://doi.org/10.1109/ISPASS.2015.7095788
18. Liu, H., Bai, J., Wang, Y., Hu, S.: BP-Miner: mining paired functions from the binary code of drivers for error handling. In: 2014 21st Asia-Pacific Software Engineering Conference, vol. 1, pp. 415–422, December 2014. https://doi.org/10.1109/APSEC.2014.67

19. Liu, H., Wang, Y., Jiang, L., Hu, S.: PF-Miner: a new paired functions mining method for android kernel in error paths. In: 2014 IEEE 38th Annual Computer Software and Applications Conference, pp. 33–42, July 2014. https://doi.org/10.1109/COMPSAC.2014.10
20. Lu, K., Pakki, A., Wu, Q.: Detecting missing-check bugs via semantic- and context-aware criticalness and constraints inferences. In: 28th USENIX Security Symposium (USENIX Security 2019), Santa Clara, CA, pp. 1769–1786. USENIX Association, August 2019. https://www.usenix.org/conference/usenixsecurity19/presentation/lu
21. Machiry, A., Spensky, C., Corina, J., Stephens, N., Kruegel, C., Vigna, G.: Dr. checker: a soundy analysis for linux kernel drivers. In: Proceedings of the 26th USENIX Conference on Security Symposium, SEC 2017, Berkeley, CA, USA, pp. 1007–1024. USENIX Association (2017). http://dl.acm.org/citation.cfm?id=3241189.3241268
22. Min, C., Kashyap, S., Lee, B., Song, C., Kim, T.: Cross-checking semantic correctness: the case of finding file system bugs. In: Proceedings of the 25th Symposium on Operating Systems Principles, SOSP 2015, New York, NY, USA, pp. 361–377. ACM (2015). https://doi.org/10.1145/2815400.2815422. http://doi.acm.org/10.1145/2815400.2815422
23. Monperrus, M., Mezini, M.: Detecting missing method calls as violations of the majority rule. ACM Trans. Softw. Eng. Methodol. **22**(1), 7:1–7:25 (2013). https://doi.org/10.1145/2430536.2430541. http://doi.acm.org/10.1145/2430536.2430541
24. Schumilo, S., Aschermann, C., Gawlik, R., Schinzel, S., Holz, T.: KAFL: hardware-assisted feedback fuzzing for OS kernels. In: Proceedings of the 26th USENIX Conference on Security Symposium, SEC 2017, Berkeley, CA, USA, pp. 167–182. USENIX Association (2017). http://dl.acm.org/citation.cfm?id=3241189.3241204
25. Wang, W., Lu, K., Yew, P.C.: Check it again: detecting lacking-recheck bugs in OS kernels. In: Proceedings of the 2018 ACM SIGSAC Conference on Computer and Communications Security, CCS 2018, New York, NY, USA, pp. 1899–1913. ACM (2018). https://doi.org/10.1145/3243734.3243844. http://doi.acm.org/10.1145/3243734.3243844
26. Wu, Q., Liang, G., Wang, Q., Xie, T., Mei, H.: Iterative mining of resource-releasing specifications. In: Proceedings of the 2011 26th IEEE/ACM International Conference on Automated Software Engineering, ASE 2011, Washington, DC, USA, pp. 233–242. IEEE Computer Society (2011). https://doi.org/10.1109/ASE.2011.6100058
27. Xu, M., Qian, C., Lu, K., Backes, M., Kim, T.: Precise and scalable detection of double-fetch bugs in OS kernels. In: 2018 IEEE Symposium on Security and Privacy (SP), pp. 661–678, May 2018. https://doi.org/10.1109/SP.2018.00017
28. Yang, J., Evans, D., Bhardwaj, D., Bhat, T., Das, M.: Perracotta: mining temporal API rules from imperfect traces. In: Proceedings of the 28th International Conference on Software Engineering, ICSE 2006, New York, NY, USA, pp. 282–291. ACM (2006). https://doi.org/10.1145/1134285.1134325. http://doi.acm.org/10.1145/1134285.1134325
29. Yun, I., Min, C., Si, X., Jang, Y., Kim, T., Naik, M.: APISan: sanitizing API usages through semantic cross-checking. In: Proceedings of the 25th USENIX Conference on Security Symposium, SEC 2016, Berkeley, CA, USA, pp. 363–378. USENIX Association (2016). http://dl.acm.org/citation.cfm?id=3241094.3241123

Find My Sloths: Automated Comparative Analysis of How Real Enterprise Computers Keep Up with the Software Update Races

Omid Setayeshfar[1], Junghwan "John" Rhee[2(✉)], Chung Hwan Kim[3], and Kyu Hyung Lee[1]

[1] University of Georgia, Athens, GA 30605, USA
{omid.s,kyuhlee}@uga.edu
[2] University of Central Oklahoma, Edmond, OK 73034, USA
jrhee2@uco.edu
[3] University of Texas at Dallas, Richardson, TX 75080, USA
chungkim@utdallas.edu

Abstract. A software update is a critical but complicated part of software security. Its delay poses risks due to vulnerabilities and defects of software. Despite the high demand to shorten the update lag and keep the software up-to-date, software updates involve factors such as human behavior, program configurations, and system policies, adding variety in the updates of software. Investigating these factors in a real environment poses significant challenges such as the knowledge of software release schedules from the software vendors and the deployment times of programs in each user's machine. Obtaining software release plans requires information from vendors which is not typically available to public. On the users' side, tracking each software's exact update installation is required to determine the accurate update delay. Currently, a scalable and systematic approach is missing to analyze these two sides' views of a comprehensive set of software. We performed a long term system-wide study of update behavior for all software running in an enterprise by translating the operating system logs from enterprise machines into graphs of binary executable updates showing their complex, and individualized updates in the environment. Our comparative analysis locates risky machines and software with belated or dormant updates falling behind others within an enterprise without relying on any third-party or domain knowledge, providing new observations and opportunities for improvement of software updates. Our evaluation analyzes real data from 113,675 unique programs used by 774 computers over 3 years.

1 Introduction

Updating software in general and applying software patches in a more specific sense is a very crucial part of maintaining an ecosystem of computers safe [6]; although regular updates alone do not guarantee complete safety, falling behind

L. Bilge et al. (Eds.): DIMVA 2021, LNCS 12756, pp. 215–236, 2021.
https://doi.org/10.1007/978-3-030-80825-9_11

for sure poses security risks [46]. Research has shown a security patch might take months to create once a vulnerability is found; it even can come after the public disclosure of the vulnerability [25], and even after the vulnerability is publicly disclosed, many users may still use older versions. These delays open the chance for attackers to exploit those vulnerabilities; For large enterprises, such risks may lead to a significant financial loss, and a negative impact on their reputation [43].

In the recent Equifax breach case, the personal information of 143 million Americans were stolen [7], and the attacker exploited a known vulnerability, whose patch was available a few months before the incident. It could have been prevented if the software was updated in time. Another study [45] shows that more than 99% of exploited vulnerabilities were used by attackers more than one year after the vulnerabilities were publicly disclosed (e.g., CVE [15]). The WannaCry ransomware also shows how missed or delayed security updates can affect enterprises, as well as individuals [6].

Having all the users keep all the programs on their computer up to date at all times is ideal, but as shown in our probe as well as [18,25], we are very far from it in the real world; even in cases where an update is installed with minimal user involvement [18]. Numerous attempts have been made to quantify how up to date a computer is, mainly by focusing on a small set of programs [49].

The software update is a complicated process that involves multiple parties and decision factors to occur such as the availability of the machine or the connection to deliver the software update (e.g., a computer isolated with an air-gap is not updated), the system-wide policy to control update behavior in an enterprise, and each machine's or software's configuration (e.g., a user can stop updater due to its annoyance of notifications). We summarize the currently unsolved challenges to understand this problem as follows.

(1) First, understanding when each software's update is created and released is important by setting the reference on the sender's side to determine how long the update takes or it has been delayed in each client machine (i.e., on the receiver's side). This is a real challenge due to the lack of standard channels. Several prior works [20,27,48] utilized this information by a connection to certain software companies [18,20]. Other works used a third party vendor, which attempts to collect this information using binaries' properties. This method typically relies on the user (or software vendors) submission of the binary executable, and thus it might not provide such information for less popular or homebrew software. Our study of a large group of 774 machines shows that only 14.2% of installed software information is available on National Software Reference Library (NSRL) [4] and 75.3% on VirusTotal [47]. There is no systematic way to obtain this information for a comprehensive set of software for general usage.
(2) Second, knowing exactly when the released software has landed in a machine is a piece of crucial information to evaluate the update process of a program in each machine. Software vendors (e.g., Google) may estimate the deployment statistics if they use update management software that reports the installation timestamps or by the usage of the software (e.g., Google Chrome) *if*

it uses network and reports its version on usage. However, many programs do not have such mechanisms implemented to evaluate the update processes. They may not use dedicated update management software relying on users to download and execute the installation package program manually. Also, programs may not use the network or do not use telemetry functions. Given numerous software programs being used in an enterprise, we observe many programs in the shadow without automated well-designed update management. Their updates solely depend on each user's alertness or the enterprise administration to initiate checks and updates. A systematic method to track the update occurrences for a comprehensive list (ideally *all*) of software is highly desired but missing.

(3) After all, there is no standard on how each software should be updated. Therefore, software vendors perform updates with their own ways and own schedules as we show in Sect. 3.2. Also, there are multiple reasons why software is incapable of updating features; legacy software (designed without updates), the programs made by a limited resource (e.g., small vendors or indie software), and the terminated or outdated programs support. All these symptoms illustrate the demand for a systematic study on how our current software is doing with updates and guidelines suggested regarding how each software should be managed and how an update management software should be designed.

In this work, we attempt to fill these gaps by creating a systematic approach to measure the update behavior of a comprehensive set of programs from all machines in an enterprise starting with individual records and summing up to show the overall patterns. This work solves the aforementioned challenges by automatically estimating (1) the release time of software and (2) the landing time of the software with a fine granularity of individual programs and individual machines in an enterprise. From these data, we could estimate how much behind the latest version each software in each machine is *without* relying on domain knowledge of developers' channels or third-party information specialized with software analysis. We take (3) multiple observations out of the real data from a real enterprise environment and provide suggestions on what would be desired properties of an update management software. Also, we deep dive on the **sloths**, that we refer to the individual software and machine behind their peers in the progress of updates inside the enterprise environment. We attempt to measure their risk in terms of the *delay* based on our inferred software versions that are available for *all* programs in our observation.

To achieve these goals, we develop FMS[1], a tool that autonomously analyzes update patterns from the collected data, detects outdated programs and machines, and produces timely notifications to administrators. Our evaluations show FMS can infer version orders with 85% accuracy. Using FMS, we have identified more than 14,690 outdated programs from 774 computers and 2,705 more programs engaged in risky behaviors.

[1] FMS is an acronym of **F**ind **M**y **S**loths, which refer to enterprise applications showing undesirable delayed update behavior.

We make the following unique contributions in the analysis of software update behaviors in a real enterprise environment.

- Systematic study of software update behavior based on real-world enterprise data; Covering a total of 113,675 programs in multiple platforms observed in an enterprise with 248 people. This result brings new observations of real-world factors in software updates.
- We propose a method to estimate software release time and update delay with only data collected inside the enterprise, without relying on software vendors' release notes or 3rd party (e.g., VirusTotal, NSRL). We enable the estimation of these information for all observed software to determine the update delay of all programs. We found the first appearance of software in a fairly large group of 774 machines can approximate software release time. We present the closeness of these two data in Sect. 3.3.
- Our approach estimates the update delay of an individual binary executable by subtracting the release time from the landing time of software update being tracked 24/7. This needs to be done individually for each software in each machine so that we can determine the delay of individual instances of software updates. It is enabled by tracking operating system (OS) events (e.g., system calls, Windows API) that access and execute each binary executable in all machines. This data enables a drill-down approach to determine the sloth in multiple layers: starting from the machine with a large update delay, we can nail down the identification of the slowest software in that machine with our fine grained individualized monitoring.

2 Observations on Enterprise Software Deployment

This research collects binary executable update records from 774 PCs and servers in an enterprise with 248 employees. This section summarizes observations from the data we collected over three years between Feb. 2017 and Feb. 2020.

Observation 1: (Complexity of Update Transitions) Software update state transitions are more complex at the client sides than the developers' views. N versions of program binary distributions can cause up to N^2 possible transitions depending on the availability and activation of updates.
Implications: Even though developers release a linear sequence of binaries, *extra* non-linear transitions appear in the software update graph that defy the versioning sequences of development due to diverse situations at the client side.

After a particular version of the software is installed, the next installed version varies depending on various factors such as the updater configuration of a particular machine, the machine's availability, connectivity, and the enterprise's policy. When there is a gap between the installed version and the new version to be installed, some software allow a direct transition of a version to another version (e.g., 1.0 to 3.0) while some other software go through the applications of all intermediate versions (e.g., 1.0–2.0–3.0). We have analyzed these behaviors of software in our observation in Sect. 4.

Observation 2: (Unusual Update Transitions) Rollbacks or regressions are not uncommon.
Implications: *Counter-intuitive* transitions such as rolling back to older versions may occur in multiple software and machines due to various situations at the client side like compatibility and functionalities.

We have observed multiple software from major vendors such as Adobe Flash and Mozilla Firefox frequently show unusual transitions. We have analyzed this observation of counter-intuitive transitions in Sect. 4.

Observation 3: (Various Update Deployment Time) Updates released get installed at clients after various delays from less than 10 minutes to several years.
Implications: In software updates, clients' roles are as important as the developers' release schedule because their configuration and choices decide *whether and when* updates get installed.

We have performed fine-grained analysis on these software delays running in an enterprise, individually measuring the delay of an individual software program in each machine. This result is presented in Sect. 4.

Observation 4: (Various Support Period of Software Update) Depending on products and vendors, we observe that the updates could be provided from no update in years to 1441 updates in three years. On average, we observe 6.4 updates for each product in our environment.
Implications: Users should be aware of the risk of end-of-support software.

We have analyzed this observation in Sect. 4. Software gets updates from developers, but its degree highly varies depending on the vendor and products. Large software vendors tend to have more extended support (presumably due to their resources). Adobe Acrobat and Microsoft Office 2010 have been supported for 11 and 9.5 years so far, respectively. Software without support poses a serious risk as vulnerabilities are discovered over time.

Observation 5: (A Long Term Software Usage) Some software gets used for a long time. Multiple programs are used as an outdated version even after when the update support is no longer provided.
Implications: Like any commodity, the software is used as far as it can perform its function. However, unlike hardware commodity, software gets vulnerabilities and becomes riskier to operate over time. Combined with the fourth observation, the software usage after the terminated support poses a high risk.

We have analyzed this usage period of software in Sects. 4 and 6.1.

3 Design of Find My Sloths

In this section, we present FMS's design, which automatically tracks and analyzes software update patterns in a real enterprise environment. FMS is composed of three main components: (1) Automated tracking of software binary information, (2) Software update inference, and (3) Software risk analysis.

3.1 Automated Tracking of Software Binary Information

Package management systems provide automated installation, upgrade, configuration, and removal of computer programs. There exist various package management systems such as Linux Advanced Package Tool [1], RPM Package Manager [38], zypper [42], portage [19], yum [8], pacman [44], Home Brew [2], MacOS App Store [12], and Microsoft Store [32], that can possibly eliminate the user's effort towards manual installs and updates.

However, prior study shows the limitations of update managers [27]. Although convenient to use, they do not provide full coverage of programs used on an everyday machine, nor do they guarantee the timely installation of updates, mainly due to inconveniences caused for the user during and after the update process. In addition, there exist software types that package managers cannot support, such as direct drop-in of a binary without an installer, custom installers that do not work with package managers, programs' self-updates, downloads of related binaries or libraries, and local compilation of programs.

In this work, we do not aim to provide yet another automated updated system, but we develop an automated and unified method to monitor software updates by leveraging OS event monitoring techniques. OS event monitoring techniques have been widely used for security analysis [9,24] or software execution diagnosis (e.g., fault diagnosis, debugging, root cause analysis) [11,16]. Our monitoring agents utilize the OS event monitoring systems, which are currently available in mainstream operating systems. In Microsoft Windows systems, we use Event Tracing for Windows (ETW) [29]. We use the Auditd system [3] for Linux operating systems. Specifically, we monitor the events regarding process execution and file modification to binary executables (e.g., executable and library files). The following table summarizes the events that we use.

Platform	Operating system events
Windows (ETW)	*WinExec, WriteFile, WriteFileEx, WriteFileGather*
Linux (Audit)	*execve, write, writev, pwrite, pwritev, pwrite64*

We install the OS event tracking system (we call them monitoring agents) in hosts, including servers, desktops, and laptops, in the organization. Our agents cover various OSes and their versions—over 30 kinds—including Windows (e.g., Windows 7, 10) and Linux (e.g., Ubuntu, Redhat, CentOS) in our prototype.

Other operating systems such as MacOS can be also supported by our system by utilizing their OS event function. Once the events are collected, the rest of the process is agnostic to the operating system itself. Tracking these OS events provides the history of execution and modification (e.g., update, patch) of all software binaries on a computer in a heterogeneous manner.

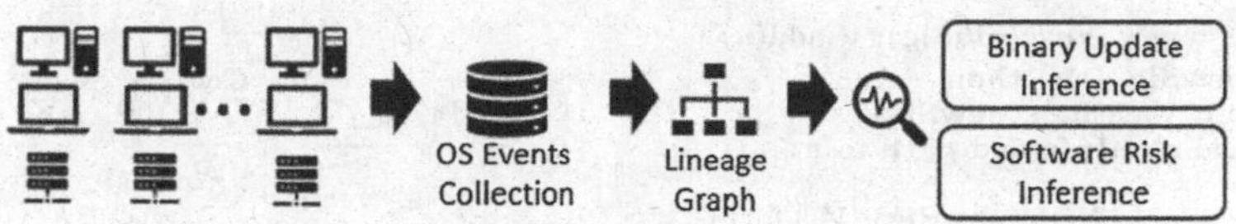

Fig. 1. Architecture of Find My Sloths (FMS).

The tracking system streams the collected events to the backend server as shown in Fig. 1. These events are stored in a database, which we use to analyze the data. Next, we explain how we use this information to infer software updates.

3.2 Software Update Inference with Binary Update Lineage Graph

Lineage Graph Generation. To track the binary update information for each software installed, we develop a lineage tracking algorithm that analyzes OS events collected by our tracking module. We identify file write events applied into binary executables and construct a binary update graph for each executable files. A file path for an executable file, which is executed, becomes a candidate for an update check. Whenever we observe a file write event applied this file candidate, this event is inferred as an update of the program.

Specifically, we first generate a graph to represent the lineage of binary updates, $G(V, E)$ where V is a set of vertices which represent the information of program binaries, including both execution history and metadata. We call this graph a *Lineage Graph*. We use a SHA256 hash of the binary, S, as the identifier of each vertex. E is a set of directed edges where each edge shows how a binary has been updated as $U(S_{old} \rightarrow S_{new})$. Each edge contains a timestamp of the update as well as the identifier of the computer that it was observed on.

Interestingly, we have observed unusual binary modification patterns in some applications, including Mozilla Firefox. To support the update without completely terminating the application, Firefox partially updates the image, reloads it in a running process, and updates the next portion of the image. It generates many bogus vertices and edges in the graph. To avoid this, we defined a time threshold, and if the sequence of binary updates happens within the threshold, we merge them in the graph and only keep the first image information. In this work, we use 99.9 percentile of the time between updates, 180 s, as an empirical threshold.

Algorithm 1. Graph Creation

```
Input: oldSig, newSig, comInfo, path
V = [], E = []
for each item in dataList do
    u = null, v = null
    if (oldSig ∈ V) then
        u = V.getItem(oldSig)
        add comInfo and path to u
    else
        u = new Node(oldSig); V.add(u)
    if (newSig ∈ V) then
        v = V.getItem(newSig)
        add comInfo and path to v
    else
        v = new Node(newSig); V.add(v)
    if ((u, v) = e ∈ E) then
        add comInfo and date to e
    else
        E.add (new Edge(u, v))
```

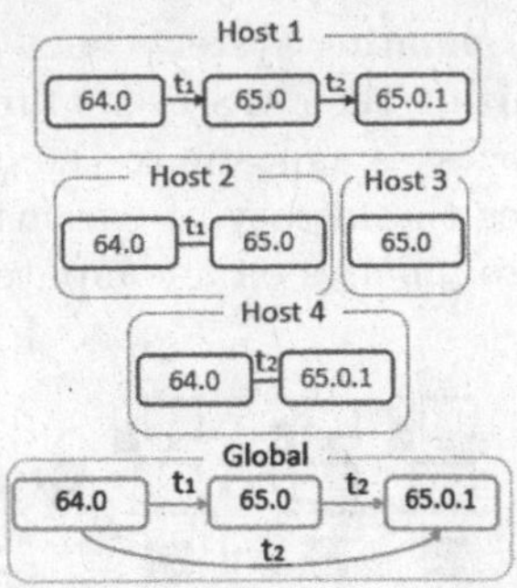

Fig. 2. Simplified graph from Mozilla Firefox demonstrates how we construct a global view of update patterns.

Global Lineage Graphs as an Enterprise Level Update Summary. We then generate the graphs for all hosts in the central server to create a collective graph and comparatively measure the risk factors for each host. We use a binary signature, S, to identify the same binary in different hosts and construct a global update graph for each application to visualize binary update patterns across hosts. It allows us to have a bird's eye view of how each program is updated, and similarities and differences of update patterns across hosts. Algorithm 1 presents how we construct global graphs.

Figure 2 demonstrates a simplified example of how we construct a global view of update patterns. In this scenario, we have four hosts that have the execution or modification history of a particular application. The application has three distinct binary signatures, the version 64.0 ($S_{64.0}$)[2], $S_{65.0}$, and $S_{65.0.1}$. *Host 1* has execution and update history where the binary has updated at t_1 from $S_{64.0}$ to $S_{65.0}$ and updated to $S_{65.0.1}$ at timestamp t_2. The binary in Host 2 has updated to $v_{65.0}$ at t_1 but never updated to $S_{65.0.1}$. Host 3 only has an execution history of $S_{65.0}$, and Host 4 does not have any sign of $S_{65.0}$, but the binary has directly updated from $S_{64.0}$ to $S_{65.0.1}$ at t_2. Note that this is simplified graphs to demonstrate, but original nodes contain metadata and execution history (e.g., timestamps when the binary has executed).

We collect graphs from each host and construct a global graph aggregating update patterns from all hosts. The global graph shows how the binary has updated, who have out-dated binary executables, and how frequently out-dated binaries have executed (we elide an execution history). We discuss how we measure the risk factors for each host using the global view in the next section.

Tracking Binary and Library Update. We detect updates based on overwriting of the binary files. These can be either by a *write* event or an *execution*

[2] This version number 64.0 is presented only for an illustration purpose. A lineage graph is constructed using binary hashes and their appearance orders without using the software's specific version numbers, which may not always available or accurate.

event which shows a new signature for the executable image. Note that not every program update changes the main executable. It is possible to update library files while the main executable stays unchanged. Most Windows applications developed by .NET framework update the manifest in the main executable even if the update is only applied to a library file [30,31], and thus FMS can detect it. However, if the update is solely through the dynamic library without updating the manifest, or main program FMS cannot detect it, and we leave it as our future work. We further discuss this issue in Sect. 9.

Table 1. NSRL Program and Version Coverage. Latest versions available for four popular programs as of the date of the writing and their corresponding records in the latest NSRL [4] release (RDS Version 2.71 - Dec. 2020) showing NSRL release is not up-to-date for several actively developed software programs.

Program name	Latest	NSRL versions	Program name	Latest	NSRL versions
Mozilla FireFox	73.0	72.0, 68.0, 61.0.1	Acrobat Reader DC	21.001.20138	N/A
Google Chrome	80.0	76.0, 49.0, 47.0	Sublime	3.2.2	N/A

Limited Reference Services. We have considered using reference libraries for software such as National Software Reference Library (NSRL) [4] or VirusTotal File Search [47] that can retrieve information of application by a hash value. They often provide known-vulnerabilities (e.g., CVE [15]) and it can be directly used for the risk prediction. Table 1 shows version information for 4 popular programs in NSRL. As shown, these references can be used with some mainstream applications, however, they often fail to provide information on less-known applications or free software distributed via source code.Also the fact that less popular programs have less disclosed vulnerabilities [5] does not mean they are more secure and they still should be monitored. We submitted all executable files installed in our enterprise to NSRL and VirusTotal database, and we found that only 14.2% of installed binary information is provided by NSRL and 75.3% of binary information is available in VirusTotal.

3.3 Software Risk Inference

In order to estimate the risk each computer or software imposes on the enterprise environment, the state of software on individual computers, as well as, the overall enterprise status as a whole have to be quantified with a score; we introduce a metric based on the *delay in update time*, that is defined as the estimated delay of the installation time behind the latest version in its software distribution.

FMS monitors the process and file events and creates lineage graphs as introduced in Sect. 3.2. From the data stream, we catch new updates as they emerges. These updates are correlated and aggregated over all the enterprise to construct the global update graph of a program. To give the administrators a better perspective, we also provide them with information on how common each program is in the enterprise and the update patterns for that particular program. Here is how FMS estimates the risk caused by the software update delay.

Inferred Versions. Relying on software vendor's release schedules or third-party services' information does not scale to cover the majority of software. Therefore, our approach determines the risk estimated by only using the measured metrics in our environment. In this scheme, the versions are determined by *temporal appearance order of signatures* relative to the prior edge nodes in an enterprise. We found that the statistical data collected from 774 machines approximate the actual order of versions with 85% accuracy. We calculate accuracy by counting the number of versions found in the correct order by FMS as compared to their respective compilation timestamp in a test set of programs related to 16,273 updates chosen randomly from Windows binary files.

Let us define a program p has a set of its signatures $V_p = \{S_{p,v,m}\}$ where v is a version and m is a host index in an organization. Among multiple signatures observed, we can find the one leading the version transitions that appear most recently compared to other versions and transitioned from one or more edge nodes of the graph. We call this version the head $\hat{v}$, and its signature is represented as $S_{p,\hat{v},m'}$ where m' is the host having this version. This signature is determined from the graph structure.

Estimated Release Time, Head Arrival Time, and Arrival Time of Updates. To estimate the update delay, we need to determine three types of timestamps. The first one is the release time, $r(S_{p,v,m})$, when the software vendor begins to distribute a new version of the software. This information is hard to obtain with comprehensive coverage of the majority of software. We estimate this information with the first appearance time of a signature, $S_{p,v,m}$, in an enterprise. The second metric is the deployment time of the latest estimated version, $d(S_{p,\hat{v},m'})$, that is the installation time of the most desirable version where the function $d(s)$ gives the installation time of a signature s. This is determined after the head signature is found from the topology of the graph. The third timestamp is the actual installation time, $d(S_{p,v,m})$, that is a specific time stamp when the software binary signature, $S_{p,v,m}$ is installed. Its absolute installation time since the release is $d(S_{p,v,m}) - r(S_{p,v,m})$.

Update Delay Metric. The update delay of software p of the current version v in a machine m behind the head $\hat{v}$ is defined as the following formula.

$$D_{p,v,m} = |d(S_{p,\hat{v},m'}) - d(S_{p,v,m})|$$

This value measures a relative delay compared to the installation of the latest version within an enterprise. Since this is calculated only by using our measurements, we can generate this risk score without any domain knowledge requirement, such as the release date and time, which is only available by developers. Such wide applicability to all programs is a unique strength of our approach. We present interesting comparative statistics showing how each software in a particular machine is doing compared to all other software instances within an organization in Sect. 4. To this end, FMS generates a daily report that outlines

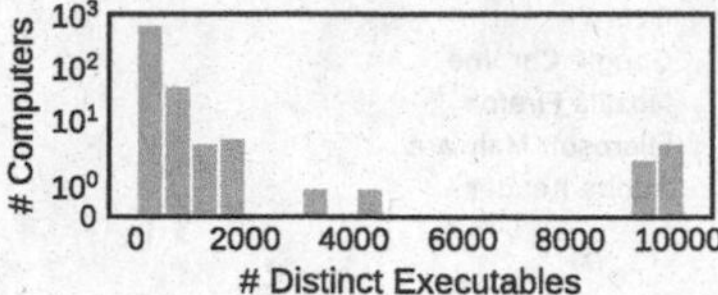

Fig. 3. Histogram over the number of computers for each unique program appearing.

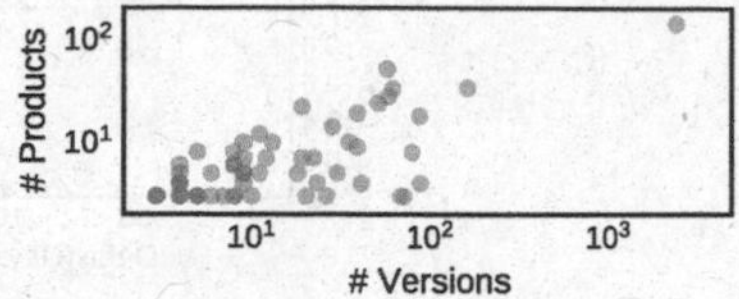

Fig. 4. Number of unique software products and unique versions observed for each vendor, each dot represents one vendor.

the state of the risk across the enterprise and the list of machines that contain outdated programs with detailed risk information.

4 Characteristics of Software Updates

Data Set. We collect binary access history (i.e., execution and modification history) from a Fortune 500 Tech company. The company has 248 full-time employees in multiple divisions, including research and technological development (RTD), maintenance, financial, and human resources. We have installed our binary monitoring module (Sect. 3.1) on 774 computers comprising *591 Microsoft Windows* and *183 Linux* machines to monitor binary execution and modifications over three years. In total, we observed 113,675 unique programs with an average of 305 observed on a computer and a total of 40,971 updates.

Binary Distribution. To better characterize the distribution of programs on computers, Fig. 3 shows a histogram for the number of unique programs in each computer. There is an average of 305 programs executed on each computer in the period of our observation.

Figure 4 shows the number of binary executables published by different publishers. We leverage the metadata from the Windows binaries to identify the publisher for each binary. We only count images that contain publisher information. This shows the imbalance between popular companies and companies with less popularity in our sample enterprise. This figure shows a sample of the meta information shown on the system's user interface. It also shows how diverse vendors are and how each one's dominance differs from the other. In this graph *Microsoft* followed by *Adobe* and *Google* have the highest number of programs.

Binary Updates. We have observed 40,971 updates of binary executables from 774 Windows and Linux computers we monitored during this study. These updates collectively introduced 11,948 new binaries to the enterprise. Updates once released are not always installed within the same period on all computers, Fig. 5 shows how each update is installed on different computers.

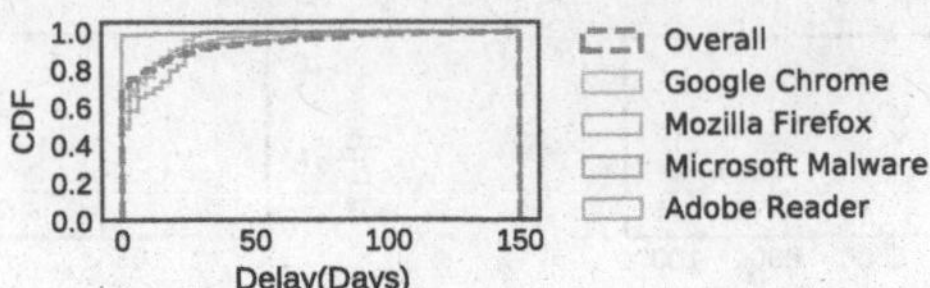

Fig. 5. CDF for the time over which each update has been applied to different computers. Multiple products are shown along with the overall list.

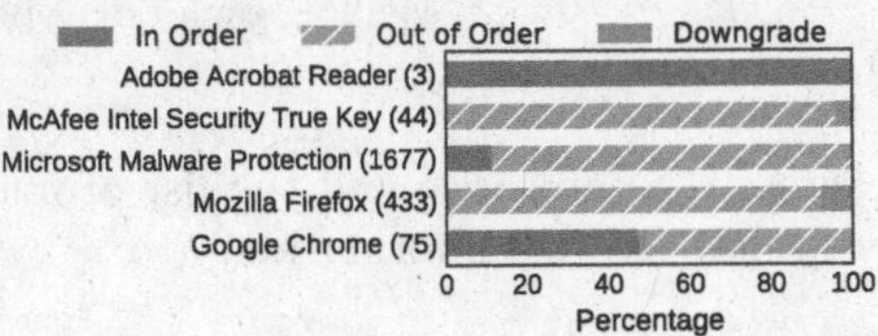

Fig. 6. Percentage of in-order and out-of-order updates for 5 different products. The number in the parentheses shows the number of updates.

Update Order Patterns. We call any update that does not follow the release order an out of order update, e.g., going from 1.0 to 3.0, skipping a known intermediate version 2.0. Furthermore, as mentioned in Sect. 2, there are a noticeable amount of downgrades observed in our dataset as well. We consider them risky behavior. Although they might have happened for reasons like a downgrade after a feature has been removed from the new version or user's choice, they could pose a risk to the enterprise. Figure 6 shows how common these out of order updates and downgrades are among some well known products. The programs in this figure observe a total of 55 downgrades. They took programs to versions with 19.7 CVEs on average at the time of downgrade.

Product Lifecycle. We study the lifecycle of programs in our observation period by their compilation timestamps which show how spread the versions we have observed are. Figure 7 characterizes each program's behaviors in terms of the number of days in which we have observed updates and the number of unique versions we have observed in our data collection. The highlighted nodes represent (0) Microsoft Malware Protection, (1–3) executable binaries included in Microsoft Windows Operating System.

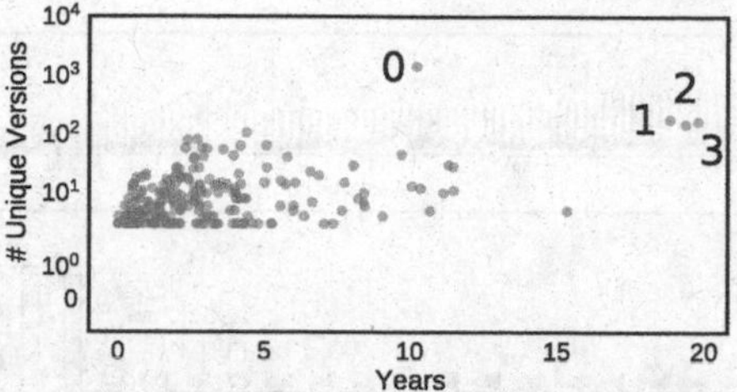

Fig. 7. The length of support and released versions. Highlighted nodes represent: 0) Microsoft Malware Protection, 1–3) Executable binaries included in Microsoft Windows Operating System.

Another part of the lifecycle is the delivery of the product to users. We observe the delay between the programs' installations and their releases in our dataset varies significantly by vendor and product. Figure 8 shows some famous vendors and their delivery performance. For example, Google has a short delay updating 89% of installations within 18 days while Mozilla has a long deployment time where some versions got installed after several months. This may have to do with the popularity of the software.

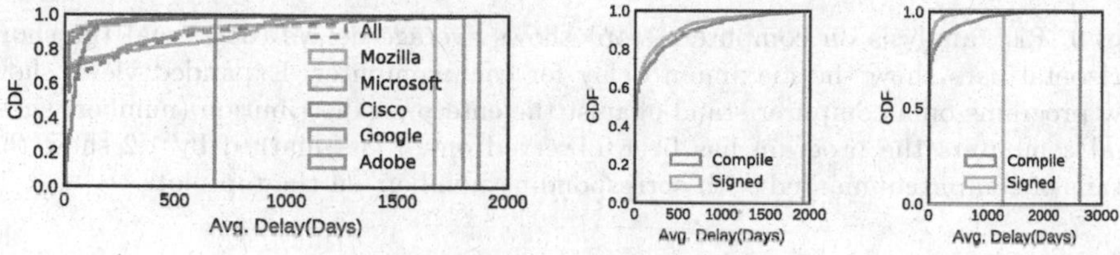

Fig. 8. CDF of days between compilation and our first observation for different vendors (**left**). Distance between compilation and signing date with our (**middle**) and VirusTotal's (**right**) first observation. Plots have been capped at 2000 days for readability.

Update Propagation. Updates are not installed on all computers at the same speed. The speed at which the update is installed across computers in the network depends on multiple factors such as the application, the user, configurations, and the vendor's delivery method. Figure 5 shows how the updates of four programs are installed compare to the overall distribution. We can see 'Microsoft Malware Protection' updates are distributed faster on the computers compared to 'Mozilla Firefox'. The vertical bars of each color represents the time when the maximum is reached.

5 Evaluation of Software Update Risk

This section presents the estimated risk determined by the delay in updates compared to peers in an enterprise environment. Figure 9 presents the estimated software update risk in our environment with three scopes from the broad view across all hosts (top) to the programs in a specific machine (bottom two).

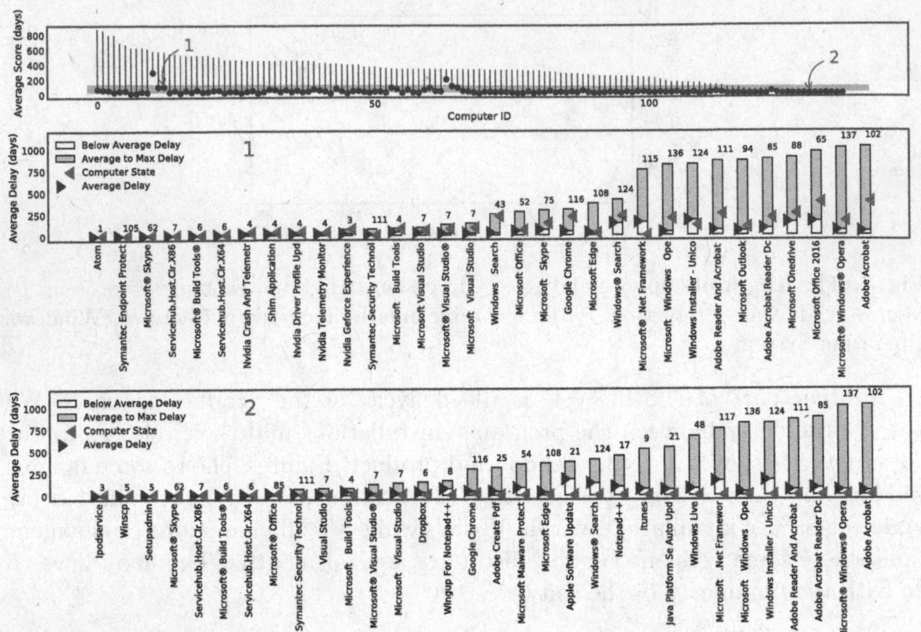

Fig. 9. Risk analysis on computers (top) shows average delays (dots) and the short horizontal bars show the maximum delay for each computer. Expanded views show how programs on a computer stand against the enterprise distribution (numbers show total computers the program has been observed on). Plots marked by 1,2 show the details of computers marked with corresponding numbers on the top plot.

Enterprise-Level View. The top figure in Fig. 9 shows the risk scores estimated for all host machines, which show an aggregated risk score for each machine. This view highlights the uniqueness of our approach *making the risk score available for all observed machines* because our approach is agnostic to OS and programs. Each vertical bar (I) shows the maximum and minimum risk scores as the top and bottom marks and the average risk score of all software within each machine as a dot in the middle. We can observe many machines have one or more highly risky programs indicated by the maximum value far away from the average, which serves a comparable score across peers. We placed a blue box to show where the averages of most machines stay. We select one sample standing out with high risk shown as a higher average (noted with the red **1** sign), and another sample of a lower risk score which stays together with peers within a blue box (noted with the red **2** sign). We provide drill-down views of these two machines with a comparison next. These two particular machines are chosen to illustrate a contrast with a comparable set of programs.

Machine-Level View. The next two figures in Fig. 9 present the views of particular hosts regarding all software programs running in them. Again, this highlights our unique view of *a comprehensive coverage of all programs' risk scores*

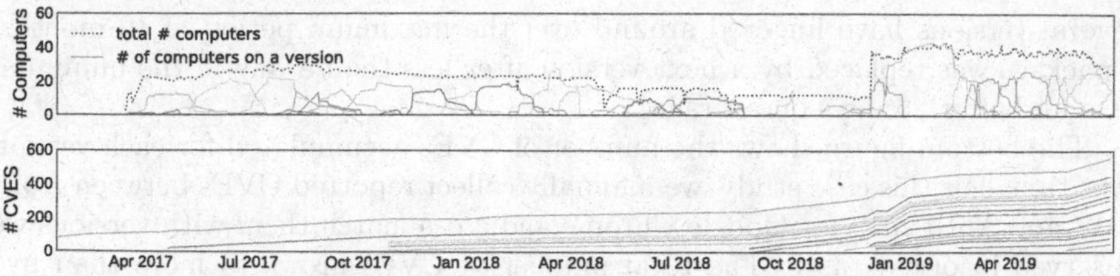

Fig. 10. Software update management of Google Chrome browser updating 75 Google Chrome versions over the period of 35 months. The top plot shows the version transitions via the deployment of each version of Chrome with respect to the number of computers. The bottom plot shows the number of CVEs discovered for each version.

because we do not rely on developers' or third-party's program metadata (e.g., reputation) to determine the risk score. Each bar represents the update status of one software in all machines. The total number of machines having this software executed is written on top of the bar. Each machine has a score of delay showing how much its version is behind the head (the latest version in an enterprise). First, the average of all delays is calculated. The number of machines having the delay shorter than the average is shown as an empty bar, and the machine having the delay longer than the average is shown as a bar with the hatches. The red horizontal lines indicate where this machine is among multiple peers. The first graph (note **1**) in the middle indicates multiple red lines are placed inside the hatch bars meaning that such software has its version more than the average delay among peers. For instance, multiple programs such as Adobe Flash player, AMD External Events, Microsoft Edge, Microsoft Outlook, and .NET framework show high risks. Administrators can use this view to spot vulnerable software. The second graph (note **2**) in comparison shows most software programs are up-to-date by having the red horizontal lines at the bottom.

6 Case Study

This section presents an instance of desirable software management and an undesirable example of a software product. These examples show how different vendors' software management policies are, highlighting what needs to be done.

6.1 An Example of a Desirable Software Management

In Sects. 4 and 5, we presented our observation on numerous shortcomings in how vendors design the software distribution policies and actions to protect their customers. We present *Google Chrome* as a desirable example with the speedy delivery of software ensuring that most of the computers are updated to the latest version in the shortest time.

Figure 10 illustrates how 75 different versions of Google Chrome have been updated. The top figure shows the deployment of each version over time. While several versions have lingered around over the maximum period of 10 months, a package was replaced by a next version after less than a day in the minimum case and after 26 days on average.

The bottom figure shows the number of CVEs accumulated for each version over time. For this case study, we manually collect reported CVEs between April 2017 and April 2019 for Google Chrome and cross-match them with versions we observed in our dataset. The total number of CVEs grows to more than five hundred for version 52.0. This data illustrates that the only solution to operate software safely is to update it with the version whose vulnerabilities are not yet discovered for the time being (although it would end up with a similar situation as the prior version). While more and more vulnerabilities have been disclosed, we can observe Google has been proactively producing new versions that replaced most of the vulnerable installations promptly.

6.2 An Example Undesirable Software Management

An opposite situation happens in another software called *Viber*. Viber is a communication app that has a desktop version. Unlike the previous case, this software vendor does not follow up with the management of software. In fact, this software is not shipped with its own updater. Therefore, a user will need to download and install the updated version by herself manually. This is a very ineffective way to manage software because of multiple reasons. First, most users are not likely to check new versions of software (e.g., by visiting the software website, etc.) with concerns about vulnerabilities. Second, even though the users may become aware of a new version (e.g., registration and a newsletter), they may not be capable of downloading a newer version and installing it.

We observe Viber installed on 4 machines, and they have been consistently executed during our observation period. Of these installations, only one machine was updated twice until Jan 2018, which leaves the machine out-dated for more than 2 years in which the application has been used regularly. During this time, 2 CVE have been disclosed that directly affected Viber Desktop and 4 more that indirectly affect the Viber platform.

Some vendors seem to improve behaviors with time, as shown in Fig. 11 for instance, Skype begins with versions not being updated and some versions lingering on for a long time in 2017, but in 2019 turns to a desirable update behavior where a majority of computers receive their updates in time. On the other hand, however, Firefox, also shown in Fig. 11 maintains bad update habits to the extent where in no time more than 10 of our sampled machines have the same version installed. Microsoft Edge has the worst performance among observed browsers. Edge versions maintain their dominant presence for more than 10 months and we observe major activity from them on these machines.

7 Lessons Learned and Our Suggestions

This section summarizes what we learned from observations and analysis of the real-world enterprise data, and we made a few suggestions for better security.

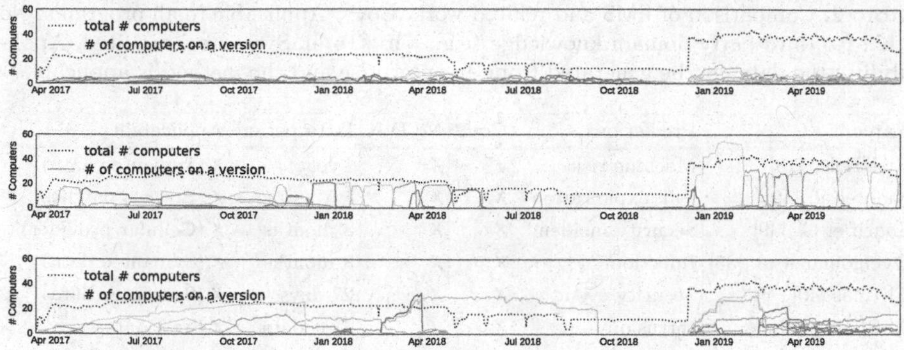

Fig. 11. Version history for Mozilla Firefox, Microsoft Skype, and Microsoft Edge from top to bottom respectively.

Minimizing Update Deployment Time. One important issue in updates is deployment time. In the end-to-end point of view, collective effort is necessary to minimize the deployment time by multiple parties including developers, system administrators, and end users.

Reliable Update Transitions. Given N versions ($s_n \in S = \{s_1, ..., s_N\}$), N^2 transition patterns may occur depending on current and next versions. When there is a gap, a direct transition to the latest can ease deployment regarding compatibility and time in subsequent updates if the update is stand-alone. If it has to be incremental, developers should thoroughly test every transition.

Software Downgrading. We have observed a considerable number of version downgrading in our data set. This is also in line with findings of [27] that users partially steer away from updates due to the issues with compatibility or features.

Automated, Enforced, Silent Delivery. We observe the effectiveness of *silent delivery* that the user has no interaction with the download and installation of the update. Google Chrome shows a successful practice of *silent delivery.*

Retirement Plan and the End of Support Notice. Proper announcement and communication of product support (e.g., a good example is the Ubuntu's LTS plan) is important to know the software's managed period. We believe that an automated method to query a program's lifespan would help the user avoid end-of-support programs.

8 Related Work

Risk Prediction and Vulnerability Assessment. RiskTeller [13] creates computer profiles based on file appearances and the general use of the machine and predicts each machine's risk based on its installed software and the usage history. RiskTeller uses external information, including VirusTotal and CVSS

Table 2. Comparison of FMS and related work. Cov∀: Applicable to all programs, No D.K.: No third-party domain knowledge (e.g., VirusTotal, Symantec) required, Applicability: the data can be generated from an enterprise and the method is applicable.

Name	Prediction	Cov∀	No D.K	Data period	Applicability
RiskTeller [13]	Machine risk	✓	✗	1 year	✗ (Symantec data)
Xiao et al. [49]	Vul. exploitation	✗	✗	1.5 years	✗ (Botnet, patches)
Sharif et al. [39]	Security incident	✗	✗	3 months	✗ (Cellular provider)
Ovelgönne et al. [35]	Infection	✗	✗	8 months	✗ (Symantec data)
Tiresias [40]	Security event	✗	✗	27 days	✗ (Symantec data)
ASSERT [34]	Intrusion	✗	✓	Test data	✗ (Test data)
Liu et al. [26]	Security incident	✗	✓	2 years	✗ (Network data sets)
Kang et al. [22]	Malware infection	✗	✗	640 days	✗ (Symantec WINE)
RiskWriter [10]	Security posture	✗	✗	1 year	✗ (Symantec data)
Find My Sloths	Vul. program risk	✓	✓	3 years	✓(General OS log)

score [15], to enable an accurate prediction. Other studies infer the risk of a computer (or mobile device) by using user behaviors of web sessions [39], distribution of binary files on the computer, the user's mobility between different ISPs [35], modeling the security-related decision-making process of users [37], and permission and internal activities of Android applications [41,50].

RiskWriter [10] and Liu et al. [26] measure the risk for an enterprise based on its externally measurable metrics such as DNS misconfigurations. Kang et al. [22] predict malware infection epidemics based on antivirus software telemetry information. Another direction of risk prediction [34,40] is to predict future security incidents based on the history of the past security-related events.

Kotzias et al. [23] studies patching landscape for the enterprise; however, the set of programs they tracks is limited to 124 well-known server and host programs for which they obtain hash and version information for the main executable. Nappa et al. [33], also studied effects of patching, threats of multiple installations of a software and the shared libraries from 10 popular programs at scale.

Unlike previous studies (Table 2), we infer update delay using only data collected inside the enterprise, without relying on external information, such as software vendors' release notes, third party metadata of software, or known vulnerabilities.

Update Development. There exist works that focus on the development side of updates that study how well developers respond to the needs for updates, including security vulnerability disclosure [25]; or the response speed of developers to new requirements of ever-changing platforms. Code change analysis [28], commit message analysis [28,36], vulnerability disclosure analysis [36,49], and versioning analysis [14] techniques have been used in these studies.

Update Deployment. Software development companies often have their solutions to deploy updates and patches effectively and promptly. For instance, Microsoft's On-Premises Update Server provides a unified interface, and it tries to minimize the network traffic by caching the update [20]. Google applies silent and automatic updates [17] to their products, including the Google Chrome web-browser. There exist studies [27,48] that evaluate the effectiveness of software update deployment models. They use a mix of user studies and monitoring a small set of programs to find the challenges stopping an effective update process. A recent study [21] identifies design flaws or malicious installations in the automated software deployment systems.

9 Discussion and Future Work

This section discusses the limitations of our work and possible improvements.

Reasons Behind Update Behaviors. In this study, we focus on identifying software update behaviors and estimating risk; however, understanding why a certain update behavior happens is a remaining challenge beyond our scope. For instance, we detect software downgrade or rollback from the lineage graph, but the reason why that decision has been made is unknown. In the future, we will conduct a comprehensive user study and a deep analysis of update management platforms to understand the reasons behind unusual update behaviors.

Grouping Updates Installed in Varied Paths. The current version of FMS detects an update of software individually based on the path where the update is installed. However, we rarely observe software that installs the update in a separate path while keeping the previous versions of the binary. It then modifies a symbolic link file to point the binary to execute. Currently, we may not correctly detect such update behaviors. We plan to implement a merging mechanism to automatically find updates in separate paths to address this limitation.

Updates By Library Modification. The current FMS cannot detect updates that only modify the library but not the main executable. We plan to improve FMS's monitoring module to enable tracking library import information at runtime. Then we will track all updates to those library files.

Leveraging Security Information. We plan to optionally incorporate standardized security information, such as code signing, to further enhance the risk estimation in FMS for certain programs whose metadata are available.

10 Conclusion

Software lifecycle management is a complex and costly process that needs the dedication of a software vendor. When it is not properly done, we find that it directly leads to risk for *every* software as vulnerabilities are discovered over time. We propose an automated approach to analyze the entire software updates in an organization comprehensively achieved by utilizing only observed metrics instead of relying on developers' or third-party software release information and metadata. Our evaluations shed light on the current industry practices on how they manage software due to high coverage of update risk assessment on total

113,675 programs' 40,971 updates in 774 machines used by real people daily. We organized our comprehensive evaluations on the current software updates practices, which suggest a list of desired design decisions on update management software to operate software securely.

Acknowledgment. We thank the anonymous reviewers and our shepherd, Juan Caballero, for their helpful feedback. This material is supported, in part, by the National Science Foundation, under grant No. OAC-1909856 and SaTC-1909856. Any opinions, findings, and conclusions, or recommendations expressed in this material are those of the authors and do not necessarily reflect the views of the NSF.

References

1. APT (Advanced Package Tool). https://ubuntu.com/server/docs/package-management. Accessed 14 May 2021
2. Homebrew. https://brew.sh/. Accessed 14 May 2021
3. Linux Audit. https://people.redhat.com/sgrubb/audit/. Accessed 14 May 2021
4. National Software Reference Library. https://www.nist.gov/software-quality-group/national-software-reference-library-nsrl. Accessed 14 May 2021
5. Top 50 Vendors by Total Number of "Distinct" Vulnerabilities. https://www.cvedetails.com/top-50-vendors.php. Accessed 14 May 2021
6. What Are Security Patches and Why Are They Important? https://www.idtheftcenter.org/Cybersecurity/what-are-security-patches-and-why-are-they-important.html. Accessed 20 May 2018
7. Why Software Updates Are So Important. https://securingtomorrow.mcafee.com/consumer/consumer-threat-notices/software-updates-important/. Accessed 14 May 2021
8. Yum. http://yum.baseurl.org/. Accessed 14 May 2021
9. Abu Odeh, M., Adkins, C., Setayeshfar, O., Doshi, P., Lee, K.H.: A novel AI-based methodology for identifying cyber attacks in honey pots. In: IAAI (2021)
10. Aditya, K., Grzonkowski, S., Le-Khac, N.A.: Riskwriter: predicting cyber risk of an enterprise. In: ICISSP (2018)
11. Ahmad, A., Saad, M., Bassiouni, M., Mohaisen, A.: Towards blockchain-driven, secure and transparent audit logs. CoRR (2018)
12. Apple: iTunes store. https://itunes.apple.com/us/. Accessed 14 Nov 2018
13. Bilge, L., Han, Y., Dell'Amico, M.: Riskteller: predicting the risk of cyber incidents. In: CCS (2017)
14. Corley, C.S., Kraft, N.A., Etzkorn, L.H., Lukins, S.K.: Recovering traceability links between source code and fixed bugs via patch analysis. In: TEFSE (2011)
15. Corporation, T.M.: Common vulnerabilities and exposures (cve®). https://cve.mitre.org/. Accessed 13 June 2019
16. Du, M., Li, F., Zheng, G., Srikumar, V.: DeepLog: anomaly detection and diagnosis from system logs through deep learning. In: CCS (2017)
17. Duebendorfer, T., Frei, S.: Web browser security update effectiveness. In: CRITIS (2009)
18. Duebendorfer, T., Frei, S.: Why silent updates boost security. TIK (2009)
19. Gentoo Foundation, I.: Portage. https://wiki.gentoo.org/wiki/Handbook:X86/Working/Portage. Accessed 14 May 2021

20. Gkantsidis, C., Karagiannis, T., VojnoviC, M.: Planet scale software updates. In: CCR (2006)
21. Han, X., et al.: SIGL: securing software installations through deep graph learning. arXiv (2020)
22. Kang, C., Park, N., Prakash, B.A., Serra, E., Subrahmanian, V.: Ensemble models for data-driven prediction of malware infections. In: WSDM (2016)
23. Kotzias, P., Bilge, L., Vervier, P.A., Caballero, J.: Mind your own business: a longitudinal study of threats and vulnerabilities in enterprises (2019)
24. Lee, K.H., Zhang, X., Xu, D.: High accuracy attack provenance via binary-based execution partition. In: NDSS (2013)
25. Li, F., Paxson, V.: A large-scale empirical study of security patches. In: CCS (2017)
26. Liu, Y., et al.: Cloudy with a chance of breach: forecasting cyber security incidents. In: USENIX Security (2015)
27. Mathur, A., Engel, J., Sobti, S., Chang, V., Chetty, M.: "They keep coming back like zombies": improving software updating interfaces. In: SOUPS (2016)
28. Meneely, A., Srinivasan, H., Musa, A., Tejeda, A.R., Mokary, M., Spates, B.: When a patch goes bad: exploring the properties of vulnerability-contributing commits. In: ESEM (2013)
29. Microsoft: About Event Tracing. https://docs.microsoft.com/en-us/windows/win32/etw/about-event-tracing. Accessed 14 May 2021
30. Microsoft: Assemblies in .NET. https://docs.microsoft.com/en-us/dotnet/standard/assembly/#assembly-manifest. Accessed 14 May 2021
31. Microsoft: Assembly Manifest. https://docs.microsoft.com/en-us/dotnet/standard/assembly/manifest. Accessed 14 May 2021
32. Microsoft: Microsoft Store. https://www.microsoft.com/en-us/store/b/home. Accessed 14 May 2021
33. Nappa, A., Johnson, R., Bilge, L., Caballero, J., Dumitras, T.: The attack of the clones: a study of the impact of shared code on vulnerability patching. In: S&P (2015)
34. Okutan, A., Yang, S.J.: ASSERT: attack synthesis and separation with entropy redistribution towards predictive cyber defense. Cybersecurity **2**, 1–8 (2019)
35. Ovelgönne, M., Dumitraş, T., Prakash, B.A., Subrahmanian, V., Wang, B.: Understanding the relationship between human behavior and susceptibility to cyber attacks: a data-driven approach. TIST **8**, 1–25 (2017)
36. Perl, H., et al.: VCCfinder: finding potential vulnerabilities in open-source projects to assist code audits. In: CCS (2015)
37. Redmiles, E.M., Mazurek, M.L., Dickerson, J.P.: Dancing pigs or externalities?: measuring the rationality of security decisions. In: EC (2018)
38. RPM: RPM package manager. https://rpm.org/. Accessed 14 May 2021
39. Sharif, M., Urakawa, J., Christin, N., Kubota, A., Yamada, A.: Predicting impending exposure to malicious content from user behavior. In: CCS (2018)
40. Shen, Y., Mariconti, E., Vervier, P.A., Stringhini, G.: Tiresias: predicting security events through deep learning. In: CCS (2018)
41. Shrivastava, G., Kumar, P.: SensDroid: analysis for malicious activity risk of android application. MTA **78**(24), 35713–35731 (2019)
42. SUSE: Zypper. https://en.opensuse.org/Portal:Zypper. Accessed 14 May 2021
43. Symantec: Internet security threat report 2017. https://www.symantec.com/content/dam/symantec/docs/reports/gistr22-government-report.pdf
44. Team, P.D.: Pacman. https://www.archlinux.org/pacman/. Accessed 14 May 2021

45. Verizon: 2015 data breach investigations report. https://iapp.org/media/pdf/resource_center/Verizon_data-breach-investigation-report-2015.pdf. Accessed 14 May 2021
46. Verizon: 2017 data breach investigations report. https://www.ictsecuritymagazine.com/wp-content/uploads/2017-Data-Breach-Investigations-Report.pdf. Accessed 14 May 2021
47. VirusTotal. https://www.virustotal.com. Accessed 14 May 2021
48. Wash, R., Rader, E., Vaniea, K., Rizor, M.: Out of the loop: how automated software updates cause unintended security consequences. In: SOUPS (2014)
49. Xiao, C., Sarabi, A., Liu, Y., Li, B., Liu, M., Dumitras, T.: From patching delays to infection symptoms: using risk profiles for an early discovery of vulnerabilities exploited in the wild. In: USENIX Security (2018)
50. Xiao, J., Chen, S., He, Q., Feng, Z., Xue, X.: An android application risk evaluation framework based on minimum permission set identification. JSS **163**, 110533 (2020)

FP-Redemption: Studying Browser Fingerprinting Adoption for the Sake of Web Security

Antonin Durey[1(✉)], Pierre Laperdrix[1,2], Walter Rudametkin[1], and Romain Rouvoy[1,3]

[1] University of Lille/Inria, Lille, France
antonin.durey@univ-lille.fr
[2] CNRS, Paris, France
[3] IUF, Paris, France

Abstract. Browser fingerprinting has established itself as a stateless technique to identify users on the Web. In particular, it is a highly criticized technique to track users. However, we believe that this identification technique can serve more virtuous purposes, such as bot detection or multi-factor authentication. In this paper, we explore the adoption of browser fingerprinting for security-oriented purposes. More specifically, we study 4 types of web pages that require security mechanisms to process user data: sign-up, sign-in, basket and payment pages. We visited 1,485 pages on 446 domains and we identified the acquisition of browser fingerprints from 405 pages. By using an existing classification technique, we identified 169 distinct browser fingerprinting scripts included in these pages. By investigating the origins of the browser fingerprinting scripts, we identified 12 security-oriented organizations who collect browser fingerprints on sign-up, sign-in, and payment pages. Finally, we assess the effectiveness of browser fingerprinting against two potential attacks, namely stolen credentials and cookie hijacking. We observe browser fingerprinting being successfully used to enhance web security.

Keywords: Browser fingerprinting · Web security · Cookies · Multifactor authentication

1 Introduction

As web usage continues to grow, web security continues to be challenged. By exploiting vulnerabilities, such as credential leaks[1] from previous hacks or phishing [10] to obtain new credentials, hackers can log into websites and harvest users' data. Additionally, websites may be vulnerable to *cookie hijacking*, which consists of extracting cookies from a user session to access their accounts. These attacks can lead to data leaks, such as username, email, physical addresses or search history [28], but also to account hijacking. Given the growth of such

[1] https://haveibeenpwned.com/.

L. Bilge et al. (Eds.): DIMVA 2021, LNCS 12756, pp. 237–257, 2021.
https://doi.org/10.1007/978-3-030-80825-9_12

attacks, *Multi-Factor Authentication* (MFA) is perceived as a reliable protection to increase web security. MFA consists in combining multiple security factors to check the identity of an authorized user. Such factors not only include user credentials, but also physical tokens, SMS codes, or dedicated mobile apps. These MFA solutions vary in price, level of security, and intrusiveness.

Among these alternatives, *browser fingerprinting* is a stateless identification technique [7,17] that accesses attributes exposed by the browser and its environment to build a unique identifier. Over the years, studies have focused on exploring new attributes, and increasing the uniqueness of browser fingerprints. More specifically, several contributions studied browser fingerprinting for tracking purposes [1,8,32], while others focused on defending against it [16,23,31]. Some contributions proposed using browser fingerprinting as a new factor in MFA solutions [2,15,29], but have not evaluated the benefits to secure online websites. Moreover, given its identification potential, browser fingerprinting is useful for bot detection [14,33], demonstrating its ability to detect undesired visitors.

In this paper, we investigate the adoption of browser fingerprinting to reinforce security on the web. Through our experiment, we intend to detect if fingerprinting is used to strengthen web security, and in which specific contexts this occurs. In particular, we target 4 types of web pages that store and process sensitive user information, namely sign-up, sign-in, basket and payment pages. Investigating these pages is a challenge as it is very hard to automate their exploration because of the sheer diversity of forms and payment processes. As such, we manually visited 1,485 pages from 446 websites belonging to 14 different categories with the aim of detecting fingerprinting scripts. By using an existing classification technique [6], we identified 169 fingerprinting scripts being used on all the secured types of pages we study, with 12 of them belonging to security-focused organizations. Finally, we study the resilience of websites adopting browser fingerprinting for security purposes by simulating two classes of attacks: *stolen credentials* and *cookie hijacking*.

The key contributions of this paper are:

- Evidence of the adoption of browser fingerprinting for security on 4 types of secure pages across various categories of websites, and a study of the browser fingerprints they extract.
- A dataset of 1,485 pages, obtained from 446 websites that include 169 distinct fingerprinting scripts;[2]
- A study of the resilience of websites that use fingerprinting to protect users from stolen credentials and hijacked cookies. In particular, we show no empirical evidence of its active use nor success in defending against stolen credentials or cookie hijacking.

The remainder of this paper is organized as follows. We give an overview of the state of the art and its limitations in Sect. 2. We introduce our dataset in Sect. 3. We analyse our results on browser fingerprinting adoption in Sect. 4. We

[2] https://zenodo.org/record/3872144.

define our attack models and evaluate them in Sect. 5. We discuss our results and its limitations in Sect. 6, before concluding in Sect. 7.

2 Background and Related Work

2.1 Browser Fingerprinting

Browser fingerprinting is a technique to identify a user by leveraging the unique combination of software configurations (*e.g.*, browser, operating system) and hardware characteristics of their device. It was first mentioned as a potential identification technique and studied in 2010 [7]. It combines a set of discriminating attributes mostly accessible from HTTP headers and JavaScript [17]. Commonly accessed attributes are the `navigator` and `screen` properties [7,18], font enumeration [22], canvas [20], audio [8], and WebGL rendering [5].

Studies. Most of the literature has focused on studying the uniqueness and stability of browser fingerprints. They report that browser fingerprinting is a powerful and stateless identification technique [7,9,18] to track users for potentially long periods of time [32]. Other studies aimed at estimating the adoption of browser fingerprinting by websites for tracking purposes. They highlighted that 3–5% of the Top Alexa 1M [1,8,22] embed browser fingerprinting scripts. However, all these studies only crawled home or random pages, thus lacking deeper insight on more sensitive pages, such as sign-up or payment pages, which demand higher security, but may require more complex user interactions to reach.

Security Usages. Bursztein *et al.* [4] argue that canvas fingerprinting can distinguish different families of browsers and uncover the use of PhantomJS to attack a website. Jonker *et al.* [14] studied the "fingerprintability" surface of bots, revealing discriminating attributes to protect websites against web scraping. They also observed that such bot fingerprinting attributes were collected by 15% of the Top Alexa 1M. Vastel *et al.* [33] mention that this technique is already used by websites to block bots. About multifactor authentication, several approaches focused on increasing web session security with browser fingerprinting [2,15,27,29]. However, these studies only cover the methodology and implementation steps, but fail to evaluate their effectiveness in production.

2.2 Multi-factor Authentication and Session Hijacking

New authentication factors are regularly proposed to secure user accounts [25]. However, studies show their adoption is slow [3], leading to compromised accounts if attacks targeting passwords are successful. Sivakorn *et al.* [28] uncovered another attack on user accounts by using cookie session hijacking to log into accounts and steal user sensitive data.

Synthesis. To the best of our knowledge, the state of the art stops either at studying browser fingerprinting from a tracking perspective or for bot detection purposes. It does not deliver any contribution to the adoptions and usages of browser fingerprinting on more sensitive pages, dealing with personal or payment data. The following sections, therefore, propose to address these limits by delivering a new study focusing on the adoption of browser fingerprinting to increase web security. Our contribution advances the state of the art by considering a dataset of 1,485 real-world sensitive pages collected from 446 domains. Unlike previous studies, we obtain this dataset by manually performing an in-depth exploration of a carefully selected set of domains, thus going beyond the surface of websites to study these sensitive web pages.

3 A Dataset of Secure Web Pages

This section reports on our methodology to build a dataset of secured web pages to study the use of browser fingerprinting for security purposes.

3.1 Websites Under Study

Secured Pages. All pages of a website are not equal when it comes to user security. While most web pages do not process sensitive data, some require careful design to deal with user personal information (*e.g.,* emails, credentials, personal details, payment card numbers). On sensitive web pages, any security breach can quickly lead to privacy leaks for the end-users and seriously affect the reputation of the website. We decided to focus on 4 types of web pages requiring personal information or requesting personal data:

1. Sign-up, which may require email, name, password, and additional personal information depending on the website.
2. Sign-in usually requests user credentials (email/pseudonym and password).
3. Payment is a page containing a specific form requesting the user to input their payment information (*e.g.,* credit card, wallet, banking information).
4. Basket refers to any page related to a shopping basket or shopping cart process, starting from adding an item up to, but not including, payment. Such pages may also request additional information, such as billing/delivery addresses.

We call these 4 types of web page *secured web pages*. To assess our results, we also collected samples from other types of pages. From these, we isolated *home pages* as it has been reported they might fingerprint 25% less [30]. We consider pages that are neither secured nor home pages to be *content* pages.

Website Categories. Previous studies crawled the Top Alexa with automated tools, thus studying a large set of homepages and resources reachable by bots. We decided to avoid the bias introduced by bots, preferring to manually browse the websites and reach deeper pages that require user interaction. Moreover, we are interested in studying the adoption of browser fingerprinting on secured pages. In this context, the diversity of websites indexed by the Top Alexa —or other ranking lists— proved to be unsatisfactory. Thus, we decided to consider a list of website categories that we estimate to be more relevant for the purpose of our study. To build this list of relevant categories, we adopted the following methodology:

- We targeted websites focused on gambling, credit card, financial and money services.
- We focused on different retail websites, such as event tickets, games, flights and transports, and accommodation booking websites.
- Finally, we added to our list job search, social network, adult, dating, institutional and governmental websites as they often request detailed personal information when creating an account.

The complete list of keywords we used to reach the websites is available in Appendix A. We mainly entered a combination of country name, category and the word '*website*' into the Google search engine, and visited the websites given on the first page of the results. We also translated the search terms into the main language of the country when we were not getting suitable results according to the country and the category, as for example, was the case for Russian websites.

3.2 Web Page Acquisition

Past studies used automated crawls to observe browser fingerprinting at scale [1,8,22]. However, relying on bot crawls introduces bias in the collected data [11,14,34] as more and more websites use defenses to block bot access [33]. Automating the registration and payment processes is also a challenge because of the high variability that can be found in related forms [13]. No unique or universal standard exists and the number of required fields can strongly differ. The coding practices may be different with obfuscated code and custom attributes, making it hard for a bot to automatically match a field with the right information. Security requirements are also different, including diverse password constraints and security questions. As the scope of this paper is not to develop a bot to automatically test these websites, we manually visited them and collected the required data via a custom web extension we developed. This strategy allows us to appropriately locate interesting secured pages and reduces the bias of being blocked by the security mechanisms in place.

3.3 Fingerprinted Page Attributes

This paper does not intend to discover new browser fingerprinting techniques, but rather to investigate the adoption of existing ones in the context of web security. As part of our data acquisition campaign, we thus focused on collecting the values of all existing attributes reported in the literature. Thus, we consider navigator & screen properties [7,18,21,22,24], fonts enumeration via `span`'s width and height measurement [22], canvas [20], audio [8] and WebGL rendering [5] and parameters [18], WebRTC [8] and bots detection attributes, including `window` properties that were considered by Jonker *et al.* [14]. Our web extension monitors access to the attributes by overriding getters of selected properties and functions. Whenever one of these attributes is accessed, the web extension collects the function or property name, the list of arguments passed if it is a function, the property's value or the function's return value, the script accessing the property or function, and the page's URL.

We manually visited the selected websites and we used a single identity we created on a popular email provider. For each visited page, we stayed at least 10 s, and manually filled each form. When asked for proof of identity, such as a valid phone number, an ID or a credit card, we provided one of the phone numbers used to create the email account. As our identity was fake, we were not able to provide a real ID (*e.g.*, a passport) when required by some websites. Given that payment pages require filling out credit card information, we used a fake credit card generator[3] to be able to validate online payment forms and make sure that we trigger most of the scripts embedded in the page. Even though the generated cards were fake and the payment processes were not completed, we bypassed many client-side verifications thanks to this technique. Yet, using fake payment data raises several issues, such as, our account could be considered suspicious and prevented from performing additional actions, and our IP address could be blacklisted and blocked for the rest of our experiment. Finally, to reduce suspicion, we used several residential IP addresses during our data collection. Although we provided websites with fake payment data, we believe the low number of payment attempts we performed on each website has had minimal impact on their operations. We did not try to harm them in any way and we canceled our baskets if any information received after the payment attempt indicated the website could validate the basket and ask for a future payment.

3.4 Resulting Dataset Description

We performed our data collection campaign from December 2019 to January 2020. We used a fresh install of Chrome 79 on Ubuntu 19.04. We always accepted the default cookie settings for pop-ups, but refused all other types of solicitations, such as geolocation, notifications, or newsletters. In total, we visited 1,485 pages across 446 websites.

Website Category and Ranking. We used the *category* keyword we put into the search engine to categorize the website. We specifically targeted bank and money-related services because of the sensitivity of the data they manipulate, visiting 85 of these websites (see Fig. 1). The country tag represents the main country the website operates in. We assign the country tag by following the result of two observations:

1. Is the website available in English or in multiple languages and translated into the user's preferred language?
2. Are the services proposed by the website available in a single country or geographic zone?

If the website is available in multiple languages or served in English, and if the website provides services to multiple countries, we use the *International* tag.

[3] https://www.creditcardvalidator.org/.

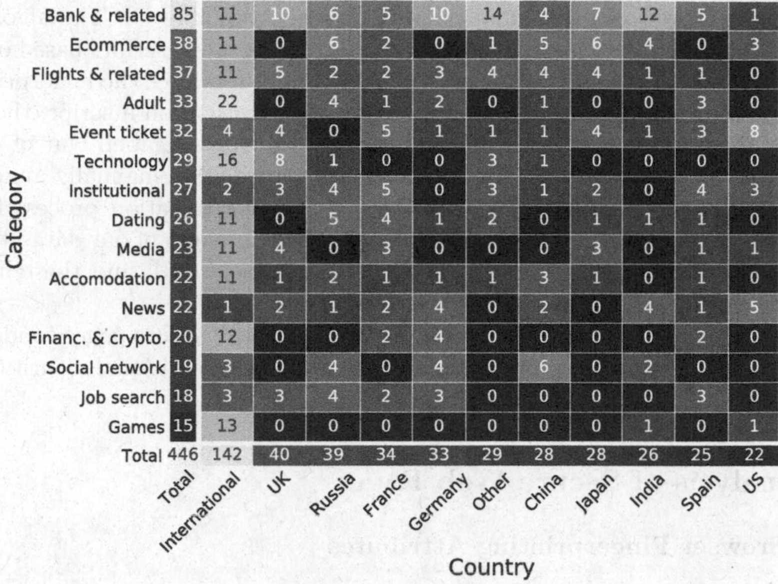

Fig. 1. Distribution of the 446 visited websites per country & category.

Otherwise, we specify the country. If the website does not operate in a listed country, we use the *Other* tag. With these rules, we tagged 142 *International* websites. The resulting distribution of visited websites per country and category is depicted in Fig. 1.

We did not aim to build an exhaustive manual dataset. However, we checked the Top Alexa rankings of the websites in our dataset. We find that our dataset is relatively well balanced across the less-than-1k (18%), 1k-10k (29%), 10k-100k (27%) and higher-than-100k (26%) Top Alexa rankings.

Page Type. We also tagged each page according to its type. By default, a page is associated to a single tag, with the exception of *home* or *content* pages that have a sign-up or sign-in embedded form that allows creating an account or authenticating without going to a specific page (44 occurrences in our dataset), and single pages that handle both account creation and authentication processes (3 occurrences in our dataset). In the case of pages containing both basket-like content and a payment form, we tagged the page as payment. If no tag matched, we used the *content* tag. Our dataset is well-balanced between secure (44%) and non-secure (56%) pages. The basket, sign-up and sign-in pages are equally present (12–13%) while payment pages represent 6% of our dataset.

Script Classification. Several studies exist to classify a real-world dataset of scripts into *fingerprinters* and *non-fingerprinters* [12,26]. All rely on both automatic and manual classification to combine efficiency and reliability. However, none of these studies provide their implementation, making them difficult to be reused. We designed and implemented an algorithm to classify the scripts of our dataset. We have made its implementation freely available [6]. The algorithm relies on a incremental process to build similarities between scripts based on the attributes they access and proposes a manual step to reinforce the fingerprinting process. When the algorithm is unable to reach a decision on a script, the user can step in to guide the algorithm and provide the correct label. Out of 4,665 scripts, the algorithm provided a label to 4,296 scripts. We manually analyzed, over several iterations, 359 of them. Overall, this classification process found 169 browser fingerprinting scripts included in 405 web pages of our dataset. The information concerning the fingerprinting scripts, their URL and the domains they were found on are available in our public dataset.

The remainder of this paper builds on this dataset of secure pages to identify scripts that collect browser fingerprints and evaluate the additional security layer provided by the browser fingerprinting technique.

4 Analysis of Secure Web Pages

4.1 Browser Fingerprinting Attributes

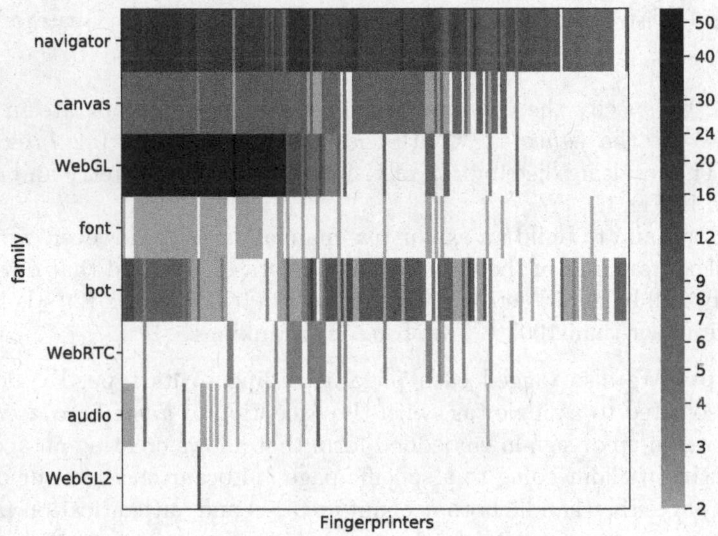

Fig. 2. Distribution of attributes families across fingerprinters.

Of the 169 browser fingerprinting scripts we classified, we observed 132 distinct fingerprinting attributes that we organized into 8 families. The family of an attribute is the parent JavaScript object calling the attribute; except for the bot attributes where we used Jonker *et al.*'s list [14]. Figure 2 reports on the distribution of the attributes per script grouped by family, showing that all attribute families are exploited in the wild. The most accessed attributes are the `User-Agent`, screen `width` and `height`, `plugins` list, and `timezone`. Even if it would be tempting to rely on these to detect fingerprinting scripts, they can be used for many other purposes, such as analytics or adjusting a website's UI to the device. In our dataset, these attributes are used by 81%, 20%, 19%, 6% and 13% of non-browser fingerprinting scripts, respectively. This illustrates the difficulty of identifying reliable attributes to detect browser fingerprinting scripts.

We analyzed the scripts that use canvas or WebGL fingerprinting. 120 scripts fingerprint browsers using canvas drawing primitives, using between 2 and 14 different drawing instructions. We found 44 different drawing sequences. Concerning WebGL fingerprinting, 54 scripts draw with WebGL primitives, using between 17 and 20 distinct drawing instructions. Only 7 drawing instruction sequences are different. Moreover, one sequence is used by 46 scripts. 54 fingerprinters enumerate fonts. The number of fonts tested ranges from 66 to 594, with 19 different sets of fonts. We observe 2 sets of fonts being largely checked by fingerprinters: a set of 82 fonts tested by 17 scripts, and a set of 66–69 fonts used by 18 scripts. Thus, even though there is a potentially unlimited combination of testable fonts, a majority of scripts use similar sets. We believe this is due to these font sets being copied from one script to another, as well as, being sufficient to capture enough uniqueness. We observed 107 fingerprinters collect at least one bot attribute. The average number of bot attributes is 5. `PhantomJS` attributes are the most collected (41% of all scripts), followed by those that detect `Headless Chrome` (18–33%) and `Selenium` (12–16%).

Finally, we observed that the most used attributes belong to the earliest identified for browser fingerprinting, like the navigator and screen properties (Eckersley *et al.* [7] in 2010) and the canvas (Mowery *et al.* [20] in 2012). More recent attributes are less present in our dataset, such as audio and WebRTC (Englehardt *et al.* [8] in 2016). We also found one fingerprinting script accessing 9 unpublished attributes from the `WebGL2RenderingContext` object which is part of the WebGL2 APIs.

4.2 Origins of Browser Fingerprinting Scripts

Regarding the adoption of browser fingerprinting for security purposes, we analyzed the scripts hosted by domains whose main goal is security. We analyzed their target markets and their presence in our dataset and identified 14 fingerprinting scripts from 12 security-focused organizations. For each of the organizations, we extracted their main purpose, and analyzed the presence of their scripts on the sensitive page types we defined. Table 1 reports on these results. All of these security scripts are present in at least one of our 4 sensitive page types.

We analyzed the attribute families collected by these browser fingerprinting scripts. All major techniques are being actively used. The navigator and screen properties are the most collected (included in 14 scripts), followed by canvas (12), bot (11), WebGL parameters (10), WebGL drawing (6), audio and font enumeration via span (5), canvas font enumeration and WebRTC (3). Access to `navigator.userAgent`, `navigator.platform` and `navigator.vendor` was

Table 1. Summary of security organizations, with the accessed attributes and the presence in the web pages of our dataset.

Organization goal	Organization name	Script # of attributes	Script presence on # domains	# pages	sign-up	sign-in	basket	payment
Payment platform	Adyen	47	1	1				✓
	CentroBill	14	1	1			✓	
	Probiller	29	1	4			✓	✓
	Razorpay	10	1	1				✓
	Secured Touch	73	1	6		✓		
Fraud prevention	Iovation	8	1	1				✓
	Nudata Security	29	2	3	✓	✓		
	Sift Science	26	10	26	✓	✓	✓	✓
	Simility	49	2	3				✓
Bot protection	Datadome	33	1	1		✓		
	Geetest	64–65	4	7	✓	✓		
	PerimeterX	69	1	3				✓

found in 13 scripts. These navigator attributes overlap, we believe that they are used to detect spoofing. Moreover, we observed 13 scripts where `screen.width`, `screen.height`, `screen.availWidth`, and `screen.availHeight` are collected. These attributes can also be used to detect spoofing, as the available sizes should be smaller than the width and height. Jonker shows this invariant can detect bots [14]. The 3 organizations that claim to protect against bots naturally collect bot attributes. PerimeterX collects 10 of them, and Datadome 5, both covering all major bot types. However, Geetest only collects 2 bot attributes, both for detecting PhantomJS.

4.3 Secured vs Non-secured Web Pages

We analysed the ratio of webpage types that include a browser fingerprinting script. We found browser fingerprinting scripts on all types of web pages. Basket (33.8%) and Sign-up (31.1%) pages fingerprint more than the average, followed by *content* (25.6%), Payment (25.3%), Sign-in (23.4%), and *home pages* (23.0%). Other studies have not targeted these specific page types and have generally relied only on home pages. Consequently, we are—to the best of our knowledge—the first study to observe the prevalence of browser fingerprinting in sensitive and secure web pages. We compared fingerprinting in secured to non-secured pages. We found 54 scripts exclusive to secured pages, 68 scripts exclusive to non-secured pages, and 47 in both.

We counted the number of fingerprinting scripts included on a page. Out of 405 pages that fingerprint, 339 pages include 1 script, 51 pages had 2 scripts, and 15 pages had 3 scripts. Out the 66 multi-script pages, (*i.e.*, 51+15), 10 had first-party fingerprinting scripts, 27 served fingerprinting scripts from a different domain, and 29 served fingerprinting scripts from both first and third-party domains. We make several hypotheses based on our observations. First, the browser fingerprinting scripts have different purposes, such as advertising or security services, and likely do not share the fingerprints they collect. Next, in the case of pages from websites being developed by several teams, they may integrate multiple browser fingerprinting scripts unintentionally. A majority of the pages with multiple fingerprinting scripts are secured pages, (35 secured versus 31 non-secure pages), although secured pages represent only 44.2% of our dataset. This result supports the statement that secured pages fingerprint more aggressively than non-secured pages.

4.4 Additional Security Mechanisms

During our data acquisition, we also marked the usage of any MFA mechanisms or bot detection techniques we found. We observed 38 pages with an MFA mechanism, the majority being sign-up pages. 3 distinct mechanisms were used during our collection: an email code or confirmation (used 19 times), an SMS code (17), and a phone call (2) in which the code to enter on the website consists of the last x digits of the calling number. The usage of an MFA mechanism for sign-up pages implies a stronger requirement for proof of identity. Because browser fingerprinting could fulfil this requirement, we compare the average number of fingerprinting attributes on these pages to other pages. We observe only 1 sign-up page that contains an MFA mechanism also embedded a browser fingerprinting script. Moreover, this webpage also included a bot detection mechanism. This means that they used both an authentication confirmation and a verification for bots. Thus, the presence of a browser fingerprinting script might be used to serve either of these purposes, as we are only observing from the client-side, we cannot conclude.

Regarding bot detection, we found 51 scripts using bot detection mechanisms: 41 ReCaptcha, 6 Geetest puzzles,[4] and 4 textual captchas. As for the MFA mechanisms, they were mainly observed in sign up pages. 2 pages were using 2 bot detection techniques: a sign-in page on an adult website and a sign-up page on an event ticket website. Half of the pages with a bot detection mechanism embed a browser fingerprinting script. This shows the interest of websites in using bot detection techniques based on browser fingerprinting.

SYNTHESIS. In this section, we explored the browser fingerprinting scripts of our dataset, their presence on the different page types we considered and the adoption of fingerprinting in combination with additional security mechanisms. More specifically, we show that browser fingerprints are effectively accessed for all the types of web pages covered by our study. We finally observed that browsers are fingerprinted slightly more aggressively on secured pages.

5 Attack Models

This section introduces two attack models we used to assess the security benefits of browser fingerprinting.

[4] https://www.geetest.com/en/demo.

5.1 Stolen Credentials

Extracting the Protected Websites. We observed in Sect. 4 that browser fingerprints are collected by websites during the authentication process. We are interested in observing any security improvements brought by fingerprinting in the case of stolen credentials. We assume that a hacker steals a user's credentials—through a data leak, a phishing page, or any other technique—and tries to authenticate into the targeted website. We reproduced this attack behaviour by trying to log into the accounts we created for this experiment. It is worth mentioning that we used a phone number or any additional information needed to create the account, but we skipped anything that was not mandatory. We assume that the attacker may use a different browser instance on a different OS, with different cookies than the victim's browser, while browsing from a different network than the network associated with the original accounts. We assume that the attacker can solve Captchas when using stolen credentials. Therefore, bot detection mechanisms are not a reliable protection in this context. We ran this attack on the 42 websites we were able to create accounts on—12 of them use a browser fingerprinting script on the sign-in page. The 42 websites are well balanced concerning the *Country* tag we defined, and mainly concern cryptocurrencies, money transfer, e-commerce, adult, event and sport tickets content. Among these websites, 16 of them belong to the Top 1k Alexa, 8 between 1k and 10k, 11 between 10k and 100k, and 7 above the Top 100k. We expect websites that collect browser fingerprints to use it them protect the accounts from stolen credentials. Our attempts to log in to the accounts with different fingerprints fell into the following 3 cases:

1. We were able to log into 37 websites without facing additional multi-factor authentication mechanisms or security warnings.
2. Three websites sent a warning message about an unknown connection to our account. These messages contained the IP address, the OS and the browser we tried to connect with.
3. Two websites asked for additional proof of identity. The first one sent an email code with additional information about the ongoing connection. The other sent an SMS code to enter to validate the connection attempt. Those 2 websites also proposed a security panel where the user can check their trusted devices.

We observe that only 5 out of the 42 websites react in a manner that strongly suggests fingerprint-based detection of known devices and browsers is being used to secure the account, namely Google, WeTransfer, (files transfer service) Skrill, Crypto and Binance (cryptocurrencies, finances or money transfer websites). 4 of them have a security panel with the authorized devices with their characteristics and all the connection attempts to log into the account.

Isolating the Triggering Characteristics. As we noticed during our previous experiment, several details, including the OS, browser and IP address, were

Table 2. Parameters and results concerning the reauthentication experiment. *Different IP, browser, device* indicates the IP address, the browser and the device were different from the ground truth respectively. * indicates the cookies from step 5 were reused in step 6 (but they differ from the ground truth cookies).

Website	MFA on sign-up pages	FP on sign-up	FP on sign-in	Authentication attempt combinations n°1 ground truth	n°2 different IP	n°3 different IP no cookies	n°4 different IP diff browser no cookies	n°5 different IP diff browser diff device no cookies	n°6 same IP diff browser diff device same cookies*
Google	SMS OTP			connection	connection	SMS OTP	SMS OTP	connection + alert	connection + alert
Skrill				connection	connection	SMS OTP	SMS OTP	SMS OTP	SMS OTP
Crypto	SMS OTP	✓	✓	connection + alert	connection + alert	connection + alert	connection + alert	connection + alert	connection + alert
WeTransfer				connection	connection	connection + alert	connection + alert	connection + alert	connection + alert
Binance	Email OTP	✓	✓	connection	connection	connection + specific alert	Email OTP	Email OTP	connection + specific alert

provided to the user to explain the warnings or requirements for additional information to authenticate. The IP address can be used to extract the approximate geolocation of the user and to detect connections from unusual networks (*e.g.*, through a cloud provider). Although not indicated, we believe the presence of previous login cookies might also be used by the website to decide to authenticate the users more easily. Their absence might reveal a device or browser change. For the 5 websites of our previous results, we tried to isolate the set of elements that trigger an additional security authentication mechanism or warning. To do so, we tried the following 6 combinations:

1. We re-authenticated with the same conditions as the ones the account was created with, to get the ground-truth.
2. We signed-in with the same browser but using a different IP address than the one used for the account creation and previous login attempt.
3. On a different IP address, using the same browser, we logged in using the browser's private mode to navigate without reusing any cookies.
4. On the same device but using a different browser, with a different IP address.
5. We then tried to reauthenticate with a different device and browser, and a different IP address.
6. Finally, we tried to log again on the same device and the same browser as the previous combination, without deleting cookies or any other stateful data, but we changed our IP address to reuse the original IP address used to create the account and log in for the ground truth combination.

We ran the above combinations in order. Browser and OS changes make the fingerprint different, contrary to IP address and cookies that do not affect the browser fingerprint. If fingerprinting is used to secure the account, we expect to observe different behaviors on the combinations where the fingerprint changes, namely combinations n°4, n°5 and n°6.

Table 2 summarizes up the results we observed according to the changes we applied to the browsing characteristics. Google, Skrill, and WeTransfer seem to be based on cookies. When they are not present, the first 2 ask for a *One Time Password* (OTP), while WeTransfer sends an alert. Crypto always has the same behavior: it allows the connection, but sends an alert. Finally, Binance have the most advanced system. First, it sends an alert about the IP address when we changed it, when browsing without cookies (combination n°3). The message did not contain any reference to device or browser changes, so we believed the website knew we were on the same device and browser. The behavior changed when we used another browser on the same device: Binance sent us an email containing an OTP and basic information about the new browser used (combination n°4). It also sent an email with an OTP when using a different device (combination n°5). When staying on the browser chosen on this second device and using the same IP address as the one used, we received an alert (combination n°6). Based on this last experiment, we make 2 observations:

- The alert message is different from the one when we changed the IP address. The message now mentions a change in the browser and device.
- We received an email alert, but we were still able to sign in. We believe this is because the cookies set by the browser were the same as the ones in the previous combination when we needed to provide an email OTP to validate the connection.

In our dataset, we see browser fingerprinting being used only once, in combination with other identifying techniques, to resist stolen credentials. As this attack is similar to a user trying to login from a fresh browser, it also illustrates the additional steps users needs to complete to sign in with a new browser.

5.2 Cookie Hijacking

Attack Design. Cookie hijacking can lead to account compromise and data leaks [28]. As browser fingerprinting can be used to identify a browser, we make the hypothesis it can be used to help tell if a cookie has been hijacked and used by a different browser. Our goal is not to study the existing ways to perform a cookie hijacking. In our attacks, we assume an attacker was able to steal cookies, no matter the method used—XSS vulnerability, insecure network exchanges, malicious JavaScript injection. Instead, we aim at studying the resilience to cookie hijacking by websites in our dataset if browser fingerprinting is used to protect the accounts. We designed 2 attacks to study cookie hijacking.

Our first attack is session cookie hijacking. It consists in trying to authenticate using cookies stolen from an existing user session. We log in to the target site on a first browser, then we extract the cookies and login page URL and insert these into a second browser. If the attack works, the second browser will be authenticated and the session will be in the same state as on the first browser. If not, the second browser will be stuck on the login page.

Our second cookie hijacking attack focuses on basket workflows. The goal is to obtain the same basket as a user by hijacking their cookies. We fill a basket with a commercial item, and visit the page summarizing the basket and its content. Similarly to the session hijacking cookie attack, we then extract the URL and cookie, and put them in another browser. If the basket content is the same on the 2 browsers, the attack is successful.

Methodology. For each website, we automated the browsing to the required pages with a Puppeteer instance. We automate the insertion of cookies and the navigation to the URL with a second Puppeteer instance. We lower the possibility to be detected as a bot by changing the fingerprint of the Puppeteer instances for them to look like Chrome 84. To do so, we reused the value of each attribute collected by fingerprinters during our manual data collection and integrated them into an extension in the Puppeteer instance that returns the corresponding value when an attribute is accessed. We also added a delay of at least one second between each action on a page.

Before studying the impact of fingerprint modification, we performed a preliminary run with and without the collected cookies to make sure that sessions could be stolen from the Puppeteer instance and that no other parameters, like `localStorage` or a hidden parameter in the URL, would impact our measurement. This way, we created a subset of websites where our attacks are successful. Finally, we ran our attack on all the websites of this subset and collected the cookies and URLs. We used different parameters and configurations of the second Puppeteer instances by running them on a different device on a different network with a different IP address. We also changed all the fingerprint attributes we monitored during our data collection by giving them values from a Firefox 72 instance with the same extension as described earlier in this section. Should a website be protected and detect the different fingerprint, we rerun the attack by modifying parts of the fingerprint to detect which attributes or combinations trigger the defense mechanism.

Results. We ran these experiments in July and August 2020. We used the 42 websites we were previously able to create an account on for the session hijacking cookie. Concerning the basket hijacking cookie attack, we used the 84 websites of our dataset containing at least a basket page—33 of them contain at least one fingerprinter on a basket page. We then ran each step of our validation process to make sure the cookies were the only variable needed to retrieve the basket or session state. The results are presented in Table 3. Because of the time gap between this experiment and the one described in Sect. 4, we were unable to fill

Table 3. Number of websites involved in each step of the validation for the session and basket cookies attacks, and results of the attack on the validated subset

	# websites			
	Session		Basket	
	FP	no FP	FP	no FP
Dataset	12	30	33	51
Cannot automate	0	5	8	8
Anti-bot triggered	2	1	3	3
Impacted by other params	3	5	6	6
Nothing sold	0	0	7	16
Validated subset	**7**	**19**	**9**	**18**
Attack works	**7**	**19**	**9**	**18**

baskets for several websites with a single item as some of them were not selling anything anymore. We believe this is likely due to the economic and societal restrictions following the Covid-19 pandemic. We ended up with a validated subset of respectively 26 and 27 websites for our session and basket cookies attacks. As explained in the methodology section, we then ran our attack and inserted the cookies on a different device on a different network with a different fingerprint and HTTP headers. With these parameters, the attacks worked on every website of our validated subset. These behaviors imply no defense mechanism was being used. Thus, browser fingerprinting is not used to protect against a session or basket cookie hijacking on the websites of our dataset.

As we did not detect any usage of additional security mechanisms, we studied the way *HTTPS* and *HSTS* are deployed and how cookies are configured to observe if their settings were secure enough to protect against traffic sniffing. If these elements are properly set, it lowers the attack surface on cookies by complicating their extraction via JavaScript and avoiding their theft from HTTP requests [28]. Over the 53 websites we tested our cookie hijacking attacks on, 52 were redirecting their traffic through *HTTPS* and 30 of these 52 websites were setting the *Strict Transport Security* response header in the browser. During the experiments, we collected and injected 1,080 cookies, 198 (18%) and 305 (28%) were `HTTPOnly` and `Secure`, respectively. We also looked at the `SameSite` parameter, observing 11 (1%) and 109 (10%) cookies have a `Strict` and `Laxist` `SameSite` policy, respectively. Even if the `SameSite` parameter is now set by default to `Laxist` since Chrome 80/Firefox 69, few websites were setting it to a secure value, indicating they were added before to all requests because of the default `None SameSite` policy.

Based on these observations, we conclude that developers put a lot of trust in cookies as their presence alone in our tests lead to direct user authentication. This trust is only possible thanks to strong security mechanisms in browsers that have grown and matured a lot in the past decade. The rise of *HTTPS* coupled with a lot of control over what can be executed on a webpage (through *CSP*, *CORS* and all their derivatives) have changed the way we come to reason about cookie hijacking and how much harder it is to pull off such an attack today. Yet, our experiment shows that if indeed cookies are stolen, none of the tested websites have any mechanisms in place to detect any irregularities. We can only hypothesize at this point that this may not be in the scope of their threat model.

SYNTHESIS. In this section, we designed 2 attack models and tested them to measure the effectiveness of fingerprinting to protect users on web pages in our dataset. We observed fingerprinting being successfully used to improve security in our first attack using credentials to log in. Concerning our second attack, we did not detect any website in our dataset that used browser fingerprinting to protect against cookie hijacking.

6 Discussion

Understanding the Intent of a Fingerprinting Script is Hard. In the case of browser fingerprinting, analyzing why a script is included in a web page and why it's accessing specific attributes is complex as there is little indication of what will be done with the collected data once it has left the device. Still, it is possible to rely on some signs to capture the intent behind a fingerprinting script, such as:

- **Accessed APIs**: depending on the goal of the script, some APIs may be picked over others. For example, anti-bot companies access well-identified bot attributes, while others interested in cross-browser fingerprinting access OS and hardware-specific attributes.
- **Number of collected attributes**: while a very high number of attributes can often be linked to a fingerprinting behavior, the numbers vary. As seen in Table 1, some third parties, like Iovation, build on only 8 attributes, while others, like Secured Touch, collect up to 73. As a lot of the state of the art in fingerprinting is interested in either uniquely identifying devices or detecting inconsistencies, it makes sense to collect as many attributes as possible. Yet, as seen with Iovation, if you have a clear goal in mind, collecting very few attributes can be enough for your purpose.
- **Execution context**: where the fingerprinting script is located can show intent. If a fingerprinting script is included in all web pages, it is probably linked with an anti-bot system but, if it is only present on a payment page, then it is likely used for fraud prevention.

Considering the above signals, it is possible to estimate how the collected information will be used, but it does not provide certainty without having access to the backend where the browser fingerprints are analyzed.

Fingerprinting is Not Being Used to Protect Individual Accounts. In Sect. 4.2, we identified third-party actors who collect a wide range of data to implement bot protection and fraud prevention. They protect a website globally against external threats. Yet, when looking at what is offered to protect users' accounts, the story seems very different. Based on our experiments detailed in Sect. 5, there is little evidence that fingerprinting is currently being used to protect individual accounts. As we detected fingerprinting scripts delivered by 12 security-oriented organizations, we would have expected them to add an additional security layer to protect users. This raises the question of the relevance of using such a script from a security organization if the final usage is not security. More generally, we tested the defenses of 42 websites by creating accounts and logging with several contexts and parameters. Apart from some warning messages with few details on the new connecting device, we found only a single website blocked access to their services when the browser fingerprint did not match. Moreover, we have not detected any usage of browser fingerprinting to protect against our second attack, the cookie hijacking. We believe these are negative results of our paper and deserves further discussion.

First, theses results raise the question of why we observed such behaviors. One concern could be the accuracy of the browser fingerprinting algorithm. While cookies and IP addresses send strong signals that websites have relied on for years, a fingerprint is, in contrast, more volatile. It can change due to a minor modification to the browser's configuration or an update. Some attributes may be deemed too unstable to be included for verification while others are much more reliable and even predictable. As detailed by Vastel *et al.* [32], browser fingerprinting techniques require constant adaptation to maintain their robustness. Another concern is user experience, as having an overly sensitive algorithm could prompt for additional checks too often, even if the user did not change their device or browser.

Deficiencies in the State of the Art. As we identify concerns about the use of browser fingerprinting in a multifactor authentication system, we believe the state of the art currently lacks studies to measure the effectiveness and reliability of MFA with browser fingerprinting. First, users would need a way to add a new fingerprint to their account to be able to connect with another device. Websites in our dataset seem to use a OTP email. We believe other options should be studied because each authentication system is different and has its own trade-offs. Also, fingerprints evolve over time, and a multifactor authentication system would must be able to tell if a fingerprint is an evolution of an already registered one or not. While solutions have been proposed to compute a fingerprint evolution [32], it has been shown to not be fast enough when confronted with a large dataset [19]. Used in an authentication context, it would require a quick decision to have negligible impact on the user experience. An interesting study has been proposed by Alaca *et al.* [2] about the requirements of a such a system, but due to the rapid evolution of the web ecosystem, the study might be outdated. Finally, the state of the art lacks an evaluation of the user experience, satisfaction and confidence when using this kind of system.

Benefits Provided by Our Dataset. We believe our manual dataset is interesting for the community for future research on browser fingerprinting. In combination with a study about the origin and causality of a change in the browser fingerprint, it could be used to better understand what information the websites is looking for. They could be interested in an attribute that concerns some specific hardware or the software detail of the device, for example, to determine whether the fingerprint is consistent. An inconsistency could reveal a possible identity theft or a fraudster. Thus, it could help understand the purpose of browser fingerprinting collection on sensitive pages. Moreover, the automated detection of multi-factor authentication mechanisms suffers from the same biases as the automated detection of browser fingerprinting, and much of the same reasoning behind this study would apply. As explained in Sect. 2, the literature lacks a study on multi-factor authentication adoption on the web. Our dataset provides information about such mechanisms and could be used as a starting point for an in-depth study on these security systems.

7 Conclusion

In this paper, we studied the adoption of browser fingerprinting for security applications. More specifically, we analyzed 4 types of secured web pages—sign-up, sign-in, basket, and payment—that process sensitive personal data. We considered the state-of-the-art JavaScript attributes and developed an extension to monitor browser fingerprinting attribute accesses. To avoid biases introduced by automated crawlers and bots, we manually visited 1,485 pages published by 446 websites, and created accounts, logged in to verify authentication procedures, and went through the payment processes where available. We labeled 169 distinct fingerprinters using an existing technique. We publicly share our secured web page dataset and the detected fingerprinters we found.[5] We observed these fingerprinters being served by all types of secured pages and various website categories. We analyzed the script providers and found 12 security-focused organizations that use browser fingerprinting in secured web pages. We measured the use of MFA systems and bot detection, showing fingerprinting is used in combination with other identification techniques. We defined 2 attack models, stolen credentials and cookies hijacking, and evaluate websites in our dataset against them. Finally, we did not observe fingerprinting being actively used to secure websites against these 2 attacks.

A Selected Search Keywords

We used the following list of keywords to get specific website types: – Bank – Money transfer service – Stock trading – Financial – Cryptocurrency – Social insurance – Taxes – Healthcare – Job search – News – Email – Adult – Dating – Metro/train/flight tickets – Flight companies – Travel agencies – Airlines – Event ticket – Sport ticket – Social network – Ecommerce – Shopping – TV channel – Streaming – Bet games – Poker – Online game.

We used the following list of countries for our experiment: – United States – Japan – Germany – France – Russia – Spain – United Kingdom – India – China

References

1. Acar, G., Eubank, C., Englehardt, S., Juarez, M., Narayanan, A., Diaz, C.: The web never forgets: persistent tracking mechanisms in the wild. In: CCS 2014 (2014)
2. Alaca, F., van Oorschot, P.C.: Device fingerprinting for augmenting web authentication: classification and analysis of methods. In: ACSAC 2016 (2016)
3. Bursztein, E.: The bleak picture of two-factor authentication adoption in the wild (2018). https://elie.net/blog/security/the-bleak-picture-of-two-factor-authentication-adoption-in-the-wild/
4. Bursztein, E., Malyshev, A., Pietraszek, T., Thomas, K.: Picasso: lightweight device class fingerprinting for web clients. In: SPSM 2016 (2016)

[5] https://zenodo.org/record/3872144.

5. Cao, Y., Li, S., Wijmans, E.: (Cross-)browser fingerprinting via OS and hardware level features. In: NDSS 2017 (2017)
6. Durey, A., Laperdrix, P., Rudametkin, W., Rouvoy, R.: An iterative technique to identify browser fingerprinting scripts (2021)
7. Eckersley, P.: How unique is your web browser? In: Atallah, M.J., Hopper, N.J. (eds.) PETS 2010. LNCS, vol. 6205, pp. 1–18. Springer, Heidelberg (2010). https://doi.org/10.1007/978-3-642-14527-8_1
8. Englehardt, S., Narayanan, A.: Online tracking: a 1-million-site measurement and analysis. In: CCS 2016 (2016)
9. Gómez-Boix, A., Laperdrix, P., Baudry, B.: Hiding in the crowd: an analysis of the effectiveness of browser fingerprinting at large scale. In: WWW 2018 (2018)
10. Anti-Phishing Working Group: Phishing activity trends report (2019). https://docs.apwg.org/reports/apwg_trends_report_q3_2019.pdf
11. Invernizzi, L., Thomas, K., Kapravelos, A., Comanescu, O., Picod, J., Bursztein, E.: Cloak of visibility: detecting when machines browse a different web. In: S&P 2016 (2016)
12. Iqbal, U., Englehardt, S., Shafiq, Z.: Fingerprinting the fingerprinters: learning to detect browser fingerprinting behaviors (2021)
13. Jonker, H., Kalkman, J., Krumnow, B., Sleegers, M., Verresen, A.: Shepherd: enabling automatic and large-scale login security studies (2018)
14. Jonker, H., Krumnow, B., Vlot, G.: Fingerprint surface-based detection of web bot detectors. In: Sako, K., Schneider, S., Ryan, P.Y.A. (eds.) ESORICS 2019. LNCS, vol. 11736, pp. 586–605. Springer, Cham (2019). https://doi.org/10.1007/978-3-030-29962-0_28
15. Laperdrix, P., Avoine, G., Baudry, B., Nikiforakis, N.: Morellian analysis for browsers: making web authentication stronger with canvas fingerprinting. In: Perdisci, R., Maurice, C., Giacinto, G., Almgren, M. (eds.) DIMVA 2019. LNCS, vol. 11543, pp. 43–66. Springer, Cham (2019). https://doi.org/10.1007/978-3-030-22038-9_3
16. Laperdrix, P., Baudry, B., Mishra, V.: FPRandom: randomizing core browser objects to break advanced device fingerprinting techniques. In: Bodden, E., Payer, M., Athanasopoulos, E. (eds.) ESSoS 2017. LNCS, vol. 10379, pp. 97–114. Springer, Cham (2017). https://doi.org/10.1007/978-3-319-62105-0_7
17. Laperdrix, P., Bielova, N., Baudry, B., Avoine, G.: Browser fingerprinting: a survey. In: TWEB 2020 (2020)
18. Laperdrix, P., Rudametkin, W., Baudry, B.: Beauty and the beast: diverting modern web browsers to build unique browser fingerprints. In: S&P 2016 (2016)
19. Li, S., Cao, Y.: Who touched my browser fingerprint?: A large-scale measurement study and classification of fingerprint dynamics (2020)
20. Mowery, K., Shacham, H.: Pixel perfect: fingerprinting canvas in HTML5. In: W2SP 2012 (2012)
21. Mulazzani, M., et al.: Fast and reliable browser identification with Javascript engine fingerprinting. In: W2SP 2013 (2013)
22. Nikiforakis, N., Kapravelos, A., Joosen, W., Kruegel, C., Piessens, F., Vigna, G.: Cookieless monster: exploring the ecosystem of web-based device fingerprinting. In: S&P 2013 (2013)
23. Nikiforakis, N., Joosen, W., Livshits, B.: Privaricator: deceiving fingerprinters with little white lies. In: WWW 2015 (2015)
24. Olejnik, Ł., Acar, G., Castelluccia, C., Diaz, C.: The leaking battery. In: Garcia-Alfaro, J., Navarro-Arribas, G., Aldini, A., Martinelli, F., Suri, N. (eds.)

DPM/QASA -2015. LNCS, vol. 9481, pp. 254–263. Springer, Cham (2016). https://doi.org/10.1007/978-3-319-29883-2_18
25. Ometov, A., Bezzateev, S.V., Mäkitalo, N., Andreev, S., Mikkonen, T., Koucheryavy, Y.: Multi-factor authentication: a survey. Cryptography (2018)
26. Rizzo, V., Traverso, S., Mellia, M.: Unveiling web fingerprinting in the wild via code mining and machine learning. In: PETS 2021 (2021)
27. Rochet, F., Efthymiadis, K., Koeune, F.A., Pereira, O.: SWAT: seamless web authentication technology. Association for Computing Machinery (2019)
28. Sivakorn, S., Polakis, I., Keromytis, A.D.: The cracked cookie jar: http cookie hijacking and the exposure of private information. In: S&P 2016 (2016)
29. Unger, T., Mulazzani, M., Frühwirt, D., Huber, M., Schrittwieser, S., Weippl, E.: SHPF: Enhancing http(s) session security with browser fingerprinting. In: AReS 2013 (2013)
30. Urban, T., Degeling, M., Holz, T., Pohlmann, N.: Beyond the front page: Measuring third party dynamics in the field (2020)
31. Vastel, A., Laperdrix, P., Rudametkin, W., Rouvoy, R.: Fp-scanner: the privacy implications of browser fingerprint inconsistencies. In: USENIX 2018 (2018)
32. Vastel, A., Laperdrix, P., Rudametkin, W., Rouvoy, R.: FP-STALKER: tracking browser fingerprint evolutions. In: S&P 2018 (2018)
33. Vastel, A., Rudametkin, W., Rouvoy, R., Blanc, X.: FP-crawlers: studying the resilience of browser fingerprinting to block crawlers. In: MADWeb 2020 (2020)
34. Zeber, D., et al.: The representativeness of automated Web crawls as a surrogate for human browsing. In: WWW 2020 (2020)

Introspect Virtual Machines Like It Is the Linux Kernel!

Ahmed Abdelraoof(✉), Benjamin Taubmann, Thomas Dangl, and Hans P. Reiser

University of Passau, Passau, Germany
abdelr02@ads.uni-passau.de, {bt,td,hr}@sec.uni-passau.de

Abstract. Virtual machine introspection (VMI) allows a monitoring application, usually running in a separate virtual machine on the same host, to peek into another guest virtual machine running on the same host, check and modify both registers and memory state of the guest. It has gained popularity in malware analysis, software reverse engineering, and intrusion detection systems. However, VMI comes with a huge overhead, which not only is a waste of resources but also can tip malware that VMI is being used.

In this paper, we present an approach to significantly enhance the performance of VMI. Our work eliminates a large number of context switches between the monitored guest system, the hypervisor, and the monitoring application. Our approach implements the management of tracing directly into the hypervisor and uses asynchronous events between hypervisor and monitoring process to minimize the performance impact of tracing without losing functionality. We show that our approach reduces the main bottlenecks of introspection by more than an order of magnitude compared to the popular approach using LibVMI and the Xen hypervisor.

Keywords: Virtual machine · Introspection · Tracing · Operating system · Debugging

1 Introduction

Virtual machine introspection (VMI) is the process of monitoring and possibly modifying the inner workings of a virtual machine (VM) execution at run-time. The hypervisor isolates the monitoring application from the monitored VM. The monitoring application typically runs in a separated VM and usually sets code breakpoints or data watchpoints in the monitored VM. When one of these interception points triggers, the monitoring application takes control of the monitored VM. In recent years, VMI has been shown to be useful for a broad range of purposes, including debugging [7], intrusion detection [10,17], malware analysis [11,16], honeypots [19], and digital forensics [24].

However, in many cases the advantage of strong isolation between monitoring application and monitored VM comes at the cost of high overheads that severely

L. Bilge et al. (Eds.): DIMVA 2021, LNCS 12756, pp. 258–277, 2021.
https://doi.org/10.1007/978-3-030-80825-9_13

degrade the performance of the monitored VM. Each hit of an interception point on code or data means that the control flow is diverted from the monitored VM to the monitoring application via the hypervisor and the operating system, causing multiple context switches. If the monitoring application observes frequently executed code or accessed data, this overhead becomes prohibitively expensive. Another factor that contributes to the performance degradation is the time spent on synchronous processing while handling the interception point.

In this paper, we present novel approaches to mitigating this severe limitation of VMI. In particular, for malware detection and analysis, minimizing the noticeable overhead also increases the stealthiness of the monitoring. Our main contribution is designing a VMI system that is flexible, secure, and fast. We do that by analyzing the main sources of overhead in current VMI implementations and eliminating them from their roots. For the purposes of this paper, we will be using the Xen hypervisor [4], as it has advanced support for VMI out of the box [2]. However, the techniques we developed can be applied to any hypervisor with sufficient VMI support. Our contributions can be summarized as follows:

1. Identifying context switches between guests and hypervisor during hypercalls and VMI events as an overhead source in VMI.
2. Identifying complex analysis in the monitoring process as another overhead source in VMI.
3. Fixing the first overhead source by creating in-hypervisor coarse-grained primitives for handling both data accesses (memory access tracers) and code execution (breakpoints).
4. Fixing the second overhead source by making the memory access tracers and breakpoints handled asynchronously using a wait-free/lock-free queue.
5. Evaluate the performance and reliability of our system when compared to other VMI implementations.

The rest of this paper is structured as follows: First, Sect. 2 surveys related prior work. In Sect. 3, we lay out all the needed background knowledge. We explain the Xen infrastructure and discuss the inner-workings of a typical VMI implementation. Section 4 analyzes in detail the causes of VMI overhead, using for illustration an infrastructure based on LibVMI. LibVMI is one of the most popular libraries for VMI, used by many introspection applications. In Sect. 5, we propose in-hypervisor tracing primitives that mitigate the shortcomings of LibVMI. Section 6 extends our design to be able to execute the vast majority of tracing algorithms without the need for doing context switches. In Sect. 7, we put our system to test. We verify the effectiveness of our proposed system in improving system performance. We show that utilizing asynchronous in-hypervisor tracing primitives can reduce performance overhead orders of magnitude.

2 Related Work

Use Cases. The use cases for which VMI has been successfully employed range from debugging over intrusion detection and prevention to malware analysis and digital forensics.

VMI can be used for debugging even if other approaches are unavailable. Normally, user-space debugging (or even kernel debugging) requires the availability of suitable interfaces and support. Mechanisms like Windows PatchGuard [22] protect the kernel from being monitored, turning debugging to be extremely complicated [18]. *Bhatt et al.* [7] have demonstrated that VMI may be very successful in introspecting Windows PatchGuard.

VMI has also been used to implement intrusion detection systems (IDS). For example, *Wishra et al.* [17] use VMI to trace system calls and apply a "bag of n-grams" approach integrated with "term frequency-inverse document frequency" to distinguish between normal and malicious activities. VMI has also been used to do real-time memory analysis as a new kind of IDS [10].

Another popular application for VMI is dynamic malware analysis. There have been multiple system designs and implementations for a complete malware analysis pipeline using VMI technology. For example, VMI can be used to classify malware families based on Windows API call traces [11], to capture the running processes of malware, detect rootkits, and analyze the sequence of system calls [16], and for building high-interaction honeypots [19].

Limitations and Performance Issues. With that being said, virtual machine introspection (VMI) has a wide range of applications in computer security. With the current implementations, the performance impact is the main issue why industry might shy away from VMI technology. It is not possible to use VMI for IDS or malware analysis in environments with real-time requirements, or when resources are scarce.

Zhao et al. proposed using hardware-assisted shadow MMU for introspection in a system which they called *ImEE*. They had an initial overhead for setting up the shadow page table. Their evaluations show that replacing LibVMI with an in-kernel framework improves VMI performance by around between 15x and 70x when compared to LibVMI [23]. However, in their benchmarking, the overhead is not clear when compared to not using introspection.

Taubmann et al. showed that compared to not using VMI, LibVMI can have overhead that goes up to around 2800% when monitoring `read`, `write`, `open`, `close`, and `exec` system call system-wide. They reduced the impact to around 60% [21] by selectively enabling system call tracing only when the right process is running. This was done by monitoring `CR3` register and using it to fingerprint processes.

This is still considered a huge overhead from the industry's point of view. The main problem with the system-wide approach is that it is extremely slow. Tracing `open`, `read`, `write` and `exec` is not uncommon in endpoint security or anti-ransomware software. Having an overhead of 60% is unacceptable by some endpoint security software. When tracing more system calls, which is usually the case, the overhead of current solutions can be expected to be even higher.

On the other hand, having a per-process tracer might be useful in some cases, but it is to be expected to reach the same overhead levels when being used to implement a system-wide IDS.

3 Background

3.1 Xen Infrastructure

Xen [4] is a bare-metal hypervisor. On top of the physical hardware, there is the light hypervisor. Its main job is to schedule the guest's access to CPU and various other resources. On top of that hypervisor, there are the guests that act as virtual machines. In Xen's terminology, these guests are called *DomU*. One of these guests is special compared to the rest. It is called *Dom0*. That specific guest has more capabilities than a normal *DomU* guest. In a typical *DomU*, the operating system can request resources from the hypervisor just the same way it would deal with normal hardware. That is also possible in *Dom0*.

However, in *Dom0*, there are special communication channels that allow the operating system to do more privileged functionalities. For example, only *Dom0* is capable of creating new virtual machines or managing the physical resources allocated per virtual machine.

There are mainly two communication channels between guests and the Xen hypervisor. The first communication channel is via hypercalls [3]. Informally speaking, the relation between guests and hypervisor when it comes to hypercalls is like the relation between user-space processes and operating system kernel when it comes to system calls. Naturally, hypercalls are synchronous. In Xen, hypercalls are used to do many things ranging from configuring events down to assisting with memory management.

The other communication channel is Xenstore [6], Xenstore is a shared storage between all guests including Dom0. The interaction between guests and Xenstore is synchronous just like a normal hypercall. However, Xenstore can be used to construct asynchronous communication channels between guests. It also provides support for transactional safety with multi-readers and multi-writers channels through Xenbus [5].

3.2 VMI Mechanics

The basic idea behind VMI is to have an introspection virtual machine that runs a monitoring application and has access to the internal state (memory, CPU, etc.) of a monitored VM as its target. For the sake of drawing a clear distinction and simplicity, we will always assume that *Dom0* is monitoring *DomU*, although it does not always have to be the case. For example, CloudPhylactor demonstrates how to move the monitoring application to a separate, isolated *monitoring DomU* [20].

VMI can use synchronous and asynchronous mechanisms [12]. Asynchronous VMI means that the monitoring application reads and analyzes the state (in particular the main memory) of the target system without direct synchronization with the target's control flow. Nevertheless, the monitor often requires a consistent view of the (concurrently executing) target system, so it is common to pause the target VM during memory access. Memory snapshots and copy-on-write (COW) techniques [9,13] can contribute to pausing the execution of the introspected *DomU* for the least possible period of time.

In synchronous VMI, introspection is based on events triggered by the monitored *DomU*. These events can range from invoking system calls, reading, writing, or executing certain memory addresses, accessing the CPU's model-specific register (MSRs), to accessing a memory-mapped IO device (MMIO). The monitoring application sets up event handlers targeting one of the running *DomU*s. As soon as an interesting event occurs within *DomU*, this event causes an interruption of the execution and a context switch to the hypervisor. Then the hypervisor switches control to *Dom0*. This technique has, for example, been utilized by LibVMI [2] and by *Taubmann et al.* [21].

4 Dissecting the LibVMI Hypervisor Interface

In this section, we analyze the code base of LibVMI[1] and the related parts in Xen hypervisor[2]. LibVMI is the de facto standard for introspection. It has full support for introspection in Xen-based virtual machines and limited support for KVM-based virtual machines. LibVMI is used to integrate introspection into Volatility[3], which is a memory forensics framework. LibVMI is also used by DRAKVUF [15], which is a dynamic malware analysis pipeline. From a top-level view, *LibVMI* provides APIs for virtual machine introspection. These APIs are used to configure event-based triggering mechanisms, access/modify memory, and control memory mapping (altp2m), as shown in Fig. 1.

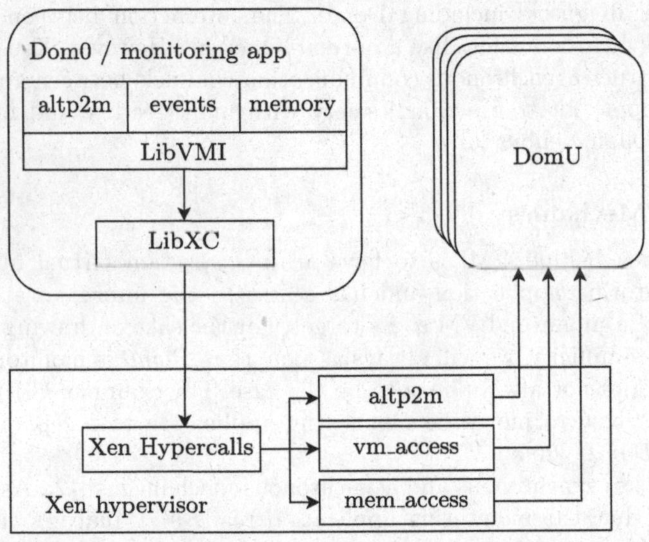

Fig. 1. Relation between LibVMI and Xen

[1] https://github.com/libvmi/libvmi.

[2] https://xenbits.xen.org/gitweb/?p=xen.git.

[3] https://github.com/volatilityfoundation/volatility.git.

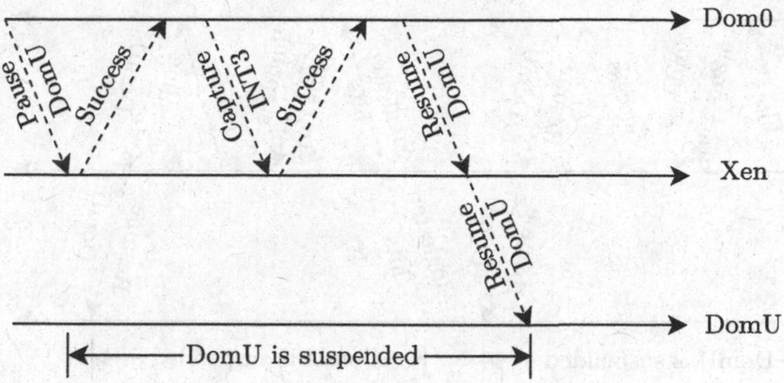

Fig. 2. Context switching when setting a breakpoint

LibXC is a thin low-level wrapper for Xen hypercalls. The motivation behind its existence is that hypercalls are vendor and configuration specific [1]. *LibXC* provides an abstraction over all the different configurations. In the set of *API* we are interested in, almost any call to *LibVMI* would have a 1-to-1 mapping to a Xen hypercall. The problem is that on almost every *LibVMI* call, there is at least one context switch from *Dom0* to the Xen hypervisor and back.

The performance overhead from these context switches can be an acceptable cost for requesting features from the hypervisor. The real problem is that intercepted events in *DomU* trigger a context switch from *DomU* to Xen, then to *Dom0*. *DomU* will have at least one (if not all) CPU cores suspended until *Dom0* finishes its introspection subroutine. That will require two context switches per CPU (pause and resume). Only after that, there will be a context switch back to the Xen hypervisor, which in turn will do a context switch back to *DomU*.

This leads to the rise of a few issues: First, introspection is slow, due to the large number of context switches. Second, any operation done in *Dom0* is not necessarily time-bounded, so there is no guarantee that *DomU* will resume after a fixed amount of time.

Aside from having performance issues, managing introspection completely from *Dom0* incurs a risk commonly ignored by research work on VMI: Should the monitoring process in *Dom0* crash for any reason, it would inevitably cause the crash of *DomU* once a monitored event is triggered, as the (synchronous) event handler is no longer available. While the main motivation behind our work is to address the first two problems, it also provides an elegant solution for mitigating the latter problem.

For the purposes of this paper, we will assume that we are dealing with a single CPU core per guest. See Dangl et al. [8] for details on how to handle additional challenges caused by multi-core guests.

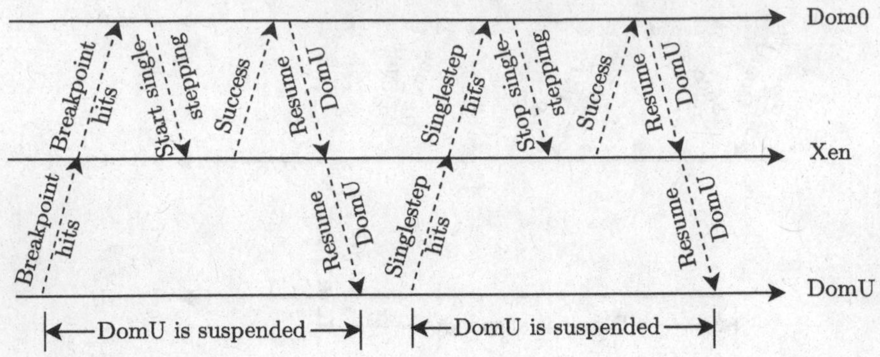

Fig. 3. Context switching when a breakpoint hits

4.1 Setting a Breakpoint

One good demonstration for the sheer amount of context switching involved per operation is by examining how breakpoints work in VMI as shown in Fig. 2. *Dom0* will first pause our *DomU* (context switches happen here) then we modify the memory content of *DomU* to replace the instruction at the address we want to break on with an `INT3`, then we configure an event listener inside the hypervisor to catch `INT3` in *DomU* (another context switching to Xen and back). After that, we resume out *DomU*. So just to configure a *DomU* breakpoint it was required to do four context switches, all during which *DomU* is being suspended.

If we take into consideration that all the operations mentioned above are hypercalls, that would imply even more context CPU cycles while *DomU* is suspended, which would be a huge performance loss.

4.2 Hitting a Breakpoint

Figure. 3 visualizes the process of processing a breakpoint hit.[4] When a breakpoint hits, Xen interrupts *DomU* and triggers the appropriate event handler in *Dom0* (two context switches). After the event handler does its arbitrarily complex introspection analysis, it would next rewrite the original data that was replaced by `INT3`, set up another event handler for single-stepping (two context switches), and resume *DomU* (2 more context switches). *DomU* only executes one instruction before it re-triggers another event for single-stepping that will be forwarded by Xen to *Dom0* (two context switches). Then *Dom0* rewrites the previously removed `INT3` and disables the single-stepping event handler (two context switches). Finally, *DomU* gets to resume its execution until another breakpoint hits.

[4] While there is a hypercall in Xen to toggle single stepping, Xen also offers the possibility to piggy-back that operation in the return ("Resume") from Dom0 to Xen. Our baseline measurements for LibVMI in Sect. 7 make use of that optimization, but nevertheless are significantly slower than our proposed optimized method.

If we are setting breakpoints on a *sendto* or *recvfrom* system calls to monitor suspicious behavior on a server, we will experience severe performance degrading because any processing on the system call (who issued the system call, or what is the data stored there) is always done by *Dom0*. So all accesses to that particular system call shall be funneled into *Dom0*. And only after that large amount of context switches, it would be possible to isolate the system calls of interest.

4.3 Memory Access Tracers as Opposed to Breakpoints

Tracing memory access (tracepoints) using *LibVMI* has a lot in common with setting breakpoints. They both share the general outline and the number of context switches. However, they differ in the nature of work done during each context switch. Instead of injecting *INT3* breakpoints, memory access tracers manipulate the memory access permissions in the hypervisor's page table.

LibVMI provides an API for switching the guest-physical-to-machine memory mapping (altp2m). This mechanism is the basis for memory tracing, as it allows creating multiple memory mapping configurations for the same guest physical memory page, with different access permissions. The memory tracer can use this to create a copy of DomU's guest physical to machine physical (p2m) map, restrict memory access on pages to be traced, and instruct Xen to use the restricted map instead of the original map.

Once a tracepoint is hit, the memory access tracer in the monitoring application would restore the original p2m table. After doing a single-step operation (for which the memory access will be enabled), the tracer would again inject the modified p2m table with restricted access.

4.4 Summary of Identified Problems

To summarize the observations from this chapter: (1) VMI as used by LibVMI (and other implementations as well) results in a significant number of context switches per monitoring action and per observed event; (2) The analysis done by the VMI monitoring application is done within the synchronous handling of events, while to monitored DomU is suspended, causing potentially long execution delays; (3) Essential state management required for handling monitoring events (such as breakpoints) is contained in the monitoring application (in Dom0 in our figures), causing the failure of a monitored Dom0 in case the monitoring application fails.

5 Hypervisor Tracers (HVT)

In Sect. 4, we demonstrated that one of the major issues of synchronous VMI is the large number of context switches between *DomU*, *Xen*, and *Dom0*. The goal of this section is to present our HVT architecture that minimizes the context switches as much as possible.

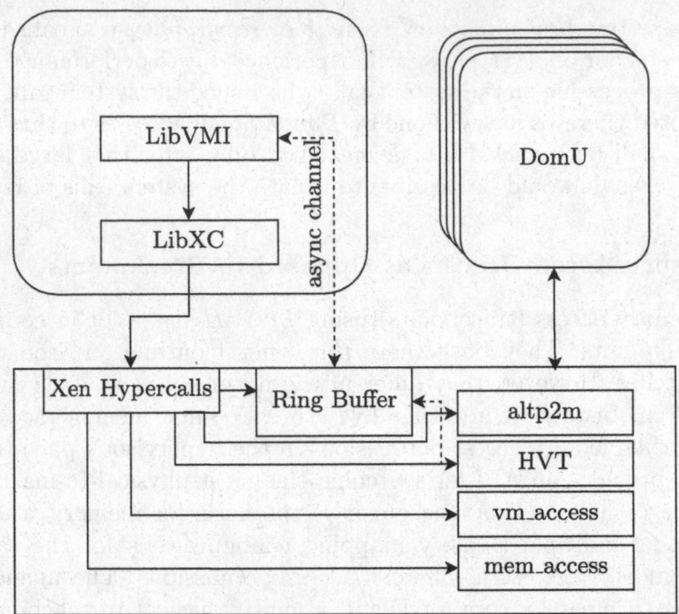

Fig. 4. HVT and asynchronous channel

Completely eliminating all context switching would remove all costs of context switching, but that is not feasible if we want to benefit from the isolation between the virtual machines and have a monitoring application in a virtual machine isolated from the introspection target by the hypervisor. So instead, our ambition is to reduce the context switches to a minimum of (a) a single interaction from monitoring application in Dom0 to the hypervisor for configuring tracing mechanisms, and (b) a single interaction from DomU to the monitoring application in Dom0 via the hypervisor for each event we want to trace in DomU.

5.1 Hypervisor Tracers Architecture

Our solution to avoid context switches creates a set of coarse-grained hypercalls for the purpose of tracing. We refer to them as *Hypervisor Tracers* (HVT). They achieve the right balance between reducing the number of hypercalls and being flexible enough for any introspection task by handling selected core parts of the introspection in the hypervisor itself. Figure 4 shows HVT and the way it interacts with the rest of Xen and *LibVMI*.

Figure 5 shows the context switching pattern in *HVT*. As demonstrated in Fig. 5a, we have only two context switches in one hypercall, which is the one needed for *Dom0* to express its interest in somehow introspecting a virtual machine using some of the tracers. Figure 5b shows that when a tracer event gets triggered, there will be only six context switches that are required to transfer control from *DomU* to *Dom0*, do single stepping and transfer control back.

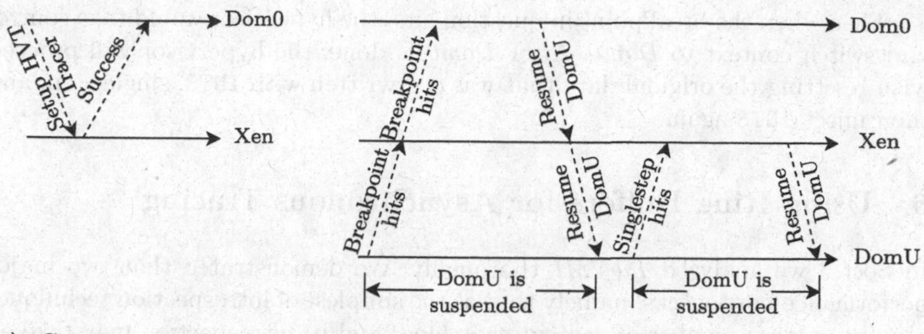

(a) Context switches when setting HVT tracer (b) Context switching when triggering HVT events

Fig. 5. Context switching in Hypervisor Tracers

We propose two tracers, each of which can be represented by a hypercall, one is the general-purpose memory access tracer, and the other is the breakpoint tracer, both of which follow the same context switching model in Fig. 5. They are described in detail in the following paragraphs.

5.2 Memory Access Tracer

The goal of the memory access tracer is to trace read/write access to main memory in the guest physical address space. When *Dom0* requests a watchpoint on a certain memory address, the hypervisor would first pause the appropriate *DomU*, then it creates alternative guest physical to machine physical mapping (altp2m) [14]. Then it sets the memory page equivalent to the memory address in question to more constraining protection. For example, a read tracer would prevent read operations on the whole memory page, and a write tracer would prevent all write operations on that page. Finally, the hypervisor resumes *DomU*.

And when memory access happens, the Memory Management Unit (MMU) triggers a page fault that is handled by the hypervisor. The hypervisor fault handler switches context to *Dom0*. After *Dom0* is done, the hypervisor will proceed with flipping the alt2pm protection to be less constrained, single step, and then re-flip the alt2pm restriction to be more constrained.

5.3 Guest Physical Breakpoint

This tracer is very similar to *LibVMI*'s original breakpoint technique, except that it follows the *HVT* rule of six context switches.

For setting a breakpoint *Dom0* would send a request to Xen via a hypercall. Xen would then pause *DomU* and overwrite the data in our guest physical address with an `INT3`, sets the appropriate interrupt event handler, and resumes the execution of *DomU* all in one hypercall.

Then when the breakpoint in question hits, the hypervisor would take control and switch context to *Dom0*. After *Dom0* is done, the hypervisor will proceed with resetting the original data that was overwritten with `INT3`, single step, and then inject `INT3` again.

6 Using Ring Buffers for Asynchronous Tracing

In Sect. 4 we analyzed *LibVMI* thoroughly. We demonstrated that two major performance bottlenecks, namely that a) the simplest of introspection techniques requires a large number of context switching, and b) introspection may take an arbitrarily long time. In Sect. 5, we addressed the former by redesigning the basic VMI primitives. In this section, we will address the latter issue.

In this section, our goal is to maximize *DomU* performance independent of the complexity of *Dom0* introspection. This way, we can implement arbitrarily complex introspection without degrading the performance. In order to guarantee independence, we designed an asynchronous data channel between Xen and *Dom0*. The asynchronous channel is a circular queue (we might also refer to as ring buffer) data structure that is shared between Xen and *Dom0*. That queue has a few basic properties:

1. It has a single producer (Xen) and a single consumer (*Dom0*).
2. It has a fixed-size buffer that is initialized at creation time.
3. The `enqueue` operation, which is performed by the hypervisor, is lock-free and wait-free. It will not be delayed for any reason.
4. The `dequeue` operation, which is performed *Dom0*, is lock-free as well. However, it is not wait-free and it might be busy-looping waiting for the hypervisor to finish writing the current entry.
5. Both `enqueue/dequeue` are guaranteed to store/retrieve non-corrupted data.
6. The `dequeue` operation guarantees event order but does not support reliability (events might be dropped). If two subsequent calls to `dequeue` returned two events E_i and E_j respectively, it is guaranteed that either there are no events enqueued between E_i and E_j, or if there were events enqueued between E_i and E_j, then they are dropped forever.

Listing 1 shows the most fundamental `Item` data structure used in our queue, representing any monitored DomU event. Aside from holding event-specific data, it holds an event-specific number `seq`. This sequence number monotonically labels events per slot in the queue. The sequence number is incremented to an odd number before an entry is modified, and incremented again to an even number after modifications have finished. All event slots in the ring buffer are initialized with `seq==0`, after adding events to all slots they all will have the value `seq==2`, and so on. This implies that each event has `seq` that is bigger than or equal to that of events triggered before it. If the sequence number is odd, the current event slot is in the middle of being overwritten and must no be read. If `seq` is even, it would imply that the current event can be read.

Listing 1. Shared data structure

```
struct Item {
    uint64_t seq;
    struct event_data data;
};
```

First *Dom0* initializes its own ring buffer by calling `DInitialize` described in Fig. 3. During this process, it requests the shared memory from Xen via hypercalling `XInitialize` described in Fig. 2. This way both *Dom0*'s and Xen's ring buffers are initialized.

As one might notice, both ring buffers share a lot in common. The `itms` member is the shared memory created by Xen and accessed by both Xen and *Dom0*. In both versions of the ring buffer, `count` refers to the storage capacity of the ring buffer. In Xen, `idx` is the index at which the next event will be written to. However, in *Dom0*, `idx` refers to the index at which an already registered event can be read.

Dom0's ring buffer has an extra member, namely `prev`. It is used to store the `seq` of previously successfully read event. Although it could have been possible to calculate it at run-time, we thought it would be more convenient to just store it.

In Xen, as shown in Listing 2, there is the `enqueue` operation that would save triggered events. It simply increments the `seq` number at the current `itm` element to be written. Then it stores the event data and again increments `seq`. Since at initialization all `seq` numbers are set to zero, it is always guaranteed that after an `enqueue`, the `seq` number will always be even while it would be odd during the `enqueue` operation.

As opposed to Xen's `enqueue`, *Dom0* has a `dequeue` operation that is slightly more involved as shown in Listing 3. First we would wait until `seq` at `itm` number `idx` is greater than or equal to `prev` which is the `seq` of last read event. Then we read the event data. But we read the `seq` before and after reading the event data, if the `seq` is an even number and did not change during copying the event data, we assume that the ring buffer did not overflow and that no race condition happened. Then we update the `prev` value as well as the `idx`.

7 System Evaluation and Benchmarking

In this section, we evaluate the performance of virtual machine tracers as well as our asynchronous channels. As memory access tracers and breakpoint tracers are conceptually very similar, we use our implementation of the HVT breakpoint tracer in this evaluation, in combination with our asynchronous event channel.

In our tests, we use the breakpoint tracer to trace the invocation of selected system calls in the introspection target (DomU). Breakpoints are placed on the system call handler function of DomU's operating system. We measure the impact on the performance of the system running within DomU. As baseline

Listing 2. Xen's side of the ring buffer

```
struct XRingBuffer {
    uint64_t idx;
    uint64_t count;
    struct Item *itms; // shared memory data structure
};
Global struct XRingBuffer xrb
procedure XINITIALIZE(uint64_t count)
    xrb.count ← count
    xrb.itms ← Allocate count × sizeof(struct Item)
    Fill xrb.itms with Zeros
    xrb.idx ← 0
    return xrb.itms to Dom0
procedure ENQUEUE(textbfstruct event_data data)
    xrb.itms[xrb.idx].seq += 1
    xrb.itms[xrb.idx].data = data
    xrb.itms[xrb.idx].seq += 1
    xrb.idx ← (xrb.idx + 1) mod xrb.count
```

Listing 3. *Dom0*'s side of the ring buffer

```
struct DRingBuffer {
    uint64_t idx;
    uint64_t count;
    uint64_t prev;
    struct Item *itms; // shared memory data structure, allocated by Xen
};
Global struct DRingBuffer drb
procedure DINITIALIZE(uint64_t count)
    drb.count ← count
    drb.itms ← XINITIALIZE(count)
    drb.idx ← 0
    drb.prev ← 1
procedure TRY_READ
    while drb.itms[drb.idx].seq mod 2 ≠ 0 do
        sleep
    data ← drb.itms[drb.idx].data
    seq ← drb.itms[drb.idx].seq
    return (data, seq)
procedure DEQUEUE
    while drb.prev > drb.itms[drb.idx].seq do
        sleep
    do
        old ← drb.itms[drb.idx].seq
        (data, new) ← try_read()
    while old ≠ new or old mod 2 ≠ 0
    drb.prev = old
    drb.idx ← (drb.idx + 1) mod drb.count
    return data
```

for our evaluation, we use two measurements: first, a system that does not use any tracing at all (ideally, we want to be close to that performance), and second, a system that uses standard *LibVMI* API for placing `INT3` breakpoints and single-stepping controlled by the monitoring application.

Our test environment is based on *Xen 4.14.0* and an Intel core i7-6700K CPU running at about 3.9 GHz, with 2 cores and 4 GB RAM for *Dom0* and 1 core and 2 GB RAM for *DomU*. *Dom0* is running Debian 10, with Linux Kernel *5.4.68*, and *DomU* is running Ubuntu *20.04.1 LTS* unmodified.

We evaluated the system performance in several different use cases: first, we used the invocation of the *getpid* system call and a network ping to localhost as microbenchmarks; second, we used the Unix Benchmark[5] for a more detailed performance evaluation with a well-known standard tool; third, we used three additional test cases that resemble two mixed CPU/IO intensive use cases (compiling the Linux kernel and extracting a *.tar.gz* archive) and a disk IO-bound use case (copying a large file).

We ran each of our own benchmark tests 11 times, ignored the first run, and calculated the average of the remaining 10 runs. We also calculated the standard deviation to show that the overhead is consistent. The reason we ignored the first measurement is that because in many cases it might be inaccurate. For example, in CPU intensive applications it would take some time before the CPU reaches maximum heat and starts throttling. At that point, it starts throttling down and the performance degrades. For IO-intensive applications, we wanted to avoid situations where we have unsynchronized IO buffers, and by ignoring the first measurement we would guarantee that the IO buffer would be full so the operating system would probably have to synchronize IO at each run at least once. For the Unix Benchmark suite, we used the average of five executions of the complete test suite in its default configuration (which internally runs each sub-benchmark multiple times).

In all our tests, the asynchronous tracer was in a league of its own when it comes to speed, consistently faster than both HVT tracing and basic tracing using standard *LibVMI*. The HVT tracer was also consistently faster than using *LibVMI* in all our tests.

7.1 Microbenchmarks: `getpid()` and `ping localhost`

First, we wanted to measure the raw overhead of the various VMI approaches with a very simple and deterministic test, without requiring the test to have meaningful computation. We created a simple program that looped 100,000 times doing a `getpid` system call and nothing else. To make sure that the real system call gets called instead of some user space implementation, we wrote the whole `getpid` test in assembly.

Our results are shown in Fig. 6a. Although measurements from this test do not necessarily reflect performance in real-world scenarios (when compared to the rest of our evaluation), it still provides clear insights on by how far is our

[5] https://github.com/kdlucas/byte-unixbench (accessed 2021-05-10).

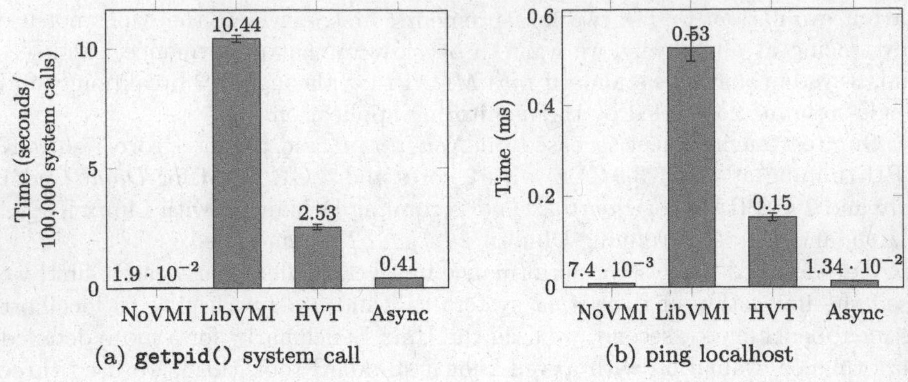

(a) `getpid()` system call (b) ping localhost

Fig. 6. VMI impact on performance for simple microbenchmarks

architecture superior to that of when introspection uses standard *LibVMI*. While our asynchronous tracer still has some overhead compared with the no VMI case (19 ms vs 410 ms), it is more than 25 times faster than standard *LibVMI*.

In a second microbenchmark, we wanted to measure the impact on a simple situation that is more realistic for real-world applications than iteratively invoking `getpid()`, while still minimizing measurement noise. As such, we benchmarked our system by observing ping time to *localhost* while having a breakpoint tracer placed on the `sendto` system call in the *DomU* guest.

As shown in Fig. 6b, breakpoints and single-stepping (which is the current implementation in *libVMI*) had the worst performance. Our HVT tracer yielded better performance than *libVMI*. Our asynchronous channel had the best performance out of all other VMI implementations, having an advantage of almost factor 40 compared to standard *LibVMI*, and less than factor 2 penalty compared to no tracing at all (NoVMI).

It is also worth mentioning that the ping test has one of the highest overhead ratios among all our test suites. That is because out of the two main operations done by the ping utility, which are `sendto` and `recvfrom`, one of them is being introspected. Other measurements that we discuss later either execute CPU-intensive tasks in the user application or perform more complex work in the Linux kernel when executing the system call. In both cases, the relative impact of system call tracing becomes smaller.

7.2 Unix Benchmark Results

For a more detailed performance evaluation, we used the Unix benchmark suite[6] in its default configuration. The suite executes 12 different benchmarks, stress-testing different parts of the system. Our detailed results (average of 5 runs) can be found in the Appendix. The numbers indicate operations executed in a

[6] https://github.com/kdlucas/byte-unixbench (accessed 2021-05-10).

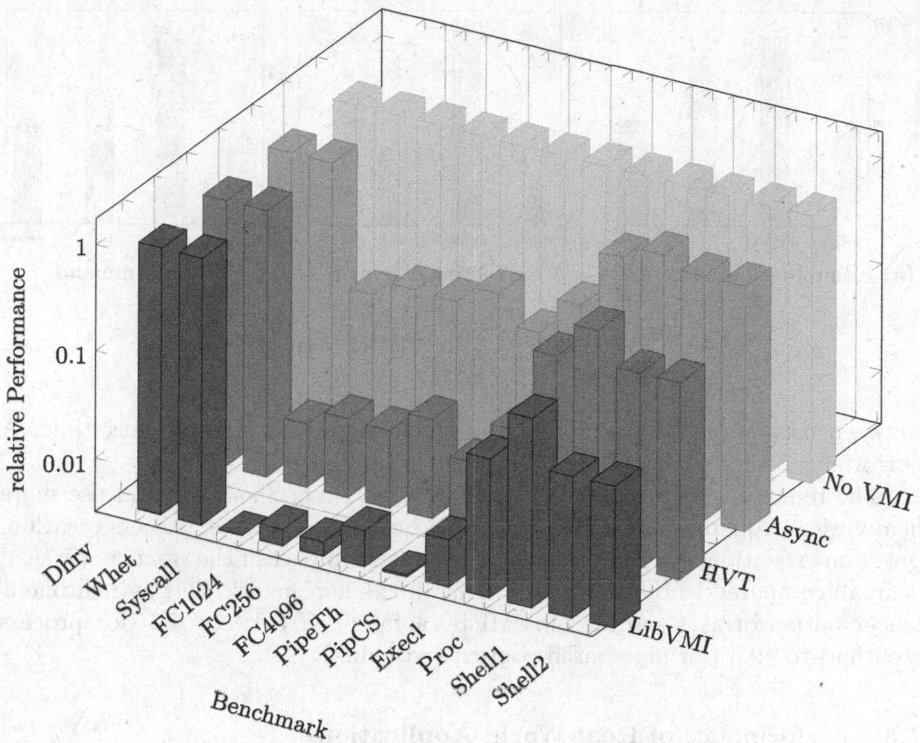

Fig. 7. Unix benchmark results (performance relative to the NoVMI case)

fixed time interval, i.e., higher values are better. For visualization in Fig. 7, we normalized all measurements relative to the NoVMI case. Relative performance is shown on a logarithmic scale.

The first two measurements (Dhrystone and Whetstone) are pure CPU measurements that (except for periodic statistics output during the benchmark run) do not make use of system calls. As expected, VMI tracing has no noticeable performance impact.

The Syscall benchmark is very similar to our previous `getpid` test, with the main difference being that it uses a mixture of multiple system calls, each with low computational complexity (`dup2`, `close`, `getuid`, `umask`): Our async tracer outperforms standard LibVMI by a factor of 23, while still a factor of 14 slower than a system without VMI tracing.

The file copy (FC$xxxx$) benchmarks as well as the pipe throughput (PipeTh) benchmarks show a performance behavior very similar to the Syscall benchmark. FC$xxxx$ first writes, then reads data from a file, with several block sizes ($xxxx$), with the total file size such that can fully be handled by the operating system's buffer cache; PipeTh transfers data between two processes. In all cases, the benchmark measures basically the performance of `read` and `write` system calls; within those system calls, the actual operation is copying a block of memory

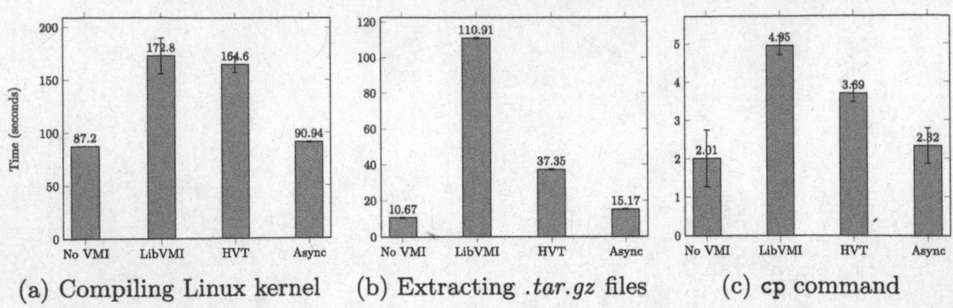

(a) Compiling Linux kernel (b) Extracting *.tar.gz* files (c) **cp command**

Fig. 8. Benchmarking with real-world applications

between user space and kernel space, which takes only a very short time. A performance very similar to Syscall is thus no big surprise.

The remaining benchmarks (PipeCS, Excel, Proc, Shell1, Shell2) use more heavy-weight operations (context switches between processes, process creation, program execution, etc.). As a result, the relative impact of the tracing overhead is small compared to the total work done in the benchmark. Our asynchronous tracer outperforms standard LibVMI by a factor of between 4.2 (for process creation) to 19.5 (for pipe-based context switching).

7.3 Performance of Real-World Applications

For an additional evaluation of performance in workloads the resemble tasks of real-world applications, we used three additional use cases: compiling the Linux kernel, extracting a large compressed file, and copying a huge file.

Compiling the Linux kernel is a mixture of IO intensive operations and CPU intensive operations. In our case, we used *kernel 5.8.13*. We compiled the kernel using `make tinyconfig`. We set breakpoints on 3 system calls *execve*, *read*, and *write*. Figure 8a shows that both of our approaches (HVT and async) are superior to *libVMI*. Compared to previous microbenchmarks, one can note that having a use-case for which parts of the workload are not being introspected (CPU workload of the compiler) did counter the overhead coming from the fact that we traced three system calls.

The experiments show that in such real-application benchmarks, the actual overhead of VMI is much smaller than in the previous benchmarks, because only a fraction of the activities in DomU are affected by the tracing. Nevertheless, the three system calls selected are system calls frequently invoked when compiling the Linux kernel. The results show that the overall overhead is down to 4% compared to the no VMI baseline, a value that should easily acceptable in most use cases, while the about 100% slowdown caused by the standard *LibVMI* approach will be prohibitively expensive in many situations such as continuous monitoring of production systems.

Another measurement we did with a CPU/IO mixed workload was extracting a compressed folder, using the Linux kernel 5.8.13 source code as example (compressed file size 170 MB). This task is composed of CPU intensive workload, that is decompressing the gzip compressed file, as well as a more IO intensive workload, which is extracting the *tar* file. For this test, we set breakpoints on all system calls that are executed by `tar`. The results we captured, as shown in Fig. 8b, was very similar to those we captured while testing the Linux kernel compilation process.

Finally, we wanted to verify that IO intensive applications would not have a huge problem with VMI. For that our last test was a pure IO process that is copying a huge file (1 GB) on disk using `cp`. As we can see in Fig. 8c, the same expected pattern emerges, *HVT* is faster than *LibVMI* and the asynchronous channel is the most efficient of them all.

Note that these results are somewhat different from those obtained using the Unix benchmark suite. For example, the difference between no tracing at all and tracing with our async tracer in the `cp` test is as small as 15%. In the `FC1024` benchmark, the corresponding difference is a factor of about 10 (i.e., 1000%). This difference can be explained by the fact that the file size in the **cp** is large, forcing the system to use real IO to the disk.

8 Conclusion

In this paper, we have examined sources for significant performance penalties when using virtual machine introspection. Using the popular *LibVMI* library in combination with Xen, two major bottlenecks in VMI operations can be identified: First, reconfiguring VMI operation as well as handling VMI events incur a significant amount of context switches. Second, the synchronous processing of observed events in the introspection target in application-level monitoring code can cause long delays in the execution of the target VM.

We reduced the impact of context switches by designing our Hypervisor Tracers (HVT). The use of HVT significantly reduces the overhead compared to standard *LibVMI*, but still the slowdown caused by VMI might be too large for some applications.

We further integrate asynchronous channels for event tracing in HVT that almost completely eliminate the tracing overhead of VMI. There is one limitation to the asynchronous channels: They can be used only for asynchronous observing what happens in the target domain (based on information included in the asynchronous events), but not for synchronous reactions to an event, as for example required for some intrusion prevention mechanisms. But for the vast set of applications for which that kind of asynchronous monitoring is sufficient, the VMI overhead is reduced to just a few percent of performance reduction, and more than an order of magnitude faster than running standard *LibVMI*.

Acknowledgements. This work has been funded by the Deutsche Forschungsgemeinschaft (DFG, German Research Foundation) – 361891819 (ARADIA).

Appendix

See Table 1.

Table 1. Unix benchmark results (average of 5 runs in default configuration, results scaled by /1000

Benchmark	No VMI	LibVMI	HVT	Async
Dhrystone 2 using register variables	54107	54048	54145	52976
Double-precision Whetstone	9.01	8.99	9.00	8.76
System call overhead	1089	3.35	13.4	77.9
File copy 1024 bufsize 2000 maxblocks	1102	4.94	19.0	109.7
File copy 256 bufsize 500 maxblocks	287	1.23	4.81	27.6
File copy 4096 bufsize 8000 maxblocks	2890	19.7	76.7	413
Pipe throughput	1500	4.95	19.8	114
Pipe-based context switching	278	2.46	9.27	48.0
Excel throughput	5.37	0.340	1.10	3.25
Process creation	13.8	2.60	6.09	10.9
Shell scripts (1 concurrent)	11.7	0.785	2.530	7.25
Shell scripts (8 concurrent)	1.54	0.105	0.340	0.960

References

1. Xen Hypercall ABI. http://xenbits.xenproject.org/docs/sphinx-unstable/guest-guide/x86/hypercall-abi.html#. Accessed 11 June 2020
2. LibVMI: Simplified virtual machine introspection (2020). https://github.com/libvmi/libvmi/blob/master/README.rst. Accessed 7 June 2020
3. Xen Hypercalls (2020). https://wiki.xenproject.org/wiki/Hypercall. Accessed 7 June 2020
4. Xen Project Software Overview (2020). https://wiki.xen.org/wiki/Xen_Overview. Accessed 7 June 2020
5. XenBus (2020). https://wiki.xen.org/wiki/XenBus. Accessed 7 June 2020
6. XenStore (2020). https://wiki.xen.org/wiki/XenStore. Accessed 7 June 2020
7. Bhatt, M., Ahmed, I., Lin, Z.: Using virtual machine introspection for operating systems security education. In: Proceedings of the 49th ACM Technical Symposium on Computer Science Education, pp. 396–401 (2018)
8. Dangl, T., Taubmann, B., Reiser, H.P.: RapidVMI: fast and multi-core aware active virtual machine introspection. In: Proceedings of the 16th International Conference on Availability, Reliability and Security (ARES) (2021)
9. Dinaburg, A., Royal, P., Sharif, M., Lee, W.: Ether: malware analysis via hardware virtualization extensions. In: Proceedings of the 15th ACM Conference on Computer and Communications Security (CCS), pp. 51–62 (2008)
10. Harrison, C., Cook, D., McGraw, R., Hamilton Jr., J.A.: Constructing a cloud-based IDS by merging VMI with FMA. In: IEEE 11th International Conference on Trust, Security and Privacy in Computing and Communications (TrustCom), pp. 163–169 (2012)

11. Hsiao, S., Sun, Y.S., Chen, M.C.: Virtual machine introspection based malware behavior profiling and family grouping. CoRR arXiv:1705.01697 (2017)
12. Jain, B., Baig, M.B., Zhang, D., Porter, D.E., Sion, R.: SoK: introspections on trust and the semantic gap. In: 2014 IEEE Symposium on Security and Privacy, pp. 605–620 (2014)
13. Klemperer, P., Jeon, H.Y., Payne, B.D., Hoe, J.C.: High-performance memory snapshotting for real-time, consistent, hypervisor-based monitors. IEEE Trans. Dependable Secure Comput. **17**, 518–535 (2018)
14. Lengyel, T.K.: Stealthy monitoring with Xen altp2m, April 2016. https://xenproject.org/2016/04/13/stealthy-monitoring-with-xen-altp2m/. Accessed 11 June 2020
15. Lengyel, T.K., Maresca, S., Payne, B.D., Webster, G.D., Vogl, S., Kiayias, A.: Scalability, fidelity and stealth in the DRAKVUF dynamic malware analysis system. In: Proceedings of the 30th Annual Computer Security Applications Conference (ACSAC 2014), pp. 386–395. ACM (2014). https://doi.org/10.1145/2664243.2664252
16. Li, C., Xiang, Y., Shi, J.: A model of dynamic malware analysis based on VMI. In: Wang, G., Zomaya, A., Perez, G.M., Li, K. (eds.) ICA3PP 2015. LNCS, vol. 9532, pp. 465–475. Springer, Cham (2015). https://doi.org/10.1007/978-3-319-27161-3_42
17. Mishra, P., Varadharajan, V., Pilli, E., Tupakula, U.: VMGuard: a VMI-based security architecture for intrusion detection in cloud environment. IEEE Trans. Cloud Comput. **8**, 957–971 (2018)
18. Reginato, L.: Updated analysis of PatchGuard on Microsoft Windows 10 RS4 (2019). https://blog.tetrane.com/downloads/Tetrane_PatchGuard_Analysis_RS4_v1.01.pdf
19. Sentanoe, S., Taubmann, B., Reiser, H.P.: *Sarracenia*: enhancing the performance and stealthiness of SSH honeypots using virtual machine introspection. In: Gruschka, N. (ed.) NordSec 2018. LNCS, vol. 11252, pp. 255–271. Springer, Cham (2018). https://doi.org/10.1007/978-3-030-03638-6_16
20. Taubmann, B., Rakotondravony, N., Reiser, H.P.: CloudPhylactor: harnessing mandatory access control for virtual machine introspection in cloud data centers. In: The 15th IEEE International Conference on Trust, Security and Privacy in Computing and Communications (IEEE TrustCom-16) (2016)
21. Taubmann, B., Reiser, H.P.: Towards hypervisor support for enhancing the performance of virtual machine introspection. In: Remke, A., Schiavoni, V. (eds.) Distributed Applications and Interoperable Systems, pp. 41–54. Springer, Cham (2020)
22. Windows Vista Security Team: An introduction to kernel patch protection (2006). https://web.archive.org/web/20061124094344/http://blogs.msdn.com/windowsvistasecurity/archive/2006/08/11/695993.aspx. Accessed 7 June 2020
23. Zhao, S., Ding, X., Xu, W., Gu, D.: Seeing through the same lens: introspecting guest address space at native speed. In: 26th USENIX Security Symposium (USENIX Security 17), Vancouver, BC, pp. 799–813. USENIX Association, August 2017. https://www.usenix.org/conference/usenixsecurity17/technical-sessions/presentation/zhao
24. Zillner, T.: Memory forensics using virtual machine introspection for cloud computing. Presented at Black Hat USA (2016)

Calibration Done Right: Noiseless Flush+Flush Attacks

Guillaume Didier[1,3,4](✉) and Clémentine Maurice[2]

[1] Direction Générale de l'Armement, Paris, France
[2] Univ Lille, CNRS, Inria, Lille, France
clementine.maurice@inria.fr
[3] DIENS, École normale supérieure, CNRS, PSL University, Paris, France
[4] Univ Rennes, CNRS, IRISA, Rennes, France
guillaume.didier@inria.fr

Abstract. Caches leak information through timing measurements and side-channel attacks. Several attack primitives exist with different requirements and trade-offs. Flush+Flush is a stealthy and fast one that uses the timing of the `clflush` instruction depending on whether a line is cached. We show that the CPU interconnect plays a bigger role than previously thought in these timings and in Flush+Flush error rate.

In this paper, we show that a naive implementation that does not account for the topology of the interconnect yields very high error rates, especially on modern CPUs as the number of cores increases. We therefore reverse-engineer this topology and revisit the calibration phase of Flush+Flush for different attacker models to determine the correct threshold for `clflush` hits and misses. We show that our method yields close-to-noiseless side-channel attacks by attacking the AES T-tables implementation of OpenSSL, and by building a covert channel. We obtain a maximal capacity of 5.8 Mbit/s with our method, compared to 1.9 Mbit/s with a naive Flush+Flush implementation on an Intel Core i9-9900 CPU.

1 Introduction

The cache hierarchy is a key component of modern CPUs, and relies on the principle of making the common case fast [3,13]. Caches have been extensively studied with respect to side-channel attacks, resulting in several primitives such as Prime+Probe, Evict+Time [24], Flush+Reload [35], and Flush+Flush [10]. These can be used to build covert channels and side-channel attacks, e.g., on cryptographic libraries. Flush+Reload is a popular choice due to ease of implementation, reliability, and reasonable requirements on x86 platforms: for example, a variety of transient execution attacks [9,15,17] used it as a covert channel.

These primitives aim to observe memory accesses from other processes, through cache timings. Flush+Reload resets the state using the x86_64 `clflush` instruction, which ensures that the latest value of a cache line is flushed back to memory, with no copy remaining in the cache hierarchy. It then makes a costly reload to check if the line is cached. Flush+Flush is a variant that uses the execution time of the `clflush` instruction itself to do the check. Flush+Flush is thus faster and stealthier, as it causes no memory accesses by the attacking process.

L. Bilge et al. (Eds.): DIMVA 2021, LNCS 12756, pp. 278–298, 2021.
https://doi.org/10.1007/978-3-030-80825-9_14

Calibration is a critical step of the attack where an attacker chooses a threshold between `clflush` hits (timing of the `clflush` instruction when the line is present in the cache) and `clflush` misses (timing when the line is absent). A sub-optimal threshold leads to errors in a covert channel or a side-channel attack. The main source of Flush+Flush noise comes from the fact that the median execution time of `clflush` hits is close to the median value for misses, whereas the distributions of load execution time for hits and misses are more separated.

Our experiments show that the timing of the `clflush` instruction actually suffers from multiple sources of variability, which impairs the threshold and the subsequent attacks. A careful analysis of these execution timings unmasks a major culprit: the CPU interconnect. We uncover the various contributions of the CPU interconnect between the attacker, the cache slice, the victim core, and the system agent accessing the main memory, and propose a method to find the topology of recent Intel CPUs. Accounting for this topology, we significantly reduce this noise, making Flush+Flush a low-noise attack primitive that remains both fast and stealthy, and, thus, a realistic alternative to Flush+Reload. Our evaluation shows that a higher number of cores and larger caches distributed in more slices increases Flush+Flush noise on modern single-socket machines.

We show that our calibration improvements to Flush+Flush improve covert channel capacity. A naive Flush+Flush implementation has a 20% error rate while our improved Flush+Flush has a negligible error rate and a bandwidth 3× higher. The latter's bandwidth is also 3 to 4% higher than Flush+Reload.

In summary, we thus make the following key contributions[1]:

1. We present a method to uncover the interconnect topology of Intel CPUs, and apply it on Coffee Lake CPUs. We explain the variation of the execution time of `clflush` caused by topology on single-socket systems (Sect. 5).
2. We measure the resulting error rate depending on the location of the attacker, victim, and cache slice accessed on single-socket machines, and analyze the differences with dual-socket machines (Sect. 6).
3. We benchmark the improved covert channel ideal capacity that results, compared with Flush+Reload and a naive implementation of Flush+Flush. We show how these improvements make Flush+Flush a reliable side-channel primitive, on par with Flush+Reload (Sect. 7).

2 Background

In this section, we describe some necessary background on CPU caches and the CPU uncore and interconnect, multi-socket systems, and cache side-channel attacks. We focus on Intel CPUs in the remainder of this paper.

2.1 CPU Caches

DRAM-based main memory is slow compared to the CPU frequency. *Caches* are smaller but faster SRAM-based memories placed in front of the main memory

[1] Code: https://github.com/MIAOUS-group/calibration-done-right.

to speed up accesses, applying the "make the common case fast" principle [13]. Caches exploit access locality to keep blocks of memory that are likely to be accessed soon. An access to a block currently in the cache is a cache hit, a fast access. Otherwise, the request gets served at the next level, until main memory.

Modern Intel CPUs typically have a three-level hierarchy. At the first level, on each core, the instruction and data memory access paths each hit their own small caches in 4–5 cycles (L1-D and L1-I). At the second level, each core has an L2 cache, that serves the L1 misses in 15–20 cycles. At the last level, the chip has a shared L3, which acts as the last-level cache and answers in 50–100 cycles, while memory takes over 200 cycles.

Cache Associativity and Eviction Policy. Caches store fixed-size chunks of contiguous memory called cache *lines*, typically 64 bytes in size. The 6 least significant bits of the address determine the offset within the line, while the remainder gives the location of the line. Caches are generally organized, from an abstract interface point of view, as an array of cache sets. Addresses are assigned to a deterministic set by a hash function that usually corresponds to a few bits of the address, next to the offset bits. Each set is composed of a fixed number of *ways*, each containing a cache line, along with metadata identifying the line cached in the way. This metadata usually comprises the coherence state (see below) and a tag, corresponding to the address bits that are not used for index and offset. The tag, index and offset can be used together to check whether the requested address is cached in this way. The number of ways is called *associativity.* A direct-mapped cache has an associativity of 1, while a fully-associative cache has a single set with as many ways as the number of lines in the cache. Most large caches associativity is of the order of 10, and a large number of sets [13].

In each set, the *eviction policy* determines what to do when a new line needs to be inserted in a set full of valid lines. Modern CPUs usually use a variant of the *least recently used* policy, that evicts the line whose last use is the furthest in the past, but the exact policy is undocumented [29].

Cache Coherence. Due to the cache hierarchy, the same memory location may be simultaneously stored in several different places. It is thus important to ensure all these locations store the same value. This is achieved using a cache coherence protocol, which enforces a Single Writer or Multiple Reader invariant. Intel uses a variation of the MESI cache coherence protocol [14], in which a line can be:

- *Invalid* (I): The cache does not store a valid value, accesses are misses and require making a request to the next level.
- *Shared* (S): The cache holds a *clean* copy of the correct value, matching the one in memory, but other caches may also own one. The line can be read with no further request, but a write requires communicating with the other caches.
- *Exclusive* (E): The cache holds the correct value, as in the shared case, but it is additionally the only cache to do so. The line can be modified (and can transition to the Modified state) without any further request to the hierarchy.
- *Modified* (M): The cache holds exclusively a modified value. The stale value in memory must be updated before this *dirty* line can be evicted from the cache.

This protocol guarantees that, for a given cache line, all cores will see the same sequence of values, but it offers no guarantee about the order in which each core sees changes to different locations. This ordering is governed by the memory consistency model. In non-server Intel CPUs, an inclusive L3 cache maintains cache coherence. It includes a copy of all lines cached in lower-level caches, and keeps track of the coherency state of each line.

Cache Slicing. The bigger SRAM is, the slower it is to access. Moreover, more cores mean higher request traffic to the cache hierarchy. To make the last-level cache scale properly with multiple cores, it is split into several slices, each associated with a core. Chips with more cores have proportionally more slices, which can proportionally serve a greater number of requests.

Physical addresses are mapped to a single slice, using a hash function. The first sliced caches simply used specific bits of addresses, similar to set indexes. However, as uncovered by Maurice et al. [20], modern Intel CPUs use a complex function, which uses the XOR of several bits of the physical address to generate each bit of the output. This was introduced in the Sandy Bridge microarchitecture, and is still present in client Skylake derivatives such as Coffee Lake. Examples of such functions are given in Appendix A. On CPUs whose number of cores is a power of two, the resulting function is linear, otherwise, a non-linear component is required [36].

`clflush` Instruction. The x86 ISA includes an instruction to flush a cache line, `clflush`. Executing this instruction causes the cache hierarchy to make sure the memory contains the latest value and evicts the cache line from all levels of cache. Such an instruction is privileged in many ISAs as its main use is in device drivers using DMA. However, x86 also *allows it in user mode*, where it can be used to manually evict lines from the cache in the unlikely case manual cache management improves performance. This instruction can thus be used in cache side-channel attacks. A significant property of `clflush` is that calling `clflush` on one core evicts it from the all of the coherency domain, usually all the cores.

2.2 CPU Uncore and Interconnect

Modern CPUs tend to have several distinct clock domains. Each core can vary its frequency independently, but there is also a significant part of the system that is not part of a core. A common clock domain is needed for the interconnection network in between the cores, the GPU, the memory, and I/O systems. This part of the core, *i.e.*, everything that is not a specific core, is called the *uncore.*

Prominent in the uncore is the core interconnect, which is not well documented by Intel apart from stating it is a bidirectional ring ([14], Section 2.4.5.3). This leaves room for several interpretations and topologies. The last-level cache is distributed among the nodes of the interconnect network, with each slice being associated with a core. While it was usually assumed that each core had exactly one slice, it no longer the case on some recent Intel systems [30].

Figure 1a is a die shot, annotated by WikiChip [1] of the 8 core Coffee Lake CPUs, this layout is used to produce among others the Intel Core i9-9900 CPU.

2.3 Multi-socket Systems

A multi-socket system is a system where several multi-core CPUs, each with its cache system, share a single physical memory space with an interconnect between the two packages. In multi-socket systems, there is no single last-level cache ensuring the coherence between the caches of the two cores. It appears that some of the ECC bits inside the DRAM are used to maintain some coherency metadata, and requests may need to flow in between the two sockets [14,22].

2.4 Cache Side-Channel Attacks

The cache hierarchy contains a global state that is shared among processes. The cache impacts timing but not the correctness of code since its memory permissions are enforced and the value it stores is preserved whether a line is cached or not. However, the time it takes to access a line leaks information to the party that performs the measurement. There are two common scenarios. First, in a *covert channel*, two processes can cooperate to communicate when they are monitored on other channels or simply when not allowed to. Second, in a *side-channel attack*, an attacker process measures which cache line an unwitting victim accesses, leaking access pattern information.

There exist two main techniques of cache attacks: Prime+Probe [18,24] and Flush+Reload [12,35]. In Prime+Probe, the attacker fills a set with her cache lines, and the victim accesses a line within that set. This causes an eviction of one of these lines, which the attacker then measures. Prime+Probe has the least requirements, as the attacker does not need to share memory with her victim, and does not require any specific instruction to evict cache lines.

However, in many settings, the attacker and victim can share read-only memory, in which case the attacker can probe a specific shared cache line. The Flush+Reload attack uses the `clflush` instruction to flush a line that may or may not be accessed by the victim, and then times how long it takes to reload it. The attacker therefore detects whether the victim accessed this line.

Flush+Flush [10] is a variant of Flush+Reload, in which the attacker times a cache line flush instead of a reload. Indeed, `clflush` takes a different time depending on whether the line is cached or not. This is however a very small variation of time, around 10 cycles, and the measurements have a large standard deviation, leading to a significant amount of noise. This attack is noisier than Flush+Reload, but faster and stealthier, as it avoids costly misses, and cannot be detected using performance counter to monitor suspicious cache misses.

One of the sources of timing variation is the scaling of the CPU frequency, for which Saxena and Panda [28] have proposed a solution.

3 Motivation

Using `clflush` as the measurement, such as in Flush+Flush, has the potential of monitoring several addresses with less interference than Flush+Reload, as flushing does not trigger the prefetcher. It is also fast, as a reload operation is slower than a flush on a miss, which Flush+Reload attacks cause frequently.

However, one point that has been overlooked for this attack is the choice of the threshold to distinguish between a flush hit and a flush miss. This threshold is crucial to avoid noise. When looking at the timings for a single address and on a single run, it appears that there is a good separation between the hits (slower) and the misses (faster), for a single-socket system. However, from one run to another, the exact threshold may change, even with a fixed frequency. The threshold also differs for different addresses.

We hypothesize that the variability is due to the complex topology of sliced caches, and that accounting for these sources of variability improves significantly the quality of the channel, especially as the number of cores grows. Our experiments show that ignoring CPU topology can result in very poor error rates, e.g., in some cases, a 45% error rate for a covert channel using a naive method for choosing the threshold. In the remainder of the paper, we show that taking into account the topology and slices to compute tailored thresholds allows us to build a side channel with an error rate well under 0.01%. Flush+Flush is therefore, contrary to what was thought before, not a noisy attack when crafted carefully.

4 Experimental Setup

We run experiments on two single socket systems:

- *4-core machine*: a Dell Latitude 7400 machine with an Intel Core i5-8365U CPU (Whiskey Lake, 4 cores, 8 threads). We have validated that it uses the cache slicing functions that were previously reverse-engineered from Sandy Bridge to Skylake [20] (see Appendix A). It runs Fedora 30.
- *8-core machine*: a Dell Precision 3630 machine with an Intel Core i9-9900 CPU (Coffee Lake, 8 cores, 16 threads). We have reverse-engineered its last-level cache hash functions (see Appendix A). It runs Ubuntu 18.04.5 LTS.

We enable hyper-threading, but disable turbo boost on those machines. The intel_pstate driver is set to performance mode on all cores, to stabilize the core frequencies. Additionally, we write a non-null value in each page before use, this prevents any optimization and involuntary page sharing involving the zero-page.

5 Topology Modeling

In this section, we investigate the factors that influence the execution time of `clflush` to improve the Flush+Flush attack, and propose a mathematical model with an associated ring topology. The only information we have from the Intel documentation is that the interconnect is a "bidirectional ring".

A `clflush` miss occurs when a cache line is not validly cached, which corresponds to a line in the I state. A line that has just been flushed is in the I state—the cache may have an entry in the I state or no entry at all, but it is

a: Intel Coffee Lake 8-core die shot. Image by Intel, annotated by WikiChip [1].

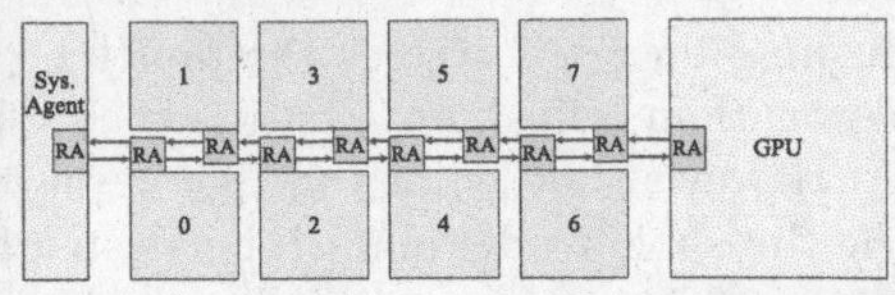

b: Proposed i9-9900/8-core topology. Each core (0 to 7, blue) has a ring agent (RA, red), handling accesses to the local L3 slice and communication over the ring. The GPU and the system agent, handling outside world communication, such as memory, also have their own RA.

Fig. 1. Core i9-9900 die shot and topology. (Color figure online)

equivalent at the cache coherency protocol level. A `clflush` hit occurs when the line is in any valid state. However, in practice in a Flush+Flush attack, the cache line of interest transitions from an I to an E state when the single victim core loads the line that has just been flushed. Therefore, the two relevant timings are `clflush` of a line in the E state for a hit, and in the I state for a miss. We study these timings depending on three parameters:

1. A: the attacker core that executes `clflush` on an address,
2. V: the victim core that accesses the address and caches it in its L1 or L2,
3. S: the core that contains the last-level cache slice that this address maps to.

V doesn't contribute to miss timing as invalid lines are not cached in any L1/L2.

Measurements and Topology. For each attacker core, Fig. 2a shows the time it takes to execute a `clflush` instruction on a cache line in the I state, depending on the slice. The first finding is that all 8 cores have a distinct timing pattern, which implies that the ring has no symmetry.[2] For each attacker, we notice that slices with a lower core number than the attacker all have the same timing, while for slices with a higher number the time increases with the distance between the attacker and the slice. Such a pattern only makes sense if the nodes are aligned in a linear fashion, and if the attacker sends a message to the slice, which then sends a message to the system agent, and then back to the slice and finally to the attacker. Consequently the miss time is more variable for attackers closer to the system agent than for one further away.

Figure 2b shows the time it takes to execute a `clflush` instruction on a cache line in the E state. Here, we notice an asymmetry in the core, which can be explained if the recall request is always sent by the slice in the same direction without knowing in which core the line is cached. We omit the graphs for other A as they only show a simple linear offset depending on $|A - S|$.

Given that the topology is described as a ring, given the die shot in Fig. 1a and our results, we thus propose the topology in Fig. 1b, with 8 cores aligned in a linear graph with forward and backward links. For a 4-core machine, similar measurements lead to a similar topology with only cores 0–3.

[2] Unlike the figure in Intel documentation [14] and the figure by WikiChip [1].

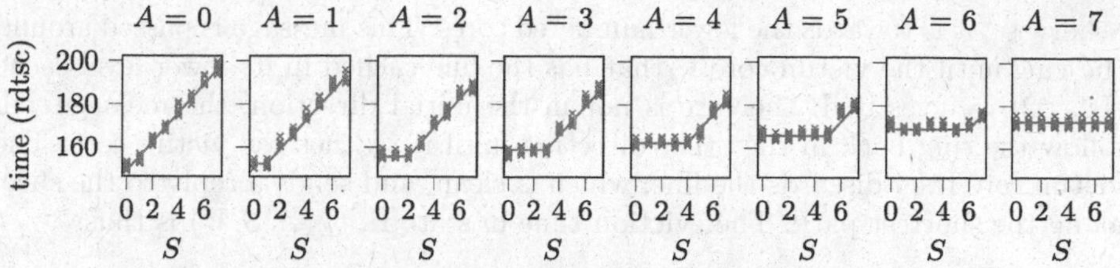

a: For a cache line in the I state, depending on its slice S for each attacker core A. There are 32 points per slice S, as we made one measurement for each attacker hyper-thread (2) and for each victim logic core (16). Victim logic core has no impact on a miss.

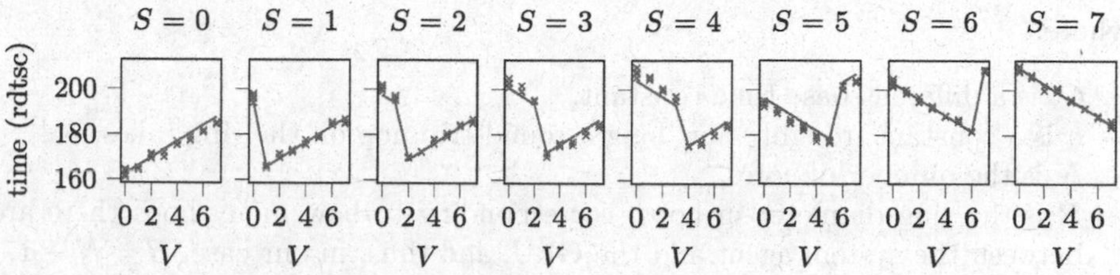

b: For a cache line in the E state, depending on the victim core V for each slice S, using a fixed attacker core ($A = 0$). There are 4 points per victim core V, one for each attacker and victim hyper-thread.

Fig. 2. Median timings of `clflush` on the 8-core machine depending on the victim core V, the slice S, and the attacker A, along with the fitted model according to our proposed topology, which corresponds to our measurements.

Mathematical Model. The above timing measurements can be interpreted within the proposed topology as follows, leading to a mathematical model that can be fitted and compared with the measurements. Misses result in a request to be sent on the ring from the core requesting the flush to the slice, which then sends a message to the memory, and then answers the same path in reverse, using each time the shortest path. The eviction time in state I, $t_I(A, S)$ is thus:

$$t_I(A, S) = C + h \times |A - S| + h \times |S - M|,$$

in which:

- C is a constant base timing,
- h is a constant corresponding to the time a round-trip hop on the ring takes,
- M corresponds to the system agent location, which is -1.

Upon receipt of a request to flush a line in the E state, the slice sends a single message along the ring, in one privileged direction. For core numbered from 0 to $\frac{n_{core}}{2}$ included, this is towards the higher numbered cores (and the GPU), otherwise, it is towards the lower numbered cores. This message is passed around the ring until the victim core V that has the line cached in its lower level cache (L1/L2) receives it. If the core is not in the initial direction, the message will follow the ring back in the other direction until it reaches the victim core. The victim core then discards the line, which is clean, and sends a reply to the slice, along the shortest path. The eviction time in state E, $t_E(A, S, V)$ is thus:

$$t_E(A,V,S) = \begin{cases} C' + h \times |A-S| + h \times |R-(V-M)| & \text{if } S \leqslant \frac{N}{2} \text{ and } V < S \\ C' + h \times |A-S| + h \times |S-V| & \text{if } S \leqslant \frac{N}{2} \text{ and } V \geqslant S \\ C' + h \times |A-S| + h \times |S-V| & \text{if } S > \frac{N}{2} \text{ and } V \leqslant S \\ C' + h \times |A-S| + h \times |M-V| & \text{if } S > \frac{N}{2} \text{ and } V > S, \end{cases}$$

where:

- C' is a different base time constant,
- h is a constant, roughly how long a round-trip hop on the ring takes,
- N is the number of cores,
- R is the ring diameter in hops, corresponding to how many hops there are between the system agent and the GPU, and thus, in our case, $R = N + 1$.

In addition to our measurements, Fig. 2a and Fig. 2b present the fitted model for the 8-core machine, which appears to explain the behavior consistently.

Summary. We have uncovered that while CPUs appeared to be arranged symmetrically in Intel's bidirectional ring, they are in fact aligned one after the other in a linear graph, with the system agent at an end and the GPU at the other end. First, the `clflush` instruction timing is always influenced by the distance between the core requesting the flush and the slice where the address lives in the last-level cache. Second, in the I state the timing will depend on the distance between the slice and the system agent, whereas in the E state, it will depend on how long a message sent along the ring will need to reach the core that currently has the line, and then go back to the slice. These finding are consistent with those by Paccagnella et al. [25].

6 Improving Error Rate Accounting for Topology

6.1 Attacker Models

We define different attacker models depending on attacker capabilities. We measure the error rate that can be achieved for each triple consisting of an attacker core, a victim core, and a slice. We also compute the average over all triples.

The attacker core can be set using the `sched_set_affinity` Linux system call. We therefore assume that the attacker always chooses the core with the lowest error rate. In some cases, the attacker may also control the victim core, e.g., if she launches the process. The victim core can always be found using the `/proc/pid` file system that gives the core affinity and the last core used.

The slice can be found using the physical address but this information is usually unavailable to an unprivileged attacker. However, when the hash function is linear, it is possible to define an equivalence class of addresses within a page that belong to the same slice. It is not possible to know which equivalence class corresponds to which physical slice *a priori*, but the pair of page and result of the hash function defines an equivalence class of virtual address with the same timing impact. We name this equivalence class $\tilde{S}$. Using timing measurements, each equivalence class can be, *a posteriori*, attributed to a precise physical slice, on a per page basis, but we do not use this attribution for our attacks.

If the attacker launches a covert channel, she can pick the addresses used to communicate, and therefore the optimal equivalence class. In a side-channel attack, the attacker cannot pick the addresses to monitor, but usually knows the equivalence class, as she knows both addresses and hash functions. We still present models where the attacker has no knowledge of the slices to compare the previous naive models with the ones that yield the best attacks.

- *Global Threshold (GT)*: The simplest model, using a single threshold that minimizes the average error rate over all triples of attacker, victim, and slice. This is a topology oblivious attacker, as in the initial Flush+Flush attack [10].
- *Best A, Known V*: The attacker knows on which core the victim is running and chooses the attacker core it runs on. The attacker computes a single threshold for all addresses, therefore ignoring the impact of cache slices.
- *Best AV*: The attacker can pick the cores both the victim and the attacker are running on, e.g., in the case of a covert channel or a side-channel attack in which the attacker launches the victim process. It ignores the impact of slices.
- *Known $\tilde{S}$*: The attacker does not know on which core she or her victim runs, but takes into account the slices, using per-slice thresholds. We use this model for comparison with the GT model.
- *Best A, Known $\tilde{S}V$*: The attacker pins her process to the best core, knows the victim core and takes into account the slices. This is a realistic attacker model. To be compared with *Best A, Known V* model.
- *Best AV, Known $\tilde{S}$*: This is the most powerful side-channel attacker, that can pin both the attacker and victim.
- *Best $AV\tilde{S}$*: This is the best covert channel attack model, where the attacker chooses the cores and an address in a slice that yields the best results.

6.2 Experimental Results on Error Rate

For each (A, V, $\tilde{S}$) we make 2^{20} measurements, 2^{19} hits (in E state), and 2^{19} misses (in I state). We time how long `clflush` takes to execute in each case using the `rdtsc` instruction and build a histogram of the execution time distribution. From these histograms, we can evaluate the number of hits and misses that would be correctly or incorrectly classified using a threshold, and determine thresholds that minimize the average error rate for each model, along with the corresponding average error rate. We present three such histograms above:

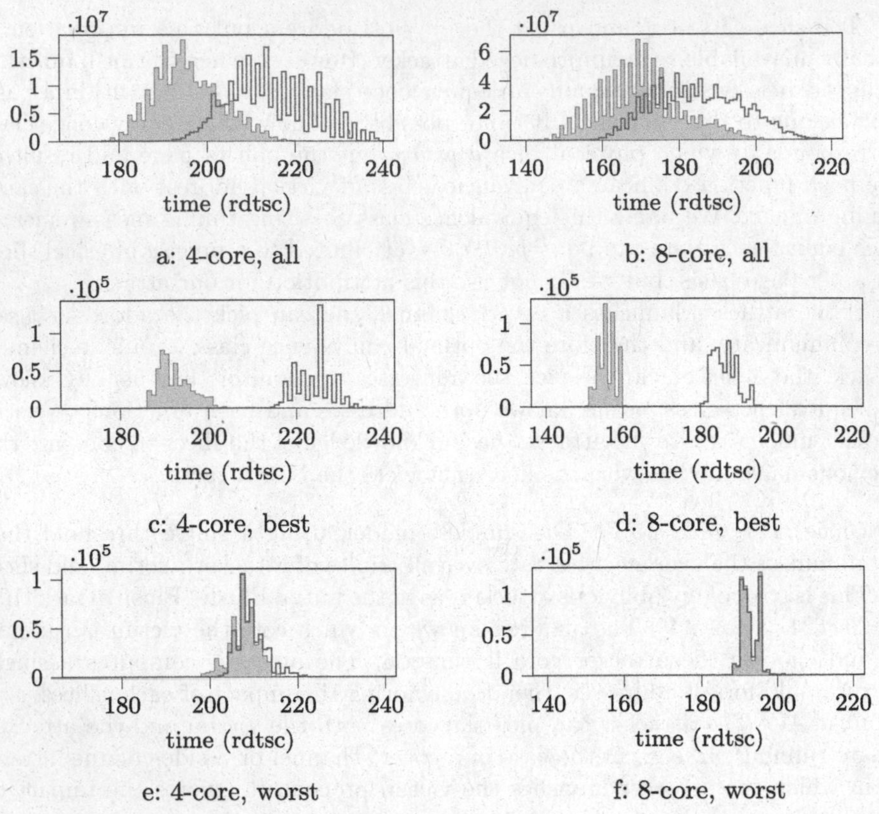

Fig. 3. Histograms for both machines of hit (outlined, red) and miss (filled, blue) `clflush` timing distributions for: – a, b: the superposition of all possible $(A, V, \tilde{S})$ triples (Average in the *GT* model). – c, d: the best possible $(A, V, \tilde{S})$ choice (*Best* $AV\tilde{S}$ model) – e, f: the worst possible $(A, V, \tilde{S})$ choice. (Color figure online)

- In Fig. 3a and 3b the histograms for all attackers, victim, and slices.
- In Fig. 3c and 3b the histograms on the best choice of attacker, victim, and slice equivalence class in the *Best* $AV\tilde{S}$ attacker model.
- In Fig. 3e and 3f the histograms on the most unfavorable choice of attacker, victim, and slice, with severe overlap between the two distributions.

Table 1 shows the results for the 4-core and 8-core machines, indicating for A, V and $\tilde{S}$ whether they are unknown, known or chosen in each case. For the 8-core machine, we observe a staggering difference between the 25% error rate of the GT attacker model, to the close to 0% error rate of the *Best* $AV\tilde{S}$ model (less than 1 error per 2^{20} measures).

Summary. Choosing the attacker and victim locations significantly improves the accuracy over the very unreliable global threshold. On top of that, using a per-slice threshold provides a further boost. However, when the victim cannot

Table 1. Results for each attacker model on the 4-core and 8-core machines. U. means Unknown, and K. Known.

	4-core machine				8-core machine			
	Error rate	A	V	$\tilde{S}$	Error rate	A	V	$\tilde{S}$
GT	14.0%	U.	U.	U.	25.1%	U.	U.	U.
Best A, Known V	6.07%	3	K.	U.	10.5%	7	K.	U.
Best AV	0.176%	7	0	U.	0.115%	7	8	U.
Known $\tilde{S}$	11.6%	U.	U.	K.	22.8%	U.	U.	K.
Best A, Known $\tilde{S}V$	3.16%	5	K.	K.	7.18%	7	K.	K.
Best AV, Known $\tilde{S}$	0.103%	7	0	K.	0.0174%	1	0	K.
Best $AV\tilde{S}$	4.96×10^{-3}%	3	3	3	0 (<2^{-20})	2	7	14

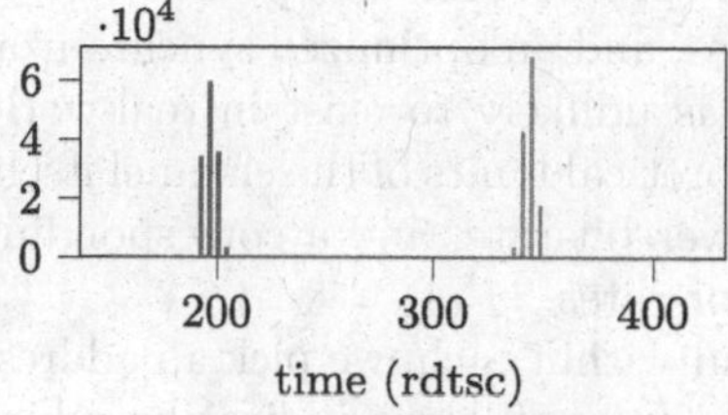

a: A and V in the same socket.

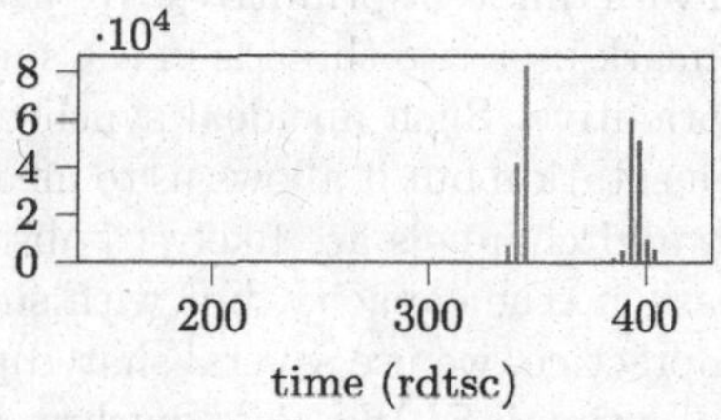

b: A and V on different sockets.

Fig. 4. Histograms of hit (red) and miss (blue, around 340) `clflush` timing distributions, for two different (A, V) pairs on a 2x Intel Xeon E5-2630 v3 machine. (Color figure online)

be chosen, accounting for slices gives a much greater boost. Lastly, choosing the best combination of attacker, victim, and slice gives close-to-perfect error rates.

6.3 The Case of Dual-Socket Machines

In dual-socket machines, there is no cache shared between all of the coherency domain. Coherence is maintained using bus snooping and using ECC bits in the DRAM to store some coherency information [14,22]. Thus, `clflush` behavior differs significantly from single-socket systems, depending on the attacker and victim location. The slice is not attached to a specific socket as each socket has its own last-level cache, and thus its contribution here was not studied in detail.

Figure 4a shows that when the victim is in the same socket, we observe that a hit is faster than a miss. This makes sense if the socket last-level cache has the coherency info of the accessed line in the E state, whereas it needs to reach out to the DRAM directory on a miss. However, when the victim is located in the other socket, *a hit is slower than a miss* as shown by Fig. 4b. This can probably be explained because more communication is required in the former case, to cause the remote core to evict and then update the DRAM directory.

Overall, if the sockets on which the attacker and victim reside are not controlled, a simple threshold model will give poor results. A dual threshold model may give good quality results, separating same-socket hits, misses and remote-socket hits, or a detailed model accounting for attacker and victim location.

7 Evaluation

In this section, we evaluate our improved Flush+Flush primitive on a covert channel and on a side-channel attack on the AES T-tables implementation.

7.1 Building a Better Channel

Protocol. We implement a framework to benchmark covert channel ideal bandwidth with different primitives. We use the same protocol for each primitive. The benchmark uses two threads in the same process, and an optimized synchronization primitive. Such an ideal synchronization is unlikely to exist in real-world implementation but it allows us to measure theoretical limits of the channel itself. Real-world channels are likely to observe a lower bit-rate, and a corresponding decrease in true capacity, but with similar error rates.

In practice, we use several shared pages, and within each, we pick an address in the optimal $\tilde{S}$. We also synchronize on a per page basis indicating which thread can currently access the page (to transmit or receive), using mutable shared memory, as the ideal synchronization primitive. Once done with a page, threads hand the page over to the other threads by flipping the per-page bit.

Implementation. We implement three covert channels with different primitives: 1. a single threshold *naive* Flush+Flush, with no core pinning (GT model), 2. a single threshold Flush+Reload that doesn't need to account for topology, and 3. a topology-aware Flush+Flush using the *Best* $AV\tilde{S}$ attacker model.

Evaluation. For each channel and machine, we evaluate its raw bit rate C, error rate p, and true capacity $T = C \times (1 + p \log_2 p + (1-p) \log_2(1-p))$ [23].

Results. We run our experiments on both machines mentioned in Sect. 4. Figure 5 shows statistics on the performance of the covert channels depending on the number of pages used, for each machine: the average error rate, the raw bit rate, and the true capacity of the resulting channel.

As shown by table Table 2, our carefully calibrated Flush+Flush yields a threefold increase in bandwidth on both machines compared to the naive Flush+Flush, and provides a bandwidth higher than Flush+Reload by 3 to 4 %. We conclude that Flush+Flush is now a compelling alternative to Flush+Reload.

7.2 AES T-Tables Attack Using Flush+Flush

AES T-Tables Implementation. The AES T-tables implementation is well-known to be vulnerable to side-channel attacks, we, therefore, use it as a benchmark to compare our Flush+Flush implementation [2,4,5,7,11,12,24,31]. We

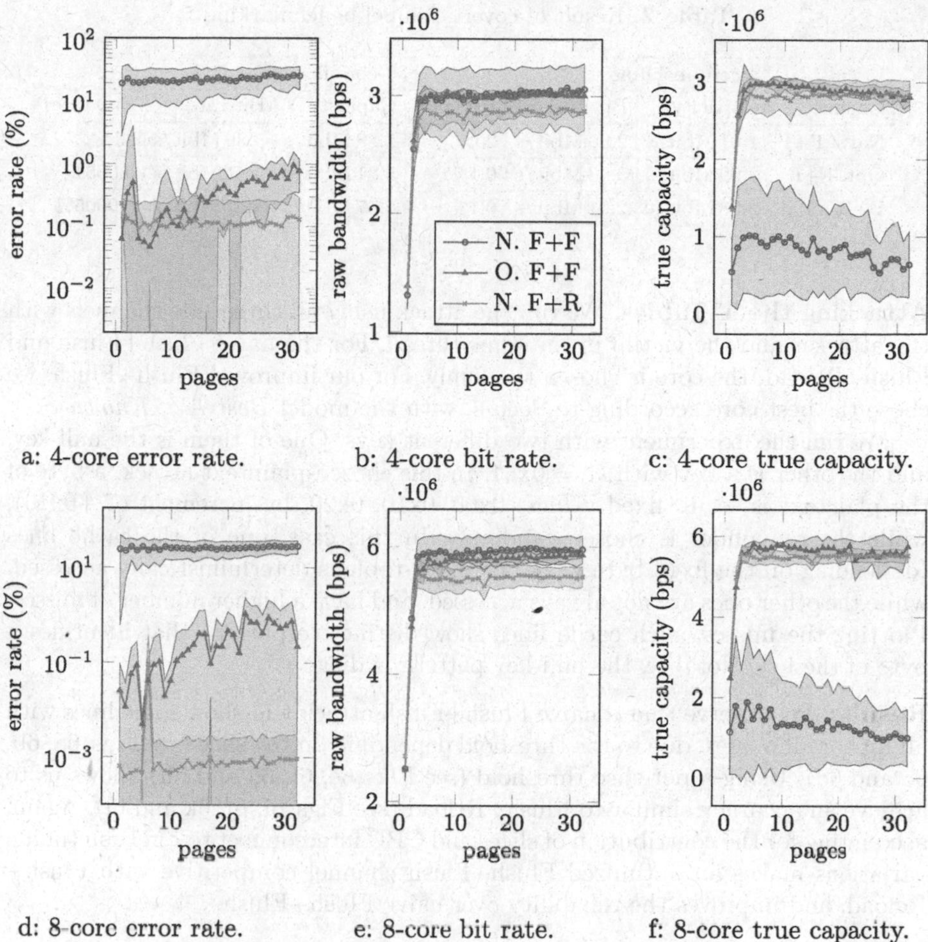

Fig. 5. Covert channel performance depending on the number of pages used.

compare our improved Flush+Flush implementation with per-slice thresholds to the naive version of Flush+Flush and to the Flush+Reload attack. We attack the OpenSSL 1.1.1g library, compiled with `no-asm` and `no-hw` to enable T-tables. For this experiment, prefetchers are enabled on both machines.

T-tables are an implementation of an AES round using lookups in tables. The lookup in the first round is $T_j[p_i \oplus k_i]$, where $0 \le i \le 16$ and j is the remainder of i divided by 4 (`j = i & 0x3`). With 4-byte elements and 64-byte cache lines, there are 16 entries per cache line, and a cache attack can only monitor the upper 4 bits of $p_i \oplus k_i$. See Osvik et al. [24] for the detailed explanation.

Table 2. Result of covert channel benchmarking

Channel	4-core machine			8-core machine		
	Capacity	Bit rate	Err. rate	Capacity	Bit rate	Err. rate
Naive F+F	1.01 Mbit/s	2.96 Mbit/s	20%	1.88 Mbit/s	5.89 Mbit/s	23%
Opt. F+F	2.99 Mbit/s	3.03 Mbit/s	0.1%	5.81 Mbit/s	5.81 Mbit/s	0.005%
F+R	2.88 Mbit/s	2.91 Mbit/s	0.1%	5.57 Mbit/s	5.57 Mbit/s	0.0005%

Attacking the T-Tables. We run the attack using all three side channels with the attacker and the victim in the same thread. For the naive Flush+Flush and Flush+Reload, the core is chosen randomly. For our improved Flush+Flush, we chose the best core according to Sect. 6, with the model *Best AV*, *Known* $\tilde{S}$.

We run the experiment with two different keys. One of them is the null key, and the other is a key with $k_0 =$ `0x51`. In this chosen-plaintext attack, a byte of the plaintext is set to fixed values (0x00, 0x10, 0x20, by increment of +0x10), while the remainder is chosen randomly. In this case, one of the cache lines (depending on the fixed byte value) of the T-table is deterministically accessed, while the other ones are not always accessed, and have a higher number of misses. Plotting the misses, such cache lines show distinctive pattern that identifies a byte of the key. Notably, the null-key pattern is diagonal.

Results. We observe that a naive Flush+Flush attack will show some lines with all hits or all misses, due to the threshold depending on the slice (see Figs. 6a, 6b, 6c and 6d). Using a per-slice threshold (see Figs. 6e, 6f, 6g and 6h) allows us to achieve an accuracy similar to Flush+Reload (see Figs. 6i, 6j, 6k and 6l). Again, accounting for the contribution of slices and CPU interconnect to `clflush` timing variations makes an optimized Flush+Flush channel competitive with Flush+Reload, and improves the reliability over naive Flush+Flush.

8 Related Work

Cache attacks are a rich field, with several primitives extensively studied and new emerging ones. The AES T-tables implementation is well-known to be vulnerable to side channels, with various ways of exploiting it. Moreover, reliable covert channels are one of the key elements for transient microarchitectural attacks.

8.1 Cache Attacks Primitives

The first cache-based attacks were published around 2005. Percival [26] attacked RSA while Osvik et al. [24] attacked AES and were the first to define the Prime+Probe primitive. The "high resolution [and] low noise" Flush+Reload primitive was defined by Yarom et al. [35], which was then automated by Gruss et al. [11] with Cache Template Attacks. Gruss et al. [10] then introduced the stealthy Flush+Flush primitive, a variant of Flush+Reload.

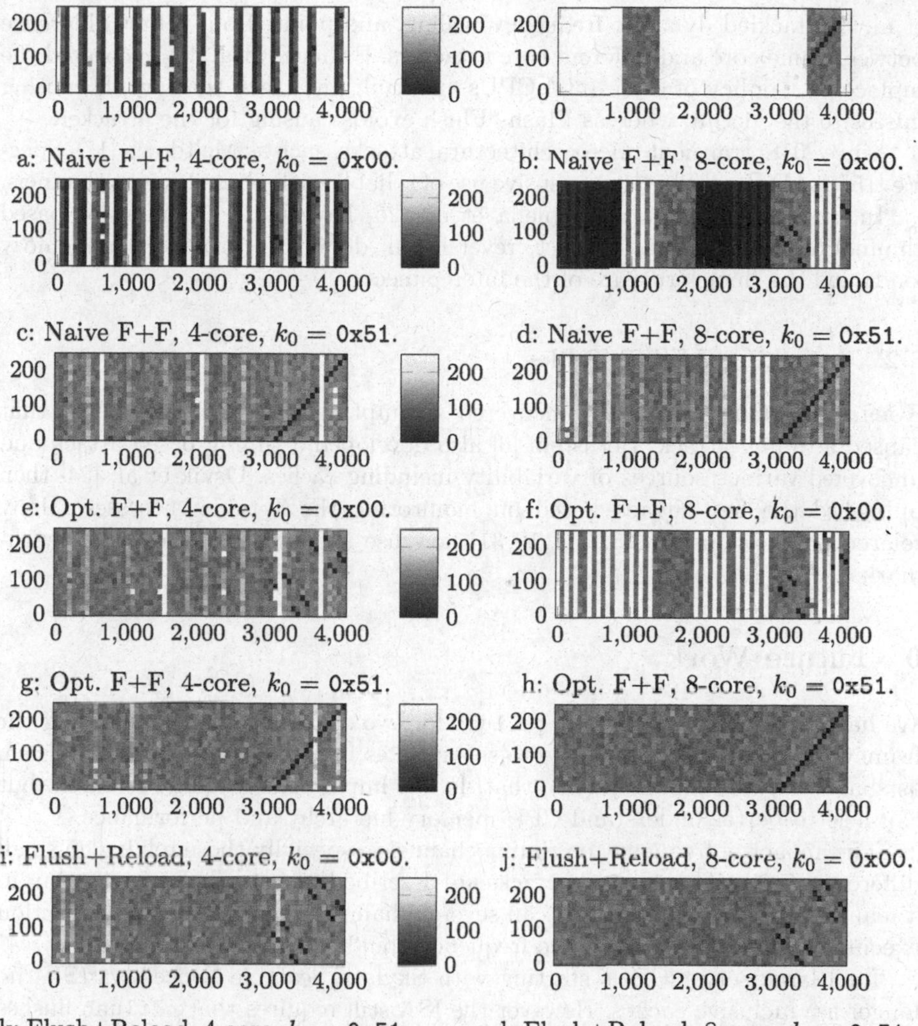

Fig. 6. Results of the T-table attack using a Naive Flush+Flush, Optimized Flush+Flush and Flush+Reload side channels. Each column represents an address and each row corresponds to a different value of the first byte of the chosen plaintext, with the remaining bytes filled randomly. The color scale cuts off lines with too many misses, T-tables that are deterministically accessed have very few misses and reveal key bits.

Cache attacks on cloud computing and virtualized environments [27,32,33], were shown to be a practical threat [18,19]. Maurice et al. [21] also studied protocols that could obtain a reliable channel on top of various primitives.

In recent years, various other primitives have been developed to adapt to evolutions in modern CPUs. Yan et al. [34] reverse-engineered non-inclusive caches directories to mount an attack on CPUs with non-inclusive caches, while Saxena et al. [28] tackled dynamic frequency scaling, and pointed out a first difference between same core and different core attackers. Briongos et al. [8] uncovered the replacement policy of some Intel CPUs and built an attack that avoids causing misses to the victim, whereas Flush+Flush avoids causing for the attacker.

Since 2018, transient microarchitectural attacks, such as Meltdown [17], Spectre [15] and Fallout [9] make extensive use of reliable cache-based covert channels.

In concurrent work, Paccagnella et al. [25] have built a contention-based channel on the ring interconnect, reversing in detail the protocol for memory loads and the finer structure of the interconnect.

8.2 Attacking AES T-Tables

Koeune and Quisquater [16] uncovered an implementation issue in AES that caused a timing attack. Bernstein [6] also developed a timing-based attack and uncovered various sources of variability including caches. Osvik et al. [24] then published the first attack based on monitoring the T-tables accesses. Many related publications [2,4,5,7,11,12,31] now use the AES T-tables as a benchmark.

9 Future Work

We have explored the timing of `clflush` for two coherence states, but using our framework, it should be possible to set-up lines in other coherence states, such as shared (S) and modified (M), that do not impact side-channel research, but can help to better understand CPU memory hierarchy and performance.

The impact of frequency on timing channels, especially those relying on small differences is significant. Most attacks are described at a steady frequency, but in a real setting, frequency scaling can severely hamper them. A model instruction execution time depending on the frequency could mitigate this variability.

Intel large server CPUs starting with Skylake Scalable Processors (SP) no longer use inclusive caches. However the ISA still requires that `clflush` flushes a cache line from all the coherency domain. It should thus be possible to use the `clflush` instruction to attack such systems, an approach that [34] has not covered. These systems also use a different topology that warrants further inquiry.

`clflush` also behaves differently on multi-socket systems, as shown in Sect. 6.3, in a way that is not always tractable with a simple global threshold model. Further work could evaluate the benefits of dual-threshold versus per $A, V, \tilde{S}$ threshold models, and the performance of channels built in this way.

10 Conclusion

The interconnect topology of Intel CPU plays a larger role than was previously known in cache attacks, and in particular Flush+Flush. A naive Flush+Flush implementation that does not account for the topology yields poor error rates, especially as the number of cores increases. We reverse-engineer this topology and study its timing impact on the `clflush` instruction. Using these insights, we significantly enhance the Flush+Flush primitive by accounting for the topology during the calibration step. Consequently, we recommend taking into account these findings into the calibration step, measuring timings for all possible combinations of attacker, victim, and home slice location, and then determining the best thresholds depending on the attacker model. Our results therefore demonstrate that the Flush+Flush primitive is as reliable as Flush+Reload, with the further advantages in stealth and being less affected by prefetcher noise.

Acknowledgements. This work has been partly funded by the French Direction Générale de l'Armement, and by the ANR-19-CE39-0007 MIAOUS. Some experiments presented in this paper were carried out using the Grid'5000 test-bed, supported by a scientific interest group hosted by Inria and including CNRS, RENATER and several Universities as well as other organizations (see https://www.grid5000.fr).

A Cache slicing functions uncovered

Our research relies on having prior knowledge of the cache slicing functions. We have updated the code base used by Maurice et al. [20] to support newer architectures and used it to uncover the slicing functions of the i9-9900 (Coffee Lake R, 8 cores) and the older i7-4980HQ (Crystal Well, 4 core Haswell with an eDRAM L4 cache), which differ from the previously known functions (see Table 3) that applied to most CPUs from Sandy Bridge to Broadwell. The CPU in our 4-core machine also uses those well known functions. The most significant bits of the functions uncovered are limited by the available memory.

This method uses performance counters located in a per physical core structure called CBox. The uncovered functions map addresses onto each CBox. However, it is suspected that starting with Skylake there are two slices within the same CBox [30], which we cannot detect with this method.

Table 3. Functions from [20] for the 2-, 4- and 8-core Xeon and Core CPU and new functions for the Intel Core i7-4980HQ and i9-9900.

		Address Bit																															
		37	36	35	34	33	32	31	30	29	28	27	26	25	24	23	22	21	20	19	18	17	16	15	14	13	12	11	10	09	08	07	06
Sandy	o_0		⊕	⊕		⊕	⊕		⊕		⊕	⊕	⊕	⊕	⊕		⊕		⊕		⊕	⊕	⊕		⊕		⊕		⊕				⊕
Bridge	o_1	⊕		⊕	⊕	⊕		⊕		⊕	⊕		⊕		⊕	⊕	⊕	⊕	⊕	⊕		⊕		⊕		⊕		⊕				⊕	
& later [20]	o_2	⊕	⊕	⊕	⊕			⊕	⊕			⊕	⊕			⊕	⊕			⊕			⊕			⊕	⊕				⊕		
(New)	o_0					⊕	⊕		⊕		⊕	⊕	⊕	⊕	⊕		⊕		⊕		⊕	⊕	⊕		⊕		⊕		⊕				
i7-4980HQ	o_1					⊕		⊕		⊕	⊕		⊕		⊕	⊕	⊕	⊕	⊕	⊕		⊕		⊕		⊕		⊕					
(New)	o_0					⊕	⊕	⊕	⊕	⊕	⊕	⊕	⊕	⊕	⊕		⊕		⊕		⊕	⊕	⊕		⊕		⊕		⊕				⊕
	o_1						⊕	⊕		⊕	⊕	⊕	⊕	⊕		⊕	⊕	⊕		⊕		⊕	⊕				⊕			⊕			
i9-9900	o_2					⊕	⊕	⊕	⊕	⊕	⊕	⊕					⊕	⊕	⊕	⊕	⊕	⊕	⊕			⊕		⊕	⊕				

References

1. Coffee Lake - Microarchitectures - Intel - WikiChip (2020). https://en.wikichip.org/w/index.php?title=intel/microarchitectures/coffee_lake&oldid=97412#Octa-Core. Last edited 3 July 2020
2. Aciiçmez, O., Koç, Ç.K.: Trace-driven cache attacks on AES (short paper). In: Information and Communications Security, ICICS (2006)
3. Amdahl, G.M.: Validity of the single processor approach to achieving large scale computing capabilities. In: Proceedings of the 18–20 April 1967, Spring Joint Computer Conference, p. 483–485. AFIPS 1967 (Spring). ACM (1967)
4. Apecechea, G.I., Inci, M.S., Eisenbarth, T., Sunar, B.: Fine grain cross-VM attacks on Xen and VMware are possible! IACR Cryptol. ePrint Arch. 2014, 248 (2014). http://eprint.iacr.org/2014/248
5. Irazoqui, G., Inci, M.S., Eisenbarth, T., Sunar, B.: Wait a minute! A fast, cross-VM attack on AES. In: Stavrou, A., Bos, H., Portokalidis, G. (eds.) RAID 2014. LNCS, vol. 8688, pp. 299–319. Springer, Cham (2014). https://doi.org/10.1007/978-3-319-11379-1_15
6. Bernstein, D.J.: Cache-timing attacks on AES (2005)
7. Bogdanov, A., Eisenbarth, T., Paar, C., Wienecke, M.: Differential cache-collision timing attacks on AES with applications to embedded CPUs. In: Pieprzyk, J. (ed.) CT-RSA 2010. LNCS, vol. 5985, pp. 235–251. Springer, Heidelberg (2010). https://doi.org/10.1007/978-3-642-11925-5_17
8. Briongos, S., Malagón, P., Moya, J.M., Eisenbarth, T.: RELOAD+REFRESH: abusing cache replacement policies to perform stealthy cache attacks. In: USENIX Security Symposium (2020)
9. Canella, C., et al.: Fallout: leaking data on meltdown-resistant CPUs. In: CCS (2019)
10. Gruss, D., Maurice, C., Wagner, K., Mangard, S.: Flush+flush: a fast and stealthy cache attack. In: DIMVA (2016)
11. Gruss, D., Spreitzer, R., Mangard, S.: Cache template attacks: automating attacks on inclusive last-level caches. In: USENIX Security Symposium (2015)
12. Gullasch, D., Bangerter, E., Krenn, S.: Cache games - bringing access-based cache attacks on AES to practice. In: S&P (2011)

13. Hennessy, J.L., Patterson, D.A.: Computer Architecture - A Quantitative Approach, 6th edn. Morgan Kaufmann (2019)
14. Intel Corporation: Intel 64 and IA-32 Architectures Optimization Reference Manual (2018). https://software.intel.com/sites/default/files/managed/9e/bc/64-ia-32-architectures-optimization-manual.pdf
15. Kocher, P., et al.: Spectre attacks: exploiting speculative execution. In: S&P (2019)
16. Koeune, F., Koeune, F., Quisquater, J.J., Jacques Quisquater, J.: A timing attack against rijndael. Technical report (1999)
17. Lipp, M., et al.: Meltdown: reading kernel memory from user space. In: USENIX Security (2018)
18. Liu, F., Yarom, Y., Ge, Q., Heiser, G., Lee, R.B.: Last-level cache side-channel attacks are practical. In: S&P (2015)
19. Maurice, C., Neumann, C., Heen, O., Francillon, A.: C5: cross-cores cache covert channel. In: Almgren, M., Gulisano, V., Maggi, F. (eds.) DIMVA 2015. LNCS, vol. 9148, pp. 46–64. Springer, Cham (2015). https://doi.org/10.1007/978-3-319-20550-2_3
20. Maurice, C., Le Scouarnec, N., Neumann, C., Heen, O., Francillon, A.: Reverse engineering intel last-level cache complex addressing using performance counters. In: Bos, H., Monrose, F., Blanc, G. (eds.) RAID 2015. LNCS, vol. 9404, pp. 48–65. Springer, Cham (2015). https://doi.org/10.1007/978-3-319-26362-5_3
21. Maurice, C., et al.: Hello from the other side: SSH over robust cache covert channels in the cloud. In: NDSS (2017)
22. Molka, D., Hackenberg, D., Schöne, R., Nagel, W.E.: Cache coherence protocol and memory performance of the intel Haswell-EP architecture. In: 44th International Conference on Parallel Processing, ICPP (2015)
23. Okhravi, H., Bak, S., King, S.T.: Design, implementation and evaluation of covert channel attacks. In: 2010 IEEE International Conference on Technologies for Homeland Security (HST), pp. 481–487 (2010). https://doi.org/10.1109/THS.2010.5654967
24. Osvik, D.A., Shamir, A., Tromer, E.: Cache attacks and countermeasures: the case of AES. In: Pointcheval, D. (ed.) CT-RSA 2006. LNCS, vol. 3860, pp. 1–20. Springer, Heidelberg (2006). https://doi.org/10.1007/11605805_1
25. Paccagnella, R., Luo, L., Fletcher, C.W.: Lord of the ring(s): side channel attacks on the CPU on-chip ring interconnect are practical. In: S&P (2021)
26. Percival, C.: Cache missing for fun and profit. In: Proceedings of BSDCan 2005 (2005)
27. Ristenpart, T., Tromer, E., Shacham, H., Savage, S.: Hey, you, get off of my cloud: exploring information leakage in third-party compute clouds. In: CCS (2009)
28. Saxena, A., Panda, B.: DABANGG: time for fearless flush based cache attacks. IACR Cryptology ePrint Archive (2020)
29. Vila, P., Ganty, P., Guarnieri, M., Köpf, B.: CacheQuery: learning replacement policies from hardware caches. In: PLDI (2020)
30. Vila, P., Köpf, B., Morales, J.F.: Theory and practice of finding eviction sets. In: S&P (2019)
31. Weiß, M., Heinz, B., Stumpf, F.: A cache timing attack on AES in virtualization environments. In: Keromytis, A.D. (ed.) FC 2012. LNCS, vol. 7397, pp. 314–328. Springer, Heidelberg (2012). https://doi.org/10.1007/978-3-642-32946-3_23
32. Wu, Z., Xu, Z., Wang, H.: Whispers in the hyper-space: high-bandwidth and reliable covert channel attacks inside the cloud. IEEE/ACM Trans. Netw. **23**(2), 603–615 (2015)

33. Xu, Y., Bailey, M., Jahanian, F., Joshi, K.R., Hiltunen, M.A., Schlichting, R.D.: An exploration of L2 cache covert channels in virtualized environments. In: Cloud Computing Security Workshop, CCSW, pp. 29–40. ACM (2011)
34. Yan, M., Sprabery, R., Gopireddy, B., Fletcher, C.W., Campbell, R.H., Torrellas, J.: Attack directories, not caches: side channel attacks in a non-inclusive world. In: S&P (2019)
35. Yarom, Y., Falkner, K.: FLUSH+RELOAD: a high resolution, low noise, L3 cache side-channel attack. In: USENIX Security Symposium (2014)
36. Yarom, Y., Ge, Q., Liu, F., Lee, R.B., Heiser, G.: Mapping the intel last-level cache. IACR Cryptology ePrint Archive (2015)

Zero Footprint Opaque Predicates: Synthesizing Opaque Predicates from Naturally Occurring Invariants

Yu-Jye Tung(✉) and Ian G. Harris

Department of Computer Science, University of California, Irvine, USA
yujyet@uci.edu, harris@ics.uci.edu

Abstract. A popular control-flow obfuscation approach used to protect software is inserting opaque predicates. However, recent research has questioned the usefulness of opaque predicates with the realization that simple heuristic attacks can effectively detect them. In this paper, we introduce a novel approach to construct opaque predicates that prevents both heuristic attacks and automated attacks by having opaque predicates *syntactically* and *semantically* resemble real predicates.

Our approach uses abstract interpretation to infer variables' value sets. From each value set, we synthesize an opaque predicate that 1) evaluates all items in its value set to the same truth value and 2) shares real predicates' common syntactic features.

Our opaque predicates syntactically resemble real predicates because they share real predicates' common syntactic features and their invariants are naturally occurring as they are inferred from the program's semantics. Previous approaches to constructing opaque predicates are susceptible to heuristic attacks because they use synthetic invariants that can inadvertently introduce unnatural code.

Our opaque predicates semantically resemble real predicates because the naturally occurring invariants they use are based on value sets. Like real predicates' variables, our opaque predicates' variables can also take on different values during runtime. From our evaluation, we show promising results that our opaque predicates can withstand automated attacks. Current state-of-the-art deobfuscation, dynamic symbolic execution, can only detect 41% of our opaque predicates.

Keywords: Opaque predicates · Obfuscation · Software protection

1 Introduction

The capability to obfuscate an executable binary with opaque predicates is prevalent, readily available in many software protection tools [9,11,12,20,24]. An opaque predicate is a disguised conditional branch instruction that uses an **invariant** to always evaluate to the same truth value at runtime in order to introduce a **dead branch** (i.e., non-executable branch). The dead branch obfuscates control-flow by pointing to non-executable code. Since an opaque predicate only

L. Bilge et al. (Eds.): DIMVA 2021, LNCS 12756, pp. 299–318, 2021.
https://doi.org/10.1007/978-3-030-80825-9_15

needs an invariant to achieve the conditional branch disguise, it can be constructed in a multitude of ways. As a result, Collberg *et al.* [33] developed a list of criteria to evaluate the quality of an opaque predicate: **potency** (obfuscation's strength *w.r.t.* manual analysis), **resilience** (obfuscation's strength *w.r.t.* automated analysis), **stealth** (obfuscation's strength *w.r.t.* detection), and **cost** (obfuscation's incurred overhead on execution speed).

1.1 Problem

Recent research [32,42] has questioned the usefulness of opaque predicates with the realization that simple heuristic attacks can effectively detect them. In other words, opaque predicates constructed using existing approaches cannot achieve high potency. For example, Sheridan *et al.* [32] dismiss the use of opaque predicates because they are able to construct highly resilient opaque predicates based on 3SAT instances that are NP-complete in the average case to detect, a significant improvement over aliased-based opaque predicates [33] which are only NP-hard in the worst case to detect [19]. However, regardless of their resilience, the opaque predicates they constructed can still be easily detected by heuristic attacks due to low potency [32].

1.2 Insight

Heuristic attacks are effective because, for opaque predicates, detection and deobfuscation are tightly coupled. Even though successful heuristic attacks do not entail deobfuscation, an opaque predicate is simple to deobfuscate once it is detected—the deobfuscation process is simply removing the dead branch from the control-flow, which subsequently removes the obfuscation (i.e., non-executable code that the dead branch points to).

To withstand removal, an opaque predicate must be stealthy as preventing detection is of the utmost importance. Of the criteria that make up the quality of an opaque predicate, stealth should be combined with potency and resilience since it is tightly coupled to both: **potency** (obfuscation's stealth *w.r.t.* manual analysis) and **resilience** (obfuscation's stealth *w.r.t.* automatic analysis). From hereon forward, any mention of either potency or resilience is *w.r.t.* stealth.

High potency prevents detection by manual analysis. To achieve high potency, we study the work by Votipka *et al.* [36], who perform observational studies on professional reverse engineers in order to understand the manual analysis process. Votipka *et al.* found that during earlier phases of manual analysis a reverse engineer commonly *scans* through the code—instead of attempting to understand each individual instruction—to identify **beacons**, or features in code that expose a program's functionality. A heuristic attack performs detection by pattern matching against beacons indicating the opaque predicates. To achieve high potency and prevent heuristic attacks, opaque predicates need to *syntactically* resemble real predicates so they do not end up as easily identifiable beacons. Syntactical resemblance to real predicates also allows opaque predicates to remain potent in clearly obfuscated code (i.e., layered with various obfuscation techniques) if the opaque predicates are applied prior to any other obfuscation techniques.

High resilience prevents detection by automated analysis. To achieve high resilience, we study prior research on automated opaque predicates detection. We found that the current state-of-the-art automated analysis approach is dynamic symbolic execution [5,27]. Dynamic symbolic execution detects opaque predicates by proving the existence of the invariant property. To achieve high resilience, opaque predicates need to *semantically* resemble real predicates such that the invariant property is nontrivial to identify.

1.3 Solution

In this paper, we introduce a novel approach to construct high-quality opaque predicates that are potent, resilient, and low cost. Our opaque predicates' invariants are naturally occurring as they are based on variables' value sets buried within the program's semantics. A **value set** for a variable contains *all possible values that variable can be assigned to* at a specific line of code. We use abstract interpretation [14] to infer correct value sets (i.e., zero false negative but possibly containing false positives). Based on correct value sets, our invariants have the following property: values that can be assigned to an opaque predicate' variable must exist in the variable's corresponding value set. From each value set, we synthesize an opaque predicate that 1) evaluates all values in its value set to the same truth value and 2) shares real predicates' common syntactic features. Because the value set is correct in that it does not contain false negatives, even if it contains false positives, the synthesized output will be an opaque predicate as it evaluates all actual possible values to the same truth value.

Our opaque predicates *syntactically* resemble real predicates and therefore ensure high potency because their invariants are naturally occurring—which avoid inadvertently introducing unnatural code—and they share real predicates' common syntactic features. In Sect. 2, we empirically identify real predicates' common syntactic features from a set of real world programs. Section 7 explains how we synthesize opaque predicates that share the common syntactic features we identified in Sect. 2.

Our opaque predicates *semantically* resemble real predicates and therefore ensure high resilience because the naturally occurring invariants they use are based on value sets. Behaviorally, a real predicate's variable can take on different values during runtime. With our opaque predicates' invariants based on value sets, our opaque predicates' invariant property becomes harder to identify since their variables also can take on different values during runtime like real predicates' variables. Section 6.1 explains why value sets we infer using abstract interpretation at the source-level (obfuscation-time) will likely not be inferred at the binary-level (analysis-time). Section 8 empirically justifies our claim for resiliency.

Lastly, our opaque predicates are low cost since their invariants are naturally occurring—so they introduce zero additional execution overheads—unlike synthetic invariants that introduce additional code to execute.

The main limitation of our approach is scalability. We rely on Frama-C's implementation of abstract interpretation [22] to infer value sets. Frama-C along with other static analysis tools in general will have difficulty performing whole-program analysis on a large codebase. This is discussed further in Sect. 9.1.

1.4 Contributions

The followings are our key contributions:

- We present a novel approach to construct high-quality opaque predicates that are potent *w.r.t.* stealth, resilient *w.r.t.* stealth, and low cost. By achieving potency, we are also able to prevent heuristic attacks that existing opaque predicates are vulnerable to.
- We show that our approach to construct high-quality opaque predicates is practical by providing a corresponding automated tool[1] to insert our opaque predicates in C source code.

2 Identifying Features of Real Predicates

To prevent heuristic attacks, we synthesize opaque predicates that share real predicates' common syntactic features. The common syntactic features that constitute our synthesis requirement are empirically identified from a set of real world programs: all 109 programs in Coreutils[2] (101254 predicates), SQLite3 database[3] (27339 predicates), Nginx web server[4] (12660 predicates), and Bluefish text editor[5] (5942 predicates). Although Coreutils are made up of 109 programs, the majority of them share part of the same codebase and hence can lead to bias [2]. This is why we also evaluate other real-world programs. Additionally, since the evaluation is based on a finite set of real-world programs, the features of real predicates identified in this evaluation might not generalize to all programs. We discuss this in Sect. 9.2 and suggest a possible remedy to further investigate in the future.

Figure 1 shows the result of our analysis to identify the features of real predicates. The analysis is performed automatically using BinaryNinja's APIs [35] on our set of real world programs' corresponding executable binaries instead of their respective source code because we want our analysis to reflect how reverse engineers perceive predicates. Since Votipka *et al.* [36] found that reverse engineers commonly scan the code prior to performing in-depth analysis, features of

[1] https://github.com/yellowbyte/zero-footprint-opaque-predicates.

[2] https://ftp.gnu.org/gnu/coreutils/coreutils-8.32.tar.gz.

[3] https://www.sqlite.org/2020/sqlite-amalgamation-3330000.zip.

[4] https://nginx.org/download/nginx-1.18.0.tar.gz.

[5] https://www.bennewitz.com/bluefish/stable/source/bluefish-2.2.11.tar.gz.

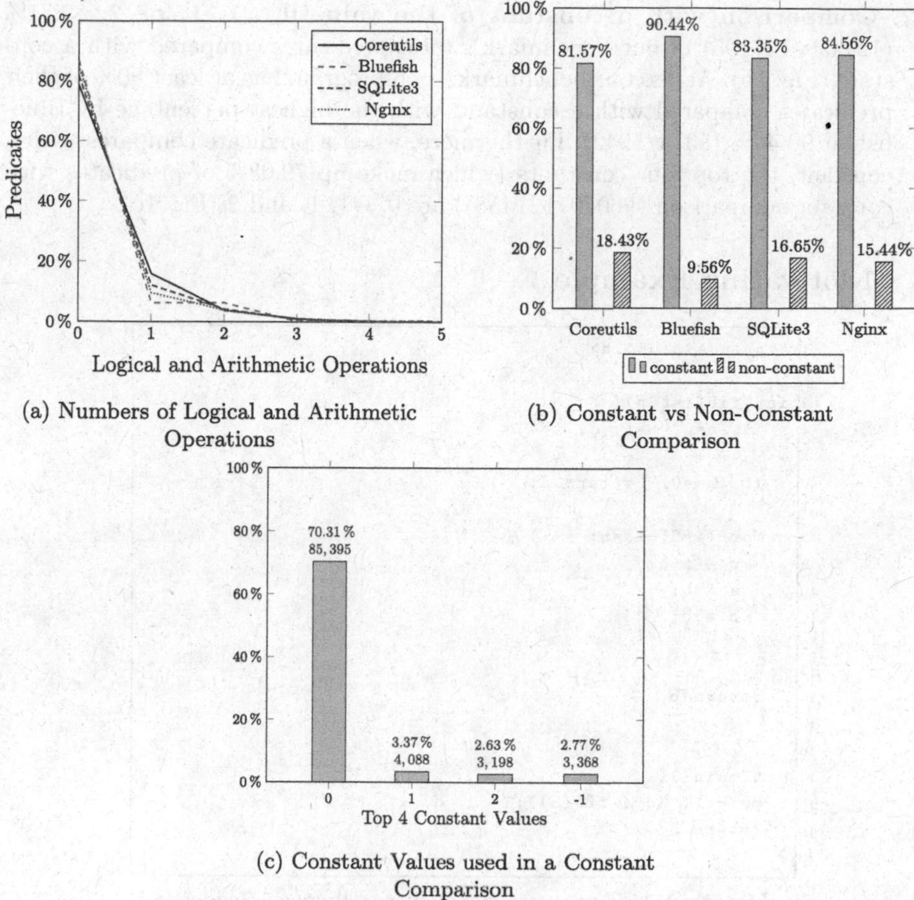

(a) Numbers of Logical and Arithmetic Operations

(b) Constant vs Non-Constant Comparison

(c) Constant Values used in a Constant Comparison

Fig. 1. Features of real predicates

code in close proximity to the invocation of the conditional branch will represent the features of real predicates as perceived by reverse engineers. As a result, we only perform analysis on basic blocks that end with a conditional branch.

Overall, our analysis at the basic block level shows that real predicates have the following common syntactic features:

F1. Zero or few logical and arithmetic operations. 80.25% (118120/147195) of our benchmark's total predicates contains zero logical and arithmetic operation (Fig. 1a), with the lowest percentage by Coreutils at 78.83% (79820/101254) and the highest percentage by Bluefish at 86.89% (5163/5942). From predicates with zero to one operation, the percentage of our benchmark's total predicates drops to 14.27% (21003/147195). The trend captured by Fig. 1a is that percentage of predicates decreases as the number of operations increases.

F2. Comparison with a constant of the value 0, −1, 1, or 2. 82.51% (121458/147195) of our benchmark's total predicates compared with a constant (Fig. 1b). Across our benchmark, each program has at least 80% of their predicates compared with a constant, with the highest percentage by Bluefish at 90.44% (5374/5942). Furthermore, when a predicate compares with a constant, the top four constants (which make up 79.08% of predicates with constant comparison (96049/121458)) are 0, −1, 1, and 2 (Fig. 1c).

3 Motivating Example

```
1  #include<stdio.h>
2
3  int fib(int n){
4    int a=0, b=1, c, i;
5
6    if (n==0)  return a;
7
8    for (i=2; i<=n; i++) {
9      c = a+b;
10     a = b;
11     b = c;
12   }
13
14   return b;
15 }
16
17 int main(){
18   printf("%d", fib(3));
19   return 0;
20 }
```

Listing 1.1. C program to calculate Fibonacci Sequence

To demonstrate how we construct opaque predicates using naturally occurring invariants, we explain the process using an implementation of the Fibonacci Sequence (Listing 1.1).

The naturally occurring invariants we use are based on variables' value sets. A variable can have different value set at different lines of code. For example, variable `c` at line 9, or more precisely after the execution of code at line 9 but prior to the execution of code at line 10, has a value set of {1,2}. However, at line 13, or after the execution of the for loop, variable `c` has a value set of {2}. An opaque predicate that shares real predicate's common syntactic features (**F1** and **F2**) for variable `c`'s value set at line 9 is `c<=0`. The opaque predicate `c<=0` satisfies the constraint that items in `c`'s value set at line 9 are equivalent when evaluated since both 1 and 2 will evaluate to Boolean false. The corresponding opaque predicate in the compiled x86 code as perceived by reverse engineers is shown in Fig. 2.

Figure 2a is the disassembly of Listing 1.1's for loop body, whereas Fig. 2b is the disassembly of the same for loop body but with the opaque predicate `c<=0`

```
mov   eax, [ebp+var_8]
add   eax, [ebp+var_C]
mov   [ebp+var_10], eax
mov   eax, [ebp+var_C]
mov   [ebp+var_8], eax
mov   eax, [ebp+var_10]
mov   [ebp+var_C], eax
mov   eax, [ebp+var_14]
add   eax, 1
mov   [ebp+var_14], eax
jmp   loc_8048446
```

(a) Without Opaque Predicate

```
mov   eax, [ebp+var_8]
add   eax, [ebp+var_C]
mov   [ebp+var_10], eax
cmp   [ebp+var_10], 0
jg    loc_804846D
.
.
.
mov   eax, [ebp+var_C]
mov   [ebp+var_8], eax
mov   eax, [ebp+var_10]
mov   [ebp+var_C], eax
mov   eax, [ebp+var_14]
add   eax, 1
mov   [ebp+var_14], eax
jmp   loc_8048446
```

(b) With Opaque Predicate

Fig. 2. Listing 1.1's for loop body with and without the opaque predicate

inserted. As shown in the disassembly (Fig. 2b), by satisfying **F1** and **F2** our opaque predicate consists of just a `CMP` instruction to set the flag for conditional branch and the conditional branch instruction `JG`. Note that in Fig. 2b the compiler compiles the opaque predicate `c<=0` to its inverse (`c>0`) so the Boolean true branch will point to the rest of the for loop body. The obfuscation is performed by the non-executable code that follows the Boolean false branch.

4 Threat Model

In our work, we provide defenses against both manual and automated attacks. The assumption we make in our threat model is that when an attacker analyzes the code, the attacker will only have access to the binary executable. In other words, we assume the original source code is not leaked. Our opaque predicates' resilience can be compromised if this assumption is not held because our approach to infer value sets takes advantage of abstract interpretation performing better analysis at the source-level (obfuscation time) than at the binary-level (analysis time) to achieve high resilience. Section 6.1 explains why value sets we inferred at the source-level (obfuscation time) will likely not be inferred at the binary-level (analysis time). In Sect. 8, we also empirically justify our claim for resilience under the condition that the original source code is not leaked.

There have been research on generic deobfuscation based on execution traces [7,41]. Those approaches can successfully deobfuscate our opaque predicates, or any other opaque predicates, since opaque predicates' obfuscation will never be part of the execution traces. However, the resulting deobfuscated program can be unreliable. There is no guarantee that the execution traces will represent all behaviors of the obfuscated program because the execution driver used to produce the execution traces may not exercise all control-flow paths.

5 System Overview

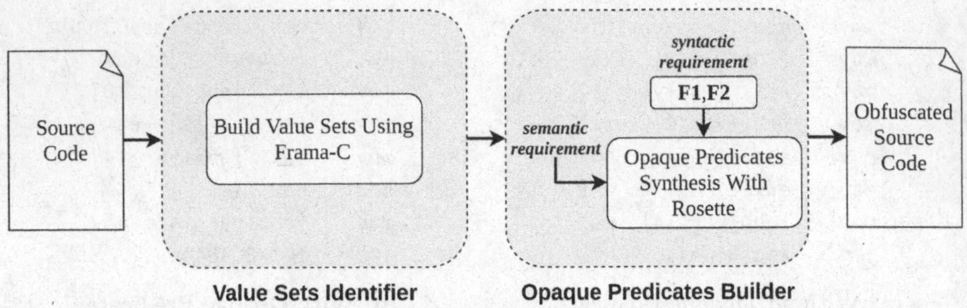

Fig. 3. Obfuscation tool overview

Figure 3 shows a global overview of how we construct opaque predicates.

In the **Value Sets Identifier** step, we identify the value sets for our opaque predicates' invariants. As a conditional branch disguise, each opaque predicate needs exactly one invariant to inject non-executable code from a dead branch. The invariants we use are based on variables' value sets at a specific line of code. We use the source-level program analysis tool Frama-C [22], particularly its value analysis plugin implemented using abstract interpretation [10], to infer correct value sets.

In the **Opaque Predicates Builder** step, we synthesize the opaque predicates using Rosette's synthesis engine [34]. For each value set, we synthesize an opaque predicate that satisfies the syntactic requirement imposed by **F1** and **F2** and the semantic requirement imposed by the value set.

6 Value Sets Identifier

To identify value sets, we use abstract interpretation because it can reason about all possible program behaviors statically to infer correct value sets. In general, statically analyzing a program to identify any interesting program property such as *is variable x constant?* using program's concrete operational semantics is theoretically undecidable and practically intractable [28]. Abstract interpretation makes analysis decidable and tractable while maintaining correctness by reasoning about program behavior in a less precise abstract domain.

6.1 Source-Level vs Binary-Level Analysis

Abstract interpretation infers more precise value sets at the source-level than at the binary-level due to the lack of signedness information at the binary-level. Furthermore, the value sets inferred at the binary-level can also be incorrect due to the lack of complete code. Therefore, the invariants we infer at the source-level (obfuscation time) will likely not be inferred by the same analyses at the binary-level (analysis time). This distinction is particularly important to assure resilience since future deobfuscation tools may adapt a deobfuscation approach based on the way we use abstract interpretation for identifying invariants to detect opaque predicates instead. We also empirically justify our claim for resilience in Sect. 8.

Lack of Signedness Information. Signedness information is not preserved through the compilation process. The lack of signedness information at the binary-level significantly hinders the possible choice of abstract domains. The original work [3] that uses abstract interpretation on binary code to infer value sets uses an abstract domain called *strided-intervals.* However, strided-intervals require the signedness of a variable. Navas *et al.* [29] and Redini *et al.* [31] both use an abstract domain based on wrapped intervals that is signedness-agnostic. However, wrapped intervals-based abstract domains do not have a lattice structure since it lacks both a least upper bound (lub) $\sqcup$ and greatest lower bound (glb) $\sqcap$ for any two wrapped intervals. To alleviate the lack of lub $\sqcup$ and glb $\sqcap$, Navas *et al.* and Redini *et al.* [29,31] create a biased pseudo-join $\widetilde{\sqcup}$ and a biased pseudo-meet $\widetilde{\sqcap}$, but the biased pseudo-join $\widetilde{\sqcup}$ is not monotonic and therefore cannot be used to compute a least fixed point. In summary, a fixed-point semantics cannot be achieved as is with abstract interpretation on non-lattice abstract domains like wrapped intervals. A solution is to use the widening operation, but each widening operation makes the analysis more imprecise by roughly doubling the wrapped intervals [29].

Lack of Complete Code. At the binary-level, we are also not guaranteed to have access to the complete code as retrieving it is an undecidable problem [38]. The lack of complete code means that the inferred value set can contain false negatives (i.e., not guaranteed to contain all possible items). One major reason hindering the retrieval of complete code at the binary-level is indirect control-flow such as x86's `JMP EAX`. Indirect control-flow makes retrieval of code difficult at both intraprocedural and interprocedural levels. Furthermore, current capabilities to identify function boundaries are lacking [1]. The retrieved code can be incorrect or incomplete if where the function ends is not correctly identified. Even though abstract interpretation guarantees no false negative, the inferred value set can still contain false negatives when the analysis is performed on incomplete or incorrect code.

In BinTrimmer's SASI [31], the authors assume the retrieval of a complete and precise control-flow graph. In the original implementation of abstract interpretation on binary code [3], the authors assume IDA Pro will correctly identify all stack and global variables. However, those assumptions will not always hold as they require complete code and complete code is not guaranteed to be retrievable. Even though binary disassembly has improved considerably in recent years [6,18,21,26], which can improve abstract interpretation on binary code, the underlying problem of a lack of complete code is still present.

7 Opaque Predicate Builder

We use program synthesis to synthesize opaque predicates that share the syntactic features of **F1** and **F2** to resemble real predicates while satisfying the constraints imposed by the invariants.

7.1 Program Synthesis Implementation

⟨*start*⟩ ::= ⟨*expr*⟩

⟨*expr*⟩ ::= ⟨*identifier*⟩⟨*op*⟩⟨*digit*⟩

⟨*op*⟩ ::= >|>=|<|<=|==|!=

⟨*digit*⟩ ::= -1|0|1|2

⟨*identifier*⟩ ::= [A-Za-z][A-Za-z0-9]*

Fig. 4. Our opaque predicates' grammar

Program synthesis involves automated techniques for generating programs from a specification [8]. The specification is defined with respect to the syntactic and semantics requirements of the program we want to synthesize. The syntactic requirement defines the space of programs to search in. Whereas the semantic requirement defines the behavior of the program to search for in the search space. Once both the syntactic and semantic requirements are specified, a search can be performed to find a program that satisfies both requirements.

We perform program synthesis with the solver-aided language Rosette [34] since it allows us to represent the syntactic and semantic requirements expressively in the programming language Racket. Once represented in Racket, Rosette then translates the requirements into logical formulae using a combination of symbolic execution and bounded model checking. With the syntactic and semantic requirements represented as logical formulae, the search for a satisfying program is performed with the Z3 SMT solver [16].

```
(define sketch
  (expr 'x [choose > < >= <= eq? neq?] [choose 0 1 2 -1]))
```

Fig. 5. Sketch of the opaque predicate grammar

```
(define (interpret p input)
  (let ([acceptable-consts (list 0 1 2 -1)]
        [acceptable-ops (list > < >= <= eq? neq?)]
        [ismember? (lambda (item lst)
                     (ormap (lambda (cur) (eq? item cur))
                     lst))])
    (match p
      [(expr _ op digit) (and (ismember? digit acceptable-consts)
                              (ismember? op acceptable-ops)
                              (op input digit))])))
```

Fig. 6. Interpreter for the sketch

Syntactic Requirement. Features **F1** and **F2** constitute our syntactic requirement since the program we want to synthesize is an opaque predicate that share the syntactic features of **F1** and **F2**. We define our syntactic requirement in formal grammar using *Backus-Naur Form (BNF)* notation (Fig. 4). The grammar shown in Fig. 4 represents the program search space. Rosette allows us to specify the syntactic requirement expressively by providing synthesis language constructs (e.g., 'choose', '??'). Those synthesis language constructs allow us to write a partial program, or sketch, that defines the program search space instead. The sketch that represents our grammar is shown in Fig. 5. As shown, we use the synthesis language construct, 'choose', to specify all possible terminal values at the corresponding position. The identifier in our sketch is fixed to the string "x" since the identifier can be easily substituted with the actual identifier after synthesis. By writing an interpreter that can execute our sketch (Fig. 6), our Rosette program can then reason about the semantic requirement that defines the behavior of the completed program we want as the synthesis output.

Semantic Requirement. Our semantic requirement is the constraint imposed by the invariant, which can be described formally as followed:

Let $\{x_1, x_2, x_3 ... x_n\}$ or $\{x_i\}_{i=1}^{n}$ be a finite sequence representing the value set for a specific variable at a particular line of code where i is the index and

```
(define always-true-expr
  (solve
   (begin
     (for ([i value-set])
       (assert (interpret sketch i)))
)))

(define always-false-expr
  (solve
   (begin
     (for ([i value-set])
       (assert (not (interpret sketch i))))
)))
```

Fig. 7. Specification of the semantic requirement

x_i is the i-th term in the sequence. We want the following logical formula to be satisfiable:

$$P(x_1) \Leftrightarrow ... \Leftrightarrow P(x_n)$$

P is a program constrained by our syntactic requirement (i.e., a syntactically correct program under the grammar shown in Fig. 4). The logical connective, $\Leftrightarrow$, represents "if and only if." For this formula to be satisfiable, every interpretation of P using items from the same value set, $\{x_i\}_{i=1}^n$, needs to evaluate to the same truth value. A synthesized P that satisfies both our syntactic and semantic requirements is essentially an opaque predicate since it always evaluates to Boolean true or always evaluates to Boolean false for every item it can be assigned to from its value set. To impose the semantic requirement in Rosette, we iterate over each item in the value set twice (Fig. 7). In one iteration, we use Racket's 'assert' construct to impose the semantic requirement that every item in the value set needs to evaluate to Boolean true ('always-true-expr') by our sketch. In the next iteration, we impose the semantic requirement that every item in the value set needs to evaluate to Boolean false ('always-false-expr') instead. If either 'always-true-expr' or 'always-false-expr' is satisfiable, it means that Rosette successfully synthesized an opaque predicate.

8 Evaluation

We did not evaluate with existing obfuscation approaches since we already differentiate from them by not introducing any beacon to enable heuristic attacks. Our opaque predicates are potent and free from heuristic attacks because they resemble real predicates by satisfying **F1** and **F2**. In this section, we evaluate our opaque predicates *w.r.t.* the other two criteria for evaluating opaque predicates' quality: resilience and cost.

We have also identified two additional criteria useful for determining the practicality of our approach: 1) the quantity of opaque predicates we can construct and 2) the obfuscation time required to construct our opaque predicates. The quantity of opaque predicates is a potential issue since the invariants our opaque predicates rely on are based on the number of value sets that can be inferred. The obfuscation time is another potential issue due to our multistage pipeline for constructing opaque predicates.

8.1 Benchmark Programs

We use a set of single file programs contained in the Frama-C open source case studies repository[6]. We use these programs as a benchmark because each of them already contains the suitable Frama-C harness [25] that enables Frama-C to analyze the program. The reason we choose single file programs is to simplify the coordination in our obfuscation pipeline. In total, our benchmark consists of 21 programs. 17 of the 21 programs belong to a case study called "bench-moerman2018" while the rest belongs to their own case study. There are more single file programs in "bench-moerman2018," however we chose a representative set of 17 programs since the other programs in the benchmark have similar code.

8.2 Evaluation Setup

Setup for Cost. To evaluate our opaque predicates' cost, we compare the execution time of the programs in our benchmark pre- and post- obfuscation. The execution time is calculated using the CPU time spent within the programs in both kernel and user modes.

Setup for Quantity and Obfuscation Time. To measure quantity, we simply count the number of opaque predicates inserted by our tool. It is possible for the opaque predicates we synthesized at the source-level to be removed by the compiler. To ascertain the number of opaque predicates in the compiled code, we purposely make our opaque predicates' obfuscation a deterministic and impossible instruction sequence, so each occurrence of the instruction sequence in the compiled code indicates one of our opaque predicates. We use the disassembler BinaryNinja to search for the instruction sequence. To measure obfuscation time, we keep track of the clock before and after the execution of our obfuscation pipeline. The obfuscation time is the difference between the two.

Setup for Resilience. To evaluate our opaque predicates' effectiveness *w.r.t.* resilience, we evaluate our opaque predicates against current state-of-the-art automated deobfuscation technique dynamic symbolic execution. In particular, we evaluate against BINSEC's implementation of dynamic symbolic execution to deobfuscate opaque predicates [5]. Additionally, we evaluate against another automated deobfuscation technique based on abstract interpretation that is implemented in BinaryNinja's OpaquePredicatePatcher [23]. OpaquePredicatePatcher detects opaque predicates by using abstract interpretation to identify predicates whose corresponding variable's value set only contains one item.

[6] https://git.frama-c.com/pub/open-source-case-studies.

Although Sect. 6.1 already explains why abstract interpretation performs better at the source-level (during obfuscation time) than at the binary-level (during analysis), we also want to empirically justify that claim since future deobfuscation tools may adapt a deobfuscation approach based on the way we use abstract interpretation for constructing opaque predicates to instead detect opaque predicates. Note that this is different from OpaquePredicatePatcher's usage of abstract interpretation. To detect opaque predicates in the way we use abstract interpretation requires evaluating each item in a variable's value set against the predicate that uses the variable. If all items in the value set evaluate to the same truth value, then the predicate is an opaque predicate. We use BinaryNinja's implementation of abstract interpretation, also used by OpaquePredicatePatcher, to implement the aforementioned new deobfuscation approach in a tool called BinValueSetEval and evaluate our opaque predicates against it.

8.3 Results

Table 1. Cost, quantity, and obfuscation time of our opaque predicates.

Program	LOC[‡]	Value Sets Quantity	Opaque Predicates Quantity	Frama-C Runtime (min:sec)	Obfuscation Time (min:sec)	Cost[§]	
						Pre- Obfuscation (seconds)	Post-Obfuscation (seconds)
2048[¶]	390	232	202	0:51	6:44	0.32	0.33
Solitaire	270	70	58	1:23	3:39	0.01	0.01
Tweetnacl-usable	858	118	111	0:06	2:52	0.09	0.09
Kilo[¶]	1045	272	54	0:42	2:57	0.43	0.43
Bench-moerman2018[*]	924	119	63	0:17	2:54	0.04	0.04

[*] The statistics for bench-moerman2018 is the accumulation of 17 programs from it.
[¶] Kilo and 2048 are both GUI programs. To calculate cost, we automate user interaction with pyautogui.
[‡] The LOC for a program does not account for spaces and code comments.
[§] The cost for each program is the average over 3 runs.

Results for Cost, Quantity, and Obfuscation Time. Aside from cost, quantity, and obfuscation time, Table 1 additionally shows lines of code (LOC) to help put the 3 aforementioned metrics into perspective. The opaque predicates quantity shown in Table 1 is the quantity found in the compiled binary. Out of the 490 opaque predicates synthesized, only two opaque predicates are removed by the compiler—program kilo and the programs in bench-moerman2018 originally synthesized 55 and 64 opaque predicates, respectively. The reason the "Value Sets Quantity" and "Opaque Predicate Quantity" columns are not equal is because not all inferred value sets satisfy the syntactic requirement imposed by **F1** and **F2**. Furthermore, we choose not to synthesize an opaque predicate when the corresponding value set only contains a zero since Frama-C will mis-identify pointer as an integer with a value set of just a zero. The reason in the program kilo we identified 272 value sets but only synthesized 54 opaque predicates is because 210 of the value sets only contain zero. Overall, we are still able to construct a sizable number of opaque predicates, with the program 2048 having the highest ratio of opaque predicates to LOC at 202 opaque predicates to 390 LOC. On the other hand, the program kilo has the lowest ratio at 54 opaque predicates to 1045 LOC due to the aforementioned reason. Even though our current tool will only construct one opaque predicate from one invariant, there is no limitation on creating multiple opaque predicates from the same invariant; this is further discussed in Sect. 9.1. Whole-program static analysis can be time-consuming. To put into perspective Frama-C's contribution to the obfuscation time, we provide statistics on Frama-C's runtime alongside the total obfuscation time. Overall, our tool's obfuscation time is acceptable as the maximum obfuscation time is less than 7 min. Lastly, our cost, or execution overheads, are nonexistent as the pre-obfuscation and post-obfuscation runtime are effectively the same. This makes sense intuitively since our opaque predicates are constructed from naturally occurring invariants that introduce zero additional code to execute in contrast to synthetic invariants.

Table 2. Resilience of our opaque predicates.

Program	Opaque predicates quantity	BINSEC¶ (#FP, #FN, #TP)	OpaquePredicatePatcher (#FP, #FN, #TP)	BinValueSetEval (#FP, #FN, #TP)
2048	202	(5, 47, 155)	(12, 200, 2)	(32, 12, 190)
Solitaire	58	(0, 55, 3)	(6, 58, 0)	(6, 58, 0)
Tweetnacl-usable	111	(20, 82, 29)	(7, 109, 2)	(8, 95, 16)
Kilo	54	(1, 53, 1)	(7, 54, 0)	(22, 48, 6)
Bench-moerman2018*	63	(5, 50, 13)	(102, 59, 4)	(103, 55, 8)
Totals	**488**	**(31, 287, 201)**	**(134, 480, 8)**	**(171, 268, 220)**

* The statistics for bench-moerman2018 is the accumulation of 17 programs from it.
¶ BINSEC's parameter, bound k, relies on user chosen value. We experimented with $k =$ 12, 16, 20, 24 as BINSEC's paper [5] states that their tool achieves favorable detection results at those bounds. In our experiment, at k = 12, 16, 20, 24 the corresponding F1 accuracy are 0.536, 0.558, 0.532, and 0.521, respectively. The table shows the statistics for BINSEC at its highest F1 accuracy when k = 16.

Results for Resilience. Table 2 shows our experimental results in respect to resilience (i.e., stealth *w.r.t.* automated deobfuscation). OpaquePredicatePatcher only identified 8 out of 488 opaque predicates and with false positives. For each program, OpaquePredicatePatcher always identified at least 6 false positives since 6 false positives occurred within functions inserted by the compiler. Specifically, they occur within the CRT startup functions that execute before and after the main function. This is why bench-moerman2018 contains significantly more false positives since it is made up of 17 programs where each has at least 6 false positives. BINSEC, on the other hand, performed better than OpaquePredicatePatcher but still only identified 201 out of 488 opaque predicates—41%. The last column of Table 2 shows the result of a new deobfuscation approach we implemented in the tool called BinValueSetEval by using abstract interpretation in the way we use it to construct opaque predicates to instead detect opaque predicates. BinValueSetEval identified significantly more opaque predicates in program 2048 (190/202 opaque predicates). However, for the other 20 programs in our benchmark, BinValueSetEval only identified 30/286 opaque predicates. BinValueSetEval also results in the highest number of false positives (171). Although OpaquePredicatePatcher and BinValueSetEval both use abstract interpretation, which guarantees an inferred value set will be correct (i.e., no false negative), an inferred value set can still be incorrect since at the binary-level the analysis could be performed on incomplete code (Sect. 6.1). With an incorrect value set, a real predicate can be falsely identified as an opaque predicate. This explains why OpaquePredicatePatcher and BinValueSet both contain false positives even though the underlying analysis is guaranteed to be correct.

9 Discussion

9.1 Limitation

Since our benchmark is small scale and part of the Frama-C open source case studies repository, it is potentially favorable for inserting our opaque predicates. For large codebases, Frama-C and static analysis in general will have difficulty performing whole-program analysis so the number of value sets we can infer from them can be significantly less than what is shown by the codebases used in our evaluation.

Overall, we are limited by the number of opaque predicates that we can construct since it is based on the number of value sets we can infer with Frama-C. One approach to alleviate the problem is to synthesize multiple opaque predicates from one value set. Currently, our obfuscation tool will only synthesize one opaque predicate from one value set. For example, if variable x will always contain a value from the set $\{1, 2, 3, 4\}$, we can construct multiple opaque predicates from the set, such as $x == 0$, $x > 0$, etc. One area of caution is that the stealthiness of our opaque predicates might be compromised if we overly use the same invariant to construct opaque predicates.

Another limitation is due to our approach of inserting opaque predicates prior to compilation since it is possible that the compiler will detect the opaque predicates and remove them accordingly from the compiled binary. In our evaluation (Sect. 8), out of 490 opaque predicates inserted at the source-level, two opaque predicates are removed by the compiler.

9.2 Future Work

Currently, the features of real predicates we identified (**F1** and **F2**) are based on a predetermined set of real-world programs (Sect. 2), but they might not characterize all programs. Future work will identify features of real predicates based on analyzing the program being obfuscated instead of generalizing the features from a predetermined set of programs.

Our mention of potency throughout this paper is *w.r.t.* stealth. Since early phases of manual analysis rely on beacons [36], we believe potency can be achieved by syntactically resembling real predicates so the opaque predicates avoid introducing beacons indicating the opaque predicates. However, we did not perform evaluation on potency. Another direction for future work is to employ human studies to assess our approach's potency.

10 Related Works

Preda *et al.* [15] have previously suggested using static analysis to construct opaque predicates from a theoretical point of view. Unlike our work, achieving resilience or potency is not their goal.

The work by Zobernig *et al.* [42] is the one closest to our work. Theirs is the only other work that shares the same sentiment that opaque predicates need to syntactically and semantically resemble real predicates. To address the resemblance problem, Zobernig *et al.* transform real predicates to resemble their injected opaque predicates using hash functions. Real predicates that compare with a constant are replaced to compare with the constant's hash value (with the predicate's variable also transformed by the hash function before the comparison). With high probability, a transformed real predicate will only evaluate to Boolean true if the original predicate evaluates to Boolean true. Opaque predicates are constructed by comparing a variable after transformation with a hash function against a random constant with the same length as the hash value. With high probability, an opaque predicate will always evaluate to Boolean false.

However, Zobernig's *et al.* approach is only able to transform real predicates that use equality comparison (==) on a constant since hash functions are not monotonic. To achieve potency, this approach needs to transform as many real predicates as possible. So Zobernig's *et al.* approach is only stealthy if the code contains many predicates with equality comparison (==) on *random* constants; if the constants used are not random, frequency analysis can be used to identify the original constant. As seen by our empirical study identifying features of real predicates (Fig. 1c), although real predicates are commonly compared with constants, majority of the constants are -1, 0, 1, or 2.

Christian Collberg, a pioneer on opaque predicates [13,33], suggests achieving potency with code diversity where multiple variants of the inserted code are created [33]. However, the practicality of that approach is in question since new variants need to be continuously developed to avoid opaque predicates inserted in the future to be identified. Furthermore, diversity introduced non-organically can inadvertently manifest beacons for heuristic attacks.

There are many works on constructing opaque predicates that primarily focus on achieving resilience. Many of those works [4,37,40] are on preventing detection by dynamic symbolic execution since dynamic symbolic execution has shown to be the most effective in automatically detecting opaque predicates [4,5,27]. Other works achieve resilience by constructing opaque predicates without the invariant constraint by allowing both branches of the opaque predicates to be reachable [17,30,39]; however, the obfuscation they can perform is limited since the basic blocks pointed to by either branch have to be semantically equivalent.

11 Conclusion

We introduce a novel approach to construct high-quality opaque predicates that are potent *w.r.t.* manual analysis, resilient *w.r.t.* automated analysis, and low cost. We achieve high potency by constructing opaque predicates that resemble real predicates. We achieve low cost by using naturally occurring invariants that introduce zero additional execution overhead. We also achieve high resilience since the naturally occurring invariants we use are value sets inferred by abstract interpretation at the source-level (obfuscation time) and the same value sets will likely not be inferred by abstract interpretation at the binary-level (analysis time) due to obstacles particular to binary-level analysis. Our opaque predicates' resilience is also justified empirically in our evaluation section by evaluating our opaque predicates against abstract interpretation and the current state-of-the-art deobfuscation technique dynamic symbolic execution. By achieving high potency, our opaque predicates are immune to heuristic attacks that existing opaque predicates are vulnerable to.

Acknowledgments. This research was supported by a generous gift from the Herman P. & Sophia Taubman Foundation. We would also like to thank the anonymous reviewers for their helpful comments and our shepherd, Sam L. Thomas, for guiding us through the revision process.

References

1. Andriesse, D., Chen, X., Van Der Veen, V., Slowinska, A., Bos, H.: An in-depth analysis of disassembly on full-scale x86/x64 binaries. In: 25th USENIX Security Symposium (USENIX Security 16), pp. 583–600 (2016)
2. Andriesse, D., Slowinska, A., Bos, H.: Compiler-agnostic function detection in binaries. In: 2017 IEEE European Symposium on Security and Privacy (EuroS&P), pp. 177–189. IEEE (2017)
3. Balakrishnan, G., Reps, T.: Analyzing memory accesses in x86 executables. In: Duesterwald, E. (ed.) CC 2004. LNCS, vol. 2985, pp. 5–23. Springer, Heidelberg (2004). https://doi.org/10.1007/978-3-540-24723-4_2
4. Banescu, S., Collberg, C., Ganesh, V., Newsham, Z., Pretschner, A.: Code obfuscation against symbolic execution attacks. In: Proceedings of the 32nd Annual Conference on Computer Security Applications, pp. 189–200 (2016)
5. Bardin, S., David, R., Marion, J.Y.: Backward-bounded DSE: targeting infeasibility questions on obfuscated codes. In: 2017 IEEE Symposium on Security and Privacy (SP), pp. 633–651. IEEE (2017)
6. Bauman, E., Lin, Z., Hamlen, K.W.: Superset disassembly: Statically rewriting x86 binaries without heuristics. In: NDSS (2018)
7. Blazytko, T., Contag, M., Aschermann, C., Holz, T.: Syntia: synthesizing the semantics of obfuscated code. In: 26th USENIX Security Symposium (USENIX Security 17), pp. 643–659 (2017)
8. Bodík, R., Jobstmann, B.: Algorithmic program synthesis: introduction. Int. J. Softw. Tools Technol. Transfer **15**, 397–411 (2013)

9. Brunet, P., Creusillet, B., Guinet, A., Martinez, J.M.: Epona and the obfuscation paradox: transparent for users and developers, a pain for reversers. In: Proceedings of the 3rd ACM Workshop on Software Protection, pp. 41–52 (2019)
10. Canet, G., Cuoq, P., Monate, B.: A value analysis for c programs. In: 2009 Ninth IEEE International Working Conference on Source Code Analysis and Manipulation, pp. 123–124. IEEE (2009)
11. Collberg, C.: The tigress c diversifier/obfuscator (2015). Accessed 14 Aug 2015
12. Collberg, C., Myles, G., Huntwork, A.: Sandmark-a tool for software protection research. IEEE Secur. Privacy **1**(4), 40–49 (2003)
13. Collberg, C., Thomborson, C., Low, D.: A taxonomy of obfuscating transformations. Technical report, Department of Computer Science, The University of Auckland, New Zealand (1997)
14. Cousot, P., Cousot, R.: Abstract interpretation: a unified lattice model for static analysis of programs by construction or approximation of fixpoints. In: Proceedings of the 4th ACM SIGACT-SIGPLAN Symposium on Principles of Programming Languages, pp. 238–252 (1977)
15. Dalla Preda, M., Giacobazzi, R.: Control code obfuscation by abstract interpretation. In: Third IEEE International Conference on Software Engineering and Formal Methods (SEFM 2005), pp. 301–310. IEEE (2005)
16. de Moura, L., Bjørner, N.: Z3: an efficient SMT solver. In: Ramakrishnan, C.R., Rehof, J. (eds.) TACAS 2008. LNCS, vol. 4963, pp. 337–340. Springer, Heidelberg (2008). https://doi.org/10.1007/978-3-540-78800-3_24
17. Drape, S.: Intellectual property protection using obfuscation (2010)
18. Flores-Montoya, A., Schulte, E.: Datalog disassembly. In: 29th USENIX Security Symposium (USENIX Security 20), pp. 1075–1092 (2020)
19. Horwitz, S.: Precise flow-insensitive may-alias analysis is NP-hard. ACM Trans. Program. Lang. Syst. (TOPLAS) **19**(1), 1–6 (1997)
20. Junod, P., Rinaldini, J., Wehrli, J., Michielin, J.: Obfuscator-LLVM-software protection for the masses. In: 2015 IEEE/ACM 1st International Workshop on Software Protection, pp. 3–9. IEEE (2015)
21. Kinder, J., Veith, H.: Jakstab: a static analysis platform for binaries. In: Gupta, A., Malik, S. (eds.) CAV 2008. LNCS, vol. 5123, pp. 423–427. Springer, Heidelberg (2008). https://doi.org/10.1007/978-3-540-70545-1_40
22. Kirchner, F., Kosmatov, N., Prevosto, V., Signoles, J., Yakobowski, B.: Frama-C: a software analysis perspective. Formal Aspects Comput. **27**(3), 573–609 (2015)
23. LaFosse, P.: Automated opaque predicate removal (2017). https://binary.ninja/2017/10/01/automated-opaque-predicate-removal.html
24. Madou, M., Van Put, L., De Bosschere, K.: LOCO: an interactive code (De)obfuscation tool. In: Proceedings of the 2006 ACM SIGPLAN Symposium on Partial Evaluation and Semantics-Based Program Manipulation, pp. 140–144. ACM (2006)
25. Maroneze, A.: Parsing realistic code bases with Frama-C (2018). https://blog.frama-c.com/index.php?post/2018/07/06/Parsing-realistic-code-bases-with-Frama-C
26. Miller, K., Kwon, Y., Sun, Y., Zhang, Z., Zhang, X., Lin, Z.: Probabilistic disassembly. In: 2019 IEEE/ACM 41st International Conference on Software Engineering (ICSE), pp. 1187–1198. IEEE (2019)
27. Ming, J., Xu, D., Wang, L., Wu, D.: Loop: logic-oriented opaque predicate detection in obfuscated binary code. In: Proceedings of the 22nd ACM SIGSAC Conference on Computer and Communications Security, pp. 757–768. ACM (2015)

28. Møller, A., Schwartzbach, M.I.: Static program analysis. Notes, pp. 3–7 (2012)
29. Navas, J.A., Schachte, P., Søndergaard, H., Stuckey, P.J.: Signedness-agnostic program analysis: precise integer bounds for low-level code. In: Jhala, R., Igarashi, A. (eds.) APLAS 2012. LNCS, vol. 7705, pp. 115–130. Springer, Heidelberg (2012). https://doi.org/10.1007/978-3-642-35182-2_9
30. Palsberg, J., Krishnaswamy, S., Kwon, M., Ma, D., Shao, Q., Zhang, Y.: Experience with software watermarking. In: Proceedings 16th Annual Computer Security Applications Conference (ACSAC 2000), pp. 308–316. IEEE (2000)
31. Redini, N., Wang, R., Machiry, A., Shoshitaishvili, Y., Vigna, G., Kruegel, C.: BinTrimmer: towards static binary debloating through abstract interpretation. In: Perdisci, R., Maurice, C., Giacinto, G., Almgren, M. (eds.) DIMVA 2019. LNCS, vol. 11543, pp. 482–501. Springer, Cham (2019). https://doi.org/10.1007/978-3-030-22038-9_23
32. Sheridan, B., Sherr, M.: On manufacturing resilient opaque constructs against static analysis. In: Askoxylakis, I., Ioannidis, S., Katsikas, S., Meadows, C. (eds.) ESORICS 2016. LNCS, vol. 9879, pp. 39–58. Springer, Cham (2016). https://doi.org/10.1007/978-3-319-45741-3_3
33. Thomborson, C., Collberg, C., Low, D.: Manufacturing cheap, resilient, and stealthy opaque constructs. In: Proceedings of the 25th ACM SIGPLAN-SIGACT Symposium on Principles of Programming Languages, pp. 184–196. ACM (1998)
34. Torlak, E., Bodik, R.: Growing solver-aided languages with rosette. In: Proceedings of the 2013 ACM International Symposium on New Ideas, New Paradigms, and Reflections on Programming & Software, pp. 135–152 (2013)
35. Vector 35: Binary Ninja: A New Type of Reversing Platform. https://binary.ninja/
36. Votipka, D., Rabin, S., Micinski, K., Foster, J.S., Mazurek, M.L.: An observational investigation of reverse engineers' processes. In: 29th USENIX Security Symposium (USENIX Security 20), pp. 1875–1892 (2020)
37. Wang, Z., Ming, J., Jia, C., Gao, D.: Linear obfuscation to combat symbolic execution. In: Atluri, V., Diaz, C. (eds.) ESORICS 2011. LNCS, vol. 6879, pp. 210–226. Springer, Heidelberg (2011). https://doi.org/10.1007/978-3-642-23822-2_12
38. Wartell, R., Zhou, Y., Hamlen, K.W., Kantarcioglu, M., Thuraisingham, B.: Differentiating code from data in x86 binaries. In: Gunopulos, D., Hofmann, T., Malerba, D., Vazirgiannis, M. (eds.) ECML PKDD 2011. LNCS (LNAI), vol. 6913, pp. 522–536. Springer, Heidelberg (2011). https://doi.org/10.1007/978-3-642-23808-6_34
39. Xu, D., Ming, J., Wu, D.: Generalized dynamic opaque predicates: a new control flow obfuscation method. In: Bishop, M., Nascimento, A.C.A. (eds.) ISC 2016. LNCS, vol. 9866, pp. 323–342. Springer, Cham (2016). https://doi.org/10.1007/978-3-319-45871-7_20
40. Xu, H., Zhou, Y., Kang, Y., Tu, F., Lyu, M.: Manufacturing resilient bi-opaque predicates against symbolic execution. In: 2018 48th Annual IEEE/IFIP International Conference on Dependable Systems and Networks (DSN), pp. 666–677. IEEE (2018)
41. Yadegari, B., Johannesmeyer, B., Whitely, B., Debray, S.: A generic approach to automatic deobfuscation of executable code. In: 2015 IEEE Symposium on Security and Privacy, pp. 674–691. IEEE (2015)
42. Zobernig, L., Galbraith, S.D., Russello, G.: When are opaque predicates useful? In: 2019 18th IEEE International Conference On Trust, Security And Privacy In Computing And Communications/13th IEEE International Conference On Big Data Science And Engineering (TrustCom/BigDataSE), pp. 168–175. IEEE (2019)

PetaDroid: Adaptive Android Malware Detection Using Deep Learning

ElMouatez Billah Karbab(✉) and Mourad Debbabi

Concordia Security Research Center, Montreal, Canada
{elmouatez.karbab,mourad.debbabi}@concordia.ca

Abstract. Android malware detection is a significant problem that affects billions of users using millions of Android applications (apps) in existing markets. Thiss paper proposes PetaDroid, a framework for accurate Android malware detection and family clustering on top of static analyses. PetaDroid automatically adapts to Android malware and benign changes over time with resilience to common binary obfuscation techniques. The framework employs novel techniques elaborated on top of natural language processing (NLP) and machine learning techniques to achieve accurate, adaptive, and resilient Android malware detection and family clustering. We extensively evaluated PetaDroid on multiple reference datasets. PetaDroid achieved a high detection rate (98–99% f1-score) under different evaluation settings with high homogeneity in the produced clusters (96%). We conducted a thorough quantitative comparison with state-of-the-art solutions MaMaDroid, DroidAPIMiner, MalDozer, in which PetaDroid outperforms them under all the evaluation settings.

1 Introduction

Android OS's popularity has increased tremendously since the last decade. It is undoubtedly an appropriate choice for smart mobile devices such as phones and tablets or the internet of things devices such as TVs due to its open-source license and the massive number of useful apps developed for this platform (about 4 Million apps in 2019 [2]). Nevertheless, malicious apps target billions of Android users through centralized app markets. The detected malicious apps increased by 40% in 2018-Q3 compared to the same period in 2017 [1]. Google Play employs a vetting system named `Bouncer` to detect malicious apps through static and dynamic analyses. Despite these analyses, many malicious apps[1] were able to bypass `Bouncer` and infect several hundred thousand devices[2]. Therefore, there is a dire need for accurate, adaptive, yet resilient Android malware detection systems for the app market scale.

1.1 Problem Statement

In this paper, we identify the following gaps in the state-of-the-art solutions for Android malware detection:

[1] https://tinyurl.com/y4qdtuy9.
[2] https://tinyurl.com/y4mckwxm.

L. Bilge et al. (Eds.): DIMVA 2021, LNCS 12756, pp. 319–340, 2021.
https://doi.org/10.1007/978-3-030-80825-9_16

P1: The accuracy of Android malware detection systems tends to decrease over time due to different factors: (1) variations in existing malware family, (2) new malware families, (3) and new Android APIs in benign and malicious apps. These factors are mostly reflected in the changes in Android API call sequences in malicious and benign apps. Nevertheless, these changes are incremental in most cases compared to the existing apps. In this context, we consider two problems: (1) The resiliency of the detection systems that use machine learning models [31] to changes over time, (2) and the possibility of automatic adaptation to the new changes [40].

P2: Android malware family attribution is an important problem in the realm of malware detection. The malware family attribution could be important essential to define the threats[3] of the detected malware [28]. However, few existing solutions [7] provide Android malware family attribution. Furthermore, these solutions rely on supervised learning where prior knowledge of the families is required [12]. However, such knowledge is hard to get and not realistic in many cases, especially for new malware families[4].

P3: Malware developers employ various obfuscation techniques to thwart detection attempts. Obfuscation resiliency is a key requirement in modern malware fingerprinting that applies static analyses. Few solutions address the obfuscation issue [36,40] in the context of Android malware detection, more specifically, the resiliency to common obfuscations and binary code transformations.

1.2 Proposed Solution

In this paper, we propose PetaDroid, an accurate, adaptive, resilient, and yet efficient Android malware detection and family clustering using natural language processing (NLP) and deep learning techniques on top of static analysis features. In PetaDroid, we aim to address the previously mentioned problems as follows:

1. Our fundamental intuition for time resiliency and adaptation is that Android apps are changing over time incrementally. Benign apps embrace new Android APIs, deprecations, and components gracefully to do not disturb the user experience. Malware developers aim to target the maximum devices by employing stable and cross-Android version APIs. We argue that PetaDroid can fingerprint malicious apps within a time window with high confidence because the application still contains enough patterns of similarity to known samples.

2. PetaDroid goes a step further in the detection process by clustering the detected samples into groups with high similarity. We *exclusively* group highly similar samples, most likely of the same malware family. PetaDroid family attribution is found upon the assumption that malicious applications tend to have similar characteristics in the Android Dalvik bytecode code. We leverage this assumption to build an automatic and unsupervised malware family tagging system using deep neural network auto-encoder for sample digest generation on top of *InstNGram2Bag* features (based on NLP bag of words). Using the DBScan

[3] https://tinyurl.com/yydg5vew.

[4] https://tinyurl.com/y8rc6q89.

[11] clustering algorithm, we cluster the *most similar samples* from the detected malicious apps.

3. PetaDroid introduces code fragments randomization during training and deployment phases to enhance the obfuscation resiliency. We artificially apply random permutations to change the order of code basic-blocks without altering the basic-block instructions. We consider a code basic-block as a possible micro-action in the app execution flows. Therefore, we randomize the app execution flows without affecting the micro-actions within the flow to emulate code transformation during the training and deployment phases. Code fragment randomization strengthens the obfuscation robustness of PetaDroid, as shown in Sect. 4.3.

1.3 Contributions and Outline

The main contributions of this paper are:

(1) We propose a novel adaptation technique for Android malware detection to automatically adapt the detection system. The proposed techniques rely on the confidence probability of the detection ensemble to collect extension training datasets from received samples during the deployment (Sect. 2.2).
(2) We propose a novel fragment randomization technique to boost the detection system resiliency to common code-obfuscation techniques. In this technique, we randomize the order of code basic-blocks without affecting the basic-blocks instructions during the training and the deployment phases (Sect. 2.2).
(3) We propose PetaDroid, an accurate and efficient malware detection and clustering framework based on code static analyses, NLP, and machine learning techniques. In PetaDroid, we propose an ensemble of CNN models on top of a code embedding model, namely *Inst2Vec*, to accurately detect malware with probability confidence (Sect. 2.2). We released the source code of PetaDroid to the community in https://github.com/mouatez/petadroid.
(4) We extensively evaluate PetaDroid to assess its effectiveness and efficiency on different reference datasets of PetaDroid under various evaluation settings (Sect. 2.1).

2 PetaDroid

In this section, we detail PetaDroid methodology and its components.

2.1 Android App Representation

In this section, we present the preprocessing of Dalvik code and its representation into a canonical instructions sequence. We seek the preservation of the maximum information about apps' behaviors while keeping the process very efficient. The preprocessing begins with the disassembly of an app bytecode to Dalvik assembly code, as depicted in Fig. 1.

```
// Object Creation
new-instance v10, java/util/HashMap
// Object Access
invoke-direct v10, java/util/HashMap
if-eqz v9, 003e
..
// Method Invocation
// * = Android/telephony
invoke-virtual v4, */TelephonyManager.getDeviceId()java/lang/String
move-result-object v11
// Method Invocation
invoke-virtual v4, */TelephonyManager.getSimSerialNumber()java/lang/String
move-result-object v13
// Method Invocation
invoke-virtual v4 */TelephonyManager.getLine1Number()java/lang/String
move-result-object v4
...
// Object Creation
new-instance v20, java/io/FileReader
const-string v21, "/proc/cpuinfo"
invoke-direct/range v20, v21, java/io/FileReader.init(java/lang/String)
new-instance v21, java/io/BufferedReader
...
move/from16 v2, v20
// Field Access
// * = Android/content/pm
iget-object v0, v0, */ApplicationInfo.metaData Android/os/Bundle
move-object/from16 v19, v0
```

Fig. 1. Android assembly from a malware sample

We model the Dalvik assembly code as code fragments where each fragment is a class's method code in the Dalvik assembly. It is a natural separation because Dalvik code D is composed of a set of classes $D = \{C_1, C_2, \ldots C_s\}$. Each class C_i contains a set of methods $C = \{M_1, M_2, \ldots M_k\}$, where we find actual assembly code instructions. We preserve the order of Dalvik assembly instructions within methods while ignoring the global execution paths. Method execution is a possible *micro-behavior* for an Android app, while a global execution path is a likely *macro-behavior*. An Android app might have multiple global execution paths based on external events. In contrast, Android malware tends to have one crucial global execution path (malicious payload) and other ones to distract malware detection systems. The malware could produce variations for the payload global execution path. However, it still depends on the micro-behavior to produce another global one. PetaDroid assembly preprocessing produces a multiset of sequences $P = \{S_1, S_2, \ldots S_h\}$ where each sequence S contains an ordered instruction sequence $S = \langle I_1, I_2, \ldots I_v \rangle$ of a class's method. In other words, P contains instruction sequences $P = \{\langle I_1, I_2, \ldots \rangle_1, \langle I_1, I_2, \ldots \rangle_2, \ldots \langle I_1, I_2, \ldots \rangle_h\}$ where the order is only preserved inside individual sequences S_i (the methods instructions). Thus, a sequence S defines a possible micro-execution (or behavior) from the Android app's overall runtime execution.

As shown in Fig. 1, the Dalvik assembly is too sparse. We want to keep the assembly instruction skeleton that reflects possible runtime behaviors with less sparsity. In PetaDroid, we propose a canonical representation for Dalvik assembly code, as shown in Fig. 2. The key idea is to keep track of the Android platform APIs and objects utilized inside the method assembly. To fingerprint

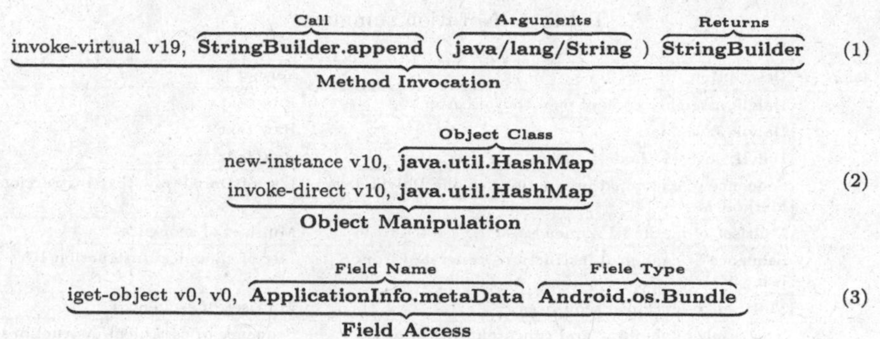

Fig. 2. Canonical representation of Dalvik assembly

malicious apps, the canonical representation will mostly preserve the actions and the manipulated system objects, such as sending SMS action or getting (setting) sensitive information objects. PetaDroid canonical representation covers three types of Dalvik assembly instructions, namely: *Method invocation*, *object manipulation*, and *field access*, as shown in Fig. 2. In the method invocation, we focus on the method call, *Package.ClassName.MethodName*, the parameters list, *Package.ClassName*, and the return type, *Package.ClassName*. In object manipulation, we capture the class object, *Package.ClassName*, that is being used. Finally, we track the access to system fields by capturing the field name, *Package.ClassName.FieldName*, and its type, *Package.ClassName*. Our manual inspections of Dalvik assembly for hundreds of malicious and benign samples shows that these three forms cover the essential of Dalvik assembly instructions.

PetaDroid instruction parser keeps only the canonical representation and ignores the rest. For example, our experiments show that Dalvik opcodes add a lot of sparsity without enhancing the malware fingerprinting performance. On the contrary, it could negatively affect overall performance, which is shown in previous solutions [29]. The final step in preprocessing a method M (see Fig. 1) is to flatten the canonical representation of a method into a single sequence S.

We keep only the Android platform related assets like API, classes, and system fields in the final method's sequence S. We maintain a vocabulary dictionary (key: value) in the form of ($Androidassets : identifier$) (for example ($Android/telephony/TelephonyManager$: 439)) of all Android OS assets (all versions) to filter and map Android assets to unique identifiers (unique integer for a given Android assets) for the method instruction sequence during the preprocessing. The output of the app representation phase is a list of sequences $\hat{P} = \{S_{c,1}, S_{c,2}, \ldots S_{c,h}\}$. Each sequence is an ordered canonical instruction representation of one method. In the following, we summarize the notations used in the rest of the paper (Table 1):

2.2 Malware Detection

In this section, we present the PetaDroid malware detection process using CNN on top of *Inst2Vec* embedding features. The detection process starts from a

Table 1. Notation summary

Notation	Description	Format
D	Dalvik assembly code of one Android App	Raw text
C	Dalvik Java Class	Raw text
M	Dalvik Java Method	Raw text
S	Sequence of extracted instructions of one Dalvik Java Method M	List of Dalvik raw text instructions
P	Multiset of methods' sequences S	Multiset of sequences
S_c	Sequence of canonical instructions generated from S using V	List of canonical instruction IDs
$\hat{P}$	Multiset of methods' sequences S_c	Multiset of sequences
P_c	The result of shuffling and concatenating of all S_c	Sequence of canonical instructions
F	Fragment is a truncated portion from P_c	List of canonical instructions
$CNNModel$	Classification model based on Convolutional Neural Network (CNN)	Deep learning model
Φ	Ensemble of classification models $\Phi = \{CNNModel_1, CNNModel_2, \dots CNNModel_\phi\}$	Set of deep learning models
y	Dataset label	Malware or not
$\hat{y}$	Prediction likelihood of the classification models $\hat{y} = \Phi(F)$	Probability
ζ	Detection threshold for the general decision strategy	Probability threshold
η	Detection threshold for the confidence decision strategy	Probability threshold

multiset of discretized canonical instruction sequences $\hat{P} = \{S_{c,1}, S_{c,2}, \dots S_{c,h}\}$. Notice that $\hat{P}$ is a multiset and not a set since it might contain duplicated sequences. The duplication comes from having the same Dalvik method's code in two (or more) distinct Dalvik classes. PetaDroid CNN ensemble produces a detection result together with maliciousness and benign detection probabilities for a given sample. To achieve automatic adaptation, we leverage the detection probabilities to automatically collect an extension dataset that PetaDroid employs to build new CNN ensemble models.

$$\hat{P} = \{S_{c,1}, S_{c,2}, S_{c,2}\} \tag{4}$$

$$\{\underbrace{S_{c,3}, S_{c,1}, S_{c,2}}_{\textbf{Shuffled sequences}}\} \tag{5}$$

$$\overbrace{\{\langle I_1, I_1, \dots I_{|Sc3|}\rangle_3, \langle I_1, I_1, \dots I_{|Sc1|}\rangle_1, \langle I_1, I_1, \dots I_{|Sc2|}\rangle_2,\}}^{\textbf{while preserving the order inside sequences}} \tag{6}$$

$$\hat{P}_c = \overbrace{\{\underbrace{I_{3,1}, I_{3,1}, \dots I_{3,|Sc3|}, I_{1,1}, I_{1,1}, \dots I_{1,|Sc1|}, I_{2,1},}_{\textbf{Fragment truncation}} \underbrace{I_{2,1}, \dots I_{2,|Sc2|},}_{\textbf{Rest}}\}}^{\textbf{Sequence concatenation}} \tag{7}$$

$$F = \overbrace{\{I_{3,1}, I_{3,1}, \dots I_{3,|Sc3|}, I_{1,1}, I_{1,1}, \dots I_{1,|Sc1|}, I_{2,1}\}}^{\textbf{on fragment size } |F|} \tag{8}$$

Fig. 3. Example of fragment generation

Fragment Detection. Fragment-based detection is a key technique in PetaDroid. A fragment F is a truncated portion from the beginning of the concatenation P_c of $\hat{P} = \{S_{c,1}, S_{c,2}, \ldots S_{c,h}\}$ as shown in Fig. 3. The size $|F|$ is the number of canonical instructions in the fragment F, and it is a hyper-parameter in PetaDroid. Our grid search for the best $|F|$ hyper-parameter result $|F| = 10k$ for the current version of PetaDroid. For a sequence $S_{c,i}$, the order of canonical instructions is preserved within a method. In other words, we guarantee the preservation of order inside the method sequence or what we refer to as a *micro-action*. However, no specific order is assumed between methods' sequences or what we refer to as *macro-action* (or behavior). On the contrary, before we truncate P_c into size $|F|$, we apply random permutations on $\hat{P}$ to produce a random order in the macro-behavior. The randomization happens in every access, whether it is during training or deployment phases. Each Android sample has $\frac{h!}{(h-k)!}$ possible permutations for the methods' sequences $\hat{P} = \{S_{c,1}, S_{c,2}, \ldots S_{c,h}\}$, where h is the number of methods' sequence in a given Android app, and k is the number of sampled sequences. The concatenation of the sampled k sequences must be greater than $|F|$.

Inst2Vec Embedding. *Inst2Vec* is based on *word2vec* [30] technique to produce an embedding vector for each canonical instruction in our sequences. *Inst2Vec* is trained on instruction sequences to learn instruction semantics from the underlying contexts. This means that *Inst2Vec* learns a dense representation of a canonical instruction that reflects the instruction co-occurrence and context. The produced embeddings capture the semantics of instructions (interpreted by geometric distances). Furthermore, embedding features show high code fingerprinting accuracy and resiliency to common obfuscation techniques [10].

Classification Model. Our single CNN model takes *Inst2Vec* features, which are a sequence of embeddings; each embedding captures the semantics of an instruction. The temporal CNN [23], or 1-dimensional CNN [42], is the working core component in the PetaDroid single classification model. We choose to build our classification models based on CNN architecture over recurrent neural networks (RNN) such as LSTM or GRU. Due to the efficiency of CNN during the training and the deployment compared to RNN. **In the training phase**, the CNN models take on average 0.05 s per batch (32 samples), which is five times faster than RNN models in our experiments. The CNN model converges early (starting from 10 epochs) compared to the RNN model (starting from 30 epochs). **In the deployment phase**, the CNN model's inference is, on average, five times faster than RNN models. Both neural network architecture gives very similar detection results in our experiments. However, our automatic adaptation technique will benefit from the efficiency of CNN models to rapidly build new models using large datasets. The non-linearity used in our model employ the rectified linear unit (ReLUs) $h(x) = \max\{0, x\}$. We used Adam [13] optimization algorithm with a 32 mini-batch size and a $3e - 4$ learning rate for 100 epochs in all our experiments. The chosen hyper-parameters are the results of empirical evaluations to find the best values.

Detection Ensemble. PetaDroid detection component relies on an ensemble $\Phi = \{CNNModel_1, CNNModel_2, \ldots, CNNModel_\phi\}$. Ensemble Φ is composed of ϕ single CNN models. The number of single CNN models in the ensemble ϕ is a hyper-parameter. We choose to be $\phi = 6$, which is a trade-off of between maximum effectiveness on malware detection with the highest efficiency possible base on our evaluation experiments.

As mentioned previously, PetaDroid trains each CNN model for the number of epochs ($epochs = 100$). In each epoch, we compute $Loss_T$ and $Loss_V$, the *training* and *validation* losses, respectively, and save a snapshot of the single CNN model parameters. $Loss_T$ and $Loss_V$ are the log loss across training and validation sets:

$$p = CNNModel_\theta(y = 1|F)$$
$$loss(y,p) = -(y \log(p) + (1-y)\log(1-p)),$$
$$Loss_T = \frac{-1}{m_{train}} \sum_{i=1}^{m_{train}} loss(y_i, p_i),$$
$$Loss_V = \frac{-1}{m_{valid}} \sum_{i=1}^{m_{valid}} loss(y_i, p_i),$$

Where p is the maliciousness likelihood probability given a fragment F (a truncated concatenation of canonical instructions P_c) and model parameters θ (Sect. 2.1). PetaDroid selects the top ϕ models automatically from the saved model snapshots that have the lowest *training* and *validation* losses $Loss_T$ and $Loss_R$, respectively.

$$\hat{y} = \Phi(x) \quad = \frac{1}{\phi}\left(\sum_{i}^{\phi} CNNModel_i(x)\right) \tag{1}$$

PetaDroid CNN ensemble Φ produces a maliciousness probability likelihood by averaging the likelihood probabilities of multiple CNN models, as shown in Eq. 1.

Confidence Analysis. PetaDroid ensemble computes the maliciousness probability likelihood $Prob_{Mal}$ given a fragment F, as follows:

$$\hat{y} = \Phi(F), \quad Prob_{Mal} = \hat{y}, \quad Prob_{Ben} = (1 - \hat{y})$$

Previous Android malware detection solutions, such as [18,31], utilize a simple detection technique (we refer to it as a *general decision*) to decide on the maliciousness of Android apps. In the *general decision*, we compute the general threshold $\zeta \in [0, 1]$ that achieves the highest detection performance on the validation dataset X_{valid}. In the deployment phase (or evaluation in our case on X_{test}), The general decision D_ζ utilize the computed threshold ζ to make detection decisions:

$$D_\zeta = \begin{cases} Malware & Prob_{Mal} > \zeta \\ Benign & Prob_{Mal} <= \zeta \end{cases}$$

PetaDroid employs f1-score as a detection performance metric to automatically select ζ and to report the general detection performance on the test set X_{test} during our evaluation, in Sect. 4. We choose f1-score as our detection performance metric due to its simplicity, and its measurement reflects the reality under unbalanced datasets. *The general decision* provides a firm decision for every sample. However, security practitioners might prefer dealing with decisions that have associated confidence values and filter out less-confident decisions for further investigations. In a real deployment, we want as many detection decisions with high confidence and filter out the few uncertain apps with low confidence probability. Unfortunately, the *general decision* strategy that has been used by most previous solutions does not provide such functionality. For this purpose, we propose the **confidence decision strategy**, a mechanism to automatically filter out apps with uncertain decisions. PetaDroid computes a confidence threshold η that achieves a high detection performance (f1-score) and a negligible error rate (false negative and false positive rates) in the validation dataset. In other words, we add the error rate constraint to the system that computes the detection threshold η from X_{valid}. In the deployment, we make the confidence-based decision as follow:

$$D_\eta = \begin{cases} Uncertain & Prob_{Mal} < \eta \ \wedge \ Prob_{Ben} < \eta \\ Malware & Prob_{Mal} >= \eta \ \wedge \ Prob_{Mal} > Prob_{Ben} \\ Benign & Prob_{Ben} >= \eta \ \wedge \ Prob_{Ben} > Prob_{Mal} \end{cases}$$

Automatic Adaptation. In this section, we describe our mechanism to adapt to Android ecosystem changes over time automatically. The key idea is to re-train the CNN ensemble on new benign and malware samples periodically to learn the latest changes. To enhance the automatic adaptation, we leverage the confidence analysis to collect an extension dataset that captures the incremental change over time. Initially, we train PetaDroid ensemble using $X_{build} = \{X_{train} + X_{valid}\}$. Afterward, PetaDroid leverages the *confidence detection strategy* to build an extension dataset X_{exten} from test dataset X_{test} from high-confidence detected apps. In a real deployment, X_{test} is a stream of Android apps that needs to be checked for maliciousness by the vetting system. The test dataset $X_{test} = \{X_{Certain}, X_{Uncertain}\}$ is composed of apps having a high-confidence decision ($X_{Certain}$ or X_{exten}) and apps having uncertain decisions $X_{Uncertain}$. In the deployment, PetaDroid accumulates from high-confidence apps over time to form X_{exten} dataset. Periodically, PetaDroid utilizes the extension dataset X_{exten} to extend the original X_{build} and later updates the CNN ensemble models. In our evaluation, and after updating the CNN ensemble, we report

updated general performance and **updated confidence-based performance**, respectively the general and confidence-based performance of the new trained CNN ensemble on X_{test}. These metrics answer the question: what would be the detection performance on $X_{test} = \{X_{Certain}, X_{Uncertain}\}$ after we build the ensemble on $X_{NewBuild} = \{X_{Certain}, X_{build}\}$? In other words, PetaDroid reviews previous detection decisions using the new CNN ensemble and drives new general and confidence-based performance.

2.3 Malware Clustering

In this section, we detail the family clustering system. PetaDroid clustering aims to group the previously detected malicious apps (Sect. 2.2) into highly similar malicious apps groups, which are most likely part of the same malware family. PetaDroid clustering process starts from a multiset of discretized canonical instruction sequences $P = \{S_{c,1}, S_{c,2}, \ldots S_{c,h}\}$ of the detected malicious apps. We introduce the *InstNGram2Vec* technique and deep neural network auto-encoder to generate embedding digests for malicious apps. Afterward, we cluster malware digests using the DBScan [11] clustering algorithm to generate malware family groups. Notice that our clustering system (DBScan [11]) requires to represent malware samples by one feature vector for each sample instead of a list of embeddings as in *Inst2Vec* for PetaDroid classification. For this reason, we introduce *InstNGram2Vec* technique that automatically represents malware samples as feature vectors without an explicit manual feature selection. *InstNGram2Vec* is a technique that maps concatenated instruction sequences to fixed-size embeddings employing NLP bag of words (N-grams) and feature hashing [35] techniques.

Auto-Encoder. We develop a deep neural auto-encoder through stacked neural layers of encoding and decoding operations The proposed auto-encoder learns the latent representation of Android apps in an unsupervised way. The unsupervised learning of the auto-encoder is done through the reconstruction of the unlabeled hashing vectors $HV = \{hv_0, hv_1, \ldots hv_{DMal}\}$ of random Android apps. Notice that we do not need any labeling during the training of PetaDroid auto-encoder, off-the-self Android apps are sufficient.

Family Clustering. PetaDroid clusters the detected malware digests $\boldsymbol{Z} = \{z_0, z_1, \ldots, z_{DMal}\}$ into groups of malware with high similarity and most likely belonging to the same family. In PetaDroid clustering: **First**, we use an **exclusive** clustering mechanism. The clustering algorithm only groups highly similar samples and tags the rest as non-clustered. This feature could be more convenient for real-world deployments since we might not always detect malicious apps from the same family, and we would like to have family groups only if there are groups of the sample malware family. To achieve this feature, we employ the *DBScan* clustering algorithm. **Second**, as an optional step, we find the best cluster for the non-cluster samples, from the clusters produced previously by computing the euclidean similarity between a given non-cluster sample and a given cluster samples. We call this step the *family matching*. In the evaluation, we report *homogeneity* and *coverage* metric for the clustering before and after applying this optional step. *DBScan*, in contrast with clustering algorithms such as *K-means*, produces clusters with high confidence. The most important metrics in PetaDroid clustering is the homogeneity of the produces clusters.

3 Dataset

Our evaluation dataset contains 10 million Android apps as sampling space for our experiments (over 100 TB) collected across the last ten years from August 2010 to August 2019, as depicted in Table 2. The extensive coverage in size (10 M), time range (06-2010 to 08-2019), and malware families (+300 family) make the result of our evaluation quite compelling.

In Sect. 4.1 and 4.2, to evaluate PetaDroid detection and family clustering, we leverage malware from reference Android malware datasets, namely: MalGenome [44], Drebin [6], MalDozer [18], and AMD [38]. Also, we collected Android malware from VirusShare[5] malware repository. In addition, we use benign apps from AndroZoo [4] dataset (randomly sampling $\approx 100k$ apps from 7.4 Million benign samples in each experiment). In the family clustering evaluation (Sect. 4.2), we use only malware samples from the reference datasets.

Table 2. Evaluation datasets

Name	#Samples	#Families	Time
MalGenome [44]	1.3K	49	2010–2011
Drebin [6]	5.5k	179	2010–2012
MalDozer [18]	21k	20	2010–2016
AMD [38]	25k	71	2010–2016
VirusShare[8]	33k	/	2010–2017
MaMaDroid [31]	40k	/	2010–2017
AndroZoo [4]	9.5M	/	2010–Aug 2019

In the comparison (Sect. 5) between PetaDroid, MaMaDroid [27,31], and DroidAPIMiner [3], we apply PetaDroid on the same dataset (benign and malware) used in MaMaDroid evaluation[9] to measure the performance of PetaDroid against state-of-the-art Android malware detection solutions.

To assess PetaDroid obfuscation resiliency (Sect. 4.3), we conduct an obfuscation evaluation on PRAGuard dataset[10], which contains $11k$ obfuscated malicious apps using common obfuscation techniques [26]. Besides, we generate over

[5] https://VirusShare.com.

[9] https://bitbucket.org/gianluca_students/mamadroid_code/src/master/.

[10] http://pralab.diee.unica.it/en/AndroidPRAGuardDataset.

100k benign and malware obfuscated Android apps employing DroidChameleon obfuscation tool [33] using common obfuscation techniques and their combinations.

To assess the adaptation of PetaDroid (Sect. 4.4), we employ the whole AndroZoo[11] [4] dataset (until August 2019), which contains 7.4 million benign apps and 2.1 million malware apps (at least detected as malicious by three vendors), by randomly sampling a dataset (100k malware and benign) in each experiment. We rely on VirusTotal detection of multiple anti-malware vendors in (metadata provided by AndroZoo repository) to label the samples. The dataset covers more than ten years span of Android benign and malware apps [4].

4 Evaluation

In this section, we evaluate PetaDroid framework through a set of experiments and settings involving different datasets.

4.1 Malware Detection

In this section, we report the detection performance of PetaDroid and the effect of hyper-parameters on malware detection performance.

Detection Performance. Table 3 shows PetaDroid *general* and *confidence-based* performance in terms of f1-score, recall, and precision metrics on the reference datasets. In the general performance, PetaDroid achieves a high f1-score 96–99% with a low false-positive rate (precision score of 96.4–99.5% in the general detection). The detection performance is higher under confidence settings. The f1-score is 99% and a very low false-positive rate (≈100k benign apps) with a recall score of 99.8% on average. The confidence-based performance causes the filtration of 1–8% low confidence samples from the testing set. In all our experiments, the confidence performance flags ≈6% on average, as uncertain decisions, which is a small and realistic value in a deployment with low false positives.

Table 3. General and confidence performances on various reference datasets

Name	General (%)			Confidence (%)		
	F1	P	R	F1	P	R
Genome	99.1	99.5	98.6	99.5	100.	99.0
Drebin	99.1	99.0	99.2	99.6	99.6	99.7
MalDozer	98.6	99.0	98.2	99.5	99.7	99.4
AMD	99.5	99.5	99.5	99.8	99.7	99.8
VShare	96.1	96.4	95.7	99.1	99.7	98.6

11 https://androzoo.uni.lu/.

4.2 Family Clustering

In this section, we present the results of PetaDroid family clustering on reference datasets (only malware apps). Malware family clustering phase comes after PetaDroid detects a considerable number of malicious Android apps. The number of detected apps could vary from $1k$ (MalGenome [44]) to $+20k$ (Maldozer [18]) samples depending on the deployment. We use *homogeneity* [34] and *coverage* metrics to measure the family clustering performance. The homogeneity metric scores the purity of the produced family clusters. A perfect homogeneity means each produced cluster contains samples from only one malware family. By default, PetaDroid clustering aims only to generate groups with confidence-based while ignoring less certain groups. The coverage metrics score the percentage of the clustered dataset with confidence. We also report the clustering performance after applying the *family matching* (optional step) to cluster all the samples in the dataset (100% coverage).

Table 4. The performance of the family clustering

Clustering metrics	DBSCAN clustering	After family matching
	Homogeneity—Coverage	Homogeneity—Coverage
Genome	90.00%—37%	79.67%—100%
Drebin	92.28%—49%	80.48%—100%
MalDozer	91.27%—55%	81.58%—100%
AMD	96.55%—50%	81.37%—100%

Table 4 summarizes the clustering performance in terms of *homogeneity* and *coverage* scores before and after applying the *family matching*. **First**, PetaDroid can produce clusters with high *homogeneity* 90–96% while keeping an acceptable *coverage*, 50% on average. At first glance, 50% *coverage* seems to be a modest result, but we argue that it is satisfactory because: (i) we could extend the coverage, but this might affect the quality of the produced clusters. In the deployment, high confidence clusters with minimum errors and acceptable coverage might be better than perfect coverage (in the case of K-Means clustering algorithm) with a high error rate. (ii) The evaluation datasets have long tail malware families, meaning that most families have only a few samples. This makes the clustering very difficult due to the few samples (less than five samples) in each malware family in the detected dataset. In a real deployment, we could add non-cluster samples to the next clustering iterations. In this case, we might accumulate enough samples to cluster for the long tail malware families. **Second**, after applying the family matching, PetaDroid clusters all the samples in the dataset (100% coverage) and homogeneity decreased to 80–82%, which is acceptable.

4.3 Obfuscation Resiliency

In this section, we report PetaDroid detection performance on obfuscated Android apps. We experiment on: (1) PRAGuard obfuscation dataset [26] (10k) and (2) obfuscation dataset generated using DroidChameleon [33] obfuscation tool (100k). In the PRAGuard experiment, we combine PRAGuard dataset with 20k benign Android apps randomly sampled from the benign apps of AndroZoo repository. We split the dataset equally into build dataset $X_{build} = \{X_{train}, X_{valid}\}$ and test dataset X_{test}. Table 5 presents the detection performance of PetaDroid on different obfuscation techniques. PetaDroid shows high resiliency to common obfuscation techniques by having an almost perfect detection rate, 99.5% f1-score on average.

Table 5. PetaDroid obfuscation resiliency on PRAGuard dataset

ID	Obfuscation techniques	General performance (%)		
		F1 (%)	P (%)	R (%)
1	`Trivial`	99.4	99.4	99.4
2	`String Encryption`	99.4	99.3	99.4
3	`Reflection`	99.5	99.5	99.5
4	`Class Encryption`	99.4	99.4	99.5
5	`(1) + (2)`	99.4	99.4	99.4
6	`(1) + (2) + (3)`	99.4	99.3	99.5
7	`(1) + (2) + (3) + (4)`	99.5	99.4	99.6
	Overall	99.5	99.6	99.4

In the DroidChameleaon experiment, we evaluate PetaDroid on other obfuscation techniques, as shown in Table 6. The generated dataset contains obfuscated benign (5k apps randomly sampled from AndroZoo) and malware samples (originally from Drebin). In the building process of CNN ensemble, we only train with one obfuscation technique (Table 6) and make the evaluation on the rest of the obfuscation techniques. Table 6 reports the result of obfuscation resiliency on DroidChameleon generated dataset. The results show the robustness of PetaDroid. According to this experiment, PetaDroid is able to detect malware obfuscated with common techniques even if the training is done on non-obfuscated datasets. We believe that PetaDroid obfuscation resiliency comes from the usage of (1) Android API (canonical instructions) sequences as features in the machine learning development. Android APIs are crucial in any Android app. A malware developer cannot hide API access, for example *SendSMS*, unless the malicious payload is downloaded at runtime. Therefore, PetaDroid is resilient to common obfuscations as long as they do not remove or hide API access calls. (2) The other factor is fragment-randomization, which makes PetaDroid models robust to code transformation and obfuscation in general. We argue that training machine learning models on dynamic fragments enhances the resiliency of the models against code transformation.

Table 6. Obfuscation resiliency on DroidChameleon dataset

Obfuscation techniques	General performance		
	F1 (%)	P (%)	R (%)
No Obfuscation	99.7	99.8	99.6
`Class Renaming`	99.6	99.6	99.5
`Method Renaming`	99.7	99.7	99.7
`Field Renaming`	99.7	99.8	99.7
`String Encryption`	99.8	99.8	99.7
`Array Encryption`	99.8	99.8	99.7
`Call Indirection`	99.8	99.8	99.7
`Code Reordering`	99.8	99.8	99.7
`Junk Code Insertion`	99.8	99.8	99.7
`Instruction Insertion`	99.7	99.8	99.7
`Debug Information Removing`	99.8	99.8	99.7
`Disassembling and Reassembling`	99.8	99.8	99.7

4.4 Automatic Adaptation

PetaDroid automatic adaptation goes a step further beyond time resiliency (100k benign and malicious apps every year). PetaDroid employs the confidence performance to collect an extension dataset X_{extend} during the deployment. PetaDroid automatically uses X_{extend} in addition to the previous build dataset as a new build dataset $X_{build(t)} = X_{build(t-1)} \cup X_{extend}$ to build a new ensemble at every new epoch. Table 7 depicts PetaDroid performance with and without automatic adaptation. PetaDroid achieves very good results compared to the previous section. PetaDroid maintains an f1-score in the range of 83–95% during all years. Without adaption, PetaDroid f1-score drops considerably starting from 2017. Table 7 shows the performance of revisiting detection decisions on previous Android apps X_{test} (benign and malware) after updating PetaDroid ensemble using $X_{build} \cup X_{extend}$, $X_{extend} \subseteq X_{test}$, where the samples in X_{extend} have been removed from X_{test}. The update performance is significantly enhanced in the overall detection during all years. Revisiting malware detection decisions is common practice in app market, (periodic full or partial scan the market's apps), which empowers the use case of PetaDroid automatic adaptation feature and the update metric.

Table 7. Performance of PetaDroid automatic adaptation

Year	No update (F1%)	General (F1%)	Confidence (F1%)	Update (F1%)
2014	98.2	97.0	97.9	99.7
2015	96.1	95.8	96.7	97.5
2016	93.0	93.3	94.8	96.4
2017	70.6	83.9	84.2	95.4
2018	54.8	87.6	91.6	93.8
2019	55.6	96.3	98.7	99.1

5 Comparative Study

In this section, we conduct a comparative study between PetaDroid and state-of-the-art Android malware detection systems, namely: MaMaDroid [27,31], DroidAPIMiner [3], and MalDozer [18]. Our comparison is based on applying PetaDroid on the same dataset (malicious and benign apps) and settings that MaMaDroid used in the evaluation (provided by the authors in [31]). The dataset is composed of 8.5K benign and 35.5K malicious apps in addition to the Drebin [6] dataset. The malicious samples are tagged by time; malicious apps from 2012 (Drebin), 2013, 2014, 2015, and 2016 and benign apps are tagged as oldbenign and newbenign, according to MaMaDroid evaluation.

5.1 Detection Performance Comparison

Table 8 depicts the direct comparison between MaMaDroid and PetaDroid different dataset combinations. In PetaDroid, we present the general and the confidence performance in terms of f1-score. For MaMaDroid and DroidAPIMiner, we present the original evaluation result [31] in terms of f1-score, which are equivalent to the general performance in our case. Notice that we present only the best results of MaMaDroid and DroidAPIMiner as reported in [31].

Table 8. Performance of MaMaDroid, PetaDroid, and DroidAPIMiner

	Peta (F1%)	MaMa (F1%)	Miner (F1%)
	General-Confidence		
`drebin& oldbenign`	**98.94–99.40**	96.00	32.00
`2013& oldbenign`	**99.43–99.81**	97.00	36.00
`2014& oldbenign`	**98.94–99.47**	95.00	62.00
`2014& newbenign`	**99.54–99.83**	99.00	92.00
`2015& newbenign`	**97.98–98.95**	95.00	77.00
`2016& newbenign`	**97.44–98.60**	92.00	36.00

As depicted in Table 8, PetaDroid outperforms MaMaDroid and DroidAPIMiner in all datasets in the general performance. The detection performance gap increases with the confidence-based performance. Notice that the coverage in the confidence-based settings is almost perfect for all the experiments in Table 8.

5.2 Efficiency Comparison

In Table 9, we report the required average time for MaMaDroid and PetaDroid to fingerprint one Android app. PetaDroid takes 03.58 ± 04.21 s on average for the whole process (DEX disassembly, assembly preprocessing, CNN ensemble inference). MaMaDroid, compared to PetaDroid, tends to be slower due to the heavy preprocessing. MaMaDroid preprocessing [31] is composed of the call graph extraction, sequence extraction, and Markov change modeling, which require 25.40 ± 63.00, 1.73 ± 3.2, 6.7 ± 3.8 s respectively for benign samples and 09.20 ± 14.00, 1.67 ± 3.1, 2.5 ± 3.2 s respectively for malicious samples. On average, PetaDroid (3.58 s) is approximately eight times faster than MaMaDroid.

Table 9. MaMaDroid and PetaDroid runtime

	PetaDroid (seconds)	MaMaDroid (seconds)
Malware	02.64 ± 03.94	$09.20 \pm 14.00 + 1.67 \pm 3.1 + 2.5 \pm 3.2$
Benign	05.54 ± 05.12	$25.40 \pm 63.00 + 1.73 \pm 3.2 + 6.7 \pm 3.8$
Average	03.58 ± 04.21	$\approx$23 s

5.3 Time Resiliency Comparison

MaMaDroid evaluation emphasizes the importance of time resiliency for modern Android malware detection. Table 10 depicts the performance with different dataset settings, such as training using an old malware dataset and testing on a newer one. PetaDroid outperforms (or obtains a very similar result in few cases) MaMaDroid and DroidAPIMiner in all settings. Furthermore, the results show that PetaDroid is more robust to time resiliency compared to MaMaDroid [31].

Table 10. Time Resiliency of MaMaDroid, PetaDroid, DroidAPIMiner.

Testing Sets	drebin & oldbenign			2013 & oldbenign			2014 & oldbenign			2015 & oldbenign			2016 & oldbenign		
Training Sets	**Miner**	**MaMa**	**Peta**	**Miner**	**MaMa**	**Peta**	**Miner**	**MaMa**	**Peta**	**Miner**	**MaMa**	**Peta**	**Miner**	**MaMa**	**Peta**
drebin&oldbenign	32.0	96.0	**99.4**	35.0	95.0	**98.6**	34.0	72.0	**77.5**	30.0	39.0	**44.0**	33.0	42.0	**47.0**
2013&oldbenign	33.0	94.0	**97.8**	36.0	97.0	**99.6**	35.0	73.0	**85.4**	31.0	37.0	**59.3**	33.0	28.0	**56.6**
2014&oldbenign	36.0	92.0	**95.8**	39.0	93.0	**98.6**	62.0	95.0	**99.4**	33.0	78.0	**91.4**	37.0	75.0	**88.9**
	drebin & newbenign			2013 & newbenign			2014 & newbenign			2015 & newbenign			2016 & newbenign		
Training Sets	**Miner**	**MaMa**	**Peta**	**Miner**	**MaMa**	**Peta**	**Miner**	**MaMa**	**Peta**	**Miner**	**MaMa**	**Peta**	**Miner**	**MaMa**	**Peta**
2014&newbenign	76.0	98.0	**99.3**	75.0	98.0	**99.7**	92.0	99.0	**99.8**	67.0	85.0	**91.4**	65.0	81.0	**82.1**
2015&newbenign	68.0	97.0	**97.1**	68.0	97.0	**97.8**	69.0	**99.0**	98.9	77.0	95.0	**99.0**	65.0	88.0	**95.4**
2016&newbenign	33.0	**96.0**	95.6	35.0	98.0	**98.2**	36.0	**98.0**	97.9	34.0	92.0	**95.2**	36.0	92.0	**98.3**

5.4 PetaDroid and Maldozer Comparison

In this section, we compare PetaDroid with MalDozer [18] to check the effectiveness of the proposed approach. Specifically, we evaluate the performance of both detection systems on raw Android datasets without any code transformation. Afterward, we evaluate the systems on randomization transformation (Sect. 2.2). Table 11 shows the effectiveness comparison between the detection systems. **First**, PetaDroid outperforms MalDozer in all the evaluation dataset without code transformation. One major factor to this result is the usage of the machine learning model ensemble to enhance the detection performance. **Second**, this gap significantly increases when we use code transformation in the various evaluation datasets. PetaDroid preserves the high detection performance due to the fragment randomization technique used in the training phase. As depicted in Table 11, the evaluation result shows the enhancement that the fragment randomization technique adds to the Android malware detection overall to enhance the resiliency.

Table 11. PetaDroid and MalDozer Comparison

	PetaDroid (F1 %)	MalDozer (F1 %)
	Raw-Randomization	Raw-Randomization
MalGenome	99.6-99.3	98.1-92.5
Drebin	99.2-99.1	97.4-91.6
MalDozer	98.5-98.6	95.2-89.3
AMD	99.4-99.5	96.1-90.1
VShare	95.8-96.0	94.2-88.1

6 Related Work

The Android malware analysis techniques can be classified to *static analysis*, *dynamic analysis*, or *hybrid analysis*. The static analysis methods [5,6,20,39] use static features that are extracted from the app, such as: requested permissions and APIs to detect malicious app. The dynamic analysis methods [8,16,21,36] aim to identify behavioral signature or behavioral anomaly of the running app. These methods are more resistant to obfuscation. The dynamic methods offer limited scalability as they incur additional cost in terms of processing and memory. The hybrid analysis [15,25], combine between both analyses to improve detection accuracy, which costs additional computational cost. Assuming that malicious apps of the same family share similar features, some methods [17,19,22], measure the similarity between the features of two samples (similar malicious code). The deep learning techniques are more suitable than conventional machine learning techniques for Android malware detection [41]. Research works on deep learning for Android malware detection are recently getting more attention [18,43]. These deep learning models are more venerable to common machine learning adversarial attacks as described in [9]. In contrast, PetaDroid employs the ensemble technique to mitigate such adversarial attacks [37] and to enhance the overall performance. In DroidEvolver [40], the authors use online machine learning techniques to enhance the time resiliency of the Android malware detection system. In contrast, PetaDroid employs batch training techniques instead of online training, which means that in each epoch t PetaDroid builds new models using the extended dataset at once. We argue that batch learning could generalize better since the training system has a complete view of the app dataset. It is less venerable to biases that could be introduced by the order of the apps in online training.

PetaDroid provides Android malware detection and family clustering using advanced natural language processing and machine learning techniques. PetaDroid is resilient to common obfuscation techniques due to code randomization during the training. PetaDroid introduces a novel automatic adaption technique inspired from [24] that leverages the result confidence to build a new CNN ensemble on confidence detection samples. Our automatic adaptation technique aims to overcome the issue of new Android APIs over time, while other methods could be less resilient and might require updates with a manually crafted dataset. The empirical comparison with state-of-the-art solutions, MaMaDroid [31] and MalDozer [18], shows that PetaDroid outperforms MaMaDroid and MalDozer under the various evaluation settings in the malware detection effectiveness and efficiency.

7 Limitation

Although the high obfuscation resiliency of PetaDroid showed in Sect. 4.3, PetaDroid is not immune to complex obfuscation techniques. Also, PetaDroid most likely will not be able to detect Android malware that downloads the payload during runtime. PetaDroid focuses on the fingerprinting process on DEX bytecode. Therefore, Android malware, which employs C/C++ native code, is less likely to be detected because we do not consider native code in our fingerprinting process. Covering native code is a possible future enhancement for PetaDroid. We consider including selective dynamic analysis for low confidence detection as future work. The latter will empower PetaDroid against sophisticated obfuscation techniques. Also, PetaDroid system needs more validation on real world deployments to check the performance as proposed in previous investigations [14,32]. Also, we need to check the correctness of the dataset split to prevent bias results as a result of *spatial bias* and *temporal bias* [32]. In Sect. 5.3 and 7, we partially addressed this issues by (1) evaluating the system on temporal splits from AndroZoo dataset and (2) employing collected samples dataset (VirusShare) in addition to multiple references datasets.

8 Conclusion

In this paper, we presented PetaDroid, an Android malware detection and family clustering framework for large scale deployments. PetaDroid employs supervised machine learning, an ensemble of CNN models on top of *Inst2Vec* features, to fingerprint Android malicious apps accurately. DBScan clustering on top of *Inst-NGram2Vec* and deep auto-encoders features, to cluster highly similar malicious apps into their most likely malware family groups. In PetaDroid, we introduced fragment-based detection, in which we randomize the macro-action of Dalvik assembly instructions while keeping the inner order of methods' sequences. We introduced the automatic adaption technique that leverages confidence-based decision making to build a new CNN ensemble on confidence detection samples. PetaDroid achieved high detection (98–99% f1-score) and family clustering (96% cluster homogeneity) performance. Our comparative study between PetaDroid, MaMaDroid [31] and MalDozer shows that PetaDroid outperforms state-of-the-art solutions on various evaluation settings.

References

1. Cyber attacks on Android devices on the rise (2018). https://www.gdatasoftware.com/blog/2018/11/31255-cyber-attacks-on-android-devices-on-the-rise
2. Mobile OS market share (2019). http://gs.statcounter.com/os-market-share/mobile/worldwide
3. Aafer, Y., Du, W., Yin, H.: DroidAPIMiner: mining API-level features for robust malware detection in Android. In: Zia, T., Zomaya, A., Varadharajan, V., Mao, M. (eds.) SecureComm 2013. LNICST, vol. 127, pp. 86–103. Springer, Cham (2013). https://doi.org/10.1007/978-3-319-04283-1_6
4. Allix, K., Bissyandé, T.F., Klein, J., Le Traon, Y.: AndroZoo: collecting millions of android apps for the research community. In: Proceedings of the 13th International Conference on Mining Software Repositories (2016)
5. Amira, A., Derhab, A., Karbab, E.B., Nouali, O., Khan, F.A.: Tridroid: a triage and classification framework for fast detection of mobile threats in android markets. J. Ambient Intell. Humaniz. Comput. **12**, 1731–1755 (2021)
6. Arp, D., Spreitzenbarth, M., Hubner, M., Gascon, H., et al.: DREBIN: effective and explainable detection of Android malware in your pocket. In: Symposium Network and Distributed System Security (2014)
7. Bai, Y., Xing, Z., Ma, D., Li, X., Feng, Z.: Comparative analysis of feature representations and machine learning methods in android family classification. Comput. Netw. **184**, 107639 (2021)
8. Canfora, G., Medvet, E.: Acquiring and analyzing app metrics for effective mobile malware detection. In: Proceedings of the 2016 ACM on International Workshop on Security and Privacy Analytics (2016)
9. Chen, X., et al.: Android HIV: a study of repackaging malware for evading machine-learning detection. IEEE Trans. Inf. Forensics Secur. **15**, 987–1001 (2020)
10. Ding, S.H.H., Fung, B.C.M., Charland, P.: Asm2Vec: boosting static representation robustness for binary clone search against code obfuscation and compiler optimization. In: Security and Privacy (2019)

11. Ester, M., Kriegel, H., Sander, J., Xu, X.: A density-based algorithm for discovering clusters in large spatial databases with noise. AAAI Press (1996)
12. Garcia, J., Hammad, M., Malek, S.: Lightweight, obfuscation-resilient detection and family identification of Android malware. ACM Trans. Softw. Eng. Methodol. **26**, 1–29 (2018)
13. Goodfellow, I., Bengio, Y., et al.: Deep Learning. MIT Press, Cambridge (2016)
14. Jordaney, R., et al.: Transcend: detecting concept drift in malware classification models. In: 26th USENIX Security Symposium, USENIX Security 2017, Vancouver, BC, Canada, August 16–18, 2017 (2017)
15. Karbab, E.B., Debbabi, M.: ToGather: automatic investigation of android malware cyber-infrastructures. In: Proceedings of the 13th International Conference on Availability, Reliability and Security, ARES (2018)
16. Karbab, E.B., Debbabi, M.: Maldy: portable, data-driven malware detection using natural language processing and machine learning techniques on behavioral analysis reports. Digit. Investig. **28**, S77–S87 (2019)
17. Karbab, E.B., Debbabi, M., Derhab, A., Mouheb, D.: Cypider: building community-based cyber-defense infrastructure for Android malware detection. In: ACM Computer Security Applications Conference (ACSAC) (2016)
18. Karbab, E.B., Debbabi, M., Derhab, A., Mouheb, D.: MalDozer: automatic framework for Android malware detection using deep learning. Digit. Investig. **24**, S48–S59 (2018)
19. Karbab, E.B., Debbabi, M., Derhab, A., Mouheb, D.: Scalable and robust unsupervised android malware fingerprinting using community-based network partitioning. Comput. Secur. **97**, 101965 (2020)
20. Karbab, E.B., Debbabi, M., Mouheb, D.: Fingerprinting Android packaging: generating DNAs for malware detection. Digit. Investig. **18**, S33–S45 (2016)
21. Karbab, E.M.B., Debbabi, M., Alrabaee, S., Mouheb, D.: DySign: dynamic fingerprinting for the automatic detection of Android malware. In: International Conference on Malicious and Unwanted Software (2016)
22. Kim, J., al. Structural information based malicious app similarity calculation and clustering. In: Proceedings of the 2015 Conference on Research in Adaptive and Convergent Systems (2015)
23. Kim, Y.: Convolutional neural networks for sentence classification. CoRR (2014)
24. Lakshminarayanan, B., Pritzel, A., Blundell, C.: Simple and scalable predictive uncertainty estimation using deep ensembles. In: Annual Conference on Neural Information Processing Systems (2017)
25. Lindorfer, M., Neugschwandtner, M., et al.: Andrubis-1,000,000 apps later: a view on current Android malware behaviors. In: Building Analysis Datasets and Gathering Experience Returns for Security (BADGERS). IEEE (2014)
26. Maiorca, D., Ariu, D., Corona, I., Aresu, M., Giacinto, G.: Stealth attacks: an extended insight into the obfuscation effects on Android malware. Comput. Secur. **51**, 16–31 (2015)
27. Mariconti, E., Onwuzurike, L., Andriotis, P., De Cristofaro, E., Ross, G., Stringhini, G.: MaMaDroid: detecting Android malware by building Markov chains of behavioral models. In: NDSS (2017)
28. Massarelli, L., Aniello, L., Ciccotelli, C., Querzoni, L., Ucci, D., Baldoni, R.: Android malware family classification based on resource consumption over time. In: 12th International Conference on Malicious and Unwanted Software, MALWARE 2017, Fajardo, PR, USA, October 11–14, 2017 (2017)
29. McLaughlin, N., et al.: Deep Android malware detection. In: CODASPY (2017)

30. Mikolov, T., Sutskever, I., et al.: Distributed representations of words and phrases and their compositionality. In: NIPS Neural Information Processing Systems (2013)
31. Onwuzurike, L., Mariconti, E., Andriotis, P., Cristofaro, E.D., Ross, G.J., Stringhini, G.: MaMaDroid: Detecting Android malware by building Markov chains of behavioral models (extended version). ACM Trans. Priv. Secur. **22**, 1–34 (2019)
32. Pendlebury, F., Pierazzi, F., Jordaney, R., Kinder, J., Cavallaro, L.: TESSERACT: eliminating experimental bias in malware classification across space and time. In: USENIX (2019)
33. Rastogi, V., Chen, Y., Jiang, X.: DroidChameleon: evaluating android anti-malware against transformation attacks. In: 8th ACM Symposium on Information, Computer and Communications Security, ASIA CCS 2013 (2013)
34. Rosenberg, A., Hirschberg, J.: V-measure: a conditional entropy-based external cluster evaluation measure. In: EMNLP-CoNLL (2007)
35. Shi, Q., et al.: Hash kernels. In: International Conference on Artificial Intelligence and Statistics (AISTATS) (2009)
36. Suarez-Tangil, G., et al.: DroidSieve: fast and accurate classification of obfuscated Android malware. In: Proceedings of the 7th ACM Conference on Data and Application Security and Privacy (CODASPY 2017), pp. 309–320 (2017)
37. Tramèr, F., Kurakin, A., Papernot, N., Goodfellow, I.J., Boneh, D., McDaniel, P.D.: Ensemble adversarial training: attacks and defenses. In: 6th International Conference on Learning Representations, ICLR 2018 (2018)
38. Wei, F., Li, Y., Roy, S., Ou, X., Zhou, W.: Deep ground truth analysis of current Android malware. In: Polychronakis, M., Meier, M. (eds.) DIMVA 2017. LNCS, vol. 10327, pp. 252–276. Springer, Cham (2017). https://doi.org/10.1007/978-3-319-60876-1_12
39. Wu, Y., Li, X., Zou, D., Yang, W., Zhang, X., Jin, H.: MalScan: fast market-wide mobile malware scanning by social-network centrality analysis. In: 34th IEEE/ACM International Conference on Automated Software Engineering (2019)
40. Xu, K., Li, Y., Deng, R., Chen, K., Xu, J.: DroidEvolver: self-evolving android malware detection system. In: IEEE European Symposium on Security and Privacy (2019)
41. Yuan, Z., Lu, Y., Wang, Z., Xue, Y.: Droid-Sec: deep learning in android malware detection. In: ACM SIGCOMM Computer Communication Review (2014)
42. Zhang, X., Zhao, J.J., LeCun, Y.: Character-level convolutional networks for text classification. In: Advances in Neural Information Processing Systems (2015)
43. Zhang, Y., et al.: Familial clustering for weakly-labeled Android malware using hybrid representation learning. IEEE Trans. Inf. Forensics Secur. **15**, 3401–3414 (2020)
44. Zhou, Y., Jiang, X.: Dissecting Android malware: characterization and evolution. In: IEEE Symposium on Security and Privacy (SP) (2012)

Spotlight on Phishing: A Longitudinal Study on Phishing Awareness Trainings

Florian Quinkert(✉), Martin Degeling, and Thorsten Holz

Ruhr-Universität Bochum, Bochum, Germany
{florian.quinkert,martin.degeling,thorsten.holz}@rub.de

Abstract. Phishing is in practice one of the most common attack vectors threatening digital assets. An attacker sends a legitimate-looking e-mail to a victim to lure her on a website with the goal of tricking the victim into revealing credentials. A phishing e-mail can use both technical (e.g., a forged link) and psychological vectors (e.g., an authoritarian tone) to persuade the victim.

In this paper, we present an analysis of more than 420,000 phishing e-mails sent over more than 1.5 years by a consulting company offering awareness trainings. Our data set contains detailed information on how users interact with the e-mails, e.g., when they click on links and what psychological vectors are used in the e-mails to convince the recipient of its legitimacy. While previous studies often used lab environments, the e-mails in our data set are sent to real users during their day-to-day work so that we can study their behavior in a genuine setting. Our results indicate a continually decreasing click rate (from 19% to 10%) with progressing awareness training. We also found some psychological vectors, including an *authoritative tone* and *curiosity*, to be more effective than others to trick a user into falling for this type of scam e-mails.

Keywords: Phishing · Measurement study · Awareness training

1 Introduction

For businesses [18] and private persons [21], phishing is still one of the most commonly used attack vectors. In phishing, an attacker sends a legitimate-looking message (often via e-mail) to a victim in order to lure her on a website under the attacker's control [11]. These e-mails have both technical (e.g., a forged link or a spoofed sender address) and psychological characteristics (e.g., an authoritarian tone or a luxurious offer) to convince victims of the message's legitimacy [14,38]. If a victim enters sensitive information (e.g., passwords or credit card information) on the attacker's website, the adversary can use it for malicious purposes, such as identity theft or financial fraud. The Anti-Phishing Working Group (APWG) announced the detection of about 147.000 phishing websites in the second quarter of 2020 [2], an increase of about 25,000 compared to the fourth quarter of 2018 [1]. Due to the popularity of this attack technique, it is crucial to understand *why* users fall for phishing and study methods that help us to educate them accordingly.

L. Bilge et al. (Eds.): DIMVA 2021, LNCS 12756, pp. 341–360, 2021.
https://doi.org/10.1007/978-3-030-80825-9_17

Previous research in this area already studied users' susceptibility to phishing [5,11] and proposed different education methods [7,26,27]. Multiple studies analyzed how psychological and technical vectors are used in phishing attacks [6,12,13,34]. These studies rely on experiments with a limited number of participants (typically students), often in a (potentially artificial) lab environment. As a result, we argue that existing work is limited in its generalizability, and it remains unclear which factors influence a victim's likelihood of falling for this type of scam e-mails in a real-world setting.

In this paper, we present a comprehensive analysis of phishing e-mails sent by a consulting company. In this paper, we refer to it as *PhishCo* as pseudonym. Clients hire PhishCo to send phishing e-mails to their employees to raise security awareness within the company. A key aspect of PhishCo's approach is to create phishing e-mails that are as close as possible to real-world phishing e-mails. For that purpose, they analyze real-world phishing e-mails and use the same techniques in their own e-mails. In particular, they use a combination of 14 different psychological and technical characteristics and customize the phishing e-mails to fit the hiring company's business.

PhishCoprovided us with a data set consisting of 429,418 e-mails sent over almost 1.5 years to employees of 77 different clients. For each e-mail, the data set contains detailed information about both the sent e-mail (e.g., used psychological and technical vectors) and the employees' interaction with it (e.g., when the provided link was clicked). The data set is anonymized and does not contain any personally identifiable information (PII) related to the employees' interaction. Unlike previous studies, the e-mails were sent to actual employees of companies belonging to a variety of industrial sectors during their day-to-day routine instead of a lab environment. Furthermore, the sent e-mails are close to real-world phishing e-mails so that we firmly believe employees likely behave similarly to when they receive a real phishing e-mail. In addition, the number of analyzed e-mails in our data set is substantially larger than previous studies, further improving the generalizability of our results.

In our analysis, we discovered an improving click rate over time. That is, employees clicked less often on the provided links in phishing e-mails in later phases, demonstrating that sending phishing e-mails to employees over a long time can be helpful to counter carelessness. Moreover, we found that the psychological vector *authority* has the most significant positive influence, i.e., employees were more likely to click on a link in an e-mail if this vector was used.

In summary, we make the following key contributions in this paper:

- We analyze a data set that is magnitudes larger than ones used in previous studies and consists of (fake) phishing e-mails that use both technical and psychological vectors to deceive users, enabling us to empirically study their influence on a large scale.
- In contrast to the majority of previous publications, we do not rely on an artificial lab environment, but gain insights into user's behavior when receiving (fake) phishing e-mails during their day-to-day routine over about one year.

- Our results show a constantly improving click rate over time, indicating that long-lasting awareness training can help users to better identify phishing e-mails.

The remaining of this paper is structured as follows: in Sect. 2, we introduce background information and present related work. Afterwards, we explain PhishCo's approach and the workflow in Sect. 3, and then present the measurement results in Sect. 4. Finally, we discuss lessons learned, limitations, and ethical considerations of our work in Sect. 5 and conclude along with recommendations in Sect. 6.

2 Background and Related Work

In this section, we describe related work which dealt with technical and psychological vectors. In addition, we present related phishing surveys.

2.1 Technical Vectors

An attacker creates a phishing e-mail that imitates a legitimate message ideally so that a victim might expect such an e-mail. For example, an attacker uses actual e-mails from the targeted company as templates, generates a similar layout, and includes company logos to let the e-mail look believable [29,35]. Moreover, an attacker can try to mimic the writing style and tone of the targeted companies' e-mails [40]. Many recipients judge incoming e-mails based on the sender's e-mail address so that spoofing this address is a preferred method to persuade victims [19]. PhishCouses comparable techniques (e.g., layout similarity, writing style, and spoofed e-mail addresses) to create believable e-mails and convince clients' employees to open the sent e-mails.

Furthermore, an attacker needs plausible domains to lure victims on websites under the attackers' control. Previous publications studied multiple technical attack techniques for that purpose, which are often referred to as *domain squatting* techniques. In *typosquatting*, an attacker creates a domain which differs from a well-known domain only by a typical typing error, e.g., `paypl.com` or `paypaal.com` [3]. A *combosquatting* domain consists of a well-known domain with added suitable terms so that the resulting domain still looks believable, e.g., `bankofamerica-security.com` or `secure-paypal.com` [23]. A domain cannot only contain Latin letters but also letters from other alphabets, such as Cyrillic. An attacker can replace one or multiple characters in well-known domain with similar looking characters from other alphabets, e.g., `bankofámerica.com`, which is referred to as *homograph domain* [33]. Registering a domain which sounds similar to a well-known domain, e.g., `guaranty-bank.com` instead of `guarantee-bank.com`, is called *soundsquatting* [30]. PhishCoregistered a set of domains using such techniques to use them in their e-mails sent to clients' employees as part of the awareness campaigns.

2.2 Psychological Vectors

Attackers do not only use technical vectors but also psychological ones, e.g., to create pressure or letting the victim feel important. Eventually, psychological vectors aim at convincing a victim to click on a link or open a provided attachment so that the attacker can, for example, collect personal information. Cialdini et al. introduce the six principles of persuasion and provide multiple examples of successful applications [9]. Similarly, Gragg analyzes triggers used to perform successful social engineering attacks and derives multiple defenses to counter these triggers [16]. Stajano et al. present principles based on real-life scams and conclude that security designers have to remember these principles in the development process [36]. Ferreira et al. combine the vectors of Cialdini et al., Gragg, and Stajano et al. to five principles of persuasion in social engineering attacks [12]. In a follow-up study, they extract the most effective elements of phishing e-mails and analyze them with regard to the previously introduced principles [13]. Van der Heijden et al. use the principles introduced by Cialdini et al. to build a classifier estimating how likely a human will fall for a certain phishing mail so that response teams in companies can prioritize incoming phishing e-mails [17]. Williams et al. conduct studies to analyze the effects of *urgency* and *authority* in e-mails [39]. PhishCouse a subset of these psychological vectors identified in prior publications for use in e-mails sent to clients' employees.

2.3 Phishing Surveys

Dhamija et al. present a user study in a lab environment with 22 participants, who classify 20 websites into legitimate and malicious [11]. Kumaraguru et al. introduce an embedded training method and a game to teach users how to identify phishing e-mails and malicious URLs [26]. In a follow-up study, Kumaraguru et al. use their training method and conduct a study with 515 faculty, staff, and students from Carnegie Mellon University, who received 10 e-mails within 28 days [25]. Caputo et al. send three phishing e-mails to 1,359 participants, show training material to a subset of them, and analyze whether it prevents participants from clicking on links in phishing e-mails [8]. Butavicius et al. ask 121 university students to classify 12 e-mails into legitimate, phishing, and spearphishing [6]. Rajivan et al. perform a two-phase experiment in which 105 participants first create phishing e-mails, which are classified in a second phase along with legitimate e-mails by 340 other participants [34]. Oliviera et al. conduct an experiment with 158 participants to understand whether younger persons or older persons have a different susceptibility for phishing attacks [31]. For that purpose, they sent spearphishing e-mails to the participants on 21 consecutive days in their day-to-day life. They concluded that older women were most prone to phishing attacks. Petelka et al. analyze the effect of different positions for suspicious URL warnings (close to suspicious URL, display on hovering the suspicious URL, deactivating the original URL and let user click it in the warning) [32]. 701 participants recruited via Mechanical Turk opened e-mails in a lab environment and answered questions about the e-mails. Wash et al. explore the influence of training users with facts about phishing or stories of previous victims to reduce the users' susceptibility for phishing [37]. They sent phishing e-mails to 2,000 faculty members out of which 26,8% clicked on a link in an e-mail. Afterwards, these participants got one form of the aforementioned phishing training. The authors inferred that facts about phishing is the more convincing form of phishing training.

While some of the previously mentioned publications already sent e-mails to actual users in their day-to-day business, they still often rely on artificial lab environments and a comparably small number of participants. In contrast, we base our survey on a much larger data set, not collected in artificial lab environments, but during day-to-day business. Hence, we believe that the observed user reaction for our data set is likely very similar to actual phishing attacks. Furthermore, PhishCo's fake phishing campaigns last for one year which is a lot longer than previous studies, enabling long-term observations. In addition, our data set covers more employees from a wider variety of industry sectors and does not focus on employees/students from one company/university. We are convinced that this aspect further improves the generalizability of our results.

3 PhishCo's Approach

In the following, we describe PhishCo's approach and how our data set is generated. We first characterize how PhishCocreates e-mail templates, followed by a description of the process when a company hires PhishCo.

3.1 E-Mail Generation

PhishCo offers awareness training and educational material in combination with sending (fake) phishing e-mails for one year. To avoid copyright infringements, the e-mails do not contain content from well-known companies, i.e., PhishCodoes not send, for example, a fake Paypal or Amazon e-mail. Instead, PhishCoanalyzes real-world phishing e-mails and creates e-mail templates which replicate typical content of phishing e-mails. PhishCocreates templates for different industrial sectors, such as *finance* or *education*, and customizes the templates for each client with respect to e-mail signatures and senders. Furthermore, each template utilizes a combination of psychological and technical vectors to convince victims of its legitimacy. PhishCo uses 14 different psychological and technical vectors in the templates, following publications on phishing and behavioral psychology discussed above. The psychological vectors include phrases drawing the victim's interest (*curiosity*) or flattering the recipient (*praise/flattering*). The technical vectors contain, for example, the use of a spoofed e-mail address (*mail address spoofing*) or domains similar to a well-known one (*domain squatting*). Table 1 provides a full list of the used vectors, which we will analyze in detail in Sect. 4.4. The majority of templates use two or three of these vectors, which we will analyze in more detail in the next section.

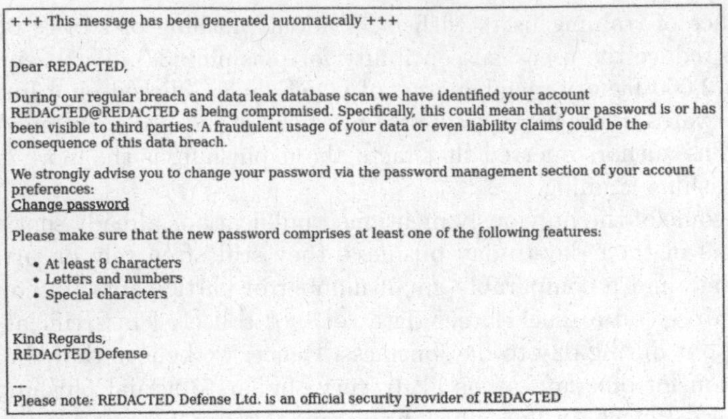

+++ This message has been generated automatically +++

Dear REDACTED,

During our regular breach and data leak database scan we have identified your account REDACTED@REDACTED as being compromised. Specifically, this could mean that your password is or has been visible to third parties. A fraudulent usage of your data or even liability claims could be the consequence of this data breach.

We strongly advise you to change your password via the password management section of your account preferences:
Change password

Please make sure that the new password comprises at least one of the following features:

- At least 8 characters
- Letters and numbers
- Special characters

Kind Regards,
REDACTED Defense

--
Please note: REDACTED Defense Ltd. is an official security provider of REDACTED

Fig. 1. Sample e-mail which has been sent to an employee of a client using the vectors *pressure/anxiety*, *trust/intimacy*, and *input mask*

Figure 1 shows an example of an e-mail that was sent to an employee as part of a campaign. The e-mail claims that the employee's account was compromised and requests a change of the corresponding password. It provides a link along with information on how to pick a new password and uses three of the aforementioned psychological and technical vectors. First, *pressure/anxiety* by pretending the employee's account was compromised and suggesting a possible data breach as a consequence. Second, the e-mail utilizes *trust/intimacy* by addressing the employee with his/her name (redacted in the example e-mail), appearing to be helpful, and pretending to be from an official security provider of the client. Third, the e-mail uses the technical vector *input mask* when the employee clicks on the *change password* link. That is, it will show input fields, asking the employee for his current password and a new one. PhishCoprevents data leakage by disabling input fields if a user actually tries to enter a password or, in other cases, similar private information. The URL uses the scheme *client-company.example.com*, i.e., a vigilant employee could detect that it is not the client's website.

Figure 2 shows a second example e-mail, which appears to be a job application. The job description is rather generic, so that most companies will likely search for applicants in this area. The e-mail uses the vector *curiosity* because the receiving employee is tempted to take a look at the documents in the attachment or dropbox (especially if the employee is working in the HR department). The vectors *attachment* and *link execution* refer to the attached documents and the link in the e-mail. The URL uses the scheme *dropbox.example.com* so that a careful employee could identify it as a link that does not lead to the actual dropbox website.

Analyzing real-world phishing e-mails and using them as basis for the sent e-mails along with using psychological and technical vectors ensures that the e-mails sent to clients' employees are close to real-world phishing e-mails. We

Dear Mr. Doe

With great interest I have seen the job advertisement for the office assistant on your website.

After eight years of work experience with a major provider of fire protection and security services, I now would like to develop professionally. I'd like to offer you numerous advantages due to my experience as an office clerk with a lot of organizational talent and a lot of experience in customer service. Please refer to my detailed application documents attached to this mail.

All documents, scans and work samples can also be downloaded via dropbox:
https://www.dropbox.com/sh/740kldjwt8usm/AAAjrtkZheapHRH8-mnsOsEa?dl=0

I'm looking forward to hearing back from you.

Kind regards
Chloe Parker

Fig. 2. Second sample e-mail which has been sent to an employee of a client using the vectors *curiosity*, *attachment*, and *link execution*

argue that analyzing the interaction of employees with these e-mails allows us to make conclusions about how users understand real-world phishing e-mails.

3.2 Workflow with Client

Clients hire PhishCo to train their employees on how phishing works, enabling them to identify malicious phishing e-mails in their day-to-day routine. Each training campaign consists of two phases (called P1 and P2 in the following) and usually runs for at least one year:

- In phase P1, which only lasts a couple of weeks, each employee receives less than five phishing e-mails.
- In phase P2, PhishCo sends less than 15 phishing e-mails to each employee distributed over the remainder of the year-long campaign.

The shorter phase P1 informs employees about the general problem of phishing, raises awareness, and allows teaching them not to fall for phishing. The longer phase P2 enables both reviewing and deepening employees' phishing understanding and knowledge. Before a campaign starts, the client notifies its employees that a phishing training will be conducted. The whole process is performed in accordance with data privacy laws, and both the data protection officer and the workers' council are made aware of the training. To ensure that the phishing e-mails reach the targeted employees, the client whitelists incoming e-mails from PhishCo.

Each e-mail sent to an employee contains a link to draw the employee's interest. If an employee clicks a link, he/she is notified that the e-mail was sent by PhishCo. Furthermore, PhishCo notes when an e-mail was sent and whether and when the link in the e-mail was clicked. Additionally, the e-mails contain a tracking pixel so that PhishCocan also log when an e-mail is opened by a client's employee.

For data protection, the collected data does not contain any information about the employee so that no personally identifiable information is stored.

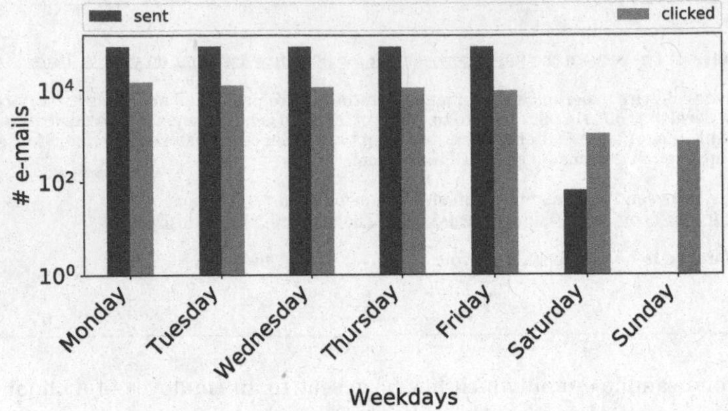

Fig. 3. Number of sent and clicked e-mails as a function of the weekday. The figure uses a logarithmic scaling on the y-axis to show that at least a small number of e-mails are clicked on Saturdays and Sundays.

Hence, neither we nor the client can link multiple e-mails to the same employee and measure the employee's performance. That is, a client cannot use collected data for disciplinary punishments or releases of employees.

4 Results

Next, we present the results of our data analysis. We start with a short description of the data set, followed by an analysis of the send and click times, the distribution among clients, the psychological and technical vectors, the click rate, and the effect of the psychological vectors.

4.1 Data Set

The data set we use for this study covers a period between November, 19th 2018, and April, 10th 2020. It consists of 429,418 e-mails sent in campaigns for 77 distinct clients. All 77 campaigns finished phase one (P1), and 14 campaigns already completed the full phase two (P2). On average, P1 lasts 20.22 days (standard deviation 9.67, minimum of 2, and a maximum of 73 days). P2 of the 14 finished campaigns lasted, on average, 285.29 days (standard deviation 115.53, minimum of 54 days, and a maximum of 372 days). The definite number of days in P1 and P2 depends on the agreement between PhishCo and the client, which explains the differences in the time periods.

4.2 Send and Click Times

Figure 3 depicts the number of sent and clicked e-mails per weekday. Note that the y-axis uses a logarithmic scaling. About 86.000 phishing e-mails are sent

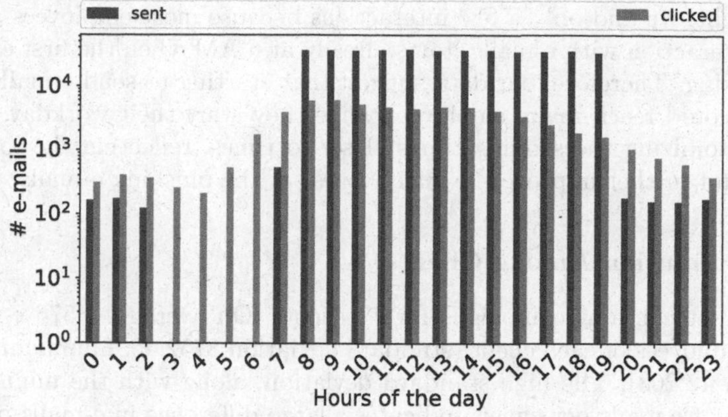

Fig. 4. Number of sent and clicked e-mails as a function of the hours of the day.

on average on a weekday. Thursday is the weekday with the lowest number of sent e-mails (85,494 e-mails), while Tuesday is the weekday with the highest number of sent e-mails (86,418). A chi-square test against a uniform distribution shows that e-mails are evenly distributed among the weekdays (p-value < 0.01). Usually, PhishCo does not send e-mails on the weekend, besides a few ones on Saturdays for testing purposes. At the beginning of the week, employees click PhishCo's e-mails more often, with numbers decreasing from Monday to Friday. Overall, the number of clicked e-mails remains in the same magnitude. Most employees work from Monday to Friday and regularly check their e-mails so that the similar distribution among workdays is not surprising. On the weekend, only a few employees click e-mails because most employees do not work during the weekend. Furthermore, PhishCo only sends a minimal number of e-mails on the weekend.

Figure 4 shows the number of sent and clicked e-mails as a function of the hours of the day. Similar to the previous analysis, we added a table to Appendix A, which contains more detailed information on the sending and clicking times of the day. E-mails are sent during working hours from 8 AM to 8 PM. Employees interact with the e-mails especially in the morning and after lunch, with clicks decreasing during the night because most employees are likely asleep.

The observed days and times are similar to the interaction with marketing e-mails reported by multiple analyses [4,20,28] and show a typical diurnal pattern. Our data set suggests that sending e-mails early in the morning and after lunch as well as earlier during the week could further improve the effectiveness of the phishing e-mails because employees handle their e-mails especially at these times. In addition, clicking e-mails at the weekend or late in the evening can have multiple reasons. For example, employees can be in a different time zone than PhishCo, which sent the e-mails, or they are working long hours. Moreover, it can indicate that e-mails are opened outside the company's infrastructure. Using private, not properly secured devices can pose a security threat. Late in the evening and at night, we find only a few interactions because most employees are likely asleep. Interaction with e-mails starts already at 6 AM when the first employees start working. Therefore, our data suggest that starting to send e-mails already at 6 AM could reach many employees while they start their workday. Furthermore, customizing the sending times closer to times, reflecting the interaction times, could further improve the effectiveness of the phishing e-mails.

4.3 Distribution Among Clients

Our data set contains campaigns for 77 clients. On average, 5,576 e-mails are sent to employees of each client (standard deviation 8752.45, minimum 103, and maximum 42,268). The high standard deviation, along with the minimum and maximum of e-mails per client, indicates a large difference in e-mails per client. The number of e-mails per client highly depends on the number of employees and the point of time in the campaign, e.g., our data set contains only very few e-mails for a small client in an early stage of a campaign. In contrast, a client with many employees will account for a lot more e-mails. The top three clients are responsible for about 25% of all sent e-mails, and the top eight clients for about 50% of all sent e-mails. The results indicate that our data set contains both big and small companies, which improves the generalizability of our analysis.

4.4 Psychological and Technical Vectors

PhishCo uses the psychological and technical vectors in e-mails with different frequencies. In some cases, clients request the usage of specific vectors, e.g., because they have been targeted with a similar vector before. Additionally, PhishCo gained experience over time, which vectors result in higher click rates. Table 1 depicts the number of sent and clicked e-mails per psychological and technical vector. Each vector was used in at least 10,000 e-mails. The most used psychological vector is *trust/intimacy*, followed by *curiosity*, and *pressure*. In case of technical vectors, *domain squatting*, *sender spoofing*, and *attachment* are most common. We will analyze how successful and promising the different vectors are along with the best combinations of vectors in Sect. 4.7. Usually, PhishCouses not only one vector in an e-mail but also combines multiple vectors to get a convincing e-mail. Table 2 shows the distribution of co-occurrences of vectors. The most common one is *pressure* and *trust/intimacy*.

4.5 E-Mail Timeline

We now analyze how fast employees click on a link after they opened an e-mail. We argue that a prolonged time between opening and clicking from P1 to P2 indicates that employees think longer about whether it is a legitimate e-mail or not. Even though the employee eventually clicked on the link, it can indicate a better understanding of how phishing works and lead to a correct decision for future e-mails.

Table 1. Overview of psychological (P) and technical (T) vectors used in e-mails sent to participants.

Vector	Description	Sent	Clicked
Pressure (P)	Urges victim to act, e.g., by giving short time to reply	178,946	14.31%
Curiosity (P)	Appealing to the recipient's curiosity, e.g., using a catchy subject	203,790	13.76%
Financial appeal (P)	Pretends a fiscal advantage for the victim, e.g., by offering a discount	35,536	7.34%
Trust/intimacy (P)	Pretends to be from a known person, e.g., by using the victim's name	280,773	9.21%
Praise/flattering (P)	Flattens the recipient, e.g., by addressing her as valuable resource	148,645	9.21%
Helpfulness (P)	Asks recipient to help, e.g., by taking part in a survey	64,288	15.15%
Authority (P)	References hierarchies e.g., pretending to be from a superior	38,616	14.13%
Attachment (T)	Contains an attachment	156,939	16.31%
Input mask (T)	Website behind link in e-mail contains an input field	104.399	17,24%
Link (T)	Tries to motivate a victim to open a link	96,538	19.40%
Bulk mailing (T)	Addressed to a larger audience, e.g., all tax consultants	12,822	9.43%
Reply/forward (T)	Forwards another e-mail, e.g., offering discounts	10,750	6.84%
Sender spoofing (T)	Pretends to be from different sender than it is, e.g., a co-worker	203,353	11.90%
Domain squatting (T)	Contains domain similar to well-known one	79,458	8.15%

As explained earlier, the opening of an e-mail is only recorded if a tracking pixel is triggered. Therefore, it is possible that employees opened e-mails but their systems blocked the tracking pixel. In such cases, we can still understand whether an e-mail was opened when a link in the e-mail was clicked. However, in the following, we focus on e-mails for which we have the opened and the clicked times to have a consistent data set. We identified 33,265 e-mails which were opened and clicked. Calculating the time between opening and clicking revealed that 753 e-mails were clicked after more than one week and 166 even after more than a month. This is noteworthy because it shows that employees sometimes click on links in phishing e-mails even after a long time has passed. As a countermeasure, companies should blacklist URLs of known phishing e-mails to prevent harm from later clicked e-mails and already handled phishing cases.

17,161 e-mails belong to P1 and 13,674 e-mails to P2. In the following, we focus on the first five minutes after opening an e-mail because we consider it to be most likely that employees did not interrupt handling the particular e-mail when the link is clicked in this time frame. In P1, 12,243 e-mails (71.34%) and in

Table 2. Co-occurences of vectors in the dataset

	Pressure	Curiosity	Financial	Trust	Flattering	Help	Authority
Pressure		65,581	14,399	169,990	189	50,883	31,357
Curiosity			10,969	131,613	4174	15,353	18,890
Financial				8379	504	773	419
Trust					3979	43,283	16,960
Flattering						0	0
Help							13,043

Table 3. Summary of sent and clicked e-mails along with click rate in relation to total, phase 1 (P1), and phase 2 (P2) numbers.

	Total	Phase 1 (P1)	Phase 2 (P2)
Sent	429,418	168,859	260,559
Clicked	59,689	32,188	27,501
Click rate	13.90%	19.06%	10.55%

P2, 9,810 e-mails (71.74%) were clicked within the first five minutes. On average, it took 1.26 min in P1 and 1.34 min in P2 from opening to clicking. That is, even though the employees eventually took a wrong decision, they spent, on average, more time on assessing the e-mails. A t-test of the average processing times in P1 and P2 led to a test statistic of -6.42 and a p-value below 0.01. Hence, the difference is significant.

In summary, our results show that links in phishing e-mails are opened even after a long time. Furthermore, constantly sending phishing e-mails leads to more time spent on a single e-mail.

4.6 Click Rate

The click rate is the percentage of e-mails in which the receiving employee clicked on the provided link. In particular, we focus on the differences between phase one (P1) and phase two (P2). We are interested in how the click rate changes between P1 and P2 because a lower click rate in P2 indicates that the employees of a client gained a better understanding of how phishing e-mails look like. Note that we cannot make a statement about the performance of single employees, as this data is not collected. Table 3 summarizes the number of sent and clicked e-mails along with the click rate for both total numbers and split between P1 and P2. In summary, it shows a decreasing click rate. In this section, we use all sent e-mails, regardless of whether the tracking pixel worked and indicated an opening of a particular e-mail because we focus on clicked e-mails to calculate the click rate. Therefore, the numbers for clicked e-mails in P1 and P2 differ from the numbers in the previous section, in which we used only e-mails which have been opened, indicated by the tracking pixel.

In total, PhishCo sent 429,418 e-mails to clients' employees, out of which 59,689 e-mails were clicked. Hence, the click rate is 13.90%. Due to the absence of large-scale academic studies analyzing such numbers for real-world phishing, it is difficult to compare the click rate with other publications. The security company KnowBe4 reported a click rate of 27% for an initial phishing test, even though it remains unclear how the click rate is calculated in that particular case [24]. The Canadian government presented an infographic saying that in 10% of phishing e-mails a link is clicked [15]. When we take into consideration that PhishCo sends highly targeted phishing e-mails where the sender is whitelisted, an overall click rate close to real-world phishing e-mails is what we expected.

Out of the 429,418 e-mails in the data set, 168,859 were sent as part of P1 and 260,559 in P2. The number of sent e-mails in P2 is higher because it lasts up to 49 weeks compared to a couple of weeks in P1. In P1, links were clicked in 32,188 (19.06%) e-mails. The click rate in P1 is (as would be expected) higher as it is an initial test of the employees' phishing awareness.

In P2, the links in 27,501 e-mails were clicked, which leads to a click rate of 10.55%. Hence, the click rate improves by about eight percentage points or 42% for e-mails sent in P2 compared with P1. A possible explanation for this drop is a familiarization with the concept of phishing and this type of scam e-mails.

In addition to the improvement from P1 to P2, we expected an ongoing improvement during P2, based on the assumption that additional e-mails increase employees' understanding of phishing. Figure 5 shows the click rate improvement as a function of three months long intervals in P2. For each e-mail, we calculated the interval in which the e-mail was sent to an employee based on the start date of P2 for the corresponding client. Afterwards, we calculated the click rate as described previously and the click rate improvement compared to P1 (for the first interval) or the previous interval (for intervals two to n). Since not all clients have already finished P2, the number of clients decreases from interval to interval. Over time the click rate not only decreases, but this positive trend intensifies over time. This effect emphasizes the importance of long term training, showing that raising awareness over a long-time is helpful. There is a positive ($r = 0.21$) significant correlation ($p = 0{,}002$) between the improvement and the interval.

Besides analyzing the overall click rate, it is interesting to see how the click rate differs per client, which we further analyze in the following. Our data set contains 77 unique clients, which have an average click rate of 12.49% with a standard deviation of 4.81. In P1, the 77 clients reach an average click rate of 15.65% (standard deviation 7.18) and in P2 an average click rate of 10.37% (standard deviation 4.97). The mean values for P1 and P2 again indicate an improvement. Comparing the average click rates of both phases, we found 61 clients who improved their click rate from P1 to P2 (minimum improvement −0.1%, and maximum improvement −26.22%). In contrast, 16 clients did not improve or decrease their click rate (minimum deterioration 0.59% and maximum deterioration 7.12%). Figure 6 shows a scatter plot with each dot representing a client. The clients' position is defined by their click rate in P1 (x-axis) and P2

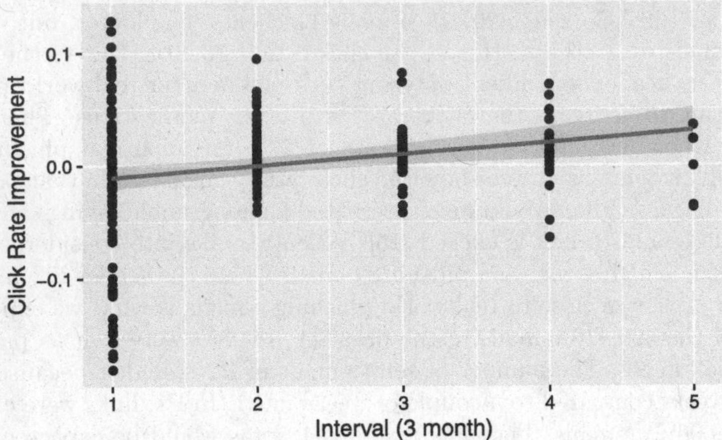

Fig. 5. Improvement compared between intervals

(y-axis). Clients below the line improved their click rate from P1 to P2. Besides the already discussed result that most clients improved their click rate, it shows that clients who did not improve their click rate are close to the line, i.e., they did not decrease their click rate much.

Our results reveal a decreasing click rate from P1 to P2. In addition, the click rate further decreases within P2, which emphasizes the importance of long-term awareness training. Finally, the sending of fake phishing e-mails proofed to be useful for the majority of clients, as 61 out of 77 improved their click rate.

4.7 Effect of Psychological Vectors

Fig. 7 shows the click rate for templates with specific vector combinations. A chi-square test shows that the clickrate and the vector combinations are statistically independent. The template with the highest click rates was comprised of text, including the psychological vectors pressure, curiosity, trust, and authority (34% click rate) as well as curiosity, trust, and authority. These e-mails all pretend to contain company internal information like updated emergency plans or training for IT security incidents as well as *CEO Fraud* [10] style e-mails. Those e-mails with the combination of curiosity, financial, trust, flattering (3%), or curiosity and help (6%) had low click rates. They mostly came from external contacts and either contained flattering invitations, e.g., for TV interviews or pretended to be customer e-mails.

Our results show a trend that confirms previous work that also found e-mails that claim to come from an "authority" to increase the click rate [39]. At the same time, our data shows that financial incentives – offering money or lucrative deals – often lead to lower click rates.

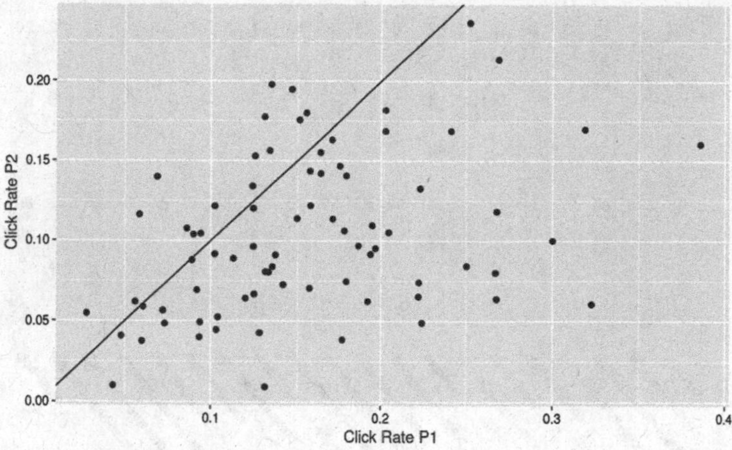

Fig. 6. Click rate in phase one (P1) (x-axis) and phase two (P2) (y-axis). Clients below the line improved their click rate.

5 Discussion

Compared to other publications, our data set is magnitudes larger than ones used in previous studies, covers longer time periods, and characterizes how employees react to phishing in their day-to-day business. In this section, we discuss our main results and compare them with previous publications.

We can confirm the results of Butavicius et al. that an authoritative tone increases the susceptibility of users to fall for phishing e-mails [6]. However, Butavicius et al. tested only authority, scarcity (similar to the vector "trust" in our data set), and social proof, which we do not have in our data set. The fact that "trust" also has a positive impact on the click rate can explain why *CEO Fraud* [10] has become so "successful" in practice. Coaxing users into giving away their information or offering financial gain, which is common in certain types of scams, is less successful in comparison. In contrast to e-mails using authority and trust, those which appear to offer financial benefits are less common in typical office situations and might, therefore, be easier to identify for many users. Furthermore, users often associate scam with a financial gain, e.g., the so-called Nigerian scam [22], so that they are more cautious. Even though some vectors led to higher click rates, we consider the variety of used vectors beneficial. Users are exposed to a wide range of phishing e-mails they might face in real world, which improves the chances that they do not click on an actual phishing e-mail when they receive it.

Additionally, our results show an improved click rate from P1 to P2 and further within P2. We did not observe an increasing click rate in later phases of P2, which could be an indicator of declining awareness. Hence, PhishCo's approach has a long-lasting effect on an employee's ability to identify phishing e-mails. Therefore, raising awareness by regularly sending phishing e-mails helps

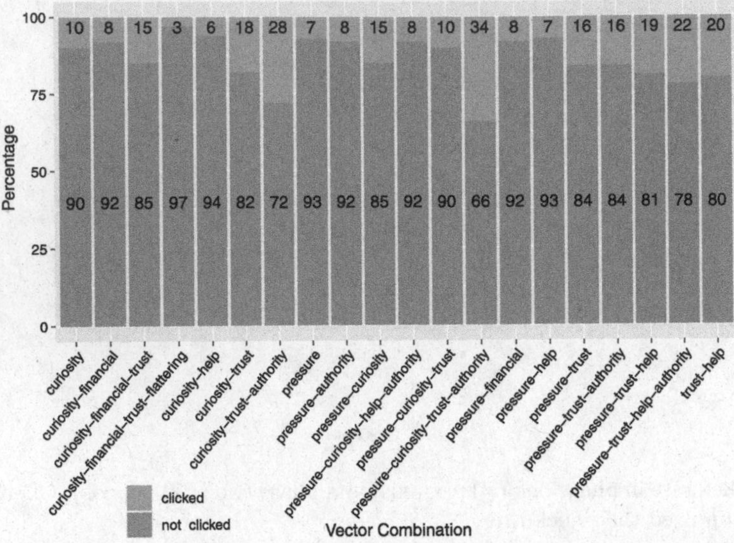

Fig. 7. Clickrates for various vector combinations

to educate employees. In contrast to our work, Oliviera et al. could not determine a connection between the day in their 21 days long study and a click on a link [31]. The time period of only 21 days might be too short to already see an increased understanding of how phishing works.

5.1 Limitations

Our data set has several constraints that limit our analysis. First, we cannot evaluate the performance on a per-employee basis because PhishCo does not provide information to connect e-mails sent to the same employee. While this could potentially lead to interesting insights, data privacy concerns outweigh the benefits. In our study, we can still examine the changing performance on a per-client basis and deduce the overall improving performance. Second, our data set contains only phishing e-mails so that we cannot infer whether employees evaluate legitimate e-mails differently, such as spending more time to decide whether it is legitimate. Third, our data set contains only e-mails sent by PhishCo, i.e., no real-world phishing e-mails. Therefore, we cannot assess the influence of PhishCo's e-mails on employees' ability to identify actual phishing e-mails. However, PhishCo replicates real-world phishing e-mails they identify in the wild so that the e-mails in our data set are as close to real phishing e-mails as possible without using actual phishing e-mails.

5.2 Ethical Considerations

Our research institution does not have an IRB for computer science so that we could not get an IRB review to perform this study. However, as noted above, the data set we received from PhishCo does not contain any personal information about single employees or clients, but only technical information about the sent e-mails and meta data about when an e-mail was opened or a link in an e-mail clicked. Additionally, PhishCoprevented the accidental collection of private information by blocking employees from entering information in input fields on landing pages. Furthermore, due to the absence of personal information, it is not possible to identify an employee receiving an e-mail or identify multiple e-mails received by the same employee. That is, neither a client nor we can assess the performance of single employees based on the collected data. While we do not have the employees' consent for our analysis, the clients in advance notify their employees that a phishing awareness training will take place. Furthermore, PhishCo informs the employee that it was a phishing e-mail sent by them immediately after the employee clicked on a link. In summary, ethical concerns were considered during our study as the data set provided by PhishCobecause is fully pseudonymized and it is not possible to make statements about employees or clients. Employees who received fake phishing e-mails had no disadvantage but got an opportunity to better understand how phishing works.

6 Conclusion and Recommendations

In this paper, we presented a detailed analysis of more than 420,000 phishing e-mails sent during more than 1.5 years as part of phishing awareness trainings performed in 77 companies. Compared to other publications, our data set is magnitudes larger than those used in other studies. Furthermore, the sent e-mails use 14 different technical and psychological vectors to create believable e-mails as close as possible to actual phishing e-mails. In contrast to multiple other studies, the e-mails were sent during employees day-to-day business instead of a lab situation. This leads to several unique insights into how people interact with phishing e-mails.

Employees continuously improve their click rate according to our results so that we recommend long-lasting awareness training instead of short-term ones. Similar to other publications, we identified the concept of *authority* as being the most successful and hence empirically confirmed this insight. Sending a variety of phishing e-mails that use different psychological and technical vectors proved to be useful so that employees are aware of different possible phishing schemes. Hence, we suggest using a diverse set of phishing e-mails, combined with current phishing trends, and phishing e-mails observed at the own institution to conduct successful phishing awareness trainings. An analysis of the interaction times revealed that employees especially interact with the sent e-mails at the beginning of the week, early in the morning, and after lunch. Therefore, we recommend focusing on these days and times to perform awareness trainings.

A Detailed Information

Table 4 provides more detailed numbers on the e-mails per hour with reference to the categories *sent* and *clicked*.

Table 4. Total number of sent and clicked e-mails along with the numbers and percentages per hour of the day.

Total # of e-mails	Sent	Clicked
	429,418	59,689
Hour 0	164 (0.04%)	307 (0.59%)
Hour 1	173 (0.04%)	406 (0.68%)
Hour 2	123 (0.03%)	366 (0.61%)
Hour 3	0 (0.00%)	257 (0.43%)
Hour 4	0 (0.00%)	212 (0.36%)
Hour 5	0 (0.00%)	533 (0.89%)
Hour 6	0 (0.00%)	1744 (2.92%)
Hour 7	540 (0.13%)	3926 (6.58%)
Hour 8	36246 (8.44%)	5955 (9.98%)
Hour 9	36026 (8.39%)	6058 (10.15%)
Hour 10	35684 (8.31%)	5191 (8.70%)
Hour 11	36515 (8.50%)	4673 (7.83%)
Hour 12	37511 (8.74%)	4429 (7.42%)
Hour 13	35836 (8.35%)	4708 (7.89%)
Hour 14	36040 (8.39%)	4694 (7.86%)
Hour 15	36217 (8.43%)	4091 (6.85%)
Hour 16	34557 (8.05%)	3317 (5.56%)
Hour 17	34642 (8.07%)	2520 (4.22%)
Hour 18	35266 (8.21%)	1880 (3.15%)
Hour 19	33208 (7.73%)	1629 (2.73%)
Hour 20	182 (0.04%)	1051 (1.76%)
Hour 21	158 (0.04%)	765 (1.28%)
Hour 22	156 (0.04%)	602 (1.01%)
Hour 23	174 (0.04%)	375 (0.63%)

References

1. Aaron, G.: Phishing activity trends report - 4th quarter 2019 (2019). https://docs.apwg.org/reports/apwg_trends_report_q4_2019.pdf
2. Aaron, G.: Phishing activity trends report - 2nd quarter 2020 (2020). https://docs.apwg.org/reports/apwg_trends_report_q2_2020.pdf

3. Agten, P., Joosen, W., Piessens, F., Nikiforakis, N.: Seven months' worth of mistakes: a longitudinal study of typosquatting abuse. In: Network and Distributed System Security Symposium (NDSS) (2015)
4. Bauer, E.: The 2017 email marketing field guide: the best times and days to send your message and get it read. https://www.propellercrm.com/blog/2017-email-marketing-field-guide
5. Blythe, M., Petrie, H.L., Clark, J.A.: F for fake: four studies on how we fall for phish. In: Conference on Human Factors in Computing Systems (CHI) (2011)
6. Butavicius, M., Parsons, K., Pattinson, M., McCormac, A.: Breaching the human firewall: social engineering in phishing and spear-phishing emails. In: Australian Conference of Information System (2015)
7. Canova, G., Volkamer, M., Bergmann, C., Reinheimer, B.: NoPhish app evaluation: lab and retention study. In: Workshop on Usable Security and Privacy (USEC) (2015)
8. Caputo, D.D., Pfleeger, S.L., Freeman, J.D., Johnson, M.E.: Going spear phishing: exploring embedded training and awareness. IEEE Secur. Priv. **12**(1), 28–38 (2013)
9. Cialdini, R.B., Goldstein, N.J.: The science and practice of persuasion. Cornell Hotel Restaur. Adm. Q. **43**(2), 40–50 (2002)
10. Cidon, A., Gavish, L., Bleier, I., Korshun, N., Schweighauser, M., Tsitkin, A.: High precision detection of business email compromise. In: Usenix Security Symposium (2019)
11. Dhamija, R., Tygar, J.D., Hearst, M.: Why phishing works. In: Conference on Human Factors in Computing Systems (CHI) (2006)
12. Ferreira, A., Coventry, L., Lenzini, G.: Principles of persuasion in social engineering and their use in phishing. In: Tryfonas, T., Askoxylakis, I. (eds.) HAS 2015. LNCS, vol. 9190, pp. 36–47. Springer, Cham (2015). https://doi.org/10.1007/978-3-319-20376-8_4
13. Ferreira, A., Lenzini, G.: An analysis of social engineering principles in effective phishing. In: Workshop on Socio-Technical Aspects in Security and Trust (STAST) (2015)
14. Fette, I., Sadeh, N., Tomasic, A.: Learning to detect phishing emails. In: World Wide Web Conference (WWW) (2007)
15. Government, C.: Phishing: how many take the bait? https://www.getcybersafe.gc.ca/cnt/rsrcs/nfgrphcs/nfgrphcs-2012-10-11-en.aspx
16. Gragg, D.: A Multi-Level Defense Against Social Engineering. SANS Institute - Information Security Reading Room (2003)
17. van der Heijden, A., Allodi, L.: Cognitive triaging of phishing attacks. In: Usenix Security Symposium (2019)
18. Ho, G., et al.: Detecting and characterizing lateral phishing at scale. In: 28th USENIX Security Symposium (USENIX Security 2019) (2019)
19. Ho, G., Sharma, A., Javed, M., Paxson, V., Wagner, D.: Detecting credential spear phishing attacks in enterprise settings. In: Usenix Security Symposium (2017)
20. Hodgekiss, R.: What our data told us about the best time to send email campaigns. https://www.campaignmonitor.com/blog/email-marketing/2019/01/best-time-to-send-email-campaigns-by-device/
21. Hong, J.: The state of phishing attacks. Commun. ACM **55**(1), 74–81 (2012)
22. Isacenkova, J., Thonnard, O., Costin, A., Francillon, A., Balzarotti, D.: Inside the scam jungle: a closer look at 419 scam email operations. EURASIP J. Inf. Secur. **2014**, 1–8 (2014)
23. Kintis, P., et al.: Hiding in plain sight: a longitudinal study of combosquatting abuse. In: Conference on Computer and Communications Security (CCS) (2017)

24. KnowBe4: Report: 2018 phishing by industry benchmarking report (2018). https://www.ciosummits.com/KnowBe4-Phishing-By-Industry-Benchmarking-Report.pdf
25. Kumaraguru, P., et al.: School of phish: a real-world evaluation of anti-phishing training. In: Symposium on Usable Privacy and Security (SOUPS) (2009)
26. Kumaraguru, P., Sheng, S., Acquisti, A., Cranor, L.F., Hong, J.: Teaching Johnny not to fall for phish. ACM Trans. Internet Technol. (TOIT) **10**(2), 1–31 (2010)
27. Lin, E., Greenberg, S., Trotter, E., Ma, D., Aycock, J.: Does domain highlighting help people identify phishing sites? In: Conference on Human Factors in Computing Systems (CHI) (2011)
28. Mailchimp: Insights from Mailchimp's send time optimization system. https://mailchimp.com/resources/insights-from-mailchimps-send-time-optimization-system/
29. Mao, J., Li, P., Li, K., Wei, T., Liang, Z.: BaitAlarm: detecting phishing sites using similarity in fundamental visual features. In: International Conference on Intelligent Networking and Collaborative Systems (INCoS) (2013)
30. Nikiforakis, N., Balduzzi, M., Desmet, L., Piessens, F., Joosen, W.: Soundsquatting: uncovering the use of homophones in domain squatting. In: Chow, S.S.M., Camenisch, J., Hui, L.C.K., Yiu, S.M. (eds.) ISC 2014. LNCS, vol. 8783, pp. 291–308. Springer, Cham (2014). https://doi.org/10.1007/978-3-319-13257-0_17
31. Oliveira, D., et al.: Dissecting spear phishing emails for older vs young adults: on the interplay of weapons of influence and life domains in predicting susceptibility to phishing. In: Conference on Human Factors in Computing Systems (CHI) (2017)
32. Petelka, J., Zou, Y., Schaub, F.: Put your warning where your link is: improving and evaluating email phishing warnings. In: Conference on Human Factors in Computing Systems (CHI) (2019)
33. Quinkert, F., Lauinger, T., Robertson, W., Kirda, E., Holz, T.: It's not what it looks like: measuring attacks and defensive registrations of homograph domains. In: Conference on Communications and Network Security (CNS) (2019)
34. Rajivan, P., Gonzalez, C.: Creative persuasion: a study on adversarial behaviors and strategies in phishing attacks. Front. Psychol. **9**, 135 (2018)
35. Rosiello, A., Kirda, E., Kruegel, C., Ferrandi, F.: A layout-similarity-based approach for detecting phishing pages (2007)
36. Stajano, F., Wilson, P.: Understanding scam victims: seven principles for systems security. Commun. ACM **54**(3), 70–75 (2011)
37. Wash, R., Cooper, M.M.: Who provides phishing training? Facts, stories, and people like me. In: Conference on Human Factors in Computing Systems (CHI) (2018)
38. Whittaker, C., Ryner, B., Nazif, M.: Large-scale automatic classification of phishing pages. In: Network and Distributed System Security Symposium (NDSS) (2010)
39. Williams, E.J., Hinds, J., Joinson, A.N.: Exploring susceptibility to phishing in the workplace. Int. J. Hum. Comput. Stud. **120**, 1–13 (2018)
40. Wright, R., Jensen, M., Thatcher, J., Dinger, M., Marett, K.: Research note–influence techniques in phishing attacks: an examination of vulnerability and resistance. Inf. Syst. Res. **25**, 385–400 (2014)

Extended Abstract: A First Large-Scale Analysis on Usage of MTA-STS

Dennis Tatang(✉), Robin Flume, and Thorsten Holz

Ruhr-Universität Bochum, Bochum, Germany
dennis.tatang@rub.de

Abstract. Nowadays, email is still the most popular communication channel of the Internet. It is based on Simple Mail Transfer Protocol (SMTP), which lacks basic security properties such as confidentiality and authenticity despite its ever-growing importance. This results in spam and frequent phishing attacks, often with spoofed sender email addresses to appear more trustworthy, as well as non-encrypted transmissions by default. To address these known problems, additional protocols such as STARTTLS have been developed. STARTTLS enables transport encryption with Transport Layer Security (TLS) for SMTP sessions between two email servers. However, an attacker can take advantage of the fact that the encryption is opportunistic and the STARTTLS command is sent in plain. Therefore, it can be stripped out of the communication, resulting in an inevitable plaintext transmission of the email message itself. This attack is referred to as *TLS downgrade*. The new Mail Transfer Agent Strict Transport Security (MTA-STS) protocol targets the prevention of TLS downgrades for incoming SMTP sessions. In this paper, we conduct the first large-scale, longitudinal measurement study on the adoption of MTA-STS. We show that it is activated by 0.0124% out of 1.76 million scanned domains, with a lower bound of 45.4% for the growth of the adoption rate within five months.

Keywords: Internet measurement · DNS · MTA-STS

1 Introduction

Email usage in private and commercial everyday life has increased continuously since its invention in 1971. Studies showed that besides information not worthy of protection, sensitive documents and data (e.g., business documents, passwords, private photos, etc.) are exchanged via this communication medium [2,19]. The foundation builds is the Simple Mail Transfer Protocol (SMTP). However, despite the ever-increasing popularity of email, it does not provide any security mechanisms (neither for the verification of communication partners nor the protection of privacy). Accordingly, emails are exchanged between email servers via SMTP unauthenticated and unencrypted by default. Increasing concerns in recent years came along with this. A solution is provided by protocols such as OpenPGP or S/MIME, which can encrypt emails end-to-end. However, this

L. Bilge et al. (Eds.): DIMVA 2021, LNCS 12756, pp. 361–370, 2021.
https://doi.org/10.1007/978-3-030-80825-9_18

requires users to take active steps when sending emails to ensure that the content of the messages is encrypted. Another limitation is that both participants must comply with all technical requirements. Therefore, Domain Name System (DNS)-based SMTP extensions such as SPF, DMARC, or DKIM are of particular importance for secure email transmission. Another SMTP extension is STARTTLS, which can be used to initiate transport encryption using Transport Layer Security (TLS) after the connection has been established. This ensures the integrity of the messages, at least during their direct transmission between the servers of the sender and recipient domain. The problem is that STARTTLS only offers *opportunistic encryption*: If one of the two communication partners does not support TLS or if an error occurs in the TLS handshake, the email is transmitted in plain text. Furthermore, TLS encryption can be prevented by actively intervening in the correspondence. Ultimately, an end-user cannot determine whether or not a given email is encrypted during transport. For several years now, domain operators can use DNS-based Authentication of Named Entities (DANE) to store the fingerprints of the X.509 certificates used by their mail servers in the DNS. This allows the servers to be authenticated and their TLS support to be implied. However, DANE requires Domain Name System Security Extensions (DNSSEC). Therefore, a new protocol called Mail Transfer Agent Strict Transport Security (MTA-STS) was standardized at the end of 2018 (RFC 8461 [14]). It aims at being able to require TLS encryption of incoming SMTP connections on the domain's mail servers. In this way, attacks on TLS encryption (TLS downgrades) as well as plain text transmissions due to lack of TLS support by the sender should be prevented. Given these shortcomings, an empirical study can shed light on the actual deployment in practice.

In this paper, we measure the distribution and relevance of the still new protocol for the first time. According to a blog post by SocketLabs, it is already widely used [20]. SocketLabs and also Google's Gmail service [12] support it since April and May 2019, respectively. For our measurement study, we implement a crawler with which the required data is gathered. The number of domains that have MTA-STS activated is also compared with the number of domains that have SPF and DMARC protocols installed. Furthermore, we examined in more detail the MTA-STS settings used in practice. Although it is possible to activate the protocol with a few simple settings, misconfigurations may occur, limiting or eliminating the desired security. In the course of the measurements, the mail servers used by the top one million domains are also examined for their STARTTLS support, which is a necessity for the use of MTA-STS. In summary, we make the following main contributions:

- We present the first large-scale study on the adoption of MTA-STS.
- We gather and analyze protocol configurations used in practice in detail.
- We discuss issues of MTA-STS itself and argue that it might be already obsolete before ever widely in use.

2 Security-Related Extensions for E-Mail

In order to solve the problems of SMTP (confidentiality as well as authentication and integrity), many different protocols have been developed in recent years.

Encryption. Encryption is used to ensure the confidentiality of transmitted data. A distinction is made between transport encryption (e.g., STARTTLS) and end-to-end encryption (OpenPGP, S/MIME). Transport encryption is relevant to our work. The standard for transport encryption is the TLS protocol. An extension that TLS uses for transport encryption of SMTP traffic is STARTTLS. It attempts a TLS handshake between the communication partners. If the handshake fails, the communication is performed without transport encryption. Therefore, it is opportunistic encryption that protects against passive attackers only. As soon as we consider active attackers, a so-called *STARTTLS downgrade attack* is possible. In the context of email communication, this attack becomes particularly important, as the opportunistic encryption achieved by STARTTLS is being circumvented, and as a result, messages can be read by third parties. It is known that this attack is used in practice by intelligence agencies, Internet service providers, and mobile phone operators [5,6]. Another extension is SMTPS. In this case, data is only exchanged after a successful TLS handshake.

Mail Transfer Agent Strict Transport Security (MTA-STS). This protocol is used to indicate support for STARTTLS. It also defines how MTA-STS compliant senders must behave if encrypted communication fails. Thus, the goal of MTA-STS is to prevent the STARTTLS downgrade attack. MTA-STS essentially consists of two components. These are a TXT resource record in the DNS and a MTA-STS policy. Both consist of key/value pairs separated by semicolons, which are used to configure the protocol for a given domain. The MTA-STS record is used to inform the sending MTA that MTA-STS is basically activated and thus a policy is available for retrieval. It consists of at least two mandatory parameters: (i) the protocol version used and (ii) an identifier (ID). It is crucial that the ID for a domain must be unique. This is because the ID enables senders to find out with a single DNS query whether their cached policy for the target domain needs to be updated. The MTA-STS policy consists of four defined keys (version, mode, mx, max_age). So far, only STSv1 *version* is supported. The possible values for the *mode* are: enforce, testing, none.

The key *mx* indicates that the corresponding mail server supports the STARTTLS command in principle. The numeric value of *max_age* indicates in seconds the maximum time a policy may be cached by the sender. The policy should not exceed the maximum size of 64 kilobytes. It must be delivered via web server using the *.well-known path* defined in RFC 8615 as media type text/plain. The generic Uniform Resource Identifier (URI) of the policy is *mta-sts.[domain].[tld]/.well-known/mta-sts.txt.*

Authentication. Integrity and authenticity are two other important protection goals, neither of which are met by SMTP. Especially against the background of possible sender spoofing and spam, not only the authenticity of the sender is important within the email infrastructure, but also that of the mail server. Protocols for authentication of the sender domain are SPF, DKIM, and DMARC. Another protocol is DNS-based Authentication of Named Entities (DANE). This prevents the impersonation of mail or web servers by fake PKIX certificates.

Reporting. The TLS-RPT protocol is defined in RFC 8460 and was developed to extend MTA-STS and DANE with a reporting mechanism [13]. The messages listed in the report can help to identify misconfigurations or even active attacks on the TLS sessions between the MTAs of both parties. In doing so, the report covers errors that occur in the areas of routing, DNS name resolution, STARTTLS parameter negotiation, or policy validation. To enable TLS-RPT, an administrator needs to set another TXT record for the policy domain at *_smtp._tls.[domain].[tld]*.

3 Measurement Approach

Crawler. Our crawler implements the following two main functions: (i) the verification of the existence of MTA-STS components (by requesting the corresponding DNS TXT records), as well as, (ii) their validation (by gathering via HTTPS accessible MTA-STS policies). We store the error handling and altering of MTA-STS and, if available, we also parse the MTA-STS policy for further analysis. In addition to crawling MTA-STS information, we also crawl STARTTLS support. For this, we also save the TLS certificates. We publish our crawler implementation after publication so that the analyses from this paper can be continued. We use for all our measurements the Tranco Top 1 Million Domain list [11] from 2019/06/21 with the ID 93J2. This means that fluctuations in the measurement results as a result of different crawled lists can be excluded.

Measurements Description. In total, we performed six regular measurements (M1-M6) and two special measurements (S1, S2) in the process of this work. We conducted the regular measurements every four weeks between June 26, 2019 and November 13, 2019. In S1, we measure a more recent Tranco list from 2019/10/27 as comparison to our list for the regular measurements. In S2, we use a Alexa list from 2019/10/31 as a basis for a further comparison.

4 MTA-STS on the Sender Side

First, we look at the extent to which MTA-STS is used by the sender, because even a high number of domains with correctly configured MTA-STS only really contributes to increased security in e-mail traffic if the sender evaluates the MTA-STS policies of the target domains in the first place. Gmail and SocketLabs are the first email service providers to support MTA-STS for both inbound and outbound email [12,20]. Since there was no information about MTA-STS support for other email providers after Internet research, we considered popular MTA software [16] and checked if MTA-STS is supported. Table 1 summarizes the results of our measurement study.

5 Empirical Measurement Results

Over all measurements, a total of 1,764,703 domains were examined for the adoption of MTA-STS. In the course of this study, all mail servers specified in

Table 1. Popular MTA-software and their MTA-STS support (✓ native; * with external plugin; ✗ none). *) MTA-software does not belong to popular software from [16]. **) Minimal version is not explicitly stated.

	Exim	Postfix	Sendmail	MailEnable	MDaemon	Microsoft Exchange	Courier*	Hurricane*
MTA-STS	*	*	✗	✗	✗	✗	✓	✓
Min. Version	4**	2.10					1.0.7	Unknown
OS	Linux	Linux	Linux	Windows	Windows	Windows	Linux	Windows

the MX records of the domains were queried to test their STARTTLS support. In total, we collected STARTTLS data from 1,397,412 mail servers (79.2%).

5.1 All Domains with MTA-STS Support

We found a total of 221 domains with MTA-STS support. For verification, we crawled them for a second time. For two domains, an error occurred when fetching the policy, leaving 219 domains supporting MTA-STS. This makes up a total of only 0.0124%. This finding contradicts a statement from SocketLabs, which states that MTA-STS is already widely supported [20]. TLS-RPT is used by 191 (87.2%) of the MTA-STS domains. Among the Tranco Top 10 domains, there is only *google.com* (1) with MTA-STS support. Four further domains are in the Top 100: *yahoo.com* (14), *live.com* (16), *office.com* (69), and *office365.com* (81).

TLDs of MTA-STS Domains. Overall, we discovered 38 different TLDs among the MTA-STS domains. The largest share with almost 38% is .com.

Geoinformation of Policy Hosts. Using the geoinformation collected during the measurements for the IP addresses of the policy hosts, the domains supporting MTA-STS can be assigned to individual countries. In total, we localized policy hosts from 27 countries across four continents. However, it needs to be restricted here that this does not necessarily mean that the corresponding domain was also registered in that country, as the server could only be hosted by a provider based there. Nevertheless, the assignment provides an overview of how, among other things, international TLDs are globally distributed and in which countries not a single MTA-STS policy server could be identified. Most are located in the USA with 106 hosts followed by Germany with 33 hosts.

MTA-STS Configuration Issues. We discovered two different configuration issues. On the one hand, invalid policy modes, on the other hand, incorrect mail server entries. In case of two Austrian domains (*fro.at* and *servus.at*), we identified the invalid *enforced* policy mode[1]. In case of four other domains, we found incorrect mail server entries in the MTA-STS policies. Table 2 provides details about the domains with incorrect mail server entries in their MTA-STS policies.

[1] We informed the domain operators and the issue was solved for both.

Table 2. Domains with wrong mailserver entries in their MTA-STS policy

Domain	MX in DNS	MX in Policy	Modus	TLS-RPT
con.com	blackhole.con.com mail.tobit.com	toma.horph.com	testing	yes
tobit.com	mail2.tobit.com mforward.dtag.de	mail.tobit.com	testing	yes
valnetinc.com	aspmx.l.google.com alt[1-4].aspmx.l.google.com	*.google.com *.googlemail.com	testing	yes
zerobounce.net	aspmx.l.google.com alt[1-4].aspmx.l.google.com	aspmx.l.google.com .aspmx.l.google.com	testing	yes

Comparison with SPF and DMARC. 215 of 219 set an SPF record, 182 set a DMARC record. 180 activated both, SPF, DMARC, and MTA-STS.

5.2 Most Recent Measurement (M6)

Next, we focus on our most recent measurement M6. For about a quarter of the crawled 1 million domains, no MX record exists. Of the remaining domains, 31.4% operate their own mail servers and 68% use external email service providers. For the remaining domains, no information could be determined (*SERVFAIL error*). By far the most popular external e-mail provider is Google with its domains *google.com* and *googlemail.com* (share of 28.3% based on the 505,609 domains that do not host their mail servers on their own). The second most popular external e-mail provider is Microsoft Outlook with the domain *outlook.com* and a share of 13.8%. The third most popular is *secureserver.com* with only 4.2%. With regard to MTA-STS, this is an important finding, as Google already implements the protocol for outgoing e-mails. In total, based on the total top 1 million domains, up to 14.3% are protected by MTA-STS, assuming the receiver domains have activated it as well.

5.3 Trend Analysis of Measurements

In the following, we consider the last three measurements and two special measurements in relation to the development of the adoption rate of MTA-STS. Figure 1 illustrates the numerical count of domains that implement MTA-STS with and without the TLS-RPT reporting protocol. An increase between M4 and M6 is clearly visible. Between the two measurements, 42 domains (+28.2%) were added. However, we checked with a t-test whether this change is a significant increase. The result was that there was no significant increase. Thus, we can argue that an increase could be seen over the last three measurements, but it is not significant and thus MTA-STS has currently not significantly increased (over the measurement period).

Next, we examine the changes in the policy modes used. Figure 2 summarizes these. Between the measurements, the number of domains using the *enforce* mode increased by 16 domains (+22.5%). However, their share decreased at the same time, as new domains were added with the *testing* mode.

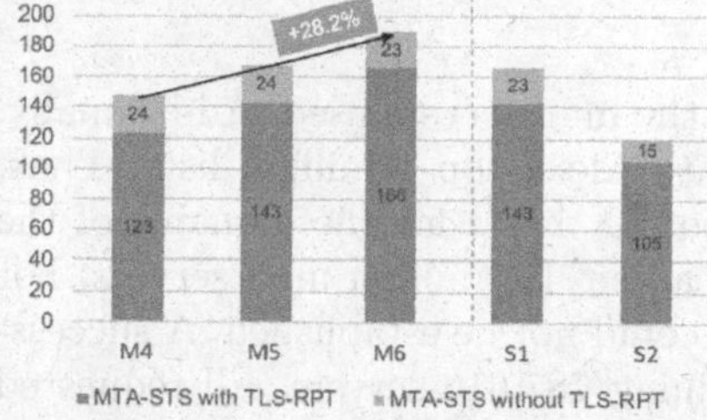

Fig. 1. Trend of M4 - M6 and comparison with S1 and S2.

	testing	none	enforce
M4	76 (51.0%)	2 (1.3%)	71 (47.7%)
M5	94 (53.4%)	3 (1.7%)	79 (44.9%)
M6	107 (54.6%)	2 (1.0%)	87 (44.4%)
S1	98 (56.3%)	3 (1.7%)	73 (42.0%)
S2	77 (61.1%)	0 (0%)	49 (38.9%)

Fig. 2. Configured policy modes distribution.

Although the adoption of MTA-STS is increasing only very slowly and not significantly, it is nevertheless positive that the number of domains protected by the enforce mode is improving.

E-mail Provider. The list of e-mail providers to be examined was compiled from an online provider list and a study [5,18]. In total we identified 111 providers with 21 different TLDs. Expectedly, the share of MTA-STS domains is the highest among the examined e-mail providers at 18.9%. Of all 111 crawled provider domains, 21 supported MTA-STS. Table 3 lists the policy configurations of the MTA-STS providers. The rank refers to our Tranco list for our regular measurements. Only 12 providers use MTA-STS in *enforce* mode. Half of them have a sufficiently long TTL of at least two weeks.

Table 3. Comparison of the MTA-STS configurations of popular e-mail service providers.

Domain	Rank	Policy	TTL	TLS-RPT
yahoo.com	14	testing	1 day	yes
outlook.com	220	testing	1 week	yes
gmail.com	376	enforce	1 day	yes
comcast.net	1,098	enforce	1 month	no
hotmail.com	1,159	testing	1 week	yes
web.de	1,197	testing	1 week	yes
mail.com	2,686	testing	1 week	yes
protonmail.com	4,332	enforce	1 week	no
gmx.com	5,476	testing	1 week	yes
riseup.net	18,770	enforce	1 day	yes
posteo.de	32,870	testing	5 min	yes
mail.de	51,330	enforce	1 month	yes
runbox.com	103,773	testing	1 day	no
mailfence.com	264,111	enforce	1 day	yes
disroot.org	322,179	testing	1 day	yes
systemli.org	896,786	enforce	1 month	yes
systemausfall.org	985,615	enforce	1 quarter	no
dismail.de	–	enforce	1 month	yes
mailjunky.de	–	enforce	1 quarter	yes
5x2.de	–	enforce	1 day	yes
schokokeks.org	–	enforce	1 week	error

5.4 STARTTLS

With the last measurement, we collected all the mail servers used. Additionally, we used mail servers from two other separate Alexa top 1 million lists. Thus, the following results do not only refer to the MX hosts for the domains of the regular measurements. In total, we crawled about 1.4 million mail servers. For 43.6% of these servers, an SMTP connection could not be established. A successful connection was established for the remaining 787,616 servers. All requested servers supported the EHLO command and, therefore, ESMTP. Compared to the results of Foster et al. [7] from 2015, the number of servers that did not offer ESMTP options STARTTLS declined by 69.6% (from 45% to 13.7%). This shows that awareness of the insecurity of the email infrastructure has improved in recent years and enhancements were implemented. The majority (86.3%) now support the STARTTLS command.

6 Discussion

Lessons Learned. Our results shows that the adoption rate increased by 28.2% in the last two measurements and by at least 45.4% over our entire measurement period. This increase looks impressive, but only 219 (0.0124%) of the approximately 1.76 million domains that were crawled in the course of this work use the protocol. 87.2% use the recommended reporting protocol TLS-RPT. In addition to this very low adoption rate, about half of the MTA-STS domains use the protocol only in test mode. Additionally, several domains with incorrect or incomplete settings could be identified. Our measurements also show that email providers implement MTA-STS significantly more often than normal domains. The customers of email service providers benefit from the adaption. The biggest problem is the server-side adaption of the protocol. It seems that so far, only Gmail and SocketLabs evaluate the MTA-STS policy of the target domain. In addition, only the MTA software Courier and Hurricane provide proprietary native support for MTA-STS. MTA-STS was developed to be used by domains for which DANE is not available. This may be the case, for example, due to a lack of DNSSEC availability. In January 2015 (three years after specification by DANE), the protocol had implemented only 128 of the then Top 1 million domains for their mail servers [22]. Between March 2018 and June 2019, an increase of 293% of DANE supported domains was identified. While in 2018, about 300,000 domains were still secured by DANE, by mid-2019, the number had already reached 1.18 million [3,4]. If a domain implements both DANE and MTA-STS, DANE must be given priority. Given the shallow adoption rate of MTA-STS and the drastic increase of DANE, the question now arises whether MTA-STS might not become obsolete shortly after its specification in 2018.

Threats to Validity and Ethical Considerations. Noe that the data is about 1.5 years old at the time of writing, but we argue that it is sufficient to show that the use of MTA-STS is low as we observed only a marginal increase. Additionally, we analyzed only a selection based primarily on one top list. However, this is always the case with measurement studies of this sort. We do not collect any personal or private data in the context of our work. All data gathered by our crawler is publicly accessible.

7 Related Work

Durumeric et al. [5] conducted a study similar to this one between January 2014 and April 2015. The authors examined the implementation of the SMTP extensions STARTTLS, SPF, DKIM, and DMARC. Also from 2015 is the study by Foster et al. [7]. Here the authors evaluated email providers in terms of TLS, SPF, and DKIM. We extend this research by the new protocol MTA-STS, which has not been analyzed yet. In a work by Holz et al. [9], SMTP servers were analyzed, among others. Google also provides current statistics on TLS encryption of SMTP connections as part of their transparency report [8]. In 2016, Hu and Wang [10] analyzed the behavior of 35 popular email providers in terms of the detection of email spoofing. Chung et al. [1] evaluated the DNSSEC infrastructure from 2014 to 2016, discovering various misconfigurations and shortcomings in key management. Schulmann and Waidner [17] confirmed the results in 2017. However, this study shows a positive development regarding DNSSEC-validating resolvers. Wander [21] quantified the DNSSEC adoption of second-level domains in the period from 2013 to 2017. Overall, a positive trend in the use of DNSSEC can be observed over the last decade. This is relevant not only for DNS security in general but also for security of email traffic, since DANE, e.g., requires DNSSEC. In a blog post from early 2015, only 128 domains are listed that supported DANE [22]. Between March 2018 and June 2019, Dukhovni and Hardaker noticed an enormous increase in DANE support [3,4]. This growth is also in line with the statistics available online from *secspider.net* [15]. We join this research field with our work and present the first study on the adoption of MTA-STS.

8 Conclusion

In this work, we measured the distribution of a young security protocol (MTA-STS) for the first time. We showed that usage is rather low, configuration errors occur, and discussed that MTA-STS is probably already obsolete due to the comparatively widespread use of DANE. For future work, the adoption of MTA-STS should be further pursued and compared with the distribution of DANE.

References

1. Chung, T., et al.: A longitudinal, end-to-end view of the {DNSSEC} ecosystem. In: USENIX Security Symposium (2017)
2. Clark, J.W., Snyder, P., McCoy, D., Kanich, C.: "I saw images i didn't even know i had" understanding user perceptions of cloud storage privacy. In: ACM Conference on Human Factors in Computing Systems (2015)

3. Dukhovni, V.: Real World DANE Inter-domain email transport. https://static.ptbl.co/static/attachments/169319/1520904692.pdf
4. Dukhovni, V., Hardaker, W.: DANE/SMTP Usage Report. https://www.isi.edu/~hardaker/presentations/2019-06-DANE-hardaker-dukhovni.pdf
5. Durumeric, Z., et al.: Neither snow nor rain nor MITM... an empirical analysis of email delivery security. In: ACM SIGCOMM Internet Measurement Conference (IMC) (2015)
6. EFF: NSA Spying. https://www.eff.org/nsa-spying
7. Foster, I.D., Larson, J., Masich, M., Snoeren, A.C., Savage, S., Levchenko, K.: Security by any other name: on the effectiveness of provider based email security. In: ACM Conference on Computer and Communications Security (CCS) (2015)
8. Email encryption in transit. https://transparencyreport.google.com/safer-email/overview
9. Holz, R., Amann, J., Mehani, O., Wachs, M., Kaafar, M.A.: Tls in the wild: an internet-wide analysis of TLS-based protocols for electronic communication. In: Symposium on Network and Distributed System Security (NDSS) (2016)
10. Hu, H., Wang, G.: End-to-end measurements of email spoofing attacks. In: USENIX Security Symposium (2018)
11. Le Pochat, V., Van Goethem, T., Tajalizadehkhoob, S., Joosen, W.: Tranco: a research-oriented top sites ranking hardened against manipulation. In: Symposium on Network and Distributed System Security (NDSS) (2019)
12. Lidzborski, N., Kardas, N.: Gmail making email more secure with MTA-STS standard. https://security.googleblog.com/2019/04/gmail-making-email-more-secure-with-mta.html
13. Margolis, D., Brotman, A., Ramakrishnan, B., Jones, J., Risher, M.: SMTP TLS Reporting. RFC 8460, September 2018. https://doi.org/10.17487/RFC8460. https://rfc-editor.org/rfc/rfc8460.txt
14. Margolis, D., Risher, M., Ramakrishnan, B., Brotman, A., Jones, J.: SMTP MTA Strict Transport Security (MTA-STS). RFC 8461, September 2018. https://doi.org/10.17487/RFC8461. https://rfc-editor.org/rfc/rfc8461.txt
15. Osterweil, E., Massey, D., Zhang, L.: Deploying and monitoring DNS security (DNSSEC). In: Annual Computer Security Applications Conference (ACSAC) (2009)
16. Mail (MX) Server Survey, 1 November 2019. http://www.securityspace.com/s_survey/data/man.201910/mxsurvey.html
17. Shulman, H., Waidner, M.: One key to sign them all considered vulnerable: evaluation of {DNSSEC} in the internet. In: USENIX Symposium on Networked Systems Design and Implementation (NSDI) (2017)
18. Sieg, S.: Serverlist. https://dismail.de/serverlist.html
19. Snyder, P., Kanich, C.: Cloudsweeper: enabling data-centric document management for secure cloud archives. In: ACM Workshop on Cloud Computing Security Workshop (2013)
20. SocketLabs Becomes the First Email Service Provider to Embrace MTA-STS Encryption. https://www.socketlabs.com/press/socketlabs-becomes-the-first-email-service-provider-to-embrace-mta-sts-encryption/
21. Wander, M.: Measurement survey of server-side DNSSEC adoption. In: Network Traffic Measurement and Analysis Conference (TMA) (2017)
22. Zorz, J.: More DANE/DNSSEC/TLS Testing From Go6lab. https://www.internetsociety.org/blog/2015/06/more-dane-dnssec-tls-testing-from-go6lab/

Centy: Scalable Server-Side Web Integrity Verification System Based on Fuzzy Hashes

Lizzy Tengana(✉), Jesus Solano, Alejandra Castelblanco, Esteban Rivera, Christian Lopez, and Martin Ochoa

Appgate, Inc., Bogota, Colombia
{lizzy.tengana,jesus.solano,alejandra.castelblanco, esteban.rivera,christian.lopez,martin.ochoa}@appgate.com

Abstract. Providing integrity guarantees for websites rendered on a user's browser is a crucial security property for web applications. There are several ways to tamper with data being received or rendered on the client side, including browser hijacking, malicious plugins, cross-site scripting attacks and manipulation of data in transit. Detecting such attacks is important for content providers in order to generate alerts and prevent further attacks. Detection of website integrity is a challenging task, due to the heterogeneity of possible attacks. In this work we present an approach to detect integrity attacks that is designed to scale to millions of clients while offering high accuracy. Our approach is based on a fine grained analysis of website internal components and a clustering technique. Such clustering allows for an efficient automatic and semi-automatic classification of client-side content (such as scripts, forms, iframes, etc.). This approach is partially implemented in a productive system and is evaluated on a real-world dataset belonging to a sample of tens of thousands unique visits. We show that we can achieve up to 98.7% accuracy on real data based on a labelled prefix, and up to 99.4% compression ratio on incoming to-be-classified client-side content. To the best of our knowledge, we are the first study to show a scalable and practical clustering system for web integrity detection.

Keywords: Web integrity · Clustering · Fuzzy hashes

1 Introduction

Modifying a website with the objective of tricking a victim into performing specific malicious actions (for instance a transaction that benefits an attacker) or to steal private information (session IDs or login credentials) are examples of popular attacker goals [18,19]. Different attack techniques achieve these purposes, such as malware attacking browsers, tricking victims into installing malicious plugins and cross-site scripting, among others. As a consequence, browser vendors are constantly updating and patching their software to prevent some of the

L. Bilge et al. (Eds.): DIMVA 2021, LNCS 12756, pp. 371–390, 2021.
https://doi.org/10.1007/978-3-030-80825-9_19

above mentioned attacks, and web-developers must strive to prevent vulnerabilities in their software to avoid possible attack vectors.

Current solutions designed to deal with web application content integrity are thus scattered and prevent particular attack vectors, in a cat-and-mouse fashion. Client-side solutions, such as plugins that check for cross-site scripting [23,27] cannot be enforced at large by a service provider, since they rely on user's individual responsibility and security awareness. In a similar fashion, older browser versions might be vulnerable to browser-hijacking or drive-by-download attacks [9,26]. Techniques to minimize server-side vulnerabilities usually do not provide strong guarantees and hidden vulnerabilities might remain exploitable by attackers [21]. Moreover, users might use outdated or vulnerable browsers without their knowledge, which lies outside of the enforcement capabilities of a service provider. In this scenario, a generic approach that is not tailored to any particular attack vector would have the advantage of coping better with novel attacks, while helping to enforce the fundamental integrity requirement.

To motivate our approach, consider the sequence diagram in Fig. 1. A client, authenticated to a service, requests a given URL to the service provider. The server replies with the intended content, which essentially will be interpreted as a tree structure (DOM, for Document Object Model). This content is altered by an attacker, using an arbitrary integrity attack vector (such as manipulation in transit, cross-site scripting, or an attack to the victim's browser). For instance, an attacker may add a malicious script, which will be a new leaf to the DOM tree. The attacker might have different objectives, a common one is credentials (session) filtration for harvesting and reselling or to carry other attacks subsequently. If the integrity attack is detected in real time, the service provider might take the preventive action of blocking the victim's account to avoid attacks. Note that this is a race condition, and the attacker might be successful at carrying out further malicious activity before any action can be taken. On the other hand, swift preventive measures will prevent many attacks from happening.

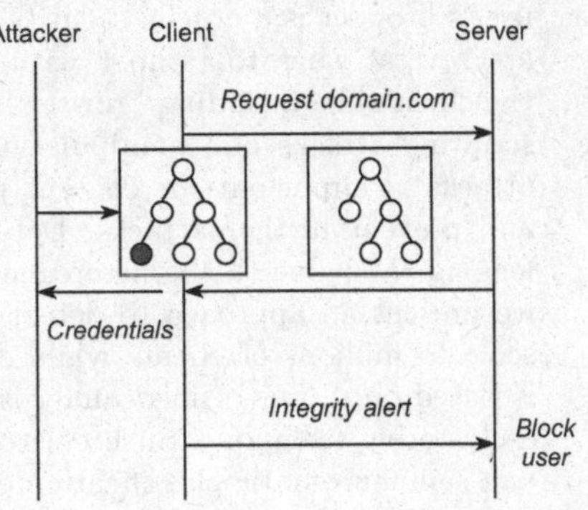

Fig. 1. Example of integrity attack.

In this work we propose Centy, a centralized system to detect integrity attacks on web applications that is designed to be scalable and agnostic to any concrete attack vector. We achieve this by placing a monitor on the client side, which sends back the rendered DOM into a verification module on the server. There, the *web-atoms* (i.e., forms, scripts, iframes and other elements in the DOM) are compared against the intended content sent by the service provider. This is challenging since modern sites are often very dynamic, so there are potentially some minor differences (IDs, variable names, regions, language). The verification system must thus be resilient to small changes while also being able to detect malicious injections or modifications. We tackle this problem by creating an online clustering system that efficiently find similarities among HTML-nodes using Local Sensitive Hashing and HTML-node structural signatures (i.e., Abstract Syntax Trees). The goal of our work is thus to make the process of semi-automatically label atoms cost-efficient.

Our system is evaluated on a productive environment serving various customers and hundreds of thousands of users. We are able to measure the effectiveness and scalability of our approach on real-life data. We show that we can achieve up to 98.7% accuracy on real data based on a labelled prefix, and up to a 99.4% compression ratio (Eq. 1) on incoming to-be-classified web-atoms.

In sum, we make the following novel contributions:

- We propose an integrity verification system that labels similar DOM contents and detects possible threat clusters, regardless of the attack vector, or technique used to break the integrity of a website.
- We evaluate our approach on realistic data containing over 300K DOMs.
- We show that this approach scales in terms of computational and classification resources while providing a high accuracy.

The rest of the paper is organized as follows. In Sect. 2 we review fundamental definitions of browser internals, fuzzy hashes and abstract syntax tree. We outline our approach in Sect. 3. In Sect. 4, our implementation is evaluated in terms of classification accuracy, work-load compression and system overhead. Finally, we discuss related work in Sect. 5 and conclude in Sect. 6.

2 Background

2.1 Document Object Model (DOM) Integrity

The document object model consist of a standard interface for the representation of objects in a tree-structured document, mainly used for HTML, allowing the use and manipulation of these objects. Through this interface it is possible to access the structure of the document and make modifications in both its form and content [31].

Any illegitimate DOM alteration can be considered an integrity attack ultimately threatening user security. With the DOM sitting on the client-side, a web server is powerless to defend a user from these attacks as the completeness and accuracy of the data cannot be assured on an infected browser. The user keeps unwittingly performing genuine interactions with an otherwise trustworthy interface, only to encounter a deceiving form prompting the user to input the login credentials, for instance, or to download malware to the user's machine.

A compromised DOM may be due to man-in-the-browser attacks [11], browser hijacking [23], any flavor of cross-site scripting [20,21], or manipulation of data in transit [28]. In terms of integrity, plenty of sources could provoke changes on a DOM, thus analyzing DOM variations may lead to the characterization of their sources. In fact, knowing all possible legitimate states of a DOM in an authentic client/server communication, any unrecognized alteration represents an anomaly.

2.2 Abstract Syntax Tree (AST)

An AST is a graph representing the syntax structure of a given source code. Each node of this tree structure contains the construction objects within the source code such as loops, conditional statements, binary operations, etc. ASTs are generated through a parsing process usually during the translation and compiling stages. This type of structuring is useful when performing semantic analysis of source code. In addition to allowing the analysis of code operation, ASTs reduce possible ambiguities always present in the syntax of the source code, mainly due to the behavior of the component elements in function of the context in which they are used. For instance, binary operators that act differently depending on the type of variables on which they are executed. Furthermore, AST representations are then useful for the comparison between two given source codes, because it is able capture the overall logic of the operations in both codes independently of the context and the programming language used for each one.

2.3 MinHashing and LSH

One of the most used approaches to determine the similarity between two or more documents, including HTML documents and source code, is achieved by measuring its Jaccard similarity. This is defined for two sets as the size of intersection divided by the total number of elements in their union, meaning: $J(C_1, C_2) = \frac{|C_1 \cap C_2|}{|C_1 \cup C_2|}$ for a pair of sets C_1 and C_2.

Then, in order to compare a pair of documents, a process known as MinHashing can be applied to them to determine if they are similar, but not necessarily identical. The first step consists in transforming these documents into their set representations or $k - shingles$, where sliding windows of substrings of length k are taken from a document and grouped into a set. A MinHash is an independent permutation of the set representation of a document. A MinHash signature over a document a fixed size vector of MinHash functions on its $k - shingles$ such that if the Jaccard similarity between the document signatures is high, the documents themselves are likely to be similar as well.

As for the LSH [17], it enables a sub-linear search for similar documents using a technique that approximates the Jaccard similarity of two documents. The LSH indexes MinHash signatures in a process that maps them into buckets containing documents with high probability of being similar. More details can be found in [25].

2.4 DOM Monitoring

Monitoring changes in the DOM can be made through tools such as the *MutationObserver API* [5] (provided in most modern web browsers [1]) which analyzes a DOM tree and sends an alert through a callback function according to established parameters in the DOM observer method. When changes occur to the scripts, forms and other DOM nodes, they can be collected and analyzed with our approach in order to determine whether the alterations are malicious or not.

Other tools based on the *MutationObserver API*, such as *DOM observer* [2], add more features to enhance the change detection performance; these kind of tools are even able to create alerts against potentially dangerous changes in the DOM and thus take reactive measures against them. However, the previously mentioned tools require third-party software to be installed on the client-side, which makes them virtually impossible to enforce at large scale.

2.5 System and Attacker Model

Centy can be integrated in any client/server web architecture. It assumes a JavaScript monitor can be shipped to the client tied to a legitimate web page, and communicated to the verification system on the server, monitoring only the website it is attached to. We also assume that if a web page is served but its monitor does not send the DOM back, the monitor has been attacked (heartbeat functionality). Besides, we assume the monitor relies on software protection mechanisms that make tampering with the monitor logic difficult (such as obfuscation and software protection methods).

We assume an attacker wants to manipulate the way a victim renders a target website, thus compromising the page integrity. For instance, if the victim interacts with a banking application, an attacker wants to trick the user to perform apparently legitimate transactions or wants to harvest authentication credentials. We assume that although an attacker might be aware of our DOM monitoring mechanism, they cannot tamper with its logic or disable it without the verification server noticing. We acknowledge there could be advanced attackers in a position to bypass this mechanism but we argue that the cost/benefit of doing so might deter them to do it. Also, recent efforts in trusted computing can more effectively protect this type of logic on the client side, such as SGX for Javascript [15], Fidelius [12] and ProtectIOn [10].

3 Approach

Our main goal is to minimize the complexity of inspecting every client's DOM for integrity attacks when analyzed on the server-side. Thus, we don't want to build a classifier for every possible threatening scenario, but instead, we seek to leverage the collection of rendered versions of the same web page to detect integrity attacks. We aim at reducing the problem into one of distinguishing legitimate DOM components with small tailored changes (majority) from unknown risky components (minority). Therefore, we are interested in answering the following general research question **GRQ: Can collective analysis of DOMs generated from the same web source be suitable for detecting integrity attacks as they occur?** In order to reach better understanding of the performance of our approach we propose a set of result-oriented research questions which lead to valuable insights about the research problem.

- **RQ1:** Could a centralized system accurately detect integrity attacks given the evolving nature of threats?

- **RQ2:** How to design a centralized system that efficiently manages the search and classification of HTML elements?
- **RQ3:** Is it possible to guarantee the scalability and sustainability of such system over time?

In order to answer our research questions we propose a framework to efficiently abstract, analyze and classify the independent rendered versions of the same web page source code. To accomplish this, we send a client-side DOM monitor to collect web page information when the service is requested by a user. We design a *DOM Parser* which not only extracts the relevant elements from the DOM, but it can also add information about their context. The elements generated by the *DOM Parser* feed the core module of our integrity verifier. This module is a clustering system that enables the efficient search of similar web atoms and the prioritization of unknown elements for classification.

In this way, the effort required to perform fine-grained detection of integrity attacks on a certain DOM can benefit several other users who encounter similar threats. Our approach was conceived to handle real-life data (i.e. millions of entries per day) in an effective and scalable procedure.

An overview of the proposed system to detect integrity attacks (e.g. cross-site scripting, defacement) from the server-side is depicted on Fig. 2 and explained in detail throughout this section.

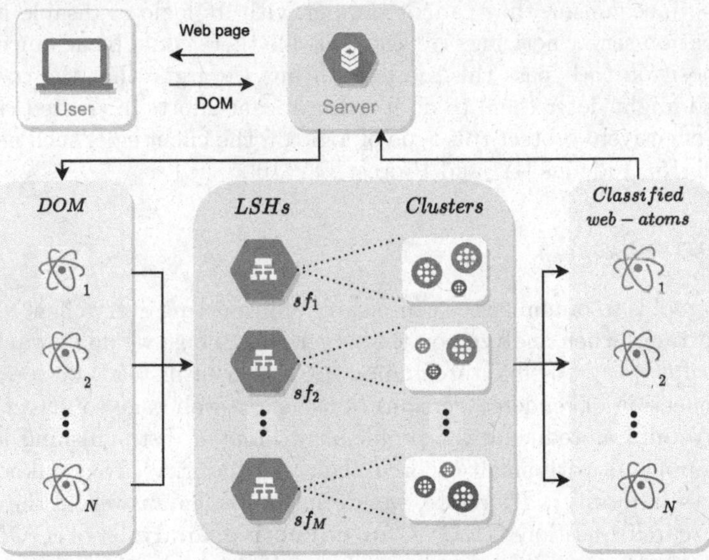

Fig. 2. Outline of Centy: an integrity verification system's design. Centy is designed to efficiently classify web-atoms from a client's DOM as 'safe' (green), 'malicious' (red) or 'unknown' (gray) by taking advantage of the knowledge gained from previously classified web atoms. In the end, the server will be able to take further actions if some DOM element is compromising the integrity of the service request. (Color figure online)

3.1 DOM Monitor

The rendered version a user has on a web page at any given time is represented by its HTML DOM. Since we would like to verify if a specific web page was rendered without being compromised on the client-side, we collect the DOM directly from the user by sending a JavaScript function appended to the legitimate web page. This function acts as a DOM monitor sending back the user's DOM when triggered. The monitor follows customizable rules to decide when to collect a DOM, such as every t seconds and/or due to reactive DOM changes.

From a privacy perspective, the client-side monitor is concerned only with the website which it is attached to (that is, the one that includes the JavaScript function described above). The monitor cannot collect the DOM from the other websites the user visits. Furthermore, as the monitor acts as a security supplement on a website, the service provider is already in possession of any sensitive information being served to client.

3.2 HTML DOM Parser

The DOM Parser works by simply traversing the HTML DOM tree structure. When a collected DOM enters the centralized system, each relevant node is extracted as well as its context and assembled into what we call a *web-atom*. A web-atom represents one of the following HTML DOM nodes: a script, a form, an iframe or a single HTML element (input tag, button tag, etc.). Our system focuses on these node types because unintended changes on them can actually pose a threat to the user. We also extract additional contextual elements from the DOM, that is, metadata such as the timestamp and the source URL in which the HTML node was collected (Fig. 3).

To find commonalities among web atoms, we craft what we call *structural features*. A structural feature is meant to abstract a core property of some HTML node type which will be used as a similarity criteria when grouping web-atoms together. Examples of these features can be the AST for *script* elements, domain name for URLs, action field for forms or input description (i.e. 'Username', 'Password') for input tags.

Web Atom

HTML-node attributes:

* Content.
* Structural feature.
* MinHash signature over content.

Context attributes:

* URL protocol and domain.
* Timestamp.

Fig. 3. Web-atom structure.

For every web-atom, the appropriate structural feature is computed and the atom's content field is serialized in a way that allows to take a literal MinHash signature over it. A script tag with JavaScript code, for instance, will have its AST as the structural feature and its MinHash signature will be generated by extracting the shingles from the code string (content).

3.3 Online Clustering System

The clustering algorithm is permanently receiving all sorts of web-atoms and determining whether they are known to the system. To perform this task efficiently, the clustering system aims to generate a small number of clusters exhibiting common characteristics among HTML-nodes and their features while providing a righteous classification to its matches, hence, maximizing cluster cohesiveness and minimizing the execution time of the overall classification.

As web-atoms arrive in an online fashion, each of them can be similar to a previously seen one and therefore, match with a pre-existing cluster or, if a web-atom is sufficiently different (by certain threshold), it can start a new cluster on its own right.

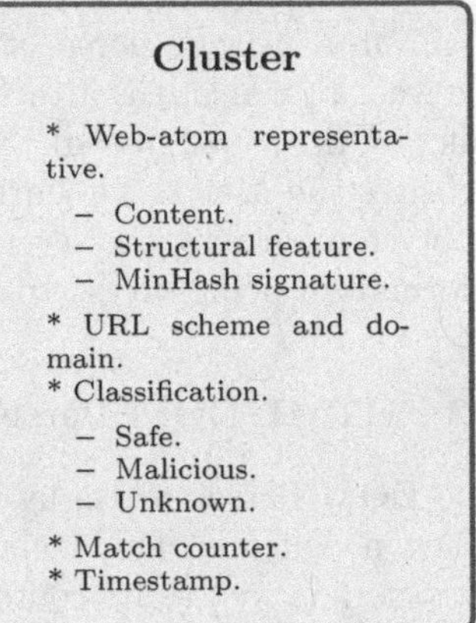

Fig. 4. Cluster structure.

The first web-atom in a cluster is automatically taken as the cluster representative, meaning this web-atom will encompass key characteristics to be matched by future incoming web-atoms according to a predefined similarity criterion. To deem a fresh web-atom similar to a cluster representative, the following two conditions must be met: they must have the same structural feature and the similarity between their MinHash signatures must exceed a given threshold.

The selection of structural features is not trivial. These features need to represent distinctive characteristics among web-atoms of the same type and be broad clustering criteria as well. In this way, the number of different features remains small over time in the context of our integrity verification system. A good example of such feature is the tree representation of the abstract syntactic structure of source code (AST) because two scripts with the same AST are likely to have the same behavior even though their literal source code may differ (e.g. different values for the same variables). In case of monitoring a web application, the clients receive mostly the same scripts with some expected customizations, which means the ASTs of the scripts collected afterwards will be resilient to those changes and consequently, the number of different ASTs in the system is expected to remain low.

Structural features can vastly abstract web-atom content and are powerful patterns for clustering highly dissimilar elements. However, they can be overly coarse when it comes to classifying web-atoms as safe or malicious. Then a subclustering stage is added to make sure web-atoms with the exact same structural feature, but with substantially different syntax are not grouped together. This additional stage is necessary to counterbalance possible biases introduced by structural features when handling edge cases. Hence, the subclustering consists on leveraging the capabilities of Locality-Sensitive Hashing (LSH) to parameterize the similarity matching, thus, tailoring the clustering criteria to any special case as needed.

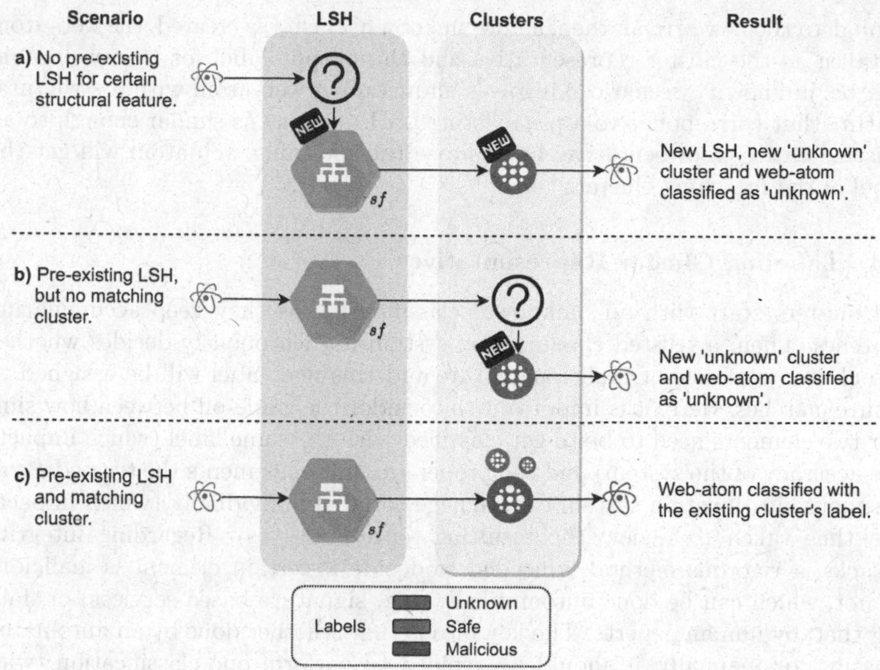

Fig. 5. Clustering scenarios for each web-atom in a DOM. LSH_{sf} is the LSH indexing all cluster representatives that share the same structural feature (sf).

As explained in Sect. 2.3, an LSH indexes MinHash signatures over the target elements to support efficient querying of similar items based on a specified threshold. Hence, to enable the MinHashing on web atoms, the next step is to serialize them in such a way that they can be easily compared with others that share the same structural feature. An LSH per structural feature is built to provide enough room for optimizing individual parameters (e.g. similarity threshold, number of permutations, number of buckets etc.) depending of the characteristics of the HTML node to be analyzed, as a *one-size-fits-all* LSH configuration is unlikely to suit enough cases in this static analysis.

In short, this system receives web-atoms and outputs one of three labels: 'unknown', 'safe' or 'malicious'. In detail, the main clustering scenarios are depicted in Fig. 5. Scenario *a* occurs when there is no LSH for an incoming web-atom's structural feature, then, such LSH is created to index a new cluster representative (i.e. the incoming web-atom) while both the new cluster and web-atom are labelled as 'unknown'. Notice this is the case in the beginning, when the very first web-atom arrives. In this manner, the system does not require any previous knowledge to be initialized as it is able to group and classify web-atoms as they come.

Scenario *b* occurs when there is an LSH corresponding to the incoming web-atom's structural feature but none of its indexed cluster representatives is similar enough to the new arrival, then, a new 'unknown' cluster is created, the web-atom is taken as the cluster representative and the output label for that web-atom will be 'unknown'. Scenario *c* involves an incoming web-atom with a structural feature that corresponds to a pre-existing LSH and that is similar enough to an existing cluster representative; in this case the incoming web atom will get the label of the matching cluster.

3.4 Labeling Cluster Representatives

All clusters start with an 'unknown' classification as they keep accumulating matches. Then, a trusted classification system asynchronously decides whether the cluster is of safe or malicious nature and this new label will be assigned to future matches. Here, it is important to consider the trade-off between how similar two elements need to be to get classified with the same label (which impacts the accuracy of the system) and the proper amount of elements the trusted asynchronous classification system can manage to label individually (which impacts the time taken to review the resulting representatives). Regarding integrity attacks, a rigorous method is needed to decide if certain element is malicious or not, which can be done automatically (e.g. signature based services) or, failing that, by human experts. The key idea is that whether done by an automated classifier or manually, it should be avoided to perform one classification twice for similar elements and thus, setting the right threshold to balance efficiency and accuracy is crucial to prevent system overload.

One advantage of our approach is that we can choose the scope of the classification to be on a cluster-by-cluster basis (fine-grained) or by grouping clusters sharing the same structural feature (coarse-grained). That is, there are cases where the structural feature fairly determines the maliciousness of web-atoms, then it is not necessary to classify the clusters individually, but to extend the structural feature classification to all of them will suffice.

Finally, the outcome of the integrity verification system is the vector of labeled web-atoms for every single DOM. If any web-atom from a client's DOM is labeled as malicious, an alert is raised to the server so it can take further actions to protect the user from the specific attack. The appropriate server response could be to ask the user for a one time password, to send a notification of suspicious activity by email, to terminate the user session, etc.

3.5 System Limitations

Centy can detect if web atoms have slight content or structure variations, but it cannot determine whether a *never-before-seen* web-atom is an attack attempt or a benign entry. However, in our approach, unknown web-atoms are automatically clustered. Moreover, automatic clustered items are easier to be reviewed and classified by either an algorithm or a human experts. If a cluster happens to be an attack, an alert will be raised for each previous occurrence. Notice that those alerts could have a delay, after a particular client has been affected. Centy does not have a way to immediately respond to these never-before-seen attacks that are not similar to anything the system encountered in the past, but it will surely be able to detect unknown inputs and produce timely alerts to the server once the attack cluster has been classified as such, by an automated system or by human experts.

The syntactic analysis performed by Centy is better suited for modifications involving several characters because, despite the LSH parameters being configurable, aiming to catch small but potentially malicious modifications (i.e. 1 byte) would lead to an explosion in the cluster number and the benefits of clustering would vanish. Moreover, there is a wide range of web attacks which may have no impact on the DOM such as phishing, cross-site request forgery (CSRF), clipboard hijacking, and social engineering. Web attacks leaving no footprints on the DOM are out of the scope of this work.

4 Evaluation

To evaluate how our approach answers our research questions, we implemented a centralized system based on a subset of all relevant HTML nodes: *script tags*. We picked script tags for the evaluation because malicious code injections can easily alter a client's DOM. Nevertheless, the same evaluation can be extended to any other HTML node. Script tags can contain either source code (usually in JavaScript) or a URL pointing to an external scripting file. In the former case, the structural feature chosen was the abstract syntax tree (AST), which is expected to have minor variations among clients and to be relatively stable in the same web page over time. In the latter case, the concatenation of protocol and domain name was selected as the structural feature because it facilitates the identification of cross-origin threats.

4.1 Datasets

We use four datasets to evaluate our approach. Three of them belong to real banking environments that were accessible in virtue of a partnership with the data owners and where sensitive information was properly anonymized beforehand. The first dataset is a manually labeled set of HTML script tags collected from users of 'bank A' web service for over 2 years. The human experts in charge of the labelling considered criteria such as if a script was a legitimate bank resource, if it contained adware, if it was reported in malware search engines like VirusTotal, if the source domain was reported as malicious in public records, if the code was obfuscated and the nature of the resources fetched or the information sent by any script request.

The next two datasets consist of a sample of raw DOMs collected from users of two highly visited web services respectively in the span of a year. Specifically, we sampled up to 100 DOMs per hour from users navigating to login and transactional pages from each web service throughout 2020. The last dataset contains malicious JavaScript samples obtained from public repositories: Hynek Petrak [24], GeeksOnSecurity [14], and additional samples were downloaded from VirusTotal [30]. The details of the datasets are summarized in Table 1.

Table 1. Summary of the datasets for evaluation.

Dataset	Content	Labeled	Time frame	Size	Classification	
					Safe	Malicious
Bank A	Script tags	Yes	2.5 years	60, 375	53,311	7,064
Bank B	DOMs	No	1 year	133, 940	–	–
Bank C	DOMs	No	1 year	142, 627	–	–
Malicious	JavaScripts	Yes	-	41, 819	–	41,819

4.2 Performance Metrics

Addressing **RQ1** about the accuracy of our solution and **RQ2** about its efficiency and scalability, the following metrics are used on the available datasets:

- Classification accuracy when testing incoming web-atoms against a labeled dataset.
- Average processing time to analyze DOMs and web-atoms.
- Compression is the fraction of incoming web-atoms that were clusterized and represented by a single web-atom in system with respect to the total amount of web-atoms (Eq. 1).

$$\text{Compression} = \frac{|\text{Web Atoms}| - |\text{Clusters}|}{|\text{Web Atoms}|} \tag{1}$$

Where $|Clusters|$ is the number of clusters created in a particular time period by the system (i.e. the final number of relevant HTML instances to be classified), and $|Web\ Atoms|$ is the initial number of HTML nodes incoming to the system (i.e. before being clustered by Centy).

In Eq. 1, if all web-atoms were different from each other structurally and content-wise, the number of clusters would be equal to the number of atoms, hence the Compression would be 0%, and consequently all incoming atoms would have to be individually evaluated. On the other hand, if there were similarities among the incoming atoms, the number of clusters would be smaller than the number of incoming atoms, the Compression would increase, and therefore fewer atoms would have to be evaluated, which is the goal of our system. The effectiveness of the our approach is given by the incoming web-atoms' compression ratio accomplished, in other words, how much the workload decreases after the original workload is processed by the integrity verification system.

Additionally, the clusters are labeled into three categories: *safe*, *malicious* and *unknown*. The *unknown* label is assigned to clusters which have not been yet classified. In that sense, for the first two known labels, namely *safe* and *malicious*, if an incoming web atom is similar enough to fit into one of them, its classification is straightforward. But for clusters with *unknown* label, a web-atom representing the cluster must be sent to an asynchronous classifier. Henceforth, our results include clusters with *unknown* label as a measure of how many clusters represent the classification workload remaining for the asynchronous classifier.

4.3 Accuracy and Efficiency

There is a trade-off between accuracy and efficiency of the integrity verification system. The higher the similarity threshold, the less web-atoms will be match together in clusters, therefore the accuracy of each cluster label propagated to its highly similar matches will increase at the expense of having to classify more of those smaller clusters. In Fig. 6 we have depicted an illustration of cluster's distribution for different similarity thresholds.

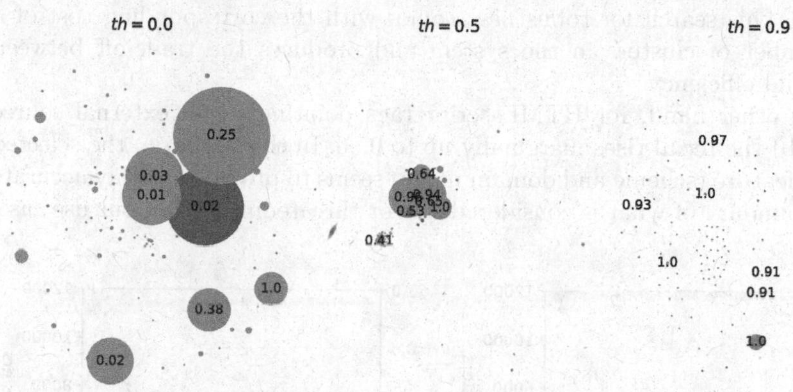

Fig. 6. Illustration of cluster distribution on the labeled dataset using Fruchterman-Reingold force algorithm. Green and red circles represent safe and malicious clusters respectively. The size of the circles represent the quantity of web-atoms that matched with the cluster representatives. The number inside the circles is the average similarity between each incoming web-atom and its cluster representative. (Color figure online)

Notice that in a real scenario each cluster needs to be asynchronously classified, and a flood of requests could exceed an acceptable response latency from the classifier. Hence, it is crucial to find the balance between the strictness of the similarity threshold and the amount of clusters the asynchronous classifier can handle. In the best case, there are automated tools that can be rapidly queried for safe or malicious coincidences (e.g. VirusTotal), on the contrary, a human expert could investigate an occurrence and assess its threatening potential in a time-consuming, but highly reliable operation.

To gain insights about the effect of parameter selection in our use case, we performed a sensitivity analysis on the similarity threshold using the labeled dataset from bank A. Figure 7 shows the system performance and the clusters created for different similarity thresholds. Given the fact that there are ostensibly more safe samples (negative class) than malicious samples (positive class), we highlighted in Fig. 7 the probability that a positive sample is marked as such (recall). Moreover, it can also be observed how moving along the threshold axis impacts the number of clusters in the system. In both graphs it is evident how the performance of the system dramatically increases when grouping similar items together beyond their structural feature (*threshold* > 0.0). Notice, however, that for the HTML script tags containing JavaScript (Fig. 7a), the recall swings between 0.77 and 0.95 for low similarity thresholds, which calls into question the selection of such low thresholds to be a reasonable similarity requirement when comparing source code, despite their apparent good performance. Delving into this fluctuation, it could seem that a similarity threshold of 0.2 works better than others, but its performance explainability borders on luck rather than the effectiveness of this measure. Now, zooming into the higher thresholds, an steady increase in accuracy can be observed from 0.6 on, which are much more reliable thresholds. This search for robustness comes with the corresponding cost of a higher number of clusters in the system and produces the trade-off between accuracy and efficiency.

On the other hand, for HTML script tags pointing to an external source file (Fig. 7b) the recall rises marginally up to 0.96. In this scenario, the selected structural feature (scheme and domain name) seems to provide a highly accurate decision boundary of what is considered safe or threatening within our use case.

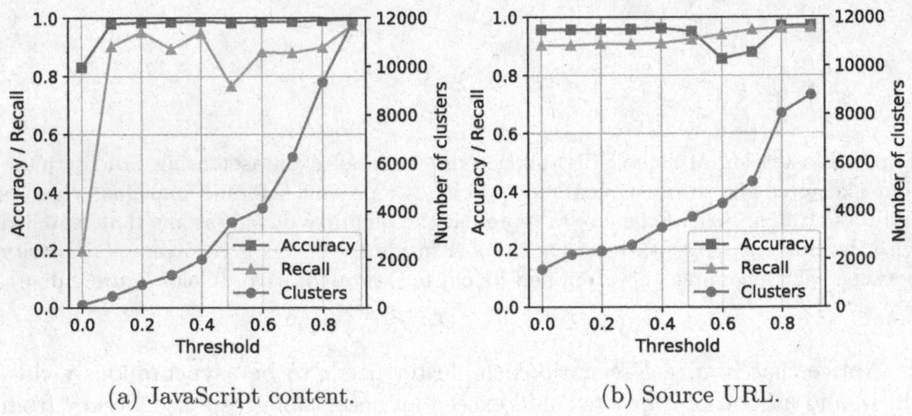

(a) JavaScript content. (b) Source URL.

Fig. 7. Accuracy, recall and the number of clusters over time in the classification of HTML script tags in the labeled dataset of Bank A.

4.4 Scalability

For testing the scalability of our approach and its sustainability over time (**RQ3**), we used the datasets from bank B and bank C (both unlabeled). The goal is to evaluate the performance of all of the modules of the integrity verification system from a sample of the real flow of client sessions in highly visited websites. In order to make our evaluation more realistic, a set of malicious JavaScript dataset was included into the system at initialization. Each malicious JavaScript file was considered as if its source code came in an script tag from the monitored web service, thus, the 41819 scripts in the dataset were condensed in 24306 unique artificial web-atoms which formed 10370 clusters with *malicious* label.

Then, the DOMs from the banking web services were loaded into the system in the order indicated by their reported timestamp. A fixed similarity threshold of 0.6 was established for comparing the MinHash signatures when querying the different LSHs for simplicity. Figure 8 shows that for both banks B and C, as DOMs timely arrive in the system, the amount of clusters remains steadily low relative to the amount of unique web-atoms identified. Specifically, the compression rate of incoming web-atoms to clusters exceeds 97% for both banks after 25 days (Fig. 9). As mentioned, it is interesting to see not only the incoming web-atom compression rate, but also the rate relative to unique web-atoms identified by the system because it highlights the variety of scripts present in clients' DOMs; this compression rate exceeds 87% for both banks after 25 days.

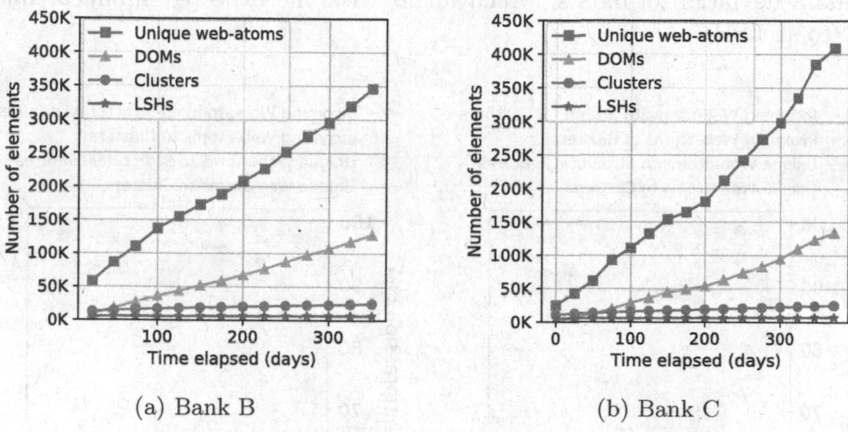

(a) Bank B (b) Bank C

Fig. 8. Number of elements in the system over time.

Another interesting compression rate is the one from web-atoms into structural features, which indicates how many web-atoms share the same underlying structure. The compression rate of incoming web-atoms to structural features exceeds 94% for both banks after 25 days, and the compression rate for unique web-atoms to structural features exceeds 70% for both banks after 25 days. These results confirm the intuition that even in real dynamic web pages, most of the HTML nodes from client DOMs can be grouped into few structural representations, meaning it is possible to separate the known *safe* elements from the *unknown* ones that could pose a threat to the integrity of a client's rendered version of a legitimate web page.

Now the question is, how feasible it is for an asynchronous classifier to label the remaining *unknown* clusters in a timely manner? At the end of the clustering phase, bank B and C had 28 and 30 massive clusters (>30,000), which can be considered as a semi-automatic heuristic to label them as safe. Both banks had 10370 malicious clusters at initialization from which none of the banks reported coincidences. Finally, for the unknown clusters left to be classified,

Bank B formed 14778 and Bank C formed 15131. In the most time-consuming scenario, human experts are required to manually inspect cluster representatives for possible integrity threats. Based on the experience of the labeled dataset from Bank A, we estimate an analyst would take between 30 s to 10 min to classify a web-atom as *safe* or *malicious*. To put it in perspective, if a team of 10 analyst were to review the remaining 15131 clusters of bank C, assuming they work 8 h per day, they would finish the classification of the unknown clusters in around 16 days.

Regarding the cost of DOM collection, the DOM monitor on the client-side runs in the background after all the regular web page elements are loaded and thus, it doesn't interfere with the user experience. As for the average web-atom processing time, regardless of the similarity thresholds, it was 0.02 s with a standard deviation of 0.02 s, which aligns with the expected sublinear query time to an LSH.

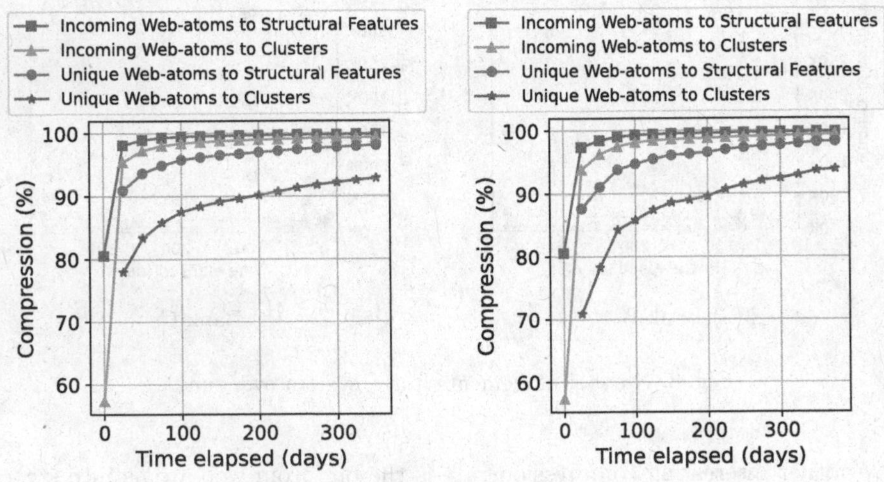

Fig. 9. Compression of web-atoms over time.

4.5 Discussion and Threats to Validity

In this section we have evaluated our proposed approach on various datasets containing data of the real flow of user session in banking environments. We have evaluated two scenarios: (1) a dataset containing manually labeled data by experts, in which we were able to measure labelling accuracy (safe vs malicious) and its relation to the number of clusters formed; (2) two unlabeled datasets of DOMs from real user sessions to evaluate the full workflow of Centy in terms of the compression ratio reached by our approach. As shown throughout this section, after our approach is applied the workload for semi-automatic analysis becomes manageable since Centy could greatly decrease it by up to 99.4%. This fosters quality in the analysis as well as an improved cost-benefit ratio.

In regard to validity, first, our approach is constrained by the same drawbacks of static analysis since LSH does not capture the semantics of the elements of the DOM. For instance, Centy is better suited for detection of modifications involving several characters, rather than detection of special cases where small modifications (i.e. 1 byte) can be considered malicious, because setting the LSH parameters to such fine-grained detection may lead to an explosion in the number of clusters and therefore diminish the benefits of clustering. Second, the accuracy of the system is highly dependant on the manually devised structural features which oftentimes require expert knowledge as well as trial an error for them to be as scalable as the ones shown for this evaluation. Third, in case some cluster gets missclassified, the error could propagate faster to the subsequent web-atoms than in individual evaluation. Fourth, our system is not able to predict the classification of unknown web-atoms, only to detect if an incoming one is similar to a previously classified cluster. This means zero-day attacks could bypass this detection. However, our system is still able to single out the attack as its own cluster and an analyst can have a chance to actually unveil it, which can be an advantage rather than a severe limitation. The prediction of malicious web-atoms based on the classified ones is going to be considered in future work.

5 Related Work

The rise of defaced or malicious injections to legitimate websites in the past decades has motivated the development of systems that detect significant changes to website content integrity [8,13,33]. Such systems employ diverse methodologies to detect attacks such as cross-site scripting and malicious plugins. Multiple resources can be monitored to extract insights from the integrity of the web applications, in this review we focus on systems that perform DOM based analysis as a complement or an alternative to other analysis such as network-traffic analysis, text-based analysis, visual similarity or manual black-listing, among other approaches [29,32]. Considering that the analysis of website similarities is crucial for the phishing detection problem, even more with the rise of asynchronous and dynamic content technologies [4], previous studies have proposed varied methods for near-duplicate recognition.

Xiang et al. [32] proposed a method called CANTINA+, where they filter website duplicates by comparing the SHA1 hashes of a pre-processed HTML input against a previously known list of phishing sites, they report a 99.64% accuracy for near duplicate detection in a set of 2219 sites, however, one to one comparison could compromise scalability of the method. In the work performed by Bagban et al. [7] the web-pages DOM are extracted, then MinHash and LSH algorithms are applied to the DOM shingles in order to assign a cluster for each document, and based on that cluster. They determine if the corresponding web-page is related to a given web template or is not, computing their similarity in a method that works even for heterogeneous web sites. In the best setting, they achieved a recall of 0.6 and a f1-score of 0.75, different from them, our system is centralized and could benefit from DOMs observed in other users.

Similarly, Ben-bassat et al. [4] presented a methodology where MinHash and LSH are used to analyze DOM similarity and accelerate the duplicate content search between web pages. The method extracts the DOM tree of the web page in a particular state s, the accuracy of detecting similar states in real world applications such as Github, Facebook and Netflix were in the range of 78% to 82%. This approach was proposed for website testing purposes rather than for phishing detection. For security purposes Abed et al. [6] proposed a method in which a MinHash technique is used as a data integrity check between a sender and a receiver of a message by using the MinHash function to generate public and private keys in RSA and AES data encryption protocols.

Also, Hunt et al. [16] presented a method using MinHashing and LSH to determine the similarity between DOM objects, compression or accuracy are not disclosed. Different from those studies, our work presents a methodology to monitor client-side website integrity from the server-side. The proposed method integrates a structural signature (i.e. AST) analysis with a clustering system, to generate a scalable, efficient process and detect malicious activity from thousands of users.

Regarding the classification module that determines new cluster labels for unknown inputs, the use of machine learning algorithms to classify unknown malicious websites, based on individual DOM features, is widely addressed in literature. The CANTINA+ method [32] defined three groups of high-level web-page and DOM features to train a classifier, the 15 HTML-based features are based on pre-defined rules that detect bad forms, bad action fields, non-matching URLs and out of position domain strings. They achieved an accuracy of 93.47% for phishing detection of unknown inputs with Bayesian Networks.

Also, Gangi et al. [22] trained a random forest classifier that achieved a balanced classification accuracy of 90.2% for a total of 100 infected pages and 92.4% for 693 clean pages. Finally, Zhuang et al. [3] also presented a phishing model that integrates URL and DOM features, several classifiers for each feature (e.g. Naive Bayes and SVMs) are integrated with a hierarchical clustering system, they validated their approach with a large dataset comprising around 204000 websites from a production environment, accuracy was in the range of 96.4 to 98.7%. Notice that our approach achieved a classification accuracy of 98.7% over in-the-wild data.

In sum, to the best of our knowledge, our work is the first to show an accurate, scalable and practical clustering system for web integrity compromise detection evaluated on production data.

6 Conclusions

In this paper we present a system design, Centy, that allows a system provider to check for integrity of an intended web site on the client's end. This approach generalizes to diverse attack types, since it is not tailored to a particular attack technique. Furthermore, we show that Centy (using a combination of fuzzy hashes and abstract syntax trees, scales for semi-automatic analysis) achieves up to 98.7% accuracy while compressing incoming web-atoms up to 99.4%. This is obtained by evaluating our approach on production data belonging to two different sites from the banking domains. Finally, we show that our approach offers a good trade-off between classification accuracy and scalability.

References

1. Can I use... Support tables for HTML5, CSS3, etc. https://caniuse.com/. Accessed 28 Nov 2020
2. DOM-observer: An abstraction for Mutation Observer with some extra features. https://github.com/jstoolkit/dom-observer
3. Zhuang, W., Jiang, Q., Xiong, T.: An intelligent anti-phishing strategy model for phishing website detection. In: 2012 32nd International Conference on Distributed Computing Systems Workshops. 51–56 (2012). IEEE
4. Ben-Bassat, I., Rokah, E.: Locality-sensitive hashing for efficient web application security testing. arXiv.2001.01128 (2020)
5. MutationObserver - Web APIs—MDN. https://developer.mozilla.org/en-US/docs/Web/API/MutationObserver
6. Abed, S., Waleed, L., Aldamkhi, G., Hadi, K.: Enhancement in data security and integrity using minhash technique. Indones. J. Electr. Eng. Comput. Sci. **21**(3), 1739–1750 (2021)
7. Bagban, T.I., Kulkarni, P.J.: Template based clustering of web documents using locality sensitive hashing (LSH). In: Iyer, B., Deshpande, P.S., Sharma, S.C., Shiurkar, U. (eds.) Computing in Engineering and Technology. AISC, vol. 1025, pp. 567–584. Springer, Singapore (2020). https://doi.org/10.1007/978-981-32-9515-5_54
8. Chen, Q., Snyder, P., Livshits, B., Kapravelos, A.: Improving web content blocking with event-loop-turn granularity Javascript signatures. arXiv (May 2020)
9. Cova, M., Kruegel, C., Vigna, G.: Detection and analysis of drive-by-download attacks and malicious Javascript code. In: Proceedings of the 19th International Conference on World Wide Web, pp. 281–290 (2010)
10. Dhar, A., Ulqinaku, E., Kostiainen, K., Capkun, S.: Protection: root-of-trust for IO in compromised platforms. In: Proceedings 2020 Network and Distributed System Security Symposium. Internet Society (2020)
11. Dougan, T., Curran, K.: Man in the browser attacks. Int. J. Ambient Comput. Intell. (IJACI) **4**(1), 29–39 (2012)
12. Eskandarian, S., et al.: Fidelius: protecting user secrets from compromised browsers. In: 2019 IEEE Symposium on Security and Privacy (SP), pp. 264–280. IEEE (2019)
13. Fajardo, I., Deiro, C.: Systems and methods for detecting and addressing html modifying malware - US.9798875 (2017)
14. GeeksOnSecurity: Malicious Javascript Dataset. https://github.com/geeksonsecurity/js-malicious-dataset. Accessed 3 Jan 2021
15. Goltzsche, D., Wulf, C., Muthukumaran, D., Rieck, K., Pietzuch, P., Kapitza, R.: TrustJS: trusted client-side execution of Javascript. In: Proceedings of the 10th European Workshop on Systems Security, pp. 1–6 (2017)
16. Hunt, A.: Using hash signatures of DOM objects to identify similarity - US.9686283 (2017)

17. Indyk, P., Motwani, R.: Approximate nearest neighbors: towards removing the curse of dimensionality. In: Proceedings of the Thirtieth Annual ACM Symposium on Theory of Computing, pp. 604–613 (1998)
18. Kapravelos, A., Grier, C., Chachra, N., Kruegel, C., Vigna, G., Paxson, V.: Hulk: eliciting malicious behavior in browser extensions. In: 23rd USENIX Security Symposium (USENIX Security 14), pp. 641–654 (2014)
19. Kirda, E., Kruegel, C., Vigna, G., Jovanovic, N.: Noxes: a client-side solution for mitigating cross-site scripting attacks. In: Proceedings of the 2006 ACM Symposium on Applied Computing, pp. 330–337 (2006)
20. Klein, A.: Dom based cross site scripting or XSS of the third kind. Web Appl. Secur. Consort. Artic. **4**, 365–372 (2005)
21. Lekies, S., Stock, B., Johns, M.: 25 million flows later: large-scale detection of DOM-based XSS. In: Proceedings of the 2013 ACM SIGSAC Conference on Computer & Communications Security, pp. 1193–1204 (2013)
22. Moniruzzaman, M., Bagirov, A., Gondal, I., Brown, S.: A server side solution for detecting webinject: a machine learning approach. In: Ganji, M., Rashidi, L., Fung, B.C.M., Wang, C. (eds.) PAKDD 2018. LNCS (LNAI), vol. 11154, pp. 162–167. Springer, Cham (2018). https://doi.org/10.1007/978-3-030-04503-6_16
23. Nikiforakis, N., Meert, W., Younan, Y., Johns, M., Joosen, W.: SessionShield: lightweight protection against session hijacking. In: Erlingsson, Ú., Wieringa, R., Zannone, N. (eds.) ESSoS 2011. LNCS, vol. 6542, pp. 87–100. Springer, Heidelberg (2011). https://doi.org/10.1007/978-3-642-19125-1_7
24. Petrak, H.: Javascript Malware Collection. https://github.com/HynekPetrak/javascript-malware-collection. Accessed 3 Jan 2021
25. Rajaraman, A., Ullman, J.D.: Mining of Massive Datasets. Cambridge University Press, Cambridge (2011)
26. Rieck, K., Krueger, T., Dewald, A.: Cujo: efficient detection and prevention of drive-by-download attacks. In: Proceedings of the 26th Annual Computer Security Applications Conference, pp. 31–39 (2010)
27. Sun, F., Xu, L., Su, Z.: Client-side detection of XSS worms by monitoring payload propagation. In: Backes, M., Ning, P. (eds.) ESORICS 2009. LNCS, vol. 5789, pp. 539–554. Springer, Heidelberg (2009). https://doi.org/10.1007/978-3-642-04444-1_33
28. Tekli, G.: A survey on semi-structured web data manipulations by non-expert users. Comput. Sci. Rev. **40**, 100367 (2021)
29. Varshney, G., Misra, M., Atrey, P.K.: A survey and classification of web phishing detection schemes. Secur. Commun. Netw. **9**(18), 6266–6284 (2016). https://doi.org/10.1002/sec.1674
30. VirusTotal: Malware Querying Service. https://www.virustotal.com. Accessed 3 Jan 2021
31. w3 schools: JavaScript HTML DOM. https://www.w3schools.com/js/js_htmldom.asp
32. Xiang, G., Hong, J., Rose, C.P., Cranor, L.: Cantina+: a feature-rich machine learning framework for detecting phishing web sites. ACM Trans. Inf. Syst. Secur. (TISSEC) **14**(2), 1–28 (2011)
33. Zhang, M., Meng, W.: Detecting and understanding JavaScript global identifier conflicts on the web. In: ESEC/FSE 2020 - Proceedings of the 28th ACM Joint Meeting European Software Engineering Conference and Symposium on the Foundations of Software Engineering, pp. 38–49. Association for Computing Machinery Inc., New York (November 2020)

Author Index

Printed in the United States
by Baker & Taylor Publisher Services

Printed in the United States
by Baker & Taylor Publisher Services